AMERICA'S
Favorite
INNS,
B&Bs
& SMALL HOTELS
Sixteenth Edition

New England

States Covered in This Edition

Connecticut   New Hampshire
Maine   Rhode Island
Massachusetts   Vermont

Also in This Series

America's Favorite Inns, B&Bs & Small Hotels, U.S.A. and Canada

America's Favorite Inns, B&Bs & Small Hotels, The Middle Atlantic

America's Wonderful Little Hotels & Inns, The Midwest

America's Wonderful Little Hotels & Inns, The Rocky Mountains and The Southwest

America's Favorite Inns, B&Bs & Small Hotels, The South

America's Favorite Inns, B&Bs & Small Hotels, The West Coast

AMERICA'S
Favorite
INNS,
B&Bs
& SMALL HOTELS

Sixteenth Edition

New England

Edited by Sandra W. Soule

Associate Editors:
Nancy P. Barker, Elyse Brown, Carol Dinmore
Betsy Nolan Sandberg, Hilary Soule

Contributing Editors:
Suzanne Carmichael, Rose Ciccone, Gail Davis, Nancy
Debevoise, Linda Goldberg, Betty Norman, Pam
Phillips, Joe Schmidt, Susan Schwemm, Diane Wolf

Editorial Assistants:
Rachel Brown, Tyler Sandberg

St. Martin's Griffin
New York

This book is dedicated to the people who take the time and trouble to write about the hotels and inns they've visited, and to my children—Hilary and Jeffrey—my husband, and my parents.

ISBN 0-312-19561-3

First Edition: December 1998

10 9 8 7 6 5 4 3 2 1

Maps by David Lindroth © 1996, 1994, 1992, 1991, 1990, 1989, 1988, 1987 by St. Martin's Press

Contents

Acknowledgments

I would again like to thank all the people who wrote in such helpful detail about the inns and hotels they visited. To them belong both the dedication and the acknowledgments, for without their support, this guide would not exist. If I have inadvertently misspelled or omitted anyone's name, please accept my sincerest apologies. I would also like to thank my wonderful colleagues Nancy Barker, Carol Dinmore, Elyse Brown, Betsy Sandberg, Suzanne Carmichael, Rose Ciccone, Nancy Debevoise, Gail Davis, Linda Goldberg, Betty Norman, Pam Phillips, Susan Schwemm, and Diane Wolf; and to faithful respondents Peg Bedini, Carol Blodgett, Donna Bocks, Judith Brannen, Sherrill Brown, James and Pamela Burr, Marjorie Cohen, Dianne Crawford, Lynne Derry, Gail DeSciose, Brian Donaldson, Sally Ducot, Ellie and Robert Freidus, Connie Gardner, Gail Gunning, B.J. Hensley, Lisa Hering, Emily Hochemong, Tina Hom, Stephen Holman, Linda Intaschi, Christopher Johnston, Keith Jurgens, Arleen Keele, Peggy Kontak, Bradley Lockner, Bill MacGowan, Myra Malkin, Pat Malone, Celia McCullough, Mark Mendenhall, Michael and Dina Miller, Carolyn Myles, Eileen O'Reilly, Marilyn Parker, Julie Phillips, Adam Platt, Penny Poirier, Jill Reeves, Stephanie Roberts, Glenn Roehrig, Duane Roller, Marion Ruben, Lori Sampson, Conrad and Nancy Schilke, Joe and Sheila Schmidt, B.J. and Larry Schwartzkopf, Robert Sfire, Fritz Shantz and Tara O'Neal, Nancy Sinclair, Mary Jane Skala, Ruth Tilsley, Susan Ulanoff, Wendi Van Exan, Marty Wall and Kip Goldman, Hopie Welliver, Tom Wilbanks, Beryl Williams, Rose Wolf, Karl Wiegers and Chris Zambito, Susan Woods, and the many others who went far beyond the call of duty in their assistance and support.

Introduction

Reading the Entries

Each entry generally has three parts: a description of the inn or hotel, quotes from guests who have stayed there, and relevant details about rooms, rates, location, and facilities. Please remember that the length of an entry is in no way a reflection of that inn or hotel's quality. Rather, it is an indication of the type of feedback we've received both from guests and from the innkeepers themselves.

Wherever a location is of particular tourist interest, we've tried to include some information about its attractions. In some areas the magnet is not a particular town but rather a compact, distinct region. Travelers choose one place to stay and use it as a base from which to explore the area. But because this guide is organized by town, not by region, the entries are scattered throughout the chapter. When this applies, you will see the name of the region noted under the "Location" heading; check back to the introduction for a description of the region involved. Cross-referencing is also provided to supplement the maps at the back of the book.

The names at the end of the quotations are those who have recommended the hotel or inn. Some writers have requested that we not use their names; you will see initials noted instead. *We never print the names of those who have sent us adverse reports, although their contributions are invaluable indeed.*

Although we have tried to make the listings as accurate and complete as possible, mistakes and inaccuracies invariably creep in. The most significant area of inaccuracy applies to the rates charged by each establishment. In preparing this guide, we asked all the hotels and inns to give us their 1999–2000 rates, ranging from the least expensive room in the off-season to the most expensive peak-season price. Some did so, while others just noted the current rate.

Some of the shorter entries are marked "**Information please**" or "**Also recommended**." These tend to be establishments that are either too large or too small for a full entry, or about which we have insufficient information to complete a full entry.

Please remember that the process of writing and publishing a book takes nearly a year. *You should always double-check the rates when you make your reservations; please don't blame the inn or this guide if the prices are wrong.* On the other hand, given the current level of inflation, you should not encounter anything more than a 5% increase, unless there has been a substantial improvement in the amenities offered or a change of ownership. Please let us know immediately if you find anything more than that!

If you find any errors of omission or commission in any part of the entries, we urgently request your help in correcting them. We recognize that it takes extra time and effort for readers to write us letters or fill in report forms, but this feedback is essential in keeping this publication totally responsive to consumer needs.

The Fifteen Commandments of Vacation Travel

We all know people who come back from a vacation feeling on top of the world, and others who seem vaguely disappointed. Here's how to put yourself in the first category, not the second.

1. Know yourself. A successful vacation is one that works for the person you are, not the person you think you should be. Confirmed couch potatoes who resent having to walk from the far end of the parking lot will not find true fulfillment on a trek through the Himalayas. If privacy is a top priority, a group tour or communal lodge will turn fantasy into frustration. Acknowledge your own comfort levels. How important is it for you to be independent and flexible? Structured and secure? How essential are the creature comforts when it comes to sleeping, eating, and bathing? Would you rather have one week of luxury travel or two weeks of budget food and accommodation? And remember that while your personality doesn't change, your needs do. The type of vacation you plan for a romantic getaway is totally different from a family reunion.

2. Know your travel companions. Adjust your plans to accommodate your travel partners. Whether you are traveling with friends, spouse, children, and/or parents, you'll need to take their age, attention span, agility, and interests into account. If you're traveling with the kids, balance a morning at an art museum with an afternoon at the zoo; if you're spending time with elderly parents, make sure that they can stroll a country lane while you go rock-climbing; if your group includes skiers and non-skiers, pick a resort that has appealing shops and other activities.

3. Plan ahead: anticipation is half the fun. Enjoy the process. The more you know about an area you're going to visit, the more fun you'll have. Skim a guidebook; get a calendar of events; write to the local chambers of commerce and tourist offices; read a novel set in the region; talk to friends (or friends of friends) who have been there recently.

4. Don't bite off more than you can chew. Keep your itinerary in line with the amount of time and money available. Focus on seeing a smaller area well, rather than trying to cover too much ground and seeing nothing but interstate highways. Don't overprogram; allow yourself the luxury of doing nothing.

5. Avoid one-night stands. Plan to stay a minimum of two nights everywhere you go. A vacation made up of one-nighters is a prescription for exhaustion. You will sleep poorly, spend most of your time in transit, and will get only the smallest glimpse of the place you're visiting. If it's worth seeing, it's worth spending a full day in one place.

6. Travel off-season. Unless your vacation dates are dictated by the school calendar, off-season travel offers many advantages: fewer crowds, greater flexibility, and a more relaxed atmosphere. Learn to pick the best dates for off-season travel; typically these are the weeks just before and after the rates change. Off-season travel offers big savings, too; for example, most ski areas are delightful places to visit in summer, and offer savings of 50% or more on accommodations.

7. Book well ahead for peak-season travel. If you must travel during peak periods to popular destinations, make reservations well in advance for the key sites to avoid aggravation, extra phone calls, and additional driving time.

8. Take the road less traveled by. Get off the beaten path to leave the crowds behind. Instead of booking a room in the heart of the action, find a quiet inn tucked in the hills or in a neighboring village. If you visit the Grand Canyon in August, at the height of the tourist season, stay at the North Rim, which attracts 90% fewer visitors than the South Rim.

9. Ditch the car. Sure you need a car to get where you're going. But once you're there, get out and walk. You'll see more, learn more, experience more at every level, while avoiding crowds even at the most popular destinations. We promise. Car travel is an isolating experience, even when you're in bumper-to-bumper traffic.

10. Hang loose. The unexpected is inevitable in travel, as in the rest of life. When your plans go astray (and they will), relax and let serendipity surprise you. And keep your sense of humor in good working order. If possible, travel without reservations or a set itinerary.

11. Carpe diem—seize the day. Don't be afraid to follow your impulses. If a special souvenir catches your eye, buy it; don't wait to see if you'll find it again later. If a hiking trail looks too inviting to pass up, don't; that museum will wait for a rainy day.

12. Don't suffer in silence. When things go wrong—an incompetent guide, car troubles, a noisy hotel room—speak up. Politely but firmly express your concern then and there; get your room changed, ask for a refund or discount, whatever. Most people in the travel business would rather have you go away happy than to leave grumbling.

13. Remember—being there is more than seeing there. People travel to see the sights—museums and mountains, shops and scenery—but it is making new friends that can make a trip memorable. Leave a door open to the people-to-people experiences that enrich travel immeasurably.

14. Don't leave home to find home. The quickest way to take the wind out of the sails of your trip is to compare things to the way they are at home. Enjoy different styles and cultures for what they are and avoid comparisons and snap judgments.

15. Give yourself permission to disregard all of the above. Nothing is immutable. If you find a pattern that works for you, enjoy it!

Inngoer's Bill of Rights

Although nothing's perfect, as we all know, inngoers are entitled to certain reasonable standards. Of course, the higher the rates, the higher those standards should be. So, please use this Bill of Rights as a kind of checklist in deciding how you think a place stacks up on your own personal rating scale. And, whether an establishment fails, reaches, or exceeds these levels, be sure to let us know. We would also hope that innkeepers will use this list to help evaluate both the strong points and shortcomings of their own establishments, and are grateful to those who have already done so.

The right to suitable cleanliness: An establishment that looks, feels, and smells immaculate, with no musty, smoky, or animal odors.

The right to suitable room furnishings: A firm mattress, soft pillows, fresh linens, and ample blankets; bright lamps and night tables on each side of the bed; comfortable chairs with good reading lights; and adequate storage space.

The right to comfortable, attractive rooms: Guest rooms and common rooms that are as livable as they are attractive. Appealing places where you'd like to read, chat, relax.

The right to a decent bathroom: Cleanliness is essential, along with reliable plumbing, ample hot water, good lighting, an accessible electric outlet, space for toiletries, and thirsty towels.

The right to privacy and discretion: Privacy must be respected by the innkeeper and ensured by adequate sound-proofing. The right to discretion precludes questions about marital status or sexual preference. No display of proselytizing religious materials.

The right to good, healthful food: Fresh nutritious food, ample in quantity, high in quality, attractively presented, and graciously served in smoke-free surroundings.

The right to comfortable temperatures and noise levels: Rooms should be cool in summer and warm in winter, with windows that open, and quiet, efficient air-conditioning and heating. Double windows, drapes, and landscaping are essential if traffic noise is an issue.

The right to fair value: Prices should be in reasonable relation to the facilities offered and to the cost of equivalent local accommodation.

The right to genuine hospitality: Innkeepers who are glad you've come and who make it their business to make your stay pleasant and memorable; who are readily available without being intrusive.

The right to a caring environment: Welcoming arrivals with refreshments, making dinner reservations, providing information on activities, asking about pet allergies and dietary restrictions, and so on.

The right to personal safety: A location in a reasonably safe neighborhood, with adequate care given to building and parking security, as well as the highest standards of fire safety, as well.

The right to professionalism: Brochure requests, room reservations, check-ins and -outs handled efficiently and responsibly.

The right to adequate common areas: At least one common room where guests can gather to read, chat, or relax, free of the obligation to buy anything.

The right of people traveling alone to have all the above rights: Singles usually pay just a few dollars less than couples, yet the welcome, services, and rooms they receive can be inferior.

The right to a reasonable cancellation policy: Penalties for a cancellation made fewer than 7–14 days before arrival are relatively standard. Most inns will refund deposits (minus a processing fee) after the deadline only if the room is rebooked.

The right to efficient maintenance: Burnt-out bulbs and worn-out smoke detector batteries are the responsibility of the innkeeper—not the guest. When things go wrong, guests have the right to an apology, a discount, or a refund.

Of course, there is no "perfect" inn or hotel, because people's tastes and needs vary so greatly. But one key phrase does pop up over and over again: "I felt right at home." This is not written in the literal sense—a commercial lodging, no matter how cozy or charming, is never the same as one's home. What is really meant is that guests felt as welcome, as relaxed, as comfortable, as they would in their own home.

What makes for a wonderful stay?

We've tried our best to make sure that all the inns listed in this guide are as special as our title promises. Inevitably, there will be some disappointments. Sometimes these will be caused by a change in ownership or management that has resulted in lowered standards. Other times unusual circumstances will lead to problems. Quite often, though, problems will occur because there's not a good "fit" between the inn and the guest. Decide what you're looking for, then find the place that suits your needs, whether you're looking for a casual environment or a dressy one, a romantic setting or a family-oriented one, a vacation spot or a businessperson's environment, an isolated country retreat or a convenient in-town location.

We've tried to give you as much information as possible on each property listed, and have taken care to indicate the atmosphere each innkeeper is trying to create. After you've read the listing, request a copy of the establishment's brochure, which will give you more information. Finally, feel free to call any inn or hotel where you're planning to stay, and ask as many questions as necessary.

Inn etiquette

A first-rate inn is a joy indeed, but as guests we need to do our part to respect its special qualities. For starters, you'll need to maintain a higher level of consideration for your fellow guests. Century-old Victorians are noted for their nostalgic charms, not their sound-proofing; if you come in late or get up early, remember that voices and footsteps echo off all those gleaming hardwood floors and doors. If you're going to pick a fight with your roommate, pull the covers up over your head or go out for a walk. If you're sharing a bath, don't dawdle, tidy up after yourself, and dry your hair back in your room. If you've admired the Oriental carpets, antique decor, handmade quilts, and the thick fluffy towels, don't leave wet glasses on the furniture, put suitcases on the bed, or use the towels for removing make-up or wiping the snow off your car. After all, innkeepers have rights, too!

Hotels, inns . . . resorts and motels

As the title indicates, this is a guide to exceptional inns, B&Bs, and small hotels. Generally, the inns have 5 to 25 rooms, although a few have only 2 rooms and some have over 100. The hotels are more often found in the cities and range in size from about 50 to 200 rooms.

The line between an inn or hotel and a resort is often a fine one. There are times when we all want the extra facilities a resort provides, so we've added a number of reader-recommended facilities. We've also listed a handful of motels. Although they don't strictly fall within the context of this book, we've included them because readers felt they were the best option in a specific situation.

What is a B&B anyway?

There are basically two kinds of B&Bs—the B&B homestay and the B&B inn. The homestay is typically the home of an empty nester, who has a few empty bedrooms to fill, gaining some extra income and pleasant company. B&B inns are run on a more professional basis, independently marketed and subject to state and local licensing. Guests typically have dedicated common areas for their use, and do not share the hosts' living quarters, as in a homestay. We list very few homestays in this guide. Full-service or country inns and lodges are similar to the B&B inn, except that they serve breakfast and dinner on a regular basis, and may be somewhat larger in size; dinner is often offered to the public as well as to house guests. The best of all of these are made special by resident owners bringing the warmth of their personalities to the total experience. A B&B is *not* a motel that serves breakfast.

Rooms

All guest rooms are not created equal. Although the rooms at a typical chain motel or hotel may be identical, the owners of most of the establishments described in this book pride themselves on the individuality of each guest room. Some, although not all, of these differences are reflected in the rates charged.

More importantly, it means that travelers need to express their needs clearly to the innkeepers when making reservations and again when checking in. Some rooms may be quite spacious but may have extremely small private baths or limited closet space. Some antique double beds have rather high footboards—beautiful to look at but torture for six-footers. Most inns are trading their double-size mattresses in for queens and kings; if you prefer an oversize bed, say so. If you want twin beds, be sure to specify this when making reservations and again when you check in; many smaller inns have only one twin-bedded room. If you must have a king-size bed, ask for details; sometimes two twin beds are just pushed together, made up with a king-size fitted sheet.

Some rooms may have gorgeous old bathrooms, with tubs the size of small swimming pools, but if you are a hard-core shower person, that room won't be right for you. More frequently, you'll find a shower but no bathtub, which may be disappointing if you love a long, luxurious soak. If you are traveling on business and simply must have a working-size desk with good lighting, an electric outlet, and a telephone jack for your modem, speak up. Some rooms look terrific inside but don't look out at anything much; others may have the view but not quite as special a decor. Often the largest rooms are at the front of the house, facing a busy highway. Decide what's important to you. Although the owners and staff of the hotels and inns listed here are incredibly hard-working and dedicated people, they can't read your mind. Let your needs be known, and, within the limits of availability, they will try to accommodate you.

Our most frequent complaints center around beds that are too soft and inadequate reading lights. If these are priorities for you (as they are for us), don't be shy about requesting bedboards or additional lamps to remedy the situation. Similarly, if there are other amenities your room is lacking—extra pillows, blankets, or even an easy chair—speak up. Most innkeepers would rather put in an extra five minutes of work than have an unhappy guest.

If you really don't like your room, ask for another as soon as possible, preferably before you've unpacked your bags. The sooner you voice your dissatisfaction, the sooner something can be done to improve the situation. If you don't like the food, ask for something else—since you're the guest, make sure you get treated like one. If things go terribly wrong, don't be shy about asking for your money back, and be *sure* to write us about any problems.

What is a single? A double? A suite? A cottage or cabin?

Unlike the proverbial rose, a single is not a single is not a single. Sometimes it is a room with one twin bed, which really can accommodate only one person. Quite often it is described as a room with a standard-size double bed, in contrast to a double, which has two twin beds. Other hotels call both of the preceding doubles, although doubles often have queen- or even king-size beds instead. Many times the only distinction is made by the number of guests occupying the room; a single will pay slightly less, but there's no difference in the room.

There's almost as much variation when it comes to suites. We define a suite as a bedroom with a separate living room area and often a small kitchen, as well. Unfortunately, the word has been stretched to cover other set-ups, too. Some so-called suites are only one large room, accommodating a table and separate seating area in addition to the bed, while others are two adjacent bedrooms which share a bath. If you require a suite that has two separate rooms with a door between them, specify this when you make reservations.

Quite a few of our entries have cabins or cottages in addition to rooms in the main building. In general, a cabin is understood to be a somewhat more rustic residence than a cottage, although there's no hard-and-fast rule. Be sure to inquire for details when making reservations.

Making reservations

Unless you are inquiring many months in advance of your visit, it's best to telephone when making reservations. This offers a number of advantages: You will know immediately if space is available on your requested dates; you can find out if that space is suitable to your specific needs. You will have a chance to discuss the pros and cons of the available rooms and will be able to find out about any changes made in recent months—new facilities, recently redecorated rooms, nonsmoking policies, even a change of ownership. It's also a good time to ask the innkeeper about other concerns—Is the neighborhood safe at night? Is there any renovation or construction in progress that might be disturbing? Will a wedding reception or bicycle touring group affect use of the common areas during your visit? If you're reserving a room at a plantation home that is available for public tours, get specifics about the check-in/out times; in many, rooms are not available before 5 P.M. and must be vacated by 9 A.M. sharp. The savvy traveler will always get the best value for his accommodation dollar.

If you expect to be checking in late at night, *be sure to say so;* many inns give doorkeys to their guests, then lock up by 10 P.M.; often special arrangements must be made for late check-ins, and a handful of inns won't accept them at all.

We're often asked about the need for making advance reservations. If you'll be traveling in peak periods, in prime tourist areas, and want to be sure of getting a first-rate room at the best-known inns, reserve at least three to six months ahead. This is especially true if you're traveling with friends or family and will need more than one room. On the other hand, if you like a bit of adventure, and don't want to be stuck with cancellation fees when you change your mind, by all means stick our books in the glove compartment and hit the road. If you're traveling in the off-season, or even midweek in season, you'll have a grand time. But look for a room by late afternoon; never wait until after dinner and expect to find something decent. Some inns offer a discount after 4 P.M. for last-minute bookings; it never hurts to ask.

Payment

The vast majority of inns now accept credit cards. A few accept credit cards for the initial deposit but prefer cash, traveler's checks, or personal checks for the balance; others offer the reverse policy. When no credit cards are accepted at all, you can settle your bill with a personal check, traveler's check, or even (!) cash.

When using your credit card to guarantee a reservation, be aware that most inns will charge your card for the full amount of the deposit, unlike motels and hotels which don't put through the charge until you've checked in. A few will put a "hold" on your card for the full amount of your entire stay, plus the cost of meals and incidentals that you may (or may not) spend. If you're using your card to reserve a fairly extended trip, you may find that you're well over your credit limit without actually having spent a nickel. We'd suggest inquiring; if the latter is the procedure, either send a check for the deposit or go elsewhere. If you have used American Express, Diners Club, MasterCard, or Visa to guarantee your reservation, these companies guarantee if a room is not available, the hotel is supposed to find you a free room in a comparable hotel, plus transportation and a free phone call.

Rates

All rates quoted are per room, unless otherwise noted as being per person. Rates quoted per person are usually based on double occupancy, unless otherwise stated.

"Room only" rates do not include any meals. In most cases two or three meals a day are served by the hotel restaurant, but are charged separately. Average meal prices are noted when available. In a very few cases no meals are served on the premises at all; rooms in these facilities are usually equipped with kitchenettes.

B&B rates include bed and breakfast. Breakfast can vary from a simple continental breakfast to a full breakfast. Afternoon tea and evening refreshments are sometimes included as well.

MAP (Modified American Plan) rates are often listed per person and include breakfast and dinner; *a 15% service charge is typically added to the total.* Full board rates include three squares a day, and are usually found only at old-fashioned resorts and isolated ranches.

State and local sales taxes are not included in the rates unless otherwise indicated; the percentage varies from state to state, city to city, and can reach 20% in a few urban centers, although 10 to 15% is more typical.

When inquiring about rates, always ask if any off-season or special package rates are available. Sometimes discounted rates are available *only* on request; seniors and AAA members often qualify for substantial discounts. During the week, when making reservations at city hotels or country inns, it's important to ask if any corporate rates are available. Depending on the establishment, you may or may not be asked for some proof of corporate affiliation (a business card is usually all that's needed), but it's well worth inquiring, since the effort can result in a saving of 15 to 20%, plus an upgrade to a substantially better room.

A number of companies specialize in booking hotel rooms in major cities at substantial discounts. Although you can ask for specific hotels by name, the largest savings are realized by letting the agency make the selection; they may be able to get you a discount of up to 65%. **Hotel Reservations Network** (8140 Walnut Hill Lane, Dallas, Texas 75231; 800–96–HOTEL) offers discount rates in over 20 U.S. cities plus London and Paris; **Quikbook** (381 Park Avenue South, New York, New York 10016; 800–789–9887) is a similar service with competitive rates.

Express Reservations (3800 Arapahoe, Boulder, Colorado 80303; 800–356–1123) specializes in properties in New York City and Los Angeles. For California, try **San Francisco Reservations** (22 Second Street, Fourth Floor, San Francisco, California 94105; 800–677–1500, or **California Reservations** (3 Sumner Street, 94103; 800–576–0003).

Another money-saving trick can be to look for inns in towns a bit off the beaten path. If you stay in a town that neighbors a famous resort or historic community, you will often find that rates are anywhere from $20 to $50 less per night for equivalent accommodation. If you're traveling without reservations, and arrive at a half-empty inn in late afternoon, don't hesitate to ask for a price reduction or free room upgrade. And of course, watch for our ¢ symbol, which indicates places which are a particularly good value.

If an establishment has a specific tipping policy, whether it is "no tipping" or the addition of a set service charge, it is noted under "Rates." When both breakfast and dinner are included in the rates, a 15% service charge against the total bill—not just the room—is standard; a few inns charge 18 to 20%. A number of B&Bs are also adding on a service charge, a practice which sits poorly with us. If you feel—as many of our readers do—that these fees are a sneaky way of making rates seem lower than they really are, let the innkeeper (and us) know how you feel. When no notation is made, it's generally expected that guests will leave $1–3 a night for the housekeeping staff and 15% for meal service. A number of inns have taken to leaving little cards or envelopes to remind guests to leave a tip for the housekeepers; most readers find this practice objectionable. If you welcome a no-tipping policy and object to solicitation, speak up.

While the vast majority of inns are fairly priced, there are a few whose rates have become exorbitant. Others fail to stay competitive, charging top weekend rates when a nearby luxury hotel is offering a beautiful suite at a lower price. No matter how lovely the breakfast, how thoughtful the innkeepers, there's a limit to the amount one will pay for a room without an in-room telephone, TV, or a full-size private bathroom. One B&B has the nerve to charge $125 for a room with shared bath, then asks you to bring your own pool towels during the summer (it's not listed here!).

Deposits and cancellations

Nearly all innkeepers print their deposit and cancellation policies clearly on their brochures. Deposits generally range from payment of the first night's stay to 50% of the cost of the entire stay. Some inns repeat the cancellation policy when confirming reservations. In general, guests canceling well in advance of the planned arrival (one to four weeks is typical) receive a full refund minus a cancellation fee. After that date, no refunds are offered unless the room is resold to someone else. A few will not refund *even if the room is resold,* so take careful note. If you're making a credit card booking over the phone, be sure to find out what the cancellation policy is. We are uncomfortable with overly strict refund policies, and wish that inns would give a gift certificate, good for a return visit, when guests are forced to cancel on short notice.

Sometimes the shoe may be on the other foot. Even if you were told earlier that the inn at which you really wanted to stay was full, it may be worthwhile to make a call to see if cancellations have opened up any last-minute vacancies.

Minimum stays

Two- and three-night minimum weekend and holiday stays are the rule at many inns during peak periods. We have noted these when possible, although we suspect that the policy may be more common than is always indicated in print. On the other hand, you may just be hitting a slow period, so it never hurts to call at the last minute to see if a one-night reservation would be accepted. Again, cancellations are always a possibility; you can try calling on a Friday or Saturday morning to see if something is available for that night.

Pets

Very few of the inns and hotels listed accept pets. When they do we've noted it under "Extras." On the other hand, most of the inns listed in this book have at least one dog or cat, sometimes more. These pets are usually found in the common areas, sometimes in guest rooms as well. *If you are allergic to animals, we strongly urge that you inquire for details before making reservations.*

Children

Some inns are family-style places and welcome children of all ages; we've marked them with our 🐾 symbol. Others do not feel that they have facilities for the very young and only allow children over a certain age. Still others cultivate an "adults only" atmosphere and discourage anyone under the age of 16. We've noted age requirements under the heading "Restrictions." If special facilities are available to children, these are noted under "Facilities" and "Extras." If an inn does not exclude children yet does not offer any special amenities or rate reductions for them, we would suggest it only for the best-behaved youngsters.

Whatever the policy, you may want to remind your children to follow the same rules of courtesy toward others that we expect of adults. Be aware that the pitter-patter of little feet on an uncarpeted hardwood floor can sound like a herd of stampeding buffalo to those on the floor below. Children used to the indestructible plastics of contemporary homes will need to be reminded (more than once) to be gentle with antique furnishings. Most importantly, be sensitive to the fact that parents—not innkeepers—are responsible for supervising their children's behavior.

State laws governing discrimination by age are affecting policies at some inns. To our knowledge, both California and Michigan now have such laws on the books. Some inns get around age discrimination by limiting room occupancy to two adults. This discourages families by forcing them to pay for two rooms instead of one. Our own children were very clear on their preferences: although they'd been to many inns that don't encourage guests under the age of 12, they found them "really boring"; on the other hand, they loved every family-oriented place we visited.

Porterage and packing

Only the largest of our listings will have personnel whose sole job is to assist guests with baggage. In the casual atmosphere associated with many inns, it is simply assumed that guests will carry their own bags. If you do need assistance with your luggage, don't hesitate to ask.

If you're planning an extended trip to a number of small inns, we'd suggest packing as lightly as possible, using two small bags rather than one large suitcase. You'll know why if you've ever tried hauling a 50-pound oversize suitcase up a steep and narrow 18th-century staircase. On the other hand, don't forget about the local climate when assembling your wardrobe. In mountainous and desert regions, day- and nighttime temperatures can vary by as much as 40 degrees. Also, bear in mind that Easterners tend to dress more formally than Westerners, so pack accordingly.

Meals

If you have particular dietary restrictions—low-salt, vegetarian, or religious—or allergies—to caffeine, nuts, whatever—be sure to mention these when making reservations and *again* at check-in. If you're allergic to a common breakfast food or beverage, an evening reminder will ensure that you'll be able to enjoy the breakfast that's been prepared for you. Most innkeepers will do their best to accommodate your special needs, but be fair. Don't ask an innkeeper to prepare a special meal, and then, when it's being served, say: "I've decided to go off my diet today. Can I have the luscious peaches-and-cream French toast with bacon that everyone else is eating?"

In preparing each listing, we asked the owners to give us the cost of prix fixe and à la carte meals when available. An "alc dinner" price at the end of the "Rates" section is the figure we were given when we requested the average cost of a three-course dinner with a half bottle of house wine, including tax and tip. Prices listed for prix fixe meals do not include wine and service. Lunch prices, where noted, do not include the cost of any alcoholic beverage. Hotels and inns which serve meals to the public are noted with the ✕ symbol.

Dinner and lunch reservations are always a courtesy and are often essential. Most B&B owners will offer to make reservations for you; this can be especially helpful in getting you a table at a popular restaurant in peak season and/or on weekends. Some of the establishments we list operate restaurants fully open to the public. Others serve dinner primarily to their overnight guests, but they also will serve meals to outsiders; reservations are essential at such inns, usually 24 hours in advance.

A few restaurants require jackets and ties for men at dinner, even in rather isolated areas. Of course, this is more often the case in traditional New England and the Old South than in the West. Unless you're going only to a very casual country lodge, we recommend that men bring these items along and that women have corresponding attire.

Breakfast:

Breakfast is served at nearly every inn or hotel listed in this guide, and is usually included in the rates. Whenever possible we describe a typical breakfast, rather than using the terms "continental" or "full" breakfast.

Continental breakfast ranges from coffee and store-bought pastry to a lavish offering of fresh fruit and juices, yogurt and granola, cereals, even cheese and cold meats, homemade muffins and breads, and a choice of decaffeinated or regular coffee, herbal and regular tea. There's almost as much variety in the full breakfasts, which range from the traditional eggs, bacon, and toast, plus juice and coffee, to three-course gourmet extravaganzas.

We've received occasional complaints about breakfasts being too rich in eggs and cream, and too sweet, with no plain rolls or bread. A dietary splurge is fun for a weekend escape, but on a longer trip we'd advise requesting a "healthy breakfast" from your innkeeper. You can be sure that they don't eat their own breakfasts every day! Equally important to many guests are the timing and seating arrangements at breakfast. Some readers enjoy the friendly atmosphere of breakfast served family-style at a set time; this approach often enables innkeepers to serve quite spectacular three-course meals. Other readers much prefer the flexibility and privacy afforded by breakfasts served at tables for two over an extended time period.

Lunch:

Very few of the inns and hotels listed here serve lunch. Those that do generally operate a full-service restaurant or are located in isolated mountain settings with no restaurants nearby. Many inns are happy to make up picnic lunches for an additional fee.

Dinner:

Meals served at the inns listed here vary widely from simple home-style family cooking to gourmet cuisine. We are looking for food that is a good, honest example of the type of cooking involved. Ingredients should be fresh and homemade as far as is possible; service and presentation should be pleasant and straightforward. We have no interest in the school of "haute pretentious" where the hyperbolic descriptions found on the menu far exceed the chef's ability.

Drinks

With a very few exceptions (noted under "Restrictions" in each listing), alcoholic beverages may be enjoyed in moderation at all of the inns and hotels listed. Most establishments with a full-service restaurant serving the public as well as overnight guests are licensed to serve beer, wine, and liquor to their customers, although "brown-bagging" or BYOB (bring your own bottle) is occasionally permitted, especially in dry counties. Bed & breakfasts, and inns serving meals primarily to overnight guests, do not typically have liquor licenses, although most will provide guests with set-ups, i.e., glasses, ice, and mixers, at what is often called a BYO (bring your own) bar.

Overseas visitors will be amazed at the hodgepodge of regulations around the country. Liquor laws are determined in general by each state, but individual counties, or even towns, can prohibit or restrict the sale of alcoholic beverages, even beer.

Smoking

The vast majority of B&Bs and inns prohibit indoor smoking entirely, allowing it only on porches and verandas; a few don't allow smoking anywhere on the grounds. Larger inns and hotels usually do permit smoking, prohibiting it only in some guest rooms, and dining areas. Where prohibitions apply we have noted this under "Restrictions." We suggest that confirmed smokers be courteous or make reservations elsewhere. If there is no comment about smoking under "Restrictions," those allergic to smoke should inquire for details.

Physical limitations and wheelchair accessibility

We've used the well-known symbol ♿ to denote hotels and inns that are wheelchair accessible. Where available, additional information is noted under the "Extras" heading. Unfortunately, what is meant by this symbol varies dramatically. In the case of larger hotels and newer inns, it usually means full access; in historic buildings, access may be limited to the restaurant and public rest rooms only, or to a specific guest room but not the common areas. *Call the inn/hotel directly for full details and to discuss your needs.*

If you do not need a wheelchair but have difficulty with stairs, we urge you to mention this when making reservations; many inns and small hotels have one or two rooms on the ground floor, but very few have elevators. Similarly, if you are visually handicapped, do share this information so that you may be given a room with good lighting and no unexpected steps.

Air-conditioning

Heat is a relative condition, and the perceived need for air-conditioning varies tremendously from one individual to the next. If an inn or hotel has air-conditioning, you'll see this listed under "Rooms." If it's important to you, be sure to ask when making reservations. If air-conditioning is not available, check to see if fans are provided. Remember that top-floor rooms in most inns (usually a converted attic) can be uncomfortably warm even with air-conditioning.

Transportation

A car is more or less essential for visiting most of the inns and hotels listed here, as well as the surrounding sights of interest. Exceptions are those located in the major cities. In some historic towns, a car is the easiest way to get there, but once you've arrived, you'll want to find a place to park the car and forget about it.

If you are traveling by public transportation, check the "Extras" section at the end of each write-up. If the innkeepers are willing to pick you up from the nearest airport, bus, or train station, you'll see it noted here. This service is usually free or available at modest cost. If it's not listed, the innkeeper will direct you to a commercial facility that can help.

Parking

Although not a concern in most cases, parking is a problem in many cities, beach resorts, and historic towns. If you'll be traveling by car, ask the innkeeper for advice when making reservations. If parking is not on-site, stop at the hotel first to drop off your bags, then go park the car. In big cities, if "free parking" is included in the rates, this usually covers only one arrival and departure. Additional "ins and outs" incur substantial extra charges. Be sure to ask.

If on-site parking is available in areas where parking can be a problem, we've noted it under "Facilities." Since it's so rarely a problem in country inns, we haven't included that information in those listings. Regrettably, security has become an issue in most cities. Never leave anything visible inside the car; it's an invitation for break-in and theft.

Christmas travel

Many people love to travel to a country inn or hotel at Christmas. Quite a number of places do stay open through the holidays, but the extent to which the occasion is celebrated varies widely indeed. We know of many inns that decorate beautifully, serve a fabulous meal, and organize all kinds of traditional Christmas activities. But we also know of others, especially in ski areas, that do nothing more than throw a few token ornaments on a tree. Be sure to inquire.

Is innkeeping for me?

Many of our readers fantasize about running their own inn; for some the fantasy will become a reality. Before taking the plunge, it's vital to find out as much as you can about this demanding business. Begin by reading *So You Want to Be an Innkeeper*, by Pat Hardy, Jo Ann Bell, and

Mary Davies. Hardy and Bell are co-directors of the Professional Association of Innkeepers, International (PAII—pronounced "pie") which also publishes *Innkeeping Newsletter,* various materials for would-be innkeepers, and coordinates workshops for aspiring innkeepers. For details contact PAII, P.O. Box 90710, Santa Barbara, California 93190; 805–569–1853, or visit their Internet website at www.paii.org. Another good book is *How to Start and Run Your Own Bed & Breakfast Inn* by long-time innkeepers Ripley Hotch and Carl Glassman, covering everything from financing to marketing to day-to-day innkeeping responsibilities ($14.95; Stackpole Books, P.O. Box 1831, Harrisburg, Pennsylvania 17105; 800–732–3669). Another excellent source, especially in the East, are consultants Bill Oates and Heide Bredfeldt. Contact them at P.O. Box 1162, Brattleboro, Vermont 05301; 802–254–5931, to find out when and where they'll be offering their next prospective innkeepers seminar. Bill and Heide are highly respected pros in this field and have worked with innkeepers facing a wide range of needs and problems; Bill's newsletter, *Innquest,* is written for prospective innkeepers looking to buy property. An equally good alternative is Lodging Resources Workshops, 98 South Fletcher Avenue, Amelia Island, Florida 32034; 888–201–7602. Director Dave Caples owns the Elizabeth Pointe Lodge in Amelia Island, and has been conducting workshops throughout the U.S. since 1992. Last but not least is *Yellow Brick Road*, a well-established newsletter that recently changed its focus to provide "insight for aspiring innkeepers." Subscriptions are $45 annually; single copy, $8. Contact Bobbi Zane, P.O. Box 1600, Julian, California 92036; 760–765–1224.

For more information

The best sources of travel information in this country and in Canada are absolutely free; in many cases, you don't even have to supply the cost of a stamp or telephone call. They are the state and provincial tourist offices.

For each state you'll be visiting, request a copy of the official state map, which will show you every little highway and byway and will make exploring much more fun; it will also have information on state parks and major attractions in concise form. Ask also for a calendar of events and for information on topics of particular interest, such as fishing or antiquing, vineyards or crafts; many states have published B&B directories, and some are quite informative. If you're going to an area of particular tourist interest, you might also want to ask the state office to give you the name of the regional tourist board for more detailed information. Most states have toll-free numbers; call 800–555–1212 to get the numbers you need. If there's no toll-free listing, call the information operators for the relevant states, and ask them to check for the number under the state's capital city. Many states have also established websites on the Internet; use search engines to see what you can find.

You may also want to contact the local chamber of commerce for information on local sights and events of interest or even an area map. You can get the necessary addresses and telephone numbers from the inn or hotel where you'll be staying or from the state tourist office.

If you are one of those people who never travel with fewer than three guidebooks (which includes us), you will find the AAA Tour Guides to be especially helpful. The guides are distributed free on request to members, and cover hotels, restaurants, and sightseeing information. If you're not already an AAA member, *we'd strongly urge you join before your next trip;* in addition to their road service, they offer quality guide books and maps, and an excellent discount program at many hotels (including a number listed here).

Guidebooks are published only once every year or two; if you'd like to have a more frequent update, we'd suggest one of the following:

Country Inns/Bed & Breakfasts (P.O. Box 182, South Orange, New Jersey 07079; 800–877–5491), $23, 6 issues annually. You know what they say about a picture being worth a thousand words. A must for inngoers.

The Discerning Traveler (504 West Mermaid Lane, Philadelphia, Pennsylvania 19118; 800–673–7834 or 215–247–5578), $50, 6 issues annually, $8 single copy. Picks a single destination in the New England, Mid-Atlantic, or Southern states and covers it in real depth—sights, restaurants, lodging, and more. The authors have published three delightful books on the subject as well.

Easy Escapes (P.O. Box 120365, Boston, Massachusetts 02112–0365), $47, 10 issues annually, $6 single copy. Covers inns, hotels, and resorts in the U.S. and the world; exceptionally honest and forthright. Each issue usually covers one or two destinations in a breezy, informal style.

Harper's Hideaway Report (P.O. Box 300, Whitefish, Montana 59937), $125, 12 issues annually. Covers the best (and most expensive) inns, hotels, resorts in the U.S. and abroad.

The Internet: Those of you with on-line access will want to check out the huge amount of travel information found on the World Wide Web. Start with our own website, at http://www.inns.com, where you'll find thousands of listings and photographs. From there, take a look at some of the other inn directories, as well as the many sites devoted to state and regional travel information. Of equal interest are the chat rooms and bulletin boards covering bed & breakfasts; you can find them on the Internet as well as on the proprietary services like America on Line and the Microsoft Network.

Where is my favorite inn?

In reading through this book, you may find that your favorite inn is not listed, or that a well-known inn has been omitted from this edition. Why? Two reasons, basically: In several cases, establishments have been dropped because our readers had unsatisfactory experiences. Feel free to contact us for details. Other establishments have been omitted because we've had little or no reader or innkeeper feedback. This may mean that readers visiting these hotels and inns had satisfactory experiences but were not sufficiently impressed to write about them, or that readers were pleased but just assumed that someone else would take the trouble. If the latter applies, please, please, do write and let us know of your experiences. We try to visit as many inns as possible ourselves, but it is impossible to visit everyplace, every year. So please, keep those cards, letters, and telephone calls coming! As an added incentive, we will be sending free copies of the next edition of this book to our most helpful respondents.

Little inns of horror

We try awfully hard to list only the most worthy establishments, but sometimes the best-laid plans of mice and travel writers do go astray. Please understand that whenever we receive a complaint about an entry in our guide we feel terrible, and do our best to investigate the situation. Readers occasionally send us complaints about establishments listed in *other* guidebooks; these are quite helpful as warning signals.

The most common complaints we receive—and the least forgivable—are on the issue of dirt. Scummy sinks and bathtubs, cobwebbed windows, littered porches, mildewed carpeting, water-stained ceilings, and grimy linens are all stars of this horror show.

Next in line are problems dealing with the lack of maintenance: peeling paint and wallpaper; sagging, soft, lumpy mattresses; radiators that don't get hot and those that make strange noises; windows that won't open, windows that won't close, windows with no screens, decayed or inoperable window shades; moldy shower curtains, rusty shower stalls, worn-out towels, fluctuating water temperatures, dripping faucets, and showers that only dribble, top the list.

Food complaints come next on this disaster lineup: poorly prepared canned or frozen food when fresh is readily available; meals served on paper, plastic, or worst of all, styrofoam; and insensitivity to dietary needs. Some complaints are received about unhelpful, abrasive, or abusive innkeepers, with a few more about uncaring, inept, or invisible staff. Complaints are most common in full-service inns when the restaurant business preoccupies the owners' attention, leaving overnight guests to suffer. Last but not least are noise headaches: trucks and trains that sound like they're heading for your pillow, and being awakened by the sound of someone snoring—in the next room. More tricky are questions of taste—high Victorian might look elegant to you, funereal to me; my collectibles could be your Salvation Army thriftshop donation. In short, there are more than a few inns and hotels that give new meaning to the phrase "having reservations"; fortunately they're many times outnumbered by the many wonderful places listed in this guide.

Pet peeves

Although we may genuinely like an inn, minor failings can keep it from being truly wonderful. Heading our list of pet peeves is inadequate bedside reading lights and tables. We know that there is not always room for a second table, but a light can always be attached to the wall. For reasons of both safety and comfort, a lamp should be at every bedside. Another reader is irked by inadequate bathroom lighting: "I think it must be an innkeepers' conspiracy to keep me from ever getting my makeup on properly." *(SU)* Other readers object to overly friendly innkeepers: "The innkeeper chatted with us all during break-fast, and was disappointed that we didn't plan to go in to say goodbye after we loaded up the car. Innkeepers should remember that the guests are customers, not long-lost relatives." *(KW)* Another common gripe concerns clutter: "Although pretty and interesting, the many col-lectibles left us no space for our personal belongings." And: "Instruc-tions were posted everywhere—how to operate door locks, showers, heat, air-conditioning, and more." Anything you'd like to add?

Criteria for entries

If this guide to the inns and hotels of the U.S. had included all the en-tries appearing in our regional editions, this publication would have totaled over 2,000 pages. So how did we manage to condense the in-formation to about 500 pages? With great difficulty. First of all, in areas of strong traveler appeal, where there are many inns, we included full write-ups on just a handful of places, covering the others more briefly under the "**Also recommended**" heading. That part was relatively easy. Secondly, we did not include the inns in towns well off the beaten path. We felt that for a country-wide guide, attention must be focused on key tourist and business centers. That required some really tough deci-sions, since it meant excluding many of our favorite places. If you plan any in-depth exploring of a particular region, please consult the ap-propriate regional edition for optimal coverage.

Unlike many other guides, inns cannot pay to be listed in this book. All selections are made by the editors, based on guest recommendations and personal visits. Entries are written and compiled by the editors, not the inns. When we update a regional guide, inns that received full en-tries in the previous edition, and that will also appear in the new edi-tion are charged a processing fee to help defray our research costs. There is no fee for new entries, and no fee for listing in our *U.S.A. & Canada* edition. If we receive significant complaints or insufficient rec-ommendations about a particular property, we omit their listing. As al-ways, what matters most to us is the feedback we get from you, our readers.

About our name

We've changed our name from *America's Wonderful Little Hotels & Inns* to *America's Favorite Inns, B&Bs & Small Hotels*. Why? First, we felt that it better reflects what we're all about. Properties listed here are *your* favorites—if you don't like them, we don't include them. Since the ma-jority of our entries are inns and B&Bs, the new title better reflects their importance. Last but not least, reasons connected with the copyright were also a factor.

Important Note on Area Codes

Telephone area codes are changing faster than a two-year-old's attention span. Although we've tried to incorporate all the new ones in our listings, many numbers were still in the "to be decided" state at press time. *If you dial a number listed here and get an announcement that it's not in service, we urge you to call the information operator and see if that region has been assigned a new area code.* Please forgive the inconvenience!

Free copy of INNroads newsletter

Want to stay up-to-date on our latest finds? Send a business-size, self-addressed, stamped envelope with 55 cents postage and we'll send you the latest issue, *free!* While you're at it, why not enclose a report on any inns you've recently visited? Use the forms at the back of the book or your own stationery.

Key to Abbreviations and Symbols

For complete information and explanations, please see the Introduction.

¢ Especially good value for overnight accommodation.
♦♦ Families welcome. Most (but not all) have cribs, baby-sitting, games, play equipment, and reduced rates for children.
✗ Meals served to public; reservations recommended or required.
✠ Tennis court and swimming pool and/or lake on grounds. Golf usually on grounds or nearby.
♿ Limited or full wheelchair access; call for details.
Rates: Range from least expensive room in low season to most expensive room in peak season.
Room only: No meals included; European Plan (EP).
B&B: Bed and breakfast; includes breakfast, sometimes afternoon/evening refreshment.
MAP: Modified American Plan; includes breakfast and dinner.
Full board: Three meals daily.
Alc lunch: À la carte lunch; average price of entrée plus nonalcoholic drink, tax, tip.
Alc dinner: Average price of three-course dinner, including half bottle of house wine, tax, tip.
Prix fixe dinner: Three- to five-course set dinner, excluding wine, tax, tip unless otherwise noted.
Extras: Noted if available. Always confirm in advance. Pets are not permitted unless specified; if you are allergic, ask for details; *most innkeepers have pets.*

We Want to Hear from You!

As you know, this book is effective only with your help. We really need to know about your experiences and discoveries. If you stayed at an inn or hotel listed here, we want to know how it was. Did it live up to our description? Exceed it? Was it what you expected? Did you like it? Were you disappointed? Delighted? Have you discovered new establishments that we should add to the next edition?

Tear out one of the report forms at the back of this book (or use your own stationery if you prefer) and write today. *Even if you write only "Fully endorse existing entry" you will have been most helpful.*
Thank You!

Connecticut

The Griswold Inn

As small as Connecticut is, the state has several areas of interest to tourists, which are where the best inns tend to be found. Because the listings for each area are scattered throughout this chapter (listed alphabetically by town), here are a few notes on the different regions. (Check the "Location" heading for each entry.)

Connecticut River Valley: Although the Connecticut River extends far past Connecticut all the way to northern Vermont, the area we're describing starts just below Middletown and extends south about 25 miles to the river's mouth at Old Lyme/Old Saybrook. Due to a happy accident of nature—a sandbar at the mouth of the river prevented deep-draft ships from entering—commercial traffic after the 1840s went to deep harbors such as New Haven. Consequently, these unspoiled river towns retain much of their early character.

Area attractions include the Goodspeed Opera House at East Haddam, Gillette Castle at Hadlyme, Florence Griswold Museum in Old Lyme, and the antique shops and train and riverboat rides starting in Essex. It's about a 2½-hour ride from New York and Boston, and only 45 minutes from Hartford.

For inns in this area, see **Chester, Clinton, Deep River, East Haddam, Essex, Ivoryton, Madison, Old Lyme, Old Saybrook,** and **Westbrook.**

Fairfield County: Although it's better known for high-priced real estate than tourist attractions, this pretty part of New England is closest to New York City and its airports. Its inns are convenient for weekend getaways from the city, and good places for a first or last night's stay if you're touring New England.

For inns in this area, see **Greenwich** and **Ridgefield.**

Litchfield Hills: Litchfield Hills occupies the northwest corner of the state and used to be known as the foothills of the Berkshires. This area was a popular summer retreat 100 years ago; many of the places we list were built either as inns or as private mansions during that period. Today the area still offers beautiful lakes, mountains, and picturesque villages and is only 2 to 2½ hours from New York City. A full range of recreational pleasures is available, from tennis, golf, hiking, and canoeing to cross-country and downhill skiing, plus a number of art and antique shops, summer theater, and concert programs. Rates are highest in summer and during October fall foliage, when two-night weekend minimums are the rule.

Reader tip: "If you're traveling north from coastal Connecticut to the Litchfield Hills area, take Interstate 684 to Route 22 in New York State, or Route 8 from Bridgeport. Route 7 often has heavy traffic and congestion, with tantalizing snippets of superhighway." *(RSS)*

For inns in this area, see **Lakeville, New Milford, New Preston, Norfolk,** and **Salisbury, Connecticut,** plus **Great Barrington, North Egremont, Riverton,** and **Sheffield, Massachusetts.**

Mystic/Eastern Connecticut Shore: From Madison up to the Rhode Island border at Westerly, the Connecticut shore offers many lovely towns and beaches. Areas of major interest are Mystic, with its maritime museum and aquarium; Groton, with the USS *Nautilus* National Submarine Memorial and Connecticut College Arboretum; New London, home to the US Coast Guard Academy, and home port to the tall ship *Eagle*; Ledyard with the immensely popular Foxwoods Casino on the Mashantucket Pequot Indian reservation; and Stonington Borough, one of the prettiest coastal villages in Connecticut. This area is 125 miles northeast of New York City, 100 miles southwest of Boston.

For inns in this area, see **Mystic/Old Mystic.**

Northeastern Connecticut: If it's possible to have an "undiscovered" section of a state as small as Connecticut, then this area wins first place—even its tourist council calls it "The Quiet Corner." Area attractions include wineries, herb farms and greenhouses of note, as well as such historic sites as the home of Nathan Hale, America's first spy, and a museum devoted to the history of textiles. Those who love antiques will enjoy its many shops. For more information contact the Northeast Connecticut Visitors District, P.O. Box 598, Putnam, CT 06260; 203–928–1228 or 800–CT–BOUND.

Peak-season rates along the shore generally run from May or June through October. Off-season rates are considerably lower and represent an especially good value during April and May, when the weather is usually just right for sightseeing.

BETHEL

Information please: Just south of Danbury in southwestern Connecticut is the **Tailoring Inn** (40 Durant Avenue, 06801; 203–778–8740), named for the tailoring talents of Italian-born owner Franco Rossi, and his American-born wife Geri. Two well-equipped suites are available.

Rates, including a continental breakfast, range from $75–110. Children are welcome. "Friendly innkeepers, comfortable accommodations, delicious food with great espresso." *(TC)*

CHESTER

For additional area inns, see **Deep River, East Haddam, Essex, Ivoryton, Madison, Old Lyme, Old Saybrook,** and **Westbrook.**

The Inn at Chester 🏃 ✕ ⚲
318 West Main Street, 06412

Tel: 860–526–9541
800–949–STAY
Fax: 860–526–4387
E-mail: innkeeper@innatchester.com
URL: http://www.innatchester.com

In 1778 John Parmelee built a farmhouse for his family along the Killingworth Turnpike in Chester. In 1982 this same house, and a barn transported to the property, became the Inn at Chester; two new wings for guest accommodations were added later. Innkeeper Deborah Moore bought and re-opened the inn in 1992 and has won rave reviews for the fine meals served in the inn's Post and Beam Restaurant, housed in the barn with its massive stone fireplace and period chandeliers. Under the creative hand of chef Lorelei Reu-Helfer, the dinners include such entrées as duck breast with apple and sweet potato gratin, rack of lamb with Brussel sprouts and fennel, and salmon with roasted tomato coulis. Dunk's Landing offers lighter fare in a tavern setting. Deborah, a retired Merchant Marine officer, vowed never to have a nautical theme to her inn, but her mementos are slowly finding their way to this room.

"Quiet but convenient setting, well back from the main road. Pleasant grounds with pond and flowers. Efficient and pleasant management. Charming dining room with appealing menu. Delightful breakfast buffet of breads, muffins, coffee cakes, bagels, juice, and fruit, enjoyed on the enclosed sun porch. Surprisingly good fitness equipment. Comfortable guest room with Williamsburg-style decor; good bathroom amenities. Small-inn feel despite its size." *(Janeen LaFaver)* "Superb, leisurely dining. Enjoyed the antique puzzles in the bar." *(Gina Miller)* "Breakfast included muffins, scones, bagels, and breads." *(Mary Belle)* "The Colonial-style guest rooms have Eldred Wheeler reproduction furniture and queen-size canopy or twin-size beds. Outdoor activities are numerous, but one can just as easily borrow a book from the library, and settle in a chair by the 20-foot fireplace and read all afternoon." *(Mrs. George Ainsworth)* "Large airy common areas with exposed wooden beams; even the hallways are spacious with sofas and chairs under skylights, and little corners with chairs and lamps." *(Abby Humphrey)* "Lots of space and privacy in this small hotel." *(MW)*

Open All year.
Rooms 1 3-bedroom guest house, 1 suite, 42 doubles—all with full private bath, telephone, TV, desk, air-conditioning. 2 with fireplace. Guest house with 3 fireplaces, 2 sitting rooms, dining room, kitchenette.

Facilities Restaurant, tavern with music Thurs.–Sat. evenings, dining room with fireplace, living room with fireplace, piano; library with fireplace, board games; game room with pool table, exercise room with sauna, conference rooms. 12 acres with tennis, lawn games, bicycles, hiking, cross-country skiing, ice-skating. Nearby lake for swimming, boating; CT River for boating. 20 min. to downhill skiing.
Location CT River Valley. 30 m S of Hartford. 5 m from town. From I-95, take Exit 69 (Rte. 9). Go N on Rte. 9 to Exit 6. Turn W on Rte. 148, go 3.2 m to Chester.
Restrictions Smoking restricted in dining room.
Credit cards Amex, MC, Visa.
Rates B&B, $215 suite; $105–185 double. Extra person, $25. Holiday weekend minimum stay. Alc lunch, $10; alc dinner, $35–50; tavern, $8–15. Package rates.
Extras Wheelchair access; some rooms equipped for disabled. By prior arrangement: airport/station pickups; pets; crib, babysitting.

CLINTON

For additional area inns, see **Chester, Deep River, East Haddam, Essex, Ivoryton, Madison, Old Lyme, Old Saybrook,** and **Westbrook.**

Captain Dibbell House ¢
21 Commerce Street, 06413

Tel: 860–669–1646
Fax: 860–669–2300
URL: http//www.clintonct.com/dibbell

Just crossing the century-old wisteria-covered footbridge that leads to the Captain Dibbell House will put you in the mood for a relaxing visit at the shore. Built in 1866, this house has been owned by Ellis and Helen Adams since 1986. Furnishings include a comfortable mixture of antiques, family heirlooms, auction finds, and New England artwork and crafts. Breakfast includes fresh fruit and juice, cereal, home-baked muffins, scones or coffee cake, plus such entrées as baked French toast with sausage, or perhaps buttermilk waffles with bacon. Other thoughtful touches include fruit baskets, afternoon treats, fresh flowers (in season), bathrobes, twice-daily housekeeping, and turndown service with chocolate pillow treats.

"Beautiful setting with a large, private, fenced yard, complete with a gazebo where we enjoyed our breakfast. The guest pantry is well-stocked with glasses and a small refrigerator filled with cold drinks. Ellis bakes delicious cookies and scones." *(Richard & Holly Benton)* "Helen Adams was a wonderful hostess, acquainting me with the house, and making sure I was comfortable. Tucked under the eaves, the delightful Garden Room has lots of plants, unusual ceiling angles, double wedding ring quilt, a wooden bench, a white wicker rocker, sun pouring in the windows with hunter green wooden slatted shutters, and a welcoming atmosphere. I also liked the Morning Room, with a huge bay window, a white iron bed, blue wallpaper, and red accents, for a spacious, nautical feel. The Captain's Room was more traditionally Victorian with a queen-size brass bed, lace curtains, a dried flower arrangement above the bed, and an antique washbasin. Off the comfortable sitting room is the breakfast room, where we enjoyed a baked egg dish with delicious, melt-in-your-mouth buttermilk scones, baked by Ellis." *(Abby Humphrey)*

"Helen and Ellis know when guests want to chat, and when they want privacy. Breakfast included melon, coffee cake, strata, and sausage. Ellis bakes delicious afternoon cookies—chocolate chip one day, oatmeal raisin the next. A cat motif runs throughout the decor; two beautiful Abyssinian cats have the run of this spotlessly clean house. Our room had a small but modern bathroom and a firm, comfortable bed." *(John Corcoran)* "Quiet side street, yet close to the main one; first-rate B&B with lots of character." *(Elizabeth Dakin)*

Open April–Dec.
Rooms 4 doubles—all with private bath, radio, air-conditioning, ceiling fan.
Facilities Living room with fireplace, TV, games; breakfast room. Guest refrigerator, bicycles, beach towels & chairs. ¾ acre with gardens, gazebo. Swimming, sailing nearby.
Location CT shore. 38 m S of Hartford, 25 m E of New Haven. Walk to town & beach. From I-95, take Exit 63 to Rte. 81 S to stoplight at intersection of Rtes. 81 & 1. Go through light (Library Lane), go right onto Commerce St. to inn immediately on right.
Restrictions No smoking. No children under 14.
Credit cards Amex, MC, Visa.
Rates B&B, $85–105 double, $65–85 single. Corporate rates. Discount for 3-night stay.
Extras Airport/station pickups.

DEEP RIVER

For additional area inns, see **Chester, Clinton, East Haddam, Essex, Ivoryton, Madison, Old Lyme, Old Saybrook,** and **Westbrook.**

Riverwind Inn
209 Main Street, 06417

Tel: 860–526–2014

In 1983, Barbara Barlow left her native Smithfield, Virginia, for Connecticut. She discovered the abandoned 1750s farmhouse that is now Riverwind, and spent almost a year restoring it, doing nearly all the work herself. Her husband Bob Bucknall joined her in 1987, and completed a four-room addition, preserving the traditional feel of the original building. The decor includes an extensive collection of New England and Southern country antiques—quilts, jugs, basket, and much more, artfully displayed throughout the entire inn. Barbara notes that the inn's "best features are the decor and the large number of common rooms, affording ample space for privacy or socializing." Breakfast is served from 9–10:30 A.M. at guests' choice of large table or small tables, and consists of Smithfield ham, an egg casserole or perhaps French toast, fresh fruit and juice, and such baked treats as coffeecake, trifle, or biscuits.

"Hearts and Flowers is our favorite room, from the heart motif in the stained glass window to the thoughtful extras—the bathrobes, soaps, Poland Spring water, and mint chocolates. Delicious breakfasts. Lots of area activities, plus great restaurants. Barbara decorates beautifully for Christmas, too." *(Marilyn Parker)*

Open All year.
Rooms 1 suite, 7 doubles—all with full private bath and/or shower, radio, clock, air-conditioning. 6 with ceiling fan, 2 with balcony/deck.
Facilities Dining room, parlor, keeping room, study; all with fireplace; piano in parlor; guest refrigerator, porch. 1 acre.
Location S CT; CT River Valley. ½ hr. NE of New Haven; ¼ m to center of town. Take I-91 or I-95 to Rte. 9 (Exit 69 from I-95). Take Rte. 9 to Exit 4. Go left on Rte. 154 to inn 1.5 m on right.
Restrictions No smoking in bedrooms. Children 12 and over.
Credit cards MC, Visa.
Rates B&B, $155 suite, $105–185 double. Extra person, 50% more. 2-night weekend minimum. Tips appreciated.
Extras Train station pickups.

EAST HADDAM

For additional area inns, see **Chester, Clinton, Deep River, Essex, Ivoryton, Madison, Old Lyme, Old Saybrook,** and **Westbrook.**

Bishopsgate Inn　　　　　　　　　　*Tel:* 860–873–1677
7 Norwich Road, 06423　　　　　　　　　*Fax:* 860–873–3898
　　　　　　　　　　E-mail: ctkagel@bishopsgate.com
　　　　　　　　　　URL: http://www.bishopsgate.com

A Colonial-style home built in 1818 by a local merchant and shipbuilder, Bishopsgate was restored as an inn in 1985, and has been owned by the Kagel family—Colin Senior and Jane, plus Colin Junior and his wife Lisa—since 1995. Breakfast is served at the dining room table between 8 and 10 A.M., and might include waffles, baked eggs, soufflés or perhaps omelets or quiche, plus pastry and fruit. A recent winter dinner menu consisted of feta and walnut spinach salad with basil dressing, baked salmon with rosemary garlic mashed potatoes and roast winter vegetable, with raspberry cheesecake for dessert.

"Welcoming atmosphere and unpretentious warmth allow guests to feel like family. Wonderful Christmas decorations." *(Stuart Leyton)* "Immaculately maintained inn." *(Lee Toole)* "Tasty home-cooked breakfast. Beautifully decorated old home." *(Anne & Win Patterson)* "Comfortable beds with featherbeds. The hosts brought refreshments to our room upon our arrival. Lively conversation with our hosts during our delightful breakfast, thoughtfully prepared." *(Angeline Crancy)* "A clean, bright inn within walking distance of the Goodspeed Opera House. Ample parking." *(Richard Calilli)* "Magnificent four-poster bed. We needed only a match to light our in-room fireplace. Service with a smile; friendly, informative hospitality, with careful attention to detail; excellent value." *(Michelle A. & Frederick A. Warburton)*

Open All year.

Rooms 1 suite, 5 doubles—all with full private bath and/or shower, radio, clock, air-conditioning. 4 with fireplace, 1 with deck, sauna.

Facilities Dining room, living room with fireplace, library/den with books/games. 1.25 acres with gardens, off-street parking. Hiking, mountain biking, riverboat cruises on CT River nearby.

Location Lower CT River Valley. 2.5 hrs. from NYC, Boston. Historic district. Take I-95 to Exit 69 to Rte. 9. From Rte 9 take Exit 7 to East Haddam. Go left at 1st blinking light. Go right at 1st light & follow Rte. 82 over bridge 1½ blocks to inn on left. From Hartford, take I-91 S to Rte. 9. Go S on Rte. 9 to Exit 7 & follow directions above.

Restrictions No smoking. Children 5 and over. Traffic noise possible in front rooms.

Credit cards MC, Visa.

Rates B&B, $140 suite, $95–115 double. Extra person, $15. 2 night weekend minimum. By advance reservation: box lunch, $10–15; alc dinner, $25–40.

Extras Train station pickups with advance notice. Pets possible by prior arrangement only.

ESSEX

A most appealing town, Essex is home to the Connecticut River Museum, the Essex Steam Train and Riverboat ride, and a delightful Main Street, perfect for strolling, with many intriguing shops.

For additional area inns, see **Chester, Clinton, Deep River, East Haddam, Ivoryton, Madison, Old Lyme, Old Saybrook,** and **Westbrook.**

The Griswold Inn ¢ ⭒ ✕
36 Main Street, 06426

Tel: 860–767–1776
Fax: 860–767–0481

Built as an inn in 1776, the Griswold claims to be America's oldest continually operating inn, and is a longtime reader favorite. In its long history, the Gris has been owned by only six families; in 1995, it was purchased by three brothers, all Essex natives: Gregory, Douglas, and Geoffrey Paul. The decor is eclectic, with an exceptionally fine collection of maritime art and antiques from many periods; some guest-room floors have a "port or starboard list," a few are quite small. The Tap Room, where lively music—from sea chanteys to Dixieland—rings out nightly, was originally built as a schoolhouse in 1738, but was pulled to this location by a team of oxen in 1801. The Griswold serves hearty American food; the Sunday Hunt Breakfast is a tradition dating from the War of 1812. The breakfast for overnight guests includes fresh fruit and juice, cereal, English muffins, coffee and tea, served in the library.

"The rooms are quaint, cozy, and comfortable—some with exposed rough-hewn rafters." *(Betty Norman)* "The inn serves excellent and abundant portions of food in the attractive dining rooms (the Library was our favorite). The tavern is inviting, a gathering place for locals as well as guests. Our room in the annex was tiny but cozy and well decorated, with flowered print wallpaper, simple curtains, and a white bedspread. We especially liked the rustic Garden Suite, with a loft bedroom.

Their wonderful-smelling soap is made from a century-old recipe." *(Sally Ducot)* "Lovely, spacious guest room." *(Tina & James Kirkpatrick)* "Packed to the rafters on a Saturday night with banjo players and a great sing-along." *(William Gerhauser)*

"An old favorite that is only improving under new owners. Careful attention to detail. Although we had the last room available, the effective air-conditioner provided ventilation and sound-proofing. Quality mattress, pillows, towels. Freshly wallpapered; new sink and toilet; good bedside lights. Good water pressure in the shower; ample hot water. The restaurant is a New England classic, with a pub-type bar and a variety of interesting dining rooms. Pleasant, intelligent waitress. Complimentary corn relish and herbed cottage cheese spread and crackers. Delicious sausage sampler on sautéed spinach as a first course, followed by salmon with leeks and crabmeat. An excellent value." *(Nancy Barker)*

Open All year. Restaurant closed Christmas Eve & Day.

Rooms 13 suites, 17 doubles—all with private bath, telephone, air-conditioning, clock/radio. 8 suites with fireplace, 1 with wet bar, some with desk. Some rooms in annexes.

Facilities Restaurant, tavern with live entertainment, lounge with TV, library; fireplace in all public rooms.

Location CT River Valley. From I-95, take Exit 69, Rte. 9 N, to Exit 3. Go left at end of ramp, then right at light. Go to stop sign; take Middle Rd. to bottom of hill. Bear right at rotary onto Main St. to inn ¼ m on right.

Restrictions Restaurant/bar noise in some rooms. No smoking in guest rooms.

Credit cards Amex, MC, Visa.

Rates B&B, $135–185 suite, $90–115. Extra person, $10; no charge for children under 6. Alc lunch, $10–15; alc dinner, $20–35; Sunday brunch, $12.95; children's menu.

Extras Station pickups. Crib; babysitting by arrangement. French spoken.

GLASTONBURY

Butternut Farm ¢
1654 Main Street, 06033

Tel: 860–633–7197
Fax: 860–659–1758

If you have business in Hartford but prefer the warm atmosphere of a 1720 farmhouse to a chain hotel, take a short drive to Glastonbury and the Butternut Farm. This classic Colonial home was carefully restored by Don Reid, who exposed the boarded-up fireplaces, stripped the wide-board pine floors, and furnished the inn with fine 18th-century Connecticut antiques. The keeping room decor features an extensive collection of antique tools, fabrics, and pewter, herbs drying near the immense fireplace, and small fur pelts, just like any Colonial citizen would have; comfortable wingback chairs provide a cozy spot for studying them at leisure. The living room is more formal, with wood paneling around the windows, an Oriental rug, antique cherry highboy and table; blue and white Delft china is displayed on the walls.

"Combines authentic Colonial history with all modern comforts. Reading in bed was a pleasure with the clip-on lights on each side of our comfortable pencil-post bed; the bathroom had a good lighting, a nightlight, and a wall-mounted hairdryer. Plenty of private little spaces throughout the house for relaxing; the guest kitchen is fitted to look like an old pub. Breakfast included fresh juice, an herb-cheese omelet made from just-laid eggs, and toast with goat cheese and tomato jelly. Wonderful menagerie in the barn; four sweet Abyssinian cats live in the house (but don't shed)." *(NB, also MM)* "Comfortable, wonderful furnishings, helpful host, tasty breakfast." *(Virgina Baggett)*

Open All year.
Rooms 2 suites, 3 doubles—all with private bath and/or shower, telephone, radio, air-conditioning. 3 with fireplace, 2 with TV, 1 with refrigerator, desk. 1 suite in barn.
Facilities Keeping room, living room, dining room; each with fireplace, 1 with TV; guest kitchen, screened sun room. 2 acres with patio, herb gardens, lawn games. Barn with goats, chickens, pigeons, ducks, pheasants, geese, pigs, llama.
Location Central CT. 5 m SE of Hartford. Take I-91 or I-84 to Rte. 2 & exit at Glastonbury. Inn is on Main St., 1.6 m S of town, at corner of Whapley Rd.
Restrictions No smoking.
Credit cards Amex.
Rates B&B, $70–90 suite, double. Extra person, $15.
Extras Babysitting. French, some Italian & German spoken.

GREENWICH

If Greenwich is the starting point for your New England tour, you'll find a community that's an unusual (and expensive) mix of New England coastal village, suburban commuter town, and corporate headquarters. Greenwich celebrated its 350th anniversary in 1990, and history buffs can find a taste of the town's past at the Bush-Holley House and General Putnam's Cottage. Also worth a visit is the recently renovated Bruce Museum. Among corporate headquarters, Pepsico in neighboring Purchase, New York, is a standout; open to the public, its beautifully landscaped grounds are studded with museum-quality sculptures by Henry Moore, Brancusi, Calder, and many more.

Greenwich is located in Fairfield County, 29 miles northeast of New York City, just off both I-95 and the Merritt Parkway.

Information please: Under the new ownership of Rick and Cindy Kral in 1998 is the **Cos Cob Inn** (50 River Road, Cos Cob, 06807; 203–661–5845), just minutes from I-95 and all of Greenwich and Stamford. Overlooking the marinas of the Mianus River, close to Long Island Sound, this century-old mansard-roofed Victorian home has 14 guest rooms, combining period charm with such mod cons as private bath, TV/VCR, voice mail, data port, and air-conditioning; many have kitchenettes. A continental breakfast is served to guests in the common room. B&B double rates range from $99–189, suites to $279.

The Homestead Inn ✖
420 Field Point Road, 06830

Tel: 203–869–7500
Fax: 203–869–7502

The Homestead was built in 1799 by Augustus Mead; in 1859 it was sold and converted into an inn. Architecturally, it was transformed from a Colonial farmstead into a Victorian Italianate Gothic house, complete with distinctive belvedere and wraparound porches. In 1978, the Homestead was restored as an elegant hostelry, and was purchased by Theresa Carroll and Thomas Henkelmann in 1997. Guest rooms are found in both the original home, as well as in converted out-buildings. Rooms in the former have a more genuine historic feel, while the newer rooms tend to be more spacious, with modern baths, and better sound-proofing. The inn, set in the beautiful Belle Haven residential area—full of lovely old Victorian homes—is convenient to the interstate and to downtown Greenwich. The Homestead is also well known for its French restaurant, "Thomas Henkelmann," which has garnered praise from local and national media. Under the supervision of master chef Thomas, breakfast choices range from eggs Benedict to brioche French toast. Lunch entrées might include striped bass with mushroom risotto and grilled veal with basil tomato fondue; dinner possibilities are Dover sole with artichoke purée and rack of lamb with herb crust.

"Our room was superior in every sense. Good reading lamps, terry bathrobes, huge towels, bidet, and all the shampoos and bath salts one could use." *(MAA)* "We had an exceptional dinner with two standout entrées of amazingly flavorful lamb and veal. Servings were generous, and both dishes were individually garnished with a variety of perfectly prepared vegetables. Service was attentive and professional, never intrusive or familiar." *(SWS)* "We stayed in the General's Suite, a comfortable room with lovely facilities." *(Mr. & Mrs. K.C. Keller)* "Evening conversation on the veranda is special. A steaming cup of strong black coffee, ready before 7 A.M., sets the stage for early morning contemplation of the dew glistening on the grass of the expansive front lawn. Then breakfast in the enclosed front dining porch. Especially good bran and corn muffins." *(John Blewer)* "A sophisticated country inn; excellent housekeeping, food, service." *(MP, also Pam Phillips)*

Open All year. Restaurant closed Labor Day & New Year's Day.

Rooms 6 suites, 14 doubles, 3 singles—all with private bath and/or shower, telephone with call waiting/voice mail/data port; radio, TV, desk, air-conditioning. 8 rooms and suites in the "Inn Between," and 3 in the "Cottage."

Facilities Bar, restaurant, common room, meeting room, porch. Three acres with gardens, lawn furniture and terrace. Large park, tennis, golf nearby.

Location 1 m from town center. From NY, take I-95 to Exit 3. Turn left at bottom of ramp. Go to 2nd light, turn left onto Horseneck Lane. At end of road, go left onto Field Pt. Rd. to inn on right.

Credit cards Amex, DC, MC, Visa.

Rates Room only, $250–300 suite, $150–185 double, $110 single. Alc breakfast $10–16; alc lunch, $35–55; alc dinner, $55–75.

Extras Three working fireplaces in the restaurant. Crib. German, French, Spanish, Arabic, and Portuguese spoken.

Stanton House Inn ¢   *Tel:* 203–869–2110
76 Maple Avenue, 06830   *Fax:* 203–629–2116

Stanton House is an imposing Colonial-frame house, built around 1840 and enlarged in 1890 under the supervision of noted architect Stanford White. It remained a private residence until 1937, when Nora Stanton Barney converted it into a hotel, naming it after her grandmother, feminist reformer Elizabeth Cady Stanton. After a period of decay, Tog and Doreen Pearson restored this fine old mansion as a B&B in 1985. Rooms are bright and cheery, decorated with Laura Ashley– and Waverly-style fabrics and period furnishings, many with queen- or king-size beds. A complete fire sprinkler system enhances guests' safety. Available from 7–8:30 A.M. weekdays, and 8–10:30 A.M. on weekends, the self-service breakfast buffet includes juice, coffee, tea, yogurt, granola, cereals, home-baked muffins, Danish, bagels, and fruit.

"Charming rooms, warm atmosphere, personal service, excellent housekeeping, convenient location. The Pearsons make you feel as if you are a guest in their own home. Each room is different; #20 and 39 are my favorites." *(William Theodore Federici)* "A charming, spotlessly clean inn with a warm, friendly atmosphere. Ideal for business and vacation travelers. Wonderful grounds and pool; ample parking." *(Richard Varney)* "Ideal for either the business traveler (room #22, 24) or for a romantic get-away (room #14). The best continental breakfast I've had anywhere. This is the cleanest and most organized inn I've stayed in. Great pool and grounds for the warmer months." *(Richard Varney)* "Located on a relatively quiet street, surrounded by equally lovely older homes, churches, and schools. Our suite (#25), was located on the second floor with windows facing the side yard so we didn't get any street noise. The room had yellow-and-white striped Waverly wallpaper and charming furniture. Tog was delighted to provide restaurant suggestions, excellent travel advice, and directions." *(Nancy Schultz)* "A staff member checked often and replenished breakfast supplies as needed. Convenient location; friendly, helpful staff." *(Peg Bedini)*

"Wonderfully located near a classic New England stone church, yet only a short walk to Greenwich shops and restaurants. Rooms vary in size, but all are spotless and cheerful. One of my favorites is on the top floor, looking both south and east with four windows, a seating/reading alcove, old-fashioned claw-foot tub in a windowed bathroom, queen-size four-poster bed, nice writing secretary, and large closets." *(Richard Lutzy, also SWS)*

Open All year.
Rooms 1 king suite with kitchenette, 7 mini-suites, 12 doubles—20 with private bath and/or shower, 2 rooms sharing 1 bath. All with telephone/voice mail, radio, TV, desk, air-conditioning, fan. Some with refrigerator, pull-out sofa; 2 with fireplace.
Facilities 2 parlors with fireplace, dining room with fireplace. Fax, copier. Off-street parking. 2 acres with garden, patio, swimming pool.
Location ¼ m to town center. Take Exit 4 off I-95. Go N on Indian Field Rd. about 1 m to Rte. 1 (Putnam Ave.). Go left about 1 m to Maple Ave. (Look for

large gray stone Second Congregational Church on right.) Take sharp right just before church, go approx. 100 yds. to inn on left.

Restrictions No children under 7.
Credit cards Amex, Discover, MC, Visa.
Rates B&B, $179 suite, $120–159 mini-suite, $89–115 double. Extra person, $20. 2-night weekend, holiday minimum.
Extras French, Spanish spoken.

HARTFORD

For additional area entries, see listings under **Bristol, Farmington, Glastonbury,** and **Simsbury.**

Information please: A short walk from the Mark Twain House is **The 1895 House** (97 Girard Avenue, 06105; 860–232–0014), a Colonial Revival home with bay and Palladian windows. Thoughtful in-room touches include fruit, cookies, candy, and terry-cloth robes. Breakfast, served at guests' convenience, consists of fruit, juices, muffins, or toast, and such entrées as Mexican brunch pie or French toast with ricotta cheese. Three guest rooms are available at B&B double rates of $70–85.

A small luxury hotel, **The Goodwin Hotel** (1 Haynes Street, 06103; 800–922–5006 or 860–246–7500) is based in the renovated downtown residence of turn-of-the-century financier J.P. Morgan. Behind the hotel's landmark brownstone façade is a four-story barrel-vaulted atrium, plus 136 guest rooms handsomely furnished in period decor. Pierpont's, the hotel's acclaimed restaurant, specializes in American regional cuisine served in elegant surroundings, while the America's Cup Lounge offers lighter fare and cocktails amidst rich woods, leathers, maritime paintings, and books. Double rates range from $149–229; ask about weekend and promotional rates.

Six miles north of Hartford is **The Charles R. Hart House** (1046 Windsor Avenue, Windsor 06095; 860–688–5555), a century-old Queen Anne mansion, beautifully restored with Victorian antiques and rich Bradbury & Bradbury wallpapers. The double rate of $65–109 for the four guest rooms includes a full breakfast. "Gracious hospitality, lovely decor, excellent breakfast." (*Rose Ciccone*)

IVORYTON

Copper Beech Inn ✕   *Tel:* 860–767–0330
46 Main Street, 06442   *Fax:* 860–767–7840
        URL: http://www.copperbeechinn.com

The Copper Beech Inn was built about 100 years ago by a wealthy ivory merchant. As the town's name suggests, ivory was once its principal product and source of income. The sprawling mansion derives its current name from the enormous copper beech tree that spreads over the front lawn.

Eldon and Sally Senner bought the inn in 1988 and have worked hard to maintain and improve it. They expanded a side porch to create a Victorian-style conservatory for quiet seating or pre-dinner cocktails, and rejuvenated the gracious terraced English gardens with thousands of spring-flowering bulbs. The inn is well known for its restaurant, offering country French cuisine in an elegant, formal setting. A recent dinner began with artichokes, spinach, and goat cheese wrapped in pastry served with a tomato-mushroom cream; followed by breast of pheasant; and concluded with mango and coconut sorbets served with a compote of grilled pineapple.

"Ivoryton is a peaceful town featuring wonderful old homes and the Ivoryton Playhouse. A perfect base for exploring Connecticut's historic seaport towns, minutes away from Essex on the Connecticut River and close to Goodspeed Opera House and Gillette's Castle." *(Maria Schmidt)* "The breakfast buffet of fresh fruit and juice, cereal, croissants, and assorted pastries was served in the same dining room as dinner. The attentive innkeepers ensured that supplies were ample. We had a spacious room in the carriage house, with a four-poster bed, couch, table, a Jacuzzi in the bathroom, and a deck in back. Pretty grounds, too." *(Lynda Worrell)*

"Our upstairs room in the carriage house had access to a porch overlooking the quiet hillside. The vaulted ceilings were supported by old barn beams." *(June Horn)* "Our spacious room at the back of the main house was quiet and relaxing." *(Mrs. Michael Cromis)* "My spacious room upstairs in the main house had wing chairs, a rocker, plants, a bay window, and plenty of closet space." *(Melissa Robin)* "The public areas and guest rooms are well appointed and carefully maintained, with fresh flowers and live plants. The comfortable guest rooms have good reading lights, lovely sheets and quilts, comfortable mattresses, and current magazines. Dinner is expertly prepared, and most entrées have wonderful sauces. The vegetarian entrées are complex and delicious—perhaps glazed root vegetables with grilled polenta and black bean purée. The service is professional, friendly, and personable; desserts are extraordinary." *(Holiday Collins)*

Open Closed 1st week of Jan., Dec. 24–25. Restaurant closed Mon., also Tues. Jan.–Mar.

Rooms 13 doubles—all with private bath and/or shower, air-conditioning, fan, telephone/fax link, clock/radio. 9 with Jacuzzi, TV, balcony or deck. 2 with desk. 9 rooms in carriage house.

Facilities Restaurant, lounge, parlor with books; conservatory; antique shop with collection of Chinese porcelain. 7 acres with gardens. Tennis, swimming, boating, fishing nearby.

Location Lower CT River valley. 30 m E of New Haven. 30 m W of Mystic, CT. 3 blocks from center of town. From I-95 take Exit 69 to Rte 9. At Exit 3, turn left and go 1¾ m to inn.

Restrictions Light sleepers should request rooms away from street and restaurant. No smoking. "Facilities not well suited for children under 10." Room #1 has a small tub, no shower.

Credit cards Amex, DC, MC, Visa.

Rates B&B, $125–180 double. Extra person, $30. 2-night weekend/holiday minimum. Alc dinner, $50–60.

Extras Restaurant wheelchair accessible with lavatory equipped for disabled. Some Portuguese, Spanish spoken.

MADISON

Just 18 miles east of New Haven is the charming Long Island beach town of Madison. Once a summer getaway for the well-to-do, it is now an inviting community year-round.

Information please: The only inn in town with a private beach and a fishing pier, the **Madison Beach Hotel** (94 West Wharf Road, 06443; 203–245–1404) has 32 rooms on four floors, all with water-view balconies. B&B double rates range from $70–225, depending on season, size of room, and view. Guests can relax on rocking chairs on the old-fashioned porch, and a choice of two restaurants, one more casual than the other. "Charming beach-side atmosphere. The Crow's Nest, on the upper deck, offers good food and entertainment." *(Joan & Tom Nolan)* "Exceptional lobster bisque." *(Nora Jean Downey)*

Tidewater Inn
949 Boston Post Road (Route 1), 06443

Tel: 203–245–8457
Fax: 203–318–0265

When the Boston Post Road was just a rutted dirt track, the Tidewater served as a welcoming stagecoach stop for exhausted passengers. Restored as an inn in 1986, it still extends an invitation to weary travelers, whether they're looking for a homey respite on a business trip, or a relaxing weekend getaway at the shore. Jean Foy and Rich Evans purchased the inn in 1996, and have furnished it with both antiques and reproduction pieces. For a special occasion, book the Curtis Cottage Suite, complete with its own antique-furnished sitting room, bedroom with a king-size bed with a carved teak headboard, a stocked entertainment kitchen, and a bathroom with a double Jacuzzi and oversize shower.

Weekdays, business travelers are accommodated with a breakfast of juice, coffee, tea, and such home-baked treats as pineapple muffins and apricot nut bread, served from 7–8:30 A.M., while regular guests can enjoy a more leisurely schedule. A typical breakfast might include melon and kiwi, California egg puff with sausages, and English muffins; or blueberry muffins and apple oatmeal waffles with hot spiced fruit and bacon. The meal is served at guests' choice of large or small tables, from 8:30–9:30 A.M.

"Charming decor, excellent service, delicious breakfast. The hospitable owners gave us some excellent ideas of what to do in Madison." *(Dave & Sue Cronin)* "Ample parking; good restaurants nearby." *(Jack & Nancy Curnow)* "Quiet hillside setting, with an inviting garden patio. The front hall is dramatically wallpapered with a deep navy background and floral design. The living/dining area offers comfortable seating in front of the fireplace, and breakfast tables next to a large bay window. Our first-floor room was furnished with twin beds, a night table and reading light, and ample storage space, with nightlights and toiletries in the bathroom. Jean served us a breakfast of coconut fruit compote and Belgian waffles with sausage. Ample information on area activities and restaurants." *(Betsy Sandberg)* "Comfortable and homey, with a fire always burning." *(Paul Miller)*

Open All year.

Rooms 1 cottage, 8 doubles—all with private shower and/or tub, telephone, clock, TV, air-conditioning. 5 with desk, 2 with fireplace. Cottage with kitchenette, double whirlpool tub.

Facilities Dining room, living room with fireplace, guest refrigerator. 1½ acres with English garden. Off-street parking. Beaches, state park nearby.

Location One hr. from Hartford, 1½ hrs. from New York City, 2 hrs. from Boston. From Boston: Rte. 95 S to exit 62. Left off ramp onto Hammonasset Connector. Right at light onto Rte 1. Inn is 1 ¼ m on right. From New York: Rte. 95 N to exit 61. Right off exit ramp onto Rte 79. Left at third light onto Rte. 1. Inn is 1 m on left.

Restrictions No smoking. Children over 7.

Credit cards Amex, MC, Visa.

Rates B&B, $80–160 double. Extra person, $20. 2-night summer weekend minimum. Midweek corporate rate, $65 single (continental breakfast).

MYSTIC/OLD MYSTIC

For information on area activities, see the chapter introduction.

Mystic is located in southeastern Connecticut, 130 miles northeast of New York City, and 90 miles southwest of Boston.

Reader tip: "J.P. Daniels is our favorite restaurant in the area, but we also had an excellent meal at Bravo, Bravo on Main Street in Mystic." *(Rose Ciccone)*

Information please—in town: Overlooking Mystic Harbor and Long Island Sound is the **The Inn at Mystic** (Rtes. 1 & 27, Mystic, 06355; 860–536–9604 or 800–237–2415 or www.innatmystic.com). This 68-room inn, motel, and restaurant complex sits on 14 landscaped acres, with gardens, tennis court, swimming pool, and hot tub; it borders a river where guests may take a canoe or rowboat out for a free ride. Guest rooms are furnished with Colonial reproductions, and double rates range from $70–235.

Located in downtown Mystic, near the famous Mystic Pizza is the **Six Broadway Inn** (6 Broadway, Mystic, 06355; 800–44–MYSTIC or 860–536–6010; www.visitmystic.com/sixbroadway), restored in 1977 by Joan and Jerry Sullivan. Each of the five guest rooms have a private bath and air-conditioning, plus queen-size beds; three have a river view and one has a private porch. B&B double rates range from $150–225. "Guest rooms with luxurious European linens and Victorian antiques. Helpful, professional innkeepers. Enjoyable afternoon cider and homemade bread." *(AC)*

House of 1833 🛏 ♿   *Tel:* 860–536–6325
72 North Stonington Road, Mystic, 06355   800–FOR–1833
                           URL: http://www.visitmystic.com/1833

Four imposing Doric columns topped by a simple strong pediment, framed by mature shade trees and plantings create the initial elegant impression of the House of 1833. Entering this Greek Revival mansion, built by Elias Brown in 1833, you'll find the equally elegant decor tempered by the warmth of owners Carol and Matt Nolan, who restored the house as an inn in 1994. The uncluttered, sophisticated antique and reproduction furnishings highlight both the spacious common areas and guest rooms, from the formal front parlor with a Belgian marble fireplace to the charming Peach Room, complete with a canopy bed, a double whirlpool tub in the bath, and private porch overlooking the pool and tennis court.

Breakfast is served at 9 A.M., although Carol and Matt encourage guests to come down to breakfast a little early for a chat while the meal is being prepared. A typical meal might start with an elaborate fruit plate, followed by baked custard, French toast with fresh raspberry sauce, sausage, and homemade muffins. Matt—a professional musician—plays the piano during the second course, setting a romantic atmosphere. Carol also notes that the swimming pool is quite large and private, so that guests are able to enjoy quiet time even when several couples are there. The tennis court was constructed in 1994, and is kept in excellent shape by Matt, an accomplished player.

"Perfect inn for an overnight romantic getaway. Elegantly decorated with crystal chandeliers, marble fireplaces, and a grand piano accenting the couches and wing-back chairs. The lovely Peach Room has French provincial side chairs, an Eastlake marble-topped lady's dressing table, and a peach-curtained queen-size canopy bed with matching comforter. The fireplace was ready for lighting, and a vase of fresh flowers sat on a small table nearby. A separate entrance led to a small porch with wicker seating that looked over the swimming pool and tennis court. The bathroom has a wonderful double whirlpool tub, set into an oversize shower area, so you could step from the tub to the shower. The romantic Cupola Suite on the third floor is furnished with a draped four-poster canopy bed, a woodburning stove, love seat, and such thoughtful touches as sherry and fresh flowers. A flight of stairs leads to the cupola, where you can sit with a glass of wine to watch the sun set. Beautiful open kitchen with Italian tiles, and wide-planked oak flooring. Hot cider and cookies were set out here in the evening for a bedtime snack. Breakfast included a lovely fruit plate, pumpkin muffins, and puff pancakes with apple, cinnamon and brown sugar topping, and bacon." *(Rose Ciccone)* "The Nolans tempt their guests with cookies and lemonade in summer, cider and brownies in winter. Loved the hand-painted murals of the Mystic waterfront in the dining room and on the curved spiral staircase wall." *(Linda Phillipps)* "Charming inn, delightful innkeepers, beautiful decor, immaculately clean, delicious food, inviting swimming pool." *(Bobbie Silverman)*

Open All year.

Rooms 5 doubles—all with private bath and/or shower, clock, air-conditioning, fireplace or woodstove. 2 with whirlpool tub, porch.

Facilities Dining room, living room with fireplace, music room with piano, organ, fireplace; deck. Piano played at breakfast, from 4–7 P.M., on request. 3 acres with pool, HarTru clay tennis court, croquet. Bicycles. Off-street parking.

Location Take Exit 90 off I-95. Go N on Rte. 27 to Old Mystic Country Store; bear right at stop sign; continue approx. ½ m to inn on right. 3 m from downtown Mystic.

Restrictions No smoking. Children welcome midweek.
Credit cards MC, Visa.
Rates B&B, $95–225 double. 2-night weekend minimum.
Extras Limited wheelchair access. Mystic train station pickup.

Old Mystic Inn 🛏 ♿   *Tel:* 860–572–9422
58 Main Street, P.O. Box 634   *E-mail:* omysticinn@aol.com
Old Mystic, 06372

The Old Mystic Inn was built in 1794, restored as a B&B in 1986, and purchased by Mary and Peter Knight in 1991. The original chestnut and pine flooring and woodwork were all retained in the restoration, complemented by modern baths, four-poster canopy beds, and wicker furniture. The Carriage House was built in 1988, and combines reproduction Colonial furnishings with Victorian accents.

"Careful attention to detail throughout the inn. The Herman Melville Room was beautifully appointed, restful, and well coordinated, with a comfortable canopy bed, its own thermostat, and a private porch with stairs to the back lawn. The bed and bathroom linens were of exquisite design and comfort. Relaxed, friendly innkeepers, solicitous about our well-being and enjoyment, but never intrusive." *(Wayne Le Blanc)* "Homey but uncluttered; clean and fresh. Homemade chocolate chip cookies always available on the entry table. I was invited to use the kitchen to make an early-morning cup of tea. Wonderful breakfast at 8:30 A.M.; friendly atmosphere with Peter and Mary serving and conversing. It's clear they really enjoy being innkeepers." *(Leigh Robinson)* "Inviting, spotless guest rooms and common areas. Both Mary and Peter—a retired Episcopal priest, did everything possible to make us comfortable; their hearts are as warm as the stories they tell." *(Marilea Schlobohm)* "My room was attractively decorated for Christmas with ivy and mistletoe around the mirror; wreaths on the doors, a small Christmas tree on the dresser; and poinsettias on the desk and nightstand. Breakfast was good and plentiful, served at separate tables." *(Bill Novak)* "An interesting blend of old and new. The Knights reside in the carriage house, so they are always available if assistance is needed." *(Barbara Stack)*

"Peter is down-to-earth, funny, and knowledgeable about the area. Our lovely room was large and bright, with a four-poster bed covered by a patchwork quilt and contrasting floral sheets in shades of mauve, pink, blue, and green. Our room, as was the rest of the inn, was decorated with pretty handcrafted items—grapevine wreaths, candle holders, and baskets. Highlights include the beautiful inlaid hardwood floors and the stencil work. Families are welcome in the carriage house—children even have a separate play area. We had French toast made with challah bread, and baked ham; another favorite is the eggs Benedict with crab. Mary and Peter have a wine and cheese party each Saturday evening; it's informal and fun because of their skill at getting people together." *(Rose Ciccone)*

Open All year.
Rooms 1 suite, 7 doubles—all with private bath, air-conditioning, line for computer. 2 with whirlpool tub, 3 with fireplace, 1 with balcony/deck. 4 rooms in annex.

Facilities Dining room, keeping room with fireplace, TV; library; 3 unscreened porches. ¾ acre with lawn games, swing set, gazebo. Bicycle rental. Boating, fishing, swimming nearby.
Location Eastern CT shore. Take Exit 90 off I-95. Go N 1½ m on Rte. 27 to inn on right. 1½ m to Seaport; 3 m to downtown Mystic; 6 m to Foxwoods Casino.
Restrictions No smoking.
Credit cards Amex, MC, Visa.
Rates B&B, $95–145 suite, doubles. Extra person, $20–35. Tipping encouraged. 2-night weekend minimum. Corporate rates available.
Extras Limited wheelchair access. Airport/station pickups.

Red Brook Inn 👭

P.O. Box 237, Gold Star Highway
Route 184, Old Mystic, 06372

Tel: 860–572–0349
E-mail: rkeyes1667@aol.com

Composed of the Haley Tavern, circa 1740, and the Crary Homestead, circa 1770, the Red Brook Inn gives guests an authentic taste of Connecticut's Colonial past; not surprisingly, it's listed on the National Register of Historic Places. Ruth Keyes restored the inn in 1981, and is still its owner and innkeeper. The guest rooms are decorated with period furnishings, stenciled wide plank floors, and canopy beds with hand-embroidered linens. Breakfast is served in the keeping room at guests' choice of large tables or small, from 8:30–10 A.M., and might include fresh fruit and juice, pancakes and sausage. Rates also include afternoon coffee, tea, and cider.

"Our spotless, spacious room had a queen-size canopy bed plus a twin-size bed; linens were crisp. The ample common areas were furnished with interesting antiques, and included the tavern (for guests only), and both a gentlemen's parlor and a ladies' parlor. The knowledgeable innkeeper explained the fascinating utensils used in the open hearth cooking." *(Pat Borysiewicz)* "Beautifully furnished with antiques, beautiful linens on the canopy beds; handsomely stenciled wide-plank floors." *(Janet Thompson)* "A lot of effort has gone into preserving this inn. I enjoyed reading how the innkeeper had purchased the Haley Tavern at an auction and had it disassembled and moved piece by piece to its current location, where it was reassembled exactly as it had been. Delicious breakfast of pecan waffles and sausage, served before a crackling fire in the huge hearth." *(Pat King)*

Open All year.
Rooms 10 doubles—all with private bath and/or shower. Some with fireplace, whirlpool tub; radio, clock, air-conditioning, fan on request. Rooms in 2 buildings.
Facilities Keeping room with fireplace, 2 parlors, tavern room with TV, games, guest refrigerator. Terrace. Dining room, living room, porch. 7 acres with gardens, lawn games. Tennis, golf, water sports nearby.
Location 7 m E of New London; 3 m N of Mystic. From I-95, take Exit 89, Allyn St. Go N 1.5 m to light at Goldstar Hwy (Rte. 184). Turn right (E), & go slowly to next corner. Go left up driveway & follow arrow to Haley Tavern.
Restrictions No smoking. "Carefully supervised children who appreciate antiques are welcome." BYOB.
Credit cards Amex, Discover, MC, Visa.

Rates B&B, $95–189 double, $75–169 single. Extra person, $25. Reduced rates for children. 2–3 night weekend/holiday minimum.
Extras Train/bus station pickups. Crib.

Stonecroft &
515 Pumpkin Hill Road, Ledyard, 06339

Tel: 860–572–0771
800–772–0774
Fax: 860–572–9161
E-mail: stoncrft@concentric.net
URL: http://www.stonecroft.com

A Georgian Colonial home built in 1807, Stonecroft is surrounded by meadows, woodland, and stone walls. Opened as an inn in 1995, owners Joan and Lynn Egy report that "we try to create an environment that refreshes our guests in body, mind, and spirit. We provide the highest quality cotton sheets, terry robes, oversize towels, fine toiletries, and aromatherapy bath salts." Public rooms include the Great Room with its nine-foot wide fireplace; the Red Room for intimate fireside conversation, and for quiet pursuits; and the Snuggery, once the birthing room and now a small library. In 1998, they completed the Grange, a restored post and beam barn, housing six guest rooms, a lounge, and a dining room. Rooms are decorated in American, English, or French country style, and have either queen- or king-size beds. If you'd prefer B&B&B (bed & breakfast & boat), plan to spend a night on *Zephirine*, an antique wood motor yacht.

In cool weather, breakfast is served by the dining room fireplace; in summer, guests dine on the terrace. Coffee and juice are ready at 8 A.M.; the meal is served at 9 A.M. One day, the menu might be broiled grapefruit, cranberry scones, and crêpes with ricotta filling and fresh strawberry coulis; and the next, cherry crisp with crème fraîche, shirred eggs with chives, maple sausage, toast, and raspberry coffee cake. Special diets are accommodated with advance notice. Dinners are served by prior reservation, and a recent winter menu consisted of crab and avocado rolls, shrimp with rosemary, salad, duck breast with prunes and brandy, and apple-pear tart for dessert.

"Warm hosts who truly open their home to their guests. I felt like I was visiting friends." *(Bari Meltzer)* "Spotless and inviting; the plumbing is in excellent working condition. Wonderful food, generous servings. Joan and Lyn go out of their way to meet your needs." *(LL)* "Close to Stonington, Mystic, and Foxwoods, with a peaceful farm setting." *(Robert Mitchell)* "The Stonecroft room has a hand-painted wraparound mural of the grounds as they might have appeared in the 19th century; the tiger maple reproduction furniture includes a king-size canopy pencil-post bed. The Buttery is the oldest room, with the original doors and beams. Plants and fresh flowers are strategically placed throughout the common and guest rooms. The Egys serve wine in the Great Room each afternoon so people can come together. At breakfast, orange juice and coffee were set on the sideboard; we sat together at the dining room table and enjoyed melon and blueberries, muffins and cornbread, herb omelets and Canadian bacon." *(Rose Ciccone, also Terry Banks)* "Not a detail is overlooked: bathroom nightlights, huge, thirsty

41

towels, the finest quality sheets, and excellent bedside lighting. Immaculately clean and uncluttered." *(Nancy & Bruce Barker)*

"Beautifully decorated house with bright cheery common rooms. The dining room is my favorite, with a graceful arrangement of grapevines and dried flowers framing the windows. Our room had a working fireplace, a lovely painted dresser, and a comfortable king-size bed with down comforter. Guests are tempted by such goodies as pistachio nuts, gourmet jellybeans, biscotti, and fruit. Another nice touch was the classical music or jazz which played softly in the background." *(Rhonda Vogelzang)* "Loved the wide-board floors—some as much as 22 inches wide." *(Craig Seeley)*

Open All year.
Rooms 2 suites, 8 doubles—all with full private bath, clock, air-conditioning. 9 with fireplace, 6 with double whirlpool tub, towel warmer, telephone; 1 with terrace. 4 in main house; 6 rooms in renovated barn; 1 on boat.
Facilities Dining room, living room with TV, sitting room, lounge—all with fireplaces; library, porch, stone terrace. Barn with exercise track, horseshoes, darts. 6½ acres with croquet, cross-country skiing. 42-foot sailing sloop for charter. Equestrian center next door. Beaches, fishing, hiking nearby.
Location Mystic/E CT shore. 1 hr. E of Hartford; 1½ hrs. S of Boston. 2½ hrs. NE of New York City. 10 min. to downtown Mystic. Take I-95 to Exit 89. Go N on Allyn St. Continue N; turns into Cow Hill Rd., then turns into Pumpkin Hill Rd.
Restrictions No smoking. Children over 10.
Credit cards MC, Visa.
Rates B&B, $99–250 double. Extra person, $25. 2-night weekend, holiday minimum. Summer packages for mid-week and full week.
Extras Wheelchair access; 1 room/bath specially equipped. Airport/station/marina pickups.

NEW HAVEN

Home to Yale University and many outstanding museums, theaters, and medical facilities, New Haven is located about 90 minutes drive northeast of New York City, and about 45 minutes south of Hartford.

Reader tip: "Although it has much to offer, New Haven is a city with typical urban problems. Be street-smart, and ask for advice if unsure about safety issues." *(MW)*

Also recommended: For a luxury B&B, try the **Three Chimneys Inn** (1201 Chapel Street, 06511; 203–789–1201; www.threechimneys inn.com/), an 1847 Victorian "painted lady," restored as an inn in 1988 and re-opened under new ownership in 1997. B&B double rates for the ten guest rooms range are $160, including a full breakfast; all have private baths, queen- or king-size four-poster beds, TV, and telephones with modem hookups; some have fireplaces. "A delightful experience, just a block from Yale. Appealing dining room for breakfast; cozy library for relaxing in the afternoon." *(MP)*

Information please: Adjacent to the Yale campus is **The Colony** (1157 Chapel Street, 06511-4892; 203–776–1234), an 86-room hotel. The

$99–109 double rate includes guest privileges at a nearby health club. Yale's Payne Whitney gymnasium.

For an additional area B&B, see **Wallingford.**

NEW LONDON

Long a prosperous seaport, New London is a good base from which to explore the eastern Connecticut shoreline, and is the jumping off point for summer ferries to Block Island. It's also home to the U.S. Coast Guard Academy and Connecticut College. Although a number of historic homes have been restored as museums, drama buffs will head for Monte Cristo Cottage, boyhood home of Eugene O'Neill.

Also recommended: A waterside choice is the 1902 **Lighthouse Inn** (6 Guthrie Place, New London, 06320–4206; 860–443–8411 or 888–443–8411), a 51-room waterside inn and restaurant, overlooking Long Island Sound. The inn is popular for weddings and other functions, so ask for details when booking. An elaborately carved spiral staircase leads to some of the guest rooms in the original 1902 mansion, and furnished in period reproductions. Double rates range from $75–255. "This small hotel has pleasant rooms overlooking the well-manicured grounds or the water. Spectacular azalea hedge borders the fountain at the inn's entrance. Exceptional food and ambience in the restaurant and pub." *(Linda Jennings)*

NEW MILFORD

Also recommended: A handsome Colonial-style home built in 1850, the **Barton House** (34 East Street, Route 202, 06776; 860–354–3535) offers two guest rooms, each with queen- or twin-size beds, private bath, TV, and air-conditioning, at B&B double rates of $95. Owners Rachel and Ray Barton serve breakfasts of fresh fruit and juice, home-baked breads and muffins, and such entrées as Bailey's French toast, frittata, or pancakes. "Delightful proprietors; ideal balance of privacy and chatting time." *(Paul & Sue Marinaro)* "Beautifully landscaped grounds, appealing little town. Delicious breakfasts, elegantly served." *(Debra & John Aniano)* "Though the B&B is located on a main street, our room was quiet and restful." *(Mrs. Louis Vargo)* "Lovely old farmhouse within walking distance of the town square." *(Renee Cantwell)* "My room was clean, comfortable, well-outfitted, quiet and pleasant. Friendly innkeepers." *(John Naus, S.J.)*

For an additional area inn, see **Woodbury.**

The Homestead Inn ¢ 🕴   *Tel:* 860–354–4080
5 Elm Street, 06776   *Fax:* 860–354–7046

The Homestead Inn is close to the village green, and dates back 145 years; the adjacent motel annex is called Treadwell House. Many small shops, the town library, churches, and restaurants are within walking distance. Peggy and Rolf Hammer have owned the Homestead since 1985 and have worked hard to spruce up their welcoming inn while keeping its rates affordable.

"The Hammers go all out to ensure their guests' comfort and enjoyment, whether they're visiting for pleasure or business. Warm and cozy, an inviting and unpretentious in-town inn. Spacious, casual, welcoming common areas. The second-floor guest rooms are decorated with warm, inviting color schemes and floral prints; one has a bay window looking out to the village green. New Milford is an appealing little town, and makes a fine, affordable base for area touring." *(SWS)* "My four-year-old daughter enjoyed playing with the toys available in the common area. The front porch was a great place to sip coffee in the morning while looking out to the town square. On summer Saturday mornings, a small farmers' market sets up in the square—an easy walk." *(Mary Walter Midkiff)*

"The surrounding area is full of recreational activities and is an antique shopper's dream." *(Carolyn Myles)* "Windows that open, plenty of storage space in closets and dresser, caring innkeepers who are sensitive to the guests' needs and schedules." *(Bill Hemings)* "The presence of their beautiful golden retriever and two cats added to the homey atmosphere." *(John & Gretchen Pokorny)* "Our simple room in the motel annex had ample room for two, with a table and chairs, bureau, nightstand, and double bed—all in pine. The immaculate bathroom offered plenty of hot water and thick towels. The serve-yourself breakfast included melon, apples, bananas, cereal, orange juice, muffins, English muffins, whole-grain bread, coffee, and ten types of tea." *(Linda Alpert & Marc Karell)*

Open All year.

Rooms 14 doubles—all with private bath and/or shower, telephone, TV, desk, air-conditioning; 6 rooms in motel adjacent to house.

Facilities Living room with fireplace, piano, TV; breakfast room with games, toys; porch, gardens. Boating, fishing, swimming, downhill and cross-country skiing nearby.

Location NW CT, Litchfield Hills. 15 m N of Danbury. Center of town. Follow Rte. 202 across bridge, up to village green. Go left to top of green, go right on Elm to inn on left, adjacent to hospital.

Restrictions No smoking in common areas. Traffic noise possible in front rooms. Some bathrooms quite small.

Credit cards Amex, Carte Blanche, DC, Discover, MC, Visa.

Rates B&B, $80–105 double, $70–95 single. Extra adult in room, $10; extra child, $6. 2-night weekend minimum May–Oct., & holidays.

Extras Crib.

NEW PRESTON

Set in the Berkshire Hills, New Preston's key attraction is Lake Waramaug, an inviting spot for swimming, fishing, and boating in summer, and skating in winter. Other area activities include hiking to the top of

Pinnacle Mountain for views reaching to Massachusetts and New York, canoeing, bicycling, golf, and horseback riding; in winter, there's sledding, plus cross-country and downhill skiing. Many plays and concerts are offered in the summer, along with craft fairs, and the supply of antique shops is plentiful year-round.

New Preston is located in northwestern Connecticut, 45 miles west of Hartford and 85 miles north of New York City. From NYC, take Hutchinson River Pkwy. to I-684 N, then I-84 E to Exit 7 onto Rte. 7. In New Milford take Rte. 202 (formerly Rte. 25) to New Preston. From Hartford, take I-84 W to Farmington to Rte. 4 to Rte. 118 to Litchfield. Take Rte. 202 to New Preston, then left on Rte. 45 to Lake Waramaug.

Rates are highest here in summer, and on weekends year-round, and are considerably lower midweek from November through May.

Information please: Renovated in 1995 is **The Birches Inn** (233 West Shore Road, New Preston, 06777; 860–868–1735 or 888–590–7945 or www.thebirchesinn.com), an inn since the 1940s. Guests are welcome to relax on the deck, or enjoy the inn's private beach on Lake Waramaug. B&B double rates for the eight guest rooms from $95–300, and include continental breakfast, afternoon tea and snacks, and evening wine and cheese. The inn's restaurant offers a creative and imaginative menu, and is winning rave reviews; plan on spending about $35 per person.

Boulders Inn ✕ 🛪 ♿
Route 45, 06777

Tel: 860–868–0541
800–55–BOULD
Fax: 860–868–1925
E-mail: boulders@bouldersinn.com
URL: http://www.bouldersinn.com

Set in the hills overlooking Lake Waramaug, the Boulders was built in 1895 as a private residence. Converted to an inn 45 years ago, the inn was purchased by Kees and Ulla Adema in 1988, assisted by their son, Eric, the inn's talented chef. Rooms in the inn are handsomely appointed in country decor with antiques and handmade quilts, while the rebuilt carriage house has a pleasing mix of antiques and contemporary furnishings. The cottages were recently renovated, adding new bathrooms, some with whirlpool tubs, and decks with lovely views of the lake. Breakfast includes a buffet of freshly squeezed orange juice, both fresh and dried fruit, yogurt, and lemon poppy seed muffins, orange walnut scones, or other pastries from the inn's bakery. Daily entrées might be a choice of ham and Swiss cheese omelets or cinnamon French toast; eggs any style are always available. Elegant, leisurely dining is a highlight at the Boulders; a recent dinner included an appetizer of jumbo scallops in a crispy potato purée with a sweet and sour blood orange sauce; sesame-seared yellowfin tuna with wasabi whipped potatoes, Oriental vegetables, and ginger cream sauce; and fresh fruit tart with apricot glaze. The wine list includes about 400 wines, with two dozen available by the glass.

"Appealing location, set back from the road with attractive landscaping and good lighting from the parking lot to the main entrance.

Our carriage house room had a cathedral ceiling, Shaker-style four-poster bed, fireplace, comfortable seating areas, an antique bureau, quality bath amenities, and a good supply of fluffy towels. The living room in the main house is inviting, with lots of polished woodwork, a lively mix of floral fabrics, antique lamps, overstuffed sofas, and beautiful vistas of the lake through large windows. The renovated, circular porch offers an equally good view.

"Breakfast is hearty, starting off with a buffet of fruit, juices, granola, yogurt, and freshly made muffins and breads, followed by a cooked-to-order hot entrée—I especially liked the omelets with fresh herbs and the waffles with fresh berries. For a magnificent view of the Litchfield Hills, follow Kees's directions up the small mountain behind the inn; it's an energetic 45-minute climb, but it's worth it." *(NB)* "We walked the entire seven miles around the lake, as a soft snow fell. Later, couples gathered in the living room, reading, listening to the softly playing classical music, or talking quietly." *(Mary Beth O'Reilly)* "Our lovely cottage room had a deck with a lake view, charming country-style furnishings, and a delicious plate of home-baked cookies." *(SWS, also MC)*

Open All year. Restaurant open Thurs.–Sun, Jan.–April, except holiday weekends; Memorial Day weekend through Oct. 31, restaurant open Wed.–Mon.

Rooms 8 cottages, 2 suites, 7 doubles—all with private bath and/or shower, telephone, air-conditioning. Some with desk, double whirlpool tub. Cottages with deck, refrigerator, fireplace. Carriage House rooms with fireplace, refrigerator.

Facilities Restaurant, living room with fireplace, library/TV den with fireplace, terrace, game room with pool table, darts, piano, antique pinball machine. 27 acres with swimming, canoeing, sailing, paddleboats, tennis court, bicycling, hiking.

Location On Lake Waramaug, 7 m N of New Milford.

Restrictions No smoking in guest rooms, cottages, dining room. Children under 12 by arrangement.

Credit cards Amex, MC, Visa.

Rates B&B, $150–275 double. Extra person, $25. MAP, $225–325 double, $200–350 single. Extra person, $50. 15% service. 2–3 night weekend minimum. Alc dinner, $35–40.

Extras Wheelchair access to restaurant, 1 guest house. Dutch, German, French, Spanish spoken.

NORFOLK

Norfolk is an interesting old town and the summer home of the Yale School of Music, which holds chamber music concerts from mid-June to mid-August. It's a good base from which to explore the wonderful old towns of Litchfield Hills, with their numerous art galleries, antique shops, artisans' workshops, and Colonial mansions, not to mention the sheer beauty of the countryside. Outdoor activities include fishing, hiking, canoeing, swimming, tubing, downhill and cross-country skiing.

Norfolk is located in northwestern Connecticut, one hour northwest of Hartford via Route 44.

Information please: A Federal-style home, **Greenwoods Gate** (105 Greenwoods Road East, Route 44, 06058; 860–542–5439) has four inviting suites, each with antique furnishings and private bath. B&B double rates range from $150–250, include wake-up coffee and juice, a full, creative breakfast, and evening wine and cheese. George Schumaker is the welcoming, well-traveled innkeeper. "Careful attention to detail, with such extra touches as in-room sherry and brandy, and wonderful toiletries for the bath. Exceptional hospitality." *(DLG)* Additional comments appreciated.

Angel Hill B&B

Tel: 860–542–5920

54 Greenwoods Road East (Route 44 East) *E-mail:* dgritman@snet.net
P.O. Box 504, 06058 *URL:* http://www.angelhill.com

In today's fast-paced world, we all need a guardian angel to watch out for us. You can be sure of finding at least one at Angel Hill B&B, where owners Donna and Del Gritman have taken care to sprinkle them artfully throughout the decor. Built in 1800, Angel Hill was restored by the Gritmans as a B&B in 1994. Donna reports that "our goal is to provide individual hospitality; we try to make each room a tranquil oasis with no details forgotten." Guest rooms are decorated with soft floral patterns; most have queen-size canopy beds, and one has a king/twin combination. Breakfast is served from 8:30–10:30 A.M.; a typical morning might bring oven-puffed crêpes with caramelized apples and currants, fresh-baked muffins and breads, bacon or sausage, and fresh fruit. Yogurt fruit parfaits are available for light eaters.

"Del and Donna were available and accommodating, helping us plan outings and highlighting maps for us. Impeccable housekeeping; comfortable lights for reading, yet never harsh. Fluffy pillows, cozy quilts; excellent water pressure and lots of hot water." *(Courtney Turay)* "Soft music plays throughout the house; fires burn in the great room. The delightfully warm hostess provides homemade snacks in the butler's pantry." *(Diane Jarett)* "Breakfast, garnished with fresh flowers from the garden, was served at our choice of time and location—in our room, on the porch, or in the gazebo." *(Melissa Heilweil)* "Wonderfully decorated, welcoming atmosphere, immaculate housekeeping. The Gritmans think of everything to make your stay a delight." *(NE)* "Lavishly decorated house with many collectibles; beautiful home design and gardening books. Chamber music played softly through the day. Hosts are wonderfully respectful of guests' privacy." *(Gayle Reasoner)* "Every toiletry one could possibly need and a profusion of thick towels. Spectacular breakfasts." *(Kathleen Walsh)* "Warm, friendly hosts. Romantic Victorian atmosphere with candles and soft lighting. All rooms have garden views." *(Sue Coventry)* "The wraparound porch is ideal for relaxing, reading, and enjoying a cold drink." *(Judy MacDonald)*

Open All year.
Rooms 2 suites, 2 doubles—all with full private bath, cassette player, clock, fan. 2 with whirlpool tub, working fireplace, desk, air-conditioning. 3 with TV; VCR on request. Carriage house.
Facilities Dining room; living room with fireplace, stereo, books; library; guest pantry, screened porch. 8 acres with gazebo, lawn games, brook.

Location 5-min. walk E of town green. From NYC: Take I-84 E to Waterbury, then Rte. 8 N to Winsted. Go right at exit onto Rte. 44 W to Norfolk & inn on left.
Restrictions No smoking. Children 10 and older.
Credit cards None accepted.
Rates B&B, $125–180 double. Extra person, $20. 2–3 night weekend/holiday minimum. Fireplace rooms higher in fall, winter. 20% midweek discount for 2-night stay.

Manor House *Tel:* 860–542–5690
69 Maple Avenue, 06058 *Fax:* 860–542–5690
E-mail: tremblay@esslink.com
URL: http://www.manorhouse-norfolk.com

The Manor House is a large Victorian-era Tudor, with lots of chimneys, beautiful woodwork, and mullioned windows, surrounded by spreading lawns and large shade trees. Innkeepers Diane and Henry Tremblay have owned the Manor since 1985 and provide a casual atmosphere for a relaxing visit. "Spacious third-floor suite, decorated beautifully with Victorian furnishings. Breakfasts at Manor House are consistently delicious and satisfying; we usually linger over pots of tea. The sun room, with a view of the gardens, is an ideal place to curl up with a book, or chat with the other guests. Good location for early morning or after-dinner strolls." *(Judy MacDonald)* "Careful attention to detail from the Victorian dress items displayed throughout the house to the floral sprays hung on each bedroom door. Magnificent Tiffany windows. Scrumptious breakfasts served from 9–10 A.M., with lemon-chive eggs Benedict, orange waffles, and homemade blueberry pancakes. Convenient location, peacefully set back on a side road, ensuring a quiet night's sleep." *(Cathy Mitchell)* "Meticulously clean, warm and friendly owners and staff, and yummy breakfasts." *(Risa Silvia)* "We stayed in the Lincoln Room, with a fireplace, wonderful bed, and antiques." *(Ken Krumenacker)* "Popcorn appeared after a long walk; a full cookie jar at 2 A.M.; endless supply of perfect pancakes at breakfast; staff pointing out a robin's nest; an unexpected upgrade to a double Jacuzzi room. Exceptional privacy." *(Erika Batdorf)*

"The rooms are ample in size, with comfortable beds and modern plumbing." *(Kristen Fernandez)* "The Jacuzzi tub blended well with the Victorian decor." *(Kimberly & VanEric Stein)* "The spacious Spofford Room has a comfortable king-size bed and fireplace." *(Karen Marder)* "A lovely 1898 mansion in a quiet location near the village with pretty gardens and ample parking. Delightfully decorated in a cozy, warm, homey way, with lots of antiques and memorabilia. Excellent service and housekeeping." *(Mr. & Mrs. Edmund Bilhuber)* "Cozy yet spacious; old-fashioned atmosphere with modern amenities. The innkeepers are charming and engaging. We had fun exploring the grounds and discovering the inn's innumerable treasures." *(Susan Qaddoumi)* "Breakfast was served in a large, sunny dining room with gorgeous stained-glass and leaded windows and exquisite woodwork that could only have come from a home crafted in the late 1800s. Hank's oatmeal and his Portuguese bread are delicious." *(Marilyn Brisendine)* "A fire at night, popcorn to munch, tea and coffee always available. Great restaurants minutes away." *(Amy Fisher)*

"Authentic Tiffany windows create a rainbow of hues in the dining and living rooms." *(Robert Romagnoli)* "The Country French Room has a queen-size bed, a day bed, a wing chair, ample lighting, and walls decorated with interesting Victorian artifacts. The wood-paneled bathroom had a skylight, an oversize bathtub, and an old-fashioned dressing table fitted with a sink." *(Martha Moore)* "Each night Hank made sure that the fireplace in our beautiful little room was ready to light." *(Lisa Capeuso)* "Superb breakfast of blueberry pancakes, bacon, juice, German strudel, and unlimited coffee." *(EG)* "The sunny dining room has two full-size dining tables, and pretty china collections." *(June Horn)*

Open All year.
Rooms 1 2-bedroom suite, 8 doubles—all with private bath and/or shower, desk, fan. Some with fireplace and/or balcony. 2 with double Jacuzzi tub, 1 with double soaking tub.
Facilities Dining room, library, living room with piano, games; sun porch, gazebo. 5½ acres with perennial gardens, raspberry and blueberry bushes. Trail, carriage, sleigh, hay wagon rides. 5 min. to private lake for swimming, fishing, canoeing.
Location 5 min. walk to town. From NY, take I-84 to Danbury (exit 7) and take Rte. 7 N to Rte. 44. Go E to Norfolk.
Restrictions No smoking. Children 12 and over.
Credit cards Amex, Discover, MC, Visa.
Rates B&B, $125–225 double. Extra person in room, $20. No tipping. 20% senior discount midweek. 2–3 night weekend, holiday minimum.
Extras Elevator for disabled. French spoken. Station pickups.

NORWICH

Information please: Come to the **Fitch-Claremont House** (83 Fitchville Road, Bozrah, 06334; 860–880–0260) for the history of a house built in 1790; for its location, just a few miles west of Norwich and convenient to area casinos and Mystic; plus wine-tasting at the surrounding Old Fitch Farm Vineyard. Each of the four guest rooms has a private bath, fireplace, in-room telephone and TV. B&B double rates of $100–175 include such seasonal breakfast treats as blueberry buckle, apple coffee cake, or raspberry cream pastry.

OLD LYME

Old Lyme has a reputation as an art colony and is the home of the Florence Griswold Historical Museum, with an excellent collection of American Impressionist paintings, the Lyme Art Association Gallery, and many fine antique shops.

Also recommended: Three miles north of Old Lyme, east of Chester and Deep River is **Hidden Meadow** (40 Blood Street, Lyme, 06371; 860–434–8360), dating back to 1760, and expanded in the Colonial Revival style in 1925. Rates for the five guest rooms range from $95–135 and include a full breakfast. "The house has a fascinating history. Attractive, comfortable guest rooms; relaxing breakfast on the patio." *(Marilyn Parker)*

For additional area inns, see **Chester, Clinton, Deep River, East Haddam, Essex, Ivoryton, Madison, Old Saybrook,** and **Westbrook.**

Bee and Thistle Inn ✗
100 Lyme Street, 06371

Tel: 860–434–1667
800–622–4946
Fax: 860–434–3402
URL: http//www.beeandthistle.com

Longtime innkeepers Bob and Penny Nelson, assisted by their son, Jeff, and daughter, Lori, describe their inn as "a relaxing getaway, in a gracious warm setting, appealing to sophisticated adults." The Bee and Thistle serves breakfast, lunch, and dinner daily, and brunch on weekends, and menus change with the seasons. The breakfast menu includes raspberry crêpes, beef and bacon hash, artichoke-dill omelets, and popovers filled with scrambled eggs, bacon, and cheese. Lunch favorites range from crab cakes to smoked chicken salad, and dinner entrées might include grilled shrimp with garlic couscous and tomato pesto, rack of lamb with potato flan, duck with mushroom risotto, and veal with lemon sage. From November through May, a proper English tea is served three days a week in the parlor or garden porch, including finger sandwiches, scones, and desert.

"Wonderful location, next door to the Florence Griswold Museum, and an easy drive to the Goodspeed Opera House. Lovely rooms with canopy beds. Relaxing grounds with flower gardens and river views." *(Marilyn Parker)* "Exceptional dinner; creative menu, fine service, lovely atmosphere. Be sure to make reservations." *(SWS)* "One of the least expensive, our room was quite small but lovely; we had a chance to see many of the others, and especially liked Rooms #1, #2, #5, and #11 in this well-maintained inn. We had a drink in the inviting bar, then a superb dinner which included homemade scones with honey, delicious salad with raspberry vinaigrette, wonderful clam chowder, trout, and an apple tart with ginger ice cream. The accommodating innkeepers offered us iced tea to take down to the river, where we relaxed and read." *(Trudy Selib)* "The bathroom was small but well supplied with lotions and soaps, and large, fluffy towels. The dinner menu was inventive, the atmosphere incredibly romantic with a harpist." *(Pamela Carafello)*

"Built in 1756, the building was moved several hundred feet away from the road about 65 years ago; various wings and porches were also added over the years." *(EL)* "The immaculate cottage has a sitting room with a fireplace and sofa bed, a bedroom with a dressing room, kitchen stocked with coffee and tea, a TV room with a brick floor and floor-to-ceiling windows opening onto a large deck, a private garden, and a path down to a private dock on the river. Private and quiet." *(William Gerhauser)*

Open Closed 1st 2 weeks in Jan.

Rooms 1 cottage, 11 doubles—all with private bath and/or shower, desk, air-conditioning, fan. Cottage with TV, kitchen, fireplace.

Facilities Restaurant with guitarist and harpist on weekends. 2 parlors with fireplace, bar; porches, library with books. 5½ acres with gardens. Swimming, boating, tennis, golf nearby.

Location E CT shore. Midway between NYC and Boston. 30 m E of New Haven. In historic district. From I-95 N, take Exit 70. Go left off ramp to 2nd traffic light, turn right (Rte. 1 E). Go to "T" in road & turn left to inn on left. From I-95 S, take Exit 70, turn right off ramp, third bldg. on left.

Restrictions Smoking in parlor only. No children under 12. Restaurant noise possible in two rooms until 11 P.M. on weekends.

Credit cards Amex, DC, MC, Visa.

Rates Room only, $215 cottage, $75–210 double. Extra person, $15. Alc breakfast, $5–7 (extra charge for breakfast in bed). Alc lunch, $20; alc dinner, $40–50; afternoon tea, $13; Sunday brunch, $15. Tips welcome.

OLD SAYBROOK

Information please: For a resort hotel, check out the renovated **Saybrook Point Inn** (2 Bridge Street, Route 154 South, 06475; 860–395–2000 or 800–243–0212; www.saybrook.com), located where the Connecticut River meets Long Island Sound. Double rates for its 63 guest rooms range from $135–375; facilities include a restaurant, banquet rooms, spa and fitness center, and marina.

For additional area inns, see **Chester, Clinton, Deep River, East Haddam, Essex, Ivoryton, Madison, Old Lyme,** and **Westbrook.**

Deacon Timothy Pratt House B&B 👫 ♿   *Tel:* 860–395–1229
325 Main Street, 06475   *Fax:* 860–395–4748
                         E-mail: Shelley.nobile@snet.net

Innkeeping and old house restoration have two important qualities in common—both are labors of love. Both elements are clearly in evidence at the Deacon Timothy Pratt House, built in 1746, and listed on the National Register of Historic Places. Shelley Nobile purchased the house in 1995, and has worked hard to restore it. She is delighted to share the history of her inn and town with her guests; the restoration is documented in a photo album and scrapbook. In addition to the many fireplaces typical of an 18th-century home with a central chimney, original details include the wide-board floors with hand-forged nails, hand-hewn beams, vertical beaded board and raised-panel wainscoting, stenciled walls, and hand-forged door latches.

Continental breakfast is available between 7 and 10 A.M.; there's one seating for the full breakfast, at a time agreeable to all guests. A typical menu includes muffins and fresh fruit; Belgian waffles or perhaps eggs Benedict; and ham, bacon, or sausage. Complimentary sherry is served in the evening.

"Quiet yet convenient location within walking distance of local shops and restaurants. Shelley, an electrical engineer, has lovingly restored this 1746 Colonial home with the help of her fiancée, who is in the construction business. Extensive grounds, with a charming old-fashioned rope swing in the back yard. The breakfast table was beautifully set with linen, sterling silver, crystal, fresh flowers, and candles. The meal started with a bowl of fresh fruit, yogurt, juice, muffins, and cinnamon buns, followed by heart-healthy, heart-shaped, blueberry pancakes. The comfortable living room has a Mount Vernon decorating theme, carried through to the blue and white wallpaper. Vases of fresh flowers highlight the decor. Our room was done in a deep wine color with a wallpaper ceiling border. The queen-size bed was a light pine as was the armoire that hid a TV, CD player, and a selection of CDs; good reading lights were positioned on each side of the bed. The wood was laid in the fireplace, ready to be lit. The windows had room-darkening shades, topped with swags. Our bathroom has plenty of surface space, good quality towels, and glycerin soap." *(Rose Ciccone)*

"Beautifully and authentically restored. Impeccably clean. Friendly atmosphere." *(George Smith)* "Lots of little extras, stacks of pillows for extra comfort." *(Gail Thorpe)* "As a professor of architecture, I especially appreciated the care and sensitivity with which the proprietor renovated and decorated this handsome old structure. The wood-burning fireplaces, wide-board painted floors, dried floral arrangements, and period furnishings create an atmosphere of authenticity and comfort. Shelley and Ray were gracious and thoughtful hosts, from accommodating our special dietary restrictions, to making sure that we had accurate directions to the local hiking trails, beach walks, antique shops, and restaurants. Breakfast at the formal mahogany dining table, set with silver and china, was delicious, abundant and elegant, neither stuffy nor pretentious." *(Leslie K. Weisman)*

Open All year.
Rooms 1 suite, 2 doubles—all with full private bath, clock, air-conditioning, fan, wood-burning fireplace. Some with telephone, desk, TV, radio, CD player, data port. 1 with whirlpool tub (planned for 1999).
Facilities Dining room with fireplace, living room with fireplace, TV/VCR, stereo; guest refrigerator, laundry. ¾ acres with gardens, hammock, swing, picnic tables, off-street parking, 1 m to skiing, hiking, golf, tennis, beaches; passes provided.
Location CT River Valley at Long Island Sound. Less than 2 hrs. from NYC and Boston, MA. 50 min. S of Hartford, Providence RI airport. Historic district; ¼ mile to town green.
Restrictions No smoking.
Credit cards Amex, MC, Visa.
Rates B&B, $125–140 suite, $125 double, $110 single. Extra person, $15 adult, $10 child. Corporate, government, midweek rates. $15 less for continental breakfast. 2-night weekend minimum May–Oct.
Extras Limited wheelchair access. Train/bus station pickups. Crib.

SALISBURY

Salisbury is located in northwestern Connecticut, at the junction of Routes 41 and 44. Explore the stores and antique shops of this village, or use it as a base to explore the area's many lakes and mountains; activities include hiking, canoeing and kayaking, fishing, swimming, golf, and tennis, with downhill and cross-country skiing in winter. Car racing is a few miles south at Lime Rock, open from July through October. A number of summer music programs are within an easy drive, and Tanglewood, in Lenox, Massachusetts, is just 24 miles north. This area has almost as many prep schools as antique shops, so reservations during parents' weekends and graduation can be tough to find.

Also recommended: Owned by Juliet Moore, **The White Hart** (Village Green, 06068; 860–435–0030) is a historic 19th-century inn, with a popular restaurant and tavern, inviting front porch, and 26 guest rooms. Double rates range from $85–190, and rooms are furnished similarly with period reproductions and chintz florals. "Small hotel privacy. Our lovely room was done in blue and white, with mauve accents, a canopy bed, and a fireplace. On an earlier visit, a smaller room was less satisfactory. Exceptional veal at dinner." *(RSS)*

For additional area inns, see **Lakeville, Connecticut,** and **Sheffield, Massachusetts.**

Under Mountain Inn ✕ ♿   *Tel:* 860–435–0242
482 Undermountain Road (Route 41), 06068   *Fax:* 860–435–2379

"This inn is under Bear Mountain, one of Connecticut's 'loftiest' peaks at 2,300 feet; after one of Peter and Marged Higginson's full English breakfasts, guests will want to follow the nearby Under Mountain Trail to its peak, to ensure that they'll have room for afternoon tea and shortbread, served from 4–5 P.M., plus the American and English dinners prepared nightly by chef Peter. The oldest parts of the inn date back to the early 1700s, with the wide boards and uneven floors you'd expect. The common rooms and the bedrooms are highlighted with antiques; five guest rooms have canopy beds (most queen-size). My two favorite rooms are the corner rooms at the front of the inn, one with a king-size canopy bed. Most appealing is the cozy pub with its 250-year-old paneling, found hidden in the attic when the inn was restored. Just across the road is a pretty lake and a country road that invites strollers and joggers. The Higginsons have owned the inn since 1985 and are friendly and relaxed innkeepers." *(SWS)*

"Relaxing and rejuvenating. A beautiful area of Connecticut, close enough for a perfect weekend getaway. The rooms are bright, quiet, well-maintained, and attractively furnished. Marged is a charming hostess, most attentive to her guests, while Peter is the quiet man-behind-the-scenes, serving up delicious English meals, with generous portions." *(Richard Boas)* "The English atmosphere, the excellent food, and fine service brought back memories of our cruise on the *QEII.*" *(Marcela Dios)* "Nicely prepared and presented meals, even steak and kidney pie prepared for American palates. We used the inn as a base for day trips, antiquing in the treasure trove of area shops." *(John Blewer)* "Peter's English heritage permeates the inn with the many books on England and afternoon tea at four." *(Phyllis Fredericks)* "Exudes warmth and country inn hospitality from the minute you walk through the door." *(Jedd Savel)*

Open All year.

Rooms 7 doubles—all with private bath and/or shower, air-conditioning.

Facilities Living room with games; 3 dining rooms with fireplaces; pub; library with British books, books-on-tape, videos. 3 acres with croquet; lake nearby for swimming, canoeing; horseback riding. 15–20 min. to downhill and cross-country skiing. 40 min. to Tanglewood.

Location 4 m N of village center on Rte. 41.

Restrictions No smoking. Not suitable for children under 6.

Credit cards MC, Visa.

Rates MAP, $170–200 double, $115–150 single, plus 7% service. Extra person, $50. Senior discount midweek. 2–3 night weekend/holiday minimum. Midweek/weekend, theme packages. Christmas, New Year's 3-night packages, MAP, $595–725 double.

Extras Restaurant wheelchair accessible.

TOLLAND

Set halfway between Hartford and Sturbridge, Tolland remains a traditional New England town, with many buildings clustered around the central town green. Founded in 1715, Tolland has long served as a resting point for travelers on the Old Post Road from New York and Boston.

Area activities include bicycling, golf, swimming, fishing, and boating, plus cross-country skiing and ice-skating.

Tolland is located in northeastern Connecticut, just ½ mile from Interstate 84, 25 minutes southwest of Sturbridge Village, 25 minutes northeast of Hartford, and 15 minutes northeast of the University of Connecticut at Storrs.

Also recommended: An 1840 Colonial-style home set on three acres, the **English Lane B&B** (816 Tolland Stage Road, 06084; 860–871–6618 or 888–871–6618; EnglishLane@compuserve.com) offers two guest rooms, each decorated with English florals, queen-size beds, antiques, and private baths. Breakfast is included in the $65–75 double rate, and consists of fruit, homemade breads or muffins, and a hot entrée, served in the chestnut-beamed dining room or in the gazebo. In the evening, guests can relax with a cup of tea or a glass of port in the parlor, or enjoy a video in the cozy den. "Delicious breakfasts, charming antique decor. Owners Rick and Sheryl King are excellent hosts, and made us feel right at home." (*Brenda Dasher*)

Old Babcock Tavern B&B ¢
484 Mile Hill Road (Route 31), 06084

Tel: 860–875–1239
Fax: 860–870–9544
E-mail: babcockbb@juno.com

When Barb and Stu Danforth purchased the Old Babcock Tavern in 1967, this historic building, dating back to 1720, was in sad shape indeed. In 1984, with many years of restoration work behind them and the satisfaction of being listed on the National Register of Historic Places, the Danforths opened their house to B&B guests. A hearty breakfast of fruit or juice, eggs and bacon or sausage, herb-seasoned home fries, home-baked muffin and apple pie or coffee cake is served, as is a welcoming tray of tea and cookies. The Danforths feel that they are ideally suited for "herb people, as we are just three miles from famous Caprilands Herb Farm, and antiques people, because we are near many shops and auctions."

"Warm and attentive owners, excellent service, beautifully furnished rooms. Breakfast was exactly what we wanted after a relaxing night's sleep." *(William Lukas)* "The Danforths shared their stories about the inch-by-inch authentic Colonial restoration of the house. Barb has collected pottery, glass, and old utensils, all displayed around the tavern. We stayed in the 'ballroom,' the largest guest room, with a wide-board floor, double canopy bed, a ¾ bed, sofa, and dresser. The South Room is medium-sized and sunny, with a peg board for hanging up clothes. We breakfasted beside a roaring fire, on hearty home fries, eggs, light pumpkin/blueberry muffins, and apple cake." *(June Horn)* "Barbara welcomed us with wine and cheese, making us feel right at home." *(Judith Brannen & Larry Machum)* "All is well kept, immaculate, and furnished primarily with genuine antiques. The delightful Danforths suggested an excellent place for dinner and even made our reservations." *(Nora & Bob Weed, also Larry Schwartz)*

Open All year.
Rooms 3 doubles, 1 single—all with private bath, fan, 1 with desk.
Facilities Tap room with fireplace, breakfast room with fireplace, sitting room with evening slide presentation on request. 1 acre with herb gardens.
Location N central CT. From I-84, take Exit 67 (Coventry). Follow Rte. 31 S 2 m to first stop sign. Inn on right corner.
Restrictions No smoking. Children 12 and over.
Credit cards None accepted.
Rates B&B, $70–85 double, $45 single. Rates include 12% tax. Extra person, $20–30. Tipping discouraged.

The Tolland Inn ¢   *Tel:* 860–872–0800
63 Tolland Green (Route 195)   *Fax:* 860–870–7958
P.O. Box 717, 06084   *E-mail:* tollinn@ntplx.net

A convenient location makes this historic B&B well worth a stopover. "Stephen and Susan have done an admirable job of renovating the entire inn themselves. The dining room has a beautiful long cherry table built by Stephen, where breakfast is served from 8–9:30 A.M. The menu changes daily, and might include fresh fruit salad and juice, granola, yogurt, oat scones with maple butter, orange-walnut French toast, and apple tarts. The formal living room has a charming tea cart that Stephen made with real bicycle wheels. Tea and good home-baked cookies are set out for guests to nibble before and after dinner. Guest rooms vary in size, and attractive wallpapers, handsome beds, and some antiques. The ground-floor guest room has a queen-size mahogany canopy bed (made by Stephen), fireplace, and hot tub. Guests can relax on the curving veranda with rocking chairs overlooking the peaceful back yard." *(SWS)*

"Surrounded by quaint old homes, right on the village green. Our private hall bath was spacious, with gleaming hardwood floor, claw-foot tub, and charming hand-stenciling. Steve's skill as an artisan is evident throughout the house; Susan's innkeeping heritage is shown in both her culinary expertise and graciousness. The family atmosphere around the table and the friendliness of the hosts soon draw guests into easy conversation." *(Betty & Bill Clough)*

Open All year.

Rooms 2 suites, 5 doubles—all with private shower and/or bath. 1 suite with hot tub, 1 with fireplace. Some with TV, air-conditioning.

Facilities Living room, dining room, kitchen with fireplace, sun porch/tea room with fireplace, meeting room, veranda. 1 acre with grape arbor, gardens.

Location From I-84, take Exit 68 to Rte. 195 N into Tolland; inn is on town green on left after stop sign..

Restrictions No smoking. No children under 11. Light traffic noise in front rooms.

Credit cards Amex, DC, MC, Visa.

Rates B&B, $70–130 double, $60–120 single. Some weekend/holiday minimum stays. Afternoon tea; call for rates/times.

WALLINGFORD

Also recommended: If you're visiting Choate, or prefer a pastoral setting to downtown New Haven, consider the **High Meadow B&B** (1290 Whirlwind Hill Road, 06492; 203–269–2351 or hmbandb@mail2.nai.net), a 1742 home moved by owners Bob and Nancy Charles to this quiet hillside, with views of farmlands, ponds, and wildflowers. Wide floorboards and raised paneling contrast handsomely with the Charles' art collection, gathered during their years with the Peace Corps in Thailand. The B&B double rate for the two guest rooms, each with private bath, is $95; also available is a two-bedroom guest house. "The inn offers magnificent views and inviting walking paths, yet is convenient to both I-95 and I-91. The house is cozy and comfortable, with marvelous antiques, Thai artifacts, and handsome paintings done by Nancy and her family. The guest rooms have abundant pillows, comforters, towels, lovely quilts, and immaculate bathrooms. Bob is an accomplished cook and warm host, providing excellent breakfasts, beautifully presented on heirloom china, crystal, and silver. Locally smoked bacon is hard to resist, as are the homemade bran muffins, country eggs, baked blueberry French toast, wonderful coffee, and even homemade tomato juice. Excellent restaurants are nearby, and Bob is happy to make reservations and give directions." *(Judith Murray)*

WASHINGTON

Also recommended: For a special occasion splurge, consider the **Mayflower Inn** (Route 47, Washington, 06793; 860–868–9466), a luxurious country hotel. The library has leather club chairs, myriad classics and mystery novels; the living room has Oriental rugs and comfortable seating areas accented with fine artwork. Imported linens, down comforters, and custom-blended toiletries are the appropriate complement to the king-size four-poster canopy beds and antiques found in the 25 guest rooms. Baths are fitted with marble, mahogany wainscoting, Limoges sinks, and deep tubs. The inn's restaurant utilizes local New England produce, from both land and sea. Double rates are $250–415, suites to $620, exclusive of meals. "Food, accommodations, and service for our wedding were all perfect." *(Tina Chen)*

WESTBROOK

Also recommended: The **Water's Edge Inn** (1525 Boston Post Road, 06498; 860–399–5901 or 800–222–5901) is a restaurant, inn, and 100 guest-room condo-complex, originally dating back to the forties, when it was a popular summer retreat. The restaurant overlooks the water and specializes in seafood, while the hotel rooms are done in period decor. Resort facilities include tennis courts, indoor and outdoor swimming pools, hot tub, and a small private beach for swimming. "We stayed in a condo with clean, contemporary furnishings, one private bedroom and a second one in the loft. We were able to walk out to an island at low tide—a neat experience, as the island was pretty far out. Delicious Sunday brunch in the restaurant, overlooking the water. Great shopping at the discount outlet mall nearby." *(Amy Phillipps)* B&B double rates range from $110–210; many packages available.

WESTPORT

The Inn at National Hall ✕ 👭
Two Post Road West, 06880

Tel: 203–221–1351
800–NAT–HALL
Fax: 203–221–0276
E-mail: nathall@ibm.net
URL: http://www.integra.fr/relaischateaux/nationalhall

When National Hall was built in 1873 on the shores of the Saugatuck River, sailing sloops docked right in front and were loaded with onions and other local produce for shipment to New York City. In those days, the First National Bank of Westport was housed on the first floor, the local newspaper on the second, and the town's meeting hall on the third. The building saw a variety of commercial uses over the years, but was completely run down by 1987 when it was purchased by Arthur Tauck of Westport-based Tauck Tours; the painstaking reconstruction of the building as a small hotel took nearly five years. Now this Italianate building, with a cast-iron and brick façade, is listed on the National Register of Historic Places.

Many guest rooms have 18-foot ceilings; some have loft bedrooms and sweeping river views. All are lavish, each individually decorated, with extravagant use of rich silks and heavy cottons; furnishings include imported English antiques and 19th-century antique reproductions. Local artists created the elaborate stenciling and hand-painted murals throughout the building. Each room has a different decorative motif painted on the walls, from murals of an Indian rajah to a room with Egyptian lotus and scarab motifs. The inn is also home to the Restaurant at National Hall, featuring creative New England and international cuisine. Rates include your choice of a European continental breakfast, morning paper, and turndown service.

"They say you can't judge a book by its cover, and this holds true for the simple exterior and setting of this hotel, as well as the trompe l'oeil books painted on the elevator wall. Wonderful accommodations; exceptional food and service in the restaurant. Overall, a worthwhile splurge." *(NB)*

Open All year.
Rooms 7 suites, 8 doubles—all with full private bath, telephone, radio, clock, TV/VCR, desk, air-conditioning, refrigerator. 1 with fireplace. In-room fax on request.
Facilities Restaurant, living room with fireplace, books, honor bar; breakfast room; meeting facilities, business services; room service. Downtown setting on Saugatuck River, with boardwalk, fountain. Complimentary use of YMCA.
Location SW CT. 54 m NE of NYC, 68 m SW of Hartford. National Hall Historic District; west bank of Saugatuck River. Walking distance to shops, restaurants. Near beach.
Restrictions No smoking.
Credit cards Amex, DC, MC, Visa.
Rates B&B, $345–575 suite, $195–395 double. Alc lunch, $18; alc dinner $35–50.
Extras Crib. Babysitting. Member, Relais & Chateaux. AAA Five Diamond Award.

WOODBURY

The Everview Inn 🏃   *Tel:* 203–266–4262
339 Hoophole Hill Road, P.O. Box 557, 06798

If you avoid B&Bs for fear of being trapped in small fussy rooms with small fussy furnishings, then Everview is the perfect place for you. Taking its name from the panoramic vistas of the surrounding rolling Litchfield Hills, Everview offers dramatic contemporary architecture that's nearly as expansive as the view. From the 1,000-square-foot, two-story great room with a fifty-foot-high glass wall and cathedral ceiling, to the generously sized guest rooms, to the extensive grounds, there's ample room to relax. The handsome, eclectic furnishings are over-sized and comfortable—no fear of breaking a delicate antique chair not really intended for sitting. Sue Baer and her husband Vincent Simone built Everview as a private home in 1986; Sue opened it as a B&B in 1997.

Breakfast is served at the dining room table between 8 and 9:30 A.M., and might include melon with yogurt and berries, blueberry corn muffins, and honey wheat bread, followed by a vegetable frittata. Edible landscaping surrounds the house and enlivens the morning meal. Although guests are welcome to spend their day at the inn, enjoying the views, gardens, and swimming pool, Sue notes that within a few miles are myriad antiques shops, the Gertrude Jekyll gardens, and first-rate dining at the Good News Café.

"Worth a visit for the views alone—especially at sunset or when there's a rainbow. Comfortable and well-run inn with a gracious, welcoming hostess." *(R. Ragaini)* "Our room was very private and well equipped, with a spectacular bathroom." *(Thomas & Elizabeth Maloof)* "The grounds were pristine, the house was stunning, and the generous breakfast buffet was excellent. Abundant towels and toiletries; excellent housekeeping." *(Jay Ramras)* "Marvelous views; friendly, accommodating innkeeper. Wonderful breakfast of home-baked breads, fresh squeezed juice, homemade jams, just-picked strawberries. Easy to reach down a country lane, yet enjoys a peaceful, quiet, and serenely pastoral setting. Convenient parking, ample privacy." *(Diane Sorey)* "Beautiful view of the moonrise over the hills. Spacious, comfortable suite." *(Keith Gott)* "Luxurious bathrooms with lots of extras. Sue helpful with touring advice and restaurant reservations." *(Kathleen Pomerantz)*

Open All year.

Rooms 1 suite, 2 doubles—1 with full private bath, 2 rooms share 1 bath. All with telephone. 2 with clock, TV, air-conditioning. 1 with radio.

Facilities Dining room; living room with fireplace, piano, TV/VCR, stereo; porch. 5 acres with gardens, patios, decks, swimming pool. Hiking, downhill, cross-country skiing nearby.

Location Litchfield County. 25 m NE of Danbury; 10 m NW of Waterbury. Take I-84 to Exit 15. Go E on Rte. 6 to Rte. 47. Go left onto 47 N for 1.8 m; then left onto Hoophole Hill. Watch for inn sign 1.6 m on left.

Restrictions No smoking.

Credit cards Amex, Discover, MC, Visa.

Rates B&B, $175–210 suite, $100–125 double, $95–120 single. Extra person, $10.

Extras Airport/station pickups. Pet, babysitting by prior arrangement.

We Want to Hear from You!

As you know, this book is effective only with your help. We really need to know about your experiences and discoveries. If you stayed at an inn or hotel listed here, we want to know how it was. Did it live up to our description? Exceed it? Was it what you expected? Did you like it? Were you disappointed? Delighted? Have you discovered new establishments that we should add to the next edition?

Tear out one of the report forms at the back of this book (or use your own stationery if you prefer) and write today. *Even if you write only "Fully endorse existing entry" you will have been most helpful.*

Thank You!

Maine

Five Gables Inn, Boothbay Harbor

Coastal Maine has long been one of the foremost tourist areas in the Northeast, with its striking rock cliffs and innumerable coves and sheltered inlets. The coastline is so curving, in fact, that it supposedly twists through 3,000 miles to cover a distance of 240 miles as the crow flies. Inland Maine brings other, quieter pleasures of wooded mountains and peaceful lakes. The Lakes Region, about 100 miles northwest of Portland, in the White Mountains along the New Hampshire border, combines relatively easy accessibility with inviting small towns and villages. North of Route 2, the (human) population density diminishes rapidly, with the exception of winter visitors tackling the challenging ski slopes at Sugarloaf, or those making the pilgrimage to the northern terminus of the Appalachian Trail. If getting away from the crowds is your preference, amble up Route 1 north of Ellsworth to discover relatively undeveloped, un-touristy Maine. Here you can explore roads leading south from Machias to Roque Bluff State Park, and take Route 191 through sleepy Cutler and on to the fishing village of Lubec. From here cross over to Campobello Island (Canada) to visit picture-postcard villages and FDR's famous "summer cottage." For the more adventurous, head north to explore remote Aroostook County's virgin lakes as well as Baxter State Park's imposing Mt. Katahdin, then try out your college French in border towns such as Fort Kent and Van Buren.

By the way, if you've ever wondered why the natives refer to going "Down East" when the rest of the world thinks of it as "up north," we're glad to report that it dates to sailing days, when the prevailing coastal winds out of the northwest made the trip from Boston to Bar Harbor an easy trip *east*, going *down* wind.

Peak season in Maine runs from mid-June to mid-October, and rates are significantly higher during these months. Two-night to three-night minimum stays on weekends and holidays are the rule. Many coastal inns are open only from May through October, although a few stay in operation year-round. If you can get away in September, the chances are you'll have great weather and fewer crowds. Rates at most coastal inns are lower in May, June, September, and October, and are lowest during the winter months.

Reader tips: "I toured the coast from Camden to Blue Hill to Deer Isle in early November. Although the foliage season was over, Maine's beauty was still breathtaking, with views of tall evergreens silhouetted against the deep blue sky, and the sun sparkling on the water. The complete lack of crowds and traffic more than compensated for the fact that some inns, shops, and restaurants were closed." *(SWS)* "The black flies can attack with a vengeance in June; if possible, visit during another month, but bring bug repellent for any warm weather visit." *(MW)*

AUGUSTA

Straddling the Kennebec River in central Maine, Augusta is the state capital, easily accessed via I-95. Although we have no in-town recommendations, following are two nearby inns.

Reader tips: "Not far from the Lakes region, the charming river town of Hallowell is an antiquer's paradise, with many interesting shops and handsome architecture." *(Emily Hoche-Mong, Anne Sullivan)* "The River Café in Hallowell serves excellent, authentic Lebanese food." *(Suzanne Carmichael)*

Also recommended: About ten miles northwest of Augusta is **Home-Nest Farm** (Baldwin Hill Road, Fayette; mailing address, Box 2350, Kents Hill, 04349; 207–897–4125), owned by Arn and Leda Sturtevant. Accommodations are offered in three buildings: Josiah's Place, the main residence, dating from 1784, the Lilac Cottage, and the Red Schoolhouse, both built in 1830. Guests prepare their own breakfast from larders well-stocked with fresh eggs, hot or cold cereals, milk, bread, butter, jam, juice, and hot beverages. B&B rates are $60–105, and include use of the owners' canoes. "Beautiful rural setting, with sheep grazing in the meadows, lakes and ponds, and distant mountains. Our spacious apartment was in the East Wing of Josiah's Place, and had a parlor with TV, a sitting room with a fireplace, a well-equipped kitchen, and a bedroom with a queen-size four-poster bed, wide-board floors, and country antiques. The two cottages were equally spacious and charming. Genuine 18th-century farm; a terrific value." *(SC)* "Beautiful grounds. Rustic accommodations in the Lilac Cottage, with a comfortable bed and functional bath. Delicious breakfast muffins. Ideal family getaway; excellent weekly rates." *(GB)*

Maple Hill Farm B&B ¢ ♿
Outlet Road, RR 1
P.O. Box 1145, Hallowell, 04347

Tel: 207–622–2708
800–622–2708
Fax: 207–622–0655
E-mail: info@MapleBB.com
URL: http://www.MapleBB.com

Built in the 1890s, Maple Hill Farm has been owned by Scott Cowger since 1992, with Vince Hannan assisting as manager. Scott notes that "we offer personalized service, immaculately clean accommodations, and a relaxed country-farm atmosphere. We are easygoing hosts and are delighted to help guests explore our area, from a visit to the State Museum or Capital building—where I am a state representative—to little known local hiking trails, or a visit with our own menagerie of farm animals (llama, pony, draft horses, sheep, goats, cows, and chickens). Breakfast is served from 7–9 A.M., chosen from a menu of blueberry or buttermilk pancakes, thick-sliced French toast, eggs Benedict, hot oatmeal, or eggs-to-order from the farm's own chickens."

"Appealing food, ambience, and staff; popular for business meetings." *(Ann Conway)* "Our room was pretty, clean, and pleasant. Thoughtful, friendly owners. Coffee, tea, and iced tea were always available. Big old maples sheltered the front yard and the pasture." *(Anne Sullivan)* "Scott and Vince made me feel right at home during an extended stay; they are friendly, pleasant, personable, professional, and accommodating. Their inn has an excellent reputation for hosting weddings and meetings. Guest rooms are in the original farmhouse as well as in a newer wing." *(Elizabeth O'Neil)* "Careful attention to detail. Excellent meals prepared for our business group." *(Louise Smart)* "Our huge, uncluttered room had a window seat, bedside tables with reading lights, and pleasant views of the surrounding fields. Breakfast was delicious and beautifully served." *(EM)* "Perfect location for anyone wanting to do genealogical research at the Augusta Archives. Our spacious room had a whirlpool tub, plus efficient air-conditioning during an unusual hot spell. Great blueberry pancakes. Our hosts were very knowledgeable about area restaurants." *(Gary & Gail Boyle)* "For guests who may have forgotten something, the bathroom had a thoughtful basket of toiletries with a note asking you to leave a modest payment." *(SC)*

Open All year.

Rooms 1 suite, 6 doubles—all with full private bath and/or shower. 3 with whirlpool tub, balcony/deck. All with telephone, radio, clock, TV, desk, air-conditioning, in-room thermostat, ceiling fan, refrigerator, balcony/deck.

Facilities Dining room, living room with fireplaces; library with books, organ, TV/VCR, stereo; porch; wedding/small conference facilities. 130 acres with fields, woods with trails for hiking, cross-country skiing; lawn games; hot tub planned for 1999. Adjacent to Jamies Pond Wildlife Area. 1 m to lake swimming, canoeing, fishing.

Location Central ME, Capital area, 4 m SW of Augusta. From I-95 N, take Exit 30; from I-95 S, take Exit 30A. Stay in left lane on exit ramp for Rte. 202 W. Go immediately left & turn onto Whitten Rd. Follow sign to Maple Hill Farm on Outlet Rd.

Restrictions No smoking. Children 8 and over preferred.

Credit cards Amex, CB, DC, Discover, MC, Visa.

Rates B&B, $100–130 suite, $70–125 double, $60–115 single. Extra person, $12. AAA, senior discount. 2-night minimum some summer weekends.

Extras Wheelchair access; bathroom specially equipped. Some French spoken.

BAR HARBOR

Bar Harbor is Mt. Desert Island's main town. It's where you'll find most of the island's shops and restaurants; in season (mid-May to mid-

October), it's the center for a wide variety of shows, lectures, festivals, and theater. From the center of town, it's a short drive to the Bluenose Ferry to Nova Scotia, and to Acadia National Park. The Bangor Airport is 45 miles to the northwest, and Boston is about a 5-hour drive. From the south, take I-95 north to I-395 at Bangor. Follow I-395 to Route 1A. Take 1A to Ellsworth to Route 3 east to Mt. Desert Island and Bar Harbor.

Bar Harbor's popularity dates to the turn of the last century, when millionaires from John D. Rockefeller and J.P. Morgan built "cottages" for the brief summer season. Unfortunately, many of these mansions were destroyed in a devastating fire in 1947. Most of the island is occupied by Acadia National Park, a Rockefeller legacy of breathtaking beauty. From the top of Cadillac Mountain to the road along the shore, you'll find extraordinary vistas at every turn. The park is honeycombed with innumerable trails for hiking and wide carriage paths for jogging, strolling, horseback riding, bicycling, and cross-country skiing. Unfortunately, it's hardly a secret: Acadia is the second-most-visited national park, after the Smokies. August is the busiest month; if you can visit the area in June, or better yet, in September, you'll avoid most of the crowds and still have good weather. Aside from the park, area activities include golf, tennis, swimming, as well as whale-watching and kayaking.

Rates are highest from mid-June to mid-October; off-season rates are typically $50–100 less (reflected in the lower number in our range of rates). Many of Bar Harbor's inns have a two-night minimum stay throughout the summer and early fall; a one- or two-night deposit is typically required to confirm your reservation. Some inns also require full payment for the *entire* stay at check-in.

Reader tips: "Especially recommended is eating at one of the lobster pounds on the island. You pick out a lobster and it is cooked right in front of you. You then proceed with your plate out to picnic tables on the pier, piled high with lobster traps, and surrounded by lobster boats. A real New England experience. We also suggest getting up very early to see the sunrise at the top of Cadillac Mountain—they say it's the first place in the U.S. from which to view the dawn—and returning at night with a bottle of wine and a hunk of cheese to enjoy the sunset." *(SP)* "Parking is a problem in season; we were glad our inn was within walking distance of shops and restaurants." *(EHM)*

Also recommended: For luxurious accommodations, a breathtaking setting overlooking Frenchman's Bay, and a convenient location just two blocks from town, consider the **Balance Rock Inn** (21 Albert Meadow, 04609; 207–288–2610 or 800–753–0494). This shingle-style mansion built in 1903 offers two luxurious two-bedroom suites, at B&B double rates of $125–435, depending on room and season. "Sumptuously decorated; rates include a lavish buffet breakfast, as well as afternoon tea. We took our breakfast out to the covered back porch where we could view the ocean. Amenities include a swimming pool, exercise room, and a prime location on the shore path." *(Ginny Watkins)*

A good resort alternative is the **Bar Harbor Inn** (Newport Drive, Box 7, 04609; 207–288–3351 or 800–248–3351), "a sprawling seven-acre complex on a scenic point just east of town. Rooms are found in the original building, the oceanfront lodge, and the motel. Best of all is the harbor view of ships and boats coming and going." *(Duane Roller)* "Good food and service; generous continental breakfast buffet. Superb views from our ocean lodge room. Great location, close to shops and restaurants." *(Carol & Gil Abernathy)* A total of 130 units are available, with rates ranging from $69–265, depending on view, room size, and season.

The **Manor House Inn** (106 West Street, 04609; 207–288–3759 or 800–437–0088), a 22-room mansion built in 1887, has long been owned by Down East native Mac Noyes. Beautifully furnished throughout with Victorian decor, stained- and leaded-glass windows, period reproduction wallpapers, and lace curtains, the inn has 12 guest rooms and 2 cottages. Double rates of $85–175 include a full breakfast and afternoon tea. "Beautiful inn, terrific location, scrumptious food, friendly dining arrangement that encourages meeting others." *(Jennifer Worden)*

Offering superb views of Frenchman's Bay is **The Tides** (119 West Street, 04609; 207–288–4968; www.barharbortides.com), an 1887 Greek Revival mansion, with four beautifully furnished and well-equipped guest suites. B&B double rates range from $95–275, including a full breakfast and afternoon refreshments. "Excellent location on a quiet residential street, a few minutes' walk to town. Breakfasts served on the veranda overlooking sweeping lawn, gardens, and bay." *(Suzanne Scutt)* "At night you can snuggle in front of the fireplace, watching the moonlight dance on the bay." *(Kent Anders & Deborah Anderson)*

A Tudor-style house built in 1885, **Ullikana** (16 The Field, 04609; 207–288–9552), has rooms decorated with French fabrics and wallpapers, complemented by local prints and paintings. Despite a quiet setting overlooking meadows and Frenchman's Bay, it's just a minute's walk to town. "Spacious rooms and baths. Longtime owners Helene Harton and Roy Kasindorf were warm, knowledgeable, and informative. Helene prepared a wonderful breakfast of fresh banana muffins, fruit with Grand Marnier, mushrooms over fresh puff pastry, and good, strong coffee. Loved their dog, Zoe." *(Mary & Jim White)* B&B double rates for the 10 guest rooms range from $110–190 double, including breakfast and refreshments.

For additional area entries, see listings for **Southwest Harbor,** also on Mt. Desert Island, plus the nearby towns of **Blue Hill, Castine, Corea,** and **Hancock.**

Black Friar Inn ¢
10 Summer Street, 04609–1424

Tel: 207–288–5091
Fax: 207–288–4197
E-mail: blackfriar@acadia.net
URL: http://www.blackfriar.com

In the 1980s, the Black Friar was completely redone with all new plumbing and wiring, using old materials to reconstruct this old house in an old-fashioned yet creative way. The large and sunny common room is used for breakfast and afternoon tea, while the cozy wood-paneled pub is especially appealing on chilly evenings. Breakfast is served between 8 and 9:30 A.M., and might include orange-cranberry juice, baked apples, and eggs baked with bacon and home fries, or perhaps blue-berry-stuffed French toast. One guest room has a mantle and mirror as the headboard for its queen-size bed; in another, the headboard was made from an old door set on its side and a section of banister and balustrade, attached to the ceiling by an old porch post. Although the suite has a king-size bed and fireplace, most guest rooms are small, but all have a queen-size bed, closet area and/or a dresser, and excellent lighting. Guests are uniformly delighted with the quality mattresses and plumbing, good food and atmosphere, and most of all, by the pres-ence of Perry and Sharon Risley, the warm and welcoming owners, along with inn dog, Falke, a Brittany spaniel.

"The highlight of our Maine trip, from our first phone call to the thank-you postcard sent to our home. After our arrival at the inn, Perry spent time with us, describing the sights, and sharing his books and tapes on Acadia. Not only did he recommend restaurants, but men-tioned several to avoid. All questions, from sea-kayaking to glider flights were answered with pleasure. The tasty breakfasts included gin-gerbread waffles and broiled grapefruit." *(Doug & Sandy Jenkins)* "Ex-ceptional hospitality, beautiful renovation, mercifully uncluttered, with spotless housekeeping. The Risleys are informative and interesting but never pushy or overbearing." *(Mildred & Byron Fox)* "Just a short walk to all Bar Harbor spots." *(Jeff & Linda Lee)* "The Risleys gave us exact instructions for finding the inn, and room descriptions so we could choose just what fit our needs. The inn is immaculate, attractive, and comfortable, and complete with a friendly, well-mannered, and well-trained dog." *(Marjorie McClure)* "The stained-glass window cast a rosy glow over the room; the ceiling fan kept us cool and comfortable." *(Melody Miller)* "Perry offered us wine each evening before dinner, and was pleased to keep us company. Breakfast was always punctually served, and Sharon was always ready to top off our coffee mugs. Her pistachio biscotti were a perfect afternoon treat." *(Helen Hsu)* "Appre-ciated the personal attention with planning meals and hikes." *(Carol & Larry Phillips)* "The Risleys even helped us with reservations at our next B&B." *(Jeannie Doran)*

"The inn's size and congenial atmosphere is conducive to socializ-ing with interesting guests from all over. Quiet but convenient in-town location." *(Elizabeth & Sean Singh)* "Different breakfasts every day from dill-poached eggs to spinach quiche; recipes shared gladly." *(Ann Liv-ingston)* "Whether you need a rain poncho or binoculars for whale-watching, the Risleys are always there to help." *(Helen Lee)* "Perry built a fire in the Pub Room in the afternoon where guests congregate to chat over wine, tea, and snacks." *(Vickers & Richard Myers)* "Sitting areas felt like home with helpful books about the area." *(Angela Freeman Smith)* "We felt cared for, yet our privacy was respected." *(Barb Floria)* "Good toiletries, fluffy towels, and extra pillows; excellent fruit at breakfast." *(Susan & Joe Winner)* "We stayed in Room 1 which was well decorated and comfortable. Excellent breakfasts, different each morning of our week-long stay. Perry and Sharon joined us for conversation over a pre-dinner glass of wine." *(Mr. & Mrs. K. Woodall)*

Open May–Nov.

Rooms 1 suite, 6 doubles—all with private bath and/or shower, radio, ceiling fan, air-conditioning, hair dryer. 1 with fireplace.

Facilities Common room with TV, books, games; pub with fireplace; 3rd floor deck; garden; off-street parking. Off-season fly-fishing, sea-kayaking. 1 block from ocean. Tennis, golf at nearby club.

Location Center of town. Take Rte. 3 to Bar Harbor to Cottage St.; turn left onto Summer St., immediately after municipal building.

Restrictions No smoking. Children 12 and over.

Credit cards Discover, MC, Visa.

Rates B&B, $150 suite, $95–120 double. 2-night minimum mid-June–mid-Oct. Off-season discounts.

Extras Local airport/bus pickups.

Cleftstone Manor　　　　　　　　　　　　*Tel:* 207–288–4951
92 Eden Street, 04609　　　　　　　　　　　　888–288–4951
　　　　　　　　　　E-mail: cleftstone@acadia.net
　　　　　　URL: http://www.acadia.net/cleftstone

Cleftstone Manor is an 1884 three-story mansion, perched on a terraced hillside, and was one of the few original "cottages" to survive the 1947 fire which devastated Millionaire's Row. Common areas and guest rooms are decorated with antiques and period pieces to create an atmosphere that is both inviting and elegant. The inn has been owned since 1997 by Kelly and Steve Hellmann, who are taking care to ensure guest comfort by providing good lighting at bedsides and in bathrooms, with uncluttered spaces for guests to set down personal items.

Breakfast is served from 8–9:30 A.M. at tables for four, with a different menu every day: perhaps quiche Lorraine, wild blueberry pancakes, pineapple muffins, and blueberry crumb cheesecake one day; followed by baked tomatoes, eggs and smoked mozzarella in phyllo cups, banana walnut pancakes, and blueberry bread the next. Rates also include such afternoon treats as iced tea and lemonade in summer, hot tea and cider in winter, with chocolate chip cookies, plus evening tea and wine, cheese and crackers.

"Kelly and Steve are natural innkeepers who set a tone of friendliness throughout the inn." *(Dr. & Mrs. Richard Symons)* "The Hellmanns are committed to doing the little things that make their guests feel pampered and welcome. Although there is a lot to do in Bar Harbor, we enjoyed just reading in a quiet nook, playing chess, or talking in the garden. Guest rooms are beautifully decorated and well-kept. Outstanding breakfasts, delightful afternoon lemonade and cookies." *(Lynn Lohman)* "We felt at home and comfortable; when we weren't using them, we kept our bikes in the basement. It's a short walk to downtown Bar Harbor, which meant that the inn is away from all the noise." *(Mariano Garcia)* "Wonderful breakfasts of pancakes or French toast, fruit cobblers, fresh fruit, cereal, bagels, English muffins, and more kept us fueled for a full day of hiking." *(Victoria Scire-Banchitta)* "We were delighted with the Prince of Wales and the Sherlock Holmes Rooms." *(Mary Bermingham)* "Especially nice in May—no crowds, low rates." *(Lisa Bodenhorn)* "We really enjoyed the romantic Romeo & Juliet Room with English antiques, a king-size bed, and working fireplace (with a love seat strategically placed in front of it)." *(John & Nancy Schultz)* "Guests are asked to write comments on the menus of local restaurants, which makes choosing a restaurant much easier. Tea is served from 4–5 P.M., and wine, cheese, crackers, cookies, or grapes are offered in the evening." *(Alice Sharf & David Steshko)* "Steve and Kelly were so accommodating, and have two darling cats." *(BBR & KR)*

Open May–Oct.

Rooms 16 doubles—all with private bath and/or shower, air-conditioning, clock/radio. Most with desk; some with balcony/deck; 5 with fireplace.

Facilities Living room, breakfast room, dining room with fireplace. Wicker sun room with games; library, writing room. 1 acre with formal garden.

Location Rte. 3; 1 m to center of town; 600 ft. to Nova Scotia ferry. "When entering village, look for huge brown mansion on right, up hill." Adjacent to large motel.

Restrictions No smoking. No children under 8. Traffic noise in some rooms.

Credit cards Discover, MC, Visa.

Rates B&B, $100–185 double. Extra person, $20. 2-night minimum stay July, August.

Coach Stop Inn ¢
Route 3, Bar Harbor Road
P.O. Box 266, 04609

Tel: 207–288–9886
E-mail: tcombs@acadia.net
URL: http://www.maineguide.com/
barharbor/coachstop

Although most of Bar Harbor's inns occupy turn-of-the-century mansions, the Coach Stop Inn dates back to the turn of the previous century. Built in 1804, it long served as a stagecoach stop and tavern. In 1995, it was bought by longtime Maine innkeepers Kathy and Tom Combs, who restored this Cape Cod–style Colonial home. The ceilings have exposed hand-hewn and pegged beams; the original floors are wide-planked pine. Antique and country furnishings are enhanced by a collection of antique coach prints, plus Waverly, Schumacher, and other designer fabrics and wallpapers.

Breakfast is served from 8–9 A.M. at individual tables, and includes fresh fruit and juice, cereal, home-baked goods, breakfast meat, plus such daily specials as Colonial bread pudding with warm maple syrup, vegetable frittata, blueberry corn pancakes, or stuffed French toast with sautéed apples. Rates also include afternoon iced tea or apple cider, and wine and a tempting snack.

"A wonderful find and an excellent value, with cheerful, well-decorated rooms and knowledgeable, friendly innkeepers. The public rooms have the original, pine wide-board floors; the comfortable sitting room has red wallpaper above white wainscoting, hand-hewn beams, a TV in an antique bureau, a comfy sofa, and a fireplace which was lit in chilly weather. It's a bright, sunny room with fresh flowers, books and menus, and other local information; Tom is a park ranger so there's lots of information on Acadia. If you express an interest, Kathy has fascinating information about the house.

"Our first-floor suite had a living room with wall-to-wall carpeting topped with Oriental rugs, a brick fireplace, exposed ceiling beams, white walls accented with a floral wallpaper border, and a colorful, dazzling quilt. The bedroom had a queen-size bed, done in pink, green, and cream-colored linens. The bath was modern, with a small tub/shower unit and a pedestal sink; towels were arranged in a big white wicker. The cozy second-floor guest room is tucked under the eaves, but has a spacious sitting room with comfortable seating and an old dollhouse holding a selection of magazines. Its bathroom has an old-fashioned claw-foot tub with shower, a pedestal sink, and a mirror that resembles a house window, with mullions. The newer addition has three guest rooms. Room 2 has its own porch with two white-wicker chairs overlooking a small garden area, and is creatively decorated, using old wide floorboards as wainscoting, a fireplace mantel as a headboard, and stenciled nightstands with table lamps. Generous breakfast highlighted by delicious blueberry coffee cake and homemade blueberry and cranberry jams." (*Suzanne Carmichael*)

"Kathy Combs welcomed us warmly and showed us around the inn, explaining about breakfast, afternoon refreshments, local restaurants, special activities, and what to do in Acadia National Park. She did this all with such charm that we felt right at home. Kathy's breakfasts were as delightful as the company, and were a fun time to share travel stories with the other guests. After a day of exploring, we always made sure to be back around 5:00 P.M. to enjoy the wine and hors d'oeuvres, served in an inviting room with a fire crackling in the fireplace. After browsing through the binder with the menus of local restaurants, we sometimes ended up going out for dinner with other guests. Our room was beautifully decorated—comfortable, clean, and quiet. The inn is perfectly located for exploring Acadia." (*Maaike van Es-Oosting*)

Open Mid-May–late Oct.
Rooms 2 suites, 3 doubles—all with full private bath and/or shower, clock, fan; 1 with TV, desk, fireplace. Some with private entrance, porch/patio.
Facilities Common room with fireplace, TV, stereo, books; guest refrigerator. 3 acres with apple trees, gardens, arbors, outdoor seating. 2 m to Acadia National Park.
Location 5 m from downtown Bar Harbor. From Ellsworth, take Rte. 3 to Bar Harbor. At Thompson Island Bridge bear left. Inn is on left, 4 m from bridge. From Nova Scotia ferry, make right onto Rte. 3. Inn is on right approx. 5 m from ferry.
Restrictions No smoking. Children 6 and over.
Credit cards Amex, Discover, MC, Visa.
Rates B&B, $75–129 suite, $49–99 double, $44–94 single. Children free in parents' room.

Graycote Inn	*Tel:* 207–288–3044
40 Holland Avenue, 04609	*Fax:* 207–288–2719
	E-mail: graycote@acadia.net
	URL: http://www.graycoteinn.com

Take a restored 1881 Victorian home in a convenient yet quiet location, decorate it with a light, airy Country Victorian style, furnish it with guest comfort in mind, add warm and welcoming innkeepers, season liberally with delicious breakfasts and afternoon tea, and voilà—the Graycote Inn, owned by Roger and Pat Samuel since 1996. Originally built for the first rector of St. Savior's Episcopal church, Reverend Christopher Leffingwell, Graycote became a guest house in the 1950s, and was restored as a B&B in 1986.

Coffee and tea are ready for early risers at 7 A.M. Breakfast is served at tables for two, or four, on the breakfast porch or at the dining room table, and is different each day. The meal always includes juice, fruit, a hot entrée, and a home-baked treat. Favorite dishes include apple-cranberry crisp, strawberry soup, oatmeal or blueberry muffins, orange pecan pancakes, or chili-cheese casserole. Rates also include afternoon lemonade or mulled cider, coffee and tea, with brownies or perhaps scones, cheese and crackers or cucumber sandwiches.

"Roger welcomed us warmly, and gave us a helpful orientation to the inn and area. He answered our questions, putting us at ease. The inn is attractively decorated and landscaped, and feels uncrowded and spacious inside and out. The Samuels were a wealth of information on the island and local activities, and recommended their favorite places for hiking, bicycling, and jogging. On a rainy day, we enjoyed a tour of the lobster hatchery, where we saw the life cycle of the lobster from the egg to the point where baby lobsters are released to the sea. The generous, creative breakfasts included tasty breakfast burritos, served with fresh-sliced fruit. The period furnishings enhance its turn-of-the-century charm. We enjoyed sipping a glass of wine and sharing a glimpse of the past. Roger honestly explained the pros and cons of various Bar Harbor establishments, steering us to restaurants that met our tastes, and directing us to great late-night jazz in a small club a short walk away." (George & Laurene Willett) "Fantastic breakfasts, with no duplicates during a week-long stay. Ideal location on a side street at the edge of town with plenty of parking. Lovely gardens with lots of perennials. After a day of hiking or boating, we loved to relax on the porch, nibbling one of Pat's delicious cakes, sharing experiences and exchanging dinner experiences with the other guests." (Thelma Shoneman) "Our Frenchman's Bay Room was huge, with everything provided to make it cozy. Loved having early morning coffee delivered to our door." (Allan & Nancie Jones)

"A typically thoughtful touch was the hot chocolate waiting outside our door in the morning." (Nancy & Mark Akers) "We loved relaxing in the hammock on the lawn, or playing croquet." (Laura Daillak) "Warm, friendly, open-minded hosts. Attractive, comfortable rooms, spacious but cozy, with great fireplaces in winter." (Adam Baacke) "Warmly professional from arrival to departure. Accommodations were roomy, beautifully decorated and furnished, spotless, and comfortable. The innkeepers anticipated our every need, even lending us jackets for watching the sunset on Cadillac Mountain." (Louis Sarosdy) "Pat was truly concerned about dietary restrictions, and planned breakfasts accordingly. Delicious orange-pecan pancakes; equally tasty afternoon treats. Comfortable beds, too." (Betty Chelmow)

Open All year.
Rooms 2 suites, 10 doubles—all with private bath and/or shower, radio, clock. Some with TV, desk, air-conditioning, fan, fireplace, sun porch/balcony. 2 two-bedroom suites in carriage house.
Facilities Dining room, breakfast porch, guest refrigerator; living room with fireplace, grand piano, games, books; porch. 1 acre with off-street parking, croquet, hammocks. Laundromat adjacent.
Location 4 blocks to center of town. 5-min. drive to Acadia National Park entrance. From stop sign at junction of Rte. 3 & Rte. 233, go left onto Mt. Desert St. Take 1st left onto Holland Ave. to inn on right.
Restrictions No smoking. Children over 10.
Credit cards Amex, Discover, MC, Visa.
Rates B&B, $135–200 suite (sleeps 4), $65–155 double, $60–145 single. Extra person, $20. 2-night minimum in season & holiday weekends.
Extras Local airport pickups. Basic French, German spoken.

Hearthside ¢
7 High Street, 04609

Tel: 207–288–4533
E-mail: hearth@acadia.net

Hearthside is a three-story Victorian home with cheerful red awnings and bright flower boxes. Owners since 1987, Barry and Susan Schwartz have fully renovated the house and have decorated the rooms with both antiques and traditional pieces. Guest rooms are done in country Victorian decor; all have queen-size beds. Susan's buffet breakfasts include homemade muffins and granola, fresh fruit, juice, and a main dish—perhaps stuffed French toast, quiche, omelets, or ham-and-cheese strata. Rates also include afternoon lemonade and cookies.

"Ideal location, within easy walking distance of downtown, yet on a quiet residential street. Susan and Barry make you feel so comfortable in their home, and are always ready to chat or offer guidance on activities and restaurants. Susan's breakfasts and afternoon snacks are first-rate." *(Ann Ranger)* "The Schwartzes balance genuine hospitality with guests' need for privacy." *(Annette Hanson)* "Beautifully appointed rooms with scrupulous attention to detail. Excellent breakfasts with something for everyone." *(Patricia Kay)* "The Winston Churchill Room is decorated in shades of blue and mauve, with Churchill mementos placed throughout—including his portrait and bust, pipes, and samples of his writing." *(SC)* "Susan and Barry combine light-hearted banter with a thorough knowledge of the area; the places they suggested to visit are not found in the guidebooks." *(Helen Richardson)* "The charming Emily Dickinson Room is decorated in deep Victorian mauves and greens. Susan and Barry shared their collections of kaleidoscopes, teddy bears, and books." *(Mrs. Regina Kockmaruk)*

Open All year.
Rooms 9 doubles—all with private bath and/or shower, fan, clock, air-conditioning. Some with fireplace, whirlpool tub, balcony.
Facilities Dining room, living room with fireplace, books, games. Guest refrigerator. Porch. Off-street parking.
Location From Rte. 3, go left on Mt. Desert St., left again on High St. to inn on left.
Restrictions No smoking. Children 10 and over.

Credit cards MC, Visa.
Rates B&B, $65–135 double. 2-night minimum in season, holidays.
Extras Airport pickups. Limited French, German.

The Inn at Canoe Point
P.O. Box 216, 04609

Tel: 207–288–9511
Fax: 207–288–2870
E-mail: canoe.point@juno.com
URL: http://www.innatcanoepoint.com

Nancy and Tom Cervelli, who bought the Inn at Canoe Point in 1996, previously owned the Kingsleigh in Southwest Harbor (see listing) for six years. The Cervellis note that "you will never realize that busy Bar Harbor is just two miles away. Lounge on the decks, read in the Ocean Room, walk among the trees, or sit on the rocks and watch the boats sail by." Breakfast is served from 8–9 A.M., and includes fruit juices, muffins or coffee cake, fresh fruit or maybe apple crisp, and a daily special—perhaps eggs Benedict and home fries, blueberry pancakes, or spinach-mushroom quiche. Afternoon refreshments include cheese and crackers, cookies and brownies, and perhaps iced tea and lemonade, or hot cider and cocoa.

"To have a good time, a guest need do no more than sit in the living room or on the deck and stare at the ocean. But Nancy and Tom aren't content to let it go at that. They have made, and are continuing to make, improvements to the inn's facilities. And their style of personal service makes this special location even more so. The Garden Room is a lovely small room with a great water view; everything was in excellent condition and beautifully maintained. Breakfasts are imaginative and delicious. As long as the Cervellis own this inn, we can't imagine staying anywhere else in Bar Harbor." (JF)

"At first, all you see of the inn is a tasteful sign on a road and the beginning of an inviting little lane. Turning in, you come to the inn at the end of the road, an 1889 Tudor cottage set in the pines and rocks just above the water." *(Mrs. James Todd)* "Perfect location—five minutes from Bar Harbor and seconds from the National Park." *(Yvonne Stoner)* "All the rooms are comfortable and beautifully appointed. The Master Suite has a fireplace and a private deck; the Garrett Suite has the wonderful sunrise view. Little touches include coffee on the upstairs landing at 7 A.M.; Nancy's lemon French toast at breakfast; tea on the deck in the afternoon or in front of a roaring fire in winter. It's so pristine and quiet, we felt like we were miles from civilization." *(Denise Dixon)*

"Tom and Nancy love sharing their favorite restaurants, hiking trails, and bicycling routes. Humor is always abundant, and guests love to socialize." *(Doug & Marylou Benzel Jr.)* "We walked along the beach, and read books on the deck." *(Edward Rogers)* "Our room's lighting was excellent, with a small Tiffany-style lamp to keep on as a nightlight. Breakfast and snacks are served in the Ocean Room, which has a large fireplace, a spectacular view, and pleasant background music. We enjoyed countless cups of hot cider in front of a blazing fire as the rain came down outside. Tom mapped out a perfect tour of Acadia for us." *(Stephanie Roberts)* "While located just off the main highway leading into

Bar Harbor, the inn is secluded from the road by its lower elevation and setting among tall trees. The property is situated on the water and is within easy walking distance of the main entrance to Acadia National Park. Excellent and creative breakfasts are served on the outdoor deck, weather permitting." *(Ellis Locher)*

Worth noting: This inn is deservedly popular. Book well ahead in season to avoid disappointment.

Open All year.
Rooms 2 suites, 3 doubles—all with private shower and/or bath, radio/clock, fan. 3 with desk. 2 with fireplace, deck, private entrance.
Facilities Breakfast room with fireplace, living room with fireplace, piano; ocean room with fireplace, library, deck. Guest refrigerator. 2 acres on waterfront.
Location 2 m from Bar Harbor, 1 m from Nova Scotia Ferry. From Ellsworth, take Rte. 3 approx. 15 m toward Bar Harbor. Just beyond the village of Hulls Cove, watch for entrance to Acadia National Park on right. ¼ m past entrance, watch for inn driveway on left.
Restrictions No smoking. Children 16 and over.
Credit cards Discover, MC, Visa.
Rates B&B, $120–245 suite, $80–175 double.
Extras Airport pickup.

The Maples Inn ¢
16 Roberts Avenue, 04609

Tel: 207–288–3443
Fax: 207–288–0356
E-mail: maplesinn@acadia.net
URL: http://www.acadia.net/maples

Built in 1903, the Maples Inn combines tranquility and convenience, with a location on a quiet residential street, yet within easy walking distance of all shops, restaurants, and the waterfront; Acadia National Park is a five-minutes' drive away. The inn was purchased in 1998 by Tom and Sue Palumbo, who left corporate life behind to fulfill their dream of becoming innkeepers. They were frequent visitors to Mt. Desert Island for the past twenty years, and now enjoy sharing their love of the island with their guests. Guest rooms, each named for a different tree, have antique and reproduction furnishings, and down comforters; the English Holly Room has a four-poster queen-size bed with matching antique dressing table, while the White Birch Suite has a queen-size pewter bed and a separate sitting room with a fireplace. Tom's breakfasts range from sautéed berries in puff pastry, maple ham and leek quiche, oatmeal loaf, and bacon; to pineapple boats with strawberries and kiwi, blueberry-stuffed French toast, and lemon yogurt bread, and maple sausage. In the afternoon, tea and cookies are served on the front porch or in front of a cozy fire in the parlor.

"Tom and Sue have a real affinity for innkeeping! Prompt and delicious breakfasts of quiche and pastry one day, blueberry-stuffed French toast the next." *(Julie Cloninger)* "A pleasant and restful stay. The Red Oak is a cozy room with a huge, comfortable queen-size four-poster bed, abundant with decorative pillows. We immediately felt welcome and at home." *(Dan & Terri O'Neill)* "Tom and Sue made our stay pleasurable, with friendly, helpful hints as well as cozy, well-appointed rooms. Tom's gourmet breakfast was a plus, too!" *(Marlys Davis)* "The air is always scented with baking bread or cookies. A tidy little basket in our room was filled with those little necessities—safety pins, Band-aids, etc." *(Pat Bacon)* "From the spectacular breakfasts and warm hospitality to the carefully decorated rooms, the Maples Inn is a top value in coastal Maine." *(Josephine Schuda)* "A perfect, quiet, romantic honeymoon visit." *(Scott Shaw)* "Located in a quiet neighborhood, close to beautiful churches, within walking distance of town. Pick up a book from the library, fix a cup of tea, and sit by the fireplace to rest your soul." *(Ryoko Asakura)* "We enjoyed the convivial porch, the reading lamps, the Ralph Lauren towels, the choice of pillows, and the restaurant and sightseeing recommendations." *(Linda Leavell)* "The White Birch Suite was beautifully furnished and immaculate." *(Paul Michaelson)*

Open Feb. 1–Dec. 15.
Rooms 1 suite, 5 doubles—all with private shower, radio, fan. 2 with desk, 1 with fireplace, deck.
Facilities Parlor with fireplace; dining room, porch. Off-street parking.
Location Center of town. Turn left on Cottage St., go 4 blocks to Roberts Ave. & turn right to inn on left.
Restrictions No smoking. Children 8 and over.
Credit cards Discover, MC, Visa.
Rates B&B, $95–150 suite, $60–115 double. Extra person, $15.

Mira Monte Inn ♿
69 Mount Desert Street, 04609

Tel: 207–288–4263
800–553–5109
Fax: 207–288–3115
E-mail: mburns@acadia.net
URL: http://www.acadia.net/mira_monte

This rambling Victorian home was built in 1864 and was named Mira Monte ("behold the mountains") in 1892 by its then-current owners who came from Philadelphia each summer. Longtime owner Marian Burns has extensively furnished the inn with antiques and period reproductions, with lace curtains and flowered wallpapers. Equal attention has been lavished on the exterior, with masses of flowers blooming in perennial gardens throughout the summer season and comprising bouquets for each room. Insulated windows and air conditioning minimize the effect of any traffic noise. Marian notes that: "We especially enjoy visitors who stay with us for several days, walking or bicycling along the carriage trails, taking nature hikes with the park rangers, enjoying our library and the lively conversations at breakfast and during afternoon wine and cheese."

"If you want to socialize you can join in singing at the library piano, or chat over wine and cheese before the fire; if privacy is preferred, retreat to the serenity of your room, build a fire in your own fireplace, or gaze out into the garden. Marian, a Maine native, is a fount of historical information and, as a former science teacher, is knowledgeable about local flora and fauna." *(Dara Blackstone & Shigeru Hayashi)* "Well-run, relaxed, and comfortable, with a fine, friendly staff. Each room balances a sense of history with modern conveniences. Marian goes out of her way to help guests find activities and sights off the beaten track." *(Karen & Eric Keller)* "The lovely West End Room has a private entrance and back porch. Marian has mastered the art of being helpful without being intrusive, and is pleased to share her wealth of knowledge with her guests. The breakfast buffet is served on a beautiful antique sideboard, and includes freshly baked muffins with Maine blueberries, home-baked coffee cake, fresh fruit, waffles, eggs, oatmeal, and granola; the selection varies daily. You can share the company of fellow guests, or enjoy breakfast on your own balcony or porch. The spacious grounds allow you to relax in peaceful solitude." *(Sandra Labaree)*

"Our spacious, homey room was quiet, and the bed most comfortable. At breakfast we chatted with the other guests while enjoying delicious homemade breads and muffins." *(Daniel Comiskey & Suzanne McConnell)* "Beautiful old house with lots of porches; comfortable places to sit in the common rooms; lots of good area information. Our quiet room overlooked the garden and had both a small private porch and a fireplace. Convenient location within walking distance of town. Marian is a wonderful innkeeper." *(Emily Hoche-Mong)* "Our package rate included a choice of such activities as mountain bike rentals, a glider ride, and a whale-watching cruise." *(Kevin Harbison)*

Open May 1–Nov. 1.
Rooms 3 suites, 13 doubles—all with private bath and/or shower, telephone, clock/radio, TV, desk, air-conditioning, fan. Some with double whirlpool tub, balcony or deck, fireplace, kitchenette. Three 1- or 2-bedroom suites in adjacent building.
Facilities Living room with fireplace, library with fireplace, piano, TV/VCR; dining room, porch, deck. 1½ acres with gardens, terraces, lawn games.
Location Center of town.
Restrictions Light sleepers should request rooms away from street. Smoking on balconies only.
Credit cards Amex, DC, Discover, MC, Visa.
Rates B&B, $200 suite, $125–160 double. Extra person, $15. 2-night minimum. Tipping envelope. Four-night & off-season packages.
Extras Wheelchair access; two rooms specially equipped.

BATH

The "City of Ships," Bath was a major port in the early 1800s, and has been an important shipbuilding center for 200 years. Be sure to visit the Maine Maritime Museum to see how ships were built in the old days; at the Bath Iron Works, modern-day frigates are still being constructed. The mansions built by prosperous sea captains and merchants still line the city's streets; one of them, the Sewell House, displays an excellent collection of marine art and ship models. Nearby Popham Beach and Reid State Park both offer pleasant beaches and woodland hiking. Also available is golf, tennis, and river- and ocean-fishing. If you need a break from too much relaxation, head down the road to Freeport for an afternoon shopping frenzy. Bath is located in mid-coastal Maine, about 20 minutes northeast of Freeport, 45 minutes northeast of Portland, and about 2½ to 3 hours north of Boston's Logan Airport.

Reader tips: "Explore the historic district of old shipbuilders' homes, with its narrow streets, wonderful architecture, and well-tended gardens." *(Becky Nielsen)* "We highly recommend the Georgetown Coop Fish Market for a great lobster dinner on the docks. We took a pleasant evening stroll through the downtown area—some intriguing shops." *(Marilyn Sharp)* "We were pleased with our choice of Bath as a base for touring mid-coastal Maine; B&B rates are very reasonable compared to other towns, and the town itself has enough to do for a full day of exploring." *(MW, also Elizabeth & Herbert Smith)*

Also recommended: A 1790 Georgian-style home in the heart of Bath's historic district, the **Packard House** (45 Pearl Street, 04530; 207–443–6069 or 800–516–4578; www.mainecoast.com/packardhouse) is owned by Debby and Bill Hayden. Each of the three guest rooms have a private bath, and the B&B double rate ranges from $65–90, including a breakfast of pancakes, French toast, or eggs, with sausage, fruits, and home-baked goods. "The Haydens are friendly but do not intrude, and are always ready to help guests find the best restaurants, local events, sights, and more. Guests enjoy great conversations over Debby's delicious breakfasts. Rooms are immaculate and decorated with quiet charm; our favorite is the spacious suite, with a comfortable sitting room." *(Catherine Peterson)* "Attention to detail ranges from ample blankets and pillows, to water glasses and good reading lights, to perfect mattresses and ample hot water." *(Carol Cosmar)* "Quiet, side street location; beautiful collections of china and silver, paintings and books. The private bathrooms have fluffy towels, plenty of hot water, and pretty soaps. Breakfasts are a highlight. Debby is a great cook, and Bill is an engaging host, making sure coffee cups are never empty." *(Becky Nielsen)*

For additional area inns, see **Boothbay Harbor, Brunswick,** and **Freeport.**

Fairhaven Inn ¢ 👫
North Bath Road, RR 2, P.O. Box 85, 04530

Tel: 207–443–4391
888–443–4391
Fax: 207–443–6412
E-mail: fairhvn@gwi.net
URL: http://mainecoast.com/fairhaveninn

Frenetic crowds can easily quash dreams of a relaxing summer vacation on the Maine coast. Better to find a lesser known destination, and an inn with a peaceful country setting for better results and more reasonable prices. The Fairhaven Inn, purchased by former guests Susie and Dave Reed in 1995, is just such a place. Built in 1790, this weathered, shingled Colonial home was expanded many times over the past 200 years. Prior to buying the inn, the Reeds owned a pastry shop in Washington, D.C.; Susie tells us that "I'm happy to share recipes, and give occasional pre-breakfast baking lessons." The breakfast menu varies daily, but includes fruit soups, crisps or fools; hot cereal or home-made granola; and such entrées as pain perdu, vegetable hash with poached eggs and hollandaise, or cornbread with rosemary custard.

"Fully endorse entry. Suzie is a wonderful cook, and is flexible about serving times for her excellent breakfasts. We enjoyed visited with the friendly fellow guests in the tavern area." *(Gail M. Boyle)* "Many inviting places to curl up with a book." *(Laura Senier)* "Rooms are comfortable with down comforters and beautiful country views. We enjoy watching the birds at the feeders during breakfast—served according to guests' schedules." *(Judy Taylor)* "The Reeds are pleasant and accommodating. The Oak Room is comfortable with a small bathroom." *(Herbert Smith)* "The Reeds' concern for their guests' enjoyment shows in all the little touches—a bowl of popcorn set next to me as I read in the large living room at night; the glass of wine brought to my room after I returned from a hectic day; finding all the snow swept from my car before departure. The house is clean, spacious, and well-decorated. The inn is located in a rural area, good for hiking or just relaxing, a short distance from the town of Bath, a quaint and friendly place. But the best part about Fairhaven is the Reeds themselves." *(Ruth Maderski)*

"Situated on the side of a rocky hill, the beautiful vista encompasses trees, grasses, and flowers, and bits of the Kennebec River. In the summertime, the front lawn is peppered with lounge chairs for quiet relaxation. This lovely inn has spacious public rooms, good lighting, with classical music playing softly on the stereo. We stayed in the large and cheery Maple Room, with a comfortable queen-size bed." *(John Blewer)* "Two magnificent and uncrowded beaches nearby." *(Brian Yellin & Janice Nolan)*

Open All year.

Rooms 1 suite, 7 doubles—6 with private bath and/or shower. 2 with maximum of 4 people sharing bath. All with clock/radio, fan.

Facilities 2 dining rooms, 1 with fireplace; "tavern" with fireplace, TV, guest refrigerator; library, porch, patio. 16 acres with lawns, hiking/cross-country skiing trails, swings, lawn games. Golf next door; water sports, beaches nearby.

Location 20 m N of Freeport, 30 m S of Boothbay Harbor. 2½ m from Bath center. On High St. go N 1.5 m, turn left onto Whiskeag Road, go 1.2 m, turn right on North Bath Rd. Go .3 m to inn on left.

Restrictions No smoking.

Credit cards Discover, MC, Visa.

Rates B&B, $80–120 suite, double, $50–65 single. Extra person, $15; infants free. 2-night weekend minimum May 15–Oct. 31. Winter weekend package.

Extras Bus station pickups. Crib, babysitting by arrangement. Pets by arrangement; $10 per stay.

The Inn at Bath ♿   *Tel:* 207–443–4294
969 Washington Street, 04530   *Fax:* 207–443–4295
                              E-mail: innkeeper@innatbath.com
                              URL: http://www.innatbath.com

After 25 years on Wall Street, Nick Bayard decided it was time for a new lifestyle, and changed from the capital-intensive mode of an investment banker to the labor-intensive world of innkeeping—a switch from high-tech to high-touch. He purchased this 1810 Greek Revival home in 1989, and in the past ten years, has done a superb job of restoring, renovating, and refurbishing the inn, assisted by longtime manager Barbara Wilson. The decor is elegant but uncluttered, with 18th- and 19th-century antique furnishings and designer fabrics. Several guest rooms have queen-size canopy or four-poster beds, while others have king-size beds (convertible into twins). The romantic River Room is the renovated hayloft of the old attached stable and has hand-hewn ceiling beams, wide-pine floorboards, and a wood-burning fireplace, while the Captain's Cabin has a Jacuzzi for two overlooking the wood-burning fireplace. Several guest rooms can be modified to create two-bedroom family suites.

Breakfast is typically served from 8–9 A.M., but a continental breakfast is also available for early risers and late sleepers. Hot cereal, homemade granola, and English muffins are on the menu, but most guests prefer the daily special—perhaps blueberry pancakes, scrambled eggs, or banana French toast. Rates also include afternoon tea and coffee, and drink set-ups in the evening.

"A meticulously restored Greek Revival home. My favorite is the River Room with views of the Kennebec River. Waking up to Nick's banana French toast or Barbara's blueberry pancakes is a great start to the day. Nick will forever be remembered by my young son for providing Captain Crunch cereal in lieu of oatmeal. We enjoy meeting the other guests in the well-appointed dining rooms, at tables set with antique silver, although one can also have a breakfast tray in one's room. Nick and Barb offer helpful referrals to local restaurants and attractions." (Margaret Cavalli, also Pamela Humphrey) "Nick is a stickler for detail, and each room is impeccably decorated, never overdone, always tasteful and comfortable." (RPR) "Warm and friendly atmosphere. From the initial greeting to our reluctant departure, we always feel welcome and special. Nick is well-informed about area activities and can get dinner reservations at the best places." (Eleanor & Harry Powers) "Gracious innkeepers and staff; the inn was a welcoming refuge in a fierce winter storm. The buildings along Washington Street are handsome and lovingly maintained; it's always a pleasure to take an evening stroll to one of my favorite local restaurants, both an easy walk from the inn." (Pamela Mensch)

Open All year.

Rooms 1 suite, 8 doubles—all with full private bath and/or shower, telephone, clock/radio/cassette player, TV. Some with double whirlpool tub, bidet, desk, air-conditioning, ceiling fan, wood-burning fireplace, refrigerator, private entrance.

Facilities 3 dining rooms, twin parlors with fireplaces, TV/VCR; guest laundry; fax/email available. 3/10 acre with gardens, off-street parking. Tennis, golf, hiking, skiing, fishing, ocean beaches.

Location Historic district, 1 block from the Kennebec River; walking distance to shops, restaurants, Maritime Museum. From Rte. 1 N, watch for Holiday Inn on right, followed by 3 gas stations. At 3rd gas station, go right at "Historic Bath" exit. Go downhill 2 blocks to light. Go left at light & go N on Washington St. for

½ m to inn on right. From Rte. 1 S, cross Carlton Bridge over Kennebec River. Take Bath exit & go right at end of bridge. Immediately bear left down a grade. At bottom of grade, bear right onto Washington St. for ½ m to inn on right.

Restrictions No smoking. Children 6 and over preferred.

Credit cards Amex, Discover, MC, Visa.

Rates B&B, $150–330 suite (sleeps 4), $75–165 double. Extra person, $15–25. Senior, children's, AAA discounts. 2-night weekend minimum in season.

Extras Wheelchair access; bathroom specially equipped. Airport/station pickups. Pets OK with prior approval. A little French spoken.

BELFAST

Settled in 1773, Belfast prospered through much of the 19th century from the fishing and shipbuilding industries. Well-to-do captains (of both sea and industry) built handsome houses for their families, and their legacy of historic homes in all styles, from Greek Revival to Italianate to Queen Anne, makes a walking tour of town a real pleasure. The restored downtown area is quite appealing; since the town is off Route 1, traffic is never heavy.

Located in mid-coastal Maine, Belfast is set on Penobscot Bay, and provides a good base for touring many area attractions. It's approximately 55 miles from Acadia National Park and Bar Harbor, as well as Augusta and Bangor, and 100 miles northeast of Portland. There's a park nearby with a swimming pool, tennis courts, playground, and a rocky beach for swimming; other outdoor activities include fishing, sailing, horseback riding, and cross-country skiing.

For additional area entries, see **Searsport** and **Stockton Springs**.

Jeweled Turret Inn ¢   *Tel:* 207–338–2304
40 Pearl Street, 04915   800–696–2304
    URL: http://www.bbonline.com/me/jeweledturret/

A grand stairway, housed in a round turret with stained- and leaded-glass panels and jewel-like embellishments, gives the Jeweled Turret its name. Laboriously restored in 1986 by Carl and Cathy Heffentrager, the inn offers such distinctive architectural features as the den fireplace, built with rocks and semiprecious stones from every state that was in the Union at the time of the inn's construction in 1898. Oak, pine, maple, and fir woodwork add to its charm. Antique furnishings, Oriental rugs, reproduction period wallpapers, and lace and chintz window treatments create an appealing Victorian atmosphere. In addition to fine coffees, teas, and cocoa, a typical breakfast might include poached lemon-cinnamon pears, German crown pancakes, or hazelnut Belgian waffles. Afternoon tea and cocoa is served in the dining room in the winter months; in summer, iced tea and lemonade awaits guests on the veranda.

"Beautiful Victorian decor, with appealing collections in the ample common areas. An inviting spot in chilly weather is the cozy den; on warm days, guests relax on the back porch or front veranda. The attractive upstairs guest rooms are uncluttered, with good lighting, ample storage space, and exceptionally beautiful woodwork throughout. Immaculate housekeeping. Delicious breakfast of bananas baked with lemon, brown sugar, and coconut; orange juice, much-too-tempting pecan scones, and blueberry sourdough waffles. Carl and Cathy have done an extraordinary job of restoration. The delicate Amethyst Turret guest room has a massive cannonball four-poster bed, with an in-room bath separated by lined lace curtains." *(SWS)*

"Beautifully restored and situated in a delightfully quaint coastal town with a rich history. Pleasant, interesting innkeepers, eager to advise us on sights and activities." *(Guy Kemmerly)* "Our room was quiet and private." *(Anna McPeake)* "Everything sparkled; even the beautiful wood floors shine. Carl and Cathy were welcoming and helpful in telling us about the house and in taking time to discuss local restaurants." *(Karen Kadushin)* "Breakfasts are outstanding; guests are offered either an 8 A.M. or 9 A.M. seating." *(Mark Mulcahy)* "At tea-time, we nibbled carrot cake, enjoying a lace-veiled view of the snow-covered yard." *(KF)*

Open All year.
Rooms 7 doubles—all with private shower and/or bath. 2 with desk, 1 with fireplace.
Facilities Dining room with fireplace, den/library with fireplace, TV; parlor, living room with fireplace, sitting room, porches with rocking chairs. ¼ acre with garden. 2 blocks from ocean. Off-street parking. 20 m to Camden Snow Bowl for skiing.
Location 2 blocks to center. From Rte. 1 N, take Northport Ave. Exit N; bear left at Church St.; go 3 blocks N on Church; turn right at Pearl to inn on corner. From Rte. 1 S, go S on High St. to traffic light. Continue straight two more blocks; go right on Pearl St.
Restrictions Smoking restricted to outside verandas.
Credit cards MC, Visa.
Rates B&B, $75–105 double, $70–100 single. Extra person, $15. Tipping "not expected." Off-season rates.
Extras Local airport/station pickups.

The Thomas Pitcher House ¢
19 Franklin Street, 04915

Tel: 207–338–6454
888–338–6454
E-mail: tpitcher@acadia.net
URL: http://www.thomaspitcherhouse.com

Thomas Pitcher, a prosperous town merchant, built this home for his family in 1873. With central heat and hot- and cold-running water, it was considered a state-of-the-art residence. Fran and Ron Kresge, who restored the house in 1992, have maintained its historical elegance with its large bay windows and handsome woodwork throughout. Three-course breakfasts are served in the spacious Chippendale dining room and a typical menu might include freshly squeezed juices, fresh fruit, lemon drizzle cake, and a ham and cheese soufflé, or German apple pancakes. Rates also include cookies or small pastries in the room, and a small chocolate treat for bedtime.

"Lovely inn, with spacious, high-ceilinged rooms, bright and airy; beautiful woodwork; some guest rooms have original built-in marble sinks. Quiet location." *(SWS)* "Excellent in all respects, with easygoing innkeepers, helpful and courteous in every way. Fascinating history of both house and town. Loved the fresh flowers, home-baked cookies; great bed—slept like a baby." *(J. Dan Frost)* "Terrific attention to detail: bath salts for the claw-foot tub, quiet fan for humid nights, comfy chairs and wonderful firm mattress. Outstanding breakfasts with homemade strawberry sauce for waffles, delicious ginger pancakes. Hosts graciously accommodated our timing." *(Jody & Bruce Davie)* "Sugar cookies in our room, our own private porch for early morning coffee." *(Joan Somers)*

"Public rooms offer lovely settings for conversations, reading, or TV. Music throughout, with consistently beautiful selections, plus a wide range of books from the classics to popular novels. Delectable, filling breakfasts. Fran and Ron are friendly, helpful, and available, yet unobtrusive." *(Mary Tazewell)* "Impeccable architectural detail and color." *(Audrey Johnson)* "Ron and Fran made us feel welcome and at home. At breakfast we each had separate coffee carafes, one decaf, one regular. The house is spotless, soothing music fills the rooms in a relaxing way, and evening homemade treats are just right for a late night snack. Your room key also opens the front door, so guests can come and go at their convenience. Common areas are always available for relaxing, and the hosts are available but not obtrusive." *(Rebecca Sucke)*

"Our bedroom was large, bright, and airy with a wonderfully comfortable bed and crisp designer linens." *(Carol & Henry Renne)* "An excellent balance of Victorian and traditional decor." *(Mr. & Mrs. Glenn Hower)* "The mouth-watering smell of freshly baked cake filled the evening air, a wonderful bedtime snack; equally inviting aromas greeted us in the morning when we were seated at the elegant dining room table, set with china, fresh linens, and flowers." *(Stephen Bird)*

Open All year.
Rooms 4 doubles—all with private bath and/or shower, clock, fan, music. 1 with desk.
Facilities Dining room, parlor with fireplace, library with TV/VCR, books; porch, deck. Off-street parking.
Location In historic district; 1 block from center of town. Take Belfast exit at intersection of Rtes. 1 & 3. Go 6 blocks E on Main St. to Cedar St. Right on Cedar St. for 1 block. Left on Franklin St. to inn.
Restrictions No smoking. Children 12 and over.
Credit cards MC, Visa.
Rates B&B, $70–90 double, $60–80 single. Extra person, $15. Off-season rates, extended-stay discounts.
Extras German, some French spoken.

BLUE HILL

Blue Hill is an old shipping town on the east coast of the Penobscot peninsula, bordering magnificent Blue Hill Bay, on the other side of which is Acadia National Park. It's 40 miles south of Bangor and an easy drive to Bar Harbor, Camden, and Rockport. Blue Hill is popular with hikers, bikers, and sailors in warm weather, and cross-country skiing and ice-skating in cold. Summertime brings first-rate concerts to Kneisel Hall. For those interested in seeing classic old boats and newly constructed ones, the Wooden Boat Museum is 10 miles to the south in Brooklin.

Blue Hill is located 40 miles south of Bangor, and 150 miles north of Portland; it's 40 minutes from Acadia National Park.

Information please: Owned by the same family since 1764, the **Oakland House Seaside Inn and Cottages** (Herrick Road, RR 1, P.O. Box 400, Brooksville, 04617; 207–359–8521 or 800–359–RELAX; www. acadia.net/oaklandhse) is a 50-acre complex, set along a half mile of private oceanfront. Operated as a hotel since 1889, the inn is currently owned by the original owner's great-grandson, Jim Littlefield, and his wife, Sally. Accommodations are available in the handsomely renovated Shore Oaks Mission–style "summer cottage," with ten bedrooms, a living room with a stone fireplace and dining room, and in 15 one- to five-bedroom cottages, scattered throughout the property; many have spectacular water views. Renovation and upgrading is an on-going process. The property includes salt- and freshwater beaches, a dock, rowboats, and miles of hiking trails. Dinner is served in the main building, over 200 years old; a typical Saturday-night menu includes salad, popovers, garden vegetable soup, prime rib or shrimp scampi, chocolate pudding or perhaps apple pie. Rates range widely with type of accommodation, length and dates of stay, but average $185 for two including breakfast and dinner in a renovated Shore Oaks room with private bath in peak season; cottages typically rent by the week in high season. "Warm, comforting breakfasts with oatmeal, lemon-ginger muffins, whole-wheat blueberry pancakes, and quiche Lorraine; ever-present homemade biscotti or cookies on the Shore Oaks sideboard; tremendous water and island views from the porch; good dinners at Oakland House." *(JU)* "Jim and Sally welcome us like family when we return for our annual summer visit." *(Marilyn Wimmergren)* Comments appreciated.

For additional area entries, see **Castine** and **Deer Isle/Stonington**.

The Blue Hill Inn ✕ ♿	*Tel:* 207–374–2844
Union Street, Route 177, P.O. Box 403, 04614	800–826–7415
	Fax: 207–374–2829
	E-mail: bluhilin@downeast.net
	URL: http://www.bluehillinn.com

A brick and clapboard building, the Blue Hill Inn has operated as a village inn since 1840, and has been owned by Don and Mary Hartley since 1987. A consistent reader favorite, guests are delighted with the inn's welcoming atmosphere, warm hospitality, and delicious food. The five-course dinner menu features local meats, fish, and produce; recent entrées included striped bass with zucchini and porcini mushrooms; pork tenderloin with rosemary and Calvados; or lobster with tomatoes, garlic, and white wine. Breakfasts are no less tasty, with fresh fruit and juice, breads and scones, and a choice of such entrées as feta cheese and tomato omelets, homemade granola with yogurt, waffles with strawberries, almond-raisin French toast, and blueberry pancakes. Equal attention is paid to the guest rooms. Beds are turned down nightly, with clean towels provided. Linens are changed daily, with flannel sheets in winter and cotton ones in summer. Fresh-brewed coffee, tea, and soda are available throughout the day. Completed in 1997 is the wheelchair accessible Cape House Suite, with cathedral ceiling, king-size bed, living area, kitchen, brick fireplace, deck, and private entrance.

"Impeccable service; it seemed that every time we returned to our room, the towels and bedding had been refreshed, and fireplace logs replaced as needed. Superb cuisine at both breakfast and dinner." *(Ron & Andrea Winson)* "Genuinely caring and hospitable innkeepers, who are always working to improve their inn. My spacious, well-equipped, easy-to-access room was right by the front door, with wood laid in the fireplace, ready to light, ample storage space in the closet and dresser, good-sized bathroom, comfortable queen-size bed, desk with a lamp, and two comfortable reading chairs with another lamp. Ample space in the parlors for relaxing and visiting with the other guests." *(SWS)* "We rarely return to an inn, preferring to try new ones, but we always come back to the Blue Hill Inn. The towels are so soft, the rooms immaculate, and the Hartleys so accommodating. My special dietary meals were met with delicious results. Beautiful area for walking." *(Terry Gray)* "The aromas of sumptuous dinners and tasty breakfasts, the soft sounds of classical music, and the comfort of a well-appointed room made the Blue Hill Inn the highlight of our trip. Elegance, class, warmth, and service." *(Donna Bradley)* "An excellent inn, professionally run. We especially enjoyed the cocktail hour and socializing with our fellow guests. Mary mapped out a lovely after-dinner stroll. One night was not enough." *(Ruthie & Derek Tilsley)*

"Competent and friendly staff who make guests feel welcome from the moment they arrive until the day they reluctantly depart." *(Ann Westbrook)* "Blue Hill is small, but lively in a relaxed way, with a number of good restaurants." *(MM)* "Lovely garden, ample and convenient parking. Information and assistance on area sights, shops, and events were readily available." *(Mary Wagner)* "At 6 P.M. guests gather in the sitting room to have cocktails in front of the fire (or in the garden in summer). The warm and friendly atmosphere soon makes it seem like a country-house party of old friends. Though there are tables for two and four, the most fun is dining at the table for eight." *(JB)* "All galleries and shops are within an easy walk." *(Arthur Avent)*

Open Mid-May–Nov. 30.
Rooms 3 suites, 9 doubles—all with private bath and/or shower, desk, fan. 4 with fireplace, 2 with air-conditioning, 1 with kitchen, TV, telephone.
Facilities Restaurant, parlor with fireplace, games, library. Chamber music in July. 1 acre with perennial gardens. Concert tickets, day sails, kayaking arranged. Bike rentals by advance notice.
Location Historic district, 1 block from center. Near village intersection of Rte. 15 and Rte. 177.

Restrictions No smoking. Not recommended for children under 13.
Credit cards MC, Visa.
Rates B&B, $90–200 suite or double, $80–160 single. MAP, $140–240 suite, double; $110–180 single. Extra person, $20–50. 15% service. 2-night minimum July 1–Oct. 15. Holiday, wine tasting, sailing packages. Corporate rates off-season. Prix fixe dinner $30. Box lunch by arrangement.
Extras Airport/station pickups. Limited wheelchair access.

Eggemoggin Reach B&B　　　　　　　　*Tel:* 207–359–5073
RR 1, P.O. Box 33A　　　　　　　　　　　　888–625–8866
Herrick Road, Brooksville, 04617　　　*Fax:* 207–359–5074
　　　　　　　　　　　　URL: http://www.eggreachbb.com

Though Maine has thousands of miles of coastline, surprisingly few of its inns have water views. A notable exception is the Eggemoggin Reach B&B, a newly built post-and-beam home in the old Maine farmhouse tradition. Comfortably decorated with antiques, traditional pieces, and pine-paneled walls, this secluded B&B offers a southwesterly panorama of the many islands across Penobscot Bay and the Camden Hills. Guests can enjoy this spectacular view from the porch that wraps around the house, and from most of its common areas and guest accommodations. The nautically themed guest quarters can be found in the main house, a carriage house, two adjacent cottages, and a recently built guest house; each cottage features wooden cathedral ceilings, an efficiency kitchen, a sitting area, and a woodstove with a Mexican-tile hearth. Owners Susie and Mike Canon built the house in 1988, opening it as a B&B in 1993. They serve a breakfast of fresh fruit, freshly squeezed orange juice, sausage or bacon, an egg casserole, cereals, and fresh breads and muffins.

"Outstanding location, on a point facing Pumpkin Lighthouse, on a tree-shaded knoll with sparkling water all around. Beautifully maintained and appointed; a superb sit-down breakfast." *(Dr. & Mrs. Edward Scull)* "Quiet location down a winding dirt road away from traffic noise. Wonderful smell of balsam mixed with the fresh sea air. We watched seals feeding, ospreys nesting, and loons calling." *(Sherry Justiss)* "Spacious, spotless, well-equipped guest rooms with individual thermostats. Inviting, relaxing living room with crackling fire in the fireplace." *(John & Barbara Smith)* "The Canons are friendly, sensitive, responsive, and well-informed about activities. Delightful breakfasts are served on the porch overlooking the water." *(Lois Swack)* "Fresh lobster brought to the door by a lobsterman, right off his boat. Susie's waffle recipe is light as a feather." *(Ilse Martz)* "A little off the beaten track, yet close to restaurants, national parks, antiquing, and quaint seaside towns." *(Lynn Chandler)*

Open Mid-May–mid-Oct.
Rooms 10 studios—all with full private baths, screened porches; many with fireplace, kitchen.
Facilities Dining room, living room with fireplace, den with fireplace, TV/VCR, stereo, books. Screened, open porches. 5½ acres with dock on ocean for boating, fishing; use of canoe and rowboat. Hiking, picnicking nearby.

Location 42 m S of Bangor. 10 min. S of Blue Hill. From Bucksport, go E on Rtes. 1/15 for 4.5 m. Follow Rte. 15 S for 14 m through Blue Hill. 4.5 m after Blue Hill, stop at a "T." Go left & continue on Rte. 15 for 2.9 m S to intersection with Rte. 175. Turn right on Rte. 175 (following the sign to Brooksville), for ½ m to the junction with Rte. 176. Bear left onto Rte. 176 for 9/10 m to intersection with Herrick Rd. Go left on Herrick Rd. & continue for 1.8 m; go right to inn entrance.
Restrictions No smoking. Children over 12.
Credit cards MC, Visa.
Rates B&B, $150–175. Extra person, $48. Lobster dinner, $25.
Extras Airport/station pickup, $30 one-way. Deep-water mooring at dock.

BOOTHBAY HARBOR

Like many Maine coastal towns, Boothbay's original reputation as a shipping port made the transition to one as a tourist center at the turn of the century. Visitors endure the inevitable T-shirt and fudge shops, and enjoy boating excursions to nearby islands, deep-sea fishing, and the Marine Aquarium on McKown's Point.

Boothbay Harbor is located in mid-coastal Maine, 30 miles north of Brunswick, and 60 miles north of Portland. Also listed in this section are inns in **Boothbay, Cape Newagen/Southport Island, Capitol Island,** and **East Boothbay**; all are within a six-mile circumference.

For additional area entries, see listings under **Brunswick, Freeport, Newcastle, New Harbor,** and **Wiscasset**.

Albonegon Inn ¢   *Tel:* 207–633–2521
Capitol Island, 04538

For a taste of old Maine, adventurous travelers seek out the Albonegon Inn, set on a private island just south of Boothbay Harbor. Described as "determinedly old-fashioned," the inn is simple but not rustic. Kim and Bob Peckham, who have owned the Albonegon since 1987, note that "the Albonegon (pronounced *al-buh-nee'-gun*) is one of the last 'island inns' of the 1800s that originally were served by steamer." Capitol Island—only ¾ mile long—is definitely a pedestrian haven; the speed limit is 10 miles per hour and bicycles may be walked, but not ridden, on the island. The breakfast buffet includes coffee, tea, and juice, plus three types of home-baked muffins and breads—perhaps peach sour cream cake, apricot corn muffins, and eight-grain bread. The inn also offers a casual dinner arrangement: they light a grill and provide chicken, steak, burgers, and hot dogs for guests to cook; chips, baked potatoes, condiments, and silverware are also supplied.

"A therapeutic return to a simpler life. The location is incredible—sounds of the surf and a distant fog horn, the smell of salt water and delicious home-baked treats, and the pleasures of rocking on the porch combine in a sensual delight. Rooms are small but adequate, with either double or twin-size beds and limited storage space." *(Ilene Wolfman)*

"A small side road led to a picturesque one-lane bridge to this private island. The narrow dirt road led us through the woods and across to a small bay, where this wonderful old hotel sits on a point jutting into the ocean. Our light, clean, simple room had a view of the sea from the bed. At night the tide was high, and the sound of the waves slapping on three sides gave us the feeling of being on a boat. This inn was built as a summer place, so walls and floors are not heavy, but we were not bothered by any noise from our fellow guests. The shared bath was not a problem, and the shower was good. Breakfast is served in a large room open to the ocean on three sides. The aromas from the kitchen of muffins baking and good coffee brewing (decaf and regular) seemed to bring everyone out early. The large and comfortable living room was well-used by the guests." *(William Hussey)*

Open Late May–mid-Oct.
Rooms 1 cottage, 1 suite, 12 doubles, 2 singles—3 with private bath and/or shower, 14 with sink in room & maximum of 6 sharing bath. 3 rooms in annex.
Facilities Living room with fireplace, library, piano, TV; dining room, porch, deck. Tennis court, croquet. Boating, fishing, swimming nearby.
Location S coastal ME. 4 m S of Boothbay Harbor (10-min. drive). From Boothbay Harbor, take Rte. 27 S to Rte. 238. Watch for inn's sign after 1½ m.
Restrictions No motorcycles or campers permitted on island. No smoking.
Credit cards None accepted.
Rates B&B, $125 suite, $75–95 double, $55 single. Extra person, $10.
Extras Babysitting by arrangement. Spanish, French spoken.

Anchor Watch B&B   *Tel:* 207–633–7565
3 Eames Road, 04538   *Fax:* 207–633–5319
                    E-mail: diane@lincoln.midcoast.com
        URL: http://www.maineguide.com/boothbay/anchorwatch

If you're coming to Maine for a taste of the sea, you'll enjoy a visit to the Anchor Watch B&B, built in 1920, and owned by Diane and Bob Campbell since 1988. Diane runs the inn, with views of islands and lighthouses, lobstermen and ducks, sunsets and seagulls, while husband Bob and son Bill captain the *Balmy Days II*, the sloop *Bay Lady*, and the *Novelty*, which will take you to Monhegan, sailing, or on a harbor tour. The nautical theme carries through to the guest rooms, named for Monhegan ferries of the past, and the artwork, painted by local artists. Breakfast is served from 8–9:30 A.M., and might include sliced oranges with raspberry sauce, baked omelets with cheddar, sausages, blueberry-pecan muffins; or perhaps fresh fruit, homemade popovers, bacon, and baked orange French toast with honey butter.

"Immaculately clean, with beautiful linens, and attractive decor. Well-maintained home. Excellent breakfasts, served on lovely china and glassware. Diane is warm, friendly, informative, and a great hostess. Delightfully private, quiet location on the water. Thoughtful touches included the fresh flowers and sherry. We were encouraged to make ourselves at home, and could use the refrigerator or make coffee. The inviting gathering room was well equipped with books and games." *(Mary Lou Hestad)* "Excellent location within walking distance of town. Delicious breakfasts served at two large tables in an inviting dining area, overlooking the water." *(Anne Finucane)* "Warm, bright, and inviting, with spectacular harbor views. Wonderful bird-watching at breakfast. Quiet location, yet just a short walk from town." *(Karen Zielsdorf)* "A beautiful green lawn leads to their private pier on the harbor, with space to sit overlooking the harbor. Rooms have comfortable chairs for reading or relaxing, with lighting to match either; they're comfortably cool in summer, and cozy warm in winter." *(Capt. J. Darrow Kirkpatrick)*

Open All year.

Rooms 5 doubles—all with full private bath and/or shower, clock/radio, fan. 1 with whirlpool tub, TV; 2 with air-conditioning, 4 with balcony.

Facilities Breakfast sun porch with fireplace, common room with TV/VCR, books, games. ½ acres with patio, off-street parking; private pier for fishing, swimming. Harbor tour discounts.

Location 5-min. walk to village. From Rte. 1, follow Rte. 27 to Oak St. into Boothbay village. Follow through village & bear right onto Commercial St. Follow Commercial to dead end. Go left on Eames to inn on right.

Restrictions No smoking. Children 8 and over.

Credit cards Discover, MC, Visa.

Rates B&B, $65–145 double, $60–140 single. Extra person, $20. 2-night holiday weekend minimum.

Five Gables Inn
Murray Hill Road, P.O. Box 335
East Boothbay, 04544

Tel: 207–633–4551
800–451–5048

Built circa 1890, the Five Gables sits on a hillside overlooking Linekin Bay. Originally a 22-room (three toilets!) summer hotel, it was extensively renovated in 1987. The fifteen guest rooms all face the bay, and are attractively furnished with reproductions, wicker, some antiques, and country touches. Most rooms have queen-size beds; one has a king-size bed, and one has twin beds that can also be made up as a king.

De and Mike Kennedy purchased the inn in 1995; the Kennedys are world travelers, and have worked everywhere from Europe to Montana to Tahiti. Mike is a graduate of the Culinary Institute of America and also spent ten years renovating Victorian homes in Atlanta. Early morning coffee is available, and breakfast is enjoyed at individual tables between 8 and 9:30 A.M. A typical morning meal might include puffed apple-cinnamon baked pancakes with cider syrup, grilled tomatoes with herbed cornmeal, grilled ham, English breakfast scones, fresh-baked whole-wheat bread, fresh-minted fruit, homemade granola, Bircher muesli, cereal, yogurt, and orange juice.

"The Kennedys are working hard to make a lovely inn even more so." *(SWS)* "De and Mike are friendly and knowledgeable about local activities. Spotlessly clean, beautifully decorated, relaxed, and unrushed. Fantastic food at breakfast, afternoon tea, and evening refreshments." *(Nancy Cowell)* "Peaceful and relaxing atmosphere; wonderful bay views." *(Anne Kollian)* "Afternoon tea and cookies were served in the comfortable common room before a roaring fire or on the porch." *(Mrs. Arthur Wahlstedt)* "Friendly atmosphere, excellent variety at each delicious breakfast. Tempting aromas of freshly baked bread and cookies." *(Ruth Birch)* "Relaxed atmosphere; well-managed inn. Our hosts provided us with excellent area information." *(S.E. Chantler)* "Baskets of fresh flowers everywhere. Our days began with breakfast in the common room by a crackling fireplace, friendly conversation, and a view of Linekin Bay." *(Linda Morin)* "Heirloom patchwork quilts; towels scented with fresh lavender; and natural soaps in the bath. Delicious fresh fruit and yogurt with muesli for breakfast." *(Sonia & Stan Nowak, also Barbara Walsh)*

"The shaded porch and the hammock overlooking the quiet cove were wonderful places to relax with a book and afternoon lemonade while hummingbirds hovered around the fuchsia, and osprey soared overhead." *(John Price)* "Picturesque, quiet location, convenient to Boothbay." *(Mark & Linda Gale)* "Guest rooms on the upper floors offer more privacy than the first-floor ones opening onto the porch, and vary in size from small to spacious." *(Pam Phillips)* "Usually the only sounds we heard were seagulls, an occasional boat, and the plaintive tolling of the bell buoys." *(Marsha & Bob McOsker)*

Open Mid-May–Oct.
Rooms 15 doubles—all with private bath and/or shower, telephone, clock/radio, fan. 5 with fireplace, 1 with desk.
Facilities Living/dining room with games, fireplace, stereo; library; wraparound veranda. ½ acre. Boating, swimming, fishing across street. 1 acre with off-street parking. Overlooking Linekin Bay for swimming, boating, fishing; two boat moorings.
Location Take Rte. 1 to Rte. 27 S to Rte. 96 through East Boothbay. Turn right on Murray Hill Rd. The inn is ½ mile on right. 3.3 m to Boothbay Harbor.
Restrictions No smoking. Children over 8.
Credit cards MC, Visa.
Rates B&B, $95–165 double. Extra person, $30.
Extras Boat moorings by reservation.

Hodgdon Island Inn ¢   *Tel:* 207–633–7474
Box 492, Barter's Island Road, 04571

Travel sometimes requires tough choices, and a visit to the Hodgdon Island Inn is no exception, reports reader *Bill Hussey:* "Our most difficult decision was where to sip our ice-cold lemonade on a sunny afternoon: on the wicker chairs on the porch, in the canopied glider by the roses, or by the sparkling swimming pool. This gracious sea captain's home is located by a quiet island, with a lawn leading down to a beautiful cove. Our lovely, spacious room had a modern bath, a king-size bed, and bay windows looking to the water. Attractive decor without fuss or clutter; friendly, efficient, unobtrusive hosts; the tasty breakfast left you full but not stuffed."

Dating back to 1800, the Hodgdon Island Inn was restored as a B&B in 1990 by Sydney and Joseph Klenk, who have furnished the inn simply with quilts and flowered comforters, Victorian and country antiques and wicker. They're happy to help guests with reservations, excursions, and travel plans, although guests are often content just to relax in the Adirondack chairs on the lawn, reading a book and watching the activity on the water. Breakfast is served from 8–9 A.M., and includes fresh fruit, homemade muffins and granola, and an entrée such as blueberry pancakes, waffles, or eggs and bacon.

"Ideal setting, a short drive from town, on quiet side road with beautiful water views. A handsome home, overlooking the water, with an attractively landscaped swimming pool." *(SWS)* "The Klenks make you feel welcome from the minute you enter their home. Immaculately clean, comfortable furnishings. We especially enjoy afternoons spent in quiet relaxation by the swimming pool. Every morning, I walk along the water and take in the beautiful views. Nearby is a nature preserve which is also great fun. Delicious breakfasts, many good restaurants nearby." *(Christiane Merrow)* "Congenial atmosphere and genuine hospitality. Set high on a knoll, the inn offers unobstructed views of a peaceful cove, with lobster and pleasure boats passing by occasionally. Joe and Sydney have extensive information on restaurants, sailing excursions, and more. Careful attention to every detail." *(Donald Finter)* "Wonderful sunset views from the porch." *(Jeannette Kaulfers)*

Open All year.
Rooms 6 doubles—all with private bath and/or shower, radio, clock, fan. 2 with balcony/deck.
Facilities Dining room, parlor with fireplace, TV/VCR, books; guest refrigerator, porch. 1 acre with chlorine-free heated swimming pool, swing.
Location 5 m to center of town. Take Maine Tpke. to Exit 9 to I-95 N. Take Exit 22 to Coastal Rte. 1 N to Rte. 27, then go S to Boothbay. After 10 m, pass the Boothbay Info. Center; continue straight past the Texaco station. Take the 2nd right onto Barter's Island Road & go 1.8 m to the inn.
Restrictions No smoking. Children over 12.
Credit cards None accepted.
Rates B&B, $65–105 double.
Extras Some Spanish spoken.

Kenniston Hill Inn ¢ ✗
Route 27, P.O. Box 125, Boothbay, 04537

Tel: 207–633–2159
800–992–2915
Fax: 207–633–2159
E-mail: innkeeper@gwi.net
URL: http://www.maine.com/innkeeper/

The Kenniston Hill Inn has welcomed travelers since the late 1790s, when David Kenniston first built this handsome center-chimney Georgian Colonial home. Set on a shady knoll, surrounded by perennial gardens and a picket fence, the inn is a five-minute drive to area attractions and activities. Guests can relax on the big front porch in warm weather, or by the open-hearth fireplace when it's chilly. Susan and David Straight have owned the inn since 1991. Rooms are decorated with antiques, handmade quilts, country wallpapers, and fresh flowers in season. Breakfasts include such Colonial favorites as blueberry pot pie, as well as peaches-and-cream French toast or hash-brown potato pie.

"Well-kept, attractive inn." *(SWS)* "Our comfortable room was tastefully decorated with a king-size bed, a rocking chair by the fireplace, a small chest, and an armoire. Fresh logs appeared daily, along with clean towels and glassware. The delicious, beautifully presented breakfasts were served in a candle-lit dining room by a roaring fire. We had broiled grapefruit, walnut and zucchini pancakes with Maine maple syrup, and sausage the first day; three-cheese pie with bacon, stuffed baked apples, and fluffy cornmeal muffins the next; followed by French toast with a hint of almond and cinnamon, topped with warm peaches. And, always, plenty of coffee. Warm, friendly, welcoming innkeepers." *(Claire & Robert Bedard)* "David and Susan are professional, courteous, helpful, and welcoming. Their advice on restaurants and attractions was excellent. Our lovely, spotless room had a jade green color scheme, a four-poster bed with matching rocking chairs, and a beautiful wardrobe and dresser." *(Beth Hampleman)*

Open All year.
Rooms 10 doubles—all with private bath and/or shower, radio, fan, deck. 5 with fireplace.
Facilities Dining room with fireplace, living room with fireplace, games; porches, patio. 4½ acres with gardens, walking paths. Swimming beaches, deep-sea and lake fishing, horseback riding nearby. Golf course borders property.
Location Midcoast ME, Lincoln County. 70 m E of Portland, 45 m E of Freeport. 2 m from Boothbay Harbor. From I-95, take exit 22 and go N on Rte. 1 to Rte. 27. Follow Rte. 27 S 10 m to inn on left.
Restrictions No smoking. No children under 8.
Credit cards Discover/Novus, MC, Visa.
Rates B&B, $69–125 double. Off-season rates.

Newagen Seaside Inn ⁋ ✕ ⚘ ⚲ 　　　*Tel:* 207–633–5242
Route 27, Southport Island, Cape Newagen　　　800–654–5242
P.O. Box 68, Newagen, 04552　　　*E-mail:* seaside@wiscasset.net

Situated at the seaward tip of Southport Island, the Newagen Seaside Inn is located six miles "out-to-sea," from the village of Boothbay Harbor. Connected to the mainland by a drawbridge, the inn is accessible by land and by water. Owners Peter and Heidi Larsen reports that "among the distinguishing features of the inn are the large, comfy public rooms and expansive grounds. These ensure the inn's well-known relaxed, unhurried atmosphere that hearkens back to its 19th century roots. A former nature preserve, the inn is a nature lover's paradise, and is bordered by the ocean on three sides; most rooms have ocean views. A country buffet is offered at breakfast; dinner might include such specialties as beef stroganoff with apples and sour cream, poached salmon with lobster sauce, and curried shrimp with linguine.

"Wonderful sense of comfort, relaxation, and peacefulness. Our favorite room has a king-size bed, veranda, and ocean view. The staff is friendly, attentive, and accommodating; the food is excellent; the grounds and beautiful and tranquil. Ideal balance of friendliness and privacy. Heidi Larsen is a marvelous innkeeper." *(Monica & Michael Weil)* "We love the fact that there are no phones, TVs, radios, or other electronic nuisances in the rooms. The inn is beautifully situated, maintained, and run." *(JM)* "The young, pleasant staff are eager to be of help.

Our room was nicely appointed, clean, and comfortable. Appealing menu with ample variety." *(Michael DeGennaro & Bernadette Davis)* "A wonderfully old-fashioned resort. You can walk around the rocky shore, watch ospreys fly in and out of their nests, or (our favorite occupation) sit on the large deck, read a book, look out at the water, and daydream. The lunch buffet is particularly appealing, with lots of choices." *(Suzanne Carmichael, also Bob Hayes)*

Open Late May–early Oct. Restaurant closed Tues.
Rooms 3 suites, 23 doubles—all with private bath and/or shower, desk. 6 with balcony, 3 with refrigerator. 4 1–4 bedroom housekeeping cottages.
Facilities Restaurant, great room with fireplace, piano, TV/VCR, games, stereo, books; bar/lounge. Evening entertainment. 85 acres with heated freshwater swimming pool, saltwater swimming pool, rowboats, 2 tennis courts, gazebo, lawn games. 1 mile of rocky shore. Nature trail, fishing. Golf nearby.
Location 6 m S of Boothbay Harbor. Follow Rte. 27 S through Boothbay Harbor. Cross drawbridge. Turn left on Rte. 238 and follow to inn.
Restrictions No smoking.
Credit cards MC, Visa.
Rates B&B, $150–200 suite, $75–180 double, $60–150 single. Extra person, $15. 10% AAA discount. 2-night minimum in-season weekends/holidays. Alc lunch, $8; Alc dinner, $20. Cottages, $750–1800 weekly.
Extras Wheelchair access. Crib. Limited babysitting.

BRIDGTON

For additional area entries, see **Center Lovell**, **Fryeburg**, **Naples**, and **Waterford**.

The Noble House ¢ **ᴎ**
37 Highland Road, P.O. Box 180, 04009

Tel: 207–647–3733
Fax: 207–647–3733

Owned since 1984 by Jane and Dick Starets, Noble House is a turn-of-the-century manor just across the street from scenic Highland Lake. Guests enjoy relaxing in the parlor or on the porch rocking chairs. Jane's breakfasts include blueberry pancakes and cheese strata, and she will gladly make dinner reservations for you at local restaurants. Aside from the lake itself, activities include shopping for crafts and antiques, the usual outdoor sports, and such nearby attractions as Shaker Village; Willowbrook, a 19th-century village; and the *Songo River Queen,* a replica Mississippi River stern wheeler.

"Delicious molasses ginger muffins for the buffet breakfast, along with a zucchini, tomato, and cheese frittata, toast, fresh fruit, and yogurt. On the second morning, we enjoyed baked French toast and English muffins. Recently refurbished, Room 1 has soft green wallpaper with a dark green and rose border, coordinating bedspread and linens, and a four-poster queen-size bed with firm mattress. A convenient basket of plush white towels is provided for guests to take swimming. The Carriage House rooms are our favorites." *(Nancy Barker)*

"Far enough from town to be quiet, close enough for convenience." *(Beth & Ed Brennan)* "Breakfast was served promptly at 8:30 A.M. (important for skiers who want to get to the slopes), in a lovely atmosphere with a crackling fire in the fireplace." *(Henry Bensman)* "We were welcomed with tea and cookies." *(Janice Roebuck)* "Outstanding features include the dock for swimming and boating; the beautifully maintained grounds and home; the welcoming hospitality; the helpful touring suggestions; the screened porches; and the comfortable furnishings." *(Stephen Bursch)*

Open June 15–Oct. 15; winter by reservation only.
Rooms 3 suites, 6 doubles—6 with private bath and/or shower, 3 with maximum of 6 people sharing bath. 3 rooms with whirlpool tub, desk. 1 with refrigerator. TV on request. 5 rooms in carriage house.
Facilities Parlor with grand piano, organ, fireplace; breakfast room, lounge with games, TV/VCR; 4 porches. 4 acres with lawns, croquet, bicycles. Private lake frontage with hammock, dock for swimming, canoe, pedal boat, fishing. 1½ m to golf, tennis, children's play equipment. 5 m to Shawnee Peak for downhill, cross-country skiing.
Location SW ME. Cumberland Cty. 20 m E of NH border, 40 m NW of Portland. Lakes Region. 40 m NW of Portland. ½ m from town. Take Exit 8 off I-95. Follow Rte. 302 NW to Bridgton. Watch for sign in park just beyond village.
Restrictions No smoking. No children under 2 on weekends in July, Aug.
Credit cards Amex, Visa.
Rates B&B, $109–130 suite, $80–99 double, $75–90 single. Extra person, $25; age 12 and under, $15. 2-night weekend minimum.
Extras Airport pickups, $40 by prior arrangement. Crib, babysitting available by prior arrangement.

BRUNSWICK

Brunswick is best known as the home of Bowdoin College, and is a charming historic town with many appealing shops and restaurants. In addition to a variety of musical and theatrical events, the college plays host to the Maine State Music Festival, performing Broadway musicals during the summer.

For additional area inns, see **Baileys Island, Bath,** and **Freeport.**

Brunswick B&B ♻
165 Park Row, 04011

Tel: 207–729–4914
800–299–4914
Fax: 207–725–1759
E-mail: inn@brunswickbnb.com
URL: http://www.brunswickbnb.com

Quilting is the art of bringing disparate shapes and patterns into a coordinated design, and makes a good metaphor for the art of innkeeping, which shares similar characteristics. When architect Steve Normand and his wife Mercie, an avid quilter, purchased the Brunswick B&B in 1991, they decided to make Mercie's quilts a decorating theme of this 1849 Colonial-style home, and picked the friendship knot pattern for their logo. Mercie notes that "Friendships are often started between us and our guests or among the guests themselves."

Breakfast is served from 8–9 A.M., and includes cereal, granola, yogurt, fruit, and perhaps Grand Marnier French toast with maple syrup and sausages; or an egg bake with cinnamon crunch coffee cake. A light continental breakfast is available midweek to accommodate business travelers.

"Both elegant and cheerful, decorated with great charm. The Normands are gracious and interesting. The appealing sitting room combines some contemporary touches with the graceful detailing of this old house. Cheerful off-white walls set off Mercie's quilts perfectly. Beautiful triple-hung windows in the living and dining areas reach from the floor almost to the ceiling. Lots of fresh flowers everywhere. Tasty breakfast of egg soufflé with mushrooms and peppers, melon, and peach-almond muffins. Even the upstairs hallway evokes a mood of nostalgia, with old-fashioned photographs and quilts. Spacious Room #3, "Baskets," has ivory-colored walls, a wall quilt in the basket pattern, a comfortable over-stuffed sofa, wood rocking chair, comfortable queen-size wrought-iron bed, and good lighting. The white cotton rug on the dark floor was immaculate. The bathroom shower had ample hot water and good pressure; nice soft towels. The Brunswick B&B really defines what is special about staying at a B&B." *(Suzanne Carmichael)* "Meticulously restored and maintained. The owners were always available, helpful, and pleasant. Convenient location and easy parking." *(Anne Angeloni)* "Innkeepers Steve and Mercie Normand instantly make you feel like you are old friends visiting for the weekend." *(Frederick & Debra Wigand)* "Set on the village green, convenient to downtown. Our charming room was done in white wicker, with good lighting and ample storage. Thirsty terry-cloth robes were a much appreciated touch after a week of camping. Delicious light breakfast of eggs, coffee cake, and fruit. Friendly owners, welcoming common area with games." *(Hilary Soule & Dave Shea)*

Open Feb. 1–Dec. 31.
Rooms 1 cottage, 1 suite, 7 doubles—all with full private bath and/or shower, telephone, radio, clock, desk, air-conditioning, fan.
Facilities Breakfast room, living room with TV, games, books; guest kitchenette, porch. 1 acre with off-street parking, gazebo, lawn games. Tennis, golf, nearby. 30 min. to state park beaches.
Location On coast, 25 m N of Portland. Historic district, on town green, 1½ blocks from Bowdoin College. Take Pleasant St. to Maine St., & go right. Take immediate left around green, then left on Park Row to inn on right.
Restrictions No smoking. Children 10 and over.
Credit cards MC, Visa.
Rates B&B, $130 suite, $90–105 double. Extra person, $15. No charge for children in parents' room. 2–3 night minimum for certain Bowdoin college events. Midweek business rate.
Extras Wheelchair access; bathroom specially equipped.

CAMDEN

Camden is one of Maine's most popular summer coastal resorts. It's about halfway up the coast, between Portland and Bar Harbor—40 miles east of Augusta, 185 miles northeast of Boston, and 414 miles northeast of New York City; take I-95 to Route 1, and follow it into the town.

A large village by Maine standards, Camden offers lots of shops and restaurants to explore (don't expect to explore them alone in season). Summer activities include tennis, hiking, swimming, sailing, water-skiing, and picnicking. There are chamber music concerts and a resident theater. The Farnsworth Collection in nearby Rockport has a fine Andrew Wyeth collection. The harbor is filled with yachts and with the two-masted schooners of the windjammer fleet. In winter, there's ice-skating and cross-country and downhill skiing within five miles. The tops of the two mountains that rise over the town, Mt. Battie and Mt. Megunticook, offer beautiful views of Penobscot Bay.

Worth noting: Most of Camden's B&Bs are on Route 1, called Elm or High Street as it passes through town. *Traffic is often heavy, so ask for a room facing away from the street if you're a light sleeper.* Most innkeepers have taken steps to minimize noise by plantings, installing double-glazed windows, air-conditioners, and white-noise machines; ask for details.

Also recommended: If you love lighthouses, then make **The Elms** (84 Elm Street, 04843; 207–236–6250 or 800–755–3567; www.midcoast. com/~theelms/) your beacon. Built in 1806, this Colonial home was purchased by Ted and Jo Panayotoff in 1994, who have named the six guest rooms (each with private bath and telephone) for New England lighthouses, decorating the inn appropriately with nautical accents and collectibles. B&B double rates of $75–105 include breakfast with puffed peach pancakes, tomato basil quiche, or perhaps apple French toast, (often accompanied by a lighthouse-shaped biscuit), plus afternoon lemonade or hot cider, depending on the season. The Panayotoffs know all about the area lighthouses, and even offer delightful lunch cruises to many which can only be seen from the water. "Homey, welcoming atmosphere; genuine hospitality; delicious, generous breakfasts and afternoon tea." *(Fred & Cherlene Wacker)* "Immaculate housekeeping; convenient location, within easy walking distance of shops, restaurants, and sights." *(Ken & Mary Patterson)* "Afternoon tea served in the bright, homey parlor. Ted made us feel right at home and took time to share a wealth of fascinating history about lighthouses." *(Nancy Wasa)* "Wonderful hosts, excellent breakfasts, immaculately clean, comfortable beds. Excellent value, with great off-season packages." *(Michelle Parks)*

Information please: Under new ownership in 1998 is the **Hartstone Inn** (41 Elm Street, 04843; 207–236–4259 or 800–788–4823; hrtstone @midcoast.com), a mansard-roofed Victorian inn built in 1835. B&B double rates for the ten guest rooms, each with private bath and telephone, four with wood-burning fireplaces, range from $75–155. Owners Mary Jo and Michael Salmon have made food a highlight of the Hartstone experience, with breakfasts of lobster and asparagus quiche, seven-grain vanilla waffles, or perhaps smoked salmon Benedict. Afternoon tea includes home-baked scones and cookies, and Chef

Michael's five course dinners ($35–45) might include pork potstickers with ginger-sesame dip; lobster corn chowder en croute, salad with avocado and blue cheese, duck with plum and scallion sauce, and berry cobbler with bourbon cream sauce. "Beautifully decorated and comfortable rooms, delicious food, hospitable innkeepers." (*Christine Blowers, also Pamela Nolan*)

For additional (and affordable) area entries, see **Rockland** and **Newcastle,** south of Camden, as well as **Belfast** and **Searsport,** approximately 20 miles north.

Blue Harbor House ¢   *Tel:* 207–236–3196
67 Elm Street, Route 1, 04843   800–248–3196
Fax: 207–236–6523
E-mail: balidog@midcoast.com
URL: http://www.blueharborhouse.com

Warm and gracious hospitality is the cornerstone of the best B&Bs, and that's just what you'll find at the Blue Harbor House, owned by Jody Schmoll and Dennis Hayden since 1989. They extensively restored and renovated their inn, a traditional Cape home built in the early 1800s and added to many times over the years; the decor is highlighted by hand-stenciled walls and colorful handmade quilts; the comfortable king-, queen-, and twin-size beds have good reading lights and bedside tables. Dennis's popular dinners include a lobster feast with lobsters and steamers, garden tomatoes, corn on the cob, and chocolate chip cookies; other days the menu might be Vidalia onion soup, spinach salad with tarragon mustard vinaigrette, poached Maine salmon, and chocolate brownie soufflé; or spicy tomato rice soup, salad with blueberry vinegar and goat cheese, grilled filet mignon, and blueberry pie. Breakfast menus change daily, and are no less tempting: perhaps baked apples with vanilla ice cream and blueberry pancakes with blueberry butter; lobster quiche with Irish soda bread; or breakfast burritos and chocolate tacos.

"Three inviting common rooms for guests to enjoy. Stenciling, plants, fresh flowers, and pretty craft items round out the decor throughout the inn, along with plenty of reading material, menus, and other tourist information. When we returned to our rooms after our lobster dinner, besides Godiva chocolates, we found a split of port with a personal note from Jody and Dennis. Dennis provides each guest with an atlas, marked for great day trips. We started at the top of Mt. Battie for a breathtaking view of Camden harbor and the coast, then followed Dennis's directions to several lighthouses, fishing villages, and a small local place with great chowder." (*Rose Ciccone, also SWS*) "Gracious hospitality, relaxing atmosphere, walking distance to harbor and shops. Our four-poster canopy king-size bed had an excellent mattress and pillows; the whirlpool tub was a real treat." (*Henrietta Sparano*)

"Our tempting breakfast consisted of morning-glory muffins and pancakes topped with blueberries, slivered almonds, warm fruit, powdered sugar, and maple syrup. Large, succulent lobster was the highlight of a delicious dinner." (*Ann Tigue*) "Jody and Dennis have scouted out interesting and out-of-the-way spots for guests to visit—whether by foot, bike, boat, or car. Impeccably clean." *(Mary W. Davis)* "Dennis's warmth made us feel like long-lost friends." *(Cheryl Feinberg)* "We were missing our own pets, and were happy to meet their well-behaved Labrador retriever, Bali, and Boots, the inn cat." *(MW)* "Immaculately clean, outstanding food, relaxing atmosphere and personable innkeepers." *(Linda and Richard Wark)* "So delightful to be welcomed with home-made brownies and lemonade." *(Irene Jacobs)* "A wonderful treat for the business traveler." *(Kathleen Power)* "Relaxing, homey atmosphere; privacy respected." *(Diane Johnson)* "Special touches included the fresh flowers, thick towels, and terry robes in our spotless room." *(Carol Yam)*

Open All year.

Rooms 2 suites, 8 doubles—all with private bath and/or shower, radio, telephone, hairdryer, robes. 8 with air-conditioning, fan. 7 with TV, 2 with refrigerator, kitchenette. 3 rooms in carriage house; 2 with whirlpool tub.

Facilities Dining room, living room, books, games; enclosed sun porch. Patio garden, lawn.

Location On Rte. 1, S of town.

Restrictions No smoking. Traffic noise masked by soundproofing.

Credit cards Amex, Discover, MC, Visa.

Rates B&B, $145 suite, $85–125 double. Extra person, $30. 2-night minimum holiday weekends. Prix fixe dinner (by reservation only), $35; beer, wine for purchase. 2-night package includes 1 dinner for two, $295–340.

Captain Swift Inn ¢ &.
72 Elm Street, 04843

Tel: 207–236–8113
800–251–0865
Fax: 207–230–0464
E-mail: swiftinn@midcoast.com
URL: http://www.midcoast.com/~swiftinn

A Federal-style home built in 1810, the Captain Swift Inn retains its original wide pine floors, chair rails, exposed beams, intricate moldings, and 12-over-12 windows. Guest rooms are furnished with period pieces and reproductions; each bed is accented by a handmade quilt. Owners Kathy and Tom Filip serve a family-style breakfast at 8:30 A.M. in the keeping room, near the old kitchen hearth (complete with beehive oven). In addition to fresh fruit and juice, favorite entrées include crustless quiche, baked apple pancakes, or banana-pecan Belgian waffles. Coffee, tea, and cocoa, plus cookies or cake are always available.

"Fully endorse entry. We stayed in a comfortable and spacious downstairs room. As in all our favorite inns, it is the innkeepers who make your stay. Tom and Kathy made us feel right at home, and joined us and the other guests at breakfast and for after-dinner chocolate cake." *(Cecile Desroches)* "Our room was spacious and immaculate, with a most comfortable bed and a first-rate shower, well supplied with shampoo and soaps. Tom and Kathy are friendly, extraordinarily helpful, wonderful conversationalists, yet never intrusive. Parking is a few steps from the door, and the harbor is an easy walk away. Exceptionally good value, too." *(Melissa & Larry Mencotti, also Ruth Anderson)* "Many of the windows have retained the original hand-blown glass, some slightly tinted. Breakfast is served in the handsome keeping room; a beautiful new kitchen has been built on to the back of house." *(SWS)* "Minor emergencies tended to with care and concern." *(Frank Scheible)* "Thoughtful amenities include hairdryers, razors, and more." *(Dorothy Rouson)* "Each time I prepare one of the recipes Kathy shared with us, it reminds me of our delightful visit." *(Julie Horrell)* "Breakfast favorites included the orange French toast, spinach pie, and baked fruit. Amazingly, each dish was low in fat, cholesterol, and salt." *(Carol Malia)* "Tom and Kathy are efficient, attentive, and immersed in hosting guests in the home they completely renovated and expanded in 1994. My sons were thrilled to find a triple-chocolate cake awaiting us when we checked in." *(KMC, also J.R. Threadgill)* "Beautifully restored home, with owners well-versed in its history." *(Helen Johnson)*

Open All year.
Rooms 4 doubles—all with private shower, radio, clock, desk, air-conditioning, fan, hair dryer, telephone with data port.
Facilities Dining room, living room, family room with books, TV/VCR; guest refrigerator, guest fax/copier; deck. 0.6 acre with off-street parking.
Location 5-min. walk from center of town. On Rte. 1 in Camden, 1.7 m N of Rte. 90 intersection. Look for inn's sign with schooner on E (right) side of road.
Restrictions No smoking. Children 5 and over.
Credit cards MC, Visa.
Rates B&B, $75–115 double. Extra person, $15.
Extras Wheelchair access; 1 bathroom specially equipped. Airport pickup.

Hawthorn Inn ♿ 👪
9 High Street, 04843

Tel: 207–236–8842
Fax: 207–236–6181
E-mail: hawthorn@midcoast.com
URL: http://www.camdeninn.com

If you think the decor of all Victorian homes is dark and heavy, you'll think again when you visit the delightfully light and airy Hawthorn Inn, purchased by Nick and Patty Wharton in 1995. From its sunny yellow exterior, to its white lace sheer curtains, to its spacious rooms, this elegant Queen Anne–style home, built in 1894, makes an excellent base for enjoying Camden and the Maine coast. Breakfast is served in the dining room at individual tables from 8–9 A.M., and includes fresh fruit and juice, homemade granola, and such creative treats as cranberry-apple muffins and potatoes baked with eggs, sour cream, goat cheese, and thyme.

"In a town filled with Colonial inns, the appealing Hawthorn is an inviting change of pace. Patty is originally from Texas, while Nick is English; both are working hard to continually improve and upgrade their inn. Patty has decorated the inn with beautiful family heirloom pieces, complimented by quality reproductions; the overall effect is sophisticated and elegant. Their beautiful springer spaniel is well-behaved and quite irresistible. While all the guest rooms are appealing, those in the carriage house are exceptionally spacious, with glass doors opening to private decks with views of Camden Harbor." *(SWS)* "Nick and Patty were friendly and helpful in suggesting restaurants and activities. The inn has lovely stained-glass windows and a wonderful turret. We visited in the winter, and had a wonderful view of the harbor lights at night, and the sun rising over the water in the morning. Breakfast was served in the sunny dining room. Convenient location, just a five-minute walk to shops and restaurants. The Camden area offered plenty to do during our week-long visit." *(Diana Etheridge)* "Warm, friendly hospitality; comfortable, homey atmosphere; immaculate accommodations." *(Pamela Johnson & Ed Hirst)*

Open All year.
Rooms 1 suite, 9 doubles—all with full private bath and/or shower. Some with whirlpool tub, TV, desk, gas fireplace, balcony/deck. All with telephone, radio, clock, TV, air-conditioning, fan. 4 rooms in carriage house.
Facilities Dining room, living room, each with fireplace; porch. 2 acres with off-street parking.
Location Historic village district, Rte. 1. Walk across back lawn to harbor. Inn is just N of public library, 4th house on right.
Restrictions Absolutely no smoking. Children 12 and over. Traffic noise possible in summer in front room.
Credit cards Amex, MC, Visa.
Rates B&B, $110–145 suite, $95–195 double. Extra person, $35. 2-night weekend/holiday minimum in season.
Extras Wheelchair access; bathroom specially equipped.

Inn at Sunrise Point &

Fire Road #9, Lincolnville, 04849
P.O. Box 1344, Camden, 04843

Tel: 207–236–7716
800–43–LOBSTER
Fax: 207–236–7716
URL: http://www.sunrisepoint.com

Waves rolling on the beach, the clang of a navigation buoy, the call of a distant foghorn. Aren't those the sounds you imagine for a Maine vacation? If you're staying at the Inn at Sunrise Point, you can open your eyes for the peaceful views of water and woods that match those sounds. Guidebook writer Jerry Levitin stayed at over 500 inns before opening his own, so he knew just what inngoers want—a balance of historic charm and modern convenience, communal guest experience and a respect for privacy, a quiet oceanfront location and an easy drive to town. A century-old home restored in 1992, the inn offers rooms and cottages with uncluttered decor in soothing shades of periwinkle, lavender, or yellow, with comfortable seating by large picture windows; light pine cabinets hide the TV and VCR. Breakfast is served at individual tables in the glass conservatory between 8:30 and 9:30 A.M., and includes fresh fruit, juice, cereal, home-baked bread, homemade sausage, and a hot entrée. In the late afternoon, tea is served by the stone fireplace in the cherry-paneled library with stone fireplace, along with such treats as hot artichoke dip, salmon on toast, trout mousse, hazelnut torte, and chocolate bittersweet cake.

"Gorgeous waterside location; beautifully furnished, immaculate, great service." *(Barbara Riso)* "Blissfully quiet and secluded. We really felt at home sitting on the wicker sofa on the porch observing the ocean." *(Ed & Rosemary McDowell)* "Romantic setting, clean and comfortable rooms; perfect location. We left our windows open and listened to the sounds of the breaking waves and the wood crackling in our fireplace." *(Candee Parkhurst)* Reports welcome.

Open Late May–late Oct.; inquire for winter/spring availability.
Rooms 3 doubles, 4 cottages—all with full private bath, telephone, clock, TV/VCR, fireplace. Most with desk, refrigerator, balcony/deck. Cottages with double Jacuzzi, wet bar, deck.
Facilities Dining room (conservatory), living room with fireplace, books, videotapes; library with fireplace; porch. 4 acres with beach.
Location 4 m N of Camden. 1 m S of Lincolnville Beach.
Restrictions No smoking. No children. BYOB.
Credit cards Amex, MC, Visa.
Rates B&B, $150–350 double. Extra person, $50. 2–3 night weekend/holiday minimum.
Extras Boat pickup.

A Little Dream B&B
66 High Street, 04843

Tel: 207–236–8742

Judging from guests' comments, the name of this B&B is accurate indeed. Owned by Bill Fontana and Joanna Ball since 1989, Joanna describes A Little Dream as a late 1800s cottage Victorian, "complete with turrets and rose arbors, decorated in a light and airy English country style. We are small and intimate and give lots of attention to our guests' needs and interests." Newly completed in 1998 is a spacious first-floor carriage house suite, complete with a large private porch with views of Curtis Island, king-size bed, gas fireplace, sitting area, soaking tub for two, and separate shower.

Inn guests choose from menus left at the door each evening, selecting breakfast times, favorite blends of coffee and teas, and full or continental breakfast. Entrées include a choice of such omelets as smoked salmon, apple cheddar, ham and brie, or perhaps banana pecan waffles with country sausage. Rates also include afternoon refreshments.

"Romantic, relaxing, and thoroughly enjoyable. Wonderful breakfasts, delightful innkeepers." *(Al & Lauren Kenney)* "Joanna is a talented designer, with wonderful collections of antique toys; she's used beautiful colors and fabrics to decorate the inn. The breakfast area felt like a garden terrace, even during a November visit, and the glassed-in side porch is both charming and private. The house was originally built as the nursery for Norumbega; children and their nannies stayed here, returning to the 'big house' for meals." *(SWS)* "Breakfast was beautifully served, with elegant place settings and silver napkin rings. Lace and frills are everywhere. Though our room was the least expensive, it was quiet, with lovely peach wallpaper, and a large toy bear who spent his days on my bed and nights sleeping on his own doll bed. Antique dresses, shoes, and hats hung on the closet doors or walls. Soft plush towels were supplied for the claw-foot tub, along with Crabtree & Evelyn bath soaps and shampoos. What really sets this inn apart is Joanna's exceptional charm, helpfulness, and hospitality." *(Sally & Tom Brown)* "Our room had a king-size Shaker pencil-post bed, with flowers garlanded around the bedposts. We were served breakfast on our private deck overlooking a Victorian castle. The owners provide first-rate recommendations for restaurants and activities." *(Cecilia & Robert List)*

Open All year. Closed Thanksgiving, Christmas, March.
Rooms 3 suites, 4 doubles—all with private bath and/or shower. 2 with gas fireplace, 4 with telephone, TV, air-conditioning, wet bar, balcony/deck in Victorian carriage house. Seasonal water views.
Facilities Dining room, living room with fireplace, books, stereo; conservatory; wraparound porch. Victorian carriage house. 2 acres with garden. Off-street parking.
Location Historic district. Follow Rte. 1 to Camden, past harbor shops. Rte. 1 becomes High St. here. Stay on High St. to #66 on left, directly across from the Norumbega castle.
Restrictions Traffic noise possible in summer in front rooms. No smoking. Not appropriate for children.
Credit cards Amex, MC, Visa.
Rates B&B, $95–195 double. 2-night weekend minimum Aug., also holidays.
Extras Italian, French, German spoken.

The Maine Stay
22 High Street, 04843

Tel: 207–236–9636
Fax: 207–236–0621
E-mail: mainstay@midcoast.com
URL: http://www.mainestay.com

Peter Smith retired from a career in the Navy to steer a ship of a different—but no less demanding—kind. In 1989, along with his wife Donny and her identical twin sister Diana Robson, he purchased the Maine Stay, built in 1802. Peter notes that "from the bubble bath beside the claw-foot tubs to the thick terry-cloth bathrobes, we have tried to anticipate guests' needs." An innkeeper's work is never done; Peter's most recent project involves creating an attic suite, building a breakfast conservatory, and restoring the barn to create an innkeepers' apartment.

Coffee is out at 6:30 A.M. for early risers, and breakfasts include egg dishes, waffles, French toast, or whole wheat pancakes with Maine blueberry syrup. In good weather, it's served on the deck overlooking the woods with Mt. Battie beyond. Most guest rooms have wide-board floors and are decorated with a mix of antiques and Oriental pieces.

"The Captain and the twins run the inn with great style and enthusiasm. They obviously care about their guests and have invested much time in suggesting walks, drives, and boat rides. The Captain's mapped itineraries include sights, events, routes, and suggested eateries. When we mentioned a hankering for a short sail, they knew the perfect small boat run by a happy and interesting couple, and arranged it all for us. We were pampered in so many ways. Never have I had such an excellent breakfast, with seconds sincerely offered. They give the word host added luster. Shops and restaurants are just an easy walk away." *(Ruthie Tilsley)*

"Wonderful antiques and quilts; friendly and comfortable. We love eating around the big dining room table, meeting new people and sharing travel advice. After breakfast, Peter brings out his folders of information sheets on coastal Maine, filled with tourist information, maps, tips on out-of-the-way places, and driving distances. He takes time with his guests, showing them around the inn, giving a little history of the house." *(Pam Phillips)* "Occasional comments would remind this dynamic trio of a song and they would spontaneously break into a barber shop rendition." *(Joan & Arnold Kerzner)* "Peter drove us to the start of a trail in Camden State Park, which ends back at the inn where homemade lemonade and cookies awaited." *(Karin & Tom Frood)*

"The spacious sitting rooms provide ample room to accommodate all guests and their varying interests. Peter Smith is genuinely friendly and sincere; guests are drawn to him like a close friend; his wife and sister-in-law are equally pleasant." *(Julie Irmischer)* "Extremely handsome building, impeccably maintained. The kitchen is the heart of the house. Guest rooms have been done with great care for guest comfort, and are mercifully free of clutter. Lovely location, combining in-town convenience with woods and nature trails right behind the inn." *(SWS)* "Wonderful breakfast of granola with yogurt, fresh fruit, quiche, and homemade muffins made with raspberries fresh from the garden." *(Susan Goldblatt)* "Our comfortable room had a large, modern bathroom and was well lit and beautifully decorated. We enjoyed watching TV downstairs in the den. Delicious, plentiful breakfast of baked apples, waffles, and sausage. Diana thoughtfully provided a computer printout with a detailed route to our next destination." *(Stephanie Roberts)*

Note: Though both are highly recommended, this Maine Stay is not affiliated with the Maine Stay listed under Kennebunkport (see entry).

Open All year.
Rooms 1 suite, 10 doubles—all with private shower and/or bath, fan. 3 with fireplace/stove. 1 with patio.
Facilities 2 parlors with fireplace, dining room, conservatory, family room with TV/VCR, videotape library; deck. 2 acres with garden, benches. Walk to state park; drop-offs at state park trail heads.
Location 85 m N of Portland. 3 blocks from harbor/center.
Restrictions Traffic noise in front rooms. No smoking. Children 8 and over.
Credit cards Amex, MC, Visa.
Rates B&B, $125–160 suite, $95–125 double. Off-season rates.
Extras Free station/airport pickups.

The Nathaniel Hosmer Inn
4 Pleasant Street, 04843

Tel: 207–236–4012
800–423–4012
Fax: 207–236–3651
E-mail: maineinn@midcoast.com
URL: http://www.nathanielhosmerinn.com

Genuine historic atmosphere, welcoming innkeepers, comfortable guest rooms, and delicious breakfasts are four excellent reasons to stay at the Nathaniel Hosmer Inn. But the fifth, and perhaps the best reason, is its convenient but quiet location, a block away from busy Route 1 traffic. Built in the 1800s, this typical New England home—with white clapboards and dark green wooden shutters—was converted into a B&B in 1985 by Dodie and Richard Schmidgall. The common rooms are beautifully furnished with early pine antiques and painted furniture.

Breakfast is served by candlelight, with fires burning brightly in the fire-places, and might include fresh fruit with grape-nut ice cream, apple-walnut or blueberry pancakes with maple syrup, and sour cream muffins or perhaps Amish friendship coffee cake.

"Ideal in-town location, an easy walk to everything, yet a block away from traffic of Route One. Exceptionally lovely common areas, with true candlelit Colonial charm. Comfortable, uncluttered, well-equipped guest rooms." (SWS) "The comfortable, immaculate Queen Room has a four-poster canopy bed and adjoining large bathroom. Rich and Dodie were accommodating and kind, from the initial phone call to the final goodbye, and were genuinely concerned about making my stay a good one. Rooms are made up and refreshed while guests are at breakfast, and evening turndown service is equally thoughtful. Inviting back courtyard and garden." (Karen Cherwinski) "We were ushered to our bedroom, with a comfortable queen-size bed, excellent pillows, and two sitting chairs with good reading lights." (Julie & Philip Fitzsimmons) "Friendly, unobtrusive owners, knowledgeable about area restaurants and activities. Superb breakfast of melon, just-baked muffins, potato-cheese casserole, and sausages. Richard thoughtfully had checked on our dietary requirements at check-in. The meal was attractively served with Richard skillfully guiding the lively conversation." (Carol Workman)

"Rich was accommodating beyond the call of duty, supplying us with a list of the flowers that we had admired in his garden and check-ing on our special dietary needs." (Maryellen & Lex Towle) "Central but quiet location. Hospitable owners and staff." (Mrs. Maggie Simmonds) "Concern for guests' comfort is paramount." (Dorothy Schwehm) "A nice alternative to the busy, mainstream inns—off the beaten path in a quiet residential area, yet still in town. Great showers—super water pressure." (Julie Irmischer) "So quiet, we heard neither other guests nor traffic." (Lucille Yachoski) "Quiet, unfussy, relaxed atmosphere." (Mary I. Rodgers)

Open All year.
Rooms 7 rooms—all with private bath. Some with air-conditioning.
Facilities Dining room, 2 living rooms with fireplaces, garden terrace. Off-street parking.
Location Historic District. 1½ blocks to center of village. Turn off Rte. 1 (Elm St.) onto Wood St.
Restrictions No smoking. Children 10 and over.
Credit cards MC, Visa.
Rates B&B, $95–140 double. 2-night weekend minimum in summer, holidays. Off-season rates, Nov.–May.

Windward House B&B ¢   Tel: 207–236–9656
6 High Street, 04843   Fax: 207–230–0433
                         E-mail: bnb@windwardhouse.com
                         URL: http://www.windwardhouse.com

Elijah Glover, a prominent lumberman and shipbuilder, constructed a handsome Greek Revival home in 1854. Restored as a B&B in 1987,

Windward House was purchased in 1995 by Sandy and Tim La Plante. The appealing guest rooms have queen-size brass, wood, or lace canopy beds.

"Sandy and Tim are enthusiastic, warm, and full of helpful information. At breakfast, they stop at every table, to see if they can help with the day's plans. We were bicycling and they provided us with maps, and suggested stops for lunch, views, historic sites, and shops. Tempting breakfasts of home-baked sweet breads, fruit, and quiches, French toast, or an egg dish." *(Joan Karter)* "Exceptional decor throughout. We were welcomed with coffee and tea, sherry and port, and a plate of cookies. Superb breakfasts with brown-sugar glazed grapefruit and feather-light yogurt pancakes." *(Barbara Heidegger)* "Homey atmosphere, with friendly innkeepers who never stop improving their inn. Careful attention to every detail." *(Uwe Heidenrich)* "Convenient parking and location." *(Fred Bollen)* "A delightful experience from the wood-burning fireplace to the superb breakfast to the opportunity for congenial innkeepers who went out of their way to make our stay comfortable, from storing bicycles, to arranging dinner reservations, to offering excellent advice." *(Michael Levin)* "Lovely house, ideally located in the village, with clean, comfortable rooms. Sandy and Tim are gracious hosts with a talent for making people feel comfortable. Lots of thoughtful touches: Crabtree & Evelyn toiletries, coffee and tea always available, fresh-baked cookies, shipping totes, and more." *(Lesley & Mark Narveson)*

"A cozy library and a separate game room with chess, checkers, and cards. Within walking distance to the harbor, Mount Battie, shops, and the restaurants." *(Pat Rowell)* "Excellent French toast with peach sauce and toasted almonds. Hot apple cider and baked treats at tea time." *(EBB)* "Attractively painted and impeccably landscaped, with a spacious backyard with trees and flower beds. The inn is located in a lovely area with mansions and restored older homes lining both sides of the street." *(Mary Welch)*

Open All year.
Rooms 8 doubles—all with private bath and/or shower. 5 with ceiling fan, 3 with Vermont Castings gas firestove.
Facilities Dining room, library, game room, living room with fireplace, porch, deck. Gardens, off-street parking.
Location On Rte. 1, 1 block N of harbor/center.
Restrictions No smoking. Children over 12.
Credit cards MC, Visa.
Rates B&B, $105–175 double.
Extras Boat/station pickups.

CARIBOU

The Old Iron Inn B&B ¢
155 High Street, 04736

Tel: 207–492–4766
E-mail: oldiron@mfx.net

Named for the hundreds of antique irons which decorate their B&B, the Old Iron Inn was built in 1910, and was restored by Kate and Kevin Mc-

Cartney in 1992. Victorian antiques highlight the uncluttered decor, and the inn's lovely oak double beds are topped with hand-stitched quilts. The McCartneys have worked hard to preserve the original charm of the house, from the oak wainscoting throughout, to the hand-dipped cedar shingles they used to restore the exterior. They're also pleased to share with visitors information about area history and activities. Kate reports that "the dominant cultural influence in this region is Acadian French, with a large population of French-speaking American Acadians, along with several Swedish communities. We have books everywhere, including specific libraries on Abraham Lincoln, aviation history, and British and American mysteries, and our reading room stocks 40 different periodicals. Kevin is a paleontologist who teaches at the University of Maine at Presque Isle, so there are lots of interesting rocks around the house, too." Breakfast is served at the dining room table at guests' convenience, and might include fruit salad, sausages, scrambled eggs with fiddlehead ferns, pain au chocolat, blueberry muffins, and chocolate-dipped strawberries; or perhaps yogurt pancakes, baked ham, hot spiced apples, and pineapple coconut muffins.

"Decorated with beautiful Victorian oak furnishings. Lots to read, from aviation to quilting. Short walk to center of town. Kate and Kevin are pleasant innkeepers, helpful in suggesting local dining and entertainment. Great breakfast of fresh fruit, juice, just-baked apple nut muffins, light and crispy yeast waffles." *(Susan Goldblatt)* "Wonderful hospitality, beautiful woodwork, intriguing collections, firm and comfortable bed, informative conversation, and delicious food." *(Bob Mathes)*

Open All year.
Rooms 4 doubles—2 with private shower/bath; 2 rooms share 1½ baths. All with clock, fan. 2 with desk.
Facilities Dining room, living room with fireplace, reading room. Monthly amateur music night. Off-street parking. Hiking, cross-country skiing, dogsledding nearby.
Location N ME, 12 m W of Canada. 3 hrs. N of Bangor, 4 hrs. SE of Québec City. 0.6 m S of Hwy 1/89 intersection. Downtown.
Restrictions No smoking. Traffic noise possible.
Credit cards Amex, DC, Discover, MC, Visa.
Rates B&B, $39–49 double.
Extras Local airport pickups. Pets possible; inquire.

CASTINE

The history of Castine goes back to 1604 when Champlain, a French explorer, charted the region. The English captain, John Smith arrived in the area just a decade later. During the American Revolution, the area was held by the British after a decisive naval battle, and the region remained a Loyalist stronghold until after the U.S./Canadian border was established further north. Through the first half of the 1800s Castine became famous as a shipbuilding port; by the second half of the century, it was discovered as a summer resort.

Much of Castine's charm is due to the numbers of beautifully restored 18th- and 19th-century Georgian and Federalist houses. "Castine's history is well documented on plaques posted throughout town." *(Pam Harpootlian)* According to *Jeff & Nan Seiden*, "Castine is a great jumping off spot for visits to Blue Hill, Bar Harbor, Camden, and the antique shops of Searsport."

Castine is located approximately 40 miles west of Bar Harbor and about the same distance south of Bangor and east of Camden; it's 3 hours northeast of Portland.

The Castine Inn ✗
Main Street, P.O. Box 41, 04421

Tel: 207–326–4365
Fax: 207–326–4570
E-mail: relax@castineinn.com
URL: http://www.castineinn.com

If you like to combine the privacy found in a small hotel with the warm atmosphere of an owner-operated inn, the sophistication of a big-city chef with the freshness of country cooking, then you'll enjoy visiting the Castine Inn. Built as an inn in 1898, it was restored in 1984, and purchased in 1997 by Tom and Amy Gutow. Amy, originally from Vermont, and Tom, hailing from Michigan, had been living in New York City, where she practiced law and he was a chef in some of New York's finest restaurants. On a visit to Castine, they fell in love with the inn, its lovely garden, wraparound porch with harbor views, and the charming dining room mural of Castine painted by artist and former innkeeper, Margaret Parker.

Although most guest rooms have either a queen-size bed or two twin-size beds, Tom and Amy spent the winter of 1998 creating a new second-floor suite at the inn. Although the lovely view of the garden and harbor hasn't changed, the new suite has a four-poster cherry queen-size bed, a sitting room with a Queen Anne writing desk, and a spacious bathroom with an antique cast-iron tub sunk beneath a tiled deck, a frameless glass shower, and two handsome sinks. Guests in this room are provided with thick terry-cloth robes and a welcome basket of fruit and water.

Breakfast is served from 8–9:30 A.M.; a typical menu includes fresh-squeezed orange juice, stewed prunes, fresh fruit, granola, apple-bread French toast with maple syrup, corned beef hash with poached eggs, and goat cheese and sage omelets. Chef Tom changes the dinner menu nightly, drawing from his diverse experience in this country and France, to create dishes with concentrated flavors and contrasting textures; local products are featured whenever possible, including Penobscot Bay crab, Deer Isle organic chicken, plus area fruits, vegetables, and condiments. Recent entrées included olive-crusted salmon with caponata; roast chicken with wild rice, spinach and garlic; scallops with celery root purée and cilantro vinaigrette; or roast lamb with eggplant and rosemary. The pub and restaurant are popular with guests and locals alike.

"The remodeled suite is accented by a blue-and-white color scheme in the sitting room and lovely new bathroom, with floral accents; it's welcoming but uncluttered. Highlights of our exceptional dinner included crab cakes with mustard sauce; gravlax with apples and cumin vinaigrette; roast chicken with baby vegetables and basil stew; steamed haddock with spinach, goat cheese, and lemon; flaky biscuits with a hint of cheese; lime mousse and kiwi with lemon crisps. Presentation and preparation were of an equally high level." *(Suzanne Carmichael)* "Quiet setting, across the street from a lovely book shop, just a short stroll from the harbor. Our spacious room had a good bath, and looked out to trees, a garden, and the harbor. First-class food and service." *(Bob & Mary Pat McLean, also Louise Donahue)* "Lavish breakfasts, imaginative cuisine comparable to the best New York City restaurants." *(Peter Gibbons)* "The Gutows are young, appealing, eager-to-please, and full of energy. Guest rooms are comfortable and meticulously clean." *(Jim & Jane Lester)* "Welcoming atmosphere with friendly owners and staff. Wonderful views from the rooms at the front of the inn; simple furnishings, extremely comfortable beds. Extraordinary food with lots of herbs and spices—not overly rich. We had box lunches prepared every day—each more delicious than the day before." *(Kathleen Browning)*

Open May–Dec.
Rooms 4 suites, 15 doubles—all with private bath and/or shower.
Facilities Restaurant, pub, living room with fireplace and games. Sauna. Wraparound porch; perennial, herb, flower gardens. Seasonal entertainment. 1 m to town beach, sailboat charters. Tennis, golf nearby.
Location 38 m S of Bangor, 18 m S of Bucksport (Rte. 1). In center of town. From Rte. 1 in Bucksport, go E 1 m to Orland, & go S on Rte. 175. Go S on 175 to Rte. 166A to Castine.
Restrictions No smoking on property. Children 8 and over welcome.
Credit cards MC, Visa.
Rates B&B, $210 luxury suite, $85–135 double.

CENTER LOVELL

This remote hamlet is set in the foothills of the White Mountains of southwestern Maine, near the New Hampshire border. It's about 60 miles west of Portland, and 25 miles east of North Conway, New Hampshire, and stretches along the shores of Kezar Lake, a beautiful glacial lake.

In addition to all the outdoor pleasures of this area, bargain hunters will enjoy the factory outlets along Routes 302 and 16 in nearby New Hampshire. Others will prefer to avoid this stretch at all costs!

Also recommended: Janice and Richard Cox won the **Center Lovell Inn** (Route 5, North Lovell Road, P.O. Box 261, 04016–0261; 207–925–1575; www.centerlovellinn.com) in a $100 essay contest—about what it will cost you to spend a night at their inn! Richard is the chef, and prepares such dinner entrées as swordfish with saffron orzo with lemon chive sauce, scallops with grilled vegetables and lemon pepper linguini, and herb-crusted rack of lamb with Port wine sauce. Breakfast includes fresh fruit, home-baked muffins, French toast, eggs, and popovers with homemade jam. Double rates for the nine guest rooms range from $60–100 double; $100–180 including breakfast and dinner. "Wonderfully spruced up with new bathrooms, new kitchen, new decor. A lovely place, and an amazing transformation." *(Elizabeth Church)*

For additional area entries, see **Bridgton, Fryeburg, Naples,** and **Waterford.**

Quisisana 👫 🐾

Tel: 207–925–3500
Pleasant Point Road (off Route 5), 04016   *Winter tel:* 914–833–0293
Winter address: P.O. Box 142
Larchmont, New York 10538

A cozy cottage, set in the woods by a beautiful lake, is a lovely escape even if that's all there is to it. At Quisisana there's more—this resort is staffed by auditioned conservatory music students from around the country, and nearly every night brings another high-quality musical performance of works from Mozart and Bach to Gershwin and Sondheim. Known for its food, Quisisana offers American-style breakfasts, lunches of creative soups, sandwiches, and salads, and dinner menus with a choice of two appetizers, entrées, and desserts: perhaps cornmeal blini, salad with Dijon vinaigrette, roast lamb with red peppers, and mocha truffle cake.

"Our cheerfully decorated, airy cabin had comfortable beds, and plenty of hot water with ample pressure. Delicious meals are served in the spacious lodge, and children are free to explore on their own. The staff, an enthusiastic upbeat group of talented musicians, charm the guests by day and perform for them by night. The guests are a marvelous blend of people with whom it is easy to share humor, books, sports, walks, and ideas. Owner Jane Orans sets the tone; without her magic touch this special community would not exist." *(Kristina Goldstein)* "There's nothing like paddling a canoe on a quiet lake at dusk and hearing a rehearsal of a Bach piano sonata float over the water. Our waitress at lunch turned into Mimi in *La Bohème* one night, and our bus boy was in *The Music Man* a few nights later." *(Jane Silverman)* "Excellent food and service by young, talented aspiring artists. Enjoyed the many rehearsals held during our opening week visit." *(ZK)* "Each morning after breakfast our comfortable cottage was again clean as a whistle. Enjoyed the cameraderie of the talented staff. The lake was warm and clear, the weather perfect." *(AM)* "Homey, relaxing setting. Excellent service for both the seniors and the youngsters in our family." *(PM)*

Open Mid-June–Aug.
Rooms 2 lodges, 47 cottages—all with private bath. Most with screened porch, some with living room, fireplace, desk.
Facilities Dining room, card room, game room, lounge, music hall with performances daily. 3 clay tennis courts, 2 sandy beaches, canoes, sail boards, rowboats, sailboats. On Kezar Lake for water sports. Golf, hiking nearby.
Location From Boston: take I-95 to Portsmouth, NH, Exit 4, Spaulding Turnpike, which turns into Rte. 16 to Conway. At Conway, go straight onto Rte. 302

to Fryeburg. Take Rte. 5 through Lovell. Continue 4 m, turn left at Turston's Garage onto Pleasant Point Rd.

Credit cards None accepted; personal checks accepted.

Rates Full board, $115–160 per person double occupancy. Extra person, $80. 15% service. One-week minimum stay in season.

Extras Crib, babysitting.

COREA

The Black Duck Inn on Corea Harbor ¢   *Tel:* 207–963–2689
P.O. Box 39, 04624   *Fax:* 207–963–7495
                                                  E-mail: bduck@acadia.net
                                    URL: http://www.blackduck.com

If you've developed a lifetime aversion to fudge and T-shirt shops, head for the tiny hamlet of Corea, one of the true few working harbors left in Maine. Restored as an inn in 1991 by Barry Canner and Bob Travers, the Black Duck Inn is a restored fisherman's home dating back to the 1880s; it's simply furnished with antiques and contemporary art. Barry notes that "our tranquil Downeast fishing village is ideal for people who love nature—not shopping. Activities include hiking, bicycling, and kayaking; it's also perfect for writing, painting, photography." Wild blueberries and cranberries grow on the property, and are included in the heart-healthy breakfasts of morning glory muffins and baked orange-glazed French toast; or eggs Black Duck, a variation of eggs Benedict, made with a spicy, low-fat sauce. Breakfast is served at 8 A.M.; guests are seated at individual tables.

"Friendly, helpful innkeepers; excellent filling but low-fat breakfasts; comfortable home with lovely antiques and fascinating antique toy collection; beautiful harbor views." *(Carol Cutler)* "Scrumptious breakfasts with blueberry buckle. In August, we pick ripe blueberries early each morning for our breakfast. After a leisurely meal and delightful conversation among the interesting guests this inn attracts, we walk along the docks by the harbor, or down to the sandy beach and Bar Island. On foggy days, we read by the woodstove, then don slickers and explore the marsh in the mist. The decor includes both country pieces and modern art. On warm days, we like to relax in the garden on lawn chairs and enjoy the harbor views. Within a reasonable drive are Bar Harbor and Acadia National Park, Campobello, and even an L.L. Bean outlet in Ellsworth. Guest rooms are spotless; housekeeping is done unobtrusively and thoroughly." *(Jeannie Bowman)*

"The Harbor Studio cottage has white-washed walls with white curtains, high ceilings, a skylight in the bath, faux finishes in bright aqua on the antique tables—and little reminders of Maine—a shell here, a lobster trap there. Our comfortable bed had a harbor view right from the pillow." *(Lark Kuhta)* "Anyone who knows the desolate stretch of Route 1 north of Ellsworth will understand the sense of enchantment as I found my way to the picturesque working harbor of Corea—a town consisting of a post office, a boat builder, and the inn. Aside from the superb location, with the harbor in front and the woods and walking paths out back, the inn's greatest assets are its two owners, Bob Travers and Barry Canner. They are friendly, helpful, and knowledgeable, yet are not overbearing or invasive. The inn is also home to friendly cats, dogs, and even a pot-bellied pig." *(Marietta Berkey)*

Open All year.

Rooms 2 cottages, 4 doubles—4 with private bath and/or shower, 2 with maximum of 4 sharing bath. All with clock/radio; 4 with desk.

Facilities Dining room; living room, TV room, sitting room—each with fireplace or woodstove; library, guest refrigerator, unscreened porch. 12 acres with gardens on Corea Harbor, Gouldsboro Bay inlet; berry-picking, walking paths. Swimming pond, beaches, kayaking, harbor fishing, cross-country skiing nearby.

Location Downeast ME. 50 m SE of Bangor, 50 m E of Bar Harbor, 80 m SW of Campobello Island. 5 m to Schoodic Section of Acadia National Park, 20 m to Petit Manan National Wildlife Refuge. From Bangor, take Rte. 395 to Rte. 1A E. In Ellsworth, turn left onto Rte. 1; from Rte. 1 in the town of Gouldsboro, turn right onto Rte. 195. Follow signs to Corea. Just after entering the village of Corea, turn left onto Crowley Island Rd. to inn 1/10 m on left.

Restrictions No smoking. Infants, children over 10 welcome. Early morning harbor sounds in some rooms in season.

Credit cards MC, Visa.

Rates B&B, $145 suite, $70–90 double. Extra person, $15. 3-night minimum in cottages. 2-night minimum holiday weekends.

Extras Danish, limited French spoken.

DEER ISLE/STONINGTON

Deer Isle is an unspoiled island in Penobscot Bay with 100 miles of road leading to the villages of Deer Isle, Sunset, Sunshine, and Stonington Harbor. The bridge connecting it to the mainland was built in the 1930s; for many years, the toll charged ensured the island's continued seclusion. There are many antique and craft shops; activities include hiking, swimming, boating, bird-watching, deep-sea fishing, golf, tennis, and musical and theatrical events. For a look at some first-rate craftspeople at work, visit the Haystack Mountain School of Crafts, where master craftsmen conduct workshops in blacksmithing, weaving, pottery, and glass.

Deer Isle is located in mid-coastal Maine, 60 miles south of Bangor and 280 miles northeast of Boston, and is accessible by bridge. To get there, take I-95 to Bangor, then go south on Route 15 through Blue Hill to Deer Isle.

Reader tips: "The bridge connecting Deer Isle to the mainland is narrow and unlit, so be careful when driving at night. This area is craft heaven, and relatively untouristed. Be sure to take a tour of the islands; our grizzled old captain was a riot. Also recommended is a walk from Stonington to the lily pond; just ask someone where it is." *(Bruce Bilmes)* "From Stonington, you can catch the mail boat to Isle au Haut and Duck Harbor at Acadia National Park for walking trails and rugged beaches." *(Annie & Andy Stickney, also CS)*

For additional area entries, see **Blue Hill**.

The Inn at Ferry Landing
Old Ferry Road, RR 1
P.O. Box 163, Deer Isle, 04627

Tel: 207–348–7760
Fax: 207–348–5276
E-mail: ferryinn@juno.com

Set on the shores of Eggemoggin Reach, the Inn at Ferry Landing dates back to the 1840s, and once served as a ferry-docking facility, general store, livery stable, and home for the Samuel Lowe family. Although the suspension bridge has replaced the ferry, and an airy and spacious living area has replaced the general store, the gorgeous views of the water and sailboats remain unchanged. Restored as a B&B in 1986, the inn was purchased in 1996 by Jean and Gerald Wheeler. Breakfast is served at the dining room table from 7:45–8:45 A.M., and might include fresh fruit and juice, bacon or ham, and such entrées as blueberry pancakes, French toast, or omelets.

"Rooms are light and airy, lovely and fresh, with Colonial decor and charming artwork. My favorite room is the suite, located above the living room, tucked under the eaves with dramatic views, a handsome queen-size brass bed, comfortable sitting area, woodstove, and a soaking tub under a skylight. The attached Mooring cottage is ideal for a longer stay. Hospitable owners." *(SWS, also Carol Blodgett)* "We left the windows open and awoke to the sound of gulls and water lapping on the shore." *(Bruce Bilmes)* "Beautiful location on the point with expansive water views of Eggemoggin Reach and the bowed bridge. The house is light, airy, and spacious." *(Janet Riehl)* "Quiet location. Our room was comfortable and homey; delicious breakfast." *(Robert Davis)* "Appealing in any season. Jean is an accomplished photographer, and her pictures of Maine enhance the lovely decor." *(Deborah Dewitt)* "Like staying with a dear friend. Jean is a perfect ambassador for this rugged and beautiful place. We stayed in the suite, and could see the bay and hear its calm waves upon the rocks without even getting out of bed." *(Kathleen McDonald)*

Open All year. Closed Thanksgiving, Christmas.
Rooms 1 cottage, 1 suite, 3 doubles—all with full private bath and/or shower, clock. Some with radio, desk, woodstove, balcony, TV/VCR. Cottage & suite attached to main house with separate entrances.
Facilities Dining room, living room with TV/VCR, woodstove, books, games; deck. 1.33 acres with beach, kayaking, sailing; off-street parking. Golf nearby.
Location From Blue Hill, take Rte. 15 S to Deer Isle & follow signs. Take 1st left after crossing causeway.
Restrictions No smoking. Children 12 and over except in cottage.
Credit cards None accepted.
Rates B&B, $110–140 suite, $80–100 double. Extra person, $16. 10% senior discount. 2-night minimum in summer; 1 week for cottage.
Extras French, some German spoken. Crib in cottage.

Inn on the Harbor &
Main Street, P.O. Box 69
Stonington, 04681

Tel: 207–367–2420
800–942–2420
Fax: 207–367–5165
URL: http://www.innontheharbor.com

If you were any closer to the water than the rooms at the Inn on the Harbor, you'd be wet. Originally built in 1880s, the inn opened in 1950, and was redesigned, rebuilt, redecorated, and renamed in 1996 (it was previously called the Captain's Quarters) by owner Christina Shipps and innkeeper Janet Snowden. Although the harbor views from the inn's windows and decks—extending over the water—are its most outstanding feature, the guest rooms, done in soft shades of cream and pale yellow, accented by muted florals, provide a soothing counterpoint. Two doors up the street from the inn is Christina's latest venture; she purchased the Austin Ice Cream building, now home to three dining experiences. The Café Atlantic is a romantic harborview dining room specializing in seafood, pasta, plus meat and poultry dishes; the Atlantic Deck, a huge outside deck on the harbor, serves lobster-in-the-rough picnic style; last but not least is the Ice Cream Window, open for treats from noon until 9 P.M. Breakfast is served in the breakfast room at individual tables, from 7:30–9:30 A.M., and includes fresh fruit and juice, homemade breads and muffins, yogurt, granola, and a daily hot entrée. Rates also include wine and sherry, served from 5:30–6:30 each evening.

"Hands-down one of the top views from any inn in the world. The exterior is freshly painted white with Colonial blue trim. Behind the inn is a large deck stretching towards the harbor, complete with picnic tables and beautifully planted flower boxes. The lobby/breakfast area has scattered Oriental rugs, a punched-tin cabinet, blue-and-white checked tablecloths, and oak chairs. Charming but not fussy. The comfortable, pretty, airy guest rooms are named for schooners. Much of the artwork is done by Chistina's aunt, Evelyn Kok, who has an art gallery next door. The Stephen Tabor has an inviting sitting area and a private deck—both ideal for watching the boats and islands—and is a very private room. The intimate restaurant enjoys the same wonderful views, with a calming decor of dark green and white. We enjoyed fresh vegetable soup, Caesar salad, herbed bread, crab cakes, lobster, and raspberry ice cream with chocolate covered raspberries. Delightful, friendly service." *(Suzanne & Don Carmichael)*

"The inn incorporates a number of buildings from earlier decades, and Christina has preserved the best of the past, while adding modern bathrooms, Stonington granite fireplaces, and private balconies. Ongoing improvements are skillfully crafted by the inn's carpenter, Glen Gray. Innkeeper Janet Snowden is an able and gracious hostess, pleased to assist with advice and information. Chef Jon Thompson has an expert flair with both preparation and presentation, making the CaféAtlantic a fine choice for lunch or dinner." *(Norman Shanklin)* "Best of all is the inn's location, set on a narrow strip of land between Main Street and Stonington's beautiful harbor, busy with fishing boats, sailboats, and Maine's windjammer fleet. At sunrise we watched the lobster boats slipping out to sea, using the binoculars thoughtfully provided by the inn, then took a morning walk, exploring the side streets and docks as the early light drifted across the water and over the town. Each guest room provides comfort and tranquility—no overdone Victoriana here. The decor is deliberately understated, so as not to compete with the views of sky and water. Our room had two large, over-stuffed armchairs set in front of the window for hours of harbor-watching; a notebook was supplied with information about the windjammers we might see and other local items of interest. The queen-size bed had a top-quality mattress and linens, and the soothing neutral colors were a perfect background for the magnificent views. Stonington is a tiny village, at the tip of a long peninsula. You feel like you are driving to the end of the earth to get there. The rolling hills and views of Penobscot Bay exemplify the best of Maine." *(MSO)* "The management takes personal interest in every guest's comfort. The food is superb and varied. Housekeeping is efficient and consistent." *(Ellen W. Douglas)* "Stonington is a working fishing community, and the day starts early for the men driving down to the docks." *(Nancy Stauffer)*

Open April 1–Jan. 1.
Rooms 3 suites, 11 doubles—all with full private bath and/or shower, telephone, TV, fan. Some with radio, desk, fireplace, refrigerator, balcony/deck. 1 cottage attached to inn; 2-bedroom suite in owner's house.
Facilities Breakfast room, espresso bar, deck with flowers. Parking in front of inn & 2 nearby lots. On harbor for boating, fishing, kayaking, sailing.
Location Mid-coastal ME. 60 m S of Bangor.
Restrictions No smoking. Children 13 and over. Traffic noise possible in 3 street-side rooms in season. BYOB to restaurant.
Credit cards Amex, MC, Visa.
Rates B&B, $100–125 suite, $95–120 double, $80–100 single. Extra person, $20. Tips welcome. Alc lunch, $15; alc dinner, $25.
Extras Wheelchair access; bathroom specially equipped. Local airport pickups.

Pilgrim's Inn ✕   *Tel:* 207–348–6615
Deer Isle, 04627   *Fax:* 207–348–7769
        E-mail: pilgrimsinn@acadia.net.com
        URL: http://www.pilgrimsinn.com

The Pilgrim's Inn is a 200-year-old inn listed on the National Register of Historic Places. Readers are delighted with its longtime owners, Jean and Dud Hendrick, its rooms, and especially the food. All rave about the delicious hors d'oeuvres, fresh fruits and vegetables, original recipes, attractive presentation, and good service (dinner nightly at 7). Breakfasts (served from 8–9 A.M.) come in for similar plaudits, especially the homemade granola and fresh Maine blueberries. Also mentioned by many are the guests themselves: "The inn attracts well-spoken and well-read visitors from all over the U.S. and Canada." *(Langevin Cote)*

"On a quiet evening, when the fog rolls in off the Penobscot Bay, the rumbling engine of a nearby lobster boat can be heard for miles. Dud and Jean's attention to detail, welcoming smiles, and unparalleled professionalism make a stay delightful and revitalizing." *(John Cullen)* "Pondside setting with plenty of room for relaxation. A busy but well-run inn with enjoyable interaction among guests." *(Ellis Locher)* "Rooms are spotless, linens crisp and immaculate." *(Chris and Edith Kressy)* "My top-floor room had an ocean view, double bed and shared bath. Good reading lights in my room, plus an excellent library." *(Pat Turrigiano)* "Fresh whole-wheat bread, wonderful soups, great salads with interesting dressings, weekly lobster bakes, wonderful salmon." *(GR)* "Spectacular setting—out one window is the mill pond, out another is an inlet leading to the sea." *(Annie & Andy Stickney)* "Antiques, handmade quilts, curtains, and wide pumpkin-pine plank floors lend homey warmth. The breakfast buffet offers homemade granola, fresh fruits, yogurt, and freshly baked muffins, plus omelets, quiches, or soufflés." *(Thomas Stark)* "The work of local artists and craftspeople is integrated into the decor." *(Linda Greenberg)* "Wonderful area for walking, visiting historic towns and innumerable craftsmen. The chef is attentive to special diet requests." *(Nepier Smith)*

"Exceptional variety of scrumptious hors d'oeuvres. It felt like a family gathering with everyone convening in front of the fire. It was fun to see the chef picking herbs from the garden just before our excellent dinner." *(Carol Blodgett)* "Friendly, knowledgeable owners and staff; quiet setting with lawns sloping down to the water; clean, attractive accommodations; excellent meals." *(Lorraine Fournier, also Sarah Woodman)* "A mecca for birders, hikers, and photographers. Incredibly relaxing atmosphere; beautifully restored." *(Jane & John Bradovchak)*

Open Mid-May–mid-Oct.

Rooms 2 cottages with kitchen, gas fireplace, private deck; 12 doubles, 1 single—10 with private bath and/or shower, 3 with maximum of 4 people sharing bath. All with desk.

Facilities Dining room, parlor, library, 2 sitting rooms with fireplaces, tap room. 2+ acres on waterfront with patio, bicycles, jogging, kayaking. Sailing, swimming beach, 2½ m.

Location In village, opposite harbor.

Restrictions No smoking. No children under 10 in inn; welcome in cottage. Advance notice required for vegetarian meals.

Credit cards MC, Visa.

Rates MAP, $150–215 double. Extra person, $60. 15% service. 10% senior discount. Weekly rates. Prix fixe dinner, $29.50. Picnic lunches. Weekly rates.

Extras Wheelchair access. Crib, babysitting.

DEXTER

Brewster Inn ⛐ 🐾 ¢   *Tel:* 207–924–3130
37 Zion's Hill Road, 04930   *Fax:* 207–924–3130
         E-mail: brewster@nconline.net
         URL: http://www.bbonline.com/me/brewsterinn

Some travelers rush up the Maine coast, sleeping each night in a different bed, and returning home exhausted. Others will prefer to settle into a comfortable, affordable inn, making it a base of operations for leisurely day trips to explore the coast, as well as Maine's equally beautiful lakes and mountains. If the latter approach appeals to you, consider the Brewster Inn, owned by Michael and Ivy Brooks since 1997. Built in the Colonial Revival style in 1934 for Ralph Owen Brewster, a Maine governor and later a U.S. Senator, and listed on the National Register of Historic Places, the Brewster was restored as a B&B in 1988, and combines 1930s-era craftmanship with a friendly, informal atmosphere. Past guests in this handsome home included Presidents Taft and Truman, U.S. Senator Margaret Chase Smith, and movie mogul Louis B. Mayer.

The decor includes the original fine woodwork, many built-in cabinets, and cut-glass and brass light fixtures, as well as Michael's extensive collection of antique radios. Guest rooms are unusually spacious, ranging from the smallest, a generous 12 by 15 feet, to the largest, at 22 by 25. Most guest rooms have a queen- or king-size bed, and several rooms have second or third beds, ideal for families. Some have 1930s-style dressers or armoires, window seats, and two have original tiling in the bathrooms. The spacious Honeymoon Suite has original wood-paneling, gas fireplace, queen-size canopy bed, and double whirlpool tub; if you like, you can have a private candlelit dinner served to your room.

Breakfast is served at individual tables, at guests' convenience, and includes fresh fruit and juice, toast and English muffins, cereal, and a daily entrée—perhaps quiche, stuffed French toast, ginger pancakes, or omelets. Coffee, tea, and cookies are always available. Sandwich and salad lunches can be ordered to go—from tuna salad to chicken—at a modest cost. Dinners are served to inn guests, and include seafood with pasta, chicken with raspberry sauce, or Thai curry beef.

"Michael and Ivy are doing a superb job. These friendly innkeepers make you feel like family. They are enhancing this gorgeous mansion, making it a homey, wonderful B&B." *(Cecile Desroches)* "Warm hospitality, comfortable accommodations, and a different, delicious breakfast each day. We enjoyed sitting in the attractive, cozy living room each evening for a night cap before bed." *(Earl & Mary Haines)* "Comfortable room, well-equipped for the disabled, with excellent parking. Immaculate throughout." *(Thomas Warren)* "My son had an especially good time, since both he and Michael enjoyed playing their guitars together." *(Richard Aronson)* "Restored with sensitivity to period and history. We had the room where Harry Truman stayed several times. A large shaded porch invites leisurely breakfasts, and the grounds are lovely." *(Robert & Rebecca Hight)* "Gracious innkeepers, present but not overbearing." *(Harmon Harvey)*

Open All year.

Rooms 2 suites, 5 doubles—all with full private bath and/or shower, clock, TV, air-conditioning. 1 with double whirlpool tub, 3 with fireplace or woodstove.

Facilities Dining room, living room with woodstove, organ; conservatory, guest refrigerator, porches. 2 acres with flower, vegetable gardens, croquet, badminton. 5-min. drive to 3-mile-long lake with canoe, rowboat available free to guests. Hiking, snowmobile, cross-country ski trails in walking distance. 9-hole golf course nearby. Fishing, whitewater rafting,

Location 1 hr. from coast & Moosehead Lake. 40 m NW of Bangor. 15 m N of I-95. From I-95, take Exit 39 to Newport. Follow Rte. 7 N to Dexter. Go left on Zion's Hill Rd. to inn on right, near Lake Wassokeag.

Restrictions No smoking.

Credit cards MC, Visa.

Rates B&B, $79–89 suite, $59–79 double, $49–79 single. Extra adult, $10; children free. 10% senior, AAA discount. Alc lunch, $4–6; alc dinner, $10–13. Corporate rates.

Extras Wheelchair access; bathroom specially equipped. Crib. Spanish, a little French spoken.

EASTPORT

Also recommended: In the easternmost city of the U.S., close to the New Brunswick border, is **The Weston House** (26 Boynton Street, 04631; 207–853–2907 or 800–853–2907), owned by Jett and John Peterson. This Federal-style home was built in 1810, and overlooks Passamaquoddy Bay. Four double and one single guest room share three baths, and the B&B double rates of $60–80 include a full breakfast and afternoon tea and sherry. "This topnotch B&B is filled with beautiful antiques. Everything is tasteful, elegant, and spotless. Terry robes are provided for the shared baths. My favorite rooms are the Audubon, with a queen-size four-poster bed, and the Weston, with a king-size bed, working fireplace, and TV; both have views of the town and Bay. The owners are refined, gracious people. The outstanding breakfast included fresh fruit, fresh-squeezed orange juice, salmon omelets, and wonderful fruit tarts. With advance notice, Jett will prepare equally tasty four-course dinners. The B&B is located just outside this quiet town in a lovely garden setting." *(Carol Blodgett)*

For additional area inns, see also **Lubec** and **Robbinstown.**

FREEPORT

Once a depressed little Maine town, known only as the home of L.L. Bean, Freeport now feels like an outdoor mall, with a variety of newly built, "New England–style" gray clapboard shops housing every brand name known to American consumers (or so it seems), interspersed with little snack bars and restaurants to refuel weary shoppers. Don't expect great bargains during the peak shopping seasons of June to December, although the January sales justify a detour. Bean's enormous store is still well worth a visit, although for bargains, go across the street and down a bit to their outlet store.

Freeport is close to Wolf's Neck State Park for fishing, boating, and swimming; in winter, cross-country skiing is nearby as well. The town is in mid-coastal Maine, 16 miles north of Portland, 125 miles northeast of Boston, and 3 hours southwest of Bar Harbor.

Worth noting: Many of Freeport's B&Bs are located on Main Street. Expect significant daytime traffic noise in any rooms at the front of a house, and be sure to inquire for details if you're a light sleeper.

Reader tips: "Tear yourself away from the shops and visit Wolf's Neck State Park, a real jewel." *(SB)* "Although there's a fantastic range of shops to visit, the best bargains were at the exception of the L.L. Bean Factory Outlet, which offered irregulars, overstocks, and off-season merchandise at sale prices. We also enjoyed Bean's Outdoor Discovery Program; we took a two-hour class in fly-fishing, held at a farm they own." *(Susan Harper)*

Also recommended: The **Country at Heart B&B** (37 Bow Street, 04032; 207–865–0512) was built in 1870 and is owned by Kim and Roger Dubay. Rooms are furnished with sturdy contemporary pieces and Shaker reproductions. "Kim is a talented crafts person, and has decorated the rooms with her many cross-stitchings, quilts, and wall-stenciling. A living room with a TV, reading material, and snacks is reserved for the guests. Delicious breakfasts of eggs and sausage with homemade cinnamon muffins, or French toast with ham and apple muffins." *(Susan Harper, also SWS)* "Though our room was small, the innkeepers were attentive and friendly, and the quiet location is only a few blocks from the shopping district." *(James & Pamela Burr)* B&B double rates for the three guest rooms, including private baths and full breakfasts, range from $65–85.

If you prefer a small luxury hotel, the **Harraseeket Inn** (162 Main Street, 04032; 207–865–9377 or 800–342–6423) combines country inn ambience with such extras as Jacuzzi tubs and steam showers, with fine dining in a full-service restaurant. "Tasty, extensive buffet breakfast; inviting library with lots of comfortable seating around the fireplace. Relaxing music played during afternoon tea. Make reservations for the popular tavern restaurant. Comfortable, attractively decorated guest rooms." *(Ann Charles)* A full buffet breakfast and afternoon tea is included in $95–245 double rates; children under 10 stay free in parents' rooms, and off-season packages are available.

The Bagley House ¢ ♁ ♿   Tel: 207–865–6566
1290 Royalsborough Road   800–765–1772
Route 136, Durham, 04222   Fax: 207–353–5878
                     URL: http://members.aol.com/bedandbrk/bagley

Dating back to 1772, the Bagley House is the oldest home in the hamlet of Durham, and has served as an inn, a schoolhouse, and a dairy farm; today its rooms are furnished with antiques, reproductions, and handmade quilts, highlighted with antique linens and china and glass collections. Purchased in 1993 by Susan Backhouse and Suzanne O'Connor, the "two Sues" describe their B&B as being ideal "for those who love peace and quiet and old homes." The kitchen, probably the oldest room in the house, is the guests' favorite. The huge free-standing fireplace has two cauldrons built into it, and a beehive bread oven. The floor has exceptionally wide pine boards, some of them "illegal," since it was against the law in Colonial days to have any board in your home wider than 23 inches; such trees automatically belonged to His Majesty, King George III, for his ships' masts. Those who like their history tempered by modern construction will enjoy a room in the adjacent carriage house, completed in 1998.

Early morning coffee is left in the upstairs hallway, and guests gather in the kitchen for a family-style breakfast at a time scheduled the night before. The meal starts with fresh fruit, juice, homemade granola and yogurt, and fresh-baked muffins. The entrée might be an egg casserole, sourdough waffles with local blueberries, maple syrup, and bacon or sausage.

"Welcoming innkeepers, comfortable room, fascinating history to the house, quiet location. Fun breakfast in the wonderful kitchen, with the innkeepers right there, cooking and chatting. A nice change from more formal inns—warm, friendly, and casual. I took a long walk on one of the country roads by there—the foliage was glorious." *(Pam Phillips)* "The two Sues know the area well and suggested great places to eat. Lots of repeat guests. The guest refrigerator is filled with fruit drinks and the bottomless cookie jar is always available." *(Mary Bauer)* "We were in a bright, cheery upstairs room, decorated in blue, with a wonderful flower-garden quilt on the bed, and some of Sue's penguin collection decorating the walls. Good bedside lighting, and individual heat controls. My favorite touch was the hot-water bottle, tucked in a soft cover trimmed in lace, tucked in our bed while we ate dinner. Coffee was set out at 7:30 A.M., followed by a breakfast in the kitchen. We had baked apples with granola and yogurt, an egg dish with home-made rhubarb chutney, English muffins and scones." *(Suzanne Carmichael)*

"Ten minutes and two hundred years from the bustle of downtown Freeport—the perfect antidote to shoppers' stress. The two Sues have delightful senses of humor, and are doing a wonderful job at this historic home. Rooms are reasonably sized, old-fashioned, simple but comfortable; some love the rustic 'unfinished' barn-like room under the eaves, others will prefer the more traditional look of the other guest rooms. Delicious chocolate chip cookies and tea." *(SWS)* "Conversation with the 'two Sues' was genuine and not forced." *(Tina Hom)* "I'm an animal lover, so Shasta Daisy, a shepherd/lab mix, made me a happy woman." *(Barbara Walsh)* "Sue and Sue make us feel like we were old friends . . . no small feat since we were traveling with a 15-month old." *(Brooke Perin)* "Perfect location for visiting Bowdoin and Bates." *(MOR)* "Enjoyed the downstairs bedrooms with extra-large bathroom; spotlessly clean, great towels." *(Peggy Kontak)*

Open All year.

Rooms 1 suite, 7 doubles—all with private bath and/or shower, gas or wood-burning fireplace, fan. 3 rooms in carriage house.

Facilities Country kitchen with fireplace, living room with fireplace, library; conference room with wood-burning stove. 6 acres with woods, gardens, berry-picking, cross-country skiing.

Location 22 m N of Portland. 6 m N of Freeport. From I-95, take Exit 20 and go N on Rt. 136 6 m to inn.

Restrictions No smoking. "Children with well-behaved parents welcome." Early morning traffic noise in some rooms.

Credit cards Amex, Discover, MC, Visa.

Rates B&B, $135 suite, $80–125 double, $65–85 single. Extra person, $15.

Extras Wheelchair access; bathroom specially equipped.

181 Main Street ¢
181 Main Street, 04032

Tel: 207–865–1226
800–235–9750
E-mail: BB181main@aol.com
URL: http://members.aol.com/bb181main/index.htm

The Creech brothers, master mariners, built this Greek Revival–style home in the 1840s. When Ed Hasset and David Cates renovated it as a B&B in 1986, they selected 181 Main Street as the name—they felt "Creech House" just did not strike the right note. After a hot summer's day of bargain-hunting, travelers will enjoy the swimming pool in the inn's large and private backyard.

"A wonderful old home, beautifully furnished and convenient to area attractions; great breakfast." *(Virginia Yedniak)* "Ed and David have extensively renovated this old cape-style home. The guest rooms are decorated with either Victorian or Colonial motifs; most have queen-size beds. The common areas are comfortable and inviting. A tasty full breakfast is served at individual tables (with seconds offered)." *(Janice & James Utt, also SWS)* "I like being able to take an early-morning cup of coffee up to my room. The breakfast is a healthy one; it's easy to go high on fruit and grains and low on cholesterol. The inn is dotted with just the right amount of antiques, and everything is clean and fresh. Parking is ample and the location is convenient." *(Catherine Brousseau)* "Delightful, welcoming hosts; delicious food; lovable yellow Lab named Mae." *(Polly Gray)* "Rooms are impeccably clean, decorated with a sophisticated touch. David and Ed have created a restful environment." *(James Lorette)*

Open All year.

Rooms 7 doubles—all with private bath, fan. 3 with air-conditioning.

Facilities 2 dining rooms, parlor, library with TV, games. 1 acre with swimming pool. Off-street parking.

Location 5-min. walk to downtown. Take Exit 20 off I-95, go E to Main St. Go left (N) on Main St. to inn (3rd house on the left).

Restrictions No smoking. Children 16 and over.

Credit cards MC, Visa.

Rates B&B, $85–100 double, $75–85 single. Extra person, $15.

Extras Airport/station pickups. French, some Spanish spoken.

White Cedar Inn ¢   *Tel:* 207–865–9099
178 Main Street, 04032   800–853–1269
        E-mail: CapandPhil@aol.com
        URL: http://members.aol.com/bedandbrk/cedar

Arctic explorer Donald MacMillan left his 1880s Victorian home in 1909, to accompany Robert E. Peary as second in command on Peary's epic trip to the North Pole. (Maine winters must have seemed balmy by comparison.) Philip and Carla Kerber, who bought and restored the White Cedar Inn in 1987, report that "our unpretentious inn is uncluttered and clean, with a relaxing atmosphere; rooms are sunny and large."

"Ideally located on the main street, within easy walking distance of Freeport shopping. The Kerbers are charming and helpful, always available but never obtrusive; there is ample quiet and privacy." *(Dr. & Mrs. Arthur A. Mintz)* "I enjoyed sitting in a rocking chair by the pot-bellied stove, browsing through the albums showing the restoration of the inn. Books, newspapers, games, tourist literature, and restaurant menus are also provided. The guest rooms are color-coordinated; if you stay in the blue room, you will have blue wallpaper, blue towels, and blue linens. All are bright, immaculate, and decorated in a modern country motif with a few antiques. Towels are big and thick, and bed linens neat and crisp. Delectable breakfasts are served in a breakfast room with three tables seating four people each. Each is set with fresh flowers, place mats, and cloth napkins. There's a choice of juice and plenty of cinnamon-scented coffee. First a fresh muffin arrives on the blueberry stoneware dishes, followed by scrambled eggs with cheese, French toast, or perhaps blueberry pancakes, garnished with Canadian bacon, sausage, or bacon, fresh fruit, and an English muffin or bagel." *(Judith Singer)* "Phil served us juice, Carla's delicious home-baked coffee cake, pancakes, and fruit." *(Marilyn Parker)*

"Early American wallpapers, dried-flower decorations, and live plants highlighted the decor. Phil is knowledgeable about the area, and suggested a wonderful trip along the coast for us." *(Jean & Craig Haley)* "The guest rooms have good lighting, and comfortable beds with down comforters." *(Dianne Crawford)* "Cordial owners; rooms are well-equipped, spotless, simply but comfortably furnished. Phil was most accommodating about preparing an early breakfast when we had to leave early for camp visiting day." *(Helen Stark, also SWS)*

Open All year.

Rooms 6 doubles—all with private shower and/or bath, desk, air conditioning.

Facilities Dining room, sun porch, living room with games, TV, books, woodstove. ¾ acres with picnic table.

Location 2 blocks N of L.L. Bean.

Restrictions No smoking. No children under 10. Traffic noise possible in front rooms.

Credit cards Amex, Discover, MC, Visa.

Rates B&B, $70–130 double. Extra person, $15.

FRYEBURG

Fryeburg is located in the Saco River Valley of Maine's southwestern lakes and mountains region, 60 miles west of Portland, and 10 miles east of North Conway, New Hampshire, and the Mount Washington Valley. S ME, at NH border.

For additional area entries, see **Bridgton, Center Lovell, Naples,** and **Waterford,** as well as **North Conway, New Hampshire.**

Acres of Austria ¢ ♿ ♥
Route 5, Firelane 48, RR 1, P.O. Box 177, 04037

Tel: 207–925–6547
800–988–4391
Fax: 207–925–6547
URL: http://www.bbhost.com/acresofaustria

For a taste of Europe on the Old Saco River, visit Acres of Austria, owned by Franz and Candice Redl since 1997. Built in 1978, this B&B makes an ideal base for canoeing on the river, exploring the area lakes, and hiking in the surrounding mountains. Cross-country skiing and snowmobiling await winter-time guests, and the outlets of North Conway, New Hampshire, are a short drive away.

Breakfast is served in the dining room at individual tables, generally between 7:30 and 9 A.M., and includes fresh fruit, juices, such homemade pastries as blackberry strudel or almond-raisin coffee cake, and a choice of the daily sweet or savory entrée—perhaps apricot crêpes or herb omelets with cheese. Franz's dinners include such traditional Austrian favorites as cucumber soup, Wiener schnitzel with parsley potatoes, and Sacher torte; or perhaps mushroom soup, beef goulash with bread dumplings, and ice cream crêpes with chocolate sauce.

"The spacious dining area has a central four-sided fireplace, with cozy tables, each set with fresh flowers, handmade needlepoint place mats, lovely dishes, crystal pitchers, and cloth napkins. The living room has huge plush velvet couches and a picture window looking out to snow-covered fields and mountains. Candace has stenciled many of the walls, and faux-painted the bathrooms, to give the look of real tile and marble; her cross-stitch pieces add to the decor. Austrian down comforters top the queen- and king-size beds. Our suite had sliding doors onto the balcony, where we were visited by birds and Jesse, a friendly German shepherd. Franz is an excellent cook; his service is fast and friendly. He served us homemade schnapps made by his uncle in Austria. Candace is warm and friendly, and bakes bread and Austrian desserts. Both were polite and friendly to us and our children." *(Joyce Wall)* "The youthful Redls are energetic, attentive, friendly, and accommodating. The breakfasts are excellent, with large portions, nicely presented. Quiet setting, well off the road; excellent value." *(John & Rebecca Rafferty & others)*

Open All year.

Rooms 1 suite, 3 doubles—all with full private bath and/or shower, telephone, radio, clock, fan. Some with refrigerator, fireplace, desk, balcony, private entrance.

Facilities Dining room with fireplace, stereo; living room with woodstove, organ, TV/VCR, video library, games; library with books in German, English; billiard room, reading room/sun room, porch. 62 with trails, gardens, meadows, woods, lawn games; ½ mile frontage on Old Saco River. Fishing, canoeing; cross-country skiing on site. Murder mystery, fondue, chocolate, and gourmet weekends; writing, needlework, and massage/holistic living seminars. Hiking, downhill skiing, tennis, golf nearby. Hot tub, gazebo planned for 1999.

Location From Rte. 302 take Rte 5N. Inn is 6.5 m N of the Fryeburg Fairgrounds, on left.

Restrictions No smoking. Children over 2.

Credit cards MC, Visa.

Rates B&B, $90–105 suite, $90–130 double. Midweek single rate, $59. Extra adult, $19; child $12. Inquire for EP, MAP rates. 10% senior discount. 3rd night discount. Lunch, dinner, $12.50–25.00; advance reservation required.

Extras Wheelchair access; 2 guest rooms specially equipped. German spoken. Airport/station pickup.

Admiral Peary House 🏃
9 Elm Street, 04037

Tel: 207–935–3365
800–237–8080
Fax: 207–935–3365
E-mail: admpeary@nxi.com
URL: http://www.mountwashingtonvalley.com/
admiralpearyhouse

Known for his discovery of the North Pole, Admiral Robert E. Peary lived in Fryeburg for several years before he left to begin surveying for the Panama Canal. Ed and Nancy Greenberg converted the Admiral's home into a B&B in 1989, decorating the rooms in a light and airy traditional style without forgetting such modern comforts as airconditioning and individually controlled heating. Nancy reports "we cater to adults who are looking for quiet, elegant accommodations. Guests who enjoy sports will find our location and facilities ideal. We are avid tennis players, and take care to keep our court in optimal condition and can arrange for lessons. We also have an outdoor spa, where guests can unwind with a therapeutic soak." Breakfast is served in the country kitchen, or on the screened porch, with white wicker chairs and tables. A recent meal included baskets of homemade muffins and breads with homemade jams, and buttermilk Belgian waffles with fruit topping; rates also include complimentary beverages. Nancy also suggests a visit during the first week of October, when the old-fashioned Fryeburg Fair, the largest in Maine, attracts hundreds of agricultural exhibitors.

"Nancy and Ed greeted us warmly and took our luggage to our room, then took us on a tour of the house. Our room, the North Pole Room, had a king-size brass bed, handmade quilt, good lighting, Palladian window, plus an immaculate bathroom with dressing table, and a supply of thick, thirsty towels. Fryeburg is a lovely, quiet New England town surrounded by lakes and close to the White Mountain National Forest." *(Phyllis & Bennett Ger)* "The prize-winning gardens are a must-see in summer." *(L. Cristiansen)*

"Our attractive, uncluttered room overlooked the quiet street, and was furnished with an antique four-poster rice bed, reproduction Queen Anne bedside chests, and crisp white swag curtains accenting the floral print wallpaper. Lighting was excellent for reading in bed, and the mattress was comfortably firm. The small bathroom was wallpapered in a burgundy and white, with ample storage space. Ample common areas; the large family room is most inviting. The canine innkeeper, Mac, a border terrier, is an absolute love, running about the large yard, always ready to retrieve a tennis ball or have his stomach scratched. Nancy and Ed are charming, funny, and skilled innkeepers who make you feel at home." *(Nancy Barker)*

Open All year.

Rooms 6 doubles—all with private shower, clock, air-conditioning. 5 with desk.

Facilities Breakfast room with woodstove; library; family room with fireplace, TV, billiard table; living room with fireplace, piano; screened porch; bicycles. 10 acres with hot tub, 2 acres of perennial gardens, tennis court (racquets available), cross-country skiing. ¾ m to Saco River for canoeing, fishing, swimming. Downhill skiing, hiking nearby. Snowshoe rentals, trail on site.

Location ⅓ m from center. Take Rte. 302 to Fryeburg. Turn on street directly across from Post Office (Elm St.) to #9, white house on right.

Restrictions No smoking. Well-behaved children welcome.

Credit cards Amex, MC, Visa.

Rates B&B, $70–128 double, $60–128 single. Extra person, $15. 10% discount for 5-night stay, except during Fryeburg Fair. Romantic Winter Getaway Weekend; Winter 7-Night contract packages.

Extras Airport/station pickups. French spoken.

GREENVILLE

One of civilization's last outposts in northern Maine, Greenville is a popular resort town located at the southern end of Moosehead Lake, and offers hiking, fishing, whitewater rafting, float plane rides, and canoeing in summer, hunting in fall, and cross-country and downhill skiing, snowmobiling, and ice fishing in winter. Greenville is located 78 miles west of Bangor, and 275 miles north of Boston.

Reader tip: "For a change of pace, try the Road Kill Café, a mini-chain with menus that sound like they've been written by Alfred E. Neuman of *Mad Magazine*. If you're in the mood for a Bambi burger or the chicken-that-didn't-make-it-across-the-road, give it a try. 'Never assume it's a raisin, notes the menu.' " *(SWS)*

For additional area information, see **Rockwood.**

Greenville Inn ✕
Norris Street, P.O. Box 1194, 04441

Tel: 207–695–2206
Fax: 207–695–2206
E-mail: gvlinn@moosehead.net
URL: http://www.greenvilleinn.com

The Greenville Inn, built in 1895 by a lumber baron, has a commanding view of Moosehead Lake's East Cove Harbor and the Squaw Mountains. Carpenters worked for ten years to complete the carved embellishments and the cherry, mahogany, and oak paneling found throughout the inn. Details include leaded-glass windows, fireplaces with carved mantels, and gas lights. Michael, Elfi, and Susie Schnetzer have been the innkeepers since 1987; Susie is also the chef. The European breakfast buffet includes homemade pastries and breads, ham, cheese, fresh fruit, and assorted cereals and yogurt. Elfi and her daughter Susie are the chefs, and a recent dinner included a choice of such entrées as lemon-basil shrimp; duck with blueberry sauce and wild rice; rack of lamb with rosemary-garlic butter; and wienerschnitzel with red potatoes.

"Beautiful mansion, with a hilltop setting offering views of the lake and mountains beyond from the charming porch, dining room, and some guest rooms. Inviting common areas, charming dining rooms. We started with a drink on the porch, looking down at the harbor, then moved inside for a delicious, well-served dinner of basil zucchini soup, halibut topped with olive-tarragon bread crumbs, and wild rice; my husband was equally pleased with his duck with orange-apricot glaze. Tasty salad, wonderful home-baked French bread. Extensive, well-priced wine list. Delicious plum strudel for dessert. An excellent restaurant, surprisingly elegant for this location." *(SWS)* "A beautifully restored mansion, with polished wood and antiques. Our room had a giant claw-foot tub, which felt great after a day of hiking or white-water rafting." *(Phyllis Salesky)*

Open May 1–Oct. 30, Dec. 1–March 31.
Rooms 6 cottages, 1 suite, 5 doubles—all with private bath and/or shower, clock, fan. Some with TV, desk, fireplace, ceiling fan, wood-stove, balcony/patio.

Facilities Restaurant, sitting rooms with fireplaces, stereo, books; porches. 5 acres with flower gardens, terrace, off-street parking.

Location ²⁄₁₀ m to center. Take I-95 to Newport, Exit 39. Follow Rtes. 7/11 to Dexter, then Rte. 23 N to Sangerville. Turn onto Rtes. 6/15 N to Greenville. In Greenville go straight through flashing yellow light. At 2nd street after light, turn right to inn on left.

Restrictions No smoking. Children over 7.

Credit cards Discover, MC, Visa.

Rates B&B, $98–148 cottage, $165–205 suite, $85–145 double. Extra person, $20. Alc dinner, $30.

Extras German spoken.

The Lodge at Moosehead Lake ✕

Upon Lily Bay Road, Box 1175, 04441

Tel: 207–695–4400
Fax: 207–695–2281
E-mail: lodge@moosehead.net
URL: http://www.lodgeatmooseheadlake.com

A visit to Maine's north woods no longer condemns you to a week of mildewed mattresses and canned ravioli. When you stay at the Lodge at Moosehead Lake, you can appreciate all the natural beauty of the wilderness while enjoying such creature comforts as a double Jacuzzi tub, terry-cloth robes, and twice-daily maid service. Roger and Jennifer Cauchi brought decades of experience in the hotel industry to this 1916 lodge, which they have restored and furnished with originality and distinction. Each of the five guest rooms has a striking hand-carved four-poster queen-size bed depicting a different animal or theme of the Maine woods or the West—moose, loon, bear—and a comfortable sitting area. Most rooms have a view of the breathtakingly beautiful lake sunsets, as do the inn's common areas. Rates include hors d'oeuvres served each evening at 5:30 in the great room, plus breakfasts of fresh fruit and juice, yogurt, cereal, home-baked breads and cakes, waffles, French toast, crêpes, or quiche. Completed in 1997 were three suites in the carriage house, complete with swinging beds with lake views, and double Jacuzzi tubs.

"Those who think 'rustic elegance' is an oxymoron will have to see this inn to believe it can be done. Wonderful lake and mountain views from all but one of the guest rooms. Inviting, spacious, generous common areas. Although there's lots to do in the area, one could easily spend a day on the veranda, pretending to read and gazing out to the view." *(SWS)* "We were warmly welcomed with shortbread cookies, which were always waiting for us in the pantry or upstairs in our room. At night, while we enjoyed dinner, our bed would be turned back, the electric blanket turned on, and the fireplace would be lit. After a great day of dogsledding, snowmobiling, or a vigorous walk in the snow, we enjoyed a relaxing soak in the whirlpool tub or glasses of wine before a roaring fire. From the living room we watched the waters of Moosehead Lake change from whitecaps to glistening ice and fresh snow." *(Paige Dominick)* "Careful attention to detail can be seen in the carefully set breakfast tables, with fine china and linens color-coordinated with the lodge's hunting motif. Our bathroom was supplied with a coffee maker, mugs, teas, coffee, creams, Caswell and Massey toiletries, hairdryer, scale, makeup mirror, ample towels, and storage space. The Cauchis were most helpful in suggesting and arranging a variety of activities, from fishing to hunting to shopping, and made equally sure we were comfortable if we just wanted to read and relax." *(Pamela Karahlios)*

"Beautifully appointed public rooms—a lounge with wonderful fireplace, dining and guest rooms overlooking the lake, spacious game room with pool table and darts. We stayed in the Totem Room for our spring retreat, with a four-poster bed with painted, carved totem poles as posts; on a winter visit, we enjoyed the Moose Room, with a large, hand-carved moose headboard. Best of all was the hospitality and attention of our hosts, Roger and Jennifer. In the spring, Roger helped arrange an out-of-season hike on Mt. Kineo requiring a boat ride; in the winter, Jennifer linked us up with two local ski touring centers for hours of outdoor fun and exercise." *(Sondra & Alex Rosiewicz)* "Wonderful cookies were served upon our return from cross-country skiing. Each evening drinks were served by a roaring fire with complimentary hors d'oeuvres. The dining room is warm and intimate, the cuisine well-presented and tasty." *(Douglas & Judith Fletcher Woodbury)*

Open Mid-May–late Oct., late Dec.–mid-March. Dinners by reservation Nov.–May, Tues.–Sat.
Rooms 5 doubles—all with full private bath, double whirlpool tub, radio, clock, TV/VCR, fan, fireplace. 1 with deck. 3 suites in carriage house with double Jacuzzi tubs.
Facilities Dining/breakfast room, living room with fireplace, great room with fireplace, books, games; library, pool table; deck. 2½ acres with lawn games.
Location Take I-95 to Newport, then Rte. 7 N to Dexter. Continue on Rte. 23 N to Guilford. Take Rte. 16 W to Rtes. 6/15 to Greenville. From blinking light in town, go 2.5 m to inn.
Restrictions No smoking. No children.
Credit cards Discover, MC, Visa.
Rates B&B, mid-June–late Oct., $275–350 suite, $175–250 double. Dinner included off-season. 2-night holiday/special event minimum. Prix fixe, $32. Canoe/floatplane, dog sled, moose safari packages.
Extras Some French spoken.

HANCOCK

Le Domaine ✗
HC 77, P.O. Box 496, 04640

Tel: 207–422–3395
207–422–3916
800–554–8498
Fax: 207–422–2316
E-mail: nicole@ledomaine.com
URL: http://www.ledomaine.com

Le Domaine is a little piece of France in Down East Maine. Longtime owner and chef Nicole Purslow credits her success to her mother, Marianne Rose Dumas, who with her father left their inn in Provence during World War II. Arriving in Hancock in 1946, they did what they knew best and started another inn. After attending the Cordon Bleu in Paris, and a bakery school in Switzerland, Nicole assumed management of the inn in 1977, ably assisted by Marjorie Peirce. The decor clearly shows a French touch, with Provençal fabric accenting Bar Harbor wicker chairs. Guest rooms, named for herbs, are simply furnished with quilted comforters and pine accent pieces. The highly praised French cuisine is complemented by a 4,500-bottle wine cellar maintained with pride by Nicole. The menu changes daily, with such entrées as lamb and eggplant with garlic and tarragon; rabbit with prunes; roasted garlic chicken; and salmon with sorrel and shallots.

"When we first arrived the tension slipped away. Margorie set the mood and pampered us throughout our visit. Accommodations are clean, bright, comfortable, and quiet. Not over done. Dinner was excellent, with outstanding bread pudding. Nicole is a brilliant chef, and takes her job very seriously. At breakfast—fresh everything: granola, fresh fruit, thick cream, wonderful baked goods, homemade jams and preserves." (*Katherine Brown & G. Wayne Schroeder*)

"Excellent cuisine and presentation; extensive wine list." (*Donald Johnson*) "We received a warm welcome from Marjorie, and Nicole came out to the small dining room several times during the evening to chat with diners. Our room had a comfortable bed, good reading lamps, and up-to-date bathroom. The lawns were neatly tended and the gardens were the source of both fresh flowers and salad greens daily." (*Barbara Wakeman*)

Open May–Nov. Restaurant open daily in Aug. Closed Tues. other months.

Rooms 7 doubles—all with private bath and/or shower, radio, desk, fan. 5 with air-conditioning, porch. Some with ceiling fan.

Facilities Restaurant with fireplace, living room with fireplace, bar, sitting room, porch, library. 90 acres with gardens, walking trails, trout pond, rowboat, badminton. Swimming, boating, fishing nearby.

Location N coastal ME. 32 m SE of Bangor, 9 m E of Ellsworth, 20 m NE of Bar Harbor. On Rte. 1, ½ m from center of town.

Restrictions Smoking restricted in dining room. "Well-behaved children over the age of 7 permitted."

Credit cards Amex, Discover, Enroute, MC, Visa.

Rates MAP, $200 double, $125 single; 15% service. B&B, $140 double, $90 single; 8% service. 2-night holiday minimum. Alc dinner, $42 plus 15% service; prix fixe menu, Thurs. night. Early season specials.

Extras Airport/station pickups, fee charged. French spoken.

ISLE AU HAUT

The Keeper's House Inn
P.O. Box 26, 04645

Tel: 207–367–2261

Here's the perfect escape for island/lighthouse fans. Jeff and Judy Burke have restored the lighthouse keeper's house on Isle au Haut, the most isolated part of Acadia National Park. They've also reconstructed the walkway that connects the house with the lighthouse, and have built a pier so that the Stonington mailboat can drop off guests.

It's not for luxury buffs—the only way to get there is on the mailboat (leaving your car behind); there are only a handful of residents' cars on the island, and no electricity in the inn (although indoor plumbing and hot water *are* among the modern conveniences). Built by the Coast Guard in 1907, the light is still operating (now automatically), and four other lights are visible at night. Along with fabulous ocean views, guests can watch the neighborhood deer, seal, and porpoises, hike in relative isolation all over the island, or visit the island's fishing village, schoolhouse, and cemetery.

Lit by gas lamps, rooms are charmingly furnished with some antiques, coastal memorabilia, and island crafts. In addition to the main house, the Burkes have restored the Oil House, a tiny white stucco building right on the water, and the second floor of the Wood Shed, a small barn beside the main house. There is no plumbing in the former, so guests follow the mossy path to the outhouse and solar shower.

Dinners of seafood or chicken are served family-style by candlelight; a recent meal included mushroom soup, salad, haddock with sour cream and dill, parsley rice, lemon basil carrots, and a choice of chocolate cake or raspberry peach pie.

"A rustic, romantic hideaway, with lots of fresh air and exercise. During the day, we hiked and bicycled around the island; at night we watched the moon reflecting off the water. We stayed in the Oil House, a short hike down a stone path. It has hardwood floors with throw rugs, a high ceiling, a double bed with a cozy down comforter, a chest of drawers, and a desk and chair. Flashlights and candles provide light, and a gas heater keeps the room warm. This single room structure has a little front porch overlooking the harbor, and a private rocky beach to play on. Next to the porch is a sink and sun shower, set in the pines. We were given the option of using the bathroom facilities in the main house, or roughing it with the sun shower and outhouse. The outhouse was very clean and rather cute, with pictures and books. The highlight of our stay was the good company and the great food. Judy is a spectacular cook. Every meal was made from scratch. Breakfast was a feast. We started with a homemade granola, juice and coffee, muffins or scones, and then peach pancakes one morning and blueberry French toast the next. Judy packed a hearty lunch to take on our hikes. In the evening we enjoyed a leisurely six-course meal. All the guests gathered in the living room of the main house to share tales of the day's adventures. Then we moved to the dining room for soup, salad, bread, main course, and a luscious dessert." *(Melissa Chenowith, also Thomas Bufford)*

"The hosts are wonderful, caring people, doing everything possible to make your stay memorable. Rooms are bright, cheerful, and immaculate; memorable views from every window. The main road (mostly gravel) is easy for walking; the trails are more rugged." *(Helen Rotvig)* "When we reached the island, Judy was waiting with a cart to transport the luggage to the Keeper's House. We chose to walk the stony road to the inn, which took about a half hour. After breakfast, you are encouraged to get out and explore the island; the island has 14 miles of road for bicycling." *(Donna Bocks)* "The lack of electricity at the inn produces a sense of coziness, camaraderie, and adventure among the guests. Remember to bring your own wine." *(Phyllis Salesky)*

125

Open May–Oct.

Rooms 1 cottage, 4 doubles with maximum of 4 people sharing bath. All rooms with desk. 1 cottage with woodstove, solar-heated shower, outhouse.

Facilities Dining room, living room with woodstove. Boathouse, dock. Bicycles. Swimming pond. 12 sq. miles of National Park; trails, beachcombing, fishing. Mainland parking, $3–5 per night.

Location Down East ME. 5 hrs. NE of Portland. Part of Acadia National Park. 7 m offshore from Stonington.

Restrictions No smoking. Not recommended for children under 5. BYOB. Dietary requests with ample advance notice.

Credit cards None accepted.

Rates Full board, $267–294 double, $217–244 single. Extra person, $75. Boat fare, $12 per person each way. 2-night minimum July, Aug.

Extras Spanish spoken. Crib.

JONESPORT

In northeastern Maine, about halfway between Bar Harbor and the Canadian border is Jonesport, a working fishing village.

Also recommended: Overlooking the waters of Moose-a-bec Reach is **Raspberry Shores B&B** (Main Street, Route 187, P.O. Box 217, 04649; 207–497–2463), a Victorian home built in the early 1900s. Guests enjoy day trips to Machias Seal Island to see the puffins, or hiking the nature conservatory trails on Great Wass Island. The three guest rooms share a bathroom, and the B&B double rate of $75 includes a full breakfast. "Hot showers, good water pressure. Comfortable beds with plenty of pillows, water views from most rooms. Delicious breakfast of fresh-squeezed orange juice, bacon, fluffy blueberry pancakes, homemade cranberry muffins, and omelets, served (in good weather) on the back deck, overlooking the water. Charming and peaceful. Geri Taylor is a friendly innkeeper, accommodating to our needs." *(Susan Goldblatt)*

KENNEBUNK

Arundel Meadows Inn ¢ ♿   *Tel:* 207–985–3770
Route 1, P.O. Box 1129, 04043   *Fax:* 207–967–4704
                                          E-mail: docmy@aol.com
          URL: http://www.biddeford.com/arundel_meadows_inn

Built in 1825, the Arundel Meadows was restored as an inn in 1986 by Mark Bachelder and Murray Yaeger. Murray, Professor Emeritus of Broadcast and Film at Boston University, now teaches at local universities; his paintings can be seen throughout the inn, along with the work of other local artists. Mark was trained as a chef by cookbook author and PBS television chef Madeleine Kamman; his breakfast menus include almond French toast and Maine crab meat breakfast pie, in addition to home-baked breads and cakes. Breakfast served at individual tables from 9–11 A.M.

"The inn's rooms are spacious, decorated with art and antiques. Our room was furnished with a queen-size bed, a love seat, a wing chair, plus a large fireplace, a stunning petrified-wood sculpture, and lovely Asian art. It had good noise insulation and was very quiet; spacious bathroom, too." *(Mary & Jim White)* "Mark provided excellent sight-seeing advice, even in mid-January, and supplied our fireplace with fresh wood each evening. An added bonus for us dedicated cat lovers, was the resident feline, Barney; he kept our bed warm while we were out and kept us company each morning at breakfast. Our two-room suite had a queen-size bed and two twins, a working fireplace, and private bath, fully stocked with soaps, lotions, and bath salts. Delicious, generous breakfasts prepared by Mark; we enjoyed chatting with him during the meal. Many restaurants within a mile's drive." *(Brenda & David Specht)* "Cozy and welcoming, with careful attention to detail. Convenient location for a peaceful, relaxing escape." *(Mr. & Mrs. Todd Hammond)* "Brightly lit, spacious, well-kept rooms. Extremely hospitable owners." *(Robert Koritz)* "Homey atmosphere. Ample opportunity to chat with the other guests in the cozy dining room." *(Janet Wohlberg)*

Open All year.
Rooms 2 suites, 5 doubles—all with private bath and/or shower, radio, clock, air-conditioning. Some with fireplace, TV, patio/balcony, private entrance.
Facilities Dining room, living room with fireplace, books; summer art gallery. 3½ acres with patio, hot tub, garden, picnic area. 5 m to beach.
Location SW ME. 25 m S of Portland. 2 m N of Kennebunk. Take Exit 3 off the ME Tpke. (I-95) at Kennebunk. Follow signs to Rte. 1 N. Go N approx. 2 m to inn on left.
Restrictions No smoking. Children 12 and over. Possible traffic noise in front rooms.
Credit cards MC, Visa.
Rates B&B, $95–125 suite, $85–100 double, $65–75 single. Extra person, $20. 2-night weekend minimum in-season & holidays. Off-season rates, $65–95.
Extras Wheelchair access to ground-floor room.

KENNEBUNK BEACH

The Ocean View   Tel: 207–967–2750
171 Beach Avenue, 04043   Fax: 207–967–5418
E-mail: arena@theoceanview.com
URL: http://www.theoceanview.com

Carole and Bob Arena describe their inn as being "the closest you'll find to a bed on the beach in the Kennebunks. Our inn is casual but elegant, whimsical and colorful, light and airy—befitting its oceanfront setting." All of the bedrooms have hand-painted furniture, some have hand-painted bedspreads and bathroom tiles. The day begins in the sunny breakfast room, with a wall of windows looking out to the water, a charming floral decorating motif, and colorful Fiesta Ware–style china. Guests sit at individual tables, and a typical meal might include baked pears dressed with yogurt, honey, and slivered almonds, followed by yogurt-based Belgian waffles, garnished with seasonal fruits and crème fraîche, and baked honey ham. If staying in one of the suites, you can opt for breakfast in bed, or on your private balcony overlooking the ocean. Rates also include afternoon refreshments, in-room robes, and beach towels.

"Sparkling clean, inside and out; beautiful, bright flowers, too. The front porch is a delightful place to relax, enjoy a cup of coffee, and take in the view. Attention to detail is evident from the individual bottles of water in each guest room refrigerator, the custom-tailored bathrobes, and the wonderfully firm yet comfortable mattresses." *(Patricia & James Cadira)* "Our oceanfront room was light and airy, decorated in pastel greens, pink, and blue. The location is convenient for shopping, nature walks, biking, and water sports." *(Susan Soviero, also Tom Wilbanks)* "We slept to the sound of the ocean every night." *(Donna Ciezki)* "Carole and Bob make guests feel truly welcome yet are never intrusive. The immaculate rooms are furnished in a contemporary and breezy style, with nice touches—two pinpoint reading lights over the bed (a must for avid readers), plenty of closet space, towels for the beach." *(Margot Anne Kelley)* "We particularly appreciated Carole's helpful recommendations and reservations for theater and dinner." *(Suzanne Scutt)*

"Cool ocean breezes on the hottest night. An early-morning walk along the beach tunes you up for breakfast." *(Roy & Ruth Baltozer)* "Only a local two-lane road and a sea wall separates this B&B from the ocean, and a sandy beach is within a short walk. This residential area is about a mile from Kennebunkport's shopping district, giving you easy access to all the sights without the crowds and traffic." *(Mary Welch)* "The breakfast room is a gem—soft ocean breezes waft through as you eat her marvelous breakfast served on beautifully coordinated china in soft pastel colors." *(Susan Tevens)* "Room #1, on the third floor, has a Palladian window giving a wonderful view of the ocean, which is echoed in the blues of the decor. You can lie in bed and pretend that you're on a cruise ship. For breakfast we had a huge goblet of fresh-squeezed orange juice, and wonderful waffles—crisp yet moist—with fresh strawberries." *(SWS)*

Open April–Dec.
Rooms 5 suites, 4 doubles—all with private bath, telephone, CD player, ceiling fan, mini-refrigerator. Some with TV, wet bar, porch/deck.
Facilities Breakfast room, living room with fireplace, TV room with books, front porch, gift shop, off-street parking. Concierge services. Ocean frontage, short walk to beach. Beach towels. Golf nearby.
Location SE ME, 85 m NE of Boston, 30 m SW of Portland. 1 m from Kennebunkport village. Off Exit 3 of ME Tpke. onto Rte. 35. Straight to Beach Ave. #171.
Restrictions No smoking. Children 12 and over.
Credit cards Amex, Discover, MC, Visa
Rates B&B, $120–250 suite, $100–180 double. Extra person, $25.
Extras Airport/station pickups. French spoken.

KENNEBUNKPORT

Kennebunkport is one of Maine's most popular resort towns, located along the coast in the southwest corner of the state. It has many sea captains' homes from the 17th and 18th centuries, as well as "cottages" built later by wealthy summer visitors. In addition to many fine gift and antique shops, art galleries, and restaurants, sights of interest include the Seashore Trolley Museum, the Brick Store Museum, and the Rachel Carson Wildlife Refuge. Visitors head to the beach for swimming, fishing, and boating; there are plenty of tennis courts in the area, and golf at the Cape Arundel course (also available for cross-country skiing in winter). Bicyclists can bring bikes along or rent them on arrival. Other activities include antiquing, golf, and whale-watching.

Kennebunkport is 264 miles northeast of New York City, 75 miles northeast of Boston, and 30 miles south of Portland. From I-95 (Maine Turnpike), take Exit 3 to Kennebunk, and turn south (left) on Route 35 into Kennebunkport.

Reader tips: "Beach passes are a necessity; most inns provide them, but ask just to be sure when booking." *(LR)* "Kennebunkport was charming and not at all as crowded or commercial as we'd expected." *(RB)* "We visited during a heat wave, and our inn, like most in town, had no air-conditioning."

Also recommended: For an intimate, luxurious, romantic getaway, you can't make a better choice than the **Captain's Hideaway** (12 Pleasant Street, P.O. Box 2746, 04046; 207–967–5711; www. captainshideaway.com), a Federal-style home built in 1808. The two exquisitely decorated guest rooms have all possible luxuries and amenities—from double whirlpool tubs to fireplaces to TV/VCR/CD players—and owners Judith Hughes-Boulet and Susan Jackson leave no pillow unfluffed to ensure their guests' satisfaction. B&B double rates range from $179–279, and include a full breakfast, plus always available hot and cold beverages, fresh fruit, and sweets. "Quiet, yet convenient location in the historic district. The Garden Room has a private entrance, and beautiful hand-painted furniture, floral wallpaper and fabrics, a queen-size antique four-poster bed with a lovely lace canopy, and a gas fireplace. The Captain's Room is done in a rich combination of forest green and burgundy, with a king-size canopy bed, and a spacious bathroom with lovely hand-painted tiles. Breakfast treats include eggs Benedict and lobster frittata. The owners are interesting and caring people, eager to make one's stay a pleasant and memorable experience." *(Carol Dinmore, also Kathy Banak)*

For additional area entries, see **Kennebunk, Kennebunk Beach,** and **Saco.**

Bufflehead Cove ♿	*Tel:* 207–967–3879
Gornitz Lane	*Fax:* 207–967–3879
P.O. Box 499, 04046	*URL:* http://www.buffleheadcove.com

Settle back in an old-fashioned Adirondack chair on the deck or porch of the Bufflehead Cove. Sip a mug of mulled cider and watch the Buf-

MAINE

flehead ducks (for whom the cove and inn are named) dive for their supper, rippling the waters that reflect the soft golds and oranges of the fall foliage. If you were to doze off for an afternoon snooze, who could blame you?

Owned by James and Harriet Gott since 1973, Harriet describes their inn as appealing "to the guest who loves warm colors, vases of fresh-cut flowers, soft classical music, magnificent views, peaceful privacy, and attention to all the details." The guest room decor includes king- and queen-size beds, wicker love seats, hand-painted and -stenciled walls, and folk art; the Balcony Room and the River Room have the best water views, but even the smallest room is comfortable and appealing. In addition to a full breakfast, rates include early-morning coffee, and evening wine and cheese.

"Enthusiastically endorse existing entry. Watching the sun rising over the water, illuminating the colorful fall foliage, was heavenly. Wonderful common room with lots of seating, good books, great fireplace. Harriet has collected beautiful art and decorative objects. Fascinating conversation with Jim Gott, a former lobsterman, concerning the fate of the lobster fishing industry. Superb location—serene and private, yet within walking distance of downtown." *(Pam Phillips, also Cecile Desroches)* "The spacious Balcony Room overlooks the water, and is beautifully furnished with a king-size brass bed, chaise lounge, a hand-painted mural, a roomy wardrobe stocked with bath robes, plus fresh flowers and bottled water. Harriet Gott is a gracious hostess, mingling with the guests over hors d'oeuvres, suggesting restaurants and making reservations, and cooking a heavenly breakfast." *(Betsy Madero)* "I was welcomed with wine and cheese. Comfortable, color-coordinated rooms with views of the cove. The superb breakfast included an orange-banana 'frostee,' blueberry pancakes, sausage, and an edible flower garnish. Quiet, private setting, yet a convenient location. Harriet offered suggestions for dinner and entertainment. Completely calm, relaxing, peaceful experience." *(Susan Goldblatt)*

Open All year. Weekends only, Jan., Feb., March.
Rooms 1 suite, 4 doubles—all with private bath, radio, fan. 4 with gas fireplace, 2 with desk, 3 with balcony, 1 with double whirlpool tub.
Facilities Dining room, living room with fireplace, books; porches, deck. 6 acres with picnic area; on river for canoeing; beach permits.
Location ½ m to center. From intersection of Rte. 35 & Rte. 1, continue E on Rte. 35 for 3.1 m & turn at inn's lane on left.
Restrictions No smoking. Children 12 and over.
Credit cards Discover, MC, Visa.
Rates B&B, $145–290 suite, $115–155 double. 2-night minimum. Picnic lunches.
Extras Limited wheelchair access.

The Captain Fairfield Inn
Corner of Pleasant and Green Streets
P.O. Box 1308, 04046

Tel: 207–967–4454
800–322–1928
Fax: 207–967–8537
E-mail: chefdennis@int-usa.net
URL: http://www.captain-fairfield.com

Captain Fairfield was a vigorous young man when he lived in this Federal home from 1813–1820, and owners Dennis and Bonnie Tallagnon have tried to maintain this lively feeling through the use of light and airy colors accenting antique and reproduction furnishings. They bought the house in 1991 after operating an inn in Vermont. Recent improvements include the renovation of several bathrooms with double soaking or whirlpool tubs, four-poster and canopy queen-size beds, new fabrics and wallcoverings, and such thoughtful touches as extra shelves in the bathrooms to increase storage space. "The living room is lovely, with a wood-burning fireplace and hand-blown panes of glass in the windows. The foyer in the front entry is illuminated by tall, leaded-glass windows. The lovely garden rooms have been redecorated with English country decor, queen-size canopy beds, and a plush toy frog to greet each guest. Great location, just uphill from the river and close to all the offerings in the town." *(Carol Dinmore)* "Highlights included the warm welcome; a jack for our modem; dinner reservations made in advance of arrival; the uncluttered surfaces in our spacious room which left ample space for our business gear; great breakfasts; hairdryer and ironing board; and the peaceful, quiet, homey atmosphere." *(BMF)* "Dennis and Bonnie are gracious hosts, with a helpful, courteous staff; immaculate housekeeping." *(Laurie Edelman)* "Impeccably maintained. Memorable details include the fresh-baked cookies; courteous, responsive, helpful staff, from the first phone call; convenient telephone area; comfortable beds and pillows; good reading lights and abundant reading materials." *(JMK)*

"In March, six historic inns of Kennebunkport host Saturday evening house parties for their guests, complete with scrumptious hors d'oeuvres and free packets of recipes. The weekend we stayed, the Captain Fairfield was the host inn, and Bonnie and Dennis served as wonderful hosts." *(Janine Lotti)* "Amenities included afternoon coffee, tea, and freshly baked cookies, and lovely sitting rooms with plenty of reading material. The breakfast table overlooked a beautiful lawn and gardens; the delicious meals were beautifully served." *(Carol Flint)* "We thoroughly enjoyed sitting with other guests at breakfast, but we also had the option of sitting at a table for two." *(Janice Donovan)* "The delightful breakfasts included homemade muffins and preserves, blueberry pancakes, poached eggs, fruits, juices, and more." *(Randon Wickman)* "Located in the quiet historic district, the inn is a short walk from the Village Green, harbor, and Dock Square shops and restaurants." *(Mary Harvey)* "At afternoon tea in the garden, guests were introduced to one another and had a chance to talk." *(Dr. Birgit Wenzel)*

Open All year.

Rooms 1 suite, 8 doubles—all with full private bath, clock/radio. 6 with fan; some with desk, telephone/modem jack, air-conditioning, porch, double whirlpool tub or soaking tub, gas or wood-burning fireplace.

Facilities Living room with games, library with fireplace, TV/VCR, piano, stereo; breakfast room with fireplace; guest kitchen. ¾ acre with breakfast patio, gardens.

Location 4 blocks from center of town. Take Exit 3 on I-95 and turn left on Rte. 35 S. Go to Lower Village, Kennebunk, and turn left on Rte. 9. Go over river and into Dock Sq. Turn right on Ocean Ave. (after monument). Go 5 blocks and turn left on Green St. Go 1 block to inn on right.

Restrictions No smoking. Children over 6 welcome.

Credit cards Amex, DC, Discover, MC, Visa.
Rates B&B, $99–235 suite, double; $89–225 single. Extra person, $25. 2-night weekend minimum. Off-season, midweek rates.
Extras Airport/station pickups by arrangement.

Captain Lord Mansion   *Tel:* 207–967–3141
Corner of Pleasant and Green Streets   *Fax:* 207–967–3172
P.O. Box 800, 04046–0800   *E-mail:* captain@biddeford.com
URL: http://www.captainlord.com

Bev Davis and her husband Rick Litchfield escaped to Kennebunkport from the advertising world in 1978. They've devoted incredible amounts of time and energy to bringing the Captain Lord Mansion back to its 19th-century elegance, while adding the modern conveniences expected by today's travelers. This Federal mansion, which dates back to 1812 and is listed on the National Register of Historic Places, is truly spectacular both inside and out. Many of the house's original architectural features have been preserved; guest rooms are spacious, immaculately clean, and individually decorated with antiques and quality reproductions. Completed in 1997 is the Captain's Suite, a first-floor river-view room, which now has a king-size carved wood canopy bed, oversize tiled shower with massage jets, as well as a whirlpool tub for two, stereo system, comfortable wing chairs in front of the gas fireplace, a Nordic Track Health Rider, and more (the Captain never had it so good!).

Breakfast is served family-style in the country kitchen, and includes fresh fruit, muesli cereal, French vanilla yogurt, home-baked muffins, and such entrées as buckwheat apple pancakes, cinnamon French toast, Belgian waffles, or vegetable quiche, plus a choice of coffees and teas.

"Rick is a most gracious host; his staff is both professional and friendly. Beautiful location, with the lawn stretching down toward the river." *(Priscilla Mason, also KB)* "The staff goes out of their way to help with dining and sightseeing information." *(James Beninath)* "We honeymooned at the inn years ago and returned to restore our beautiful memories. Fantastic lodging; impeccable service." *(Mark O'Brien)* "The focus on the customer, consistency, and attention to detail keep bringing us back." *(Michael Ostergard)* "Excellent breakfasts; useful book of local restaurant menus. Beautiful four-poster bed in the Lois Room." *(Judith & Nigel Broderick)* "Quiet, friendly, relaxed atmosphere; staff attentive but not hovering." *(Russ Lawson)* "Rick made everyone feel welcome, and facilitated conversation between guests most effectively." *(Linda Sullivan)*

"Location is excellent—walking distance to town, near the water and famed Ocean Drive." *(Pam Phillips)* "The decor tends toward the formal, with lavish linens and rugs pulling everything together. We sat in front of the sitting room fireplace sipping the inn's special Swedish glog and munching on scrumptious chocolate chip cookies. Large formal portraits of members of the Lord family stared down at us, providing great food for the imagination." *(Freda Eisenberg)* "The many antiques are complemented by good reading lights, night tables, and comfortable chairs." *(SWS)* "Eating breakfast at long tables in the big kitchen is a great way to meet people." *(Judith Brannon)* "Fully endorse entry; our favorite is the Lincoln Room." *(Ann Marie Mason, Carol Dinmore)*

Open All year.

Rooms 16 doubles—all with private bath and/or showers (3 baths are very small), hairdryer, make-up mirror, air-conditioning, desk, fan. 14 with gas fireplace, 8 with small refrigerator, 3 with double whirlpool tub.

Facilities Gathering room with fireplace, books, games; country kitchen; gift shop, conference room with fireplace, AV capability. 1 acre with gardens, outdoor seating. Walking distance to ocean, short drive to beach. Off-street parking.

Location Walking distance to village shops and restaurants. In Kennebunkport, go left at light at Sunoco station, over drawbridge. Take 1st right onto Ocean Ave., 5th left off Ocean Ave. to inn on left.

Restrictions No smoking. Children 6 and over.

Credit cards Discover, MC, Visa.

Rates B&B, $159–399 double. Extra person, $25. Midweek discounts off-season. Special packages. 2–3 night weekend/holiday minimum.

Extras Airport/station pickups, $25 round trip.

Crosstrees
(formerly Kylemere House 1818)
6 South Street
P.O. Box 1333, 04046

Tel: 207–967–2780
Fax: 207–967–2610
E-mail: crosstrees@cybertours.com
URL: http://www.crosstrees.com

A Federal-style home built in 1818 by one of Kennebunkport's founding families, Crosstrees was purchased by Dennis Rafferty and Keith Henley in 1998. Maine artist and architect Abbott Graves purchased the house in 1895, and had his art studio in the barn. Graves gave the house its name of Crosstrees for the husband and wife maple trees planted on either side of the front door. Today one of these maples remains, shading the house in summer, and bursting with brilliant color in the fall. Today, this B&B is newly remodeled and air-conditioned. Each room is decorated with lovely 19th-century antiques and reproductions; guest rooms have king-, queen-, or twin-size beds to ensure guests' comfort. Outside, it's surrounded by beautiful annual and perennial gardens, carefully planned so that flowers are blooming from May through October.

"A beautiful residential area of historic homes, within convenient walking distance of the harbor and town. Warm hospitality, conducive to meeting other guests, either in the evening over wine in the cozy living room or at the elegantly set breakfast table." *(Mr. & Mrs. Fred Cady)* "Our room was decorated with wonderful antiques, lace pillows, and curtains. Immaculate modern bathroom." *(William Harazim)* "Beautifully furnished guest room, complete with a four-poster bed." *(Peggy Griffin)* "Delicious breakfast and in-room treats." *(GR)* "Impressive attention to detail in decorating and ambience. Scrumptious little chocolates or baked goodies were left in our room." *(Janice Levenson)* "The ideal tonic for travelers in need of nurturing and comfort. The inn is spotless and beautifully furnished, with great attention to detail. Warm, hospitable owners who offered great conversation, attentiveness to our needs." *(Linda Wharton)*

Open All year.
Rooms 1 suite, 3 doubles—all with private bath and/or shower, air-conditioning, radio, desk, fan. 3 with gas or wood-burning fireplace, 1 with double whirlpool tub, TV/VCR.
Facilities Dining room, living room with baby grand piano, porch. Gardens, picnic area, art studio, off-street parking.
Location Historic district. From I-95 (ME Tpke.), take Exit 3 & turn left on Rte. 35 S. Turn left at junction of Rte. 9 (about 6 m). Go over drawbridge and through Dock Sq. Turn right at the "T" (Maine St.); go 5 short blocks to South St. and turn right. Walking distance to village center, marina, ocean.
Restrictions No smoking. Children 12 and over.
Credit cards MC, Visa.
Rates B&B, $115–195 suite, double. Extra person, $25. Off-season rates, long-stay discounts, packages.

1802 House
15 Locke Street, P.O. Box 646-A, 04046

Tel: 207–967–5632
800–932–5632
Fax: 207–967–0780
E-mail: inquiry@1802inn.com
URL: http://www.1802inn.com

While it's normal for visitors to travel to Kennebunkport, in the case of the 1802 House, the building itself had to cover some ground before its arrival in town. The original part of the inn was built in 1802 in the nearby town of Waterboro. The one-story building was dragged by oxen to its present location on Locke Street, just as sailing ships were hauled down to the Kennebunk River to be launched into the Atlantic Ocean. A second story was added to the building almost a century ago, and the building was restored as an inn in 1977. The guest rooms are located in the original part of the house, while the barn is now the dining room and country kitchen. Ron and Carol Perry purchased the inn in 1992, who have worked hard to make the inn a romantic hideaway, complementing its handsome decor with excellent food and warm hospitality.

Breakfast is served in the dining room, overlooking the Cape Arundel Golf Club, and includes fresh fruit and juice, home-baked muffins or bread, plus a daily entrée: perhaps banana walnut pancakes, eggs in pastry with mushroom sauce, potato pancakes, peach crêpes with raspberries, or asparagus cheese soufflé. A low-fat alternative is always available. Rates also include afternoon drinks—perhaps hot chocolate or iced tea, depending on the season—plus bedtime chocolates and turndown service.

"Carol and Ron Perry welcomed us with spiced hot cider next to the wood fire in the cozy parlor. The adjacent dining room has picture windows looking out to a variety of bird feeders; birding guidebooks are available, so you can enjoy identifying them. Beyond is a tranquil view of a frog pond, flower gardens, and the Cape Arundel Golf Club. The luxurious Sebago Suite has a soft cream and rose floral bedroom, with a queen-size four-poster canopy bed, a sitting room with marble-tiled gas fireplace, wet bar, TV/VCR, and CD stereo. Off of the sitting room is the Roman Garden Room, with a heated tiled floor, and a two-person whirlpool tub, surrounded by green marble tile. The private deck has a garden view. The separate bathroom has a double shower. A magnifying mirror, hairdryer, thirsty Egyptian-cotton towels, and a basket of assorted toiletries, along with two sets of robes and slippers, are provided. After a quiet and peaceful night, Carol rings a ship's bell to let you know that breakfast will be served in half an hour. We enjoyed baked apples, light lemon-ricotta pancakes, strips of bacon and home-made cranberry muffins, along with a choice of juices, coffee, and tea. The innkeepers happily shared their recipes with us, and then let us look around the kitchen. The kitchen has a wonderful barn-board ceiling, and a long wooden table for food preparation." *(Carol Dinmore)* "Careful attention to detail throughout. I loved Carol's hand-painted bathroom tiles, and the wonderful kitchen. One of the guest rooms overlooks the golf course where former President Bush played. The beauty of the inn is outweighed only by Ron and Carol's genuine warm and hospitality." *(Kathy Banak)* "Luxury and pampering on a par with the Ritz." *(Mr. & Mrs. Craig Selbrede)*

Open All year.

Rooms 1 suite, 5 doubles—all with full private bath, air-conditioning, CD/stereo system, clock/radio, TV/VCR, hairdryer, make-up mirror, bed warmers, bathrobes. Some with fireplace, double whirlpool tub; suite with deck, private entrance.

Facilities Dining room, living room with fireplace, piano books; porch. ¾ acre with gardens, frog pond, off-street parking. Golf course, cross-country skiing adjacent; tee-time reservations. Free health club passes.

Location 10-min. walk from Dock Sq. Follow Rte. 9 past Dock Sq. to North St. Go left on North St. Go left on Locke St. to inn on right.

Restrictions No smoking. Children over 12.

Credit cards Amex, MC, Visa.

Rates B&B, $199–299 suite, $119–199 double. 2-night minimum in season, also holiday, special-event weekends. Off-season packages. Tips appreciated.

Extras Limited French spoken.

The Inn at Harbor Head

41 Pier Road, Cape Porpoise, 04046

Tel: 207–967–5564
Fax: 207–967–1294

A rambling shingled home built at the turn of the century, the Inn at Harbor Head overlooks the water, and was purchased by Eve Sagris and Dick Roesler in 1998. The inn's charming antiques, fine art, and old Oriental carpets are complemented with hand-painted murals and stenciling. Many of the murals display *trompe l'oeil* effects, from the "balconied" mural of the harbor in one suite to the "blue sky" with birds flying past clouds in the Summer Suite. The dining room has an Oriental theme; breakfast is served here at 8:30 A.M., and begins with freshly squeezed juices, followed by grapefruit, raspberries, and kiwi in champagne, or perhaps bananas flambé; followed by pecan French toast or possibly herbed scrambled eggs over Canadian bacon. Dietary restrictions are accommodated with advance notice. Afternoon tea is served from 4–5 P.M., and includes freshly brewed tea with such home-baked treats as German chocolate cake or carrot cake.

"Elegant decor, yet cozy and homey. Outstanding breakfasts, beautifully presented. Sincere, energetic, likeable innkeepers." *(Horace & Rejeanne Champagne)* "Warm welcome, lovely views of gardens and lobster boats moored in the cove. Falling asleep at night you could hear a distant buoy softly sounding its warning over the water. Careful attention to detail, from the toasty bathrobes to the hairdryer. The inviting library is supplied with soft background music, board games, and reading materials. During breakfast, the soothing sounds of water trickling over rocks in the Japanese garden provided a pleasant backdrop to the conversation. Eve and Dick work together to prepare breakfast; Eve has a passion for baking and is delighted to share recipes. A quiet refuge with all the comforts one could possibly want; Eve and Dick were available, accommodating, and delightful in every way." *(Jill & Frank Fulginiti)*

"Lovely house, extensively decorated; outstanding location in a quiet neighborhood; beautiful grounds, magnificent views; charming hosts. The Harbor Suite has a fireplace and small balcony overlooking Cape Porpoise Harbor. Fresh flowers, crystal decanters of port, bottles of the inn's own label spring water, plush-white terry-cloth robes, and an assortment of shampoos, conditioners, lotions, and bath salts were provided. Coffee is set out at 7:30 A.M.; we took our mugs outside, enjoying the harbor views before breakfast. The breakfast table was set with candles, fresh flowers, china, and crystal; our fellow guests were an interesting bunch." *(Rose Ciccone)* "We had a good night's sleep in the comfortable beds, piled high with feather pillows and a down comforter." *(Mary Lynn Moyar)* "All you could hear in the quiet night was the fog horn and bell buoy." *(Paul Nared)*

Open Feb–Nov. 15; Dec. 1–15.
Rooms 2 suites, 2 doubles—all with private bath and/or shower, clock radio, air-conditioning, fan. Some with deck, Jacuzzi, gas fireplace.
Facilities Dining room, living room, library with fireplace, books, stereo; deck, patio. ½ acre with lawn chairs, hammocks. Private dock. On ocean for water sports; beach passes. Off-street parking.
Location On Cape Porpoise Harbor, 2 m E of Kennebunkport. From I-95, take Exit 3 to Rte. 35 to Kennebunkport. Go left at intersection of Rtes. 9 & 35. Cross bridge and follow Rte. 9 E through Dock Sq. to stop sign. Go right on Maine St., then left on School St. Continue on Rte. 9 about 1.5 m past school & woods. Just after Bradbury's Market, leave Rte. 9 (don't make sharp left) & go straight onto Pier Rd. to inn, .02 m on right.
Restrictions No smoking. Children 12 and over.
Credit cards MC, Visa.
Rates B&B, $205–325 suite, $130–200 double. Extra person, $50. 2-night minimum in high season and holidays.

The Inn on South Street *Tel:* 207–967–5151
South Street, P.O. Box 478A, 04046 800–963–5151
E-mail: jdowns@gwi.net
URL: http://www.innonsouthst.com

Longtime inhabitants of Kennebunkport, Jack and Eva Downs turned their early 1800s Greek Revival home into a B&B in 1982, after their children had grown and left for college. Breakfast menus vary daily, but might include fresh fruit and juice, homemade jams and bread, puffed eggs with toast, and zucchini coffee cake.

"Warm, bright, and comfortable; our favorite rooms are the Romantic and the Gibson Girl. Wonderful breakfasts of German apple pancakes with almonds and fruit, and the freshly baked breads. Eva and Jack are great storytellers and listeners." (*Kelley Meade*) "Superb breakfasts in the comfortable second-floor kitchen with harbor views. Peaceful residential location, walking distance to fine restaurants, galleries, and shops. Charmingly appointed rooms accented with Oriental antiques." (*Joan Chalmers*) "Our well-equipped room had excellent reading lamps on both sides of the bed, and by the chaise longue. Eva's lovely fresh flowers were placed in the bedroom and the bath." (*Mr. & Mrs. Bernard von Hoffman*) "Fully endorse entry. We enjoyed the second-floor sitting room with French doors opening onto a porch and ample space for sitting, reading, relaxing. Eva and Jack are experienced and gracious hosts. Delicious breakfasts with frittata one day, soufflé the next." (*Donna Kmetz, also Christine Lungren-Maddalone*)

"The immaculate rooms have comfortable beds with quality linens, piled high with pillows and bolsters. The baths are supplied with plenty of towels and imported soaps. Amenities include bowls of fruit, baskets of books and magazines, and fresh or dried flower arrangements. The Downses are cordial and helpful about making dinner reservations, sightseeing suggestions, and more." (*Georgette Mahoney*) "Once you park your car at the inn, you'll not need it again during your stay." (*Helen Wolbrom*) "Delightful afternoon lemonade and wine; glorious perennial gardens." (*Betsy Hoffman*)

Open Feb.–Dec.

Rooms 1 3-room apartment suite with fireplace, Jacuzzi, kitchen; 3 doubles— all with private bath and/or shower, radio, telephone, desk, fan. 1 with fireplace, refrigerator. Suite with kitchen, fireplace.

Facilities Country kitchen, dining area, living room with fireplace, games; balcony. Herb, flower gardens, terrace. Off-street parking.

Location From I-95 take Rte. 35 to Kennebunkport. Turn left on Rte. 9 over drawbridge and through Dock Sq. Turn right at the "T" (Maine St.); go 5 short blocks to South St. and turn right.

Restrictions No smoking. Children by prior arrangement.

Credit cards MC, Visa.

Rates B&B, \$155–225 suite, \$105–149 double, \$75–100 single. Extra person, \$25. 2-night holidays/weekends/peak season minimum. Extended stay discounts. Weekly rates.

Extras German, Spanish, Russian spoken.

Maine Stay Inn & Cottages 🏃
34 Maine Street, P.O. Box 500A, 04046

Tel: 207–967–2117
800–950–2117
Fax: 207–967–8757
E-mail: innkeeper@mainestayinn.com
URL: http://www.mainestayinn.com

They say "you can't please all the people all the time," but longtime innkeepers Lindsay and Carol Copeland sure come close. If your fantasy of the perfect inn involves climbing the steps of a suspended flying staircase in a historic Italianate mansion, built in 1860, and listed on the National Register of Historic Places, then choose one of the antique-filled rooms in the Maine Stay's original building. If you prefer the romantic privacy of your own cottage, complete with a double whirlpool tub, queen-size bed, and remote-control gas fireplace, select one of the remodeled units. And if you're traveling as a family, reserve one of the larger cottages with a fully equipped kitchen.

Breakfast is served in the dining room, although guests in the cottages can have a breakfast basket delivered to their door; at 4 P.M., tea is offered in the parlor. Menus change daily, but a typical morning brings fresh fruit cup, apple spice pancakes with Maine maple syrup, pumpkin ginger muffins, and English muffins with blueberry jam. The inn is on a quiet residential street, and the wicker rockers on its front porch invite guests to relax and watch the passing scene.

"Fully endorse existing writeup. I parked my car and walked everywhere. Lovely rooms, with a variety of accommodations to suit different needs. My lovely room had a queen-size bed and double Jacuzzi." *(Pam Phillips)* "Carol and Lindsay's friendliness and warm hospitality help set the stage for the peaceful setting." *(Paula & Michael Panik)* "Gracious, personable innkeepers who never stop remodeling and improving their inn, keeping it fresh and inviting." *(Carol Dinmore)* "We love the gorgeous rooms, the afternoon tea and pastries, the neighborhood's history, rich architecture, assigned off-street parking, and the proximity to water, shopping, and restaurants. Appealing weekend packages, too." *(Paul Grzywinski)* "Great location, within walking distance of everything. Recent renovations to the cottage rooms are lovely, with fine reproduction furnishings, beautiful wall coverings and window treatments." *(Norma LeBlanc)* "Carol and Lindsay are wonderful, welcoming hosts, always available to recommend activities and restaurants; the inn is immaculate, the breakfasts exceptional." *(Brenda & Howard Leafe)* "Although families with small children are happily accommodated in the cottages, a relaxing and elegant atmosphere is always maintained for adults." *(Jean Foy)* "The furnishings are beautiful, from the quilts to the matching curtains. A highlight of our weekend was a specially arranged maple-sugaring tour at one of the local farms." *(Mr. & Mrs. Robert Taft)*

"Service is prompt but unobtrusive. Excellent breakfast served at shared tables so guests have opportunities to meet and converse." *(Roland & Rose Sarti)* "Loved the option of a private breakfast. Our basket was always delivered promptly, and included a hot dish, fresh milk for coffee, fresh fruit, raisin bread or English muffins, and juice." *(Fritz Shantz & Tara Neal)* "Our cottage fireplace was cleaned and set up each day; plumbing and electrical systems were in excellent condition." *(Ann Steeves)* "The inn's common rooms were beautifully decorated with antiques; guidebooks, tourist information, and morning papers were available." *(Nora Corrigan)* "We climbed the curving steps of the suspended flying staircase to our suite, with a lovely sitting area furnished with antiques and a bedroom with a queen-size canopy bed. Thick, thirsty towels, lemon- and wildflower-scented soaps were welcome touches." *(Timothy & Kerry Kenney)*

Note: Though both are highly recommended, this inn is not connected with the Maine Stay in Camden, Maine (see entry).

Open All year.

Rooms 11 1–2 bedroom cottages, 2 suites, 4 doubles—all with private bath and/or shower, radio, TV, air-conditioning. Some cottages with kitchen, 9 with wood-burning or remote control gas fireplace, some with whirlpool tubs.

Facilities Breakfast room, living room with fireplace, books, stereo, porch. 1.2 acres with children's play equipment, picnic area. Cross-country skiing, golf, whale watching, fishing nearby.

Location Historic district, walking distance to town. Take Rte. 95 to Rte. 35 and go 2½ m to traffic light. Turn left & at next set of lights go right on Rte. 35. Continue 3½ m to Rte. 9 & turn left. Follow Rte. 9 over a small bridge & through Dock Sq. to top of small hill. Turn right on Maine St. & go ²⁄₁₀ m to inn on left.

Restrictions No smoking.

Credit cards Amex, MC, Visa.

Rates B&B, $85–185 cottage, $110–225 suite, $85–185 double. Extra person, $15–25; children 5–11, $10, age 4 and under free in parents' room. Crib, $10. Weekly discount. Rates higher New Year's and prelude weekends. 2-night weekend minimum. 2–3 night summer minimum in cottages. Off-season packages.

Extras Crib, babysitting.

The Old Fort Inn 🏃

Old Fort Avenue, P.O. Box M, 04046

Tel: 207–967–5353
800–828–FORT
Fax: 207–967–4547
E-mail: oldfort@cybertours.com
URL: http://www.oldfortinn.com

In 1980, David and Sheila Aldrich took an old barn and carriage house and converted the two into the Old Fort Inn. The barn, built in 1880, became the lodge, where guests gather for breakfast and conversation, while the guest rooms are found in the red brick and stone carriage house, built at the turn of the century. The buffet breakfast includes cereal and granola, fresh fruit and juice, quiche, croissants, and coffee cake, and is served poolside, weather permitting.

"Quiet, relaxing location away from the hustle and bustle, on a beautiful piece of property. The substantial, delicious, attractively presented breakfast was served at tables around the pool or on the patio. Everyone, from the owner, Sheila, who greeted us upon our arrival, to the housekeeping staff, was personable, pleasant, and eager to please. One feature, the washer and dryer, was really appreciated after a week on the road." *(Joan & Gary Goldenberg)* "Guest rooms are well decorated and extremely comfortable, with quality towels and linens, and abundant extras: candies, cookies, toiletries." *(Pauline Meyer)* "Pleasant guests and staff; warm, homey atmosphere." *(Rose Barrell)* "Colonial and Victorian decor. Comfortable beds in all sizes. The spacious baths are modern with good lighting. David and Sheila run a professional place and will bend over backward to answer your questions and help you with restaurant advice and reservations." *(Donna & Bill Beitel)* "Many amenities, good food, most pleasant innkeepers, and a warm, homey atmosphere." *(Rose Barell)*

Open Mid-April–mid-Dec.

Rooms 2 suites, 14 doubles—all with private bath and/or shower, telephone, radio, air-conditioning, TV, desk, wet bar, fan. 1 room in annex. Some with fireplace, Jacuzzi.

Facilities Lodge room with fireplace, piano; guest laundry. 3 acres with heated swimming pool, tennis court, shuffleboard, antique shop, off-street parking. 1 block from beach. Golf nearby.

Location 1¼ m from town. From I-95, take Exit 3 (Kennebunk). Go left on Rte. 35 for 5½ m. Go left at light on Rte. 9 for ³⁄₁₀ m. Turn right on Ocean Ave. for ⁹⁄₁₀ m to Colony Hotel. Go left & follow signs ³⁄₁₀ m to inn.

Restrictions No smoking. Children over 12.

Credit cards Amex, Discover, MC, Visa.

Rates B&B, $140–325 suite, double. Extra person, $25. Midweek, off-season rates. 2–3 night weekend/holiday minimum in season. Includes 1 hr. free tennis daily.

The Welby Inn

92 Ocean Avenue, P.O. Box 774, 04046

Tel: 207–967–4655
Fax: 207–967–8654
E-mail: WelbyInn@GWI.Net

A Dutch gambrel-style home built in 1900, the Welby was purchased by Allison Rowley and her daughter Merrianne Weston in 1997. Wake-up coffee is available at 7 A.M., and breakfast is served at tables in the dining room or on the sun porch at 8:30 A.M. The meal includes fresh fruit and juice, home-baked breads and muffins, and a main course. Rates also include access to the guest pantry, stocked with coffee, tea, and ice, and afternoon treats.

"One enters a spacious common room with light filtering through panoramic windows. A beautiful hand-painted tile-and-brick fireplace invites you to relax and unwind in a comfortable wing chair. An unusual antique square-shaped grand piano was restored by one of the inn's guests, and provides an ideal spot to display the owners' many family pictures. Beyond the common area are the light and cheery dining room and sun porch, where guests enjoy a delicious breakfast prepared by Allison or Merrianne." *(Carol Dinmore)* "Our room had a working fireplace, small sitting area with love seat, a queen canopy bed, and matching wallpaper." *(Rose Ciccone)* "Merrianne and Allison were extremely gracious, warm, and funny. My lovely room at the front of the house was decorated with pink, blue, and white floral wallpaper, lace curtains, and beautiful blue-and-white bedding on the four-poster bed. There was a chest of drawers, a chair with a nice quilt draped on it, two night stands with lights, and a beautiful antique armoire that gave the room lots of warmth. The bathroom was small, but perfectly adequate. For breakfast, Allison made wonderfully light and airy pancakes prepared with orange juice; also served were sausage, muffins, juice, and coffee." *(Kathy Banak)*

Open All year.

Rooms 7 doubles—all with full private shower and/or tub. All with clock/radio, fan; 1 with fireplace.

Facilities Dining room, living room with piano, family room, library with TV, guest pantry/refrigerator. Off-street parking. Beach passes.

Location Historic district, 5-min. walk to Dock Sq. & sandy beach on Parson's Way. From ME Turnpike, take Exit 3 to Rte. 35 S to Kennebunkport. Go left past Sunoco station at light. Go over drawbridge, & take 1st right onto Ocean Ave. to inn ½ m on left.

Restrictions No smoking. Children 12 and over. Traffic noise possible in front room in season.

Credit cards MC, Visa.

Rates B&B, $70–115 double. Extra person, $15. 2-night weekend minimum June 1–Oct. 30. 10% senior discount. Picnic lunches.

The White Barn Inn ✕

Beach Street, P.O. Box 560C, 04046

Tel: 207–967–2321
Fax: 207–967–1100
E-mail: Innkeeper@whitebarninn.com
URL: http://www.whitebarninn.com

For Kennebunkport's most elegant food and accommodations, your best choice is the White Barn Inn. Owned since 1988 by experienced hotelier Laurence Bongiorno, the inn's living rooms are appointed with antique and reproduction furnishings, rich fabrics and artwork. Guest rooms in the Main House are decorated with colorful fabrics, floral wallcoverings, and period antiques, while the Carriage House offers luxurious suites with four-poster king-size beds and marble baths with whirlpool tubs; rooms in the Gate House have queen-size sleigh beds and wood-burning fireplaces. Each room has terry robes, a welcoming fruit basket, fresh flowers, and European bath amenities. Breakfast includes home-baked pastries, fresh fruit, homemade granola, and freshly squeezed juices; hot entrées are available for an extra fee. Rates also include afternoon tea, evening brandy and port, and use of touring bicycles, and canoes.

The inn's restaurant is set in a magnificently restored three-story barn. Under the careful supervision of Chef Jonathan M. Cartwright, menus are changed weekly to offer the freshest of native ingredients. A recent dinner included such entrées as veal and sweetbreads with spring spinach, gratin potatoes, and cinnamon apple sauce; lamb with rosemary and port; halibut with fiddleheads and morel mushrooms; and a canneloni of basil and feta cheese on roasted tomato coulis with grilled vegetables.

"Excellent service; courteous staff; elegant, small hotel atmosphere. Our room had creatively hand-painted furniture. Breakfast was beautifully presented in a bright, cheerful room. Waiters brought beverages to the table; a buffet table offered muffins, croissants, and cereal." *(Lauren Kenney)* "Beautiful guest rooms, right down to the fixtures in the bathroom, curtains, and bedspread and antiques. The amenities are first-class, and the evening turndown and snack with fresh thick towels was an unexpected pleasure." *(GR, also Nancy Hunich)* "Suites in the Carriage House are the ultimate in comfort. Common areas in the main house are a good place to mingle with other guests." *(Pam Philips)* "The atmosphere and service have always been excellent at the White Barn, but under chef Jonathan Cartwright, the cuisine has reached new levels of excellence." *(CA)* "Fully endorse entry. Decor, food, and service were superb." *(Mary Lou Cannilla)*

141

Open All year.

Rooms 1 cottage, 8 suites, 16 doubles—all with private bath and/or shower, telephone. 12 with TV, Jacuzzi, wood-burning fireplace. 11 rooms in 3 separate buildings.

Facilities Restaurant with piano bar, breakfast room, 2 living rooms with fireplace, TV, books; meeting room, sun room, porches. Heated outdoor pool, bicycles, canoes. Swimming beach, hiking, golf, cross-country skiing nearby.

Location 5-min. walk from town. From I-95 take Exit 3 and go S on Rte. 35 7½ m to traffic light. Proceed straight through light and inn is ¼ m on right.

Restrictions No smoking in guest rooms. No children under 12. Dress code in restaurant, bar.

Credit cards Amex, MC, Visa.

Rates B&B, $350–395 suite, $160–250 double. 2–3 night weekend/holiday minimum. Off-season packages. Prix fixe dinner, $62.

Extras French, German spoken. Member, Relais et Châteaux.

KITTERY

Kittery is the first Maine town you come to if you're traveling north on I-95, and is just a mile north of Portsmouth, New Hampshire. Some travelers use it as an inexpensive base to visit Portsmouth, the beaches at York, or the outlet shops in Kittery.

Gundalow Inn ¢ ♿   *Tel: 207–439–4040*
6 Water Street, 03904

Gundalows, sailing barges that worked the river for 250 years, were a common sight when this brick Victorian home, with views of Portsmouth Harbor, was built in 1889. Renovated in 1990 by owners Cevia and George Rosol, the inn is furnished with period antiques, brass sconces and chandeliers, and Victorian art. Guest rooms have Oriental rugs, period-patterned wallpapers, brass, iron or four-poster beds, lace curtains, and bathrooms combining period decor with modern amenities. While the grounds are not extensive, flowers bloom in abundance, and guests can take a 15-minute walk across the bridge to the heart of Portsmouth. The Gundalow has long been a consistent reader favorite for its comfortable accommodations, good food, appealing location, and, most of all, its hospitable innkeepers.

"Fully endorse entry. Hospitable hosts, generous with area recommendations. Our room was charmingly decorated, supplied with all amenities. The breakfast was all we had read about and more, with fresh muffins, fruit, egg casserole, and fish cakes, served with bantering conversation by our host." *(Carol Workman)* "The inn reflects Cevia and George's warmth and graciousness. The cozy living room features an ongoing jigsaw puzzle and a very playable piano. Love the applesauce at breakfast." *(Judith & Dick MacDonald)* "Excellent restaurant recommendations. George and Cevia are genuinely interested in their guests." *(Tom Wilbanks)* "Tasty breakfasts of George's own smoked salmon, scrambled eggs, and maple-walnut scones." *(Mr. & Mrs. Frank Mac-*

Dougal) "Our third-floor room had a distant river view and a comfortable queen-size bed; the bathroom was tucked under the eaves with a European-style shower attachment for the tub." *(Lucy Hedrick)*

"Our clean and cozy room had lots of reading material, and a bathroom with an old-fashioned claw-footed tub and plenty of thirsty towels. Enjoyable breakfast of fresh-squeezed juice, homemade scones, scrambled eggs with asparagus, fish cakes with fresh vegetables, and endless cups of coffee." *(Marilyn & Richard Santoro)* "Delicious peach yogurt soup for breakfast. Homey second-floor guest room with twin beds made up as a comfortable king-size bed. Just as close to Portsmouth's historic downtown as most of Portsmouth's inns. The half-mile walk across the river drawbridge is cool and lovely, with great views." *(SWS)*

Open All year.

Rooms 6 doubles—all with private bath and/or shower, desk, ceiling fan, clock/radio. Telephone on request.

Facilities Breakfast room with fireplace, living room with piano, stereo; library, screened porch. Town green across the street. Fishing charters, whale-watch excursion boats within walking distance. 15 min. drive to ocean beaches.

Location ME seacoast. ½ m to Portsmouth, NH. From I-95 N, take Portsmouth Exit 7. Turn right on Market St. Extension and drive ⁹⁄₁₀ m into Portsmouth. Turn left on Bow St. and follow to end. Turn left on State St. and follow Memorial Bridge (U.S. Rte. 1) into ME. Immediately after bridge, make a sharp left onto Water St. Inn is 1st building on right.

Restrictions Light traffic/river noise. No smoking. No children under 16.

Credit cards Discover, MC, Visa.

Rates B&B, $80–125 double. Extra person, $20. 2-night mid-week discount Jan.–March. 2-night holiday weekend minimum.

Extras Limited wheelchair access.

LUBEC

Lubec is the easternmost town in Maine and the U.S., and sits at the edge of the Eastern Time Zone. Visit Quoddy Head State Park to see the sun rise and the candy-cane–striped lighthouse, to follow the trails along the cliff overlooking the Bay of Fundy, to see whales and dolphins, and explore the tidal pools. Moosehorn National Wildlife Refuge is a short drive away, and Campobello Island is just across the toll-free International Bridge.

Lubec is located in northeast coastal Maine, 130 miles east of Bangor, and 230 miles northeast of Portland; it's 1 mile from Campobello Island, New Brunswick, Canada. From Route 1, go east on Route 189 and follow for 11 miles into Lubec.

Also recommended: Built in 1880, **The Home Port Inn** (45 Main Street, P.O. Box 50, 04652; 207–733–2077 or 800–457–2077) is a restaurant and seven-guest-room inn, situated at the top of the hill on a tree-shaded, church-lined street. Seafood highlights the popular dinner menu, with such dishes as salmon with lemon-dill sauce, lobster pie, coquilles St. Jacques, and seafood casserole. B&B double rates range from $65–85. "Our second-floor room at the back of the inn had six windows, two beds, antique decor, a small private bathroom, and terrific views of the back bay and boating activity through salt-sprayed windows. The spacious common area was tastefully decorated with antiques, and had several comfortable sitting areas, a widescreen TV, numerous books, magazines, and games. A breakfast buffet was set up in the dining room with homemade granola, home-baked muffins, juice and fruit, coffee and tea. We had dinner two nights; the food was excellent, the prices most reasonable, and the service attentive one night, less so the next." *(CS)*

For additional area inns, see **Eastport** and **Robbinston**.

Peacock House   ♿
27 Summer Street, 04652

Tel: 207–733–2403
E-mail: peacockhouse@nemaine.com
URL: http://www.nemaine.com/peacock_house

The Peacock House was built in 1860, and was restored as a B&B in 1989 by Chet and Veda Childs. Breakfast, different each day, is offered at 7:30 and 8:30 A.M. in the dining room. In good weather, both breakfast and afternoon tea and scones are served outside.

"The Margaret Chase Smith Suite is ideal for extra space and privacy, and has large windows that make it bright and relaxing. It has a queen-size bed, a small sitting area with two wingback chairs, and antique furnishings. The private bath has a large tub, good for soaking after a long day of sightseeing. The entire inn is immaculate. The public rooms are comfortable and well decorated, with ample space for conversation with other guests, quiet places to enjoy a good book, and a separate room with a TV/VCR and a wide selection of videos. The owners take obvious pride in their inn, and are helpful but not intrusive. Breakfast is different each day; we were asked upon check-in about dietary needs and preferences. One day we had delectable pancakes with special house syrup, the next day a vegetable omelet. Excellent quantity and quality. Coffee is available at 7 A.M. for early risers." *(Nancy & Conrad Schilke)* "The owners have traveled extensively, and have taken everything they've learned to create an extremely comfortable B&B, including over thirty different breakfast menus. Our meal was excellent, and attractively served. Within walking distance of a nice restaurant." *(Ruthie Tilsley)* "Immaculate, beautifully decorated inn; fine linens. Breakfasts, prepared by Veda, were outstanding." *(Eloise Balasco)* "Extremely well maintained and clean, with plenty of common space; well-furnished rooms. Breakfast was served at two seatings at a large dining room table." *(Doris Ann Gladstone)* "The cozy Wedgwood Room is decorated in blue and white, with several Wedgwood pieces. The entire inn is furnished with well-chosen and interesting pieces from the hosts' world travels." *(Jim & Mary White)*

Open Mid-May–Mid-Oct.
Rooms 3 suites, 2 doubles—all with private bath and/or shower. Suites with TV/VCR.
Facilities Dining room, living room, family room, library with books, videos; guest pantry. Patio, garden, off-street parking. Fishing, hiking, whale-watching, golf nearby.
Location In town. 11 m off U.S. 1 on Hwy. 189.

Restrictions Children 7 and over. Smoking restricted.
Credit cards MC, Visa.
Rates B&B, $70–80 suite, double, $60–70 single. Extra person, $10. Weekly rates. Picnic lunches.
Extras Wheelchair access.

NAPLES

For additional area entries, see **Bridgton, Center Lovell, Fryeburg,** and **Waterford.**

Inn at Long Lake ¢   *Tel:* 207–693–6226
Lake House Road, P.O. Box 806, 04055   800–437–0328
E-mail: innatll@megalink.net

In pre-railroad days, the Cumberland and Oxford Canal bridged the gaps between Maine's lakes and Portland's Casco Bay. The Inn at Long Lake lies along this route, and in honor of this history, guest rooms are named after the canal boats which transported wood in one direction, molasses and rum in the other, among other products. Built in 1906 as part of a larger hotel, the four-story inn was completely restored in 1987 and was purchased in 1990 by Maynard and Irene Hincks. Rooms are individually decorated in period, with wicker chairs; some have cheerful florals, others more masculine tones. The beds have fluffy comforters, and a few have hand-stenciled headboards. Breakfast consists of coffee, juice, fruit, cereals, and muffins or pastry.

"You enter a large room with a large fireplace, overstuffed chairs, and a dining area. The rooms are clean, with individual character. The best part for me was waking up in the morning and going downstairs to the smell of fresh hazelnut coffee, and a waiting newspaper in front of the roaring fire." *(Al Konschak)* "Owners Maynard and Irene are always accommodating to our needs. The rooms are always clean and comfortable. The great room boasts a floor-to-ceiling stone fireplace and coffee always brewing. The inn has a unique, elegant, yet casual atmosphere." *(Ken & Maureen Wynn, also Janet Choy)*

"Warm and comfortable common room with a large fieldstone fireplace. Our room was attractively furnished with period pieces. We were thrilled to see a moose grazing in the field next to the inn." *(Mary & Jim White)* "Perfectly maintained, both inside and out. Our fourth-floor room was color-coordinated right down to the stenciling on the painted bathroom floor. Exceptionally clean. Continental breakfast was set up in the living room, making it easy to meet and converse with other guests." *(Judith Brannen)* "We enjoyed coffee and hot chocolate before the roaring fire in the great room. The innkeepers made us feel welcome; little extras like roses, candy, and sparkling cider reinforced their efforts." *(Joyce Thebarge, also BJ Hensley)*

Open All year.
Rooms 2 suites, 14 doubles—all with private shower and/or bath, TV, air-conditioning.
Facilities Great room/dining area with fireplace, library; porches. 2 min. walk to lake for swimming, boating, water-skiing, parasailing, fishing. Golf, hiking, bicycling nearby. 20 min. to downhill skiing, 5 min. to cross-country.

Location Lakes region. 45 min. NW of Portland, 45 min. E of Conway, NH. Close to juncture of Rtes. 302, 11, 14. From I-95, take Exit 8 to Rte. 302 W to Naples. In Naples, take 2nd rd. on left (Lakehouse Rd.) after bridge to inn on right.

Restrictions No smoking. Well-behaved children welcome.

Credit cards Amex, Discover, MC, Visa.

Rates B&B, $105–150 suite, $65–125 double; 10% discount single. Extra person, $12. Rollaway, $15. AAA, AARP discount; 10–20% 2–4 day discount. 2-night minimum in summer & holiday weekends. Special event packages. Midweek rates.

Extras Airport pickups, $50. Crib, $5. Limited Spanish, French spoken.

NEWCASTLE

For additional area entries, see **New Harbor** below.

The Newcastle Inn ✕ ♿
River Road, RR 2, P.O. Box 24, 04553

Tel: 207–563–5685
800–832–8669
Fax: 207–563–6877
E-mail: innkeep@newcastleinn.com
URL: http://www.newcastleinn.com

An 18th-century Cape-style sea captain's house, the Newcastle Inn was transformed in the early 1900s into a three-story inn with an attached carriage house. In 1995, it was purchased by Rebecca and Howard Levitan. The inn's large deck overlooks the Damariscotta River and perennial gardens, which are abundant with lupines, the inn's signature flower. In good weather, the deck serves as an outdoor dining area for breakfast, plus an evening reception hosted by the Levitans, with hors d'oeuvres and beverages. Breakfast includes juice, a fruit dish, homemade pastries, breakfast meats, and an entrée such as French toast or eggs Benedict. The dinner menu includes balanced choices of appetizers, entrées, and desserts; a recent meal included mussels in saffron cream, salad, peppered beef filet with mushrooms, and an apricot almond tart. Guest rooms are decorated individually, many with canopy or four-poster beds; the "special occasion" suite is furnished with a king-size four-poster bed, double Jacuzzi, and a fireplace in the living room. A gift of Godiva chocolates is provided with turndown service.

"The Levitans are working hard to make a wonderful inn even more so, enhancing the comfort and decor of each guest room. Rebecca loves to sew and has a great eye for color, both in paint and fabric; the inviting bar is striking with red walls and work of a contemporary Southwestern artist. Ideal location on a quiet yet convenient road, perfect for exploring Boothbay and Camden. Jasper is their irresistibly handsome Maine coon cat. " (*SWS*)

"The rooms are comfortable, the dining experiences memorable, and the innkeepers truly welcoming. Even during a power outage, their good humor and flexibility added to our enjoyment." (*Ellen & Larry Kaplan*) "Spotless and comfortably decorated. Excellent cuisine, wine lists, and a great selection of Scotch whiskies." *(PKA)* "Rebecca and Howard are cheerful, hospitable, excellent hosts." *(Nick Mills)* "Outstanding food and wine; beautifully prepared meals." *(Wendy & Gilbert Deitch)*

Open All year. Restaurant closed Mon. year-round; Nov. 1–May 31, restaurant open weekends only.

Rooms 2 suites, 12 doubles—all with private bath and/or shower, clock/radio, fan. 2 with gas fireplace, air conditioning; suites with double Jacuzzi. 6 rooms in attached carriage house.

Facilities Restaurant with fireplace, pub, living room with fireplace, books; sun porch with woodstove, deck. ½ acre on Damariscotta River with lawn, sitting areas, off-street parking. Fishing, boating, swimming, hiking, cross-country skiing nearby. 30 min. to downhill skiing.

Location Mid-coastal ME. 50 m N of Portland; 20 min. N of Boothbay, 30 min. SW of Camden. ½ m from Damariscotta historic district. Take Exit 9 off ME Tpke. (Rte. 95). Follow Rte. 95 N to Exit 22—Bath/Brunswick/Coastal Rte. 1. Continue through Brunswick and Bath. 7 m past Wiscasset, take a right onto River Rd. (look for the Newcastle Inn rd. sign). Inn is ½ m on your right.

Restrictions No smoking. Mature children 10 and over.

Credit cards Amex, MC, Visa.

Rates B&B, $175–225 suite, $95–200 double. Alc dinner, $33–40 plus gratuities. Special theme weekends.

Extras Limited wheelchair access. Station/airport pickup. French, Spanish spoken.

NEW HARBOR/PEMAQUID POINT

Reader tip: "The Pemaquid Point Lighthouse is billed as the Maine coast's most scenic (no idle boast), and the rocky shore is ideal for scrambling. Suitable restaurants, including a lobster pound, are within minutes." *(James & Pamela Burr)*

Also recommended: The **Bradley Inn at Pemaquid Point,** (361 Pemaquid Point, Route 130, HC 61, New Harbor, 04554; 207–677–2105 or 800–942–5560) is a turn-of-the-century inn with 13 guest rooms, ample common areas, a restaurant, tennis court, and a peaceful location just down the road from the Pemaquid Point Lighthouse. Most guest rooms are in a newly built wing, and have tiled private bathrooms, telephones, TV, and are furnished with antiques and period reproductions; some have views of John's Bay. Double rates range from $90–195, and include a breakfast of fresh fruit, cereal, muffins, and croissants. The inn has a cozy pub; Ships, its restaurant, specializes in seafood, and has been well received by local critics. The inn's owners are Warren and Beth Busteed; Warren grew up in the innkeeping business at the Windham Hill Inn in Vermont. "Guest rooms are lovely and immaculate. On a sunny summer morning, we enjoyed a tasty breakfast on the screened porch." *(Peg Bedini)*

Although it does not have an ocean view, the century-old **Hotel Pemaquid** (Route 130, HC-61, P.O. Box 421, 04554; 207–677–2312) is located high on the rocks, 150 yards from the coast and lighthouse, as well as a sandy beach. Converted from a farmhouse, the inn opened to guests in 1900; guest registers have been maintained ever since. Restoration of the hotel began in 1985, and the complex now includes the main hotel, surrounded by a wraparound porch, a five-unit motel, large four-unit bungalows, housekeeping cottages, and an annex. "The hotel seems immune from the tourist rush that hits nearby Boothbay Harbor. It's the sort of place where one could easily tuck away for several days. High standards; enjoyable accommodations." *(Pamela & James Burr)* "Just as pleasant on a return trip." *(JB)* B&B double rates in the hotel range from $65–135.

OGUNQUIT

Ogunquit has one of Maine's best beaches—three miles long, with fine light sand, and water that actually gets warm enough for (some) people to swim in! Walkers will enjoy the Marginal Way, a footpath that follows the tops of the rugged cliffs of this rocky coastline from Perkins Cove to the beach. Ogunquit has been popular with artists for many years, and has over twenty art galleries as well as craft and antique shops, restaurants, and a summer stock theater. Other activities include fishing, surf-boarding, tennis, golf, and cross-country skiing.

Ogunquit is 15 miles north of Portsmouth, New Hampshire, and 70 miles north of Boston.

Information please: As you would expect from its name, the **Above Tide Inn** (26 Beach Street, P.O. Box 2188, 03907; 207–646–7454; www.abovetideinn.com) has a deck extending right over the Ogunquit River, with views of the surf and tides. Each of the nine guest rooms has a private bath, air-conditioner, TV, refrigerator, and deck, and the B&B double rate ranges from $85–170, depending on the season. The inn is located at the beginning of the Marginal Way, where the Ogunquit River meets the Atlantic. It was constructed in 1980, and has been owned by Al and Maryellen Hubacz since 1994; the inn is open from mid-May to mid-October.

For a romantic, quiet setting just two miles from Ogunquit, consider the **Woodland Gardens B&B Inn** (150 Josiah Norton Road, Cape Neddick, P.O. Box 1582, 03907; 207–361–1310; www.woodlandgardens.com). As the name implies, it's surrounded by gardens, and set in the woods. The three beautifully decorated guest rooms have a private bath and TV, and the B&B double rate of $95 includes a breakfast of homemade granola, breads, and muffins, and fresh eggs compliments of the resident hens.

The Trellis House ¢   *Tel:* 207–646–7909
2 Beachmere Place, P.O. Box 2229, 03907   800–681–7909
                      E-mail: trellishouse@cybertours.com
                      URL: http://www.trellishouse.com

Built as a summer cottage in 1907, the Trellis House has a quiet location close to the Marginal Way, the beach, and town. It's been owned by Pat and Jerry Houlihan since 1993. The ample common areas and guest rooms are decorated in an inviting, uncluttered country cottage style, gracefully combining antiques and newer pieces. In warm weather, breakfast is served on the wraparound screened porch from 8:30–10 A.M., and includes fresh fruit and juice, home-baked breads or muffins, and a hot entrée.

"Charming hosts who go out of their way to please. Exquisite breakfasts taste as good as they look. A peaceful retreat." *(Jocelyne Allie)* "Plentiful breakfast with tasty ginger pancakes. Loved sipping a glass of wine by the fire. The Houlihans are perfect hosts; Pat even baked a surprise birthday cake for my husband." *(Cecile Desroches)* "On a return trip, we found that Carriage House had been renovated and redecorated; the Garden and York Rooms have fireplaces, and are beautiful and private. Pat's flowers and yard are so lovely you want to sit on the porch admiring them all day. We also visited in December; the house was beautifully decorated and festive for Christmas." *(CD, also Francois Collin)* "Relaxed, homey atmosphere; charming decor. This inviting cottage is framed by lovely gardens, with additional accommodations in the carriage house at the back of the property. The inn offers wonderful screened porch, a welcoming living room, and appealing, spacious guest rooms." *(SWS)*

Open All year.

Rooms 1 cottage, 1 suite, 6 doubles—all with private bath and/or shower, clock, air-conditioning. 2 with TV, fireplace. 1 with refrigerator.

Facilities Dining room; living room with fireplace, books; guest refrigerator; screened porch. Gardens, off-street parking. 1 block to ocean, beach, Marginal Way cliff walk. Tennis, golf nearby. 7 m to cross-country skiing.

Location ½ m from center of town. Midway between village & Perkins Cove. From Rte. 1 S turn left on Shore Rd. & follow to Beachmere Pl. Turn left to inn on right.

Restrictions Smoking on porch only. Children over 12.

Credit cards MC, Visa.

Rates B&B. $75–120 suite, double. Extra person, $25. 2–3 night weekend/holiday minimum.

POLAND/POLAND SPRING

Wolf Cove Inn Bed & Breakfast ¢ ♿   *Tel:* 207–998–4976
5 Jordan Shore Drive, 04274   *URL:* http://www.WolfCoveInn.com

Only in Maine is Poland a 15-minute drive from Paris and Norway, and perhaps only in Maine can you find a lakeside getaway that's as restful and affordable as the Wolf Cove Inn. Built as a guest house in the 1930s, the inn was purchased by Rose Aikman in 1996. Guest rooms are simply but attractively furnished, most with king- or queen-size four-poster quilt-topped beds and Oriental rugs on the hardwood floors; several have beautiful lake views. Breakfast is served in the dining room at guests' choice of large tables or small, from 7:30–9:15 A.M., and includes coffee, juice, and muffins, with choice of pancakes, eggs, or French toast, and bacon. Welcoming refreshments are served in the sitting room, porch, or grand room.

"Comfortable and welcoming, beautiful and peaceful. Best of all is innkeeper Rose Aikman, who exceeded our expectations in every way. Breakfasts were excellent and plentiful, and extras included afternoon tea and evening snacks. With the extensive gardens, sun porch, and two huge sitting rooms, you have lots of privacy and quiet. The lakeside setting makes it easy to enjoy all water sports in summer, snow sports in winter." *(Julie O'Leary)* "Waking to the sound of loons is something everyone should experience." *(John Donohue IV)* "The food is excellent, the hospitality warm, and Rose always makes us feel at home." *(James Wilburn)* "Rooms are large, bright, and comfortable. The gracious, courteous staff was knowledgeable about local sites of interest." *(Kenneth Milender)* "Tranquil, warm, and inviting atmosphere. Beautiful, quilted coverlets top comfortable beds; impeccably clean. Rose, the warm and attentive innkeeper, was pleased to provide restaurant suggestions. Thoughtful comforts include a cooler of spring water and plates of cookies and candy." *(K. Collins)*

Open All year.

Rooms 7 doubles—5 with private shower bath, 2 with maximum of 4 people sharing bath. All with clock, fan.

Facilities Living room with piano, fireplace; sitting room with TV/VCR, games; guest refrigerator, sun porch. 2½ acres on Tripp Lake; waterfront with canoes, swimming, fishing; lakeside patio, terrace, herb & flower gardens, pine grove. 10 min. to cross-country skiing, 1 hr. to downhill. Hiking, hunting, boating, golf nearby.

Location Lakes region, Androscoggin Cty. Approx. 30 m N of Portland, 12 m S of Norway, Paris; 14 m W of Auburn/Lewiston. 5 m from Sabbathday Lake Shaker Village. On Rte. 11 S, 1.2 miles from intersections of Rtes. 11 & 26. 3 m from town center.

Restrictions No smoking. Children 12 and over.

Credit cards Amex, MC, Visa.

Rates B&B, $90–150 suite, $64–95 double. Extra person, $20. 2-night minimum preferred. Weekly discount, mid-week corporate rate.

Extras Limited wheelchair access.

PORTLAND

Maine's largest city was virtually destroyed by Indian massacres in the 17th century, British bombardment in the 18th, and fire in the 19th, but has always arisen phoenix-like from the ashes. More recently, it has come back from late 19th-century urban decay to take new pride in its seaport heritage, and as Maine's cultural center, with several fine art museums and a performing arts center. Portland is located in south coastal Maine, about 45 miles north of the New Hampshire border.

Reader tips: "Summer or winter, Portland is a walker's city. The Old Port district of the city has galleries, shops, coffee houses, and is within a few blocks of the Museum of Art." *(Jeremiah Reilly)* "In the Old Port area, Street & Co. is an excellent restaurant for fresh fish and homemade pasta. A favorite with locals." *(Lynne Glaser, also NB)* "An excellent restaurant (with lots of vegetarian dishes) in the Old Port is the Pepperclub." *(Dianne Crawford)* "Portland is a lively and interesting small city. We explored an affordable antiques fair, enjoyed lively evening entertainment, and relaxed on a restful walk through a district of historic homes." *(Gail DeSciose)*

For an additional area inn, see **Saco.**

Inn by the Sea 🏃 ✕ 🦮

40 Bowery Beach Road, Route 77
Cape Elizabeth, 04107

Tel: 207–799–3134
800–888–4287
Fax: 207–799–4779
E-mail: innmaine@aol.com
URL: http://www.innbythesea.com

Blending the weathered shingle-style of an 1890s Victorian hotel with the modern amenities of today, the Inn by the Sea offers a beautiful coastal setting, with its own private boardwalk leading through the salt marsh to Crescent Beach. Built in 1986, the hotel has an unobstructed vista of the Atlantic. Guest rooms in the Main House are furnished with Chippendale reproductions and floral chintz fabrics, while rooms in the Cottages, ideal for families, are furnished informally with such Maine classics as wicker and simple pine pieces; all are accented with original art. The Audubon Room restaurant features lobster and cheese omelets, blueberry pancakes with maple syrup, and cinnamon French toast for breakfast; sandwiches, salads, burgers, and more at lunch; and for dinner, such options as tuna in a horseradish crust, portobello mushrooms stuffed with crabmeat and goat cheese, and rack of lamb with thyme and red wine.

"Appealing blend of contemporary and traditional charm. Spacious, well-equipped accommodations." *(Ginny Watkins)* "Despite a late arrival, our bed was turned down, lights on, soft music playing. Great location overlooking beach and ocean. Our suite had two TVs, phones in every room, and large closets." *(Stephanie Roberts)* "Extremely comfortable, duplex room, with balcony overlooking the grounds, which stretch all the way to the sandy beach. The kitchenette was stocked with the makings for coffee and tea, and the lighting was good throughout. The restaurant menu changes frequently, and the helpful staff altered dishes to suit our tastes." *(K.C. Keller)* "Wonderful location overlooking the Atlantic. From the spacious grounds, there is a short path down to the shore. The area is suburban, with some strawberry farms; be sure to pick some for yourselves. Excellent raspberry pancakes; good dinners, with terrific desserts." *(Bruce Bilmes)*

Open All year.
Rooms 18 2-bedroom cottages, 25 1-bedroom suites—all with private bath/shower, telephone, radio, TV/VCR, fan, kitchen, deck or balcony. 6 cottages with fireplace. Some with sunken tub.
Facilities Restaurant, lobby, library, meeting rooms; conference facilities. Outdoor heated swimming pool, tennis court, shuffleboard, gazebo, garden, lawn games. Fax, copier; 24-hour front desk. Boardwalk to Crescent Beach.
Location S ME. 10 m S of Portland, 3 m S of town. From I-95, take Exit 7 S to Rte. 1 & turn right. At Pleasant Hill Rd. turn left & go 3.3 m to end. Turn left on Rte. 77; go 3.4 m to inn on right.

Restrictions No smoking. Dress code in dining room, "Country club casual."
Credit cards Amex, Discover, MC, Visa.
Rates Room only, $129–279 suite, $159–449 cottage. 3% service on accommodations. 20% service on meals. 10% AAA discount. Alc breakfast, $4–10; alc lunch, $8–12; alc dinner, $30–45. Off-season MAP rate, $85 additional for two. Off-season packages. 2-night weekend minimum.
Extras Crib, babysitting with 24 hr. notice. French spoken.

Inn on Carleton 👫
46 Carleton Street, 04102

Tel: 207–775–1910
800–639–1779
Fax: 207–761–0956
URL: http://www.innoncarleton.com

An 1869 Victorian home, the Inn on Carleton sits on a quiet, tree-lined residential street in the historic Western Promenade neighborhood. Owners Phil and Sue Cox have furnished the spacious rooms with antiques and Oriental rugs. Breakfast includes juice, fruit, granola, yogurt, cereal, and such home-baked treats as blueberry muffins, pancakes, French toast, waffles, and quiche.

"Our large room overlooked the lovely backyard below; we had a sink in the room, and a shared bathroom nearby. Sue was friendly, and helpful with restaurant suggestions for dinner. The dining and living areas had paintings (some for sale), from a local artist, adding to the New England ambience." *(Marilyn Parker)* "Sue's warmth and caring make this a most comfortable inn. Breakfasts included blueberry pancakes, waffles, or bacon and eggs, plus home-baked muffins every day; my favorite is the raisin bran. A large bowl of fresh fruit is available throughout the day. Sue has a wonderful collection of antique linens." *(Suzanne Scutt)*

"Sue and Phil Cox are friendly and helpful, but not intrusive. The pride they take in the inn is evident; fresh flowers brighten the rooms, lovely paintings by local artists grace the walls, everything is immaculate. There's a family feeling about the place; even Tigger the cat keeps a watchful eye on the comings and goings." *(Barrie Olsen)* "Southern charm is very much in evidence; Sue really makes her guests feel welcome." *(Sharon Tomaselli)* "Parking isn't a problem, and this relatively quiet street has excellent restaurants within easy driving distance; a couple are just a five-minute walk." *(Lorraine & Gus Browne)* "Within walking distance of the restored Old Port district, the Civic Center, the Portland Museum of Art (don't miss its collection of Winslow Homers), and the Portland Performing Arts Center." *(MW)*

Open All year.
Rooms 6 doubles, 1 single—4 with private bath and/or shower, 3 with a maximum of 5 persons sharing bath. All with radio, air-conditioning. 4 with desk.
Facilities Parlor, 2 dining rooms. Off-street parking.
Location Historic Western Promenade; 10-min. walk to downtown; 15 min. to Old Port Exchange. From I-95 North, take I-295 North, to Exit 4. After crossing the bridge, bear right & follow Danforth St. ramp up hill to stop sign. Turn left onto Vaughn St.; proceed to next flashing light, at West St. Turn right. Carleton St. is 3rd left off West St. Inn is on your left, at 46 Carleton.
Restrictions No smoking. Children over 6 preferred.

Credit cards Discover, MC, Visa.
Rates B&B, $85–160 double, $65–160 single. Extra person, $20. "Tipping appreciated." 2-night holiday minimum. Weekly rate.

Pomegranate Inn &.	*Tel:* 207–772–1006
49 Neal Street, 04102	800–356–0408
	Fax: 207–773–4426

A consistent reader favorite, the Pomegranate Inn probably has the most unusual decor of any inn in New England. A stately Victorian home, it was restored as an inn in 1988 by Isabel Smiles, and is furnished with her collection of fine antiques; more surprising is its striking and sometimes humorous display of 20th-century art—a wooden cut-out butler proffers a handsome bromeliad; a Picasso-esque wooden pull-toy depicts Lady Godiva on horseback. Mrs. Smiles's daughter painted faux-finishes on columns, mantels, and moldings throughout the house, and Portland artist Heidi Gerquist Harbert created decorative murals in almost every guest room; some take their inspiration from Matisse, others from Japanese designs. Tall French doors open from the common area to an inviting city garden. Breakfasts start with fresh fruit; the menu varies daily, and might include poached eggs on homemade bread with capers, smoked salmon, and tomato; or French toast topped with rhubarb and fresh raspberries, with blueberry syrup and rashers of bacon.

"Creatively decorated by Isabel Smiles, who has an amazing sense of style. From the entertaining folk art to the unusual color combinations, nothing is overdone. We were welcomed with glasses of wine, and given excellent dinner recommendations. Our comfortable, spacious second-floor room had a king-size bed with luxurious linens, down pillows, and good reading lights, two large upholstered chairs in the sitting area. The bathroom had a claw-foot tub with hand-held shower and thick towels. The delicious, light, creative breakfast was served at the dining room table, and included raspberry French toast, sliced fruit, peach-orange juice, and coffee." (*Al & Lauren Kenney*) "Superb decor, great food, and wonderful hospitality." (*Rebecca Bernie*) "In an attractive and architecturally interesting part of Portland, a short drive from downtown." (*MM, also Eloise Balasco*) "Delicious breakfast of crêpes with apples, currants, nuts, and spices." (*Susan LaCaille*)

"When the Smiles moved to Portland they brought along an incredible wealth of good taste, sensitivity, and creativity, along with a cache of beautiful, witty, and unusual antiques and artwork. Even the table settings in the elegant dining room are gorgeous, with different antique silver at every place. Wonderful breakfast of just-squeezed fruit juice, fruit salad with yogurt, sautéed tomatoes and mushrooms on toast, and exceptional bacon." (*Lucy Price*) "Located in the beautiful residential Western Promenade area. The on-street parking was no problem." (*Nicki Brown*) "Our huge room had high ceilings and beautifully hand-painted walls, ample closet and storage space, and comfortable twin beds, fitted with the finest linens. The bathroom was spacious with a large old-fashioned sink and tub, luxurious white towels, and a night light. Even the hallways had interesting art and glossy tangerine sponge-painting on the walls." *(Lynne Glaser)*

Open All year.

Rooms 1 carriage house suite, 7 doubles—all with private bath and/or shower, telephone, radio, TV, air-conditioning. 4 with gas fireplace.

Facilities Living/dining room; 3rd-floor sitting room/library. Garden, patio, off-street parking.

Location West End. From I-295, take Exit 4 and go N on Danforth St. and continue to Vaughn St. and turn left. At Carroll St. turn right, go 1 block and turn left on Neal to inn.

Restrictions No smoking in guest rooms. No guests under 16.

Credit cards All major cards accepted.

Rates B&B, $95–175 double. 2-night holiday/summer weekend minimum.

Extras 1 room with wheelchair access.

ROBBINSTON

Robbinston is located on the opposite side of Passamaquoddy Bay from St. Andrews, New Brunswick, 12 miles southeast of Calais and the Canadian border crossing.

For additional area inns, see **Eastport, Lubec,** and **St. Andrews, New Brunswick, Canada.**

Also recommended: An elegant Greek Revival home built in 1828, the **Brewer House** (Route 1, P.O. Box 94, 04671; 207–454–2385; www.mainerec.com/brewer.html) is listed on the National Register of Historic Places. Restored as a B&B in 1991 by Estelle and David Holloway, it is furnished with fine antique furnishings, Oriental rugs, oil paintings, and many accessories. Three of the five guest rooms have private baths, and four have water views. B&B double rates range from $65–85. "A handsome house beautifully decorated with antiques. Our wonderful four-poster bed had feather pillows and a down quilt under a beautiful crocheted coverlet. Elegantly served breakfast with fresh fruit and juice, a puff pastry with apples and maple syrup, and fruited coffee cake for dessert. Congenial hosts who offered to help with luggage and travel advice." *(Carol Workman & others)*

ROCKLAND

Also recommended: On Route 1 between Camden and Rockland is **Oakland Seashore Motel & Cottages** (714 Commercial Street, Rockport, 04856; 207–594–8104), originally a seaside park operated by local trolley companies. The original dance hall now houses motel units, while the 11 cabins offer simple, affordable accommodations in a lovely, convenient setting. Double rates range from $40–110, with weekly rates available. "Although located on Route 1, it's a long drive down from the highway through pretty woods. The resort is spread out along its own private bay with lots of hiking trails and superb views. The best choice is one of the eight cabins set on a small bluff, shaded by oak and maple trees, with fabulous views of the huge rocks and pebble beach below; in the distance you can see islands, sailboats, lobster boats, and an occasional freighter. Our two-bedroom cabin, #8, was reasonably clean and comfortable, with simple, basic furnishings, wonderful water views, and cool ocean breezes." *(Suzanne Carmichael)*

Information please: Set among historic seaport buildings, the **Captain Lindsey House Inn** (5 Lindsey Street, Rockland, 04841; 207–596–7950 or 800–523–2145; www.midcoast.com/~kebarnes/) was built in 1837 and is filled with furnishings from around the world. In-season double rates for the nine guest rooms range from $100–160, including continental breakfast. Owners Ken and Ellen Barnes and their son and daughter can arrange windjammer cruises for guests. Their Waterworks Pub and Restaurant offers a variety of choices from simple pub fare to fine dining.

The Old Granite Inn (546 Main Street, 04841; 207–594–9036 or 800–386–9036; www.midcoast.com/~ogi) dates back to 1796 and was built of local granite. B&B double rates for the eleven guest rooms, most with private bath, range from $60–120, including a full breakfast; some rooms have harbor views.

For an additional area inn, see **Spruce Head.**

Lakeshore Inn
184 Lakeview Drive, Route 17, 04841

Tel: 207–594–4209
Fax: 207–596–6407
E-mail: lakshore@midcoast.com
URL: http://www.midcoast.com/~lakshore

Overlooking Lake Chickawaukie, the original structure of the Lakeshore Inn dates to 1767. Having undergone several cycles of additions and renovations, the farmhouse was most recently renovated in 1994 by its current owners, Paula Nicols and Joseph McCluskey. A colorful garden patio offers views of Dodges Mountain and the inn's small apple orchard; guests can observe deer and wildlife from the deck. Each of the guest rooms features original plank floors and a queen-size bed; all have lake views. Breakfast is served at 8:30 A.M., and includes juice, home-baked scones or perhaps apple strudel, fresh fruit, cereals, and a choice of two entrées, perhaps French toast with blueberry syrup and cheese omelets, bacon or possibly sausages.

"Paula and Joe make the Lakeshore a warm, homey, welcoming environment. The Spa Weekend was wonderful." *(Christina Sagris)* "Friendly hosts, outstanding breakfasts, comfortable and generous extras; outstanding lake view." *(JB, also Myrna Davis)* "Paula and Joe are gracious innkeepers who made us feel right at home; careful attention to detail. Superb breakfast. Our peaceful room had a view of the lake." *(Lynne & Walt Foster, also Sidney Schnall)* "Courteous, helpful innkeepers; inviting decor; immaculate housekeeping throughout." *(Gloria & Phil Rosenthal)*

Open All year.
Rooms 4 doubles—all with private bath and/or shower, clock/radio, telephone, air-conditioning, fan, hairdryer, robes. 2 with deck.

Facilities Dining room; living room with fireplace, books; sun room with fireplace, TV/VCR, games; deck. 1.7 acres with patio, hot tub/spa, orchard. ¼ m from golf. On Lake Chickawaukie.

Location Mid-coastal ME. 40 m E of Augusta, 8 m S of Camden. 2 m to town. From Portland: Take I-95 N to Coastal Rte. 1 (Brunswick/Bath) exit. Continue on Rte. 1 to State Rte. 90 (just N of Waldoboro). Turn left on Rte. 90 & go to Rte. 17. Turn right on Rte. 17 and go 3 m to inn on right.

Restrictions No smoking. Children 12 and over.

Credit cards MC, Visa.

Rates B&B. $115–125 double. Extra person, $20. 3-night minimum during Lobster Festival (usually 1st weekend in Aug.). Spa weekend packages, $399 per person.

Extras Bus station, local airport pickup. Some French, Greek spoken.

ROCKWOOD

Also recommended: "About 20 miles north of Greenville, on the west side of Moosehead Lake, is the little hamlet of Rockwood, where you can catch the little ferry to the island of Mt. Kineo, in the middle of the lake. You can hike to the top for a dramatic view of the surrounding water and mountains, play a round of golf, and enjoy a drink or light meal at the **Kineo House Inn** (P.O. Box 397, 04478; 207–534–8812), and even spend the night at this modest but inviting inn. B&B double rates are $80 in summer, $40 in winter, when guests drive across the frozen lake via snowmobile. Also available are several Victorian cottages which can be rented by the week, and which date from the era when Kineo was home to a 500-room hotel." *(SWS)*

SACO

Crown 'n' Anchor ₵   *Tel:* 207–282–3829
121 North Street, P.O. Box 228, 04072   800–561–8865
Fax: 207–282–7495

Southern Maine can be a busy place, especially in season, and the Crown 'n' Anchor makes a peaceful base from which to explore the charms of Kennebunkport or Portland, and the outlets of Kittery or Freeport. Built in 1827, and listed on the National Register of Historic Houses, this early Greek Revival home with Federal/Adamesque detailing has been carefully restored by John Barclay and Martha Forester, who purchased it in 1991. In addition to the beautiful fresh flower arrangements and elegant antique furnishings in the stately parlors, guests also enjoy John and Martha's collection of over 600 pieces of British royal family memorabilia. Breakfast is served from 7–10 A.M. at the dining room table, and includes fresh juice and fruit, home-baked bread, and such entrées as French toast, pancakes, or eggs.

"John and Martha regard fine living as an art; they know how to treat guests graciously, with discreet attention. The elegant three-course breakfasts are fresh and delicious, served by candlelight in the charming dining room. White wicker chairs on the columned porch are ideal for chatting or relaxing." *(Jeanette Carlberg Kaulfers)* "Fascinating history, friendly atmosphere, outstanding breakfast, excellent value." *(Virginia Yedinak)* "Despite the building's age, the bathrooms and other amenities are up-to-date. The innkeepers are available for questions and special requests." *(Susan & Edward Reardon)*

"We enjoyed walking in Saco's historic district, with its handsome 18th- and 19th-century homes. Meticulously restored B&B. Both early- and late-risers are accommodated at breakfast, from a menu which changes daily. The generous, delicious meal is enhanced by fresh flowers, fine china, and silver." *(Donald & Leslie Paul)* "The fried bananas are my breakfast favorite. The inn was beautifully decorated for Christmas, with a fire in the fireplace and candles on the mantle. The hosts are attentive and gracious, and have inspired me to look for coronation memorabilia for the inn's collection." *(Dick Nelson)* "Business guests are made to feel equally welcome and comfortable as those looking for a romantic getaway." *(Margaret Hassett)* "Guests are warmly welcomed by John and Martha, shown to their rooms, given instructions for their stay, and helpful suggestions of where to go, what to see, and what to do. The guest rooms are attractive, appropriately decorated in period, extremely clean, and well-lighted, with comfortable beds. Guests are invited to relax and visit with one another and the innkeepers in the parlors. The grounds are spacious and well-tended, with good lighting at the entrances and parking area." *(Josephine Poyser)* "John Barclay goes out of his way to welcome guests, and to provide information about the inn and its history. Each impeccably maintained room is named for a significant American historical figure. I always look forward to wonderful reading material throughout the inn." *(Charles Hanson)*

Open All year.

Rooms 1 suite, 5 doubles—all with private bath and/or shower, fan. 4 with desk, 2 with whirlpool tub, TV; 1 with fireplace, balcony/deck.

Facilities Dining room, double parlor, library with TV, stereo, books, games; veranda. 3 acres with lawn games, gardens. Health club privileges. Ocean beach, cross-country skiing nearby.

Location Historic district. S coastal ME. 10 m S of Portland, 12 m N of Kennebunkport. Take I-95 (ME Tpke.) to Exit 5, Saco–Old Orchard Beach. After toll, take I-195 to Exit 2-A, Rte. 1 S. Stay on Rte. 1 S to 6th traffic light (Rtes. 112 & 5). Go right onto Rtes. 112 & 5 (North St.) to inn approx. ½ m on right.

Restrictions No smoking. Children 12 and over.

Credit cards Amex, MC, Visa.

Rates B&B, $60–110 suite, double; $50–110 single. Extra person, $15.

Extras Wheelchair access; bathroom specially equipped. Some French spoken. Airport/station pickups.

SEARSPORT

Searsport is located in north coastal Maine, 42 miles south of Bangor, and 25 miles northwest of Castine. It's 2½ hours north of Portland, and

45 minutes from Augusta and Bar Harbor. Famous for clipper ships and sea captains in the mid-1800s, it's now considered a center for antiquing in Maine, and is also home to the Penobscot Marine Museum.

Reader tip: "Searsport is an excellent and affordable base for touring Camden, Blue Hill, and the Bar Harbor area. Many inns are located on Route 1, and traffic noise can be disturbing to light sleepers if a streetside room is close to the road. Ask your innkeeper for details." *(EB)*

Also recommended: A stunning example of Victorian architecture, complete with mansard roof and Italianate detailing, the **McGilvery House B&B** (134 East Main Street, P.O. Box 588, 04974; 207–548–6289 or 800–370–8555; sueo@ime.net) was built in 1860 by a prosperous shipbuilder. Each of the three guest rooms has a queen-size bed and a private bath with claw-foot tub. The B&B double rates of $70–85 include a breakfast of fresh fruit and juice, with wonderful blueberry muffins. "Beautifully furnished, convenient location, great breakfast." *(Virginia Yedniak)* "Sumptuous strawberry shortcake for breakfast. Warm and welcoming innkeeper, Sue Omness." *(Richard & Lorrie Dykstra)* "Charming atmosphere, lovely antiques. Sue kindly shared her scrumptious recipe for Ozark pudding." *(Phyllis Schwann)*

Information please: Listed on the National Register of Historic Places, **The Brass Lantern Inn** (81 West Main Street, P.O. Box 407, 04974; 207–548–0150 or 800–691–0150; brasslan@agate.net) is a Victorian home built in 1850. Located at the edge of the woods on a rise overlooking Penobscot Bay, the decor of the four guest rooms ranged from maritime treasures in the Captain's Room, to railroad collectibles in the Chessie Room. A full breakfast is included in the double rates of $65–75; blueberry pancakes are a favorite. "Clean, comfortable rooms; quality towels and linens. Pleasant, attentive, unobtrusive hosts." *(Eloise Balasco)*

For additional area inns, see **Belfast** and **Stockton Springs**.

The Homeport Inn ¢
121 East Main Street, Route 1, P.O. Box 647, 04974

Tel: 207–548–2259
800–742–5814
Fax: 978–443–6682
E-mail: hportinn@acadia.net
URL: http://www.bnbcity.com/inns/20015

Listed on the National Register of Historic Places, the Homeport is a classic Greek Revival home, topped by an enclosed cupola; it has long been owned by Dr. George and Mrs. Edith Johnson.

"The spacious rooms are comfortably furnished, with large four-poster or canopy beds and handsome armoires. Breakfast is served on a glassed-in patio area, where guests can view the grounds and gardens, extending to the ocean. Breakfasts are wholesome and satisfying, with a complete range of cereals, fresh fruit, eggs, and grains. Mrs. Johnson is especially charming, and delights in assisting her guests. The resident pets, a cat named Casper and a dog named Tina, complete the warm welcome one receives. Searsport is located between the natural splendors of Acadia National Park, and the discount shopping mecca of Freeport." *(James & Pamela Burr)* "Just as pleasant on a return trip. Convenient location, gracious hosts, engaging pets." *(JB)*

"Dr. Johnson was a wonderful host and made us feel right at home; terrific staff, too. A totally restored mansion with many Scottish decorating touches." *(Elizabeth & Herbert Smith, also Charlotte Leavenworth)* "This sea captain's mansion captures the charm and beauty of the Maine coast. Our room was quiet and peaceful, beautifully decorated, impeccably clean, and comfortable; the balcony overlooked lovely gardens and the ocean. The Johnsons were most helpful in providing information on area sights. Breakfasts were English treats with homemade scones, fresh fruit and Scottish porridge." *(Kathleen West, also Patricia Cloutier)* "Fresh flowers from the gardens adorn tables and rooms." *(T.R. Brett)* "Favorite features: warm, gracious welcome from Edith and George; fascinating home with antiques and reading material; sweeping grounds leading to the edge of Penobscot Bay; delightful evenings spent with Dr. Johnson, a great storyteller; our room with sliding glass doors looking out to the water; fascinating international guests." *(Jeanne & Barry Cole)* "Ground-floor rooms at the back of the house are spacious and quiet, with sliding glass doors looking out to the gardens and water beyond." *(SWS)*

Open All year.
Rooms 2 2-bedroom cottages with kitchen. 11 doubles—7 with private bath and/or shower, 3 with shared bath. Some with balcony.
Facilities Dining room, family room with English pub, fireplace, darts; sun room. Bicycle rentals. Oceanfront property. Sailing, tennis, golf, hiking, cross-country skiing nearby.
Location In center, on Rte. 1, on E (water) side of st.
Restrictions No smoking on 2nd floor.
Credit cards Amex, Discover, Enroute, MC, Visa.
Rates B&B, $55–90 double, $30–40 single. Extra adult, $18; extra child under 14, $6. Weekly, off-season rates. Cottages $600 weekly.

Watchtide Bed and Breakfast　　　　　　　　　　*Tel:* 207–548–6575
190 West Main Street, 04974　　　　　　　　　　　　　　800–698–6575
E-mail: watchtyd@agate.net
URL: http://www.agate.net/~watchtyd/watchtide.html

You could make Watchtide your headquarters for touring the Maine coast, making easy daytrips from Pemaquid Point (near Boothbay) to Schoodic Point (beyond Bar Harbor), but then you'd have to leave its serene and inviting sixty-foot-long sunporch, overlooking the gardens, meadows, bird sanctuary, and Penobscot Bay beyond. Originally a sea captain's home, built in 1795, it was known as the College Club Inn in the 1920s, and hosted Franklin and Eleanor Roosevelt and other luminaries. In 1994, Nancy-Linn and Jack Elliot restored Watchtide as a B&B. Guest rooms are furnished with antiques and quilts, and two have king-size beds.

Breakfast is a highlight of the Watchtide experience. Served on the sunporch at 8:30 A.M., guests sit down at two tables, laid with fine crystal and silver, for such menus as blueberry-cranberry juice or non-alcoholic mimosas; wild blueberries with lemon sorbet, or perhaps pears poached in wine; home-baked popovers with cranberry spread,

Mediterranean bread with olives, garlic, and feta cheese, or possibly oatmeal muffins or chocolate chip zucchini bread. Main courses include stuffed French toast with strawberry Grand Marnier sauce and crisp bacon; banana pancakes with pecans and maple syrup; or Maine crabmeat and cheese omelets with toasted beer batter bread. Guests are offered a choice of fresh-ground plain or flavored coffees, plus a variety of teas and hot chocolates. Rates also include afternoon refreshments, with hot coffee and tea, plus raspberry iced tea or perhaps peach lemonade, with home-baked cookies or brownies. Beds are turned down each evening with raspberry scented ice water in crystal carafes and bedside candy dishes of Bog Beans—chocolate-covered cranberries.

"Comfortable king-size beds. Incredible breakfasts, with never a repeat, using local products and seasonal produce, and unlimited coffee and tea. The immaculate bathrooms are supplied with shampoos and conditioners. Thoughtful and considerate details create a warm and comfortable atmosphere—which is exactly the attitude of the hosts, who make you feel at home and welcome. The house focuses away from the road, towards the lawn, woods, and water—lots of birds and flowers, too. Ample, convenient parking." (*Richard Belgian*) "Helpful advice and printed information sheets for area restaurants and sights made touring a pleasure. Enjoyed browsing in the Angels to Antiques shop in the barn." (*GR*) "Welcoming atmosphere, wonderful breakfasts and afternoon snacks, extremely clean, friendly, and pampering." (*Joan & Richard Hamilton*) "Rooms beautifully decorated with antiques, pillows, crystal candy dishes, and decanters. Sumptuous breakfasts— always something different—make lunch unnecessary, and afternoon tea is a delight on the enclosed porch, with its views of Penobscot Bay." (*David Berg*)

Open All year.
Rooms 4 doubles—2 with private bath and/or shower, 2 rooms share bath. All with radio, clock, fan.
Facilities Dining room, living room with fireplace, piano, library with books, TV; sunporch. 3½ acres with antiques, craft shop, lawn games. On ocean for swimming, boating, fishing. ½ m to cross-country skiing.
Location 1 m S of Searsport Village, ½ m north of Moose Pt. State Pk.
Restrictions No smoking. Children 10 and over.
Credit cards Amex, Discover, MC, Novus, Visa.
Rates B&B, $60–105 double. Extra person, $20. 2–3 night weekend/holiday minimum.
Extras Airport/station pickups. Some French spoken.

SOUTH BERWICK

Information please: Aficionados of the work of late 19th-century author Sarah Orne Jewett will want to stay in her historic hometown, just 11 miles north of Portsmouth, New Hampshire, and 15 minutes from I-95. A good base of operations is the **Academy Street Inn** (15 Academy Street, South Berwick, 03908; 207–384–5633), a handsome Colonial Revival home built in 1903, and restored as a B&B in 1990 by Paul and Lee Fopeano. B&B double rates for the five guest rooms, each with a private bath, range from $60–80, including a full breakfast.

SOUTHWEST HARBOR

Southwest Harbor is located on Somes Sound, almost on the opposite side of Mt. Desert Island from Bar Harbor (about a 15-minute drive). It's reached by taking Route 3 onto the island, then bearing right onto Route 102, then right again when 102 and 198 split.

Reader tips: "Southwest Harbor prides itself in being on the 'quiet side' of Mt. Desert Island; it's much more of a working fishing village than Bar Harbor or Northeast Harbor. The location is perfect if you dislike crowds but still wish to have ready access to Acadia National Park." *(Pamela Vollmer)* "In addition to appealing restaurants and shops, an absolute don't-miss in Southwest is the Oceanarium (207–244–7330), found in an unprepossessing old house on the docks that's been converted into a marine museum. Although we went there 'just for the kids,' the whole family was fascinated. The kids got to touch the sea cucumbers and the adults were riveted by a fascinating lecture on our favorite crustacean—the lobster." *(SS)* "Walks, hikes, kayaking, and cruising on old maritime schooners are all nearby." *(Matthew Anthony)*

Also recommended: One of Mt. Desert Island's classic inns, **The Claremont** (Claremont Road, P.O. Box 137, 04679; 207–244–5036; www.acadia.net/claremont) was built in 1884 and is listed on the National Register of Historic Places. Gorgeous views of Somes Sound and the mountains of Acadia can be had from various points throughout the complex. Guests may choose from among several accommodations—the main hotel building, two guest houses, and twelve housekeeping cottages; many rooms have recently been redecorated with improved decor, modern baths, and telephones, while other rooms have decor typical of a traditional Maine summer resort. B&B double rates range from $85–130; MAP rates $150–200. "Ideal location, with gorgeous views from our second-floor window. A welcoming fire was burning in the lobby fireplace from morning until night during our October visit. Friendly, helpful staff throughout. Our remodeled room had beautiful light wood floors and a brand-new bathroom. Some rooms have interesting antiques, and hand-stenciled chests. The breakfast buffets were generous, and the seafood at dinner was delicious. Bouquets of fresh flowers everywhere." *(Diane Bean)* "The sun shining in our windows had us up early to explore the area; at the end of the day, we felt like we were coming home to our room's simple charm. Spacious bathroom with lots of hot water, great water pressure." *(Ann Charles)* "Lovely, beautiful, gracious." *(Carol Blodgett)*

Golfers will appreciate the location of **The Heron House** (1 Fernald Point Road, 04679; 207–244–0221), right across the road from the golf course, and all will enjoy the warm hospitality provided by owners Sue and Bob Bonkowski, who take pleasure in helping guests to explore the island they know so well. B&B double rates for the three guest rooms, each with private bath, vary from $65–95 per night, and include breakfasts such as pears wrapped in puff pastry with crème anglaise, or wild mushroom frittata, garnished with edible flowers. "Charming, exceptionally welcoming, relaxed, and cheerful. After an extraordinary breakfast, take your coffee outside and relax in the lovely gardens." *(Nancy Doda)* "Delightful innkeepers, marvelous breakfasts, and fascinating fellow guests (many repeaters) make it hard to leave the breakfast table." *(Lucille Graham)*

The Inn at Southwest ¢   *Tel:* 207–244–3835
371 Main Street (Route 102), P.O. Box 593, 04679   *Fax:* 207–244–9879
E-mail: innatsw@acadia.net
URL: http://www.acadia.net/innatsw

Originally built as an inn, this Victorian home has been welcoming guests since 1884, and has been owned by Jill Lewis since 1995. Recently redecorated, with remodeled bathrooms, new carpeting, and antique wicker pieces, each of the guest rooms is named after a historic Maine lighthouse. Breakfast is served from 8–9 A.M. in the dining room or on the wicker- and flower-filled porch. Although menus change daily, a typical breakfast includes sautéed nectarines, vanilla Belgian waffles with raspberry sauce, and bacon or sausage; or perhaps poached pears in wine sauce, crab potato bake, and blueberry cornbread.

"Our room overlooked the harbor, with salt air breezes wafting through the windows. The parlor is a pleasant place to visit with other guests in the evening over tea and home-baked cookies. Jill was a great source of information on activities and restaurants." *(Jim & Laura Sawyer)* "Relaxing, quiet atmosphere. Wonderful breakfasts and afternoon cookies. Our room had a cozy down comforter on the bed, and its own thermostat. Jill has many books about the area, which we used to help us decide on the day's activities." *(Larry & Pat Edwards)* "This three-story, gray-and-white home, with a wraparound porch and black shutters, has hanging flower baskets, green lawns, and porch furniture. The cozy Owl's Head has a queen-size bed and an inviting window seat under a chapel window; thoughtful touches included the books, magazines, wooden foot massager, talc, powder, glycerin soap, and other amenities. Wonderful French toast stuffed with cream cheese and blueberries for breakfast." *(Matthew Anthony)* "The staff was pleasant, the housekeeping excellent, rooms comfortable, clean, and beautifully arranged and decorated. The inn is ideally located for sightseeing, starting with a beautiful view of the harbor." *(Steven & Susan Golembiewski)*

"A tall Victorian home with trees all around and a front porch that's perfect for the morning's first cup of coffee. Our room was cozy and beautifully decorated, complete with a photo of the lighthouse for which the room was named. We enjoyed the evening talking with the other guests in front of the fire, took a short walk to an excellent restaurant, and got a great night's sleep." *(Paul Williams)* "The parlor is comfortably furnished with several cozy couches and chairs for reading or conversing. Jill keeps the area stocked with beverages and home-baked treats from snickerdoodles to heavenly strawberry pie. Although small, the shopping area at Southwest is just steps away from the inn. The pervading sense of both inn and town is of quiet and safety. " (*Pamela Vollmer*)

Open May 1–Oct. 31.
Rooms 9 doubles—all with private shower and/or bath, clock/radio, ceiling fan. 2 with desk.
Facilities Dining room, lobby, living room with fireplace, games, stereo, piano, guest refrigerator; wraparound porch. ¾ acre overlooking harbor; off-street parking.
Location Follow Rte. 102 into town. Inn is 1 block beyond center on harbor side.
Restrictions No smoking. Children 8 and over. Summer weekend traffic noise possible.
Credit cards Discover, MC, Visa.
Rates B&B, $60–135 double. Extra person, $20.

The Island House ¢ ♦

121 Clark Point Road
P.O. Box 1006, 04679

Tel: 207–244–5180
E-mail: islandab@acadia.net
URL: http://www.acadia.net/island_house/

Opening in 1850 as Mt. Desert Island's first summer hotel, the Island House has long been the family home of Ann Bradford. Renovated as a B&B in 1984, it is simply furnished with accents from Ann's childhood years in Southeast Asia. Breakfast includes fresh fruit or juice; home-baked muffins, Danish, or coffee cake; plus eggs Florentine, vegetable omelets, or French toast with warm blueberry sauce.

"Modern facilities blended well with this historic inn. Ann and Charlie were helpful with their local knowledge: a favorite hiking trail, local restaurants, or a great spot to sit and watch the ocean." (*Patricia Poirier*) "Delicious home cooking, especially the pumpkin bread. The inn is very clean with plenty of fresh towels and ample storage space." (*Sheena Stoddard*) "The location is quiet, within walking distance of the Oceanarium, Beal's Lobster Pier, and downtown. The front porch with its rocking swing is a cool and attractive place to relax. The second-floor carriage house apartment has wood floors, lots of large windows, and a cathedral ceiling, which gives it a spacious, airy feeling. There's a pull-out couch downstairs, and a double bed in a loft reached via a steep ship's ladder. Overhead, a skylight made for a sunny awakening, and had we wanted to cook, there was a fully equipped kitchen."(*Brad Lockner, also Patricia Adams*)

Open All year.
Rooms 4 doubles share 3 baths. All with clock. 1 carriage house apt. with private bath, kitchen, radio, TV, fan.
Facilities Dining room, living rooms with fireplaces, piano, TV/VCR, stereo, books; porch with glider. 1 acre with off-street parking.
Location Across st. from harbor; ½ m to center. From Ellsworth, follow Rte. 3 S 8 m to junction of Rtes. 3 & 102. Bear right on 102 for 10 m & follow sign into SW Harbor. Turn left at light onto Clark Point Rd. Go ½ m, bearing right until you see the red, white, & blue sign on left for white house with blue/grey shutters.

Restrictions No smoking. Children over 5.
Credit cards MC, Visa.
Rates B&B, $95–165 apt. suite, $50–70 double, $50–65 single. Extra person, $25. 2-night minimum July, Aug.; 3rd night free, off-season. Additional $10 for private bath Nov.–April. Additional $10 during high season for 1-night stay.
Extras Portacrib.

Kingsleigh Inn 1904
373 Main Street
P.O. Box 1426, 04679

Tel: 207–244–5302
URL: http://www.kingsleighinn.com

Ken and Cyd Champagne Collins welcome guests to the turn-of-the-century turreted Victorian inn which they bought in 1996. The rooms are furnished with lace curtains, flowered wallpapers, and some antiques. Many have harbor views, and Room #5 offers a water view from its private balcony as well as the bed. Breakfast is served at individual tables in the dining room or on the porch, from 8–9:30 A.M., and includes juice and fruit, granola, oven-fresh coffee cake and sweet breads, and such entrées as lemon French toast with blueberry sauce, crêpes with mascarpone cheese and fresh fruit sauce, or omelets with herbed home fries. Guests are welcome to help themselves to coffee, tea, and an afternoon treat from the inn's country kitchen. On warm days, iced tea can be enjoyed from a wicker rocker on the flower-filled veranda overlooking the harbor; you can also experience the water closer up in the inn's 17-foot Old Town canoe. In cooler weather, curl up with a book in front of the living room fireplace.

"Wonderful food, accommodations, and hospitality. The resident dog, Benjamin, is warm and friendly." *(John & Sharon Bond)* "Shops and restaurants are all within easy walking distance." *(Larry & Sharon Howard)* "This beautiful home, kept in immaculate condition, is on a hill overlooking Southwest Harbor. Most extraordinary is the third-floor Turret Suite, with a large bathroom, sitting room, and a beautiful bedroom with a fireplace and windows and a turret overlooking the harbor; the views of the sunrise, and the moonlight reflecting on the sea at night, is breathtaking. The guests' sitting room is a natural conversation place while waiting for breakfast, or after coming in from dinner. Quiet music plays in the background." *(Anne & Craig Patterson)* "Immaculate housekeeping throughout the inn. Delicious breakfasts with blueberry pancakes with real maple syrup one day, and spinach egg soufflé the next. Ken and Cyd are warm hosts, pleased to share insider dining and sightseeing tips." *(Kathleen Grady)*

"My stay began with a warm welcome and a tour of the inn from Ken and Cyd, the personable innkeepers. My room was decorated with color-coordinated bedding, window treatments, and wallpaper. The bed was comfortable, and the bathroom supplied with ample hot water and plush towels." *(Susan Goldblatt)* "Careful attention to detail, from the gleaming woodwork, plush towels, fresh flowers, and inviting evening fire, to the mints left in our room." *(Bryan & Tammy Yost)*

Open All year.
Rooms 1 suite with TV, fireplace, air-conditioning. 7 doubles—all with private shower and/or bath, clock, ceiling fan. 4 with air-conditioning. 1 with desk, fireplace, TV, balcony.

Facilities Breakfast room, library, country kitchen, parlor with books, living room, fireplace, stereo, games; porch. Canoe for guest use. Swimming, boating, fishing, hiking, golf, cross-country skiing, snow-shoeing nearby.
Location 43 m E of Bangor. 100 yds. from center of town.
Restrictions No smoking. Children 12 and over. Summer weekend traffic noise possible.
Credit cards MC, Visa.
Rates B&B, $105–175 suite, $60–125 double, Extra person, $15.

The Lindenwood Inn ✕
118 Clark Point Rd, P.O. Box 1328, 04679

Tel: 207–244–5335
800–307–5335
Fax: 207–244–3460
E-mail: Lindenwoodinn@Acadia.net
URL: http://www.acadia.net/lindenwood/

Named for the stately linden trees on its property, the Lindenwood Inn, built as a sea captain's home in 1904, enjoys a quiet location on a side street by the harbor, with easy access to the municipal dock. Jim King purchased the inn in 1992; Herb Zahn is the longtime manager. The decor is contemporary, with ivory fabrics contrasting with brightly colored walls, and halogen bedside lamps; many guest rooms have water views. The breakfast of fresh fruit, baked items, and omelets, pancakes, or French toast is served at individual tables from 7:30–9:30 A.M. The creative dinner menu might include Japanese sushi rolls with lobster and roasted red peppers, roast chicken with thyme and root vegetables, and profiteroles with chocolate sauce.

"Outstanding cleanliness, warmth, and personal attention from every staff member." *(John Allen)* "Warm welcome. Contemporary, fresh, uncluttered decor. Well-appointed dining room with an excellent selection of dishes, including vegetarian. Service was impeccable. Desserts were special." *(Mary Gerhard)* "Jim King and Herb Zahn are great guys, who clearly go out of their way to make us feel welcome and comfortable. They are always there to help with directions, reservations, recommendations, and much more. The two fireplaces in the public living areas are always lit during cool weather, and help create an inviting place to curl up with a book and a cup of tea, or to enjoy conversation. The guest rooms are spacious and immaculately clean, with down comforters and pillows. Jim's personality and flair for design can be seen throughout the inn. He has a great eye for color, and interspersed throughout the house are many primitive sculptures and artwork, which he has acquired in his travels. The basic theme is comfort, and the overall effect is pleasing. The inn is made even more appealing by its excellent restaurant and its inviting swimming pool and hot tub—pleasant for a relaxing dip and a great place to congregate." *(Rich & Barbara Dixon)* "Lovely dinner, cordial staff." *(Marilyn Parker)*

Open All year. Restaurant closed Mon. off-season.
Rooms 3 cottages, 5 suites, 20 doubles—all with private bath and/or shower, telephone with data port, clock, TV, fan. Some with desk, balcony, fireplace; 1 with whirlpool tub, air-conditioning. Rooms in main inn, annexes, cottages.
Facilities Restaurant, bar, living room with fireplace, piano, TV/VCR, stereo; library, bar, porch. ¼ acre with heated swimming pool, hot tub, terrace, off-street parking. Tennis, golf, boat rentals, cross-country skiing nearby.

Location Acadia National Pk., Bar Harbor region. ¼ m from town. Take Rte. 3 to Rte. 102 to SW Harbor. In village, turn left at blinking light onto Clark Point Rd. to inn 1 m down on right.

Restrictions No smoking. Children 12 and over.

Credit cards Discover, MC, Visa.

Rates B&B, $145–225 suite, $75–155 double. Extra person, $20. 3-night minimum July 1–early Sept. Alc lunch, $10–20; alc dinner, $35–50.

SPRUCE HEAD

For additional area inns, see **Rockland**.

Craignair Inn ¢ ⁂ ✕
533 Clark Island Road, Clark Island, 04858

Tel: 207–594–7644
800–320–9997
Fax: 207–596–7124
E-mail: craignar@midcoast.com
URL: http://www.midcoast.com/~craignar/

What do Washington's Library of Congress and New York City's Brooklyn Battery Tunnel have in common with a sleepy Maine coastal village? Both were built of granite quarried here on Clark Island back in the 1920s and '30s. The Craignair Inn was built in 1929 to house quarry workers; the Vestry, which now accommodates additional guests, served as their chapel. Converted into an inn in 1938, the Craignair has been owned by Terry and Norm Smith since 1978. Favorite entrées at the inn's restaurant—popular with guests and locals alike—are bouillabaisse, prime rib, and chicken breast stuffed with spinach and feta cheese.

"Wonderful setting—the scent of pine trees mixed with salt air is incredible. The inn is simple, unpretentious, clean, and friendly, with excellent food. Last but far from least—our well-mannered dog is welcome, too." *(Nancy Williams Watt)* "A delightful experience, from my first call for directions, to a warm welcome on arrival, to our comfortable room and excellent meals." *(Mary Hope Katsouros)* "We enjoyed a wonderful wedding rehearsal dinner at Craignair, complete with old movies, then retired to our quiet room in the adjacent Vestry building. Good location for area touring, too." *(DJ)* "Attentive housekeeping. Games for rainy days, the ocean for nice ones." *(Rebecca McVeigh)* "The old-fashioned living room has overstuffed couches and chairs, and lots of books for browsing. The guest rooms are simple, but clean and pretty; ours was in the main building and had a water view. The food was reasonably priced and good; the dining room overlooks the grounds and the ocean. The inn is linked by a small stretch of land to a private island which guests are allowed to visit. We spent a morning walking along the rocks at the water's edge, gathering seashells and enjoying the smell of the sea. We returned to the inn following an inland path, past a number of old quarries, now filled with water." *(Ann Winkler)* "This unpretentious inn is charmingly decorated with items from many collections. Breakfast includes cereal, pancakes, eggs, bacon or ham, fruit, and freshly baked muffins." *(Helen Dasson)*

Open April 15–Oct. 31. Restaurant closed Oct. 12–May 21; also Sun.

Rooms 19 doubles, 3 singles—8 with full private bath, 14 with maximum of 5 people sharing bath. All with telephone. 10 with desk. Clock on request. 8 rooms in Vestry.

Facilities Restaurant, bar/lounge, library with fireplace, piano. 5 acres with shorefront, flower gardens, woods, lawn games. Saltwater quarry swimming. Hiking trails.

Location Mid-coastal ME. St. George peninsula, Penobscot Bay. 10 m S of Rockland, 80 m NE of Portland. 7.5 m S of Thomaston. From Rte. 1, Thomaston, go S on Rte. 131, then left (E) on Rte. 73. Go right (S) on Clark Island Rd. to inn on left.

Restrictions No smoking in some bedrooms.

Credit cards Amex, MC, Visa.

Rates B&B, $75–110 double, $50–55 single. Extra person, $17. Children occupying 2nd room, 25% less. Alc dinner, $15–25. 2-night minimum holiday weekends.

Extras Local airport/bus station pickups. Pets with prior approval. Crib.

STOCKTON SPRINGS

Hichborn Inn *Tel:* 207–567–4183
Church Street, P.O. Box 115, 04981 800–346–1522

If warm hospitality, good food, and comfortable accommodations are the basic layers of a B&B "cake," then a rich sense of the past is the icing which makes the experience extra special for history buffs. Listed on the National Register of Historic Places, this Italianate Victorian home was built circa 1850 by prominent shipbuilder N.G. Hichborn, and was occupied by the Hichborn family until 1939. Bruce and Nancy Suppes restored the inn in 1989, and note that their B&B has a quiet setting, away from Route 1 traffic, yet perfect for day trips to Camden, Acadia National Park, Deer Isle, and Castine. The inn's high ceilings and handcrafted woodwork are enhanced by Oriental rugs, with antique double and twin-size beds. Breakfast is served in the dining room, or on the breakfast sun porch at individual tables between 8 and 9 A.M..; the meal includes fruit juice, fresh fruit or perhaps fruit soup, crêpes or possibly Dutch babies with a choice of fillings.

"Lovely, restored home; elegant antique furnishings; delicious, healthful breakfasts, served on the plant-filled sunporch; and most importantly, friendly, gracious innkeepers who made me feel so welcome." *(Bobbie Ackerman)* "Off the beaten path, yet convenient to all the sights of mid-Coastal Maine. Excellent value, extremely peaceful." *(Donn & Ann Smith)* "Nancy is a fabulous hostess, who loves being an innkeeper, loves her guests, loves her community, and loves the history of the Hichborn family. Fine antiques are complemented by quality reproductions, and modern bathrooms. An evening in the parlor is a delight, with logs glowing in the fireplace, brandy provided by the innkeepers, two friendly Maine coon cats, stacks of new and antique books on Maine, a stereopticon to view the past, and ticking grandfather clocks. The Suppes regaled us with tales of Stockton Springs's past as a major center for the building of wooden ships, as well as the haunting experiences of this old house. Coffee and tea are set out along with the morning paper for early risers, followed by Nancy's superb breakfasts. The Hichborn is not just a place to stay, it is an experience in small-town historic Maine; Nancy grew up in coastal small-town Maine and that Bruce is a real sailor." *(Rich & Tracy Gillespie)* "Stately and old-fashioned ship captain's home, polished to perfection. The ceilings are extremely high, the long staircase elegant, the artwork lovely." *(Ruth Rappaport)* "Extraordinary attention to detail—flowers on the pillows, delicate chocolates on the bedside table, freshly squeezed orange juice at breakfast, soft classical music in the background, great dinner recommendations, and, best of all, hosts who really know how to make us feel comfortable." *(Peter Eppig)*

Open All year. Reservations required Dec.–March.

Rooms 4 doubles—2 with private shower bath, 2 rooms share 1 bath. All with clock, fan. 2 with air-conditioning.

Facilities Dining room with fireplace, breakfast sunporch, living room with stereo, books; music room with grand piano; porch. ½ acre with off-street parking. Sandy Point Beach for swimming, Penobscot Bay for water sports; golf, tennis nearby.

Location Mid-coastal ME, Penobscot Bay. 28 m SE of Bangor, 5 m NE of Searsport, 10 m NE of Belfast, 27 m NE of Camden. Church St. connects Main St. and Rte. 1. From Searsport, turn right off Rte. 1 onto Main St., then left on Church St. to inn on left. From Bucksport, turn left off Rte. 1 onto Main St. & go right on Church. From Bangor, take Rte. 1A to Rte. 1 & bear right at exit. Follow road across Rte. 1 to Church St.

Restrictions No smoking. "Not child-appropriate."

Credit cards Amex, MC, Visa.

Rates B&B, $51–95 double, $41–85 single.

Extras Airport/station pickup. Some Spanish spoken.

WATERFORD

Waterford is located in the foothills of the White Mountain National Forest near the New Hampshire border.

For additional area entries, see **Bridgton, Center Lovell, Fryeburg,** and **Naples.**

Also recommended: An 1825 farmhouse, **The Waterford Inne** (Chadbourne Road, P.O. Box 149, 04088; 207–583–4037; fax: 207–383–4037; waterfordinne@worldnet.att.net) sits on 25 acres of woods and fields—ideal for hiking and birding, and has a fine dining restaurant as well as eight guest rooms, each with private bath. B&B double rates of $75–100 include a full breakfast. The highly regarded restaurant showcases a four-course prix fixe dinner (reservations required); the menu features vegetables and herbs grown in the inn's extensive gardens. "Wonderful dinner, inviting guest rooms, lovely common areas with antique furnishings. Remote, peaceful, and truly beautiful setting. Friendly, well-traveled, knowledgeable innkeeper." *(Pam Phillips)*

WISCASSET

Reader tip: "Of the many antique shops in town, the best is the Lilac Cottage, a great place to visit, with an interesting history. The items for sale are tastefully arranged to give you the impression that the house is lived in." *(Conrad Schilke)*

Also recommended: Just a mile north of Wiscasset is the **Cod Cove Inn** (Routes 1 & 27, P.O. Box 36, Edgecomb, 04556; 207–882–9586 or 800–882–9586; www.sourcemaine.com/codcove), offering 29 well-equipped guest rooms, each with queen- or king-size beds, plus a private balcony or patio, telephone, TV, private bath, and refrigerator. B&B double rates of $79–129 include a continental breakfast, use of the hot tub and swimming pool. "A motel with style and flair, with owners who are friendly, helpful, and unobtrusive; the atmosphere is friendly and relaxing." *(Conrad & Nancy Schilke)*

The Squire Tarbox Inn ✕
Route 144, 1181 Westport Island, 04578

Tel: 207–882–7693
Fax: 207–882–7107
E-mail: squire@wiscasset.net

Caring, hands-on innkeepers; comfort without ostentation; good food prepared with love; a peaceful country setting; and a location convenient to all the Maine coast has to offer is what you'll find at the Squire Tarbox, a longtime reader-favorite. Listed on the National Register of Historic Places, this rambling clapboard Colonial farmhouse was built by Squire Samuel Tarbox; part of the building dates back to 1763. Bill and Karen Mitman have owned the inn since 1983. The inn makes a good base from which to explore coastal Maine, and a wonderful place to relax after the day's activities—pleasantly removed from the commotion of Boothbay Harbor. The Squire Tarbox is also home to a herd of friendly Nubian dairy goats—source of the inn's famed goat cheeses (served each evening as hors d'oeuvres) and of considerable guest entertainment.

The food is excellent and freshly prepared, starting with a generous breakfast of homemade bread, muffins, granola, quiche, and fresh fruit, and ending with a five-course set dinner. A typical summer meal might include a chilled carrot soup with dill, garden greens with balsamic vinaigrette, chicken stuffed with herbed goat cheese and baked in puff pastry, vegetable stir-fry, homemade pasta, and lemon mousse. Special diets are accommodated with prior notice.

"Perfectly simple and simply perfect is the best way to describe the decor of the Squire Tarbox. Our charming, airy room had good lighting and storage space, an amply sized bathroom well stocked with towels, and a private porch with Adirondack chairs and a forest view. Before dinner, we sampled the superb goat cheese and crackers in the homey barn-turned-library, attempted a puzzle and browsed through the books. The delicious dinner included spinach crêpes, Caesar salad, chicken with fresh vegetables, and a slice of chocolate sin pie—the name says it all. After the meal, we enjoyed an introduction to goat milking, complete with kid hugging. In the morning, we walked to the salt marsh, then returned to try the two swings in the barn. Karen and Bill were delightful, helpful innkeepers." *(Hilary Soule & Dave Shea)*

"Well-maintained inn with genuine Colonial charm; beautiful rural setting. Excellent dinner, welcoming ambience. Our room was large and comfortable, and we enjoyed learning about their goats and cheese-making business." *(Walt & Elinor Hermansen)* "The tiny vases of fresh flowers are typical of the Mitman's careful attention to detail. Every year improvements in safety and convenience are made, yet the atmosphere is unchanged. Good food with occasional flashes of greatness; the whey buns are a celestial experience. Opportunity for solitude along with unforced camaraderie at mealtimes. Wonderful location—isolated from the tourist scene, but close to harbors, beaches, antique shops, museums, lobster pounds, and discount outlet shopping. Observe a working farm and dairy." *(Nancy Keim)* "Loved watching the birds at the feeders, especially the orioles and the hummingbirds. And the goats stole our hearts." *(Karen Hoeb)* "Whether a guest chooses to read in front of the fire or down by the pond, watch birds from the inviting screened porch, work puzzles near the pot-bellied stove, visit the farm animals, or just watch Karen milk the goats, there is a sense of timelessness." *(Lana Alber)* "The Mitmans treat their animals with love and respect, and it shows. Our dinner favorites included the salmon in pastry crust, the melon with poppyseed dressing, the goat cheese strudel, and the chocolate pound cake with raspberry sauce. Outstanding staff." *(GF)* "Special moments during our stay included playing the player piano, enjoying an excellent fireside breakfast, rowing on a nearby river, bicycling around the inlet on the inn's two fine mountain bikes, relaxing, and dining on healthy and tasteful meals." *(Michelle & Tom Wilson)* "Rooms vary in size but all are furnished with a simple, cozy country charm." *(Pam Phillips)*

Open Mid-May–late Oct.

Rooms 11 doubles—all with private shower.

Facilities 2 dining rooms, library with puzzles, games, and books, music room with player piano, 3 parlors; all with fireplaces. 12-acre grounds include nature walk, barn animals, pond with rowboat, bicycles. Short drive to ocean beaches.

Location Mid-coastal ME. 50 m NE of Portland. On Rte. 144 between Bath & Wiscasset; 8½ m S of Rte. 1, on Westport Island.

Restrictions Smoking on weather-protected deck. Children 14 and over.

Credit cards Amex, Discover, MC, Visa.

Rates B&B, $85–167 double, $75–95 single. MAP, $143–235 double, $104–124 single. Extra person B&B, $30; MAP, $50. 12% service. Prix fixe dinner, $29 for overnight guests, $33 for dinner guests.

THE YORKS

Dockside Guest Quarters ¢ 🛉 ✕ &.
Harris Island Road, P.O. Box 205
York, 03909

Tel: 207–363–2868
800–270–1977
Fax: 207–363–1977
E-mail: info@docksidegq.com
URL: http://www.docksidegq.com

Location alone would be reason enough to stay at Dockside. Overlooking York Harbor and the Atlantic Ocean, the inn offers panoramic water views from its expansive grounds and almost all of its guest rooms. Another appealing aspect of its location is the fact that Dockside is easy to reach—only 65 miles from Boston, and convenient to all southern Maine has to offer, from water sports to outlet shopping. No less important at Dockside is the family, from the Lusty family, which has owned the inn for over 35 years, to the families who enjoy Dockside, from grandparents to toddlers. Accommodations are in the Maine House—a classic New England Cottage—and in modern multi-unit buildings at the water's edge. The Dockside Restaurant, with a water view from every table, offers a complete menu, but specializes in fresh Maine seafood.

"The Lusty family and the staff take great care in maintaining their charming and comfortable inn, and go out of their way to make guests feel at home. Our clean, attractive room had a splendid view of York Harbor. The grounds are pristine but inviting. The housekeeping staff did a marvelous job in every respect." *(Marcie & John Gordon)* "A summer breakfast on the porch, with fresh bagels, breads, muffins, fruit, cereal, and juice is an ideal start to the day. A small, intimate inn with a quiet atmosphere." *(Meredith Queenan)* "Caring and unobtrusive hosts. Serenity and beautiful sunsets bring us back each year. The restaurant serves delicious Maine cuisine and homemade desserts." *(Dr. & Mrs. H.B. Shoup)* "Immaculate accommodations, comfortable beds, and adequate kitchenette and bath." *(Dr. & Mrs. Frances B. Warrick)* "The well-kept lawn slopes gently downward to the water; tiger lilies bloom well into summer. Our duplex suite, part of the Captain's Quarters, was spacious, airy, and comfortable, with full-size kitchen essentials. Upstairs, we had two spacious bedrooms with an ocean view and a sunny, immaculate bath. Friendly, welcoming owners and staff." *(Mr. & Mrs. Robert Pressimone)* "Peaceful, quiet setting on a quiet lane, overlooking the cove. Guest rooms are simply furnished but attractive, comfortable for an extended stay." *(SWS)* "We were delighted with our newly renovated room in the Crow's Nest." *(DLG)*

Open All year. Restaurant open late May–mid-Oct.
Rooms 6 suites, 15 doubles—19 with private bath and/or shower, 2 with maximum of 4 people sharing bath. All with radio, TV, fan. Some with desk, kitchenette, porch/balcony. Rooms in Maine House and in multi-unit cottages.
Facilities Restaurant, lounge, lobby, living room with fireplace, TV, library, card-playing area. Complete wedding facilities. 7 acres with gazebo, shuffle-

board, badminton. Bicycles, fishing, boat rentals, canoes, marina. Beaches, golf, tennis, outlet shopping nearby.

Location SW ME coast, 65 m NE of Boston. 1 m to York Village. Take York exit off I-95. Take Rte. 1 to 1A to York Village, then Rte. 103 to harbor and inn.

Credit cards Checks preferred; MC, Visa accepted.

Rates Room only, $106–169 suite, $82–119 double. Extra person, $10. Crib, $7. 2-night minimum July–Sept. Reduced rates and packages Oct.–June. Continental plus breakfast buffet, $3. Alc dinner $12–25. Children's menu.

Extras Wheelchair access; some rooms specially equipped. Crib, babysitting, sandbox, games.

Key to Abbreviations and Symbols

For complete information and explanations, please see the Introduction.

¢ Especially good value for overnight accommodation.

👪 Families welcome. Most (but not all) have cribs, baby-sitting, games, play equipment, and reduced rates for children.

✗ Meals served to public; reservations recommended or required.

🎾 Tennis court and swimming pool and/or lake on grounds. Golf usually on grounds or nearby.

♿ Limited or full wheelchair access; call for details.

Rates: Range from least expensive room in low season to most expensive room in peak season.

Room only: No meals included; European Plan (EP).

B&B: Bed and breakfast; includes breakfast, sometimes afternoon/evening refreshment.

MAP: Modified American Plan; includes breakfast and dinner.

Full board: Three meals daily.

Alc lunch: À la carte lunch; average price of entrée plus nonalcoholic drink, tax, tip.

Alc dinner: Average price of three-course dinner, including half bottle of house wine, tax, tip.

Prix fixe dinner: Three- to five-course set dinner, excluding wine, tax, tip unless otherwise noted.

Extras: Noted if available. Always confirm in advance. Pets are not permitted unless specified; if you are allergic, ask for details; *most innkeepers have pets.*

Massachusetts

Deerfield Inn, Deerfield

Although there's plenty of beautiful country in between, most of our listings cluster around the East Coast—Cape Cod, Cape Ann, Martha's Vineyard, and Nantucket—and the Berkshires, in western Massachusetts.

The Berkshires: About a 2½-hour drive from New York and slightly less than that from Boston, this region of gentle mountains is known for Tanglewood—the summer home of the Boston Symphony Orchestra—Jacob's Pillow Modern Dance Theater, the Berkshire Theater Festival, the Norman Rockwell Museum, Chesterwood, the Hancock Shaker Village, and many recreational facilities. The area also features trails for hiking and lakes for fishing and swimming in summer, plenty of golf courses and tennis courts, foliage in October, and downhill and cross-country skiing in winter.

Peak season rates in the Berkshires generally apply in July, August, and October; rates are usually lower the rest of the year. Expect three- and four-night minimum-stay requirements on weekends and holidays in peak season, and book well in advance.

Worth noting: A visit to the Berkshires in season is *expensive,* so make sure you find the inn that suits your needs. Properties right in Lenox offer convenience to Tanglewood, those farther afield generally offer spacious grounds, swimming pools, and tennis courts. Prices off-season vary dramatically. Some inns drop their rates only slightly from November through April, others reduce prices by 50–75%, especially midweek, so shop around if you're on a tight budget, and don't be afraid to ask for "off-season specials."

Here's a list of towns with recommended inns in **The Berkshires:** Great Barrington, Lee, Lenox, New Marlborough, North Egremont, Richmond, South Egremont, South Lee, Stockbridge, West Stockbridge, and Williamstown.

Cape Cod: The Cape officially starts at the Cape Cod Canal, about 50 miles south of Boston, and extends out into the Atlantic like an arm, bent at the elbow at a 90° angle. Buzzards Bay is formed by the shoulder, to the south, and Cape Cod Bay by the bend of the arm, to the north. A highlight of a visit to the Cape is the Cape Cod National Seashore, with 40 miles of beach and dunes to explore; park headquarters, with guided walks and lifeguards in summer, are in South Wellfleet. Equally appealing is the Cape Cod Bike Trail, which follows the route of the old Penn Central Railway tracks for thirty miles, from Dennis to Wellfleet, past forests, ponds, marshes, and beaches.

Peak season rates on the Cape generally extend from mid-June through Labor Day, and on weekends through October. Two- and three-night minimum stays are the rule in peak season. Off-season rates vary significantly; some upscale inns keep their rates quite high all year, others discount significantly in the off-season, so bargain hunters will do well to shop around.

Reader tip: "I particularly enjoy the solitude of winter with its magnificent sunrises and sunsets. Be sure to watch the sunset on the bay side from any beach. My particular favorite, though, is Corn Hill in the winter—now that is raw beauty." *(Pamela Conrad)*

Here's a list of towns with recommended inns on **Cape Cod:** Barnstable, Brewster, Chatham, Dennis, Dennis Port, Eastham, East Orleans, Falmouth, Harwich Port, Hyannis Port, North Truro, Provincetown, Sandwich, South Dennis, Wellfleet, West Dennis, West Harwich, West Yarmouth, and Yarmouthport. See also Martha's Vineyard and Nantucket.

AMHERST

A pretty college town in Western Massachusetts, Amherst (pronounced Am´-erst) makes a good base for exploring the Pioneer Valley, home to a number of major colleges and universities (Amherst, Smith, Mt. Holyoke, Hampshire College, and the University of Massachusetts), historic places of interest from the Emily Dickinson House to Old Deerfield, and quality craft shops. For key college weekends (parents' weekends, graduation, and so on), advance reservations are essential, and prices may be higher.

Also recommended: Shaded by tall black walnut trees, and located a few minutes from the campuses of Amherst and the University of Massachusetts, **The Black Walnut Inn** (1184 Pleasant Street, 01002; 413–549–5649) is a stately Federal-style brick house. Each of the seven guest rooms is furnished with a blend of antiques and period reproductions. The Webster Room, furnished with two queen-size beds and a trundle bed, is convenient for a family stay. A full breakfast is included in the double rates of $95–125.

For additional area inns, see listings under **Leverett, Northampton, North New Salem,** and **Ware.**

Allen House Victorian Inn ¢   *Tel:* 413–253–5000
599 Main Street, 01002   *URL:* http://www.allenhouse.com

Owners Alan and Ann Zieminski offer warm hospitality and a welcoming atmosphere at Allen House. This 1886 stick-style Queen Anne home has original Eastlake fireplace mantels with ornate tilework, cherry woodwork, and period chandeliers; the Victorian decor is highlighted by antique wicker, Oriental rugs, peacock feather bouquets, and lace antimacassars. Guests dine amidst lavish Bradbury & Bradbury period wallpapers, Japanese porcelain, and paintings in a style that is reminiscent of the Victorian fascination with the Far East. Alan and Ann have given equal care to guest comfort—they have installed custom-made storm windows and central air-conditioning, to ensure a peaceful night's rest for their guests.

"Genuine Victoriana, with heavy antique furniture, appropriate accessories such as Boston ferns and umbrella stands, and the dark, authentic feel of a turn-of-the-century house. Most guest rooms have matching sets of rare Eastlake and other Victorian furniture. Lovely small bathrooms with cream tiles were installed in closets, with pedestal sinks often outside the bathroom door. We breakfasted on French toast stuffed with cream cheese, served with hot maple syrup and link sausage." *(SHW)* "Even though it was freezing cold outdoors, I was cozy under thick quilts, with ample hot water for a steaming shower." *(Isabell Morris)* "Our room was homey with lace curtains, Victorian-dressed porcelain dolls, a trinket box covered with a lace doily. The Swedish pancakes with raspberry preserves melted in my mouth." *(Janice Sirote)* "Authentically decorated and maintained. The Eastlake Room was spotless, sunny, spacious, and well appointed. Attentive and hospitable hosts, offering me an afternoon lemonade or hot tea upon arrival." *(Patricia Northlich)*

Open All year.
Rooms 7 doubles—all with private bath and/or shower, telephone, radio, desk, air-conditioning, ceiling fan. TV on request.
Facilities Dining room, breakfast room, sitting room with fireplace, TV; library with fireplace, piano; screened & unscreened porches. 3 acres with lawns.
Location 25 m N of Springfield. 45 m N of Bradley Int'l. Airport. 5 blocks from center.
Restrictions No smoking. "Well-behaved children welcome."
Credit cards None accepted.
Rates B&B, $55–135 double, $45–115 single. Extra person, $20. Children's, senior discounts. Minimum stay required college, foliage weekends.
Extras Station pickups.

BARNSTABLE

Dating back to 1637, Barnstable is a quiet and attractive village, with none of the honky-tonk found in some Cape towns. It is located on Cape Cod's north shore, 75 miles southwest of Boston, and 4 miles from Hyannis. In addition to the town beach on Cape Cod Bay, several ocean and lake beaches are within a 5-mile drive, and opportunities for golf, tennis, and hiking are easily available, as are numerous antique shops.

Reader tip: "Highly recommend the Dolphin restaurant for dinner." *(RC)*

For additional area entries, see **Yarmouthport**.

The Acworth Inn ¢

4352 Old Kings Highway

P.O. Box 256, Cummaquid, 02637

Tel: 508–362–3330

800–362–6363

Fax: 508–375–0304

URL: http://www.acworthinn.com

When you picture a classic Cape Cod inn, your first thought may be of a spacious old home with naturally weathered shingles, crisp white trim, and green shutters. Add mature evergreen plantings, overflowing flower boxes, and colorful beds of flowers, and you've just pictured the Acworth Inn, built in 1860 and bought by Cheryl and Jack Ferrell in 1994. Prior to becoming innkeepers, they had spent 30 years in corporate and military environments: Cheryl as a food service manager with Marriott, and Jack as a professor at the Air Force Academy in Colorado. Breakfasts are served from 8–9:30 A.M., and might include fresh fruit, cranberry granola, cinnamon rolls, muffins, and sour cream waffles.

"A warm welcome included refreshing glasses of cranberry spritzers. Our first-floor room in the attached carriage house had a queen-size white iron bed with Laura Ashley ivy pattern quilt and shams. The thick towels were changed twice daily. Spotless and meticulous housekeeping. The breakfast room has a fireplace to keep guests cozy on winter mornings, and sliding glass doors to the deck where tables are set on summer days. Guests sit at tables for two or four, but are close enough to chat between the tables if desired. A choice of juices is served at the table along with specially blended coffee. Entrées included an herb omelet with homemade toasted orange cinnamon bread, and heart-shaped miniature waffles with homemade syrups." *(Rose Ciccone)* "First-rate inn. Cinnamon rolls to die for." *(Susan Doucet)* "Just as special on a return visit. The elegant Cummaquid room on the first floor has a fireplace, triple-sheeted queen-size bed, and a soothing ivory color scheme. Cheryl's turndown service included chocolate-cranberry treats and a miniature rose. Rooms also have vases with fresh flowers from the Ferrell's garden. Bathroom amenities included a variety of soaps, shampoo, conditioner, body lotion, shoe mitt, cotton swabs and balls, bath gel, makeup remover pads, and a shower cap. Guests at the Acworth are made to feel like family guests and you can be as social as you wish. Cheryl and Jack offer afternoon refreshments and join guests on the deck to offer restaurant recommendations or help plan outings. Our delicious breakfast included a beautiful platter of fresh fruit, homemade granola, yogurt, just-baked almond rolls and blueberry muffins, followed by multi-grain pancakes with some homemade jam and maple syrup." *(RC)*

"Undoubtedly a labor of love; the Ferrells' hospitality is awesome." *(Jeanne King)* "Always fresh flowers and chocolates in our room. Relaxing music throughout the inn." *(Lynnette Ryan)* "Careful attention to detail, from the evening pastries to the fact that our room was cleaned while we were at breakfast." *(Nicole Fortier)* "Gracious owners who exude energy and warmth." *(Peter von Eschen & many others)* "Beautifully landscaped with flowering plants, a garden, and bird feeders outside the kitchen window." *(Ronda Hoag)* "Every conceivable comfort:

both soft and hard pillows, fluffy thick towels, thirsty robes. The innkeepers welcome you on arrival and send a thank-you note for staying." *(Abby Green)* "Cheryl and Jack made reservations for us in excellent restaurants and mapped out a tour of the prettiest spots on the Cape. The inn is located on a quiet street where you can walk for miles enjoying the scenery along the water." *(Jeanne & Thomas Russo)* "Cheryl went out of her way to accommodate my dietary restrictions." *(Holly Shaker)* "The innkeepers have decorated the house with light, airy pastel colors and hand-painted furniture." *(Carola Staiano)*

Open All year.
Rooms 1 suite, 4 doubles—all with private bath and/or shower, clock/radio, fan. 1 with TV, desk, wood-burning fireplace, refrigerator, air-conditioning.
Facilities Breakfast room with fireplace, living room, family room with TV, books, porch. Off-street parking; bicycles. Tennis, golf, swimming, fishing, boating nearby.
Location Cape Cod; north side, mid-Cape. 1½ m E of Barnstable, 4 m N of Hyannis. Center of business district. Follow Rte. 6 to Exit 6 at the Rte. 132 exit. Turn left onto Rte. 132 continuing to Rte. 6A. Turn right on 6A. Follow for exactly 4.6 m to inn on left.
Restrictions No smoking. Children 12 and over. Traffic noise possible in some rooms.
Credit cards Amex, Discover, MC, Visa.
Rates B&B, $185 suite, $85–125 double. Extra person, $20. 2-night weekend/holiday minimum. Extended stay rates.
Extras German spoken.

Ashley Manor 🏃
3660 Old King's Highway, P.O. Box 856, 02630

Tel: 508–362–8044
888–535–2246
Fax: 508–362–9927
E-mail: ashleymn@capecod.net
URL: http://www.capecod.net/ashleymn

Ashley Manor dates back to 1699, and evidence of its age can be seen in its wide-board flooring, open-hearth fireplaces with beehive ovens, and a secret passageway connecting the upstairs and downstairs suites. Donald Bain, who has owned the inn since 1986, continues to work hard on improvements and upgrades. The inviting living room has antique side pieces, richly colored Oriental rugs, and dark blue velvet couches, perfect for curling up with a book. A multi-course breakfast is served on the backyard stone patio in good weather; in cooler months, guests are seated on the Chippendale chairs in the formal dining room, complete with candlelight, fine china, and linens, before a blazing fire. Breakfasts typically include freshly squeezed orange juice, baked apples, granola, home-baked popovers, and crêpes with strawberry sauce. Candy, sherry, port, plus afternoon tea, are also included in the rates.

"Fully endorse existing entry. Donald is sweet and welcoming. Guest rooms are light and airy, beautifully decorated and well lit. The grounds are carefully maintained, and the tennis court was surrounded by flowers." *(RC)*

"We sipped coffee on the balcony of our room, then enjoyed a delicious, generous breakfast which kept us going until dinner time. A thoughtful touch is the library of recent bestsellers for guests to read at the beach or in the lovely garden." *(Mary Louise Gilbert)* "Peaceful country setting, within walking distance of restaurants and beaches. This lovely old house is warm and welcoming, well maintained and immaculately clean. Donald Bain pays careful attention to the comfort, well-being, and interests of his guests." *(Stephan Gamble)* "Friendly, humorous, knowledgeable host." *(Jean-Louis Gallani)*

"The inn is set behind a wall of hedges, well back from the road at the end of an expansive lawn, yet is just a short walk to town and Barnstable Harbor. Donald, the gracious host, is proud of his establishment and it shows everywhere—from the comfortable parlor with its crystal decanters of port and sherry, to the blazing fireplace, to the beautiful gardens planted with flowering plants, frequented by colorful birds. Each charming guest room is spotlessly clean and inviting, with a color-coordinated modern bath; many have canopy beds, whirlpools, and working fireplaces, and all have luxurious bed linens, plenty of fluffy pillows, warm comforters, and a selection of teas, coffee, and cocoa. At breakfast, freshly squeezed orange juice is always available, as is Donald's homemade granola, breads, and muffins. Crêpes are delicately arranged on a heated plate, with fresh raspberry sauce and mint garnish." *(Mindy Helman & Jim Rae)*

Open All year.
Rooms 4 suites, 2 doubles—all with private bath and/or shower, radio, coffee/tea maker, air-conditioning. 5 with fireplace, 3 with whirlpool; 1 cottage suite.
Facilities Dining room, living room with library, each with working fireplace. 2 acres with terrace, gardens, gazebo, fountain, tennis court, bicycles. Walking distance to beach for swimming, fishing. Golf nearby.
Location ½ m from village. In historic district.
Restrictions No smoking. Children over 14.
Credit cards Discover, JCB, MC, Visa.
Rates B&B, $165–180 suite, $120–140 double. Extra person in suite, 25% additional. 2–3 night weekend/holiday minimum.
Extras Airport/station pickups. French spoken.

Beechwood Inn 👪 ♿
2839 Main Street, 02630
Tel: 508–362–6618
800–609–6618
Fax: 508–362–0298
E-mail: bwdinn@virtualcapecod.com
URL: http://www.virtualcapecod.com/market/beechwood

Set on a small hilltop looking out to Cape Cod Bay, Beechwood is a Queen Anne Victorian home, built in 1853, and purchased in 1994 by Ken and Debbie Traugot. Furnished with authentic Victorian pieces throughout, the Cottage Room has a hand-painted bedroom set from the 1860s, while the Rose Room has a carved four-poster and fireplace; two guest rooms have water views, while others look out to the magnificent beech trees for which the inn is named. Breakfast is served at individual tables from 8:30–9:30 A.M., and might include banana chocolate chip muffins, honeydew melon, and French toast. Debbie's repertoire includes thirty different entrées, so you're guaranteed not to have a repeat (unless requested!). Afternoon tea is also served.

"Personable hosts offered recommendations of where to dine. Wonderful wraparound porch with rockers." *(Sandra Clark)* "Superb location; convenient yet quiet, hidden from the road by tall hedges. Two sweet golden retrievers follow the innkeepers around as they do their chores. We loved the Victorian Rose Room, with its fireplace, canopy bed, lace bedspread, and chaise lounge. The Garrett Room, with a view of Cape Cod Bay, is tucked away from the rest of the world for complete privacy; its spacious bath is one floor below. Delicious, artistically presented breakfast, with special attention to dietary needs. Best of all is the warm hospitality of Ken and Debbie, and their daughter, Morgan." *(Jennifer Irving & David Kochman)* "The Marble Room has a separate entrance off the front porch, and is done with Eastlake furnishings, a brass bed, and a marble fireplace." *(RC)*

"Warm and accommodating hosts; delightful, immaculate rooms. Scrumptious breakfasts of applesauce-oatmeal muffins, grapefruit with cinnamon sugar, and apple pancakes. Debbie cooked, Ken served, and both stayed to chat with us about the inn and the area. Careful attention to detail: matches and logs ready by the fire, a basket of bathroom necessities, fluffy towels, wine glasses and a corkscrew on the table, and even two stamped Beechwood postcards." *(Lisa Braverman & Chris Dolezal)*

Open All year.
Rooms 6 doubles—all with private bath and/or shower, refrigerator, air-conditioning, fireplace.
Facilities Dining room with fireplace; breakfast room; living room with fireplace, books; wraparound porch with rockers, glider. 1¼ acres with gardens, lawn games, bicycles. Walk to beach.
Location ½ m from center of town. From Rte. 6, take Exit 6. Turn left onto Rte. 132 N, then right on Rte. 6A E for 1¾ m.
Restrictions No smoking. Children under 1 or over 12.
Credit cards Amex, Discover, MC, Visa.
Rates B&B, $90–170 double. Extra person, $20. Children under 1 free. 2-night minimum weekends May–Oct., plus some holiday weekends. Midweek, off-season discounts.
Extras Limited wheelchair access. Station/airport pickup. Crib. French spoken.

Crocker Tavern B&B   ♿ ¢
3095 Old Kings Highway, 02630

Tel: 508–362–5115
800–773–5359
Fax: 508–362–5562
E-mail: crocktav@capecod.net
URL: http://www.capecod.net/crockertavernbnb

Built in 1754, Crocker Tavern provided refreshment and lodging to weary travelers on the Boston–Provincetown stagecoach route; during the Revolutionary War, the tavern served as Whig headquarters. Restored as an inn in 1993 by Sue and Jeff Carlson, the original woodwork, window seats, and ceiling beams are complemented by period antiques and reproductions, plus Oriental, braided, and hooked rugs; most guest rooms have queen-size canopy beds and two have fireplaces. Breakfast includes fresh fruit and juice, yogurt, cereal, and perhaps fresh-baked strawberry walnut muffins or cranberry orange scones.

"Attractive house and property. Spacious common rooms and beautifully decorated guest rooms. The hardwood floors, Oriental rugs, and beamed ceilings give a warm feeling to the house." *(RC)* "Great location; an easy walk to shops and the water. Friendly, helpful owners even offered us evening wine, sherry, and snacks. Beautifully decorated throughout with wonderful antiques, yet very comfortable. Healthy breakfasts." *(Mr. & Mrs. T. Murtaugh)* "The fireplace and candles created a cozy atmosphere in our comfortable room." *(Carol Jacobs)* "Our spacious room was well furnished, with a private bath in the hall." *(Leon & Arleen Chasson)* "The Julia Crocker Room, on the first floor on the back of the house, is a large, quiet, beautifully appointed room with a working fireplace and a queen-size bed with a remarkably comfortable mattress. Much attention has been given to the renovation of this old house; one wonders just how many feet have walked the well-worn back steps to the second floor." *(Lou Ellen M. Olin)*

Open All year.
Rooms 5 doubles—all with private shower and/or bath, radio, clock, air-conditioning. 2 with fireplace.
Facilities Dining/breakfast room with fireplace, living room with fireplace. Guest refrigerator. 3.5 acres with lawn games; beach chairs, beach towels. Harbor, beach, marina, fishing, whale-watching, golf nearby.
Location Take Rte. 6 (Mid-Cape Hwy.) to Exit 6. Go left (N) on Rte. 132 to stop sign at Rte. 6A. Go right (E) on Rte. 6A & go 2 m to Crocker Tavern on right.
Restrictions No smoking. Children over 12.
Credit cards MC, Visa.
Rates B&B, $85–130. Extra person, $20. 2–3 night stay preferred weekends/holidays.
Extras Limited wheelchair access.

Heaven on High
70 High Street, West Barnstable, 02668

Tel: 508–362–4441
800–362–4044
Fax: 508–362–4465
E-mail: heaven@tiac.net
URL: http://www.tiac.net/users/heaven

A traditional gray clapboard Cape Cod home, Heaven on High was built in 1987, and remodeled as a B&B in 1995 by Deanna and Gib Katten. The inn's hilltop location offers unobstructed views of woods, salt marshes, dunes, and beyond, Cape Cod Bay at Sandy Neck. The spacious guest rooms are handsomely furnished with traditional pieces and antiques, and have either queen-, king-, or twin-size beds. Breakfast is served from 8–9:30 A.M., in the dining room, in the country kitchen, or on the deck. In addition to fresh fruit, the meal might include potato pancakes, scrambled eggs with mushroom sauce, mango salsa, and carrot muffins; or tiramisu French toast, smoked turkey sausage, and apricot scones. Gil notes that they have added a 30-foot putting green behind their inn, so guests can practice their short green before trying one of the Cape's first-rate courses.

"Magnificent property. Attentive, helpful hosts." *(Judith & William Christensen, also Cathy & Wayne Redmon)* "Wonderful gardens and fantastic views from the rooms and the deck. Deanna's an expert cook and gardener, as is clear from the breakfasts and the gardens. Her incredible collections range from French ivory to silver, rabbits to glove stretchers, crystal to china, and much more. Lovely sponge painting, stenciling, and hand-painted murals complement the handsome furnishings. Fruit, cookies, and bottles of flavored spring water were set out for us when we returned at night." *(Rose Ciccone)* "Impressive collections throughout this immaculate house. The bright and cheerful Hearts and Flowers Room has hundreds of heart-shaped pin cushions above the bed; another wall was full of baby bonnets. Deanna and Gib go out of their way to make sure guests are comfortable, and are pleased to suggest restaurants and activities." *(Caryn Piaser)*

Open All year. Closed Thanksgiving, Christmas.
Rooms 3 doubles—all with private shower and/or bath, clock/radio, air-conditioning, mini-refrigerator, fan. 1 with private deck, fireplace.
Facilities Dining room, living room, great room with TV, deck. 1½ acres with off-street parking, putting green. 1¼ m from Sandy Neck Beach.
Location Cape Cod. 10 min. E of Sandwich, N of Hyannis. From Sagamore Bridge, take Rte. 6 approx. 10 m to Exit 5. Turn left onto Rte. 149. Follow to Rte. 6A, & go left. Follow Rte. 6A for 1 m to High St. & go left to inn, 3rd house on right.
Restrictions Absolutely no smoking. Adult oriented.
Credit cards MC, Visa.
Rates B&B, $115–145 double. 2–3 night weekend/holiday minimum.

Honeysuckle Hill Bed & Breakfast

591 Old King's Highway, Route 6A
West Barnstable, 02668

Tel: 508–362–8418
800–441–8418

From the Green Mountains of Vermont to the sparkling blue waters of Cape Cod Bay, longtime innkeepers Bill and Mary Kilburn demonstrate that hospitality is where the heart is. After 12 years as owner/innkeepers of Trail's End in Wilmington, Vermont—a contemporary ski lodge with 15 guest rooms—they decided it was time for a new challenge. In 1997, they bought Honeysuckle Hill, a Queen Anne–style home dating back to 1810 and listed on the National Register of Historic Places. Mary notes that "Madison, our resident black Labrador, is still the ultimate inn dog, and welcomes guests at the front door."

Guest rooms are furnished in antiques and white wicker, with featherbeds and Battenburg lace; most have queen-size beds and a sitting area. The bathrooms are outfitted in white marble and brass and feature big fluffy towels, English toiletries, and individual thermostats. Breakfast is served at 8:30 A.M. at guests' choice of small tables or large, and might feature Dutch baby pancakes, Captain's eggs, or Grand

Marnier French toast, plus fresh fruit and juice, homemade granola, and home-baked muffins, breads, or coffee cake.

"Mary and Bill are charming, fun, and exuberant innkeepers, and we enjoyed chatting with them on the inviting screened porch, comfortably decorated with lots of cushioned wicker furniture. The welcoming parlor has just-picked flower bouquets, a fireplace, and lots of books; a bottle of sherry is set out as well as a bowl of chocolate mints. The guest refrigerator is stocked with soda and water, and beach towels fill a convenient cupboard. The grounds are lovely, with a small fish pond and lots of flower beds. At night, the driveway and walkway are extremely well lit. Our room, Morning Glory, was done in white wicker, with a queen-size bed made up with red-and-white gingham-checked sheets, bed tables with Tiffany-style reading lamps, a loveseat and coffee table, antique trunk, and chest. Soft featherbeds and a good mattress made for a great night's sleep. Extra blankets and pillows were stocked in the large closet; attention to detail was also shown in the room-darkening shades behind the lace curtains. Immaculately clean throughout. Delicious breakfast of coffee cake, shirred eggs with Brie, bacon, and toast." (RC)

"Bill and Mary are always visible, making sure everyone is comfortable and happy." (Debra Jannetta) "Bill and Mary are kind, friendly, considerate, pleasant, fun-loving people who made our visit pleasant and entertaining. The inn's atmosphere is homey, cozy, relaxing, and peaceful. Excellent housekeeping, delicious breakfasts cooked to order." (Henry & Betty Gombeyski)

Open All year.
Rooms 1 2-bedroom suite, 3 doubles—all with private shower bath, radio, clock, air-conditioning, fan. 1 with private entrance.
Facilities Dining room, living room with fireplace, stereo, books; screened porch. 1.5 acres with off-street parking, gardens, croquet. Beach chairs, towels, umbrellas provided. 2 m to Sandy Neck Beach, hiking, canoeing, fishing, birdwatching.
Location Cape Cod. 70 m SE of Boston. 7/10 m from town. From Rte. 6 E, take Exit 5 & go N on Rte. 149 for 1 m. Go left at Rte. 6A. Go 7/10 m to inn on left. From Rte. 6A E, watch for Barnstable town line sign. Go 1.3 m & watch for inn on right.
Restrictions No smoking. Children 12 and over.
Credit cards Amex, Discover, MC, Visa.
Rates B&B, $175 suite, $115 double. 2-night weekend minimum.

BOSTON

Founded in 1630, Boston is one of America's oldest cities; its historic area is compact and easy to explore on foot. This is fortunate, considering that it is nearly impossible for the uninitiated to navigate the center city by car; the town plan was "laid out by the cows," according to legend. Boston is rich in sights and museums of all periods, from the historic Freedom Trail to the John Hancock Observatory, from the Boston Tea Party Museum to the Computer Museum. Be sure to write or call the Greater Boston Convention and Visitors Bureau, Prudential Plaza, P.O. Box 490 (617–536–4100), for details.

Reader tip: "If you want vibrant, chic, and trendy, stay on Newbury Street; if you want a quiet, residential area, walk one block north to Commonwealth Avenue, with its broad park down the center; if you want a more busy and bustling city atmosphere, walk one block south of Newbury to Boylston Street." *(Fritz Shantz & Tara Neal)*

Also recommended—luxury: It's hard to beat the view offered by the **Boston Harbor Hotel** (70 Rowes Wharf, 02110; 617–439–7000 or 800–752–7077), built on the water at Rowes Wharf. This luxury facility, built in 1987, is appointed with traditional furnishings and all the requisite amenities; of particular note is its art collection, with many historic maps and paintings. The excellent Rowes Wharf restaurant offers sweeping water views and specializes in seafood and American regional cuisine. Double rates range from $235–385; weekend packages are sometimes available. If you're coming from Logan Airport, take the water shuttle to the hotel's dock.

Readers continue to report that all standards—comfort, decor, food, and most important, staffing—have remained at the highest levels at both the **Ritz-Carlton** (800–241–3333) and the **Four Seasons** (800–332–3442). Both typically offer reasonably priced weekend packages, so call for details if you want luxury at an affordable rate.

Another fine luxury choice is the **Fairmont Copley Plaza Hotel** (138 St. James Avenue, 02116; 617–267–5300 or 800–527–4727), in the Back Bay area. Built in 1912, this French Renaissance–style hotel building was refurbished in 1992 and 1996 at a cost of millions. It offers grand and elegant common areas, plus 379 guest rooms with antique reproductions and marble baths; double rates range from $160–325. "Ask for a recently renovated room facing Copley Plaza with a view of Trinity Church." *(DLG)*

Also recommended—moderate: When every little hotel in town is full, several readers suggest trying the 977-room **Boston Park Plaza** (64 Arlington Street, 02116; 617–426–2000 or 800–225–2008), adjacent to the Public Garden: "Friendly staff, good location, ecological amenities, and great value." *(MW)* Rates range from $139–225, with weekend and off-season packages available.

A traditional turn-of-the-century hotel, the **Lenox Hotel** (710 Boylston Street at Copley Place, 02116; 617–536–5300 or 800–225–7676; www.lenoxhotel.com) underwent a $20 million renovation in 1997. The 214 guest rooms are appointed in either Colonial or French provincial decor; most have walk-in closets. The suites are large, with an elegant mix of designer fabrics, wallpaper, and furniture; some have woodburning fireplaces. Double rates range from $170–295. Although readers continue to be delighted with the hotel's convenient location, excellent sound-proofing, and efficient staff, one reader was overwhelmed by a tour group occupying the lobby.

Also recommended—budget: One of Boston's best-kept secrets is the affordable **Eliot and Pickett Houses** (6 Mount Vernon Place, 25 Beacon Street, 02108–2800; 617–248–8707; www.uua.org/ep), with a wonderful location at the top of Beacon Hill. These two 1830s brick townhouses have 20 guest rooms pleasantly furnished in period reproductions, most with a private bath and clock/radio. Guests can relax on the roof deck, watch TV in the den, and play the piano in the inn's kitchens in the living room; you'll prepare your own breakfast in the inn's kitchens; all the fixings are supplied. B&B double rates range from $85–145.

Another good choice is the affordable **John Jeffries House** (14 Embankment Road, 02114; 617–367–1866), offering 46 singles, doubles, and suites, at rates ranging from $85–145, and a fine location at the foot of Beacon Hill at the corner of Charles and Cambridge Streets. Rooms are furnished with private bath, telephone, TV, air-conditioning, and kitchenette; coffee and doughnuts are offered each morning in the double parlor. Reduced-rate parking is available at the garage next door. "Great location; quiet despite its facing the highway because of the well-made double-paned windows. My small single room was immaculate. The subway is at the front door, as is all of Beacon Hill." *(Harriet Krivit)* "Excellent location; serviceable, quiet rooms. Our room had some noise from adjacent elevator and heating system. Friendly, efficient staff; agreeable lounge." *(Caroline Raphael)*

Comprised of two adjoining four-story brick and brownstone 1880s townhouses, the **Newbury Guest House** (261 Newbury Street, 02116; 617–437–7666 or 800–437–7668; www.hagopianhotels.com) is located in the heart of Boston's fashionable Back Bay neighborhood. Each of the 32 guest rooms has a private shower bath, and the $100–145 double rate includes a continental breakfast; a limited number of parking spaces is available at $15 daily, by advance reservation. "Vibrant, chic, and trendy Newbury Street location—the hotel's chief asset. Pleasant staff, tasty breakfast of fruit, juice, cereal, muffins, pastries, and bagels, available in a breakfast room with the newspapers and CNN on the TV from 7:30–10:30 A.M. Coffee, tea, and ice were always available. Adequate but uninspired decor." *(FS)* "Excellent location. Friendly staff. Do-it-yourself breakfast." *(Caroline Raphael)*

Information please: A handsomely restored 1863 red-brick townhouse, **82 Chandler Street** (82 Chandler Street, 02116; 617–482–0408 or 888–482–0408; www.channel1.com/82chandler/) is located just off Copley Square in the historic South End. The three B&B guest rooms have a queen-size bed, private bath, telephone, and air-conditioning; two studios are ideal for week-long stays. Owners Denis Cote and Dominic Beraldi serve a family-style breakfast in their sun-filled penthouse kitchen. B&B double rates range from $110–165.

Two miles from downtown Boston is **The Bertram Inn** (92 Sewall Avenue, Brookline, 02146; 617–566–2234 or 800–295–3822; www.bertraminn.com), a half-timbered Tudor-style home built in 1907. Each of the 16 guest rooms have antique and reproduction furnishings, TV, telephone, and air-conditioning; most have a private bath. The continental breakfast can be enjoyed by the living room fireplace or on the classic front porch. B&B double rates range from $84–219.

Advance reservations are advisable but last-minute callers may be helped by the **Greater Boston Hospitality Bed & Breakfast Service** (P.O. Box 1142, Brookline, 02146; 617–277–5430), which arranges stays in inspected private homes, inns, and condominiums. Private rooms, shared or private baths, and breakfast are included; many of the accommodations offer kitchen privileges, laundry facilities, and parking. The reasonable rates generally range from $40–95. Some luxury accommodations are available.

Representing over 150 B&Bs, inns, homestays, and furnished apartments, **Bed & Breakfast Associates, Bay Colony, Ltd.** (P.O. Box 57166, Babson Park Branch, Boston, 02157; 781–449–5302 or 800–347–5088; www.tnn4bnb.com) will match your needs with a conveniently located property—perhaps a brownstone in Back Bay, or a historic home in one of the surrounding towns. Rates range from $75–175 per night; processing fees are additional.

Worth noting: Demand for accommodations in Boston is currently very high, while the supply is relatively low—not the best combination for the traveler. Just because you're paying a lot, don't expect to get a lot. Shop around for the best deals, and consider staying outside the city if appropriate.

For additional area entries, see **Cambridge, Concord, Lynn, Marblehead, Middleborough, Salem, Scituate, Southborough,** and **Sudbury**.

The Eliot 👫 ✕ ♿
370 Commonwealth Avenue, 02215

Tel: 617–267–1607
800–44–ELIOT
Fax: 617–536–9114
E-mail: hoteleliot@aol.com
URL: http://www.BostBest.com

Recognized as one of Boston's most elegant small hotels, the Eliot was built in 1925 by the family of Harvard College president Charles Eliot, and is located adjacent to the Harvard Club. Owned since 1937 by the Ullian family, the hotel was renovated extensively in 1991, and received a four-star rating from Mobil in recognition of their efforts. "We strive to provide an intimate European-style atmosphere," reports owner Dora Ullian, "and are most proud of the compliments we receive about our staff." Restaurant Clio features contemporary French-American cuisine and has received rave reviews from the local media. Entrées include glazed short ribs with corn and truffles; rack of lamb with eggplant tagine; and swordfish with lentils and shallots. The hotel's suites are furnished in traditional English-style chintz fabrics, authentic botanical prints, and antiques. French doors separate the living room from the bedrooms; all rooms have imported marble baths and plush terrycloth robes.

"A European-style hotel with a friendly, professional staff. Big, fluffy bath towels and comfy robes. Our suite was clean and comfortable, and included a small bath with Italian marble. If city noise bothers you, request an inside room." *(Pat Malone)* "Excellent Back Bay location, with all the benefits of being close to shopping on fashionable Newbury Street and to the MTA (subway). You can step outside and stroll down the charming streets of the Back Bay, complete with flowering trees in spring. Request a room on the 'Comm Ave' side for lovely views." *(NB)* "The hotel is beautiful, small, European, and intimate; I was upgraded to a spacious suite. Best of all was the staff, who were kind enough to type out directions to my appointments the next day." *(Meg Daly)* "Our suite of two attractive small rooms had a small entryway, kitchenette, plenty of lights, window seats, large botanical and hunting prints, full-length mirror, and ample seating. The bathroom had a nightlight and lots of towels." *(Jennifer Ball)* "After a long flight and a late arrival it was nice to be greeted by a welcoming, helpful staff." *(Margaret Horn)* "Intelligent, friendly front desk staff." *(Lisa Weiner)* "The helpful staff quickly met our request to change our room from one that faced Commonwealth Avenue to a quieter one. The bathroom was small, but had excellent lighting." *(Susan Ulanoff)*

Open All year.
Rooms 95 1–2 bedroom suites—all with private bath and/or shower, 2 dual-line telephones, personal fax machine, radio, 2 TVs, desk, air-conditioning, mini-bar refrigerator. Most with microwave in mini-pantry.
Facilities Restaurant, bar/lounge, function rooms. Valet parking.
Location Back Bay district. At the corner of Commonwealth & Mass. Aves.
Restrictions 71 non-smoking rooms.
Credit cards Amex, DC, MC, Visa.
Rates Room only, $225–395 one-bedroom suite; $460–550 two-bedroom suite. Extra person, $20. Children under 12 free in parents' room. Breakfast $13. Alc dinner, $40. AAA discount.
Extras Wheelchair access. Complimentary shoe shine and newspaper. Crib, babysitting. Multilingual staff.

BREWSTER

Brewster is located on the bay side of Cape Cod, north of the "elbow." It's about 12 miles northeast of Hyannis, 35 miles west of Provincetown, and is 90 miles southeast of Boston. In addition to the usual activities—swimming at 9 public beaches, fishing, golf, tennis, hiking, bicycling, horseback riding, and antiquing—nearby attractions include the Brewster Historical Society Museum, the Drummer Boy Museum, and the Cape Cod Museum of Natural History.

The Captain Freeman Inn   *Tel:* 508–896–7481
15 Breakwater Road, 02631   800–843–4664
                                        Fax: 508–896–5618
                          E-mail: visitus@capecod.net
                     URL: http://www.captfreemaninn.com

Captain William Freeman was a wealthy shipmaster who acquired his fortune in the clipper ship trade. No expense was spared when he built his home in 1866, complete with ornate plaster moldings, inlaid floors, marble fireplaces, and nine-over-nine windows. Purchased in 1991 by Carol and Tom Edmondson, the inn is decorated with Victorian antiques and artwork. An accomplished cook, Carol conducts off-season cooking classes, complete with wine tasting and a dinner party, but her guests enjoy her expertise year-round. Breakfast menus feature Cape

Cod's famous cranberries: from cranberry granola to cranberry pineapple bread, cranberry applesauce to cranberry scones. The hot entrée might be corn and cinnamon pancakes with Canadian bacon, or shrimp and prosciutto omelets; in good weather, the meal is served on the porch, by the swimming pool.

"Ideal location for everything from biking the Cape Cod Rail Trail, to browsing in nearby antique and art shops, to marveling at unbelievable sunsets while walking on the clean, quiet beaches. Hosts Carol and Tom were available but never overbearing or intrusive. Inviting screened porch, with cooling Cape breezes. Breakfasts and mid-afternoon snacks were homemade and healthy. Brewster is low-key and non-touristy, respectful of nature, beauty, and history." *(Eleanor Rulm)* "A lovely inn, beautifully decorated. Large suites with fireplaces; entertainment centers hidden discretely in armoires." *(Rose Ciccone)* "The inn is set far back from the road, making the wraparound veranda a pleasant place for breakfast or a nap. It's a short walk to the general store and Breakwater Beach." *(Steve Sennott & Ann Jordahl)* "Our favorite room has a set of French doors leading out to a private whirlpool spa on a balcony directly off the room." *(Antonietta Hallet)* "Attention to detail evident in the restaurant menus, area information, and afternoon snacks." *(Mr. & Mrs. Jay Baudier)* "Early morning coffee was greatly appreciated." *(Lauri Adley & Bill Knowles)* "Our room had a canopy bed, settee, wing chair, and a fireplace ready to light." *(Mary Bossart)* "Wonderful winter afternoon treat of homemade ginger cookies and hot cider." *(Lois Rudnick)* "From our favorite room we can look out one window to the church; out another is a spot of ocean." *(Robert & Celine Fahey)* "Finding special toiletries in the bathroom, and chocolate-dipped strawberries on our bed in the evening were added bonuses." *(James & Nancy Stockwell)*

Open All year.

Rooms 3 suites, 9 doubles—all with private bath and/or shower. Suites with telephone, TV/VCR, stereo, air-conditioning, fireplace, refrigerator, balcony, whirlpool tub. 8 rooms with fan.

Facilities Breakfast room with fireplace, parlor with games, books, audio tapes; guest refrigerator, screened-in porch. 1½ acres with swimming pool, badminton, croquet court, gardens, bicycles. On-site parking.

Location Center of town. From Brewster, turn right at intersection of Rte. 124 and Rte. 6A. Turn left on Breakwater Rd. to inn on left.

Restrictions No smoking. Children over 10.

Credit cards Amex, MC, Visa.

Rates B&B, $105–325 suite, double. Extra person, $30–35. Sat. off-season cooking class/wine tasting/dinner party. 2-night minimum in season.

The Inn at the Egg ¢ 🏃
1944 Old King's Highway, P.O. Box 453, 02631

Tel: 508–896–3123
800–259–8235
Fax: 508–896–6821
E-mail: innegg@capecod.net
URL: http://www.innattheegg.com

Located right on the town common and across from the Cape's famous Brewster General Store is the Inn at the Egg. The common has long been known as the "Egg" because of its distinctive oval depression. The inn itself has an equally rich history, dating back to 1854 when Captain Benjamin Bangs gave his home to the First Parish Church for use as a parsonage. In 1865, author and preacher Horatio Alger, Jr., lived here. It's now owned by Joan Vergnani and Diane McDonald, who have decorated the inn with a light, uncluttered look. The furnishings are eclectic, with a Colonial look in some rooms, country Victorian or contemporary in others. The guest rooms are named after historic town buildings, and contain memorabilia, both light-hearted and serious, that depict their significance. A "candlelight and crystal" breakfast is served from 8:30–9:30 A.M.; menus change daily, but might include vegetable frittata, cranberry pancakes with walnuts, or cinnamon French toast with glazed grapes.

"Incredibly hospitable, helpful innkeepers." *(Lisa Hull)* "Spotless. Delicious breakfast." *(Marjorie Curran)* "We felt the owners were still having fun running a B&B; we received a warm welcome with attention to our individual needs." *(Donna Aynesworth)* "Joan was helpful with sightseeing information. It's a five-minute walk to a beautiful, secluded beach." *(Mike Gould)* "Relaxing music played softly during the day. Easy drive to the National Seashore. Joan was personable and informative." *(Judy Mereschuk)* "A cheerful, bright, immaculate inn. Convenient parking and location. Diane welcomed us with a tray of coffee and cookies—a treat after a long day." *(Katie Moore)* "Delightful evening in front of the fire, sampling delicious chocolate cake Joan and Diane had left out for us." *(Jessie & Bill Perry)* "The family suite was the perfect spot for the four of us; there was lots of space, two bedrooms, a long hall, new bath, and a separate entrance." *(Pamela Jones)* "Welcoming notes and glasses of sherry." *(Janet Lang)*

Open All year.

Rooms 2 suites, 3 doubles—all with private bath and/or shower, TV, air-conditioning. 1 with fan, deck. 2 with private entrance.

Facilities Living room with fireplace, books; breakfast room with stereo. On-site parking. 1 acre with lawn games. ½ m to Cape Cod Bay.

Location In center of town. Take Rte. 6 to Exit 10. Turn left onto Rte. 124. Continue to end of 124 to Rte. 6A. Turn right onto 6A, then right again into first driveway.

Restrictions No smoking.

Credit cards Amex, MC, Visa.

Rates B&B, $115–195 suite, $79–115 double. Extra person, $25.

Extras Station pickups. Spanish spoken.

Old Sea Pines Inn ¢ ✕   *Tel: 508–896–6114*
2553 Main Street, P.O. Box 1070, 02631   *Fax: 508–896–8322*

Though it was founded in 1907 as the Sea Pines School of Charm and Personality for Young Women, the Sea Pines now welcomes people of *all* ages and sexes to partake of its charm. Michele and Steve Rowan bought the abandoned school in 1977 and opened it as an inn in 1981, after doing virtually all the renovation work themselves. A typical breakfast might include orange juice, honeydew melon, and eggs Benedict; or cranberry juice, grapefruit, omelets-to-order, and home-baked blueberry muffins. Seafood dominates the menu at night, and a typical dinner might be New England clam chowder; scallop, shrimp, and cod medley; salad with poppy seed dressing; and homemade strawberry shortcake.

"Peace and tranquility. The decor and relaxed atmosphere reminds me of the mood of an F. Scott Fitzgerald novel. The tasty meals are presented in the light and pleasant dining room. Steve and Micki are friendly and helpful, willing to help with suggestions for restaurants, museums, shopping, beaches, and more. Guest rooms are quiet, clean, and attractive, with comfortable beds, great showers, and claw-foot tubs with lots of hot water." *(Donna Lanigan)*

"Homemade lemonade, tea, and coffee are served in the late afternoon. The large living room, complete with a huge fireplace, has period furniture, lots of magazines and books; the equally spacious wraparound porch is well equipped with green wicker rockers, chairs and tables, and amazing floral baskets. Our room had a private bath across the hall, a working fireplace, private enclosed porch and good, solid furniture. Attractive grounds, with pine trees to screen any road noise; ample parking." *(Sandie Blackie)*

"The small double rooms with shared baths are a bargain; ours was prettily furnished with a brass bed. Our second night was in the North Cottage, which was immaculately clean, light, and airy." *(Dr. & Mrs. W. J. Moore)* "Our spotless room in the cottage unit at the back of the property had a king-size bed and a pink color scheme. Loved the hardwood floors and the long veranda with rockers. Every morning the innkeepers put a pot of coffee in the hall for early risers. A great breakfast buffet with lots of fresh fruit." *(Werner & Shirley Ziolokowski)*

Open All year.

Rooms 2 suites, 19 doubles—16 with private bath and/or shower, 5 with a maximum of 4 people sharing bath. 16 with air-conditioning, 7 with TV, 5 with fan. Some with fireplace, porch.

Facilities Dining room, bar, 2 living rooms with fireplace, wraparound porch. 3½ shaded acres. Room service available. On-site parking.

Location Take Exit 10 off Mid-Cape Hwy. (Rte. 6E) & follow Rte. 124 to end. Turn right (Main St.) & go 1 m to inn on left.

Restrictions No smoking.

Credit cards Amex, CB, DC, MC, Visa.

Rates B&B, $110–155 suite, $55–115 double. Extra person, $20. 3-night holiday, weekend minimum May 31–Oct. 15. Alc dinner, $25.

Extras Wheelchair access; some rooms equipped for the disabled. Italian, German spoken.

CAMBRIDGE

Just because Cambridge is just across the Charles River from the city of Boston don't assume that they are cut from the same cloth. Cambridge is Harvard and MIT, intellectuals and activists, street musicians and students, art cinemas, cool jazz, coffee houses, bookstores, and ethnic restaurants. For a city of just 90,000 people, 25 percent of whom are students, Cambridge has two exceptional museums, the Fogg (32

Quincy Street) with its Impressionist and Post-Impressionist paintings and the Sackler (Quincy Street and Broadway) with its Oriental and Islamic collections. Be aware that accommodations are very hard to come by during any major college event, either in Cambridge or Boston, so plan ahead—far ahead.

Also recommended: A 120-room hotel in the heart of the square, **The Charles Hotel in Harvard Square** (One Bennett Street, 02138; 617–864–1200 or 800–882–1818), is constructed of red brick in a contemporary box-on-box style, and combines a light decorative touch with a full complement of luxury amenities. Framed quilts line a stairway, original artwork adorns every room, and large windows frame a river view. Rarities, the hotel restaurant, has top ratings from local critics, while the Bennett Street Café offers bistro fare; the lounge, Regattabar, is a top jazz club. "Every amenity—from a TV and telephone in the bath, to a lap pool and the choice of two fitness centers. Friendly, polite, accommodating staff." *(Patti Ravancho)* Double rates are $225–389; suites to $599.

Information please: A lavishly restored 1892-frame Victorian house, **A Cambridge House** (2218 Massachusetts Avenue, 02140; 617–491–6300 or 800–232–9989 or www.acambridgehouse.com) is furnished throughout with beautiful antiques and rich fabrics. B&B double rates of $99–275 include breakfast, afternoon wine and cheese, tea and cookies, evening sherry, and chocolates. Sixteen guest rooms are available in the main house and in the restored carriage house. The inn is a 20-minute walk from Harvard Square, 20 minutes drive or subway ride to downtown Boston.

At the university-owned **Inn at Harvard** (1201 Massachusetts Avenue, 02138; 617–491–2222 or 800–222–TREE), built in 1991, a skylight fills the four-story Italian Renaissance–style atrium lobby with light. A custom-made Oriental rug and an ample supply of wing chairs and plump sofas give the atrium a clubby feeling, more like a living room than a hotel lobby. Most of the hotel's quiet, understated rooms overlook the university grounds, and are decorated in soft beige tones with cherry wood furnishings. Double rates for the 113 guest rooms range from $189–239.

A reasonably priced alternative is **A Bed & Breakfast in Cambridge** (1657 Cambridge Street, 02138: 617–868–7082 or 800–795–7122; doaneperry@compuserve.com), just a 5-minutes' walk to Harvard Yard, museums, shops, restaurants, and the subway. Built in 1897, the Colonial Revival house has three guest rooms on the third floor. Each has a telephone with voicemail and data port, clock/radio, and TV, but share one bathroom. Breakfast is included in the $75–125 rates, and might consist of sesame-orange spice bread, blueberry pancakes, and cranberry muffins. "Creative, light breakfasts with homemade jams. Safe neighborhood." *(Amy Magnussen)*

The Mary Prentiss Inn ♿   *Tel: 617–661–2929*
6 Prentiss Street, Cambridge, 02140   *Fax: 617–661–5989*

Listed on the National Register of Historic Places, the Mary Prentiss Inn was built in 1843 in the Greek Revival style, and was restored and expanded to open as an inn in 1992 by Charlotte Forsythe and Gerald Fandetti; their daughter-in-law Jennifer Fandetti is the manager. Rates include a full breakfast, with a menu that changes daily.

"Our lovely room featured a tiled bath with one of Charlotte's artistic masterpieces, called chardware, a Victorian crazy quilt made from broken pieces of china and glass—from teacups to watch faces—embedded in the wall. The bath itself was painted and papered in shades of green and rose. English milled soaps rested in a shell-shaped, footed antique silver dish. In the bedroom, sunlight flooded in through the original wood shutters, casting shadows over the fireplace mantle and the wide-planked floors. Yellow chintz fabrics covered the queen-size bed and skirted table, and were complemented by a vase of fresh miniature daffodils. An antique armoire concealed the TV; hidden behind louver doors was a little kitchenette. Botanical prints, antique hat boxes atop the armoire, lace curtains, Oriental rugs, a comfortable loveseat facing the fireplace, a wing chair and a tufted bench at the foot of the bed all added charm. Breakfast was served by a roaring fire in the common room, with copies of the *New York Times* and the *Boston Globe* provided. Rooms in the inn's newer section have sleeping lofts, a good choice for families." *(BNS, also Pru Bell)* "Friendly innkeepers, appealing decor, inviting deck and porch. Most guests at this in-town inn are discerning business people, academics, and parents of college students; many were from Europe. Our small suite had a separate sitting room and refrigerator, microwave and coffee maker." *(Erni Johnson, also MW)*

Open All year.
Rooms 5 suites, 15 doubles—all with full private bath, telephone, radio, clock, TV, air-conditioning. Most with kitchenette, desk; 3 with wood-burning fireplace; some with sleeping loft; 2 with Jacuzzi. Microwave on request.
Facilities Breakfast room with fireplace, stereo. Garden deck, off-street parking.
Location ½ m N of Harvard Sq. From Mass. Pike (I-90), take Cambridge/Brighton exit to Storrow Dr. W. Exit at Harvard Sq. Continue over the Charles River onto JFK St., to Harvard Sq. Continue to Mass. Ave. N. Turn right on Prentiss approx. ½ m from sq.
Restrictions No smoking.
Credit cards Amex, MC, Visa.
Rates B&B, $119–229 suite, $99–159 double. Extra person, $25. AAA discount. 2-night minimum some weekends.
Extras Limited wheelchair access.

CHATHAM

Chatham is located at Cape Cod's "elbow," on the south shore, with Nantucket Sound on one side and the Atlantic Ocean on the other. In addition to the beaches for swimming and other water sports, there is fine saltwater fishing, both amateur and commercial, tennis, golf, a railroad museum, and a 1797 wind-powered grist mill; the Cape Cod National Seashore is nearby. Chatham is approximately 90 miles southeast of Boston. To reach Chatham, take Route 6 to Route 137 South, then follow Route 28 east into town.

Worth noting: Local health department regulations limit most Chatham B&Bs to serving "continental plus" breakfasts.

Reader tip: "The Impudent Oyster offers fine dining in a casual atmosphere. Excellent menu." *(Rose Ciccone)*

Also recommended: If you prefer the atmosphere of an old-time beach resort, the **Chatham Bars Inn** (Shore Road, 02633; 508–945–0096 or 800–527–4884; www.chathambarsinn.com) combines old-fashioned elegance with a comfortable family atmosphere, attractive rooms and good food. There's a free activity program for kids in summer (including a new program for teens), and enticing theme weekends for adults in the cooler months. Economic imperatives require this resort to book a great many business groups off-season, so ask for details when booking. "Attractive location, gracious staff. The veranda, sitting rooms, lobby area, restaurant and tavern were all well-attended and comfortable." *(Rose Ciccone)* Double rates for the 150 rooms range from $100–380, depending on room and season; suites higher.

For a first-class, full-service resort, a fine choice is the **Wequassett Inn** (Pleasant Bay, 02633; 508–432–5400 or 800–225–7125; www.wequassett.com), a 104–guest room complex of 20 buildings—some dating to the 18th century, others to the 1980s—combining the weathered shingled look of Cape Cod with the attention to decor and amenities that merits a four-diamond rating from the AAA. Many rooms have been redone with quilted bedspreads and reproduction pine furnishings for a charming country look, while the resort's waterside setting is exceptionally lovely. Double rates range from $100–510, with meal plans and package rates available; ask about off-season rates, too.

Information please: Built by a prominent whaling captain in 1839, the **Moses Nickerson House** (364 Old Harbor Road, 02633; 508–945–5859 or 800–628–6972; tmnhi@capecod.net) is a stately Greek Revival home surrounded by flower gardens; the beach and village are within easy walking distance. Owners Linda and George Watts offer a full breakfast, served in the glass-enclosed dining area. B&B rates for the seven guest rooms range from $99–199.

Located on a quiet street a short stroll from town, **The Old Harbor Inn** (22 Old Harbor Road, 02633; 508–945–4434 or 800–942–4434; www.capecod.net/oldharborinn) was built in 1932 for a locally prominent doctor. Decorated in English country–style with traditional furnishings and antiques, the inn has 8 guest rooms, two of which have gas fireplaces and sitting areas; all have private baths and air-conditioning. Guests may linger over continental breakfast buffet in the sun room or the adjoining outdoor deck; it's served at individual tables between 8 and 9:30 A.M. B&B rates range from $99–199. "Casual elegance, with uncluttered rooms done in charming floral patterns. Wonderful location; a short walk and you are in the midst of the galleries and boutiques." *(Pam Phillips)*

For additional area entries, see **East Orleans** and **Harwich Port.**

The Captain's House Inn of Chatham ♿   *Tel:* 508–945–0127
371 Old Harbor Road, 02633   800–315–0728
                        Fax: 508–945–0866
E-mail: capthous@capecod.net
URL: http://www.captainshouseinn.com

The Captain's House was built in the Greek Revival style by Captain Hiram Harding in 1839. The original random-width pumpkin-pine floors, fireplaces, and antiques are complemented by four-poster and fishnet-canopied beds. In 1993, this luxurious inn was purchased by Dave and Jan McMaster. Recent improvements include the expansion of the dining room, with French doors leading to a brick patio with a small pond, as well as the addition of the Stables, with several luxury rooms with whirlpool tubs, fireplaces, and more.

Breakfast is served from 8–10 A.M. at individual tables, with a hot entrée (maybe lemon yogurt pancakes with cranberry syrup or crustless ham quiche), plus homemade breads and muffins, English muffins, raisin toast, granola, orange juice, and fresh fruit. English tea, with cream scones and jam, cakes, and cookies, all baked fresh daily, is served from 4–5 P.M.; hot chocolate, tea, coffee, and a filled cookie jar are set out each evening; and turndown service is available on request.

"Jan and Dave have a staff of young energetic students from both local schools and a hotel management school in England. Breakfast and afternoon tea are served in a lovely room with floor-to-ceiling windows on three sides, overlooking the gardens. Hanging plant baskets and the slate floor add to the feeling of dining outdoors. The fruit course was poached pears, followed by ginger pancakes with ham. An assortment of teas was available. At tea-time, English scones with raspberry jam and whipped cream were accompanied by such treats as orange spice cookies and jelly roll cake. The kitchen is open to the guests, and spring water, ice, as well as tea and coffee, are always available. The grounds are lovely, with formal, semi-walled gardens and a fountain.

"Our spacious room, the Wild Pigeon, was in the carriage house on the second floor, and had a cathedral ceiling. The queen-size lace canopy bed had reading lamps on both sides of the bed. A phone and answering machine were tucked away in a drawer to be connected if desired. The bathroom contained an assortment of shampoo, conditioners, lotions, and a hair dryer." *(Rose Ciccone)*

Open All year.
Rooms 4 suites, 15 doubles—all with private bath and/or shower, air-conditioning, telephone, hairdryer, iron, clock/radio. 13 with fireplace, 3 with oversize whirlpool tubs, robes, TV/VCR, refrigerator, coffee maker, patio/deck. Rooms in 4 buildings.
Facilities Living room with fireplace, dining room. 2¼ acres with patio, pond, gardens, fountain, croquet, bicycles. ¼ m to ocean.
Location ½ m from town. At rotary at top of Main St., turn left on Old Harbor Rd. (Rte. 28) toward Orleans. Inn on left ½ m ahead.
Restrictions No smoking. No children under twelve.
Credit cards Amex, MC, Visa.
Rates B&B, $250–325 suite, $120–275 double. Off-season rates, packages.

Cyrus Kent House Inn
63 Cross Street, 02633

Tel: 508–945–9104
800–338–5368
Fax: 508–945–9104
URL: http://www.cyruskent.com

The Cyrus Kent House has been a presence in Chatham's history since 1877. Built by a prosperous sea captain, the house is embellished with marble fireplaces, elaborate plaster moldings, and brass hardware. Sharon Mitchell Swan, who has owned the inn since 1993, offers rooms in both the white clapboard house and the carriage house. Guest rooms feature wide-board floors, most with four-poster or canopy queen-size beds. Breakfast is served at individually set tables and includes juice, a hot or fresh fruit compote, granola, yogurt, and home-baked muffins.

"Sharon has used the sense of color and style she developed as a buyer in the fashion industry to decorate the inn with elegance." *(DLG)* "Located on a quiet street, yet within walking distance of everything in Chatham. Sharon is a warm, friendly, helpful innkeeper. Rooms are beautifully decorated, quiet, and private; the breakfast is leisurely, flexible, and healthy." *(Don McKillop & Susan Davy)* "Victorian elegance." *(Wayne Byrnes)*

Open All year.
Rooms 2 suites in carriage house, 7 doubles—all with private bath and/or shower, telephone, clock/radio, TV. 4 with air-conditioning, 3 with fireplace, fan; 2 with desk, deck.
Facilities Dining room, living room with fireplace, piano; porch. 1 acre with off-street parking. Short walk to beaches.
Location Village historic district. Take Rte. 6 (Mid-Cape Hwy.) to Rte. 137, Exit 11. Go S on Rte. 137 to end at Rte. 28. Go left on Rte. 28 to center of town. Turn right at Cross St. to inn on left.
Restrictions No smoking. Children 10 and over.
Credit cards Amex, MC, Visa.
Rates B&B, $125–250 suite, $95–155 double. Extra person, $25. Senior, AAA discount. 2-night weekend minimum.

Port Fortune Inn
201 Main Street, 02633

Tel: 508–945–0792
800–750–0792
Fax: 508–945–0792
E-mail: porfor@capecod.net
URL: http://www.capecod.net/portfortune

Port Fortune was the name Samuel de Champlain gave to Chatham in 1606, and Mike and Renee Kahl decided to honor that history when they renamed and redecorated their inn in 1996. Located just 100 yards from the ocean, the inn dates back to 1910, and offers water views from its dining room and several guest rooms. The ideal location is an easy walk to Lighthouse Beach and the shops, restaurants, and galleries of Chatham village. The buffet breakfast includes freshly baked breads and coffee cake, cereals, juice, and fruit salad, and is available from 8–10 A.M. in season.

"Beautifully renovated and redecorated. The inn is comprised of two buildings: the one in front (formerly a restaurant) now houses the breakfast room and three luxurious guest rooms, all with water views; behind it is the original large Cape Cod–style shingled house. All guest rooms have been redone with new furniture, including four-poster pineapple or Shaker-style queen-size beds, and upgraded bathrooms. Our ocean-view room in the front building had two wing-back chairs with foot stools, a floor lamp, Queen Anne–style chest, bedside tables, and ginger jar lamps. Good-quality snowy-white linens with lace edging, a white Williamsburg-style coverlet, additional pillows and a hypo-allergenic mattress pillow made the bed very comfortable. Flower-print window swags matched the bed's dust ruffle and accent pillows. The room was painted pale lemon-yellow with white trim, with two nice prints on the walls. The spotless bathroom had ample amenities, storage space, and thick towels. Breakfast included coffee, tea, juices, cereals and granola, a bowl of fresh-cut apples, oranges and grapes, and two coffee cakes; the *Boston Globe* was available for guests to read. Tables for two and four are well-spaced for privacy." *(Rose Ciccone)* "I was reluctant to try a B&B for fear of in-your-face-innkeepers and overwhelming bric-a-brac. Port Fortune was a perfect choice. Ideal location, lovely uncluttered decor, and complete privacy." *(Frank Rossini)* "Outstanding location across the street from the water. Just around the corner is Main Street with its shops and restaurants. The inn is located in a tranquil residential area." *(MH, also Arlene Bowland)*

Open All year.

Rooms 2 suites, 14 doubles—all with full private bath, telephone, radio, clock, air-conditioning, fan, individual thermostat. 1 with TV, desk. 3 rooms in front building; 11 in main house. 2 suites with TV, refrigerator. Whirlpool tub may be added to some rooms in 1999.

Facilities Dining room; 2 living rooms with games, books; 1 with fireplace, guest refrigerator. 1 acre with brick patio, gardens, off-street parking. Short walk to Lighthouse Beach.

Location Take Rte. 6 (Mid-Cape Hwy.) to Exit 11; turn left onto Rte. 137 S. Continue 3 m to end at Rte. 28. Go left onto Rte. 28 (Main St.). Stay on Main St. for 4 m, through rotary & Chatham Center, to Shore Rd. Turn right onto Shore Rd. Take 1st right onto Hallett Lane, right again into the inn's parking lot.

Restrictions No smoking. Children 8 and over.

Credit cards Amex, MC, Visa.

Rates B&B, $90–180 double. Extra person, $20. 2–3 night weekend/holiday minimum. Inquire for suite rates.

CONCORD

Famous for both its history and literature, Concord remains an elegant New England town, despite the hordes of tourists who regularly descend on it. In addition to a walking tour of the homes and museums devoted to the American Revolution and authors Alcott, Thoreau, and Emerson, we'd suggest renting a canoe for a relaxing paddle on the slow-moving Concord River.

Also recommended: Just six miles west of Concord is the **Amerscot House** (61 West Acton Road, Stow, 01775; 978–897–0666) a 250-year-old farmhouse owned by Doreen and Jerry Gibson. Each of its three guest rooms has a private bath, telephone, and cable TV. The B&B double rates of $95–115 include afternoon tea with scones. "Doreen and Jeffrey made us feel like family, welcoming us with sherry and a warm fire. The electric blankets were on, the bed turned down when we returned after dinner. The delicious breakfast included perfect fruit, eggs, and sausages, and best of all, conversation with the Gibsons." *(Karen Schultz, also Betty Norman)* "Excellent dinner recommendations." *(Jan Rasmussen)* "Fresh flowers in every room; modern, functional plumbing; fluffy, heavy-weight towels." *(Donna Gates)*

For additional area entries, see **Sudbury**.

The Hawthorne Inn 🐾
462 Lexington Road, 01742

Tel: 978–369–5610
Fax: 978–287–4949
E-mail: hawthorneinn@concordmass.com
URL: http://www.concordmass.com

Longtime owners Gregory Burch and Marilyn Mudry note that their "land was once owned by Ralph W. Emerson, the Alcotts, and Nathaniel Hawthorne, and was twice surveyed by Thoreau." The inn, built in 1870, is decorated with quilts handmade by Marilyn; a varied assortment of antiques, including Sheraton, Federal, and Empire canopy beds, Empire and Victorian love seats and divans, and Windsor chairs and rockers; and a great deal of ancient and modern art, including pre-Columbian ceramics, Japanese prints, and Gregory's own sculptures. The generous, family-style breakfast is served from 8–9:30 A.M., and includes home-baked breads and muffins, jams, fresh fruit, granola, yogurt, and juice.

"A beautifully decorated and well-maintained older home. Our ample bathroom had a large sink and great water pressure. Our children were welcomed, and served juice at tea-time. There is even a secret hiding place filled with toys." *(Wendy Scully)* "The aroma of fresh baked goods lingers in the hallways. Bedrooms are charming, comfortable, and clean. Each bears a name of local significance (Walden, Concord, Emerson), and blends traditional American furnishings with modern conveniences. With each visit, there is a new work of art to command interest; a new lamp or fine piece of furniture to enhance the house." *(David Dasch)* "Innkeepers are well-informed about Concord and its history." *(Angela Foote)* "Set well back from the main road into Concord. Lighthearted, eclectic charm. Gregory and Marilyn were friendly and welcoming, as were their dog and cats. Helpful with restaurant recommendations." *(SWS)*

Open All year.

Rooms 7 doubles—all with private bath and/or shower, radio, air-conditioning. Some with telephone, desk.

Facilities Dining room, parlor with fireplace. 1½ acres with paths, meditation areas. Off-street parking. 1½ m to Walden Pond for swimming, fishing; 1½ m to Concord River for canoeing, fishing. Cross-country skiing nearby.

Location NE MA. 19 m W of Boston. ⁸⁄₁₀ m E of center in historic zone. From Rtes. 128 & 95, take Exit 30B for 3½ m. Bear right at the second blinking light. Go 1 m to inn on left, across from the Wayside.

Restrictions No smoking.
Credit cards Amex, Discover, MC, Visa.
Rates B&B, $150–215 double; $115–150 single. Extra person, $20. Reduced rates for children, families.
Extras Station pickups by arrangement. Crib, swings, treehouse, games.

DEERFIELD

Old Deerfield consists of a mile-long street of buildings dating back to the early 19th century that, since 1952, have been restored by the Historic Deerfield Foundation. Most of the buildings are lived in by staff members of the Foundation, and by faculty members at Deerfield Academy. Fourteen of the buildings are open to the public as museums.

For additional area entries, see **Leverett, Northampton,** and **North New Salem.**

Deerfield Inn ✕ ⅋ ♦
81 Old Main Street, 01342

Tel: 413–774–5587
800–926–3865
Fax: 413–773–8712
E-mail: frontdesk@deerfieldinn.com
URL: http://www.deerfieldinn.com

The Deerfield Inn was built in 1884 but was seriously damaged by fire in 1979. Fortunately, students, staff, and townspeople arrived with the firefighters and saved virtually all the inn's valuable antiques. The rebuilt inn opened in 1981, with most of its 19th-century atmosphere intact, and with modern heating, cooling, and fire safety systems. Now under the hands-on management of innkeepers Karl and Jane Sabo, the inn is in fine shape, improving each year. Dinners at the inn might include such entrées as sesame-crusted salmon with black beans, osso buco of venison with risotto, and grilled chicken over pasta with a tomato Zinfandel sauce. Formal lunches are served in the restaurant in September and October, although the coffee shop is open for lunch year-round.

The parlors and dining rooms are filled with 18th- and 19th-century antiques, while guest rooms are decorated with antiques and reproduction furnishings, accented with coordinating fabrics and wallpapers. Breakfast features a buffet with homemade granola, yogurt, cereals, sweet breads, muffins, donuts, and fruit, starting at 7:30 A.M.; from 8–9 A.M. (until 10 A.M. on weekends) a hot breakfast is served with a choice of entrées. Rates also include afternoon tea.

"The dining room is great, bordering on superb." *(Peter Overing)* "Our room was spotless, our dinner excellent." *(Mrs. Floyd Calley)* "Relaxing afternoon tea in the comfortable living room. Later, I dined by candlelight, with Vivaldi playing softly in the background." *(Marjorie Felser)* "The rooms are well-decorated with period reproduction furniture, handsome wall coverings, and coordinated window treatments. Wonderful breakfasts: excellent cheddar cheese and tomato omelet with whole-grain toast, French toast with great bread, too." *(SWS)*

"Lived up to its reputation for comfort, lovely decor, and good food. Very professional staff. It was nice to walk out of the hotel into a living museum." *(Bill Hussey)*

Open All year. Closed Dec. 24, 25, 26.
Rooms 23 doubles—all with private bath, telephone, TV, air-conditioning. 12 rooms in annex.
Facilities Restaurant, coffee shop, tavern, lobby with fireplace, 2 parlors with TV; 3 conference rooms. Fax machine. Downhill, cross-country skiing 10–20 m.
Location Central MA; 100 m W of Boston, 40 m N of Springfield. Historic Old Deerfield. From I-91 N, take Exit 24; from I-91 S, take Exit 25. Old Deerfield just off Rtes. 5 & 10 N.
Restrictions No smoking. "Children are always welcome, as long as they are kept under control. Parents are responsible for all damages."
Credit cards Amex, DC, MC, Visa.
Rates B&B, $140–206 double. Crib, $10; cot, $25. 2-night weekend minimum during peak periods. Alc dinner, $25–40.
Extras Wheelchair access; 2 rooms equipped for disabled.

DENNIS

Dennis, located in almost the geographic center of Cape Cod, has stately homes built by sea captains and summer residents, artists' studios, and the Cape Playhouse, where numerous, notable acting careers have been launched since 1927. The Cape Museum of Fine Arts, located on the grounds of the playhouse, displays the work of 20th-century Cape Cod artists.

Dennis is on Cape Cod's North Shore, on Route 6A, 90 miles southeast of Boston and 8 miles northeast of Hyannis. From Mid-Cape Highway (Route 6), take Exit 8 (Union Street) and go north 1.2 miles to Route 6A.

Reader tip: "The beaches of Dennis are two of the most beautiful on the Cape, and may even rival the pristine beaches of the National Seashore, not far away." *(Lon Bailey)*

Isaiah Hall B&B Inn 👫
152 Whig Street, P.O. Box 1007, 02638

Tel: 508–385–9928
800–736–0160
Fax: 508–385–5879
E-mail: isaiah@capecod.net
URL: http://www.virtualcapecod.com/market/isaiahhall/

Cranberries are synonymous with Cape Cod, and it may surprise you to find out the Cape's cranberry industry started right here. Built in 1857, this farmhouse was originally home to Isaiah B. Hall, builder and barrel maker. Isaiah's brother Henry cultivated the first cranberry bogs in America behind the inn. With Yankee ingenuity, Isaiah then proceeded to patent the original cranberry barrel to transport the berries. Marie and Richard Brophy restored the home as an inn in 1984 and have furnished it with antiques, quilts, and Oriental rugs.

"Everything you could want in a relaxed country B&B—a comfortable place for families, with rooms that are both casual and inviting. The light and airy common room is filled with white wicker furniture, attractive for games and casual conversation, plus there's a cozy parlor with a fireplace for chilly fall and winter evenings." *(SWS)* "Impeccably maintained, comfortable inn. Lovely grounds. Ideal location on a quiet residential street, yet a short walk to the beach, shops, Cape Theater, and restaurants." *(Joan Farquhar)* "Marie is both extremely welcoming and well-informed about local activities, attractions, and more. The rooms were delightful, the breakfast delicious, the atmosphere friendly. We sat at a large table with the other guests and shared experiences of Cape Cod." *(Rosanna Nissen)*

"The delicious breakfast always includes fresh fruit, homemade breads, granola, cereals, and juices. The beautiful garden is a delightful place for relaxing or a game of badminton or croquet." *(Beverly Carpenter)* "Marie provided helpful directions and wonderful advice about area activities. The coffee, tea, hot chocolate, and cookies available from early morning to late evening were a thoughtful touch." *(Elsie Rest)* "Fluffy towels, good bedroom lighting, an efficient breakfast setup with tasty choices, and friendly but unobtrusive hosts." *(Bill Hussey)* "The nearby beach has a gradual slope, making it ideal for children. Coffee is ready for early risers." *(Terry Stapleton)*

Open Mid-April–mid-Oct.

Rooms 1 suite, 10 doubles with private bath and/or shower. All with radio, fan, air-conditioning; most with TV/VCR, some with desk, deck/balcony; 1 with fireplace. 4 rooms in carriage house.

Facilities Dining room, parlor with TV, games, library; great room, porch. 1 acre with gardens, lawn games. ½ m from ocean beach, ¾ m from lake. Bicycle trails, golf, tennis nearby.

Location ⅓ m from village. From Union St. intersection with Rte. 6A, turn E (right) & go 3.4 m to Hope Lane (opposite cemetery & church). Turn left on Hope, to end; go right on Whig St. to inn on left.

Restrictions No smoking. Children over 7.

Credit cards Amex, MC, Visa.

Rates B&B, $156 suite, $93–128 double, $83–117 single. Extra person, $17. 10% weekly discount. 2–3 night weekend/holiday minimum June 15–Sept. 5. Midweek rates, April–June 15.

DENNIS PORT

For additional area entries, see **Harwich Port** and **West Harwich**.

The Rose Petal B&B ¢ 🛉 *Tel:* 508–398–8470
152 Sea Street, P.O. Box 974, 02639 *E-mail:* rosepetl@capecod.net
URL: http://www.virtualcapecod.com/market/rosepetal/

Leaving careers in university food service (Princeton and Rutgers) behind, Dan and Gayle Kelly restored the Rose Petal in 1986. They have decorated their home, built in 1872, with antiques and reproductions; guest rooms have been redone with queen-size brass beds, new wallpapers, linens, lace curtains, hand-stitched quilts, stenciled walls, and rugs. Breakfasts vary daily, with such daily specials as Irish eggs Benedict, apple-raspberry crêpes with whipped cream, or breakfast burritos.

"Convenient location, close to the beach. Separate, well-lighted entrances to the guest rooms. My room had a brass bed with a lovely quilt, ample lighting for reading in bed or in the wing chair, and an ironing board in the closet. My bathroom was spotless, with a wall-mounted hairdryer, and individual controls for the heat/air-conditioning. Breakfast is glorious with fresh fruit, cereal, freshly made pastries, muffins, or scones, and the featured item of the day, including my favorite, French toast with bananas foster. Flexible to my needs as a business traveler during my winter visit." *(Richelle Saunders)* "Our room was very clean and nicely furnished. Breakfast was delicious with a different entrée each morning. Fresh towels daily." *(Tatjana & Natalia Vollrath)*

"Convenient location, immaculate housekeeping. The Kellys are helpful, discreet, and friendly, making you feel at home." *(Louise Fortin)* "Extra touches include candles, fresh flowers, and luxurious bathrobes in each room. The Kellys suggested many restaurants and sights to visit." *(Ken & Judy Edge)* "Parking is handy; the house is on a fairly busy street, but our room was quiet." *(Barbara Murphy)* "Much appreciated are the firm mattresses and full-force showers. Dan and Gayle work together in the kitchen to serve wonderful breakfasts that include granola, blueberry turnovers, cranberry muffins, and other treats." *(Barbara Schaefer)* "Large, comfortable rooms; warm and light; impeccably clean." *(Beatrice Tobias)*

Open All year.

Rooms 3 doubles—2 with private bath, 1 with shared bath. All with fan, air-conditioning, hairdryer, clock/radio.

Facilities Dining room, parlor with TV, piano, guest refrigerator. ½ acre with garden, patio. Short walk to beach. Playground nearby.

Location Cape Cod. S Shore, 7 m E of Hyannis. ½ to town. Take Exit 9 off Rte. 6. Turn right onto Rte. 134. Follow to end; turn left onto Lower Cty. Rd. Go 1½ m to Sea St. and turn right, inn is 1st house on left.

Restrictions No smoking.

Credit cards Amex, MC, Visa.

Rates B&B, $55–96 double. Extra person, $12. 2-night minimum holiday weekends.

Extras Limited French spoken.

EASTHAM

Settled by the Pilgrims in 1644, Eastham is located at the "forearm" of the outer Cape, bounded on the east by the Atlantic Ocean and on the west by Cape Cod Bay, roughly halfway between Hyannis and Provincetown, 5 miles north of Orleans.

Reader tip: "The Outer Cape is quiet and beautiful, with miles of natural, unspoiled beaches, yet is still close to great shopping, beautiful villages, good restaurants, and is just off the 30-mile Cape Cod Bike Trail." *(Sue Gratzer)*

The Penny House Inn *Tel:* 508–255–6632
4885 County Road 800–554–1751
Mailing address: P.O. Box 238 *Fax:* 508–255–4893
North Eastham, 02651 *E-mail:* pennyhouse@aol.com
URL: http://www.virtualcapecod.com/pennyhouseinn

Once a prominent Eastham sea captain's home, the Penny House Inn was built in 1751, and restored as an inn in 1988 by William and Margaret Keith. The comfortable guest rooms are simply furnished with antiques, Colonial reproductions, four-poster and canopy beds, and good bedside lighting.

"Well-maintained and ideally located. Margaret is a superb hostess who serves delicious breakfasts, provides great directions, and recommends local restaurants." *(John & Margaret Vallante)* "Beautifully maintained, quiet inn. Elegantly served breakfast." *(Claudia Woodard)* "Extremely clean; beautifully decorated. Friendly, solicitous innkeeper; delicious breakfast with fresh fruit." *(Pamela Graham)* "Coffee and muffins were served immediately after we were seated, followed by omelets, bacon, grapefruit, and more muffins; the next day we had waffles, sausages, and strawberries. This renovated house feels fresh and new, with bright, modern baths." *(Mary Jane Southwick)* "Our spacious room under the eaves had a handsome wooden floor and original ceiling beams, with a queen-size sleigh bed; the different angles of the stenciled walls gave it wonderful character." *(MW)*

"Our room had a queen-size bed, wicker sofa, and a skylight in the wood-paneled ceiling. Margaret's Australian accent lends authenticity to the serving of afternoon tea and scones (off-season)." *(Bruce & Patricia Fuller)* "Margaret is a superb hostess, always bustling in and out of the kitchen, making sure everyone has plenty to eat and drink. Breakfast is served in the sunny dining room, with a potbelly stove, original wide-planked floor, and beamed ceiling." *(Maureen Garron)* "Delightful afternoon tea and scones." *(Christine Gruner)*

Open All year.
Rooms 3 suites, 8 doubles—all with private bath and/or shower, radio, clock. Most with air-conditioning. Some with desk, ceiling fan, refrigerator. 1 with fireplace.
Facilities Dining room, great room with fireplace, TV/VCR, guest refrigerator. 1½ acres with brick patio, off-street parking, lawn games. Bicycling, hiking. Near Nauset Light Beach, Cape Cod Nat'l. Seashore.
Location Follow Rte. 6 past Exit 12 & around rotary at Orleans, heading N toward Eastham/Provincetown. Inn is 5 m beyond rotary on left, across from Nauset Marsh Nursery; watch for gold pineapple on sign.
Restrictions Traffic noise possible in one room. No smoking. Children over 8.
Credit cards All major credit cards accepted.
Rates B&B, $105–175 suite, $95–150 double, $95 single. Extra person, $30. AAA, senior discount. 2–3 night weekend/holiday minimum in season.

The Whalewalk Inn
220 Bridge Road, 02642

Tel: 508–255–0617
Fax: 508–240–0017
E-mail: whalewalk@capecod.net
URL: http://www.whalewalkinn.com

Dick and Carolyn Smith, owners of the Whalewalk, realize that innkeepers "must be there whenever needed, and disappear when not. We're committed to keeping our inn spotless, yet cozy and friendly, filled with the fragrance of fresh flowers." This 1830s whaling master's home has guest rooms beautifully decorated with a light country touch—soft pink, light blue, or fresh green shades contrast with lots of white or cream colors for an uncluttered sunny look. Plump pillows, soft comforters, queen- and king-size beds, and ample bedside lighting assure comfort. Guest rooms are found in the main inn, the restored Barn, the Guest House, the Salt Box Cottage, plus the carriage house, built in 1997, with six handsome guest rooms, each with a four-poster bed, paintings by local artists, fireplace, and air-conditioning.

Breakfast menus change daily. In addition to fresh fruit and juice, the meal might consist of corn muffins, tomato and basil quiche, and scalloped potatoes; followed the next day by drop biscuits, sweet onion frittata, and orange oatmeal pie. For the virtuous, granola with yogurt and fruit are always available. Afternoon hors d'oeuvres are also served, an enjoyable time for guests to mingle and share experiences.

"Convenient location in a quiet residential area. Ample parking, immaculate housekeeping. Attention to detail is impeccable. Top-quality linens and adequate reading lights." *(Jane Chirgwin)* "Carolyn has decorated the rooms wonderfully, balancing aethestics and comfort. Our room in the new carriage house had a gas fireplace, two comfortable chairs, and a private patio; other rooms are equally appealing. Dick's breakfasts are great—hot muffins, juice, coffee, and shirred eggs with herbed home fries or possibly crusted French toast. Quiet setting, a few minutes from the water—spectacular sunsets. Friendly staff, hospitable owners." *(Lillian Fulton)* "Near picturesque Rock Harbor, this inn sits in a lovely salt meadow. Breakfast was served at umbrella-shaded tables on the slate patio, surrounded by the flower gardens." *(Shelly Senator)* "Great care was taken with breakfast, which was beautifully laid in the conservatory, a lovely light room." *(Dr. W.J. Moore)*

Open April–Nov.; some winter weekends.
Rooms 1 cottage, 4 suites, 11 doubles—all with private bath and/or shower, air-conditioning, hairdryer. 7 with kitchen, 8 with patio/balcony, 13 with gas or wood-burning fireplace, 3 with whirlpool tub.
Facilities Living room with fireplace, dining room, sun porch, garden with patio. Bicycles. ½ m to bike path, beach.
Location Take Rte. 6 to Orleans rotary. Go left on Rock Harbor Rd., right on Bridge Rd. to inn on right.
Restrictions No smoking. Children over 12. BYOB.
Credit cards MC, Visa.
Rates B&B, $200 cottage, $200 suite, $150–250 double. Extra person, $30. Off-season, extended rate discounts.

EAST ORLEANS

East Orleans is home to Nauset Beach, one of the Cape's loveliest. Come off-season to walk for miles in blissful solitude. It's located on the north shore of Cape Cod, at the "bend of the elbow," 28 miles northwest of Hyannis, 100 miles southwest of Boston.

For additional area entries, see **Chatham**.

Nauset House Inn ¢   *Tel:* 508–255–2195
143 Beach Road, P.O. Box 774, 02643   *E-mail:* jvessell@capecod.net
                                    URL: http://www.nausethouseinn.com

Diane and Albert Johnson, along with their daughter Cindy and son-in-law John Vessella, have owned Nauset House since 1982. They describe their 1800s farmhouse as a "quiet, old-fashioned country inn. Fresh flowers in each room, edible flowers garnishing breakfast plates, patchwork cats sitting on the beds, and whimsical painted furniture make Nauset House special. We also have a one-of-a-kind conservatory, with Cape Cod flowers and greenery and wicker furniture, attached to our brick-floored pub/dining room." Breakfasts feature home-baked muffins, as well as fresh fruit or juice, plus such specialties such as Portuguese omelets or blueberry pancakes; afternoon refreshments at 5:30 P.M. include wine or cranberry juice and hors d'oeuvres.

"A simple but excellent inn. Always a log fire in the living room and a family member ready to help with plans and reservations. A lovely garden area, game tables, newspapers, and a happy ambience, especially during the wine and treats. Lots of tempting choices at their excellent breakfast. Residential area, yet close to the beach and superior restaurants." *(Ruthie Tilsley)* "The cocktail hour featured tasty dips and crackers. Guests mingled, discussed dinner plans, and chatted about the next day's activities. They also have a little diary with restaurant reviews from past guests; we were encouraged to add our input. The delicious breakfast was served in a beautiful dining room with two large harvest tables, and included homemade granola and ginger pancakes with lemon sauce. Our room was beautifully decorated and provided ample closet and drawer space." *(Lynda Worrell)*

"Quiet, serene atmosphere; helpful innkeepers, who provided valuable hints on exploring the Cape. My room had a lovely homemade quilt on the bed, and walls bordered with a stencil design hand-painted by Diane and Cindy." *(Susan Tirone)* "Our room had a comfortable king-size bed and a small bath." *(AF)* "Guest rooms are small but charming, with beautiful hand-painted wall borders, furnishings, and mirrors. The conservatory is delightful, with Diane's stained-glass windows, white wrought-iron furniture, and lots of plants." *(SWS)* "Even better than we remembered it on our first visit, four years earlier, due to its wonderful innkeepers. Al went beyond the usual restaurant advice, and got us a reservation at a popular place that doesn't normally take them." *(Glenn Roehrig)*

Open April 1–Oct. 31.

Rooms 12 doubles, 1 single, 1 cottage—8 with private shower and/or bath, 6 with maximum of 6 people sharing bath; 5 rooms in carriage house and cottage.

Facilities Living room with fireplace, dining room with fireplace, conservatory, terrace. 2½ acres with picnic tables, gardens. ½ m to Nauset Beach, 3 m to bay, 2 m to lake.

Location 3 m from Orleans. Take Rte. 6 to Exit 12. Go right to 1st light; go right on Eldredge Pkwy. and straight to light. Straight across Rte. 28 (Tonset Rd.) to next light. Right on Main St. to fork in rd. at Barley Neck Inn. Bear left on Beach Rd. to inn ⁸⁄₁₀ m on right.

Restrictions No smoking. Children over 12.

Credit cards Discover, MC, Visa.

Rates B&B, $75–135 double, $65 single. 2-night weekend minimum.

The Parsonage Inn ¢
202 Main Street, P.O. Box 1501, 02643

Tel: 508–255–8217
888–422–8217
Fax: 508–255–8216
E-mail: Innkeeper@Parsonageinn.com
URL: http://www.parsonageinn.com

An authentic Cape Cod–style house dating back to 1770, with wide pine floors and low ceilings, the Parsonage served as a vicarage in the early 1800s. Expanded many times over the years, and restored as an inn in 1983, it was purchased by Ian and Elizabeth Browne in 1991. Breakfast includes Colombian coffee and a wide selection of teas, fresh fruit, cereal, and a selection of muffins, scones, waffles, French toast, or quiche. Guests can be served in the dining room, on the patio, or in their rooms.

"Beautiful, freshly decorated rooms. But the outstanding charm of this place is its owners, Ian and Liz, who seem to truly enjoy their roles as host and hostess. At the end of the day, they invite guests for wine and delicious snacks on the patio. Stories and laughs shared among the guests added to our enjoyment." *(Diana Inman, & others)* "This inn is lovingly cared for by innkeepers who seem to genuinely enjoy looking after their guests. The building is neither grand nor pretentious, but Liz and Ian make staying there a memorable experience. The spacious Barn Room is a comfortable loft room created from the original barn. Breakfast is fresh and creative, served in a sunny and comfortable dining room at tables set for two. Liz and Ian serve wine and cheese in the afternoon, and clearly enjoy entertaining their guests." *(John Felton)* "We were much impressed by the high standard of accommodations, the warm welcome extended by the owners, the professionalism of the business, and the delicious, imaginative breakfasts." *(Michael Doyle)* "Simple but charming country decor. The young English couple who own this inn are special. They learn all their guests' names, and offer some nice extra touches. Liz, a piano teacher, serenaded us with Mozart, Schubert, and Chopin." *(Helen Didriksen)*

Open All year.

Rooms 2 suites, 6 doubles—all with private bath and/or shower, clock, air-conditioning; 3 with TV, 3 with refrigerator, 1 with kitchenette.

Facilities Dining room, living room with fireplace, piano, books; guest refrigerator. ½ acre with off-street parking. 1½ m to beach.

Location 2 m from Orleans. Take Rte. 6 to Exit 12 (Rte. 6A) in Orleans. Bear right onto Rte. 6A, take 1st right onto Eldredge Pkwy. At 2nd light turn right onto Main St. Inn is 1 m on left.
Restrictions No smoking. Children over 6.
Credit cards Amex, MC, Visa.
Rates B&B, $90–125 suite, $80–115 double, $75–110 single. Extra person, $15. 2-night weekend minimum June–Sept. & all holidays.
Extras Bus station pickups.

ESSEX

George Fuller House ¢   Tel: 978–768–7766
148 Main Street, Route 133, 01929   800–477–0148
Fax: 978–447–0148
E-mail: rcameron@shore.net
URL: http://www.cape-ann.com/fuller-house

Built in 1830, the George Fuller House has retained such Federal architectural details as Indian shutters, fireplaces, and original paneling and woodwork. It was restored as an inn in 1988 by owners Bob and Cindy Cameron, who continue to improve the inn each year. Most recently, they created the Doyle Suite. On the ground floor, with a sliding glass door leading outside, is a sitting room with a fireplace, bookshelves, TV/VCR, and lots of comfortable seating; a spiral staircase leads to the bedroom, with a beautiful Palladian window facing east, overlooking the marsh. The property adjoins a salt marsh which feeds into the Essex River; in decades past, one could have seen newly launched schooners making their way to Gloucester for outfitting. Breakfasts are served between 7:30 and 9:30 A.M. at the large dining table, at individual porch tables, or in your room. In addition to fresh fruit, juice, cereal, coffee, and tea, a typical breakfast includes homemade English muffin bread with whole cranberries, ham crêpes with apricot sauce, and scrambled eggs.

"We enjoyed the privacy and spaciousness of the top-floor room, complete with breakfast in bed. Essex made a good base for day trips in Massachusetts and southern Maine." *(Susan Doucet)* "Our lovely room overlooking the salt marsh was large and bright with a cathedral ceiling and a skylight. Seven or eight seafood restaurants are within walking distance on the causeway; the town of Essex has over 50 antique stores." *(Bill Hussey, also NB)* "Our spotless room had fresh flowers, hand-made lampshades, and stenciled walls." *(Pauline Fanus)* "A special feature is the daily preference sheets we completed each night for breakfast the next day." *(Danielle Borasky)* "Our second-floor suite had the bedroom on the streetside and a sun room overlooking the marsh. The four-poster bed, facing the fireplace, had a crocheted coverlet and canopy, a set of steps to reach the high, comfortably firm mattress, and good reading lights. Attention to guests' comfort included a bathroom nightlight, excellent water pressure, and good bathroom lighting. Bob and Cindy are native New Englanders, always ready to help, yet respectful of your privacy." *(Bruce Allen)* "Excellent base for trips to Cape Ann, Rockport, Salem, and Marblehead." *(C. Reading)*

Open All year.
Rooms 3 suites, 4 doubles—all with private bath, telephone, TV, air-conditioning, fan. 5 with fireplace. 3 with balcony/deck. 1 with refrigerator.
Facilities Living room with fireplace; screened/unscreened porches. ¼ acre with perennial garden. Sailboat charter, boat tours. Tennis, golf, Cranes Beach nearby.
Location North Shore. 30 m NE of Boston. From I-95, exit on Rte. 128 (Exit 45) continue N to Exit 15. Turn left at stop sign & go 3 m. Turn left on Rte. 133. Inn is 100 yds. on right.
Restrictions Light sleepers should request back rooms. No smoking.
Credit cards Amex, CB, DC, Discover, MC, Visa.
Rates B&B, $120–135 suite, $79–98 double, $70–90 single. Extra person, $10. 2-night summer weekend minimum, also holidays, special events.
Extras Airport pickup, fee charged. Babysitting by arrangement. Wheelchair access; 1 room specially equipped (available spring, 1999).

FALL RIVER

Lizzie Borden B&B Museum   *Tel:* 508–675–7333
92 Second Street, 02721   *Fax:* 508–675–7333
       E-mail: lizziebnb@earthlink.net

If you have a taste for the macabre in lodging and history, consider staying at the Lizzie Borden Bed and Breakfast Museum, the original home of the alleged ax murderess. One of America's most infamous crime scenes, it was renovated as a museum and B&B in 1996 by Martha McGinn and Ron Evans. Martha inherited the house from her grandmother, and she and Ron painstakingly returned it to its 1892 appearance, right down to the sofa where Andrew Borden was found—murdered. While the public is invited to tour the house every half-hour from 11 A.M.–3 P.M., overnight guests receive their own personal tour.

"At precisely 8 A.M., the maid—attired in a long gray dress, white apron, and a ruffled hat—went from floor to floor ringing the bell for breakfast. The menu was similar to the Bordens' last morning meal of Johnny cakes, sugar cookies, and hot oatmeal, plus scrambled eggs with cheese, sausage patties, and fresh pears. Typical of the generous way Martha and Ron treat their guests, Ron offered to take six of us to the Borden gravesite. The very complete house tour included the basement, where one theory has it that Lizzie dropped the infamous hatchet into the privy (the tight-fisted Mr. Borden was supposedly too cheap to install indoor plumbing)." *(Chris Zambito, also MW)* "Mystery and history were emphasized, not murder and violence." *(Michelle Pizzi)* "Fascinated Lizzie buffs come to chat up the case until late in the evening. Books and tapes concerning the mystery are available to peruse or purchase." *(Jane Rimer)* "A must for anyone who likes to be scared by their own imagination." *(Leona Leonard)* "Staff is knowledgeable, friendly, and accommodating. Rooms and bathrooms are immaculate." *(Frances Patterson)* "Despite the house's history, the atmosphere is warm, welcoming, and cozy. Extensive house tour, with new theories and lots of time for questions." *(Robin Martin)* "Immaculately clean. Fantastic library. Delicious hatchet-shaped cookies." *(Nancy & Ken Griffith)*

Open All year.
Rooms 2 suites, 4 doubles—1 with full private bath. 2 on 2nd floor share bath; 3 on 3rd floor share bath. All with air-conditioning, 2 with desk.
Facilities Dining room, parlor with piano, TV/VCR, sitting room with books. Off-street parking.
Location 50 S of Boston, 20 m W of Providence, RI. From I-195, take Exit 7, Plymouth Ave. At bottom of ramp follow sign onto Rte. 81 S. At 2nd set of lights, take right onto Rodman St. (watch for Walgreen's at corner). At 1st set of lights on Rodman, go right onto 2nd st. to inn, 1.5 blocks on right, across from bus station.
Restrictions No smoking. Children 12 and over.
Credit cards Amex, Discover, MC, Visa.
Rates B&B, $150–200 suite, double. Extra person, $50. Tours, $7.50 adults, $3.50 children.

FALMOUTH

Falmouth is 72 miles south of Boston and east of Providence, on the south shore of Cape Cod's "shoulder." It's three miles north of Woods Hole, departure point for the Martha's Vineyard ferries. One delightful way to travel between Falmouth and Woods Hole is via the Shining Sea bike path; some inns have free bikes available to their guests, and rentals are easily available. Area activities include swimming, fishing, boating, bicycling, and golf.

To get to Falmouth from the south, take I-95 North to I-195 East to Route 25 (Cape & Islands exit), and over the Bourne Bridge to Route 28 South. From Boston, take Route 3 South to Sagamore Bridge Circle. Follow Route 6 West to Bourne Bridge Circle, then take Route 28 South into Falmouth.

Reader tip: "Highly recommended the Chapoquoit Grill in West Falmouth for casual dining. No reservations taken but it's worth the wait. Small menu, with many daily specials; reasonable prices and generous portions." *(Rose Ciccone)*

For additional area inns, see **Woods Hole**.

Captain Tom Lawrence House
75 Locust Street, 02540

Tel: 508–540–1445
800–266–8139
Fax: 508–457–5147
E-mail: capttom@capecod.net
URL: http://www.sunsol.com/captaintom/

The Captain Tom Lawrence House was built in the 1860s by a wealthy whaling captain. The high ceilings, hardwood floors, and magnificent circular staircase are original to the structure, but the soft colors and eclectic antiques have a European touch that is the artful work of innkeeper Barbara Sabo-Feller.

"A warm and welcoming innkeeper. Barbara pampered us, providing us with a delicious breakfast of waffles and muffins. She helpfully suggested restaurants and activities, and was wonderful with both teenagers and elderly guests. Bikes and beach chairs always available." *(Kristine Vivet, also Peggy Kontak)* "Quiet music, a fire in the fireplace, personalized service." *(Sylvie Geneau)* "Coffee and tea are set out for early risers. Breakfast (served at 9 A.M.) included fresh coffee, juice, fresh fruit cup with granola, apple crumb cake and muffins, and such favorites as seafood crêpes and Belgian waffles with homemade whipped cream and strawberries. Don't miss the beach, the bike trails, and Main Street with its quaint shops—all within walking distance." *(Lisa Lasorsa)* "Guests share in the lively breakfast table conversation; vacations are enriched by the travel information Barbara supplies." *(Tena Harris & others)*

"We were offered hot tea when we arrived, and given lots of advice about restaurants and activities." *(Abby Seixas)* "Furnishings reflect the period, with excellent reading lamps." *(Carolyn Blouin)* "Even with a full complement of guests, hot water supplies were ample." *(Craig Plunkett)* "Though the road is busy, the inn is set back 100 feet and is quiet." *(MW)* "Beautiful Victorian rooms with four-poster and lace-canopy beds, and down comforters." *(Marty Keough)* "Barbara graciously assisted us with sightseeing information and dining reservations. She had menus from many local restaurants which we loved looking through after a day of exploring." *(Janet Huesman)*

Open Closed Jan.

Rooms 1 apt. with kitchenette, TV, deck, 2 suites, 4 doubles—all with full private bath, central air-conditioning, radio, fan.

Facilities Breakfast room, living room with piano, porch. Off-street parking. 1 m to beach. Bikeway nearby.

Location 5-min. walk to town. 1 m from beach. House is 1st on right after you turn off Rte. 28 onto Locust (Woods Hole Rd.).

Restrictions No smoking. Children over 12. Families OK in apt.

Credit cards MC, Visa.

Rates Room only, $125–165 apt. B&B, $99–140 suite, $90–130 double, $75–120 single. Extra person, $30. 10% senior discount in off-season. 2–3 night minimum in high season.

Extras German spoken.

Grafton Inn Tel: 508–540–8688
261 Grand Avenue South, 02540 800–642–4069
Fax: 508–540–1861
URL: http://www.sunsol.com/graftoninn/

We're beginning to think that Cape Cod may have more inns than sand dunes, yet amazingly few of them are right on the water. If you want to overlook a beautiful beach, make a reservation at the Grafton Inn, built in 1850, and restored as an inn in 1984 by Rudy and Liz Cvitan.

"Room #7 is in the tower, on the third floor, with five windows overlooking Nantucket Sound; it's very private and is decorated with white lace curtains and soft country prints. You can watch the sun rise out of the ocean from the queen-size brass bed. We enjoyed moonlight walks on the beach across the street. The Cvitans are always there to direct guests to the best dining and entertainment, yet are never intrusive." *(Linda & Dennis Kessinger)*

"Unobstructed views of Nantucket Sound and Martha's Vineyard from our table for two in the breakfast room. Marvelous breakfasts of fresh fruit, juices, pecan rolls or muffins (cranberry, pecan, banana walnut), homemade preserves, and choices of such entrées as eggs Benedict, blueberry pancakes, apple crêpes, and French toast. We borrowed towels and beach chairs and crossed the narrow road to the beach, a peaceful place to sun, read, and swim. At lunchtime we walked down the road to the Wharf, a beach restaurant/clam bar, for a couple of cool drinks. After a day on the beach, we returned to the inn for wine, cheese, and crackers. Guest rooms in this Queen Anne Victorian are well-equipped with comfortable queen-size beds, good lighting, ample towels, and English toiletries. Our room on the second floor overlooked the garden, with a water view from the side window. It had a queen-size bed with half-canopy, good reading lights on both sides of the bed, an antique trunk, a double dresser, and a comfortable wing chair. Thoughtful touches included homemade bedtime chocolates, ample supplies of pillows and towels, cool cotton sheets, and a make-up mirror in the bathroom. The ceiling fan and ocean breezes kept us cool even during a heat wave. Owners Liz and Rudy Cvitan are charming hosts." *(Rose Ciccone)* "Just as wonderful on a return visit. Once you've parked your car (free), you never have to move it for the beach, dining, or even the ferry to Martha's Vineyard—everything is within walking distance." *(RC)* "The ideal choice for a summer visit, with a prime location across from the beach. Tasty breakfast." *(Ceci Connolly)* "Every member of the staff has the same friendly, warm personality as the Cvitans themselves." *(Carol McHugh)*

Open Feb. 15–Dec. 15.

Rooms 11 doubles—all with private shower bath, radio, clock, desk, air-conditioning, ceiling fan, telephone, TV, hairdryer, robes. 10 with ocean view.

Facilities Dining room, living room with fireplace, TV/VCR, stereo, books; enclosed porch, guest refrigerator/ice maker. Off-street parking, beach chairs, towels. Beach across street.

Location 1 m to town. Take Rte. 28 S into Falmouth to 1st traffic lights at Jones Rd. & go left onto Jones Rd. through 2 more sets of lights. You are then on Worcester Ct. Go straight to ocean & go right on Grand to inn on right.

Restrictions No smoking. Children over 16.

Credit cards Amex, Discover, MC, Visa.

Rates B&B, $75–169 double. Extra person, $35. 2–3 night weekend/holiday minimum.

Extras Bus station pickups. Limited French spoken.

Mostly Hall B&B
27 Main Street, 02540

Tel: 508–548–3786
800–682–0565
Fax: 508–457–1572
E-mail: mostlyhl@cape.com
URL: http://www.sunsol.com/mostlyhall/

Captain Albert Nye built Mostly Hall in 1849 as a wedding present for his New Orleans bride; listed on the National Register of Historic

Places, it has been owned since 1986 by Jim and Caroline Lloyd. Set well back from the road, this plantation-style home is located on the historic village green. The inn has 13-foot ceilings; grand shuttered windows; an enclosed widow's walk; a spacious wraparound porch; and hallways that dominate three floors—the source of the inn's name. A well-stocked library dominates the second-floor hallway. The guest rooms have canopied queen-size beds, with good lighting and two comfortable reading chairs. Breakfast, served at 9 A.M. on the veranda in warm weather, features low-fat stuffed French toast, eggs Benedict soufflé, or cheese blintzes with blueberry sauce, accompanied by fresh fruit and juice, breads and muffins; refreshments are served in the afternoon.

"Caroline cannot do enough for you and her cooking is heavenly." *(A. Tanner)* "Charming rooms and grounds; delightful innkeepers." *(RC)* "Caroline and Jim are welcoming yet respectful of guests' privacy. The rooms are perfectly clean and beautifully furnished. Laura's Room receives both morning and afternoon sunlight; its colors and decor are bright and cheery. Breakfast is beautifully presented by Caroline; Jim is a great raconteur, interacting with the guests, facilitating conversations, and creating a friendly atmosphere. The grounds are beautiful year-round." *(Terri Freeman)* "Excellent restaurant advice; helpful menu basket. Great library and quaint widow's walk on the top floor, now a TV room. Beautifully prepared breakfasts served with a great sense of humor by the innkeepers." *(Louisa Yue-Chan)*

Open Mid-Feb.–Dec.
Rooms 6 doubles—all with private shower, air-conditioning, radio; 5 with ceiling fan.
Facilities Dining room, living room with piano; widow's walk with TV/VCR, wraparound porch, gazebo with swing. 1¼ acres with bicycles, helmets. 10-minute bike ride to beach. Off-street parking. 3⅓ m bikeway, island ferries nearby.
Location On the village green, in historic district.
Restrictions No smoking. Persons over 16.
Credit cards Amex, Discover, MC, Visa.
Rates B&B, $95–140 double. Honeymoon packages.
Extras Station/ferry pickups. German spoken.

The Palmer House Inn ♿
81 Palmer Avenue, 02540

Tel: 508–548–1230
800–472–2632
Fax: 508–540–1878
E-mail: innkeeper@palmerhouseinn.com
URL: http://www.palmerhouseinn.com

While the term "B&B" is usually understood to mean "Bed & Breakfast," in the case of the Palmer House Inn, "Breakfast & Bed" might be a clearer reflection of this inn's focus. Breakfast is served at two seatings in the dining room with candlelight and classical music, fine china and crystal. Menus vary daily, but might include orange pineapple juice, poached pears with raspberry sauce, pineapple spice scones with whipped butter and apricot jam, potato and leek frittata; or orange banana juice, broiled grapefruit, porridge, pain perdu with orange cream and maple syrup. Afternoon refreshments are served daily; weekends in December, a three-course English tea is served from 2–5 P.M., and includes finger sandwiches, scones with raspberry sauce and clotted cream, assorted desserts, mints, and tea.

Owned by Joanne and Ken Baker since 1990, the Palmer House is a turn-of-the-century Queen Anne Victorian home, with stained-glass windows, elaborate woodwork, and antique furnishings. Guest rooms are decorated with antiques, lace doilies, old photographs, and silk flowers. The Tower Room has a queen-size brass bed and antique wicker, while Grandmother's Room has a queen-size canopy bed and lace curtains. Breakfasts vary daily, but might include orange-mango juice, fruit compote with lime sorbet, cranberry scones with orange marmalade, and herbed cheese omelets.

"Just as appealing on a return visit. We stayed in a gorgeous room in the Carriage House at the back of the property." *(Cecile Desroches, also RC)* "Ken and Joanne Baker are gracious hosts and made my stay comfortable." *(Warren Agin)* "We sampled walnut Belgian waffles, Irish oatmeal with almonds, Mexican breakfast tortillas, and German apple pancakes. Gleaming wood trim and banisters, beautiful stained-glass windows, and a lovely mix of Victorian antiques fill the house. Our room had a queen-size bed with a half canopy, pima cotton sheets, matching down comforter, and balloon swag curtains. Lovely gardens for relaxing." *(Rose & Frank Ciccone)* "Snacks awaited in our little refrigerator, and a note on the bed told us about breakfast, which was as good as promised." *(Al & Lauren Kenney)*

Open All year.
Rooms 12 doubles—all with private bath and/or shower, air-conditioning. 1 cottage suite with private bath, whirlpool tub and kitchen. All rooms with ceiling fan, radio. Some with whirlpool tub, fireplace, refrigerator, air-conditioning, TV. 4 rooms in carriage house.
Facilities Parlor with fireplace, piano, TV, books, games; dining room, lobby with gift shop, wraparound porch. Bicycles. 1 acre with gardens, off-street parking. 1 m to beach; towels provided.
Location Historic district. Follow Rte. 28 through traffic light at Jones Rd. Rte. 28 becomes Palmer Ave. at the bend. Inn is 1st house on left past shops. 1 block from village square.
Restrictions No smoking. No children under 10.
Credit cards Amex, Carte Blanche, DC, Discover, MC, Visa.
Rates B&B, $78–185 double, $68–185 single. Tipping encouraged. 2–3 night weekend/holiday/peak-season minimum. Holiday, honeymoon packages.
Extras Bus station pickups. 1 room wheelchair accessible.

Village Green Inn
40 Main Street, 02540

Tel: 508-548-5621
800-237-1119
Fax: 508-457-5051
E-mail: village.green@cape.com
URL: http://www.villagegreeninn.com/

Built in 1804, the Village Green Inn was "modernized" later in the century with porches and turrets, inlaid floors and stained-glass windows.

The inn is listed on the National Register of Historic Places and has been owned by Diane and Don Crosby since 1995. Early-bird coffee is ready at 7 A.M., and breakfast is served at 8:30 A.M. A typical meal might include juice, a fruit and yogurt parfait, glazed lemon knots, and chili-cheese egg puffs. Rates also include afternoon snacks and beverages, plus in-room fresh flowers and chocolates.

"Great location, across from the Green, within walking distance of shops and restaurants. Guest comfort is obviously a priority to the friendly innkeepers. Breakfast is served around the dining room table, where everyone is made to feel at home." *(Kathie Farlow)* "Exceptionally warm and caring atmosphere; wonderful innkeepers." *(Kendall Sanderson)* "Don came out to meet us and help with our bags. After checking in, we were offered refreshments and the choice of enjoying them in our room, or with the other guests in the living room. Guest rooms are named for historic Cape Cod figures; ours overlooked the town square, and had a queen-size sleigh bed, reading lights on both sides, two side chairs, and a dresser with area information, a tray with glasses and corkscrew, plus a dish of chocolates and a vase of fresh flowers. The wallpaper had a Wedgwood blue background with a delicate pink and white floral pattern, and was complemented by the pink comforter and white ruffled curtains. The bathroom had adequate counter space for personal items and good lighting for makeup or shaving. The Lord & Mayfair amenities included shampoo, conditioner, and lotion. In the morning, blueberry coffee cake was set along with pitchers of orange and cranberry juice. A grapefruit and strawberry fruit cup was followed by wonderful baked French toast with sautéed apples and cinnamon. Don and Diane joined the conversation after breakfast, and helped to arrange a day trip to the Vineyard for one couple, sailboat reservations for another, plus general shopping tips and restaurant recommendations. We relaxed on the front porch and read the morning papers." *(Rose Ciccone)*

"The Dr. Tripp Room is conveniently located on the first floor, with no stairs. Tempting breakfast specialties include Cape Cod bananas, breakfast ambrosia, lemon-nut bread, and cranberry crescents. Excellent location—convenient, yet quiet and peaceful." *(Suzanne Scutt)* "An immaculate and impressive three-story Victorian surrounded by a white picket fence, on a beautifully landscaped corner lot. The wrap-around porch with hanging geranium baskets and wicker furniture made it even more inviting. Located directly across from the village green, the inn is surrounded by other beautiful period mansions. The Bates Suite is named for the Falmouth native who wrote *America, the Beautiful*; it's inviting and immaculate, with a cozy sitting area." *(Toni Stone)* "Rooms are immaculate, complete with teddy bears—one of Diane's passions. Afternoon sherry and home-baked cookies are available in the parlor along with books documenting America's history (Don is a retired history/geography teacher). We borrowed bicycles and explored the Shining Sea Bikeway." *(Mark Coyle)*

Open All year.
Rooms 1 suite, 4 doubles—all with private shower and/or bath, radio/clock, TV, fan. 2 with working fireplace, 1 with desk.

Facilities Dining room with fireplace; parlor with books, games, fireplace; porches. ⅓ acre with garden, off-street parking. Bicycles, beach chairs & towels. Off-street parking. Tennis, golf nearby.

Location Historic district; on village green. In Falmouth, turn left at Queen's Byway. Go right on Hewins St. & right on Main St. to the inn.

Restrictions No smoking. Children 12 and older.

Credit cards Amex, MC, Visa.

Rates B&B, $115–150 suite, $85–130 double, $80–145 single. Extra person, $25. 2–3 night weekend/holiday minimum in season.

Extras Bus station pickup.

The Wildflower Inn	*Tel:* 508–548–9524
167 Palmer Avenue, 02540	800–294–5459
	Fax: 508–548–9524
	*E-mail:*wldflr167@aol.com
	URL: http://www.bbonline.com/ma/wildflower

If fake flowers and overly authentic Victoriana give you the willies, come to the Wildflower Inn for light and airy furnishings, enhanced by live blooms that highlight the decor, garnish the plates, and enliven the recipes. Built in 1910, the Wildflower was restored as a B&B in 1995 by Donna and Phil Stone. Each guest room has a different floral theme, complemented by colorful quilts, reflecting Donna's former career as the owner of a quilt shop. A separate loft suite has a private entrance and porch, plus a full kitchen, living room, and staircase leading to a romantic loft bedroom. Breakfast is served at 8:30 A.M. in the gathering room or on the wraparound porch, and might include a fruit smoothie, rose-petal morning cakes, homemade granola, hot almond pears with nutmeg, and sunflower crêpes with nasturtiums.

"A beautifully restored home with an inviting wraparound porch with rocking chairs. Donna and Phil were available, if needed, but once they acquainted you with the inn and all that was offered, you had your privacy. The Moonflower Room on the top floor has a platform bed built under the skylight and draped with mosquito netting, while the Jasmine Room has an Asian accent. The cheerful Geranium Room had pots of blooming geraniums, a queen-size white-painted iron bed, and white wicker furnishings. The windows have large shutters topped with swags. The flower pattern on the quilt and shams matched the luxurious sheets. The bathroom had a corner shower plus a soaking tub and ample space for personal items; shampoos, glycerin soaps, bath gels, and body lotions were supplied, along with good-quality towels and dark washcloths for makeup removal. Donna serves a fantastic, beautifully presented five-course breakfast, using edible flowers in almost every dish. We started with a smoothie of bananas, orange juice, and yogurt; followed by poached pears with cranberries, nuts, and mint; then morning glory muffins made with blueberries and roses, and served with homemade jams; our entrée was a broccoli quiche baked in a crêpe shell, beautifully garnished with chive flowers." *(RC)* "The spacious and romantic wainscoted Beach Rose Room has a rattan sleigh bed and a bathroom with an open, tiled shower, a double whirlpool tub, and a dimmer light switch and candles. Guests may help themselves at any time to coffee, tea, hot chocolate, home-baked cookies, pretzels, and more, set on a sideboard in the gathering room. Also appealing is the third-floor TV room with games and puzzles." *(Suzanne Scutt)* "Donna and Phil Stone showed us unsurpassed friendliness and hospitality. The bright, airy common room is decorated with comfortable furniture. Beautifully maintained, park-like grounds, with flowers and shrubs all around." *(Ellen Ambroziak, also Cecile Desroches)*

Open All year.
Rooms 2 suites, 4 doubles—all with full private bath and/or shower, radio, clock, air-conditioning. 5 with desk, fan. 2 with whirlpool tub. 1 with balcony/deck. 1 suite in carriage house.
Facilities Dining room, living room with gas fireplace, TV room with games; porch; guest refrigerator; wraparound porch. Off-street parking, flower gardens, fish pond, lawn games.
Location Cape Cod. Historic district. I-95 to I-195 to Rte. 25 (Cape & the Islands exit) to Rte. 28 S at Bourne Bridge. Take Rte. 28 over the Bourne Bridge & S into Falmouth; Rte. 28 becomes Palmer Ave. 5-min. walk to town. Walking distance to ferry.
Restrictions No smoking. Children 12 and over in some rooms. Inside wood shutters, air-conditioning block summer traffic noise in front rooms.
Credit cards Amex, MC, Visa.
Rates B&B, $135–160 suite, $90–145 double. Extra person, $25.
Extras Bus station pickup.

Woods Hole Passage
186 Woods Hole Road, Woods Hole, 02540

Tel: 508–548–9575
800–790–8976
Fax: 508–540–4771
E-mail: woods.hole.inn@usa.net
URL: http://www.woodsholepassage.com

Originally part of a larger estate, Woods Hole Passage is a renovated 1880s carriage house and attached barn, in a lovely garden setting. Deb Pruitt bought the inn in 1997, and describes it as "appealing to guests who want an elegant yet comfortable vacation, and who enjoy the outdoors. The grounds are spectacular with an expansive lawn, flower gardens, and an herb garden that holds the smells and tastes for our breakfasts. The great room provides a spacious gathering place bathed in sunlight from a glorious full bay window." If guests are leaving early to catch the ferry, a "breakfast-to-go" bag is left on the table and includes fruit, muffins, and juice. For those guests who don't have to rush off, a leisurely breakfast is available from 8:30–9:30 A.M. at tables for two, and includes fresh fruit with homemade bread or scones and a hot entrée.

"Each guest room is furnished with a new bathroom and a queen-size bed. Our room was done in ivory and rose, with white-painted furnishings, lace curtains and room-darkening shades, a flower print bedspread with good-quality linens, and ample storage space. Bathroom amenities included a soap and shampoo dispenser in the shower, glycerin soap at the sink, plus tissues, cotton pads, and a separate washcloth for makeup removal; a table offered space for personal items. Thoughtful touches included a supply of paperbacks and magazines. The large common room had plenty of comfortable seating, along with books, tapes, and a fireplace. Breakfast included broiled grapefruit, sticky buns, and a vegetable omelet with English muffins; in warm weather, it's served on the stone patio. The extensive grounds include a deep, wide yard with a path leading from the property to a private estate, situated on an inlet and open to walkers during the day. Deb assembled a helpful walking and driving map of the area with marked trails and roads to the beaches along Shore Drive." *(RC)*

Open All year.
Rooms 5 doubles—all with full private bath and/or shower, clock, air-conditioning, individual thermostat, hairdryer. 2 with ceiling fan. 1 with desk. 4 rooms in attached carriage house.
Facilities Dining room, living room with fireplace porch. 1.5 acres with clay tennis court, lawn games, pond, herb & flower gardens; walking trail. 15 min. walk to ocean.
Location 70 m from Boston and Providence, RI. I-95 to I-195 to Rte. 25 (Cape Cod exit) to Rte. 28 S at Bourne Bridge into Falmouth. 2 m to Woods Hole, Falmouth.
Restrictions No smoking. Children by arrangement. Occasional traffic noise possible in two rooms on summer mornings.
Credit cards Amex, DC, MC, Visa.
Rates B&B, $90–135 double, $85–130 single. Extra person, $25. 2-night weekend minimum in season.
Extras Bus station pickup off-season.

GREAT BARRINGTON

Great Barrington is located in the Berkshires of northwestern Massachusetts, at the intersections of Routes 7, 23, and 41. It's 2½ hours north of New York City, and 3 hours west of Boston, and about 30 minutes south of Lenox. Downhill skiing at Butternut and Catamount is just a few minutes away, and the town itself has many appealing shops and inviting restaurants.

For additional area entries, see **New Marlborough, Sheffield,** and **Stockbridge.**

Seekonk Pines Inn
142 Seekonk Cross Road at Route 23, 01230

Tel: 413–528–4192
800–292–4192
Fax: 413–528–1076

Wildflowers and abundant gardens surround Seekonk Pines, an 1832 clapboard farmhouse purchased in 1996 by Bruce and Roberta Lefkowitz and Bruce's mother, Rita. Decorated with period furnishings, country touches, antiques and collectibles, the inn has a pastoral feeling, yet is conveniently located for exploring the Berkshires. Roberta reports that guests especially enjoy "relaxing under the towering pine trees in the rope hammock." Breakfast is served at the dining room table between 8 and 9:30 A.M, and includes a choice of juice and cereal, plus such menus as cranberry bread, stewed fruit, and stuffed French toast with apple compote. In season, berries from the inn's gardens highlight the menu.

"Common rooms are pleasant, spacious, and attractive. Although the decor is mercifully uncluttered, I enjoyed Rita and Bruce's collections of old tools, cameras, and lunchboxes. Breakfast included fresh melon and strawberries, poached or scrambled eggs, and toasted English muffins topped with salmon." *(SWS)* "Bright and cheerful, with good bedside and bathroom lighting. Our spacious second-floor room, the Nellie French, was decorated in powder blues, with a ceiling fan, patchwork quilt, four-poster bed, beautiful marble-topped sink, curtains trimmed in lace, and stenciled designs on the walls. The guest pantry was stocked with coffee and tea, cider and soda." *(Gail Davis)* "Cozy, comfortable, and clean, with accommodating, hospitable innkeepers, who are always around if you should need something." *(Judith Mitchnick)*

Open All year.

Rooms 6 doubles—all with private bath and/or shower, radio, clock, ceiling fan. 5 with air-conditioning, 3 with desk.

Facilities Dining/breakfast room, common room with fireplace, TV/VCR, stereo, books, game table; guest pantry; porch. 4 acres with swimming pool, lawn games, picnic tables, flower/vegetable gardens. Cross-country, downhill skiing, hiking, bicycling, fishing, boating, golf nearby.

Location 2 m W of Great Barrington, at intersection of Rte. 23 & Sekonk Cross Rd. 1¼ m to S. Egremont. From Rte. 7, go W on Rte. 23 2 m to inn. From Rte. 22, go E on Rte. 23 8 m to inn on left.

Restrictions Traffic noise possible in front rooms. Children over 4 preferred. No smoking. BYOB.

Credit cards Amex, MC, Visa.

Rates B&B, $60–135 double, $40–115 single (weekdays only). Extra person, $15–20. 2–3 night weekend minimum July–Oct.

Extras Bus station pickup.

Windflower Inn 🏃
684 South Egremont Road, 01230

Tel: 413–528–2720
800–992–1993
Fax: 413–528–5147
E-mail: wndflowr@windflowerinn.com
URL: http://www.windflowerinn.com

The Liebert and Ryan families have owned the Windflower since 1980, and Gerry Liebert reports that "our inn is a family-run endeavor; we are raising the third generation of innkeepers with Jessica and Michael Ryan." Barbara Liebert is the part-time kitchen helper to her daughter, Claudia, the resident chef, and all baking is done on the premises. The large gardens are John Ryan's special interest, supplying organic berries, herbs, and other vegetables for the dining room. Breakfast includes fresh fruit, juice, cereals, homemade muffins, breads, and such entrées as wild blueberry pancakes, bacon and eggs, or a vegetable quiche in a potato leek crust.

"We arrived Friday afternoon to find tea and delicious homemade cookies. Our cozy room was furnished with antiques and comfortable country furniture; it had a wood-burning fireplace, and a private porch overlooking a charming country setting. The breakfasts were delicious, especially the homemade bread and muffins." *(Linda & David Kahn)* "Wonderful hospitality, good food, spacious rooms. Quiet country setting, yet close to restaurants and shops." *(L.A. Colton, also Anita & Marty Elias)* "Our room had a huge stone fireplace, stocked with wood and ready to light, and a comfortable four-poster bed with Laura Ashley linens." *(Maria & Joseph Tufo)*

"Defines the concept of 'country comfortable'; there's nothing stuffy or pretentious about this warm, hospitable inn. Spacious common rooms, one with tables and board games, the other with couches before the large stone fireplace. Guest rooms are comfortable and ample in size, with adequate seating and good lighting; most have antique, queen-size beds, some with canopies. Breakfast consisted of eggs to order, bacon, homemade bread, and raisin bran muffins." *(SWS)* "We had French toast with thick sliced bread for breakfast one day, and waffles the next, accompanied by juice, coffee, muffins, bacon, and cantaloupe with strawberries." *(Christine Zambito & Karl Wiegers)*

Open All year. Dinner served Thanksgiving, Christmas & New Year's Eve.
Rooms 13 doubles—all with private bath and/or shower, TV, air-conditioning. 6 with fireplace.
Facilities Dining room with fireplace, living room with fireplace, sitting room with piano, library, games; screened porch. 10 acres with vegetable & flower gardens, swimming pool. Tennis, golf across street; cross-country, downhill skiing nearby.
Location SW MA, Berkshires. 3 m W of Great Barrington/Rte. 7 on Rte. 23.
Restrictions Traffic noise in front rooms. No smoking in dining room or guest rooms; cigarettes only in living room. "Well-behaved children welcome."
Credit cards Amex.
Rates B&B, $100–200 double. Extra person, $25. 3-night holiday/weekend (July, Aug.) minimum.
Extras Crib.

HARWICH PORT

For additional area entries, see **Chatham, Dennisport, South Dennis,** and **West Harwich.**

Dunscroft by-the-Sea ♿
24 Pilgrim Road, 02646

Tel: 508–432–0810
800–432–4345
Fax: 508–432–5134
E-mail: alyce@capecod.net
URL: http://www.obs-us.com/chesler/dunscroftbythesea/

At Dunscroft, a gracious summer house built in 1920, you can fall asleep in a king-size canopy bed to the sound of the waves rolling in at a nearby, private, mile-long beach. Alyce and Wally Cunningham, owners since 1987, have created a luxurious, romantic atmosphere. Guest rooms have queen- or king-size canopy, four-poster, or sleigh beds piled high with pillows and made up with designer linens. Fine amenities are found in each bathroom, and beach and bathrobes hang in each closet. Several rooms have a Jacuzzi tub, while the honeymoon cottage has a king-size canopy bed and a living room with a fireplace.

"An enchanting stay, from the relaxing Jacuzzi to the fine linens to Alyce's superb yogurt pancakes." *(Jo Smith)* "Alyce provided us with a stack of menus from local restaurants." *(Gail Ouimet)* "The downstairs living area is spacious and tastefully decorated with an interesting variety of books, art, and personal mementos. Especially appealing are the cozy fireplace area and the screened/glassed-in porch, surrounded by a charming garden. Immaculate guest rooms, congenial service with sincere concern for guests' comfort and enjoyment. Tranquil atmosphere and excellent location near a beautiful beach and great restaurants." *(Jennifer & Chuck Baima)* "Every detail is tended to, from the plush, oversized towels to a spare pair of reading glasses." *(Andi & Duane Quinn)* "Alyce's Southern charm and gracious hospitality combined with Wally's knowledge of the area make guests feel at home, pampered, and catered to." *(Jeanne Huri)* "Beautiful Victorian-style Christmas tree, glowing fireplace and candles, and background music set the perfect mood." *(Stephen Fratalia)* "The lovely table set with fine china and crystal was equaled only by the heaping platters of hot cakes, eggs, bacon, sausage, smoked salmon, cream cheese, melon, berries, home-baked breads, and buns." *(Elayne Spiegel)*

"A delightful setting on a lovely, quiet street of green lawns and spacious gardens." *(CGE)* "Our quiet second-floor room was light and airy, with cool breezes blowing in the windows. Alyce's personal touches included romantic poetry, candles and lace, and a framed Valentine's card. Breakfast included fresh fruit compote, bacon, baked eggs or cheese soufflé, and sticky buns." *(G. Diane Whitaker)* "Guest rooms are decorated in soft florals, lace, and roses, with a Victorian or country French focus. Extra touches include chocolates, fresh flowers, comfortable chairs with reading lamps, and a desk with plenty of writing paper. Alyce's breakfasts, served from 8–10:30 A.M., are a feast." *(Sheilah Kesatie & Charles Doherty)*

Open All year.

Rooms 1 cottage, 3 suites, 6 doubles—all with private bath and/or shower, desk. Some with air-conditioning, fireplace, TV, Jacuzzi; 4 with private entrance. Clock, radio, fan on request. Cottage with kitchen, fireplace.

Facilities Dining room, living room with piano, fireplace. TV, stereo, books. Screened porch. Tennis, golf, swimming, boating, fishing nearby. Beach chairs. 500 ft. to private mile-long beach.

Location Mid-Cape; S side of Cape (Nantucket Sound). 7 m E of Chatham, 12 W of Hyannis. Take Exit 10 off the Mid-Cape Hwy. (Rte 6). Proceed S on Rte. 124 to Rte. 28. Turn left. Travel ½ m to Pilgrim Rd. on your right, alongside the large white church, in view of the water.

Restrictions Children over 12.

Credit cards Amex, MC, Visa.

Rates B&B, $155–225 cottage, suite; $115–225 double, single. Extra person, $35.

Extras Limited wheelchair access; 1 room specially equipped. Some French, Spanish spoken.

HYANNIS PORT

Reader tip: "Fantastic dinner at the Roadhouse Cafe in Hyannis; moderate prices." *(Judy MacDonald)*

The Simmons Homestead Inn 👫
288 Scudder Avenue, 02647

Tel: 508–778–4999
800–637–1649
Fax: 508–790–1342
E-mail: SimmonsInn@aol.com
URL: http://www.capecod.com/simmonsinn

Hyannis has certainly changed since Captain Simmons built his homestead in 1820, but the warmth and hospitality of a well-liked inn has remained the same. After 160 years as a private home, the Homestead was converted into an inn in 1987. Innkeepers Bill Putman and Betsy Reney have furnished with Colonial antiques, enlivened by many plants and his extensive collections of brass, wood, enameled, and cloth birds and animals—from macaws to elephants to giraffes. The second-floor landing is home to the hoods from his old race car and Paul Newman's, a motor, and radio-controlled model airplanes. A simple but filling breakfast of fresh fruit, juice and coffee, scrambled eggs or pancakes, and bacon is served from 7:30–9 A.M.; Bill notes that if you don't like the food, "beer is always available."

"Endless supply of wood for the fireplaces. Bill and Betsy recommend excellent restaurants and make dinner reservations." *(Noreen Manzo)* "The Rabbit Room has polished floors, scatter rugs, easy chairs, lace curtains, and bunnies everywhere. Its bathroom was equally wonderful with an original cast-iron bath and quantities of fluffy towels. Guests gather in the common area each evening to enjoy complimentary wine and Bill's entertaining stories. It was difficult to tear yourself away and go out for the evening. Breakfast was served in the dining room, where the guests sit around one large table and chat about the previous day's experiences while eating Betsy's fabulous breakfasts. Complimentary hot and cold beverages are always available on a self-service basis." *(Claire & Craig Johnson)* "You couldn't meet two friendlier people than Bill and Betsy; they were the highlight of our stay. Plenty of hot water for the bath tub." *(Evelyn Sulli)* "Each guest room has an individual animal decorating theme: parrots, fish, rabbits, giraffes, elephants, and more. Warm innkeepers directed us to the best beaches." *(Allen Sisson)*

"Being a smoker of cigars and pipes, it was nice to find an inn where I can enjoy those pleasures. The innkeeper was a fount of knowledge about Cape Cod, providing maps and excellent suggestions." *(Joseph Landolfi)* "Even though check-out time was long past, no one wanted to leave. The guests were all chatting, laughing, and kibitzing with the innkeeper. We got a chuckle out of the sign in the kitchen which states 'The Innkeeper is Always Right.'" *(RC)* "The inn is convenient to town and a couple of blocks from the Kennedy compound." *(R.B. & Patty Clark)* "Bill has written directions to the area, including what is good and what is not." *(JMB)* "The Elephant Room has a queen-size four-poster bed with canopy, fireplace, and Queen Anne's chairs; elephant art accents the decor." *(Karen Mason)*

Open All year.
Rooms 1 2-bedroom suite, 12 doubles—all with private bath and/or shower, radio, fan. Some with wood-burning fireplace, desk. 1 with deck.
Facilities Common room with fireplace, stereo, library, games; dining room with fireplace, piano, TV/VCR; billiard room. 1.5 acres with croquet, pond. 10-speed bicycles, beach chairs and towels. ½ m to beach; golf, tennis nearby.
Location ½ m from town. From Rte. 6, take Exit 6 to Rte. 132 S. Go 1½ m to Sheraton. Turn right on Bearses Way. Go 100 yds., turn right again on Pitchers Way. Follow to end (approx. 2½ m). At stop sign at Scudder Ave., see inn on right.
Restrictions No smoking in guest rooms; fine elsewhere. "Kids are welcome. Drinking, smoking, and carousing are perfectly acceptable, possibly encouraged. Tank tops on guys (tacky) are not. Don't let the cats inside."
Credit cards Amex, Discover, MC, Visa. 5% surcharge.
Rates B&B, $300 suite (sleeps 4), $120–200 double, $100–180 single. Extra person, $10–20. 2–3 night holiday/weekend minimum in season. Discount for 4-night stay.
Extras Airport/station pickups. Dogs permitted with prior approval.

LEE

Lee is located in the Berkshires of western Massachusetts, 130 miles west of Boston, 130 miles north of New York City, 55 miles southeast of Albany. It's about 6 miles south of Lenox, and three miles northeast of Stockbridge.

Also recommended: A renovated 1885 schoolhouse, the **Chambery Inn** (Route 20, Main & Elm Streets, P.O. Box 319, 01238; 413–243–2221 or 800–537–4321; www.berkshireinns.com) has nine rooms, six with fireplaces and all with whirlpool baths. Rates range from $75–265, depending on day of week and season; the Monday–Wednesday rate of $75–99 is one of the best values in the Berkshires. "Restored in 1990, the original classrooms are now spacious suites with king-size canopy beds and sitting areas. The continental breakfast is delivered to your room as requested between 8 and 9:45 A.M. No common areas." *(SWS)* "Our suite had a double Jacuzzi tub, CD system, 35-inch TV screen, VCR, refrigerator, coffeemaker, and fireplace. Breakfast was delivered fresh to our room each morning. Pleasant innkeeper and staff." *(CD)*

For additional area entries, see also **Lenox, South Lee, Stockbridge,** and **West Stockbridge.**

Applegate   *Tel:* 413–243–4451
279 West Park Street, RR 1, P.O. Box 576, 01238   800–691–9012
                                                  Fax: 413–243–4451
                                    E-mail: applegate@taconic.net
                                    URL: http://www.applegateinn.com

Years ago Rick Cannata and Nancy Begbie-Cannata fell in love with the Berkshires, and spent many vacations here, exploring its B&Bs. In 1990 they found this large Colonial Revival home with dramatic two-story pillars and decided to create their own inn, using their experiences as a guide. Taking its name from the old apple orchard that surrounds the inn, the Applegate is furnished with quality Colonial reproductions and Oriental rugs; teddy bears and dolls add a whimsical touch. Rates include a breakfast of freshly squeezed orange juice, cereal, yogurt, fruit, breads and muffins, coffee, and tea with silver candelabras; afternoon wine and cheese; and bedside chocolates and brandy.

"Warm atmosphere, exceptional hospitality and attention to detail. We became engaged over the weekend and returned to our room to find champagne awaiting us." *(Kim Griffinger)* "Loved both the steam shower for two, the king-size bed, and fireplace in spacious Room #1." *(Ann & Bill Thibaud)* "Delightful little touches include wine and cheese at 5:00, plus bedtime brandy and chocolates." *(Marthe & Steven Hemsen)* "A wealth of entertainment options at the inn. Nancy and Rick offered wonderful dinner recommendations." *(Gwen Goltzman & Ron Zaczepinski)* "Generous little touches included a makeup removal towel, cotton balls, and Q-Tips; down pillows and comforters; large, soft towels." *(Jennifer Laterra)* "The French room was beautifully decorated with a great fireplace. Wonderful guest comment book on local restaurants." *(Mike & Julia Dubisz)*

"Nancy provided menus from at least 25 local restaurants." *(Kimberly Adams)* "I stopped by to visit during the off-season. Everything looked perfect, yet the innkeepers were busy scraping and painting, ensuring that this lovely inn stayed in tiptop shape. The rooms are handsome and well decorated in dramatic colors, from the deep green and rose of the suite, to the lovely Lavender Room, to the rich jewel-tones of Room #6, the smallest room, done in deep green florals (an excellent value). The dining room has several tables, allowing seating for both couples and groups of guests. Convenient location, yet away from traffic noise." *(SWS)* "The large, well-maintained grounds give the inn a quiet, secluded environment." *(Bonnie & James Surma)* "Extra touches include fresh flowers, classical music, a carafe of brandy in each room, and coffee served in lovely antique cups." *(Mary Jean & David Nelson)*

Open All year.

Rooms 6 doubles—all with private bath and/or shower, radio, air-conditioning. 1 with steam shower. 2 with fireplace. Carriage house apartment with living room, kitchen, 2 bedrooms, bath with Jacuzzi, deck.

Facilities Dining room with fireplace, living room with fireplace, stereo, piano, library; TV/game room, screened porch. 6 acres with swimming pool, bicycles. 5 m to cross-country skiing, 14–20 m to 5 downhill ski areas. Golf and tennis directly across street at country club.

Location W MA, Berkshires. 130 m W of Boston, 130 m N of NYC, 55 m SE of Albany. 3.5 m from Stockbridge, ½ m from center of town. From I-90, take Exit 2, bear right on Rte. 20 into town. Go ½ m past 1st stop sign to inn on left, across from golf course.

Restrictions No smoking. Children over 12 welcome.

Credit cards MC, Visa.

Rates B&B, $1,000 apt. (weekly), $95–230 double. Extra person, $30. Tipping encouraged. 2–3 night weekend/holiday minimum. 10% weekly discount. Off-season rates. New Year's, wine-tasting, special event weekends; mid-winter packages.

Extras French spoken.

Devonfield 🏃
85 Stockbridge Road, 01238

Tel: 413–243–3298
800–664–0880
Fax: 413–243–1360
E-mail: inkeeper@devonfield.com
URL: http://www.devonfield.com

The original Devonfield, built by a Revolutionary War soldier, was razed, then rebuilt in 1928 by John Bross Lloyd. During the summer of 1942 it was the residence of Queen Wilhelmina of the Netherlands, her daughter, Princess Juliana, and her granddaughters. The inn has been owned by Sally and Ben Schenck since 1994. Breakfast is served at individual tables from 8–10 A.M., and includes fresh fruit and juice, granola, home-baked muffins, and a hot entrée—perhaps pancakes with apples, pears, and walnuts with maple syrup.

"Sally and Ben continually improve their warm and efficient B&B. Favorite features include the pool and tennis on the grounds, the nine-hole golf course almost across the street, and the proximity to Lenox and Tanglewood." *(Stephen & Sue Fisher)* "Convenient but quiet country setting. The Schenks are gracious, friendly, and unobtrusive. Tasty breakfasts. Public rooms are large and comfortably furnished, offering a wide selection of books, magazines, and music." *(Marjorie Spector)* "Beautiful home in a relaxing, picturesque setting. Comfortable rooms with plenty of sunlight and mountain views. Hosts go above and beyond to make guests feel welcomed." *(Victoria Muradi)* "Lovely grounds with old trees and wide grassy meadows. Exceptionally clean and well-maintained." *(Edna Berk Kuhn)* "Warm greetings, hot tea, calming music, large windows to admire the grounds and mountains beyond. Having a TV room and guest pantry added to the feeling of being in your own home. Our room had a fireplace, unlimited wood supply, and an antique four-poster bed." *(Nicole Swetland)*

"Large, varied book and magazine collection. The terrace overlooks the sweeping lawns, and mountains beyond. The swimming pool was a welcome relief after a long drive. Bathrooms have good towels and quiet plumbing." *(Ruth & David Bernhardt)* "Elegant, spacious common areas, with comfortable seating and appropriate lighting. Guest rooms are light and airy, furnished with traditional pieces; many have been recently redone with floral wallcoverings, and most have hardwood floors with area rugs, ample storage space, and good lighting. Delightful owners." *(SWS)* "We sat on the outside swing and watched the moon rise." *(JG)* "Caring, gracious innkeepers; immaculate house and grounds. Ample common areas, tasty breakfasts." *(Michael & Dina Miller)* "Plenty to read of local interest, and lots of comfy nooks for reading." *(Joanne Little)*

Open All year.
Rooms 1 cottage, 3 suites, 6 doubles—all with full private bath, air-conditioning. 2 with whirlpool tub, 5 with TV, 4 with wood-burning fireplace. Cottage with kitchen.

Facilities Dining room; living room with fireplace, books; TV room; stocked guest pantry, porch. 25 acres with off-street parking, heated swimming pool, tennis court, lawn games, cross-country skiing; bicycles. Golf, skiing, hiking nearby.

Location From Mass. Pike, take Exit 2. Bear right on Rte. 20 to Lee. At 1st stop sign, do not bear right around the park. Stop at stop sign & go straight onto W. Park St. (becomes Stockbridge Rd). Continue 9/10 m to inn.

Restrictions No smoking. Children 10 and older July & Aug.; any age rest of the year.

Credit cards Amex, MC, Visa.

Rates B&B, $120–260 suite, $70–195 double. Extra person, $20. 10% weekly discount. 3-night minimum summer weekends, 2-night minimum foliage weekends.

Extras Pets off-season in cottage.

LENOX

Lenox is most famous for Tanglewood, the summer home of the Boston Symphony, in residence from mid-June through August. Call 617–266–1492 for schedules and ticket information. Also in Lenox is the Mount, a restoration of Edith Wharton's house; Shakespeare is presented at the Mount's outdoor amphitheater from July to October.

Rates are highest from late May through October, and 2–3 night weekend minimum stays are the rule; during Tanglewood season, weekend rates generally apply Thursday through Sunday nights. When reading through the rates noted in the following pages, be aware that the off-season rates are *half* the peak-season rate—an excellent value. On the other hand, a peak-season visit will cost you about $185 per night with service and tax (for two) for a charming—but not at all luxurious—room with a continental breakfast. If you must pay these prices, make sure that you're getting a decent breakfast and afternoon tea, too!

When you need a culture break, you'll find that there are lakes nearby for fishing, swimming, and boating, along with tennis courts and golf courses. In winter, there's plenty of cross-country and downhill skiing nearby. Lenox is in the Berkshires, 7 miles south of Pittsfield, approximately 10 miles west of the New York border, 40 miles east of Albany, and 150 miles north of New York City.

Reader tip: "I'd suggest visiting Lenox during the second or third week of September, when the midweek rates are quite low, but the weather is lovely." *(MW)*

For additional area entries, see also **Lee, Richmond, Stockbridge,** and **West Stockbridge.**

Amadeus House *Tel:* 413–637–4770
15 Cliffwood Street, 01240 800–205–4770
Fax: 413–637–4484
E-mail: info@amadeushouse.com
URL: http://www.amadeushouse.com

Named to capture the feeling of Lenox as a music haven, Amadeus House includes good music as a major part of one's stay—from the extensive library of recordings and books to the naming of each guest room after a famous composer. Guests are encouraged to "pick up a baton and conduct a symphony in the living room." Built in 1820 and "Victorianized" in the late 1800s, the Amadeus House has been extensively restored by John Felton and Marty Gottron since they bought it in 1993.

"Lovely, quiet neighborhood. The cordial, helpful innkeepers made us feel right at home and were always ready with a map or advice on things to do or places to eat. The Bach Room is a large, impeccably clean room on the second floor. Delicious, tempting breakfasts and afternoon tea." *(Jan Kenney)* "First-rate suggestions for hiking, dining, and more. The convenient in-town location allowed us to walk to shops and restaurants." *(Helen Stark)* "Exceptional hospitality. Everything as described in your book, and more." *(Helen & John Van Roy)* "The well-equipped rooms are light and airy. Conscientious, caring innkeepers." *(SWS)* "The Brahms Suite is spacious, incredibly clean, with a comfortable bed and large bath. Questions about restaurants, antiquing, or sightseeing were answered with pleasure. Great breakfast muffins." *(Zsuzsi & Lenny Entrabartolo)* "Close to Tanglewood and within walking distance of shops and excellent restaurants." *(AM)* "Excellent CD collection of classical music and jazz." *(Timothy Moran)* "The Mozart Room has a comfortable bed and relaxing atmosphere. Breakfast was superb, as were the afternoon treats. Their black lab, Bravo, is a fine inn dog." *(Dudley Alleman)*

"We had a great night's sleep in the cozy, comfortable Sibelius and Schubert Rooms. Loved the robe provided." *(Vivian Ottenberg)* "Many extras—fresh flowers, sweets in the sitting areas, and chocolates in our room prior to retiring." *(Karen Millett)* "Tea at 5 P.M. with hot-from-the-oven gingerbread was a treat. Breakfast consisted of grapefruit and orange slices, juice, freshly baked poppy seed muffins, and homemade apple waffles." *(Adrean Abrams)* "John met us in the driveway and helped with our luggage. Immaculate bathrooms with lots of towels and good water pressure in the shower. Breakfast different every morning, with low-fat choices as well." *(Lisa Witkowski)* "Painted in handsome cream with tan and green accents, with a wonderful wraparound porch, grand old rockers, and bright geraniums." *(Ellen Schecter)* "Warm and loving attention to details: a guest's needs, sweet rooms, smooth operation, and a deep love of music." *(Jane Wyatt Goodwin)* "The porches are a wonderful place to rock and read and watch the world go by. Dining, shops, and entertainment within walking distance." *(Jean Hyatt)*

Open All year.

Rooms 1 suite, 7 doubles—6 with private bath and/or shower, 2 with a maximum of 4 people sharing. All with radio, clock, fan. 3 with air-conditioning. 2 with deck. 1 with telephone, desk, fireplace, refrigerator.

Facilities Dining room, living room with fireplace, stereo, books; guest refrigerator, unscreened porch; fax privileges. ½ acre with off-street parking, lawn games. Walk to restaurants, shops, hiking, cross-country skiing.

Location 1 block to town center. From I-90 (Mass. Pike), take Exit 2. Follow Rte. 20 through Lee to Rte. 183 (Walker St.) to Lenox. At the monument in Lenox

(Main St./Rte. 7A) turn right. Go 2 blocks & turn left onto Cliffwood St. to 3rd house on left.

Restrictions No smoking. Children over 10.

Credit cards Amex, Discover, MC, Visa.

Rates B&B, $100–195 suite, $65–155 double. Extra person, $20. Tipping encouraged. 3-night weekend minimum. July/Aug.; 2-night holiday weekend minimum off-season. Midweek discount; off-season dinner packages. 10% weekly discount. Box lunches, suppers.

Extras Station pickups.

Birchwood Inn	*Tel:* 413–637–2600
7 Hubbard Street, 01240	800–524–1646
	Fax: 800–637–2600
	E-mail: detoner@ben.net
	URL: http://www.bbonline.com/ma/birchwood

The oldest building in Lenox, Birchwood dates back to 1764, and is listed on the National Register of Historic Places. Although it served as a tavern in the late 1700s, it was a private home for most of its history, and took on its present appearance during the ownership of the Dana family, who occupied it from 1885 to 1953. Renovated as an inn in 1891, Birchwood has been owned by Joan, Dick, and Dan Toner since 1991. Breakfast is served at individual tables from 8:30–10 A.M., and includes a buffet of fresh fruit and juice, yogurt and cereal, followed by such entrées as eggs Benedict, huevos rancheros, mushroom cheese omelets, or gingerbread pancakes.

"The combination of the delicious muffins and the classical music in the background make breakfast a wonderful experience." *(Marge Callahan)* "The Toners are marvelous hosts, creating a cozy, warm environment." *(Denise & Merton Thompson & others)* "Birchwood offers atmosphere, scenery, peace and quiet, good food, and comfortable yet sophisticated surroundings. This handsome home is perched on top of a hill, surrounded by meticulous landscaping. We were served wine and cheese each evening in the huge library by the gracious innkeepers, and enjoyed a game of Scrabble in front of the fireplace. A smaller room with a TV and fireplace provided an additional common area for relaxing or browsing through restaurant menus." *(Carolyn Levine)* "The porch was a favorite spot for morning coffee and the newspaper, a cool drink in the afternoon, or an evening cordial." *(Mary Ann & Frank Brody)*

"Dick Toner is a retired brigadier general and he and Joan have traveled extensively, as can be seen from the wonderful pieces of furniture, china, jade figurines, screens, and rugs. The dresser and armoire in our room were custom-made in Korea—beautifully detailed with bronze hinges and trim. A fire was laid for us each night; all we had to do was light the match. The walk-in closet provided ample storage space, and the large bathroom was well supplied with towels and toiletries. At breakfast, we helped ourselves to fresh blueberries, hot muffins, and fresh crusty bread; Joan served us eggs chasseur one day, and ham and cheese omelets the next. Dick and his son Dan share the cooking duties; Joan keeps the conversation going, offering advice on area activities and sights." *(Rose Ciccone)* "Every detail added to the comfort of our room—a comfy and romantic canopy bed, upholstered chairs, and a large, deep old-fashioned tub. " *(Greg & Linda Schumacher)* "Room #10 on the third floor had a comfortable bed and two back rests for reading in bed. The dining room was bathed in sunlight, with the tables spaced perfectly for privacy or conversation, as desired." *(Nancy Mitchell)* "Beautifully decorated and festive at Christmas. Wonderful teddy bear collection." *(Janice Zeltzer)*

Open All year.

Rooms 2 suites in carriage house with desk, air-conditioning, kitchen, private bath. 10 doubles—8 with private bath and/or shower, 2 with maximum of 4 people sharing bath. All with telephone, radio/clock, fan. Some with TV, fireplace, air-conditioning.

Facilities Dining room with fireplace; living room with fireplace; den with fireplace, stereo, TV/VCR, games; 3,000-volume library with fireplace; porch. 2 acres with lawn games; Kennedy Park adjacent.

Location In historic district. From Mass. Pike (I-90), take Exit 2, Lee. Go W on U.S. Rte. 20 5 m. Go left on SR 183 to Lenox Center. Go right at monument (Main St./Rte. 7A) to top on hill & inn on right at corner of Main & Hubbard, across from Church on the Hill.

Restrictions No smoking. Children over 12.

Credit cards All major.

Rates B&B, $125–210 suite, $60–210 double. Extra person, $20. Tipping encouraged. 3-night weekend minimum July & Aug. 2–3 night minimum holiday weekends & Oct. weekends. 10% weekly discount; midweek & corporate rates.

Extras Some French, German spoken.

Blantyre ✕ 木 よ

16 Blantyre Road, P.O. Box 995, 01240

Tel: 413–637–3556
Fax: 413–637–4282
E-mail: hide@blantyre.com
URL: http://www.blantyre.com

Built at the turn of the century, Blantyre is a lavishly restored Tudor-style mansion, reminiscent of a grand Scottish manor. Rates include a breakfast of coffee, fresh fruit, and breakfast breads; full breakfast is available at an additional charge. Three-course prix fixe dinners are served in the paneled dining room, with a selection of several appetizers, entrées, and desserts. A spring menu included such entrées as sea bass with spinach and risotto, rabbit with turnips and lemon thyme, and duck with endive and wine, tomato, and chive sauce. The extensive wine list offers many complementary choices. Standards at Blantyre are very high, as are the prices and reader expectations: "expensive but worth it" is the on-going consensus.

"Waiting for us in our spotless room in the Carriage House were a complimentary bottle of Evian, a fresh fruit basket, and a tray of assorted cheeses. Two thick terry robes hung in the closet. Breakfast, which can be taken in your room or in the beautiful conservatory in the main house, includes fresh-squeezed juices and seasonal fruit, warm croissants, muffins, and imported jams. All are presented in a dignified and efficient manner." *(Mrs. Eileen Yudelson)* "Perfectly manicured grounds and a museum-like collection of antiques. Our room had a crocheted spread on the queen-size bed, a huge bath with everything from towel warmers to the strongest shower I've ever had. Meals were superlative, from canapés in the Main Hall where we ordered before entering the dining room, to the dessert with 'Happy Anniversary' inscribed in chocolate. The staff is superb; Roderick Anderson, the long-time resident manager, is one of those people who does his job so well, and enjoys it so much, that you cannot help but admire him." *(Mark Traub)* "Elegant and formal, though the staff goes out of their way to be warm and friendly." *(Mimi Cohen)* "Food was fabulous. A return to the gilded era." *(BNS)* "Caring, unobtrusive, unpretentious service. Superb dining." *(EE)*

Open Mid-May–early-Nov. Restaurant closed Mon.
Rooms 6 suites, 17 doubles—all with private bath and/or shower, telephone, radio, TV, desk, air-conditioning; 7 with fireplace. 8 rooms in main house, remainder in Carriage House and cottages.
Facilities Dining rooms; parlors; music room with pianist, harpist evenings; conservatory. 85 acres with flower gardens, heated swimming pool, 4 tennis courts, Jacuzzi, exercise room, sauna, 2 tournament-sanctioned croquet courts, walking paths.
Location 2–3 miles from town, Tanglewood. ½ m from Rte. 20. From Stockbridge, go N on Rte. 7 to 2nd light (5 m), turn right on Rte. 20, ½ m to Blantyre. From Lee, take Exit 2 off Mass. Pike, go W on Rte. 20 to inn on right.
Restrictions No children.
Credit cards All major.
Rates $325–700 suite, $265–485 double. 10% service. Extra person, $50. Rate includes continental breakfast; full breakfast, $8–14; alc lunch, $30–40. Prix fixe dinner, $70, plus 18% service. Picnic baskets, 24-hr. notice, $30–75. 2-night weekend minimum.
Extras Limited wheelchair access. French spoken. Airport/station pickups, $90. Member, Relais et Châteaux.

Brook Farm Inn
15 Hawthorne Street, 01240

Tel: 413–637–3013
800–285–POET
Fax: 413–637–4751
E-mail: innkeeper@brookfarm.com
URL: http://www.brookfarm.com

Given the motto of the Brook Farm Inn, "There is poetry here," this entry should perhaps be written in iambic pentameter, or at least rhyming couplets, but straightforward text will have to suffice. The inn has a library of 1,500 books, containing 750 volumes of poetry, with another 70 poets recorded on tape. Brook Farm is a 100-year-old Victorian home, purchased in 1992 by Joe and Anne Miller.

"Accommodating, sociable innkeepers." *(JMC)* "Welcoming atmosphere with books and music, delicious food, enchanting rooms, and pleasant guests; Bob the cat is a true treasure." *(Kristina Brown & Dale Brunelle)* "The Miller's breakfasts kept us going for most of the day. Enjoyed all books, puzzles, magazines, and games, plus afternoon tea and scones." *(Robert Fiordaliso)* "Off the main street, with easy access to town. The well-stocked guest pantry enables guests to make themselves at home." *(Lisa Taylor)* "Attention to detail ranges from the lounge chairs outside for sunning and reading, to the hall basket with new toothbrushes, lotions, and more, for those of us who have forgotten something." *(GR)* "Our large, beautifully appointed room had a queen-size canopy bed and fireplace." *(Tom Pedulla)*

"Decorated throughout with lovely wallpapers, fabrics, and carpeting, plus renovated bathrooms. The largest rooms are located on the second floor, although the Garret (Room #9) on the third floor has lots of space for a queen-size bed and two twin beds; it has Waverly floral fabrics, and a cathedral ceiling with exposed beams." *(SWS)* "Each room has an assortment of journals, puzzles, and books." *(Shawne Goodrich)* "Breakfasts served promptly at 8:30 A.M., with piping hot coffee, fresh fruit, tasty breads, cereal, and a hot entrée." *(Cathy Reitz)* "Our room was bright and sunny, decorated with blue-and-white striped wallpaper, white wicker furniture and a comfortable queen-size bed; the wood was laid in the red brick fireplace, needing only a match to light. Joe hosts an informal poetry reading during afternoon tea and scones; the atmosphere is casual, with guests feeling free to stay or just enjoy their tea and depart." *(Maria Posella)* "Smaller tables are available, but most guests enjoy meeting around the beautiful refectory table to enjoy the wonderful buffet breakfasts." *(Mary Henrich)* "Young chamber music players entertained us at Sunday breakfast." *(Rachel Epstein)* "A jigsaw puzzle in progress, a bowl of apples, and a plate of cookies made us feel at home." *(Elizabeth Kelley)*

Open All year.

Rooms 12 doubles—all with private bath and/or shower, telephone, air-conditioning, ceiling fan. Some with desk, fireplace.

Facilities Library with fireplace, books, games, stereo; breakfast room with guest refrigerator; guest pantry. 1¼ shaded acres with small swimming pool.

Location ³⁄₁₀ m from town. From Rte. 7 N in Lenox, go left onto Rte. 7A (Kemble St.) to Walker St. (Rte. 183), & go to statue at town center. Bear left, then turn left onto Old Stockbridge Rd. Turn right at Hawthorne St. to inn. Walking distance to Tanglewood.

Restrictions No smoking. Children over 14. No pets.

Credit cards Discover, MC, Visa.

Rates B&B, $80–200 double. Extra person, $20. 3-night weekend minimum late June–early Sept. & some holidays; 2-night weekend minimum in Oct. 10% weekly discount. Packages.

Extras Free station pickups.

The Gables Inn 𝒯	*Tel:* 413–637–3416
81 Walker Street (Route 183), 01240	800–382–9401
URL: http://www.gableslenox.com

In the 1880s, Lenox was the inland Newport. The Gables, originally known as Pine Acre, was one of the original Berkshire cottages, and was home to Mrs. William C. Wharton, mother-in-law of Edith Wharton, the novelist. Edith Wharton lived at Pine Acre for two years while her own cottage, the Mount, was being built. Many of her short stories were written here, presumably in the eight-sided library. The Gables, a Queen Anne–style cottage, was bought and restored by Mary and Frank Newton in 1985. The decor includes both Victorian antiques and traditional pieces from the 1920s and 1930s, are enhanced by the Newtons' collection of art and books. Rates include a full breakfast, available from 8–10 A.M., plus afternoon wine.

"Inviting common areas; enjoyed the swimming pool and tennis court. Strong, dark colors and solid furnishings gave our spacious room a handsome masculine look, a welcome change from the lace and frills at many inns." *(RSS)* "Our third-floor gable room had a comfortable bed, attractive bathroom, and an ample supply of blankets and other necessities." *(Jan & Dave Blankenship)* "The staff was always available to help with any request." *(Lynn Lovett)* "Delighted with the recently renovated and beautifully furnished Teddy Wharton suite." *(Andrew Morton)*

Open All year.

Rooms 4 suites, 17 doubles—all with private bath and/or shower, radio, air-conditioning. Some with desk, wood-burning fireplace, TV/VCR, refrigerator, deck.

Facilities Breakfast room, living room, dining room—all with fireplace. Library with fireplace, books. Heated swimming pool, tennis court, garden. Off-street parking.

Location From Mass. Pike (I-90), take Exit 2 (Lee). Go W on Rte. 20 to Rte. 183 W to Lenox to inn on right (opposite Kemble St.). Historic district; 1½ blocks to center.

Restrictions No cigar smoking. No children under 12.

Credit cards Discover, MC, Visa.

Rates B&B, $160–210 suite, $80–160 double. Extra person, $20. 3-night weekend minimum July, August.

Extras Station pickup available. Spanish spoken.

Gateways Inn ✗ ♿
51 Walker Street, 01240

Tel: 413–637–2532
888–GWAY-INN
Fax: 413–637–1432
E-mail: gateways@berkshire.net

The "house that Ivory Soap built" was originally the summer home of Harley Procter of Procter and Gamble fame. Built in 1912, it's been an inn for the past 50 years, and was purchased by Fabrizio and Rosemary Chiariello in 1996. The guest rooms have queen- and king-size four-poster, canopy, or sleigh beds; many have Oriental rugs on gleaming hardwood floors. The Suite was a favorite of the late Boston Pops conductor, Arthur Fiedler. A continental breakfast is served at individual tables from 8:30–10 A.M. Dinner menus change frequently; on a recent night, the entrées included roasted red snapper with braised romaine, white beans, and tomato vinaigrette; beef tenderloin with Swiss roesti potatoes, and fennel gratin; and chicken with goat cheese and asparagus.

"Extensively, expensively restored to attain its original elegance as well as provide the modern comforts and conveniences today's guests prefer. Ongoing redecoration and renovation is bringing every aspect of the inn to a high standard. Fabrizio is a charming host who works hard to ensure his guests' comfort. The inn's elegant tone is set by the beautiful mahogany staircase, designed by Stanford White, and illuminated by a skylight. The equally elegant dining room has candles on the tables, chandeliers, and Oriental rugs on the hardwood floors. Our dinner was outstanding, with appealing variety and creativity. Presentation was excellent and the accompaniments were individual to each entrée. The terrace is used in nice weather for al fresco dining. One redecorated guest room was beautifully decorated with king-size sleigh bed, club chairs, and a deep rich color scheme. Our attractive room had period reproduction furnishings, flower print wallpaper with matching fabrics in yellow and rose. The king-size four-poster bed was triple sheeted with yellow-and-white striped cotton sheets. Swing-arm brass lamps on either end table made reading in bed a pleasure. Housekeeping throughout the inn was excellent. The continental breakfast buffet included juice, fresh fruit, cereal, and muffins; coffee, yogurt with dried peaches, and toasted bagels or English muffins were brought to the table, along with butter, Rosemary's homemade jams and cream cheese." *(Rose Ciccone)* "Beautifully decorated rooms; superb meals. Rosemary and Fabrizio were accommodating hosts, providing a welcoming, peaceful atmosphere. Spotless housekeeping; soft and inviting lighting. All new plumbing, heating, and cooling systems meant that all worked well, with in-room temperature controls and only clean, fresh smells. Safe, convenient parking." *(CDM)* "Casual or formal—Gateways is comfortable either way. Innkeepers go out of their way to accommodate guests." *(TD)*

Open All year. Restaurant closed Mon., also Tues. off-season.

Rooms 1 suite, 11 doubles—all with full private bath and/or shower, telephone, radio, clock, TV, air-conditioning. Some with gas fireplace; 1 with whirlpool tub, desk.

Facilities Restaurant, breakfast room with fireplace; dining terrace. Off-street parking, tennis court.

Location Historic district. 1.5 m to Tanglewood. From S, take Taconic Pkwy. or Rte. 22 N to Rte. 23. Go E on 23 to Great Barrington. Go N on Rte. 7 N to Stockbridge & Lenox. At 1st light in Lenox, go left onto Rte. 7A, Kemble St. Go to stop sign and go left to inn on right. From Mass. Pike, take Exit 2. Bear right to Lee, MA (Rte. 20/Housatonic St.). Go through town until Rte. 20 merges with Rte. 7 after a few miles. Stay in left lane, and turn left at 1st light onto Rte. 183 (Walker St.). Go towards center of town to inn on right.

Restrictions No smoking. Children 12 and over.

Credit cards All major cards accepted.

Rates B&B, $225–380 suite, $75–170 double, $165–240 single. Extra person, $40. 5% service (rooms). 2–3 night weekend/holiday/foliage minimum.

Extras Wheelchair access; bathroom specially equipped. Spanish spoken.

The Rookwood Inn 🏃

11 Old Stockbridge Road, 01249

Tel: 413–637–9750
800–223–9750
Fax: 413–637–1353
E-mail: innkeepers@rookwoodinn.com
URL: http://www.rookwoodinn.com

Dating back to 1825, the oldest portion of Rookwood was originally a tavern with lodgings. In 1880, it was moved to its current location by a New York family who expanded it as a Victorian cottage, complete with gables and turrets. Taking its name from an eclectic style of Victorian pottery, the Rookwood Inn is a "painted lady" done in shades of cream and gold, with gray-green and dark red accents. Amy Lindner-Lesser and Stephen Lesser have owned the inn since 1996, and have furnished it with English and American antiques, Oriental rugs, and period wallpapers, as well as their personal collections of antique handbags and Wallace Nutting prints.

Breakfast is served at individual tables from 8–10 A.M., and chef Steve prides himself on his health-conscious breakfast menu, using low-fat milk and cholesterol-free eggs. In addition to hot and cold beverages, fresh seasonal fruits, yogurt and cereals, the hot entrée might be challah French toast, fruit cobbler, or frittata Mexicana with mushrooms, onions, and roasted peppers. Afternoon tea is served with sweets or tea sandwiches, occasionally accompanied by live music.

"Our cozy room at the back of the house was shaded by large trees. It had a comfortable queen-size canopy bed flanked by two small end tables with reading lights and clock radio. The floral quilt and wallpaper were nicely set off by the white lace curtains, canopy, and trim. Each guest room has seating for two; some have a small sofa bed, ideal for families. In the Tower Room, steps lead to a turret with a skylight and daybed, ideal for a third person, or an exceptionally romantic hideaway. The heart-healthy breakfast is served in the dining room in winter, on the veranda in the summer, or can be brought to your room. We enjoyed a mushroom strata and a pear crisp. In the Victorian parlor, guests are encouraged to play the grand piano; the living room has a pump organ from the late 1800s. The two porches are well supplied with newspapers and lots of comfortable wicker seating. Afternoon tea is served each day at 4 P.M., with hot tea, lemonade, and iced herbal tea, plus healthy home-baked goods." (Rose Ciccone)

"Innkeepers Steve and Amy are gregarious without being overbearing, providing excellent service and amenities. They are knowledgeable about the area, its activities, and restaurants, and encourage their guests to interact at breakfast and afternoon tea." (Liz Winfield & Sue Spielman) "Great location and hospitality. Comfortable beds, great water pressure. Afternoon tea included home-baked treats like yogurt-fudge pastry puffs." (Virginia & Courtney Hale) "Shops and restaurants in easy walking distance. The low-fat breakfasts were especially appreciated." (June Kluglein) "Steve and Amy provide warmth, hospitality, and charm, along with lovely rooms, delicious homemade breakfasts, and a serene getaway." (Heather Angstreich) "The Lessers are totally committed not only to their inn but to Lenox." (Sally O'Grady) "Warm and friendly, neither pretentious or stuffy." (Teri & Joe Vitti)

Open All year.

Rooms 2 suites, 19 doubles—all with private bath and/or shower, clock, air-conditioning. Some with desk, ceiling fan, fireplace, balcony/deck, telephone, TV, refrigerator.

Facilities Dining room; living room with piano, TV/VCR, fireplace, stereo, books; porches. Occasional live music at teatime. 1 acre with gazebo, croquet, off-street parking. Tennis, golf, skiing, hiking nearby.

Location ½ block to center of town. From Mass. Tpke. (I-90), take Exit 2 (Lee). Go right onto Rte. 20 W. Turn left onto Rte. 183. Proceed to large monument in Lenox; bear left to inn on left.

Restrictions No smoking. Well-supervised children welcome.

Credit cards Amex, Discover, MC, Visa.

Rates B&B, $150–300 suite, $75–240 double, $65–225 single. Extra person, $25. No charge for children under 12. 2–3 night weekend/holiday minimum. Off-season packages.

Extras Bus station pickup. Crib; babysitting by arrangement. Spanish spoken; some German.

LEVERETT

For additional area entries, see **Amherst, Deerfield,** and **North New Salem.**

Hannah Dudley House Inn   *Tel: 413–367–2323*
114 Dudleyville Road, 01054

Now a part of the town of Leverett, Dudleyville acquired its name because it was almost entirely populated by Dudleys. One of these founding families built what is now the Hannah Dudley House in 1797. Restored as an inn in 1992 by Daryl and Erni Johnson, this Colonial home has six working fireplaces and wide-plank floors. Breakfast is served family-style at 8:30 A.M. in the dining room, and includes fresh fruit and juices, homemade granola, home-baked pastries, breads, or muffins, and perhaps pancakes, apple crisp, or a soufflé. Guests are welcomed with snacks, wine, and soft drinks. Occasionally, the Johnsons serve complimentary lobster dinners on Wednesday and Saturday nights in the summer, and hors d'oeuvres or design-your-own-pizza in winter. As a complement to his past career as a landscape designer, and his current one as innkeeper, Daryl is also an artist, using hand-crafted wood and metal, plus antique farm equipment to create wind chimes and sculptures to enhance the inn's grounds.

"Scrumptious breakfasts with flaky pastries, tasty muffins, fresh fruit, and a daily special, enhanced by lovely presentation and caring service. Gorgeous property with hiking trails, benches, ponds, immaculate pool, all within a historical setting." *(Jane Baldridge)* "Attention to detail evident in the fresh fruit in our room, the loan of picnic utensils, Daryl's beautiful and creative wind chimes, and the peaceful grounds—we loved the resident beavers. Daryl and Erni are wonderful, inspirational people." *(Rita & Todd McGee)* "Charming and whimsical guest rooms; one with a frog theme, another with a dragon theme. Thoughtful touches included the soft, thick terry robes, and an always-available supply of juices, soda, fruit, and crackers." *(Pamela Johnson)* "The hospitable innkeepers gave us a hand with the luggage." *(Helene Wilder)*

"This historic house has been carefully and tastefully restored, preserving its past while offering all modern amenities: comfortable beds, modern baths, spacious armoires and chests, and windows with panoramic views. The expansive grounds include woods to hike, landscaped lawns, horse paddocks, a pristine swimming pool, and a pretty Japanese tea garden complete with a frog pond." *(Glenda White)* "We enjoyed the extra pillows and the views from the many-windowed Frog's Den." *(Linda Nordell)* "Dragon's Lair has a beautiful four-poster bed, blazing fireplace, gliders to rock away stress, and a clean, pretty, new bathroom. Delicious breakfasts with Hannah's bananas and pancakes with strawberry rhubarb sauce. Wonderful, down-to-earth, smart, service-oriented innkeepers. Impeccable housekeeping. A little out-of-the-way, but well worth the effort. Great hiking trails, gorgeous swimming pool, lovely plantings." *(Susannah Rabb Bailing)*

Open All year.

Rooms 1 suite, 3 doubles—all with private bath and/or shower, clock, desk, air-conditioning, fan, refrigerator, robes. 2 with fireplace.

Facilities Dining room with fireplace; living room with fireplace, piano, stereo, books, games; guest microwave. 100 acres with gardens, swimming pool, hiking trails, ponds for fishing/ice-skating, lawn games. Fishing on property. Cross-country skiing nearby.

Location N-central MA. Pioneer Valley Hills. 45 min. N of Springfield. 2 hrs. W of Boston. From I-91 N, take Exit 24 (Conway, Deerfield). Right at ramp; right again on Rte. 116 S. Go 2 m & go left on Rte. 47 N. Follow 5 m to end at Rte. 63. Cross over Rte. 63, to N. Leverett Rd. Take N. Leverett Rd. 3.7 m to Moore's Corners. On right is Village Co-op. Take Dudleyville Rd. (right fork just past the Co-op). Continue 1 m to inn sign on left.

Restrictions No smoking. Children over 12.

Credit cards MC, Visa.

Rates B&B, $185 suite, $125–155 double. 2-night weekend minimum late-Sept.–early Nov.; mid-May–mid-June. 15% discount Mon.–Thurs., June–Sept.

LYNN

For additional area entries, see **Marblehead** and **Salem.**

Information please: In neighboring Swampscott is **Cap'n Jack's Waterfront Inn** (253 Humphrey Street, Swampscott, 01907; 781–595–7910 or 800–958–9930; www.capnjacks.com). The 25 rooms, including eight suites and apartments, are located in three buildings; facilities include a swimming pool and hot tub. Double rates of $60–135 include breakfasts of fresh fruit and juice, coffee, and coffee cake. "Rooms are clean and comfortable, all with TV and refrigerator; many have fantastic water views. Several restaurants, coffee shops, and bakeries are a short walk away for meals. The patio provides a scene of waves crashing on the rocks, and a skyline view of Boston. Within a few hundred feet are miles of ocean beach for swimming and walking." *(Ernest White)*

Diamond District B&B Inn 🛉   *Tel:* 781–599–4470
142 Ocean Street, 01902–2007   800–666–3076
Fax: 781–599–4470
E-mail: diamonddistrict@msn.com
URL: http://www.bbhost.com/diamonddistrict

One of New England's oldest towns, Lynn's growth came in the 19th century, when it was America's shoe-manufacturing center. One successful factory owner, P.J. Harney, built this Georgian mansion in 1911, in a neighborhood named for the prosperity of its inhabitants. In 1989, Sandra and Jerry Caron restored it as a B&B, naming it the Diamond District B&B to reflect its regained status as a local jewel. They have furnished the house with antiques and Oriental rugs, complementing the original claw-foot tubs, pedestal sinks, cabinets, light fixtures, woodwork, and hardwood floors. A candlelight breakfast is served from 8–9:30 A.M. at your choice of the larger Chippendale table or smaller tables, and includes fresh fruit, homemade muffins and scones, a choice of meat, and an entrée that might be Belgian waffles, lobster quiche, eggs Florentine, or ham-and-cheese omelets.

"The house is large and attractive; our room was ample and so was the bathroom, well supplied with thick, fragrant towels. Easily reached from the Boston airport. Attractive gardens. Fine water views and lovely breezes from the huge back porch." *(Emily Hoche-Mong)* "Excellent breakfasts with waffles one day and French toast the next, plus fresh juice, fruit, and muffins." *(Ann Baker)* "Well-lit, well-marked parking area. The living room has the original Mexican mahogany woodwork, and is a collector's delight, with vintage art, musical instruments, and an 1895 rosewood Knabe concert grand piano. In acknowledgment of Lynn's history in the footwear business, a subtle shoe theme can be found throughout the house. Our large first-floor room had excellent lighting and a comfortable bed. Quality linens and towels. At breakfast, the sideboard was set up with carafes of coffee, juice, granola, and muffins; we were served delicious peach-stuffed French toast with peach syrup and bacon." *(NB)* "One block from the beach, precisely where I wanted to be. Inventive breakfasts that accommodated my diet." *(Dean Weber)* "Jerry showed me the entire inn and what it had to offer, and provided me with a detailed map of the surrounding area." *(Joseph Woytach)* "Beautifully appointed rooms, many with ocean views, lovely service." *(Lucille Wendel & others)*

Open All year.

Rooms 3 suites, 8 doubles—9 with private bath and/or shower, 2 with maximum of 4 people sharing bath. All with telephone, clock/radio, TV, desk, air-conditioning. Some with ceiling fan, fireplace, whirlpool tub, deck, refrigerator.

Facilities Dining room with fireplace; living room with fireplace, piano, books; beach umbrellas, towels; guest refrigerators. ½ acre with croquet, gardens. 1 block to 3-mile beach for swimming with bicycling, walking paths.

Location N Shore. 8 m NE of Boston. Historic district. 1 m from town. 1 block to Boston bus. From Logan Airport, take Rte. 1A N 7.3 m over Gen. Edwards Bridge to Lynn. Continue straight (7 lights) to overhead sign, "Swampscott-Marblehead," then bear right toward ocean and rotary. Go ⅔ around rotary along ocean. Go ⁹⁄₁₀ m through 1 light & blinking light. Go left on Prescott Rd. & right on Ocean St. to inn on right.

Restrictions No smoking. "Inn not child-proofed."

Credit cards Amex, CB, DC, Discover, Visa, MC.

Rates B&B, $145–225 suite, $90–140 double. Extra person, $20. Senior, AAA discount midweek. 2-night holiday minimum, also Sept., Oct.

Extras Crib.

MARBLEHEAD

Historic Marblehead was famous in Colonial times as a sailing capital; today's visitors enjoy the water views, appealing shops and restaurants, and historic buildings. Marblehead is located on the North Shore, 15 miles northeast of Boston and Logan Airport, and 4 miles east of Salem.

Information please: Just a block from the Marblehead Harbor is the **The Harbor Light Inn** (58 Washington Street, 01945; 781–631–2186; www.harborlightinn.com), two connected 18th-century homes, owned by Peter and Suzanne Conway since 1986. The inn takes its name from Marblehead's famous harbor light, which you can see from the widow's walk. Rates of $95–275 for the 21 suites and double rooms include a breakfast of fruit, freshly baked breads, and yogurt.

Overlooking Marblehead's picturesque harbor and rocky coastline, **Oceanwatch** (8 Fort Sewall Lane, 01945; 781–639–8660; oceanwatch @shore.net) was restored as an inn in 1996 by owners Diane and Paul Jolicoeur. The Victorian-era landmark includes three guest rooms, each with a king-size bed, private bath, telephone, and TV. A continental breakfast is included; in the evening guests are invited for sherry in the observatory atop Oceanwatch, affording views from Gloucester to Plymouth. B&B double rates range from $130–175.

A Victorian home overlooking the bay, **Spraycliff on the Ocean** (25 Spray Avenue, 01945; 781–744–8924 or 800–626–1530), has seven guest rooms, five with striking ocean views. B&B double rates of $175–200 include a light continental breakfast, and use of the inn's bicycles. "Beautiful rooms, attentive innkeepers, ideal location." *(EJ)*

Built in the 1840s, **Stillpoint** (27 Gregory Street, 01945; 781–631–1667 or 800–882–3891) sits on a quiet street in Marblehead's Old Town, a few minutes' walk to antique shops, restaurants, and seaside activities in Crocker Park. In good weather, a breakfast of juice, fresh fruit, cold cereal, yogurt, and homemade breads and muffins is served on the deck overlooking the garden and Marblehead Harbor. Double B&B rates for the three guest rooms range from $70–90. An equally appealing choice is the neighboring 1840 **Harborside House** (23 Gregory Street, 01945; 781–631–1032; www.shore.net/~swliving/); the two guest rooms share a bath, and the $70–80 double rates include breakfast and afternoon tea.

MARTHA'S VINEYARD

Martha's Vineyard is a 20-mile-long island, located 5 miles south of Woods Hole in Cape Cod, and 80 miles south of Boston. It is easily reached by air from LaGuardia Airport or White Plains, NY; Bridgeport, CT; New Bedford and Boston, MA; or by a 45-minute ferry ride from Woods Hole or a longer one from Hyannis. Its beautiful beaches— many of them free—offer full surf on the south side of the island, and gentle waves along the state beach between Edgartown and Oak Bluffs. Swimming, fishing, and sailing are always popular, as are horseback riding and bicycling. A 15-mile bicycle path leads along the water and through the woods.

The Vineyard is a popular and crowded place in the summer, so make car reservations for the ferry three to six months in advance. You can also rent a car after you arrive, but again, advance reservations are essential. If you're staying at an inn in Edgartown or Vineyard Haven, you can manage quite well without a car at all; in the up-island towns, such as Menemsha or West Tisbury, it's essential. Rates are highest in July and August, and two- and three-day minimum stays are the rule; a number of inns charge peak season rates from early June through mid-October. We urge you to visit in September or October for sunny weather minus the crowds.

All the towns on the island, except for Edgartown and Oak Bluffs, are dry; when you're going out to dinner, bring your own wine, and the staff will be happy to chill and serve it for you.

Information please: Like many area homes, the **Ashley Inn** (129 Main Street, Edgartown, 02539; 508–627–9655; www.vineyard.net/biz/ashleyinn) is a former sea captain's home, and was built in 1860. Located within walking distance of town, the inn has ten guest rooms, each with private bath, some with air-conditioning; a continental breakfast is included in the $75–250 rates. "Cozy sitting room with lots of books about the island and New England. Friendly, knowledgeable innkeeper; adequate accommodations. I had to leave early for an appointment, and would have appreciated early-bird coffee and muffins." *(SG)* "Passed down through generations of the Crowell family until it was renovated as an inn in 1983 by the Hurley family. Spacious property with pretty gardens and an expansive back yard with lounge chairs, hammocks, and ample parking. Bright and cheerful, with attractive decor and fresh flowers." *(Rose Ciccone)*

One block from the beach and a five-minutes' walk from downtown is the 75-year-old **Pequot Hotel** (19 Pequot Avenue, Oak Bluffs, 02557; 508–693–5087 or 800–947–8704). The simply furnished rooms have private baths and air-conditioning. Ideal for families is the apartment suite with two bedrooms, a sitting area, kitchen, and bath. A continental breakfast is included in the double rates of $65–165. "While furnishings are modest, the prices are affordable by island standards. Comfortable queen-size bed. The staff is friendly and helpful, and further renovations are planned." *(RC)*

The Charlotte Inn ✕
27 South Summer Street
Edgartown, 02539

Tel: 508–627–4751
Fax: 508–627–4652

The Charlotte has a well-deserved reputation as the most elegant inn on Martha's Vineyard. Each guest room is decorated differently, but all have beautiful European antiques, original paintings and engravings, and brass lamps. Rich, dark-colored wallpapers contrast handsomely with the light-colored carpets and window trim in the main inn.

Gery and Paula Conover bought the Charlotte Inn in 1970, and have gradually expanded it from the original Captain's House, built in 1860, adding suites in the Carriage House and guest rooms in the 200-year-old Garden House, the Summer House, and the Coach House; Carol Read is the general manager. Rates include a breakfast of coffee, juice, and homemade muffins. The inn's restaurant, L'Etoile, serves excellent French cuisine in a beautiful setting. Although the menu changes frequently, a recent choice of entrées included lobster with parsnip and chive custard, pheasant on broccoli rabe, and rack of lamb with spring greens.

"Fully endorse entry. The rooms are wonderful, the grounds are absolutely beautiful, the common rooms are elegant, and the excellent staff can constantly be seen delivering drinks, freshening flowers, and more. Our second-floor room in the Summer House was done in green and white, with lovely woodwork, antique furnishings, and silky green wallcovering. Fabric patterned in white dogwood on an ecru background was used for padded headboard, bed tables, and draperies. Linens, pillows, and the down comforter were all top quality. The opulent bath was as large as our bedroom. A marble-topped table held a vase of fresh flowers, silver brushes, and a book; other amenities included generous men's and women's toiletries, terry robes, and a heated towel rack. Towels were changed in the morning and again at night when the bed was turned down. A small alcove held a cabinet with a variety of books, a Bose Wave radio, a selection of CDs, and a silver tray with a bottle of port and glasses. The semi-private porch was perfect for relaxing. Dinner at L'Etoile was outstanding, with appetizers of veal terrine and lobster and scallop bisque; entrées of rack of lamb and lobster; and desserts of pumpkin crème brûlée and a fruit tart. Coffee was accompanied by a liqueur and a plate of shortbread cookies, truffles and chocolate-covered pecans. Breakfast is brought to your room or served in the terraced dining room. Served to our table were coffee, juice, and a tray with toast, croissant, bagel, coffee cake, and muffins. More than ample and all freshly made." *(Rose & Frank Ciccone)*

"Excellent location on a quiet lane, just off one of Edgartown's main shopping streets. The grounds are a lovely expanse of well-tended greenery, and the antique-filled rooms are exceptionally handsome. The restaurant feels much like a greenhouse—it's light and airy with lots of glass, plants, and even a little waterfall." *(SWS)* "Our room had a private terrace that opened to the English garden. The staff attended to every need but were almost invisible." *(Margaret Horn)* "Quite possibly the most relaxing 48 hours we've ever spent. Quiet room, impeccable taste." *(GR)*

Open All year. Restaurant closed Jan. 2–Feb. 14.

Rooms 2 suites, 23 doubles—all with full private bath, radio, fan, air-conditioning. 16 with TV. Most with telephone, desk. 5 with fireplace. Guest rooms in 5 buildings.

Facilities Restaurant, art gallery. Living room in Garden House with fireplace, TV; sitting room in Main House. Outside sitting areas, decks, porches, gardens. Walking distance to tennis, beaches, charter fishing. Public parking diagonally across the street.

Location 15-min. ride from the ferry. ½ block to Main St. Follow signs to Edgartown. Turn right onto S. Summer St. (after Town Hall). Inn ½ block down on left.

Restrictions No cigars, pipes, or heavy cigarette smoking. Children over 14.
Credit cards Amex, MC, Visa.
Rates B&B, $395–650 suite, $175–450 double. 2-night weekend/high-season minimum. Full breakfast, $9. Prix fixe dinner, $56.

Crocker House Inn   *Tel:* 508–693–1151
12 Crocker Avenue, P.O. Box 1658   800–772–0206
Vineyard Haven, 02568   *E-mail:* crockerinn@aol.com

The Crocker House Inn is a charming turn-of-the-century Victorian home with red cedar shingles and gingerbread trim, set on a quiet residential side street in the village of Vineyard Haven, just a short walk from the ferry, beach, restaurants, shops, and more. The inn was purchased by Jynell and Jeff Kristal in January of 1998 and has been tastefully redecorated with bright and refreshing colors. Some rooms have water views, sitting areas, and private porches and entrances. The top floor room can accommodate four, and offers a deck and views of the Vineyard Haven Harbor.

"Restful, charming, and immaculate, with a convenient location. Tasty breakfasts served from 8:30–10 A.M., with homemade granola, fresh fruit, and different kinds of homemade muffins every day; great chocolate chip cookies to eat on the porch." *(Judy MacDonald)* "Cozy, homey, and comfortable. Excellent water pressure in the shower." *(Cathleen Jaffe)* "Attractive rooms, ample towels; light refreshments readily available." *(Andrew DePalma)* Comments appreciated.

Open All year.
Rooms 8 doubles—all with private bath and/or shower, air-conditioning, deck.
Facilities Breakfast room, living room, porch. Bike rentals. Tennis, golf, swimming pool, beach, public park nearby. Off-street parking.
Location 150 m E of Boston. 5-min. walk from ferry. 1 block from Main St. From ferry, go to Main St. & turn right. Go right again on Crocker Ave. to inn (2 blocks on foot).
Restrictions No smoking. Children over 13.
Credit cards Amex, MC, Visa.
Rates B&B, $95–245 double. Extra person, $20. 3-night August minimum.

The Hanover House   *Tel:* 508–693–1066
10 Edgartown Road, P.O. Box 2107   800–339–1066
Vineyard Haven, 02568   *Fax:* 508–696–6099
E-mail: ronkay@vineyard.net
URL: http://www.freeyellow.com/members4/hanoverhouse/

A gambrel-roofed cottage built in the 1920s, the Hanover House has been an inn since 1934; Ron and Kay Nelson bought it in 1992. Guest rooms are furnished with vintage or reproduction beds, quilts, antique bureaus, and good bedside lighting. Breakfast is served from 8–10 A.M. at individual tables, and includes homemade muffins, coffee cake, and toasting bread with jams and jellies, plus juice, coffee, tea, and cocoa.

"Our quiet suite was set back from the road; it had a spacious, cathedral-ceilinged living room with comfortable sofa, a television placed on an antique sewing machine stand, and plenty of books and magazines. The four-poster, queen-size wrought-iron bed had a wonderfully firm, comfortable mattress; the well-equipped bathroom had fluffy towels. A private patio added to the romance and seclusion. Our breakfast of orange juice, herbal teas, freshly brewed coffee, and delicious homemade baked goods made it hard to stay on a diet. Ron and Kay were friendly, thoughtful, and caring." (*Amy Silverman*) "Our immaculate room was tidied daily, including fresh flowers. It had good reading lamps, comfortable seating, a suitcase stand, and nicely coordinated wallpapers and curtains. Friendly, personable innkeepers." (*Valerie Myers*) "We enjoyed the camaraderie among the guests." (*Nicholas & Eileen Pappas*) "Superb location; friendly, warm, professional innkeepers; immaculate, attractive furnishings." (*J. Conrad MacQuarrie*)

Open March–Dec.

Rooms 3 suites, 12 doubles—all with private shower and/or tub, radio, clock, TV, air-conditioning. 10 with deck, 4 with fan, 1 with desk. 2 suites in carriage house with kitchenette, private deck or patio.

Facilities Breakfast room with stereo; decks. ½ acre with 5 off-street parking spaces.

Location 3 blocks to town. From ferry, go left. Turn right at next intersection. Bear left at next corner & turn left on Edgartown Rd. Inn is 3rd house on left.

Restrictions Absolutely no smoking. Children welcome in certain rooms; inquire for details.

Credit cards Amex, Discover, MC, Visa.

Rates B&B, $140–280 suite, double. Extra person, $15–20. 3-night minimum for holidays & for suites.

Hob Knob Inn   ♿ ♀

128 Main Street, P.O. Box 239, Edgartown, 02539

Tel: 508–627–9510
800–696–2723
Fax: 508–627–4560
E-mail: hobknob@vineyard.net
URL: http://www.hobknob.com

Named after the estate that belonged to its owner's grandparents, the Hob Knob Inn is a Gothic Revival home dating back to 1860 and was purchased by Maggie White in 1995; it was previously known as the Governor Bradford Inn. After extensive refurbishing, the airy and spacious guest rooms are now appointed with luxurious down comforters and pillows, with cotton bedding; many have king-size beds. Decorated with select antiques, English chintz fabrics, fresh flowers, rooms overlook the inn's gardens or Edgartown's quaint streets.

Breakfast is served in the two dining rooms, at individual tables, from 8:30–10 A.M, and includes a buffet of fresh fruit and juice, cereals and home-baked breads and muffins, plus a choice of omelets, berry pancakes, poached eggs with tomato, Canadian bacon, and English muffin, or the daily special. Afternoon tea often includes home-baked scones and pitchers of lemonade served on the spacious porch. Rates also include fresh flowers and the morning paper, delivered to your door.

"Beautifully decorated and inviting common areas and guest rooms." *(RC)* "Maggie and her decorator have done a wonderful job of making Hob Knob a place of distinction. The marvelous living room is enhanced by a fireplace and one-of-a-kind antiques, a sunlit Garden Room opens out to the English garden terrace, and the spacious porch is ideal for afternoon and evening enjoyment. Each bedroom is individually designed with a decorator's flair from the upholstered headboards to the coordinating dust ruffles, throw pillows, and accents. The helpful staff is quick to provide guests with newspapers, cups of coffee, or extra pillows; these local residents really know the island and are pleased to share their knowledge. Our visit included a harbor tour aboard the Hob Knob Boston Whaler, complete with a picnic lunch made by the chef. Delicious breakfast with home-baked muffins and scones, locally made jams and jellies, and excellent French toast. Herbs picked from the garden enhanced many of the dishes. In the afternoon, the staff treated us to mouth-watering cookies and first-rate tea in the Garden Room. A decanter of excellent port is available to guests as well." *(Mary Crawford)*

Open All year.

Rooms 3-bedroom guest house, 16 doubles—all with full private bath, telephone, Bose Wave radio, clock, TV, fan. Some with desk, refrigerator, modem/data port.

Facilities 2 dining rooms, living room with fireplace, garden room with books; porches; exercise room. Meeting facilities. Patios, gardens, off-street parking. Extra charges for bicycles; Boston Whaler for charter fishing trips, sunset cruises; picnic baskets; clambakes; massage therapy.

Location 2 blocks from heart of village.

Restrictions No smoking. Children under 1 or over 12.

Credit cards Amex, MC, Visa.

Rates B&B, $125–375 double. Extra person, $30. 2–3 night weekend/holiday minimum. 10% AAA discount off-season. Picnic baskets, $15–40 per person; clambake, $50 per person.

Extras Wheelchair access; bathroom specially equipped. Crib; babysitting by arrangement.

Thorncroft Inn &
460 Main Street, Vineyard Haven, 02568

Tel: 508–693–3333
800–332–1236
Fax: 508–693–5419
E-mail: kgb@tiac.net
URL: http://www.thorncroft.com

A secluded, luxurious, couples-oriented country inn, Thorncroft was built in 1918 and has been owned by Lynn and Karl Buder since 1981. Breakfast is offered at two seatings, 8:15 and 9:30 A.M., served at individual tables for two; if you prefer, have a continental breakfast in bed, delivered at 9 or 10 A.M. On one morning, enjoy a cheese strata; the next, almond French toast; and on a third day, scrambled eggs with sausage and buttermilk biscuits. In 1996, the Buders constructed a private, secluded cottage, with a double Jacuzzi tub, fireplace, four-poster king-size bed, and a fully accessible bathroom.

"Beautiful inn with traditional furnishings, plush carpets, immaculate bathroom. Amenities include bathrobes, coffee delivered to the room on a silver tray, Boston newspaper at the door, postcards and envelopes already stamped, and headphones for the television. Private, romantic escape." *(Louisa Yue-Chan)* "Room #14 is our favorite, with a two-person Jacuzzi and wood-burning fireplace. Throughout the inn, rooms are furnished with beautiful period antiques. Innkeepers Karl and Lynn Buder provide exceptional attention to detail. Turndown service and twice-daily maid service ensure that your room is always in order. Convenient, quiet location, a pleasant walk to the shops and restaurants of Vineyard Haven in one direction; in the other, an inviting stroll past the West Chop Lighthouse to gaze at the spectacular views of the ocean beyond." *(David & Frances Labossiere)* "Warm, hospitable owners, always plenty of real firewood available. Our favorite rooms are the two with private hot tubs." *(Glenn Morris)*

Open All year.

Rooms 1 cottage, 14 doubles—all with private bath and/or shower, telephone, radio, clock, TV, air-conditioning, hairdryers, irons, ironing boards, flashlights, bathrobes. Most with wood-burning fireplace. Some with private hot tub or double Jacuzzi, balcony/deck, refrigerator, desk. 5 in carriage house.

Facilities 2 dining rooms, 1 with fireplace; 2 living rooms, 1 with fireplace, 1 with refrigerator. 3½ acres with ample off-street parking. Golf nearby.

Location 1 m to ferry. By car: from ferry dock, go left to stop sign & turn right. Take next left onto Main St. to inn 1 m ahead on left. On foot: go straight ahead off ferry dock to Main St. & go right.

Restrictions Absolutely no smoking. Children over 15.

Credit cards Amex, CB, DC, Discover, EnRoute, MC, Visa.

Rates B&B, $160–450 double. 3-night weekend minimum summer, holiday weekends.

Extras Cottage wheelchair accessible. Some French, Spanish spoken.

The Tuscany Inn ✕

22 North Water Street, P.O. Box 2428
Edgartown, 02539

Tel: 508–627–5999
Fax: 508–627–6605

While the white clapboard exterior of this 1893 ship captain's home is distinctly Victorian, the interior of the Tuscany Inn reflects the heritage (and decorating skill) of Laura Scheuer, a native of Tuscany, and her husband Rusty. An inn since 1931, it was purchased and restored by the Scheuers in 1993. Breakfast is served at individual tables, from 8:30–10 A.M., or on the patio, weather permitting. A typical summer menu includes entrées such as frittata, buttermilk blueberry pancakes, and French toast. Continental breakfast is served off-season. The inn restaurant, La Cucina, exhibits Tuscan flair with such entrées as halibut with potato and leek ragout; roast salmon with fennel and onion; tomato-basil egg noodles; and rosemary-and-lavender marinated lamb chops with cannelini beans and oven-dried tomatoes.

"Traditional furnishings, with warm colors; there's an inviting library for sitting and reading. Our third-floor room, with a view of the harbor, had a king-size bed and ample bath with Jacuzzi tub. Laura and Rusty have done a magnificent job of restoration; they also make everyone feel welcome and at home." *(J. Van Rooyen)* "A little jewel, in pristine condition, totally updated, and charmingly decorated by Tuscan native Laura Scheuer, who has given it the feel of an Italian country inn. The breakfast room has displays of Italian pottery, and afternoon cappuccino and biscotti are served on the patio. Central location." *(Mary Beth O'Reilly)*

Open March 15–Dec. 31. Restaurant open Memorial Day–Sept.

Rooms 8 doubles—all with private shower and/or tub, air-conditioning. 3 with whirlpool tub. TV on request.

Facilities Restaurant, dining room with fireplace, living room with fireplace, library, porch. ½ acre with off-street parking, patio, gardens, fountain, hammock. Golf nearby.

Location Historic district. From ferry, follow signs to Edgartown. Follow Main St. to Water St. Turn left on Water St. & go 1 block to Winter St. to inn on corner.

Restrictions Some traffic noise possible. No smoking. Children over 8.

Credit cards Amex, DC, MC, Visa.

Rates B&B, $90–375, double. Extra person, $25. 2-night minimum. Off-season Tuscan cooking packages.

Extras Italian spoken.

MIDDLEBOROUGH

Zachariah Eddy House *Tel:* 508–946–0016
51 South Main Street, 02346 *Fax:* 508–947–2603
E-mail: zacheddy@aol.com
URL: http://www.bbhost.com/zacheddyhouse

Location, lobster, and history are three appealing aspects of the Zachariah Eddy House. If you're looking for an affordable base of operations for touring Boston, Cape Cod, Newport, and Providence, you'll be pleased to learn that it's less than 35 miles from each of those destinations. If it's lobster that you crave, you'll be tempted by dinners of just-caught crustaceans. And if you're fascinated by American history, then you'll enjoy learning about a home dating back to 1831. Named for its original owner, a noted 19th-century attorney and associate of John Quincy Adams and Daniel Webster, the Zachariah Eddy House was built in the Greek Revival style, and was renovated in the late 1800s with Colonial Revival detail. Owners Cheryl and Bradford Leonard have lived here since 1977; in 1995, they opened their home as a B&B. Middleborough's historic district has just been named to the National Register of Historic Places, and was a part of the original Plimoth Colony; it's also home to the Tom Thumb Museum.

The Leonards serve a hearty and creative breakfast from 8–10 A.M. in the dining room or side porch. In addition to fresh fruit and home-baked breads and muffins, the meal might include bread pudding, Yankee scramble with bacon, new potatoes, and New England baked beans; or perhaps strawberry peach compote, baked apple pancake, lobster and red pepper omelet, and sausage casserole. Summer dinners include produce from the Leonards' garden, and lobster and clams that they catch themselves. Guest rooms are attractively decorated with king-, queen-, and full-size beds, plus Victorian antiques. Of particular interest is one of the bathrooms, originally built as a private chapel, and still featuring a magnificent stained-glass window.

"Cheryl is a caring and attentive innkeeper. She and Brad are delightful and we spent a couple of hours chatting with them on the lovely porch. Their comfortable house has beautiful inlaid patterned wood floors. Our bedroom shared a large full bath with double sinks; robes and plenty of large, plush towels are provided. Our appealing room had a turret with a window seat, and fascinating curved windows and oak trim. Extraordinary breakfast with fresh fruit with yogurt and granola, blueberry muffins, baked apple pancakes, and vegetable omelets with a sausage casserole." *(Rose Ciccone)* "Everything we were promised was there—and then some—from the fabulous breakfasts prepared at our convenience to the warm hospitality and our beautiful room. We were welcomed with glasses of wine and bowls of clam chowder on a stormy night. Excellent information and directions to assist with our daily explorations." *(Julie Hebert)*

"Our room was accented with antique toys, which made for interesting conversation." *(Julie & Al Fenner)* "Delectable all-you-can-eat lobster dinners." *(Beth Young)* "Exceptional lobster omelets. Ideal balance of privacy and hospitality." *(Pat McCormick)* "Elegant decor yet homey and comfortable. We could breakfast at the dining room table, or on the beautiful porch overlooking the flower garden and a copper beach tree." *(Priscilla Boehm)* "Spacious, well-appointed, and attractive rooms. Our hosts understand the fine art of conversation without being intrusive." *(Paul Busick)* "The innkeeper went way out of her way to obtain passes and give directions to places we wished to visit. Many antique shops within walking distance. The porch was a peaceful spot to relax in the evening, and is furnished with white wicker." *(Mrs. Raymond Bowman)* "Gorgeous woodwork, etched glass, and stained-glass windows. Brad took us out on the boat to pull up lobster pots; we ate the catch that evening in the elegant dining room." *(Martha Eddy)*

Open All year.

Rooms 3 doubles—1 with private hall bath, 2 with maximum of 4 sharing bath. All with clock, TV, air-conditioning, robes. 2 with ceiling fan; 1 with desk, data port.

Facilities Dining room, double parlor with fireplace, TV/VCR; porch with swing, deck. ¾ acre with lawn games. Tennis, golf, water sports nearby.

Location SE MA, 35 m S of Boston, 30 m E of Providence, RI, 35 m NE of Newport, RI, 20 NW of Cape Cod, 15 m W of Plymouth. From I-495, take Exit 4. Go N on Rte. 105 (S. Main St.) for 1 m to the inn, just S of Town Hall. Historic district.

Restrictions No smoking. Children 10 and over preferred. Air-conditioning masks possible summer traffic noise in front room.

Credit cards Amex, Discover, MC, Visa.

Rates B&B, $75–125 double, $75–110 single. Extra person, $15 Senior, AAA discount. 2-night weekend July–Oct., Thanksgiving, Christmas. Prix fixe dinner, $16–25.

Extras Airport/station pickups.

NANTUCKET

Nantucket, a relatively small island about 7 by 15 miles, located 25 to 30 miles south of Cape Cod in the Atlantic Ocean, was settled in the late-17th century by theological nonconformists who were not welcome in the Puritan Massachusetts Colony. The island thrived as a port for fishing and whaling ships and the profits earned were often invested in stately saltbox or Federal-style houses which still stand clustered cheek-to-jowl in the town of Nantucket. With the decline of the whaling industry, modern development bypassed the community; when it was once again "discovered" by sailors and summer vacationers, the unspoiled Colonial architecture became part of its allure. Strict preservation laws now restrict development, and all new houses must have unpainted clapboard, which weathers to that unique shade known as "Nantucket gray." Lovely beaches encircle the island and between the communities of Siasconset (pronounced "Sconset") to the east and Madaket to the west you'll find 7,700 non-contiguous acres of open land, including a nature sanctuary, windswept moors, and cranberry bogs. Of particular interest on rainy days is the Nantucket Whaling Museum and the Peter Foulger Museum covering Nantucket history.

Peak season (when the population can swell from 4,000 to 40,000) runs from Memorial Day through Labor Day weekend although spring, fall, and Christmas are becoming increasingly popular. During July and August, expect crowds, high rates, and minimum-stay requirements at all inns. If you're making last-minute plans and aren't having any luck at the inns recommended here, call the Nantucket Information Bureau (25 Federal Street; 508–228–0925); they can tell you where rooms are available.

You can fly to Nantucket from New York, Providence, Boston, New Bedford, or Hyannis, or take the ferry from Hyannis, or Oak Bluffs (Martha's Vineyard). Reservations are essential in peak season, and should be made several months in advance for cars, but almost all innkeepers recommend leaving your car on the mainland, if possible. Most inns listed below are within a short distance of the ferry dock, in the town of Nantucket itself. *In-season parking is a problem in Nantucket Town.* New visitors to the island should familiarize themselves with a map before they start out cross-island on a bicycle (rental shops abound) as distances can be deceiving.

Nantucket is expensive. Prices for everything on the island are higher; fuel for heating and electricity must be brought in on barges, and most food and other commodities make the trip on the ferry, adding to their cost. Where we have identified an inn with the ¢ symbol, it indicates that a few of their rooms are more economically priced *for the island*, yet they are still more than you would pay on the mainland.

When calling for reservations, take the time to shop around, and make sure you're getting the best value for your money. Understand what the total cost will be, and what is included in the price, i.e., light or hearty continental breakfast, afternoon tea or evening refreshments. And let us know what you discover!

Reader tips: "Highly recommend a visit to Nantucket midweek in late October, or even early November. The weather was lovely, the crowds were small, and the room rates were exceedingly reasonable. If you don't mind a bit of uncertainty, you can save even more if you wait until your arrival to look for a room—most inns have irresistible 'walk-in' rates—but don't ever try this on a weekend." *(SWS)* "The Brotherhood of Thieves is a fun pub with evening entertainment and appealing decor. The Atlantic Café is also a good choice for late-night fare." *(Sally Ducot)* "Something Natural was our favorite for lunch. We enjoyed the slide film *Nantucket Seasons on the Island* to see what it is like the rest of the year." *(Glenn Roehrig)*

Also recommended: The "grand dame" of Nantucket inns, the **Jared Coffin House** (29 Broad Street, 02554; 508–228–2400 or 800–248–2405; www.nantucket.net/lodging/jchouse) is comprised of the Jared Coffin House (1845), two attached wings built in the 1700s and in 1857, two 19th-century buildings (the Henry Coffin and the Harrison Gray) less than 50 feet away, and the Daniel Webster House, built in 1968. Two restaurants, the Tap Room and Jared's, offer casual and more formal dining. Some rooms have been renovated more recently than others, others can be noisy in season, so get details when booking. A full breakfast is included in the $100–225 double rates; there are 60 guest rooms (30 with a queen-size canopy bed). "Enjoyed the food, service, ambience, and excellent value at the midweek off-season seafood buffet." *(SWS)* "Our favorite rooms are in the Harrison Gray House, offering antique decor, lots of common space for guests, and quiet atmosphere." *(DLG)*

An attractive 90-room motel-style property particularly appropriate for families, **The Beachside** (30 North Beach Street, 02554; 508–228–2241 or 800–322–4433) is located midway between town and Jetties Beach, about a ten-minute walk in either direction. Although not right on a beach (despite its name), a swimming pool provides an added benefit for the younger set. The double rates of $95–225 include a continental breakfast.

Cliff Lodge (9 Cliff Road, 02554; 508–228–9480) was built in 1771 on a hill overlooking Nantucket Harbor, and was renovated two centuries later in an English country–style, with Laura Ashley wallpapers, splattered-paint floors, and white eyelet bedding. Half the rooms have water views and the widow's walk provides the second highest observation spot in town. Double rates $65–250 for the eleven guest rooms (each with private bath) include a breakfast of juices, fresh fruit, cereal, and homemade muffins. "A pleasant walk to town. Lovely views of the harbor from the deck and garden. Inviting common areas downstairs, charming guest rooms upstairs." *(SWS)*

A restored sea captain's mansion, **Four Chimneys** (38 Orange Street, 02554; 508–228–1912) offers ten luxurious guest rooms, each with a simple private bath. Continental breakfast and afternoon snacks are included in the double rates of $150–275. "A comfortable yet elegant home away from home, conveniently located four blocks from the center of town. The nightly hors d'oeuvres and chocolate mints were a nice touch." *(Mary Beth O'Reilly)*

Built in the late 1770s, the **Union Street Inn** (Seven Union Street, 02554; 508–228–9222 or 800–225–5116; www.union-street-inn.com/)

has a convenient in-town location and genuine historic charm, with antique furnishings, original wide-plank floors, raised wood-panel walls, and fireplaces. One of the few B&Bs licensed to serve a full breakfast, the inn serves fresh fruit and cereal, plus French toast, pancakes, or eggs in the dining area or on the lovely garden patio, with views of Stone Alley and the gilded church tower and town clock. B&B double rates for the twelve guest rooms range from $80–245. "Hands-on resident owners; great location, especially off-season; authentic Colonial appeal; beautifully maintained." *(SWS)*

Information please: Built in the mid-19th century, **The Wauwinet** (120 Wauwinet Road, P.O. Box 2580, 02584; 508–228–0145 or 800–426–8718) is one of Nantucket's few waterfront inns; after a multimillion dollar restoration, it is now also the island's most expensive. The decor of the 35 guest rooms and cottages includes antique pine armoires, iron or wicker headboards, sisal carpeting, and fresh flowers. The inn's lawns sweep down from the porch to the harbor on one side; to the other, it's a 50-yard walk to the dunes and the Atlantic beyond. B&B double rates $195–725 (suites to $1,400) include a full breakfast, twice-daily maid service, use of the mountain bicycles, tennis courts, and boats, plus jitney service to Nantucket Town, eight miles away. Topper's, the inn's restaurant, combines American cooking with regional specialties. "Magnificent setting with beautifully landscaped grounds and water views. Both the common areas and the guest rooms are lush and stunning." *(SWS)* "Although we had booked the least expensive room for our midweek off-season visit, we were thrilled to be upgraded to one of their best!" *(MW)*

Ideal for couples or families, the **Wharf Cottages** (New Whale Street, P.O. Box 1139, 02554; 508–228–4620 or 800–ISLANDS) offer studios and one-, two-, or three-bedroom waterfront cottages right on the docks in the Nantucket Boat Basin. Each cottage offers a private deck and fully equipped kitchen. For those traveling by water, boat slips can be arranged. Rates range from $210–525, depending on the season and size of cottage. Under the same management is **The White Elephant** (Easton Street, P.O. Box 1139, 02554; 508–228–2500 or 800–ISLANDS), a 56-room hotel and cottage complex about three blocks north. From the private terrace, guests have a commanding view of the busy harbor. A private harborside pool and clay tennis courts are among the amenities. Double rates range from $200–650.

Centre Street Inn ¢ &.

78 Centre Street, P.O. Box 262, 02554

Tel: 508–228–0199
Fax: 508–228–8676
E-mail: inn@nantucket.net
URL: http://www.centrestreetinn.com

Longtime Nantucket vacationers Sheila and Fred Heap decided to make the island their year-round home when they bought the Centre Street Inn in 1994. Built by a Nantucket whale-oil trader in 1742, and an inn since 1875, the inn is decorated by the Heaps with a light and airy look, with Waverly, Ralph Lauren, and Laura Ashley floral and gingham fabrics, and antique, English pine, white-washed, and white wicker furnishings. Sheila notes that "our delightful shared-bath guest rooms make a Nantucket vacation quite affordable; the money saved can be used to enjoy some of the island's fine dining!" Breakfast is served from 8:30–10 A.M. at the dining room table, and includes fresh fruit and juice, with yogurt-and-granola fruit parfaits, home-baked breads and muffins, and locally roasted coffee. Rates also include afternoon refreshments.

"Excellent location on a quiet residential street in the historic district. Both common areas and all guest rooms—from the smallest to the largest—are fresh and inviting with charming decor, thoughtful touches, and constant upgrading. Sheila has done a wonderful job of honoring the building's history and heritage without stuffiness or formality. Caring, hands-on innkeepers." (SWS) "The decor includes beautiful stenciling and wall-painting, charming quilts, and a spring-green color scheme with gentle florals. The relaxing atmosphere encourages guests to congregate happily in the two comfortable downstairs living rooms, chatting away like old friends." (Patricia Niece, also MW) "Sheila has combined the flair of an interior designer, with the warmth and comfort of your own home." (Mary Kevin Wald) "Welcoming, accommodating innkeepers. Breakfast is a time to meet the other guests and to share island experiences and to enjoy wonderful baked goods. The Heaps' abundant socializing skills make evening gatherings equally pleasant. Improvements are seen with every visit. Fred and Sheila are devoted to their beautiful inn and to their guests' enjoyment." (Tom & Margie Dwyer) "Fred and Sheila take a personal interest in their guests, and are always available for advice on restaurants, shops, walks, and bike trails. The cheerful staff keeps the inn spotless. Even their dogs are wonderful, although I am partial to Brita—Murphy and Toby regard me as a necessary nuisance." (Noel Ryan) "Pampering touches include the fine linens and bath soaps. We enjoyed drinking tea in the side garden." (Toby Kerans)

Open Mid-April–early Dec.

Rooms 1 suite, 10 doubles, 2 singles—7 private shower bath, 6 rooms with maximum of 4 people sharing bath. All with radio, clock, fan. 5 with fireplace.

Facilities Dining room, living room, guest pantry. Brick patio, gardens, cedar table, Adirondack chairs. 10–20 min. walk to harbor beaches.

Location Residential historic district. 10-min. walk to shops, restaurants. Shuttle stop nearby. Short walk to ferry. From ferry dock, take Broad or Main St. & turn right onto Centre St. to inn, 7th house on left beyond Congregational Church, at corner of Centre & Lily. 7-m taxi ride from airport.

Restrictions No smoking. Children 8 and over.

Credit cards Amex, MC, Visa.

Rates B&B, \$115–195 suite (sleeps 4); extra adult, \$30; extra child, 20. \$65–175 double; \$45–75 single. 2–3 night weekend/holiday/peak season minimum. Tipping envelopes.

Extras Wheelchair access; bathroom specially equipped.

Cliffside Beach Club ♀ ✕
32 Jefferson Avenue, 02554

Tel: 508–228–0618
800–932–9645
Fax: 508–325–4735
URL: http://www.cliffsidebeach.com

Nantucket's sea captains didn't much care much about having a water view when they returned home—why would they after months or years at sea? But most of us "landlubbers" want nothing more from a beach vacation than to go to sleep at night, and awaken in the morning to the sight, sound, and smell of the ocean just outside our door.

Originally built in 1924 as a private beach club, Cliffside once had 400 changing cabins for guests to switch from silk suits and top hats to bathing costumes. The transition to a beach resort began in the 1970s with the construction of several apartments, and was recently completed with the renovation of the lobby and construction of new guest rooms and suites. A fully equipped health club was completed in 1998; it's located in a separate building, with saunas, massage room, weight and aerobic machines, and a hydrotherapy spa. The inn's exterior is traditional, with weathered cedar shingles, redwood trim, and pine decks, while the handsome interior has cathedral ceilings with 60-year-old beaded hemlock, custom-milled cedar, and heart pine from Boston's Old South station; furnishings were designed and built by Nantucket craftsmen, complemented by soft lighting and local artwork to complete the elegant but casual look. Longtime owners Monique and Robert Currie tell us that "most of our rooms and all the common areas view the beach and the sea. We have casual but well-appointed rooms offering our guests all the expected amenities, including terry-cloth robes, and Crabtree & Evelyn toiletries." Rates include a breakfast of coffee, tea, juice, muffins, and fresh-baked breads.

"Located on a white, sandy beach, Cliffside provides newspapers from New York and Boston with breakfast. It also has a waterside restaurant that serves lunch and dinner. An enjoyable walk to town and great shopping." *(Kevin Micchelli)* "Beautiful beachside setting in posh residential area." *(SWS)* "Artfully decorated with antiques, unique paintings, fresh flowers, and beautiful plants. Soothing music playing in the background. Tasty breakfast to eat in the lobby; we like to take a tray back to our deck and watch the beach come alive. We always get a room with a deck right on the beach." *(John & Nancy Swayne)* "The Curries are assisted by a staff whose enthusiasm and love for their jobs are evident from their cheerful faces and willingness to help. Promptly at 4:30 P.M., the chairs and the umbrellas from the beach club are put away and the beach club members depart. Sheer bliss is sitting on the deck watching the sunset, while relaxing with a glass of wine." *(Carolyn Viani)* "The housekeeping and service are first-rate. Quiet, serene comfort in a beautiful setting." *(Tal Smith)*

Open Memorial Day weekend–mid-October. Restaurant open mid-June–mid-Sept.

Rooms 4 suites, 23 doubles, 1 cottage, 1 apt.—all with private bath and/or shower, telephone, radio, clock, TV, air-conditioning, fan, refrigerator. Most with balcony/deck. 1 with fireplace.

Facilities Lobby with fireplace, piano; restaurant, bar/lounge, health club. Pavilion. 4 acres with private swimming beach, swings, off-street parking, bicycles. Beach service with umbrellas, chairs, beach towels.

Location N shore. Less than 1 m from center of town. Located directly on beach.

Credit cards Amex.
Rates B&B, $360–1,170 suite, $195–475 double. $395–595 3-bedroom apt., $470–795 cottage. Extra person, $25. Alc lunch, $8–12; alc dinner, $18–30. 5.3% service.
Extras Cribs. Babysitting. French spoken.

Martin House Inn   *Tel:* 508–228–0678
61 Centre Street, P.O. Box 743, 02554   *E-mail:* martinn@nantucket.net
               URL: http://www.nantucket.net/lodging/martinn

White wicker furniture and an inviting hammock adorn the porch of the Martin House Inn, built in 1803 and operated as an inn since the 1920s. Debbie Wasil bought the Martin House as well as the adjacent Centerboard Guest House (see below) in 1998. The inn is furnished elegantly with period antiques and Oriental carpets; guest rooms have four-poster or canopy beds. Breakfast, served at the dining room table from 8:30–10 A.M., includes fresh fruit, homemade granola, and home-baked muffins. Afternoon tea and coffee are also available.

"Fine location on a quiet street in the historic district, close to restaurants, shops, and galleries. Friendly, helpful innkeeper; comfortable yet luxurious inn. We enjoyed our breakfast on the veranda just outside the dining room. Our immaculate room was spacious, tastefully decorated with a four-poster bed; a decanter of sherry and candies were an unexpected but thoughtful touch." *(Sandie Blackie)* "Charming inn, spacious common areas and guest rooms. Breakfast is served at the handsome dining room table, or can be taken out to the porch, done in white wicker, with a tempting hammock. All the guest rooms are fresh and inviting; while small, the top-floor rooms are cozy and appealing, and an excellent value." *(SWS)* "Inviting common areas, where guests feel comfortable just hanging out. In the summer, the breezy porch offers ample seating areas, plus an irresistible hammock, perfect for reading or napping. The well-maintained backyard is also ideal for sunning on days when the beach is too windy. In chilly weather, a fire is always going in one or both of the downstairs fireplaces." *(Veronica Leger)*

Next door is Debbie's other inn, **The Centerboard Guest House** (8 Chester Street, 02554; 508–228–9696), a mansard-roofed Victorian home built in the late 1800s. Antiques and reproductions share space with hand-painted murals and stained-glass panels; baths are fitted with marble and brass. B&B double rates for the six guest rooms range from $110–185, and include a breakfast of homemade breads and muffins, cereals, and fresh fruit; also available is an English manor–style suite ($185–325), with a mahogany fireplace, Oriental rugs, a seven-foot high canopied bed, and a double Jacuzzi tub. Each guest room has a private bath, TV, refrigerator, and air-conditioning. "Quiet but convenient location. Light, summery, charmingly eclectic beach cottage decor, an appealing change from the usual Colonial or Victorian styling. My favorite room is done in the softest of pastels, with a white peeled log queen-size bed angled into a corner, and a misty Nantucket countryside wall mural behind it." *(SWS)*

Open All year.
Rooms 11 doubles, 2 singles—9 with private shower and/or tub, 4 with maximum of 6 people sharing bath. All with radio, clock, fan. 3 with desk, fireplace. 1 with refrigerator. 1 with balcony.
Facilities Dining room, living room with fireplace, piano, TV, books, stereo; guest refrigerators; porch. ⅓ acre with gardens; covered bike rack.
Location Historic. From Main St., turn right on Centre St. to inn on right.
Restrictions No smoking. Children over 5.
Credit cards Amex, MC, Visa.
Rates B&B, $55–175 double; $40–65 single. Extra person, $25. 2–3 night weekend, high-season minimum.

The Pineapple Inn   ♿   *Tel:* 508–228–9992
10 Hussey Street, 02554   *Fax:* 508–325–6051
E-mail: pineappl@nantucket.net
URL: http://www.nantucket.net/lodging/pineappleinn

In Colonial America, pineapples were rare and expensive; sharing one was seen as a sign of exceptional hospitality. As a result, the fruit itself came to be a symbol of hospitality, and the same holds true today for the Pineapple Inn. Purchased, renovated, and redecorated in 1997 by Caroline and Bob Taylor, the inn was built in 1838 by whaling ship captain Uriah Russell. Complementing antique charm with modern comfort, they have decorated with handmade four-poster queen- and king-size canopy beds from the Eldred Wheeler Company, Ralph Lauren linens, goose-down comforters, handmade Oriental carpets, white marble baths, and a balance of reproduction furniture and 19th-century antiques. Caroline notes: "Our guests can start the day with a cappuccino, freshly squeezed orange juice, a fresh fruit cup, bircher muesli or cold cereal, and tempting home-baked pastries." Breakfast is served from 8–10 A.M. at the dining room table, or at one of the tables on the garden patio.

"Professional, personable, and gracious owners. The Taylors' warm welcome, the staff's attention to our needs, and the delightful breakfast added to the pleasure of our stay. The rear patio area, with its flower-lined walkway and softly bubbling pineapple-topped fountain made a delightful setting for the well-served, healthful breakfast. The renovation was done with sensitive attention to architectural detail, and the decor created a comfortable, luxurious, yet authentic period atmosphere." *(Roger & Bobbi Suddleson)* "Comfortable and relaxing." *(Erica Darling & Lewis Goldstein)* "While not large, our room was decorated to maximize the space." *(MW)* "The bed was exceptionally comfortable." *(Lisa Rechter)* "Special sheets, immaculate housekeeping, elegant breakfasts. The hosts were gracious about special requests, from an afternoon cup of tea in our room, to early morning travel plans." *(Lisa Rubenstein, also Hillary Weireter)* "Ideal in-town location, within walking distance of restaurants, shops, harbor, but tucked away on a quiet side street." *(Dr. & Mrs. Patrick Riccardi)* "Outstanding service. Delicious homemade biscuits with a cinnamon topping for breakfast." *(Robert Moreau)* "Bob and his wait-staff, particularly Mac, are experienced at serving folks; we were pleased to be served breakfast, instead of lining up at a buffet. They were happy to share recipes, too. Housekeeping was efficient but unobtrusive." *(Maureen & Dan McIntyre)* "Our breakfast favorite were the cinnamon biscuits. Exceptionally courteous, attentive staff." *(Bob & Judi Moreau)*

Open May–mid-Dec.
Rooms 12 doubles—all with full private bath and/or shower, telephone with voice-mail/data port, TV, desk, air-conditioning.
Facilities Dining room, living room with fireplace and stereo, garden patio with fountain; bike racks.
Location Historic district. 3–4 blocks from ferry.
Restrictions No smoking. Children 10 and over.
Credit cards Amex, MC, Visa.
Rates B&B, $75–250 double. Extra person, $50. 2–3 night weekend/holiday minimum.
Extras Wheelchair access; bathroom specially equipped.

Seven Sea Street Inn
7 Sea Street, 02554

Tel: 508–228–3577
Fax: 508–228–3578
E-mail: seast@nantucket.net
URL: http://www.nantucket.net/lodging/seast7/

Matthew and Mary Parker welcome guests to their red oak post-and-beam guest house. Built in the sturdy Federal-style of old Nantucket, complete with rooftop widow's walk and Colonial-style furnishings, the inn offers such modern comforts as up-to-date plumbing, queen-size canopy beds, and in-room amenities. Matthew reports that three favorite features of their inn are "the lovely views of Nantucket harbor at sunset from the deck of the widow's walk, the whirlpool room, and our quiet, convenient location in the historic district." Their knowledge of the island is extensive, as lifelong residents, and as owners and editors of *Nantucket Journal*, a quarterly publication about local activities and interests.

"The owners are friendly and hospitable, pleased to assist with dinner reservations, sightseeing information, and beach-going advice. The inn is done all in natural woods and is immaculate. We enjoyed a breakfast of fresh fruit salad, juices, and our fill of home-baked cranberry, corn, and bran muffins. The Parker family also owns several other inns on the island." *(Dottie & Frank Scarfone)* "For those of us who like to look at historic houses but not live with sloping floors, low ceilings, and oddly placed bathrooms, Seven Sea Street is ideal, with a simple floor plan, recent construction, and tasteful Colonial-reproduction decor." *(Bruce Allen)* "Matthew assembled and finished all the guest room furniture himself, from four-poster to canopy beds. Each room has its own color theme, with coordinating handmade quilt and braided rugs." *(NB)* "The second floor had a living room and library combination with comfortable chairs, a sofa, and wood stove. Fantastic harbor view from the widow's walk." *(Richard & Irma McCarthy)* "Quiet but convenient location, on a little street close to shops, restaurants, and the harbor. Attractive, well-equipped, comfortable inn. Those who have trouble with steps will appreciate having the dining room and several guest rooms on the ground floor, just a step or two up from the street." *(SWS)*

251

Open All year.
Rooms 1 apartment, 1 suite, 7 doubles—all with private shower, telephone, TV, air-conditioning, desk, refrigerator, robes. 2 with gas stove/fireplace.
Facilities Breakfast room with fireplace, 2 common rooms with woodstove, books; Jacuzzi room, patio, rooftop deck. Limited off-street parking. Beaches for swimming, surf casting nearby.
Location Historic district. On Sea St. between N. Water and S. Beach Sts.
Restrictions No smoking. Children over 7.
Credit card Amex, Discover, MC, Visa.
Rates B&B, $165–265 apartment, $125–235 suite, $75–195 double, $65–155 single. Extra person, $20. 2–3 night weekend, holiday minimum. Midweek, weekly discounts off-season.
Extras French spoken.

Sherburne Inn   *Tel:* 508–228–4425
10 Gay Street, 02554   *Fax:* 508–228–8114
            E-mail: sherinn@nantucket.net
      URL: http://www.nantucket.net/lodging/sherburne

Although most of us find the ocean air to be energizing and invigorating, the Nantucket climate was not as salutory for an interesting 19th-century experiment. In 1835, three local businessmen founded the Atlantic Silk Company, complete with a factory and steam-powered looms; they hoped to supplant imports from France and India with their high-quality fabric. Unfortunately, the mulberry trees needed by the silkworms did poorly in the island's fogs and sandy soil, and the factory closed in disgrace in less than a decade. A section of the factory was converted into lodgings in 1845, and was restored as an inn in 1994 by Dale Hamilton and Susan Gasparich. Reflecting another aspect of Nantucket's history, they named the inn after the island's original name, Sherburne, after the English homeland of some of the early settlers. Each guest room is furnished with queen- or king-size beds and mementos of the whaling era. Breakfast is served from 8–10 A.M., and includes a buffet of breads and muffins, fresh fruit, and juice. Guests can enjoy Susan's home-baked treats in front of the living room fireplace, or take a tray to the garden, deck, or their room.

"Delightful hands-on innkeepers, Dale Hamilton and Susan Gasparich, always improving their inn, from the addition of central air-conditioning to enhancements of the decor." *(SWS)* "The inn is tucked away on a quiet residential street behind the main area, but only a block's walk to the center of activity. Quiet but convenient location. Delightfully decorated with period furnishings and original artwork that Susan and Dale have collected. At breakfast, I enjoyed the different varieties of fruit, juices, baked-that-morning-by-Susan muffins or coffee cake, English muffins or bagels, breads, and jams. Meticulous housekeeping, from the bathrooms to the brass, silver, and tabletops." *(Joseph Nameche)*

Open All year.
Rooms 8 doubles—all with full private bath and/or shower, telephone, radio, clock, air-conditioning, ceiling fan. 1 with TV, fireplace, refrigerator, balcony/deck.

Facilities 2 parlors with fireplace, TV; guest refrigerator; patio. Flower garden. On-street parking. Massage therapy.
Location Historic district. 2 blocks from Main St.
Restrictions No smoking. Children 6 and over.
Credit cards Amex, MC, Novus, Visa.
Rates B&B, $65–200 double. Extra person, $25. 3-night weekend/holiday minimum.
Extras German spoken.

Stumble Inne ¢
109 Orange Street, 02554

Tel: 508–228–4482
800–649–4482
Fax: 508–228–4752
E-mail: romance@nantucket.net
URL: http://www.nantucket.net/lodging/stumbleinne

So many inns have dignified and historically authentic names these days, that it's quite charming to find one that doesn't take itself so seriously. The Stumble Inne (we almost wish there was an adjacent tavern called the Stagger Oute) was named by the woman who converted it into an inn in 1976. Built in 1704, the inn was purchased by Mary Kay and Mal Condon in 1985. Guest rooms are fresh and inviting, with simple island charm; most have queen-size beds. The Condons also offer rooms decorated in Laura Ashley fabrics and linens at the nearby Spring Cottage, which has luxuriously equipped suites with country Victorian decor.

"Mary Kay and her staff are friendly and helpful, even giving us a ride to the ferry when we couldn't get a taxi. Breakfast is served with the guests sitting around a large table, and we enjoyed comparing notes on restaurants, activities, and more. Since we like walking, especially in the evening after dinner, we appreciated the pleasant walk along quiet residential streets back to the inn." *(Glenn Roehrig, also SWS)* "Our breakfast basket, complete with fresh flowers, was delivered to our room each morning." *(Ginny & Chet Snook)* "I was traveling on business, and Mary Kay went out of her way to accommodate my needs." *(Linda Webber)* "Warm and friendly from the minute we arrived. The innkeepers were responsive to our needs, from beach towels to information. Homey and welcoming, from the common rooms to our light and airy guest room, complete with a queen-size bed, sitting area, an extra daybed and a nook with a refrigerator, an ice bucket, and wine glasses. Breakfast was served in two seatings and encouraged conversation among the guests." *(Doreen DeTucci)* "We have found Mary Kay and Mal to be welcoming each and every time we have visited." *(Marianne Johnson)* "We enjoy everything from the backyard that Mel has filled with hydrangeas to the breakfasts that we look forward to all year." *(Maggie & Bob Althen)*

"With beach plum jelly simmering on the kitchen stove, and classical music drifting through the common rooms, the inn couldn't be more pleasant. The spacious guest rooms have four-poster or canopy double- or queen-size beds. A short early morning walk to see the sunrise brought us to a beautiful marsh, complete with herons. The casual atmosphere is restful and well worth the walk to town." *(Pam Phillips)*

"Excellent breakfasts of fresh fruit and juice, granola, cereal, and home-baked muffins, shared with other guests around the large table in the dining room." *(Claire Theroux)* "Even the bathrooms are interesting. Ours had a glass case in the wall containing some old photos and small bottles found between the walls of the inn during remodeling." *(Pat Borysiewicz)*

Open April–Dec.
Rooms 3 suites, 6 doubles—all with private shower and/or bath, radio, fan, air-conditioning, TV/VCR. Suites with telephone, desk.
Facilities Breakfast room with fireplace, sitting room with fireplace, TV/VCR, books, video library. Gardens. Beach nearby for swimming, fishing, windsurfing, sailing.
Location 15-min. walk to Main St.
Restrictions Traffic noise possible in season in front rooms. No smoking. No children under 5.
Credit cards Amex, MC, Visa.
Rates B&B, $135–250 suite, $90–215 double. Extra adult, $30; extra child, $10. 3-night minimum high season, weekends mid-season.

NEWBURYPORT

At the far northeastern corner of Massachusetts, just five miles south of the New Hampshire border and 38 miles north of Boston, is the historic town of Newburyport. Founded in 1640, it was the fourth largest town in America at the time of the Revolution. A disastrous fire in 1811 laid the town bare except for the brick Federalist buildings that line the streets of the historic district today, but prosperity continued via the shipbuilding and manufacturing industries through the 19th century. By the 1950s, the downtown was rundown and boarded up, but was saved from the wrecking ball by vociferous community groups.

Now restored, the town offers two interesting museums, Cushing House, a handsome mansion with an eclectic but fascinating historical collection, and the Custom House Maritime Museum, devoted to Newburyport's shipbuilding industry. Equally appealing is a walking tour of its historic homes, attractive shops and galleries, and waterfront boardwalk and park along the Merrimack River. If you need some fresh air to blow away the cobwebs of history, drive out to Plum Island, a nature preserve with beautiful beaches and miles of hiking trails.

For an additional area inn, see **South Hampton, New Hampshire.**

The Windsor House *Tel:* 978–462–3778
38 Federal Street, 01950 888–TRELAWNY
Fax: 978–465–3443
E-mail: tintagel@greennet.net

Built as a wedding present in 1786 by a Colonial officer for his bride, the Windsor House was designed as a combination residence and ships' chandlery. The original hoist is still in place (and in working condition) in the inn's attic. In renovating the Federal-style home, longtime owners Judith and John Harris have given each room a decor reminiscent of its original purpose, combining period and reproduction furnishings, with such modern comforts as good bedside lighting and queen- or king-size beds. John's upbringing on the Cornish coast of England is reflected in the hearty English breakfasts and afternoon tea with Cornish shortbread, tea cakes, and scones. Windsor House is a longtime reader favorite; all are delighted to have discovered Newburyport's rich history, inviting restaurants and sights, and the Harrises' exceptional hospitality.

"John and Judith are quintessential innkeepers and wonderful raconteurs. English memorabilia is found throughout the inn; each item has a story. You enter through a brick courtyard, open the door, and ring a ship's bell to let the owners know that you have entered. Breakfast is served at the kitchen table, and consisted of orange juice, coffee or tea, fresh melon, and eggs-to-order, sautéed mushrooms, baked beans, tomatoes, and English muffins. The Merchant Suite, a roomy, high-ceilinged room, easily accommodated our family. The dishes of candy found throughout the inn, along with the friendly dog and cat, rated highly with our two sons."(*Betsy Sandberg*)

"The spacious Library Suite on the third floor was comfortable and quiet. About five o'clock each evening, tea was served in the living room with an assortment of treats, different each day: a delicious spinach dip or a cream cheese and chutney spread, butter cookies, Dutch apple pie or marble cake, fresh fruit. Delightful, charming owners; a memorable visit." (*Bill Novack*) "Helpful packet of area information. Pleasant living room; good breakfast; exceptionally friendly and helpful innkeepers. The inn is on quiet street, a short, inviting walk to the center of town." (*MM*) "Delightful English atmosphere, just minutes from the waterfront." (*Harvey Goldstein*) "Worth returning just to sit around the huge breakfast table and listen to John and Judith tell stories." (*Bill Hussey*)

Open All year.

Rooms 4 doubles—all with private bath and/or shower, telephone, fan, fireplace.

Facilities Breakfast room, living room, dining room—all with fireplace. Living room with TV/VCR, stereo, books; meeting room. Courtyard with garden, terrace.

Location 2 blocks from center. From I-95, take Rte. 113 exit & go E on Rte. 113 for 1 m. Turn right onto High St. & go 2 m to Federal St. Turn left. Inn is 5 blocks down on left, across from Old South Church.

Restrictions No smoking. Children by arrangement.

Credit cards Amex, Discover, MC, Visa.

Rates B&B, $135 double, $99 single. Extra person, $35. 2–3 night weekend/holiday minimum. Off-season, corporate rates. Specialized tours to Britain.

Extras Bus station pickup. Pets by arrangement.

NEW MARLBOROUGH

The Old Inn on the Green & Gedney Farm ✕ ᴄ̧ ♚ *Tel:* 413–229–3131
Village Green, Route 57   800–286–3139
Mailing address: Star Route 70, 01230   *Fax:* 413–229–8236
                                                    E-mail: brad@oldinn.com

New Marlborough dates back to 1739; the town developed along one of the first roads linking eastern and western Massachusetts. One of the oldest buildings on the town green, built in 1760, had long served the village as an inn, tavern, store, and post office. In 1979, husband-and-wife team Bradford Wagstaff and Leslie Miller restored the building, now a part of a historic district listed on the National Register; Michael Smith is the inn's manager. The restaurant is downstairs, with a few guest rooms upstairs. Most guests stay at Gedney Farm, ²/₁₀ of a mile away. Built at the turn of the century to house Percheron stallions and Jersey cattle, the gambrel slate and cedar roofs of this Norman-style barn now shelter two-level suites with granite fireplaces, Turkish rugs, and whirlpool tubs. At dinner-time, Gedney Farm guests can drive or follow a footpath through the meadow back to the inn. An adjacent horse barn now serves as a wedding and conference facility. Rates include a breakfast of home-baked muffins and bread, jams, juice, and coffee; specialties include sticky buns, fruit tarts, and biscotti.

The inn is well-known for its cuisine; on Saturday nights there is a limited choice prix fixe menu, published seasonally with each evening's meal described in detail; à la carte dinners are available on other nights. A recent spring dinner included portobello mushroom and eggplant caviar; veal with asparagus and potato gratin; and chocolate almond torte.

"Architecturally unique; pleasant service." (Nancy Lampe) "A perfect dinner. The fireplace in our room was a real boon on a rainy weekend." (T. Fisher) "Unusual and charming; innovative restoration, with fabulous artwork in the common areas. Good breakfast; helpful staff; wonderful whirlpool tub." (Frances Garnley) "Wonderful Colonial atmosphere in the restaurant with candlelight, dried flowers, and hand-painted murals. At Gedney Farm, the courtyard area between the two barns is set up in warm weather for breakfast. The guest rooms at Gedney Farm form a separate structure within the barn; several of the handsomely tiled bathrooms have Plexiglas ceilings so you can see 'out' to the original barn roof. The rooms themselves are sculptural in their dramatic design and use of space and color, and many are simply furnished with four-poster beds, Windsor chairs, and atmospheric lighting; some have unusual interior balconies." (SWS) "Delicious French toast and strawberries for breakfast; excellent dinner." (Donna Bocks) "The linens are first-rate, the rooms are spotless. The well-presented breakfast included coffee, pastries, and granola." (Anita Dichter) " Tasty, elaborate dinner recipes; lovely staff. Enjoyed the sculpture exhibition in the field behind the barn." (Annette Holloway)

Open All year. Restaurant closed Mon.–Wed., Nov. 1–July 1.
Rooms 5 suites, 13 doubles—all with private bath and/or shower, telephone. 10 with fireplace, 6 with whirlpool tub. 13 rooms in converted barn; 5 in old inn.
Facilities Restaurant, tavern, conference center. 50 acres with woods, meadow, wetland. Lake swimming, cross-country, downhill skiing nearby.
Location S Berkshires, SW MA. 10 m E of Great Barrington, 2½ hrs. from NYC. From Great Barrington, take Rte. 23 E for 3.4 m to Rte. 57. Bear right, go 5.7 m to inn. From Norfolk, CT, take Rte. 272 N, bearing right to Rte. 57 to inn.
Restrictions Children over 14 preferred.
Credit cards Amex, MC, Visa.
Rates B&B, $225–285 suite, $120–205 double. Extra adult, $40, extra child, $20. 2-night summer weekend, holiday minimum. Prix fixe dinner (Sat. only), $48,

plus tax and service; alc dinner, $35. Wine-tasting dinners, $70. Mid-week summer specials; spring, winter weekend packages.

Extras Gedney Farm with wheelchair access. Crib, babysitting. Airport/station pickups for fee. French, Spanish spoken.

NORTHAMPTON

Located in west central Massachusetts, the Northampton area makes a fine base for visiting one of the five colleges in the Pioneer Valley, looking at fall leaves along the Connecticut River, or concentrating on Northampton itself, with its many intriguing restaurants, shops, and Victorian buildings. Advance reservations are *essential* for parents' weekends and graduations, so plan accordingly.

Also recommended: Built in 1872, the **Lupine House** (185 North Main Street, Route 9, P.O. Box 60483, Florence, 01062; 413–586–9766 or 800–890–9766) was opened as a B&B in 1996 by Evelyn and Gil Billings, and is located just three miles from downtown Northampton and Smith College. Breakfast includes a variety of homemade breads and granola, plus fresh fruit; special dietary needs are easily accommodated. Lupine House is open from mid-September to early June; during the summer, the Billings run a B&B in York Beach, Maine. Each of the three guest rooms have a private bath, desk, and clock/radio. The B&B double rate is $75. "A peaceful retreat. Each room is provided with a white sound machine, offering various sounds from ocean waves to a stream." *(Hannah Sikerski)* "Our room was modern and comfortable, down to the bowl of Hershey's Kisses and bathrobes. Breakfast was at eight, with everyone sitting down together." *(Judy & Dick Plotz)* "We especially enjoyed the low-fat muffins. Ideal location for the five-college area." *(Elizabeth & Peter Valiando)* "Hosts provided great directions and touring suggestions. Modest surroundings, exquisitely clean and homey." *(Mary Pettigrew)* "Healthful homemade breakfast." *(Lynda Brennan & Donald Watson)*

For additional area entries, see **Deerfield** and **Leverett**.

Clark Tavern Inn Bed and Breakfast　　　　*Tel:* 413–586–1900
98 Bay Road, Hadley, 01035　　　　　　　　　　*Fax:* 413–587–9788
　　　　　　　　　　　　　　　　E-mail: mrcallhn@aol.com
　　　　　　　　　URL: http://members.aol.com/mrcallhn

One of the joys of travel in New England is seeing the area's genuinely historic homes. Massachusetts has many restored museum villages, such as nearby Old Deerfield, where a visit will give you a taste of the Colonial past. But far better than a brief tour is the chance to stay overnight in a historic home such as Clark Tavern Inn, whose early visitors included the Minutemen on their way to the Battle of Concord. Even better is the fact that you can enjoy history without sacrificing modern comfort—from modern baths, cable television (hidden in antique cabinets), telephones, and even data ports for your modem. As innkeeper Ruth Callahan notes, "I had always dreamed of having an historic inn where guests would feel as if they had stepped back in time, but I vowed never to sacrifice their comfort to do so." Mike and Ruth are Pioneer Valley natives, knowledgeable about all area activities, and especially interested in hiking, animals, and the environment.

Built in 1740, this Georgian Colonial saltbox home was restored by Ruth and Mike Callahan in 1995. In addition to spacious guest rooms, appointed with queen-size canopy beds, antiques, and period reproductions, the inn offers large, inviting common areas and extensive grounds. Breakfast is served from 8–9:30 A.M. and can be enjoyed at individual tables in the dining room, on the patio, or in bed. Menus are left on guests' beds each evening, and guests are encouraged to select their favorites, as well as the time and setting for their candlelit breakfast. A recent selection included baked pears, cranberry nut bread, and oven-puffed pancakes with banana topping; cereal, eggs, toast, and bacon or sausage are always available as well.

"Beautifully decorated and immaculately clean; gracious hospitality, fascinating information about the inn's history; excellent directions." *(Susan & Kevin Hunt)* "Ruth and Mike really care about their inn and their guests." *(Joan & John Sica)* "We felt as though we had stepped back in time two centuries—but with better food, more comfortable beds, and modern plumbing! Our cozy room had a queen-size canopy bed and a wood-burning fireplace. Each morning we woke up to outstanding breakfasts, delivered to our room. The spiced baked apple was yummy, the peach yogurt even better, and best of all were the waffles. We spent evenings in the living room, playing chess and doing puzzles by the enormous blazing fireplace. The three friendly cats kept us company." *(Joanna Grand & David Marlin)* "Magnificent restoration; delightful innkeepers. Attention to detail includes a supply of toiletries you might have forgotten to pack, and a stocked guest pantry." *(Helen Robin)*

Open All year.

Rooms 3 doubles—all with full private bath and/or shower, telephone, radio, clock, TV/VCR, air-conditioning, fan, data port. 2 with wood-burning fireplace.

Facilities Dining room, living room with fireplace, games, stereo; guest refrigerator, screened porch. 1 acre with swimming pool, gardens, water garden, hammock, croquet. ½ m from Ct. River marina for boat, canoe rentals. Hiking, cross-country, downhill skiing nearby.

Location 2 m from Northampton, Amherst; ½ m from center of Hadley. From I-91 S, take Exit 20 & go left at 1st light. Go 1 m & turn left at light onto Rte. 9 E, past Coolidge Bridge into Hadley. Bear right to Rte. 47 S & go straight for 1.1 m. After blinking yellow light, inn is 2nd driveway on left. From I-91 N, take Exit 19. Go right onto Rte. 9, & follow as above.

Restrictions No smoking. Children 12 and over.

Credit cards All major credit cards.

Rates B&B, $115–155 double, $105–145 single. Extra person, $20. 2–3 night college weekend/holiday minimum.

Extras Minimal Spanish spoken.

PRINCETON

Fernside Bed & Breakfast ♿
162 Mountain Road, P.O. Box 303, 01541

Tel: 978–464–2741
800–545–2741
Fax: 978–464–2065
E-mail: fernside@msn.com

While both eastern and western Massachusetts have inns by the score, options in the central part of the state have been pretty slim, making Fernside an especially delightful discovery. Just an hour west of Boston, the inn is located on the eastern slope of Mt. Wachusett (*gesundheit!*), the state's second highest mountain—just over 2,000 feet. The area is ideal for hiking or skiing, apple-picking or antiquing, although once you've settled in with a good book on the deck at Fernside, with its views of Boston in the distance, you may decide a nap is all you really need.

Fernside is a Federal-style home, built in 1835 by Captain Benjamin Harrington. Operated as a tavern and boarding house for Harvard professors and students in the late 1800s, it was purchased in 1890 by the Girls Vacation House Association of Boston and served as an affordable summer vacation house for working women for over 100 years. In 1994, Jocelyn and Richard Morrison restored it as an inn, preserving its historic charms while adding modern bathrooms, insulation, windows, and more. The guest rooms are individually decorated with antiques and period reproductions, queen-size four-poster beds, Oriental rugs, and down comforters. Breakfast is served in the dining room from 7:30–9:30 A.M.; a recent menu started with fresh fruit cup and warm cranberry scones and offered a choice of poached eggs on toast with herbed butter, Red Bliss potatoes, and chicken-apple sausage; crêpes stuffed with baked apples; or homemade granola with fresh fruit.

"Lovely mountainside setting. Lavish and elegant restoration." (*Jenny & Nick Littlefield*) "Old-fashioned hospitality. In the summer, guests may enjoy the spacious outside deck and its view; in winter, you can toast by the living room fireplace. Delicious and abundant breakfasts." (*Clarissa Townsend*) "Quiet, easy to find and reach. Warm and attentive innkeepers." (*Katy & Doug McDonald*) "Always a fire burning, tea and muffins ready, warm and welcoming innkeepers." (*Josephine Kaestner*) "Our room was nicely furnished with original watercolors and spotlessly clean." (*Ann Ryan-Small*) "Ideal balance of warmth and elegance; spacious guest rooms with comfortable sitting areas; ample common areas for relaxing, too. Excellent breakfast of fruit cup, garnished with nasturtiums, scrambled or poached eggs to order, whole wheat toast and yummy scones. Not overly sweet, thank goodness. Excellent restaurants nearby." (*SWS*) "After a day of business in the Worcester area, I was thrilled to return to my mountain aerie." (*MW*) "I visited the inn with an older woman (a 96-year-old retired pathologist) who had worked at Fernside when it was a vacation home for women. We were the first guests as it opened as a B&B; it is first-class in charm, quality, and hospitality." (*Anne Carlson*)

Open All year.
Rooms 2 suites, 4 doubles—all with full private bath and/or shower, radio, clock. 4 with working fireplace, 1 with air-conditioning.
Facilities Dining room, living room, family room, library; each with fireplace. Porches, deck. 7 acres with lawn games; cross-country skiing, hiking. Downhill skiing, hiking, swimming, fishing, golf, tennis nearby.
Location Central MA. 55 m W of Boston, 15 m N of Worcester, 10 m S of Fitchburg. From Rte. 190 take Exit 5 to Rte. 140 N. Go 2¼ m to Rte. 62. Take Rte. 62 W for 4 m to Princeton Center. Go right on Mountain Rd. for 1.5 m to inn on right.
Restrictions Absolutely no smoking. Children 12 and over.
Credit cards All major.
Rates B&B, $135–155 suite, $105–155 double, $95–155 single. Extra person, $50. 2-night holiday minimum.
Extras Wheelchair access; bathroom specially equipped. Train, plane, bus pickups.

PROVINCETOWN

The first landing point of the Pilgrims, Provincetown sits at the very tip of Cape Cod. It later developed as an art colony, and is best known as a summer beach resort. It's also a starting point for many whale-watching cruises—don't forget to take your Dramamine.

Reader tips: "P'town in season is a bit much. Fall, though, is another story—rates drop, the pace slows, and the atmosphere is relaxed and friendly." *(MW)* Also: "Much of Provincetown is gay and proud of it. Our visiting Kansas cousins were goggle-eyed at the transvestites in leopard leggings and spike heels." *(HS)*

Information please: We'd like to know what you think of the **Watermark Inn** (603 Commercial Street, 02657; 508–487–0165), traditional in appearance but with modern-balconied suites and contemporary decor. Rooms have a bedroom, living/dining room, full bathroom and kitchen, telephone and TV. Strong points include its setting directly on the water, overlooking the bay, and its location on Provincetown's quieter east side. Double rates are $115–300. "Helpful, accommodating owners; delightful getaway." *(MW)*

For additional area entries, see **Eastham, North Truro,** and **Wellfleet**.

The Black Pearl B&B ¢ &.   *Tel:* 508–487–6405
11 Pearl Street, 02657   *Fax:* 508–487–7412
E-mail: blkpearl@capecod.net
URL: http://www.provincetown.com/blackpearl/

Years ago, a major motel chain ran an ad campaign entitled "no surprises," guaranteeing you the identical experience in any of their rooms. B&Bs are just the opposite. The Black Pearl, for example, is a sea captain's house built in 1840. Although you might expect traditional Colonial furnishings with a few nautical accents, the decor is a delightful surprise. When Paula Post and John Gair bought the inn in 1995, they added extensive sound-proofing and insulation, private baths and fire-places, then invited friend and artist-in-residence Linda Singer to transform each room into an original work of art, using hand-painted murals, stenciling, and textured wall finishes. Paula notes that "Provincetown is the oldest continuous art colony in the U.S., and we feel that our approach is in keeping with the spirit of Provincetown."

Breakfast is served at individual tables, during the accommodating hours of 8:30–11 A.M., and includes homemade spice granola, yogurt, fresh fruit, orange juice, and Paula's home-baked treats—perhaps buttermilk scones with lemon curd, raspberry cream cheese coffee cake, harvest grain bread, or peanut butter sesame bread with homemade sour cherry jam. Chocolate chip cookies or brownies are available every afternoon, and tea makings are always available.

"Literally steps away from restaurants, shops, night clubs, and the beach, yet far enough from peak-season crowds to ensure a quiet night's sleep. Although parking is ample, you may never need to get in the car during your visit. Our favorite rooms include the Sunny Brook, with twin beds and a skylight, and the southwestern Mesa Verde, with a queen-size bed and a fireplace. The Southwestern theme extends to the Indian-style patterns on the sheets, to the traditional folk art over the fireplace, to the Nevada-based novels of J.A. Jance. Dresser and closet space are ample, and the beds are most comfortable. Other rooms include the Lullwater Suite (handicapped accessible with an outside deck), the Constantinople Room in bold colors with Middle-Eastern theme murals, and the tranquil, tropical Micronesia Room. Guests enjoy socializing in the living room, or relaxing by the fire to read up on the history of Provincetown and the Cape. John and Paula are knowledgeable about all local attractions and activities, and provide menus of most area restaurants and a log of past guests' dining reviews." *(Chris Garamella & Mike Sodins)* "Each day a new fire was laid in our fireplace, with extra wood for those of us who like a good fire. Scrupulously clean. Paula and John learned we were wine lovers, and provided us with a carafe, wine glasses, and corkscrew before we even asked. They enjoy being innkeepers, and are fun to talk with, yet allow guests complete privacy." *(Barbara Kingsborough)*

Open Mid-March–Dec. 31.
Rooms 1 cottage, 1 suite, 4 doubles—all with full private bath and/or shower, clock/radio, fan, robes, beach towels. Some with whirlpool tub, fireplace, TV/VCR, desk, air-conditioning, refrigerator, data port. 1 with balcony/deck.
Facilities Dining room, living room with fireplace; guest refrigerator, porch. Off-street parking.
Location Cape Cod. 120 m SE of Boston. Historic district. 5-min. walk to town center. From Rte. 6, take 2nd Provincetown exit (left at stoplight onto Conwell St.). At end of Conwell, turn left onto Bradford St.; Pearl St. is 1st right.
Restrictions Absolutely no smoking. Children 12 and over.
Credit cards MC, Visa.
Rates B&B, $115–175 suite, $55–150 double. 2–3 night weekend/holiday/peak-season minimum.
Extras Wheelchair access; bathroom specially equipped. Airport, bus station pickup.

REHOBOTH

Perryville Inn ¢ 👫
157 Perryville Road, 02769

Tel: 508–252–9239
800–439–9239
Fax: 508–252–9054

The Perryville Inn was originally built as a Colonial farmhouse in the 1820s; in 1897 the existing structure was raised to the second and third floors, and a new Victorian-style first floor added. Tom and Betsy Charnecki restored and opened the inn in 1985. Breakfast is served between 7 and 10 A.M., and includes guests' choice of juice, fresh fruit, cereal, hot beverage, and muffins, sticky buns, or croissants.

"Our room had a canopy bed and a homemade quilt. Although the inn is decorated with antiques, it is unpretentious, comfortable, and homey. The Charneckis make sure you are comfortable and serve you breakfast, but are never intrusive. They're hospitable, informative, flexible innkeepers." *(Cecelia Anderson)* "Delightful, comfortable, friendly, and attractive. Charming country setting, yet a convenient base for touring Providence and southeastern Massachusetts." *(Diane Wolf)* "Wonderful hosts, peaceful setting, charming service. Be sure to try the sticky buns." *(David Oprava)*

"Warm and inviting, simply decorated with a mixture of brass, sturdy antiques, and colorful, locally sewn patchwork quilts. Extras included fresh-cut flowers, complimentary wine, beer, and soft drinks, and assistance with travel plans. Our favorite bedrooms were the four-poster canopy bedroom and the room with the brass bed. Spotless bathrooms, with ample hot water. Breakfast was served each morning at our convenience in the dining room, and we enjoyed visiting with our hosts and the other guests." *(Beth & Earl Tweed, also SWS)*

"A basket of toiletries and notions is available in case you forgot something. Outside a beautiful pink dogwood in bloom reached all the way up to my bedroom window. My room was immaculate, the mattress was firm, and the pillow full, with extra pillows and blankets in the closet." *(Renee Cohen)* "Irresistible homemade honeybuns at breakfast." *(Jane Grossman)*

Open All year.
Rooms 1 suite, 3 doubles—all with private bath and/or shower, radio, desk, air-conditioning.
Facilities Dining room, 2 sitting rooms with piano, books, games, puzzles; screened porch. 4½ acres with trout stream, fishing pond, and woods. Tandem bicycles. Golf course across street, tennis, horseback riding, cross-country skiing, hot-air-ballooning nearby.
Location SE MA. 8 m E of Providence, RI, 45 m S of Boston, 40 m N of Newport, RI, 25 m W of Plymouth. From I-95 N, take I-195 E to Exit 1 in MA. Go N 2 m on Rte. 114A to Rte. 44. Go right (E) 5 m to Rte. 118. Go left (N) ½ m to Perryville Rd. Go left 1½ m to the inn. From I-95 S, take Exit 3A to Rte. 123. Go E 2 m to Rte. 118. Go S 8 m to Perryville Rd., as above.
Restrictions No smoking.
Credit cards Amex, Discover, MC, Visa.

Rates B&B, $85–95 suite, $65–95 double, $55–85 single. Extra person, $10. Family, children's rates. 2-night minimum during high season.
Extras Crib, babysitting, play equipment. Some French spoken.

RICHMOND

For additional area entries, see **Lenox, North Egremont, Stockbridge,** and **West Stockbridge.**

The Inn at Richmond
802 State Road, Route 41, 01254

Tel: 413–698–2566
888–968–4748
Fax: 413–698–2100
E-mail: innatrichmond@taconic.net
URL: http://www.innatrichmond.com

What could be more country than leaning over a paddock fence, watching colts frisking in the meadows? What could be more relaxing than lolling in a hammock with a good book or gliding in a swing admiring a spectacular mountain sunset? What could be more Berkshires than fine dining and wonderful music in Lenox? You can easily enjoy all this if you stay at the Inn at Richmond, a handsome farmhouse dating back to 1774, and restored as a B&B by Jerri and Dan Buehler in 1994. Behind the house is a large Shaker barn, relocated to this site in the 1920s. Champion Morgan horses are boarded here, and guests are welcome to watch demonstrations of training exercises in preparation for shows.

Breakfast is served at individual tables at 9 A.M., garnished with homegrown herbs and flowers in season. A recent menu included orange juice, granola, yogurt, applesauce spice muffins, strawberries and pineapple with lemon mint glaze, and frittata with asparagus, mushrooms, sweet peppers, and gruyere cheese. Another morning might feature sourdough bread with roast onions, pecan bread, and lemon cottage cheese pancakes with warm raspberry syrup. Complimentary coffee and tea, port, sherry, and soft drinks are always available.

"The Buehlers are warm, welcoming, and eager to please their guests." *(Barbara Kurshan)* "Convenient location, on an easy-to-find yet lightly traveled road." *(SWS)* "Peaceful setting, yet close to Lenox, Stockbridge, and all area activities. We were welcomed warmly, given a tour of the inn, and shown to our room. Nothing is too much trouble for the Buehlers; they are a mine of information about restaurants and activities. They keep the inn spotlessly clean, have unobtrusive but excellent help, and run the inn professionally but with warmth and good humor. The inviting guest rooms are individually decorated with antiques and reproductions, queen- or king-size beds, and good lighting; the carriage house and cottage are perfect for an extended stay, and have well-equipped kitchens. Delicious, beautifully presented breakfasts with freshly baked breads and pastries." *(Renee Samson)* "The main house offers ample rooms to relax, including a wonderful library with an attached sun room overlooking the countryside." *(Joan Merrill)*

Open All year.

Rooms 2 suites, 4 doubles, 1 cottage, 1 carriage house—all with private bath and/or shower, telephone, clock/radio, TV, air-conditioning. 3 with fireplace, 2 with fully equipped kitchen.

Facilities Dining room; library with fireplace, piano, stereo, books; parlor with stereo; garden room with guest refrigerator; greenhouse. 27 acres with stable, gardens, reflecting pool, fields, trails for walking and snowshoeing. Lake swimming, hiking, bicycling, downhill, cross-country skiing nearby.

Location W MA. Berkshires. 7 m W of Lenox. From NYC, take Taconic Pkwy. to Rte. 295. Go E (right) on 295. Follow to end. Go N (left) on Rte. 41 & go 1 m to inn on left.

Restrictions No smoking. Children over 10.

Credit cards Amex, MC, Visa.

Rates B&B, $155–250 suite, $110–185 double. Extra person, $25. 3-night weekend minimum July, Aug., holidays. Off-season & midweek promotions. Inquire for weekly rates for cottage, carriage house.

Extras Arrangements can be made for station pickup.

ROCKPORT

Rockport is on Massachusetts's "other" cape—Cape Ann, with a coastline more like that of Maine than Massachusetts, yet only 40 miles northeast of Boston. To get there, take Route 128 north until it ends at a set of traffic lights, then pick up Route 127 to the center of Rockport. Rockport has one of the country's oldest artist colonies, along with dozens of craft and antique shops. Other activities include golf, hiking and bicycling, and of course swimming, fishing, schooner and lobstering trips, boating, and whale-watching in season—from April through October.

Rockport is a "dry" town, so bring your wine from Gloucester; restaurants will gladly chill and serve it for you, charging a modest corkage fee.

Reader tip: "For a real change of pace, drive about ten miles south along the coast to Magnolia, home of Hammond Castle, built in the 1920s by millionaire inventor John Hammond. An enormous structure, it mixes eccentric whimsy with exceptional European antiques and is well worth a visit. We'd also suggest leaving Rockport's congestion behind, and heading out to Halibut Point Reservation to hike through the woods and along the shore." *(NB)*

For additional area entries, see **Essex.**

Addison Choate Inn ¢
49 Broadway, 01966

Tel: 978–546–7543
800–245–7543
Fax: 978–546–7638
URL: http://www.cape-ann.com/addison-choate

The Addison Choate Inn is a Greek Revival home, built in 1851, and converted into an inn in 1963. Knox and Shirley Johnson, who bought the inn in 1992, have decorated with a mixture of antiques and reproductions, with original art. Rates include a breakfast of homemade granola, fresh fruit and juice, with home-baked breads, muffins, and coffeecake, plus afternoon tea. The third-floor Celebrations Suite is furnished in white wicker with a queen-size canopy bed, and overlooks Rockport and the ocean beyond. Two apartment suites are available in the renovated stable, complete with post-and-beam construction, stained-glass windows, a sleep sofa on the main floor, a queen-size bed in the loft, and a fully equipped kitchen. Responsive to guests' needs, the Johnsons have made sure that each guest room has good reading lamps and a sitting area with comfortable wicker chairs. We heard from many of the Johnson's guests; while all were delighted with the accommodations, food, and setting, most felt that best of all was the innkeepers' exceptional hospitality and service.

"Immaculately maintained and charmingly furnished, with exquisite flower beds surrounding the house." *(EG)* "Convenient location, close to the waterfront and shopping." *(Diane Woehl)* "Breakfasts and afternoon tea were delicious and of the highest quality." *(Donna Ferrara-Kerr)* "Bright flower boxes line the porch railing." *(Nancy & Bill Pollock)* "All praise to Knox and Shirley whose warm and gentle personalities are a treasured memory of the U.S." *(Michael Umm)* "Inviting swimming pool in the private yard under the trees." *(Dorothy Singer)* "Our Stable House Suite was more than comfortable; the beds were perfect, and all the little extras were there—toiletries, kitchen supplies, even postcards for mailing." *(M. Colleen Zirkelbach)* "Wish we could have brought the bed home; I've never slept so well." *(Alex & Hilary Workman)* "The comfortable Chimney Room has a queen-size lace canopy bed, sitting area, plenty of closet space, and a private bath. The fireplaced dining room is a pleasant place for breakfast in chilly weather; in summer, most guests eat at tables-for-two on the inviting porch. The Johnsons have converted a first-floor closet into a handy information booth, stocked with local brochures and two telephones for guest use, one of which is a portable." *(John Felton & Martha Gottron)* "Warm hospitality from our first meeting." *(Max Roehl)* "Innkeepers the most helpful we've ever met. Delicious freshly ground coffee." *(Karen Hirsh)* "A beautifully restored inn reflecting the hosts' expertise in interior and landscape design. Well-chosen artwork adds to the charm of the rooms." *(Marita Lindlau)* "Superb referral system to area attractions." *(Mary Winther)* "Again and again we noticed the cleanliness; housekeeping was unobtrusive. We appreciated the cushioned wicker chairs, the extra table for our computer, a selection of bed pillows, and delicately perfumed glycerine soap." *(Eleanor Schmidt)*

Open All year.
Rooms 3 suites, 5 doubles—all with private bath and/or shower, air-conditioning, clock/radio, hairdryer. 2 suites in Stable House with kitchen, TV.
Facilities Dining room with fireplace, living room with fireplace and books; TV room with videos of local places of interest; porch. Off-street parking, swimming pool, gardens.
Location 2 blocks to town center/harbor. Take Rte. 128 to Gloucester. From Gloucester, take Rte. 127 to Rockport. At five-corner intersection, take 127A (Broadway). Go 1½ blocks to inn on right and park in back.
Restrictions No smoking. Children over 12.

Credit cards Discover, MC, Novus, Visa.
Rates B&B, $105–135 suite, $85–105 double, $60–110 single. Extra person, $15.
Cottage, weekly $670. $2 daily gratuity suggested. 2–3 night weekend/holiday
minimum in season. Weekly rates for suites.
Extras Afternoon tea, train station pickups, trip itineraries.

Rocky Shores Inn & Cottages ¢ 👫

65 Eden Road, 01966

Tel: 978–546–2823
800–348–4003

URL: http://www.rockportusa.com/rockyshores/

Built as a seaside summer home by a wealthy Texan in 1905, Rocky
Shores was converted into an inn in 1948; its rustic shingled cottages
were built at that time. It was bought by Renate and Gunter Kostka in
1980, who note: "Some of our rooms are done in light colors and white
wicker, others with Victorian antiques, but all have fresh flowers,
sweets, and first-class housekeeping." Rates for inn guests include a
breakfast buffet of juice, cereal, fruit, yogurt, jams, assorted breads,
coffee, and tea.

"Serene, beautiful, and gracious, with hospitable innkeepers." *(Karen
Brown)* "Beautiful guest rooms with spectacular ocean views." *(Nancy
Mauloin)* "Our second-floor room had a private balcony with a splendid panoramic ocean view. Ample privacy; easy parking." *(Larry &
Rita Pelland)* "Attractive curtains, fresh flowers, and wonderful local
paintings." *(Muriel Borne)* "Renate, Gunter, and their staff have a great
knack for making guests feel welcome. The location is one of the prettiest on Cape Ann; the grounds are spacious, the cottages and rooms in
the inn are clean, airy, and comfortable; the breakfasts are generous and
delicious." *(Mrs. Martha Falls)* "We watched the sun come up over the
twin lighthouses on Thatcher Island. Guests awaken to the aromas of
fresh-baked pastries and just-brewed coffee." *(Willard & Helen Reed)*
"The dining room has a lighthouse view, crisp linens, and fresh flowers on the tables. The cabins are simply furnished in '50s-style maple,
with homey touches such as matching tablecloths and kitchen curtains
and fresh flowers on arrival." *(Charles & Betty Fay)*

Open May 1–Nov. 1.
Rooms 11 2–3 bedroom cottages, 11 doubles—all with private bath and/or
shower, TV, fan. 3 with air-conditioning. Cottages with kitchen.
Facilities Dining room, living room, sun room, porches. 3 acres.
Location N Shore. 30 m NE of Boston, 3 m N of Gloucester. 2 m from town.
From Rte. 128 take Rte. 127 to downtown Rockport. Turn right on Rte. 127A (also
called South St. & Mt. Pleasant St.) & go 2 m to Eden Rd. Turn left & continue
to inn.
Restrictions No smoking in guest rooms or breakfast room. Children welcome
in cottages.
Credit cards Amex, MC, Visa.
Rates B&B (inn rooms only), $84–117 double, $81–114 single. Extra person,
$10. Cottages (for 4–6 people), $850–1055 weekly. Extra person, $35 per week.
2-night minimum in cottages as available.
Extras German spoken.

Seacrest Manor　　　　　　　　　　　*Tel:* 978–546–2211
99 Marmion Way, 01966　　　　　　　　*URL:* http://www.
　　　　　　　　　　　　　　rockportusa.com/seacrestmanor/

"Decidedly small, intentionally quiet" is the way Leighton Saville and Dwight MacCormack describe the 1911 seaside manor house they've owned since 1973. They go on to explain: "Peace and quiet are prime commodities here, along with attention to detail. We offer advice and reservations for trips, activities, shopping, and meals. Guests enjoy our extensive prize-winning gardens, magnificent views, and comfortable lawn and deck furniture. During the last five years our rooms have been fully refurbished, with plush carpeting throughout."

Breakfast is served at individual tables from 7:30–9:30 A.M., and includes fresh-squeezed orange juice ("if we don't squeeze it, we don't have it"), along with Irish oatmeal with chopped dates, and such entrées as French toast, corn fritters, pineapple/coconut pancakes, or bacon and eggs, plus English teas, coffees, and hot chocolate. Rates also include afternoon tea, served at 4 P.M.; free daily newspapers, evening turndown service, men's shoeshines, bathroom amenities, and fresh flowers throughout.

"Beautiful gardens and ocean views. Quiet and peaceful, yet within walking distance of town via the ocean path. Helpful and sincere owners and staff, dedicated to making your stay the very best it can be." *(Joyce & Richard Hyatt)* "The staff and owners were involved, available, and engaging. Great art displayed at the inn." *(Ed & Nancy Nasief)* "I heard cheery laughter in the kitchen as breakfast was being prepared, the fire was set and glowing in the dining room, each table was beautifully laid, and the care with which breakfast was served was simply delightful. The views of two lighthouses and the sea, the gardens and the pines, and the loveliness within the inn add to its gentle charms." *(Kay Lyou)*

"Spectacular gardens. Our room had a wonderful view of Rockport Harbor and Cape Ann; a freshly cut rose in a vase set on the bureau was a thoughtful touch. I loved dozing in the hammock, awakening to gaze out to the ocean. Fascinating collections of antiques, books, paintings, and bunnies." *(Valerie Elmore)* "Inn dog Bailey was friendly and entertaining. Our favorite spot is the patio facing the water with great views and cool breezes." *(James Mendori)* "Our spacious room had comfortable furnishings and a wonderfully large bathroom and bathtub. Delicious, filling breakfasts of cinnamon oatmeal, French toast, eggs, and bacon. Excellent tips on restaurants and area sights." *(Jonathan & Kim Howard)* "Pleasant atmosphere, quiet location, congenial owners. Ice and glasses were brought to our room with a dish of mints. In the evening the bed was turned down and chocolates were left on a pretty dish with a note; the newspaper was at our door every morning." *(Carolyn & Burton Panetta)*

Open April–Nov.
Rooms 8 doubles—6 with full private bath, 2 rooms with maximum of 4 people sharing bath. All with clock/radio, TV, hairdryer. 7 with desk, 3 with balcony.
Facilities Dining room with fireplace; living room; library with books, fireplace;

porch, terrace. 2 acres with off-street parking. Bicycle rentals. Nature preserve across street.

Location 1 m from town. Less than 5 m from the N end of Rte. 128, just off Rte. 127 (alternate).

Restrictions No smoking. Children not encouraged. No check-in after 9 P.M.

Credit cards None accepted.

Rates B&B, $98–146 double. 10% service. 2-night minimum in season; 2–3 night weekend/holiday minimum.

Extras Station pickups. Some French spoken.

SALEM

Founded in 1628, Salem has many historic attractions. It's infamous for the Witch Trials of 1692, but it is also the home of Hawthorne's House of the Seven Gables. Two major museums, the Peabody Museum and the Essex Institute, are fascinating reminders of the town's importance as a port in the late 1700s. The former started with the trinkets sea captains brought back from their voyages, while the latter encompasses the reconstruction of houses dating back to the 17th century. Salem is located on the North Shore, 18 miles northeast of Boston, and about a 45-minute drive from Boston's Logan Airport. Boston and the North Shore are easily accessible from Salem via commuter rail.

Foliage and Halloween combine to make October the busiest month for visiting Salem; rates are highest and advance reservations are a good idea. Although nearly all guest rooms in Salem's B&Bs have private baths, many have been built into closets and are quite small—ask for details when booking.

Reader tip: "Many Salem B&Bs are in working-class areas. Salem is a real city and not a picturesque spot reserved for the upper middle class." *(WH)*

Information please: More reports are needed on all Salem's lodging options. Built in 1845 for Amelia and Edward Payson, the **Amelia Payson House** (16 Winter Street, 01970; 978–744–8304) is a fine example of Greek Revival architecture. Located in the historic district, Salem's major attractions are only steps away. A continental breakfast is served family-style and includes fresh fruit, home-baked muffins and scones, cereals and yogurt. B&B double rates range from $65–125. "Friendly innkeepers, spotless housekeeping, homey atmosphere. Pink seems to be a favorite color." *(EE)*

The **Hawthorne Hotel** (On the Common, 01970; 978–744–4080 or 800–729–7829; www.hawthornehotel.com) is a restored Federal-style hotel with 89 guest rooms, a restaurant, and pub; it's within walking distance of all Salem's museums, historic attractions, shopping, and the harbor. The hotel is being renovated by the new management—be sure to ask for a renovated room. Double rates range from $82–172, suites are $150–285. "Friendly staff, newly redone room, fine dinner." *(Walt Hermansen, also BJ Hensley)*

Built in 1808, the **Morning Glory Bed & Breakfast** (22 Hardy Street, 01970; 978–741–1703) is a Georgian Federal home located directly across the street from the House of Seven Gables. The third-floor deck offers views of the harbor. An expanded continental breakfast and afternoon tea are included in the rates of $85–120. The inn has four guest rooms, each with private bath; one has a telephone and data port, another has a fireplace.

Once used as a school house, **The Suzannah Flint House** (98 Essex Street, 01970; 978–744–5281 or 800–752–5281; www.salemweb.com/biz/suzannahflint) is adjacent to Salem Commons. Built around the turn of the 18th century, this Federal-style B&B offers three guest rooms, each with a private bath, antique furnishings, Oriental rugs over the original hardwood floors, TV/VCR, and a decorative fireplace. B&B double rates of $55–115 include continental breakfast. "A comfortable inn, with a wonderful location right off the Commons in the heart of old Salem, within walking distance of all sights. Inviting courtyard and breakfast room. The inn is very clean, beds and chairs were comfortable, and the rooms have lots of light; the compact bathrooms were built into closets. Simple breakfast of fruit, juice, coffee, cereal, and sweet bread or rolls. The innkeepers are friendly and accessible, but unobtrusive." *(Elizabeth Houdek)*

For additional area entries, see **Gloucester, Lynn, Marblehead,** and **Rockport.**

SANDWICH

Founded in 1639, Sandwich is the oldest town on Cape Cod, and offers plenty to interest both children and adults. In addition to a walking tour of the village and its historic buildings (several are open to the public), visitors will enjoy the Sandwich Glass Museum, displaying the work which made the town famous in the 19th century, and the nature center and separate museum dedicated to the famous children's writer Thornton Burgess, author of the Peter Cottontail stories. Also worthwhile is Heritage Plantation, a 76-acre open-air museum devoted to different aspects of American life; for collectors of all ages, Yesteryears Doll and Miniature Museum is a don't-miss.

Sandwich is located on Cape Cod, approximately 3 miles west of the Cape Cod Canal and 20 miles northeast of Hyannis. From Bourne Bridge, continue on Route 6A into town.

Worth noting: Most of the B&Bs in Sandwich are on its appealing main street, and are buildings of similar size and style. In most, both common and guest rooms are fairly small, typical of the period. For safety reasons, most innkeepers use Duraflame-type logs in guest rooms with working fireplaces.

Captain Ezra Nye House ¢
152 Main Street, 02563

Tel: 508–888–6142
800–388–2278
Fax: 508–833–2897
E-mail: captnye@aol.com
URL: http://www.captainezranyehouse.com

Built in 1829 by a packet ship captain, the Ezra Nye House has been owned by Elaine and Harry Dickson since 1986. They've restored the house with a pleasing mixture of period antiques and contemporary art, as well as their handsome collection of Oriental art and Chinese porcelain. Guest rooms are painted in soft pastels with hand-stenciling, each with an individual appeal—a queen-size canopy bed or sleigh bed, or a white wicker king-size bed. Breakfast is offered at two seatings in the peak season. Menus change daily, and might include orange juice, goat cheese soufflé, apple raisin muffins, and home-baked Irish soda bread one day, followed by perhaps grape juice, baked apples, buttermilk pancakes with bacon, and homemade granola.

"Convenient location within walking distance of most points of interest." *(Jane & Richard Kidney)* "Elaine and Harry are friendly hosts, attentive to guests' needs. Homey, peaceful atmosphere throughout the inn. Comfortable beds. Breakfast consisted of orange juice, freshly brewed coffee and tea, homemade orange muffins, and Swedish pancakes with fresh Vermont syrup." *(Susan Goldblatt)* "Lovely Colonial home—understated but true to the era with fine furnishings. Much to see in this area, including the Heritage Plantation." *(Rose Ciccone)* "Immaculate, warm, and cozy, with a variety of helpful Cape Cod maps and guidebooks." *(Melinda Stendardo)* "The Dicksons are friendly and helpful but allow guests to enjoy the quiet and cozy town of Sandwich. Elaine's breakfasts give the day a great start." *(Stacy Foreman)*

"Our bedroom had a white canopy bed, white wicker chairs, blue antique furniture and curtains." *(Emil & Betsy Lenz)* "The sitting area provides comfortable seating for conversation, reading, or watching television." *(Dolores Grant)* "Excellent location, with the Dan'l Webster across the street for dinner." *(Craig MacMillan)* "Elaine and Harry are wonderful hosts. The delicious breakfasts were enhanced by the lively conversation of our fellow guests." *(Sammie & Jack Turner)* "Lighting options ranged from candles to bright reading lights." *(Kelly Blanchard)* "The bathroom was spotless with an old-fashioned claw-foot tub and skylight." *(Anna Pendino)*

Open All year.
Rooms 6 doubles—all with private bath and/or shower, fan. 1 with fireplace.
Facilities Living room, fireplace; family room with library, TV/VCR, fireplace; porch, deck. 4 blocks to tennis. 5 m to Sandy Neck Beach.
Location Center of town.
Restrictions No smoking. Children over 10 preferred.
Credit cards Amex, Discover, MC, Visa.
Rates B&B, $85–110 double. 2-night holiday, weekend (Memorial Day–Nov. 1) minimum.
Extras Airport/station pickups. Spanish spoken.

The Dan'l Webster Inn 🏃 ✕ ♿
149 Main Street, 02563

Tel: 508–888–3622
800–444–3566
Fax: 508–888–5156
E-mail: dwi@capecod.net
URL: http://www.danlwebsterinn.com

The Dan'l Webster dates back to 1692, and was operated as a tavern and inn through much of its history. In 1915, it was named for one of its most famous regular guests. The historic building was destroyed by fire in 1971 and rebuilt in Colonial style. The Catania family, owners of the inn since 1980, have renovated and expanded it to an adjacent property, the Fessenden House, built in 1826. The Dan'l Webster is a good choice for travelers who want the mood of a historic inn with the conveniences of a small hotel.

"Exceptional service from every member of the staff, who feel like part of an extended family. Excellent dining and an extensive wine list. Ample parking and a strategic location for those wishing to visit nearby historic sites." *(Patricia & James Donovan)* "Lovely landscaping, with flowers everywhere. Our favorite room is #31, but all are spacious, comfortable, and in excellent condition, with chairs just right for sitting and reading, and extra pillows and blankets. Bathrooms are shiny clean with plenty of big fluffy towels. Ice is delivered to your room in the evening, and coffee awaits early risers in the gathering room." *(Roger Dennis, Jr.)* "Meals are elegant, the food is always good (great sandwiches served in the pub), the staff cordial, the innkeepers warm and friendly, and the guest rooms comfortable." *(Hopie Welliver)* "The owner was helpful with information about restaurants, antiques, and auctions. Our room, with a working fireplace, was furnished with numerous antiques including a canopy bed, trunk, and antique chest." *(Gail Owings)* "Endorse existing entry. A pleasant small hotel, with clean, comfortable rooms and good food." *(Pat Borysiewicz)* "Delightful dinner in the plant-filled Conservatory, with wonderful salad and striped bass from the Catania's Aquafarm. The apple-cranberry bread pudding is a special dessert treat." *(DLG)*

Open All year. Closed Christmas Day.
Rooms 9 suites, 37 doubles—all with full private bath, telephone, radio, TV, desk, air-conditioning. Some with fireplace or whirlpool tub. Guest rooms in several buildings.
Facilities Restaurant, tavern, gift shop. 5 acres with flower gardens, swimming pool, gazebo. Health club, golf privileges.
Location Historic district. Take Rte. 6A to 3rd light, turn right on Jarves St. At end, turn right onto Main St. to inn.
Restrictions No smoking in some guest rooms. No pets.
Credit cards Amex, DC, Discover, MC, Visa.
Rates Room only, $89–199 suite, double. Extra person, $10. MAP, $170–280 suite, double. No charge for children under 12. 2-night weekend/holiday minimum. Alc breakfast, $7; alc lunch, $7–15; alc dinner, $22–45.
Extras Wheelchair access; some guest rooms equipped for disabled. Spanish, French, Portuguese, Italian, spoken. Crib.

The Summer House ¢ 　　　　　　　　　　　　*Tel:* 508–888–4991
158 Main Street, 02563 　　　　　　*E-mail:* sumhouse@capecod.net
　　　　　　　　　URL: http://www.capecod.net/summerhouse

Built in 1835 in the Greek Revival style, the Summer House was purchased by Phyllis and Erik Suby in 1998. The breakfast room was once the formal parlor and makes a dramatic picture with Chinese red walls, white woodwork and shutters, and a hand-painted black-and-white checkerboard floor; the adjoining parlor is more subdued with antique Victorian furnishings grouped around a black marble fireplace. Guest rooms have antique furniture, hand-stitched quilts, heirloom linens, and Cape Cod–painted hardwood floors. Breakfast is served between 8–9:30 A.M., and a typical menu includes fresh fruit and juice, followed by French toast stuffed with ham and cheese and strawberry-rhubarb cobbler; or perhaps asparagus and sun-dried tomato quiche with raisin oatmeal scones. Afternoon tea and cakes are served in the sun porch, or in the garden.

"Our spacious room had a fireplace and king-size bed. Outstanding hospitality. Fires were started for you at whatever time requested. Delicious breakfast of fresh fruit, bacon, and eggs, any time you desired." *(Brian Sanders)* "Outstanding location; excellent value. The accommodating owner prepared (at our request) a vegetarian, sugar-free breakfast of oatmeal with cinnamon and multi-grain toast." *(Marjorie Krems)* "Relaxing sun room and living room. Friendly, flexible, helpful innkeepers." *(GR, also Matt Corcoran)* "The owners are always on hand for a chat or to advise on places of interest. Appealing decor. Generous breakfasts, with seconds offered." *(Mrs. A. Payne)* "Convenient in-town location, yet quiet at night. Inviting backyard with flowers, sitting area, and enticing hammock." *(Diana Inman)* "Wonderful flowers everywhere, from the pink roses by the front door, to the begonias and geraniums on the sun porch, to the perennials surrounding the patio."*(MW)*

Open All year.
Rooms 5 doubles—all with private bath and/or shower, fan. 4 with fireplace.
Facilities Breakfast room with fireplace, parlor with fireplace, games, books; sun porch, patio. ½ acre with herb, flower gardens, hammock. Golf, tennis, beach, cross-country skiing nearby.
Location Historic district.
Restrictions No smoking. Children 6 and over.
Credit cards Amex, Discover, MC, Visa.
Rates B&B, $65–105 double. Extra person, $10–15. 2-night weekend/holiday minimum June–Oct.
Extras Free station pickup.

SCITUATE

Reader tips: "Scituate is a delightful town south of Boston, formerly a fishing village and still home to lots of lobster boats. It makes a good base for exploring Plymouth and Duxbury, and for day-trips (by car) to Boston. We enjoyed walking around the harbor and out along the causeway to a residential district. We had dinner at the Barker Tavern, and enjoyed outstanding swordfish." *(NB)* "The new Scituate Golf Links are something special. 'Links' means natural, i.e., *rough* roughs, environmentally appropriate grasses—with minimum use of fertilizers and pesticides—and a fabulous, but challenging design." *(IG)*

The Allen House ♿
18 Allen Place, 02066

Tel: 781–545–8221
Fax: 781–565–8221
E-mail: allenhousebnb@worldnet.att.net
URL: http://www.allenhousebnb.com

Christine and Iain Gilmour purchased this 1905 gabled merchant's home in 1989 and remodeled it as a B&B. They describe their inn as "a home full of personality, with classical music, and two cats." Its common areas contain antique and reproduction furnishings, Oriental rugs, hardwood floors and moldings, and French doors with scroll-carved headers. A sunny porch off the dining room overlooks busy Scituate Harbor. Breakfast includes fresh fruit and juice, home-baked muffins or breads, plus such entrées as pan-fried trout almondine with lemon, or orange and macadamia nut waffles topped with honey, syrup, or cream. With advance warning, dietary restrictions can be accommodated. Guests are occasionally treated to afternoon tea with cakes, pastries, or scones, served between 5 and 6 P.M.

"The Gilmours are a delightful English couple; Christine is an accomplished chef and Iain a talented classical pianist. We were treated to Iain's music while we were served tea on the porch. Our room in the addition was called Peggotty, after a beautiful cove in Scituate. Christine's English-country decorating is beautiful and the grounds resemble an English garden." *(Martha Mahan)* "Well-equipped bathrooms with plenty of towels, soap, lights, mirrors, shelves, and linens. The attractive addition has an inviting library and guest pantry. The screened porch is most appealing for breakfast, with interior window boxes overflowing with colorful annuals. At breakfast, a variety of antique china was used for each course. Our delicious breakfast began with fresh fruit and muffins, then juice and scrambled eggs with broiled tomatoes and whole-grain toast. Wheelchair accessibility is sensitively provided via a well-designed access ramp, and a spacious room off the library, with a king-size bed, good lighting, lots of windows, and roll-in shower." *(Nancy Barker)* "Our room had a harbor view; a thunderstorm lit up the sky as we watched from the picture window. The Gilmours have created a warm and caring home, and are welcoming but unobtrusive. At breakfast, they were available to help guests plan their day, and if need be, pack a lunch." *(Martin & Jane Schwartz)*

Open All year. Closed mid-March–early April.
Rooms 6 doubles—all with private bath, radio, fan. 1 room with TV.
Facilities Dining room with fireplace, living room with fireplace, TV, games, parlor with books; guest pantry; screened porch. Porch, flower gardens, lawns. Off-street parking. Fishing, boating, swimming, golf, nearby.
Location 30 m SE of Boston. Town center.
Restrictions No smoking. Children age 12 and over.
Credit cards Amex, Discover, MC, Visa.
Rates B&B, $69–169 double.
Extras Wheelchair access; 1 room specially equipped. Some French, German, Spanish spoken.

SOUTH DENNIS

For additional area entries, see **Chatham, Dennisport, Harwich Port,** and **West Harwich.**

Captain Nickerson Inn ¢ 👫
333 Main Street, 02660

Tel: 508–398–5966
800–282–1619
Fax: 508–398–5966
URL: http://www.bbonline.com/ma/captnick/

Built in 1828, the Captain Nickerson Inn was rebuilt in the Queen Anne style by Captain Miller Nickerson in 1879, and was restored as a B&B in 1993 by Patricia and David York. Guest rooms are named for the captain's ships, and the charming decor combines wide-board pine floors and Oriental rugs with both Colonial and Victorian furnishings. The charming Elizabeth Room has a white iron queen-size bed, blue floral curtains, and white wicker rocking chair and table, while the elegant Bridal Room has a rice-carved queen-size four-poster bed and cherry-wood furnishings. Breakfast is served at individual tables from 8:30–9:30 A.M., and includes fresh fruit and juice, cereal, home-baked muffins or pastries, plus eggs, pancakes, or French toast; crêpes are a Sunday morning specialty.

"Friendly, accommodating hosts who gave us great recommendations on restaurants and activities; excellent directions." *(Tania Malik)* "Our comfortable room was well-appointed and spotless. Robes were provided for our journeys to the large bath. A guest fridge was located near our door for cold drink storage. Pat provided a helpful notebook of pertinent local information in our room; additional materials were available in the front hall." *(Margaret Marsett)* "Quiet setting, away from the hustle-bustle; we even heard crickets at night. Warm, country hospitality. Pat and Dave went out of their way to accommodate our early departure by serving us breakfast, well before the usual time. Firm comfortable beds; powerful shower heads in the bath." *(Lucy Scott)* "Helpful hostess; exceptionally clean; ample privacy." *(Joan Decelle)*

Open All year. Closed Thanksgiving, Christmas, certain weeks in Jan., Feb.
Rooms 5 doubles—3 with private shower and/or bath, 2 with maximum of 4 people sharing bath. All with clock/radio, air-conditioning, robes. 4 with ceiling fan, writing table.
Facilities Dining room with fireplace, living room with fireplace, TV/VCR, games, videotapes; guest refrigerator, porches. ½ acre with off-street parking, swing set, lawn games. Complimentary bicycles. Beaches, golf, tennis, bicycle trail, boating, horseback riding nearby.
Location Cape Cod. Take I-195 or I-495 to Rte. 25 across Bourne Bridge. Take last exit off rotary to Rte. 6 E. Take Exit 9 & bear right off ramp onto Rte. 134. At 3rd set of lights, go right onto Upper Cty. Rd. At 4-way stop, go left onto Main St. to inn ¼ m on right.
Restrictions No smoking. Air-conditioning masks possible traffic noise in some rooms.
Credit cards Discover, MC, Visa.

Rates B&B, $65–95 double; $60–90 single; Extra person, $15; crib, $10. 2–3 night minimum in-season/holiday weekends.
Extras Hyannis station/airport pickups, $10. Crib; babysitting by arrangement.

STOCKBRIDGE

"The lovely village of Stockbridge is where Norman Rockwell lived and worked; don't miss the display of his famous magazine covers at the Norman Rockwell Museum. In addition to Tanglewood, another Stockbridge attraction is the Berkshire Theater Festival." *(Irving Litvag)*

Stockbridge is located in the Berkshires, just seven miles south of Tanglewood, summer home of the Boston Symphony, and five miles southwest of Exit 2 of the Massachusetts Pike.

For additional area entries, see **Great Barrington, Lee, Lenox, North Egremont, South Egremont, South Lee,** and **West Stockbridge.**

The Inn at Stockbridge	*Tel:* 413–298–3337
Route 7, 30 East Street	888–466–7865
P.O. Box 618, 01262	*Fax:* 413–298–3406

E-mail: innkeeper@stockbridgeinn.com
URL: http://www.stockbridgeinn.com

The Inn at Stockbridge is a white-pillared Georgian Colonial-style home built in 1906, and purchased by Alice and Len Schiller in 1995. In 1997, the Schillers added a cottage house, housing four luxury suites with whirlpool tubs, gas fireplaces, televisions, and VCRs. Both common and guest rooms are generally large and graciously proportioned, and are furnished with Queen Anne reproductions, brass accents, and chintz and velvet fabrics. The lovely tree-shaded grounds include a forty-foot swimming pool. Breakfasts are served at the large table in the beautiful dining room; afternoon cheese and wine are offered as well. In addition to fresh fruit and juice, breakfast includes freshly baked triple-berry coffee cake, cinnamon buns, or perhaps pumpkin nut bread, plus such entrées as Belgian waffles with fresh strawberries, baked French toast with orange-apricot Grand Marnier sauce, or cheese and ham soufflé.

"The Kashmir Room in the cottage was spacious and exceptionally comfortable, with a king-size bed and inviting whirlpool bath for two. This beautifully furnished room was immaculate, with every amenity, including shampoo and hand creams in the bath. Lighting was ample for reading, with conveniently placed light switches. Housekeeping was excellent but unobtrusive; the breakfast delicious; and the owners very knowledgeable about area activities, hiking trails, and restaurants." *(Elaine Berkenwald & Stanley Klughaupt)* "Comfortable elegance; hospitable host and hostess. Delicious breakfast of fresh fruit, fresh-squeezed juice, homemade waffles, and muffins. Great location, close to all Berkshire attractions." *(Martin Steinberg)* "Elegant dining room and parlor; inviting sitting room." *(Rose Ciccone, also SWS)* "We like to read in bed, and appreciated the good, tall lamps set on large night tables." *(PS)* "Lovely, comfortable rooms; enjoyable 5 P.M. wine and cheese; accommodating, understanding owners." *(Amy Kargauer)*

Open All year.

Rooms 4 suites, 8 doubles—all with private bath, radio, telephone, air-conditioning. Some with gas fireplace, TV/VCR, whirlpool tub, desk. 4 suites in cottage house.

Facilities Living room with piano, fireplace; fax; library with books, fireplace; TV lounge, porch, deck. 12 acres with swimming pool. Tennis, golf, skiing nearby.

Location Berkshire Cty. 12 m S of Pittsfield. 45 m E of Albany. 1 m to center on Rte. 7. From Mass. Pike (I-90), take Exit 2 in Lee. Take Rte. 102 into Stockbridge. Go right at 1st major intersection onto Rte. 7 N. Go 1.2 m to inn on right (watch for sign; inn not visible from road).

Restrictions No smoking. No children under 12. Traffic noise might disturb light sleepers.

Credit cards Amex, MC, Visa.

Rates B&B, $125–260 suite, $95–220 double. Extra person, $30. 2-night weekend minimum. 3-night minimum summer/holiday weekend, special event. New Year's Eve 3-night gala, off-season packages.

Extras Free bus station pickups.

The Red Lion Inn ⅰ ✕ ⅰ

Main Street, 01262

Tel: 413–298–5545
Fax: 413–298–5130
E-mail: innkeeper@redlioninn.com
URL: http://www.redlioninn.com

The Berkshires may now have more inns than antique shops (imagine!), but there is only one Red Lion, a wonderful old hotel of great charm and character. It's a tribute to its longtime owners, the Fitzpatricks, and its management, headed by Brooks Bradbury, that reader reports are consistently so positive. Founded in 1773, the Red Lion burned to the ground in 1896; soon rebuilt, it has since been enlarged and renovated many times, and is furnished with antiques and period reproductions. If you're traveling with friends or family, ask about the inn's annex houses, with a quiet location on the streets behind the inn; if you'd like a romantic escape, reserve the Firehouse, with an enormous common area on the ground floor, and luxurious bathroom and bedroom on the second.

The Red Lion is also a delightful place to eat. Although menus change frequently, a recent dinner included such entrées as roast halibut with parsley risotto; beef tenderloin with mushrooms and leeks; and braised artichokes with red lentils.

"Longtime owners, the Fitzpatrick family continually maintains and upgrades the inn. Our room had furnishings original to the hotel, but had been redone with new fabrics, wallpaper, and paint; feather pillows were on the firm beds, with extra foam ones in the closet. Equal attention to detail can be seen in the flowers which bedeck the inn during the summer; we were told that keeping them blooming is a full-time job. Standouts at dinner were the freshly steamed corn-on-the-cob and the apple pie. Fun Victorian ambience: the original birdcage elevator, assorted antique paintings, sideboards, and sofas lining the long halls—

even a glass case filled with century-old hats and shoes (the original lost and found, perhaps)." *(SWS)*

"The main dining room offers casual elegance, the tavern is cozy and romantic, and the Lion's Den is a great place for a light meal in an intimate atmosphere; excellent cappuccino, too." *(Sally Ducot, also MW)* "The staff was unfailingly cheerful and helpful." *(NB)* "Our room had twin beds with crisp white linens and lovely old spreads. Two rocking chairs with a reading lamp were by the window and an old pine desk held writing materials and information about Stockbridge. Plenty of electrical outlets and good lighting. Breakfast of fresh squeezed grapefruit juice, fresh muffins, and bagels was delivered punctually to our room. Most impressive is the constant care and updating." *(Wendy Van Exan)* "On a beautiful summer afternoon, there is no nicer place to be than rocking on the front porch of the Red Lion." *(William Gerhauser)*

Open All year.
Rooms 27 suites, 93 doubles—most with private bath and/or shower, 18 with shared bath. All with air-conditioning, telephone, TV, and desk. 18 rooms in adjacent buildings.
Facilities Restaurant, bars, tavern, TV rooms, living rooms, meeting rooms; automatic elevator. Live music in bars, restaurant. Courtyard, gardens, swimming pool, tennis court, exercise room.
Location SW MA, Berkshires. Center of town.
Restrictions Traffic noise in some rooms; light sleepers should ask for a courtyard room. Minimal interior soundproofing. Parking can be tight when inn is full. No smoking in dining rooms, most guest rooms. Most rooms accessible by elevator.
Credit cards Amex, CB, DC, MC, Visa.
Rates Room only, $167–350 suite, $97–165 double, $65–155 single, plus $2 daily housekeeping charge. Extra person, $20. B&B rates. Full breakfast, $5–10. Alc lunch, $9–20; alc dinner, $25–40. Children's menu. Off-season midweek packages Nov.–mid-May. Holiday menus, programs.
Extras Limited wheelchair access; 1 room specially equipped. Japanese, Spanish, German spoken. Crib, babysitting.

STURBRIDGE

For additional area entries, see **Tolland, Connecticut.**

Publick House Historic Inn ✕ ♿ 👪
P.O. Box 187, Route 131
On the Common, 01566
Tel: 508–347–3313
800–PUBLICK
Fax: 508–347–5073
URL: http://www.publickhouse.com

Founded in 1771 by Colonel Ebenezer Crafts, the Publick House is now a large complex, including the original inn with 16 guest rooms furnished in Federalist Colonial style, plus several restaurants and shops. The 225-year-old slanted floors and exposed beams of the Publick House give a feeling of history to guest rooms furnished with four-poster acorn beds, fluffy pillows, firm mattresses, and period reproductions. The inn's restaurants share the same kitchen; extensive buffet breakfasts are served weekends in the main dining room, originally the stables and carriage house. Next door is Chamberlain House, with four suites and similar reproduction Colonial decor. In the same compound is the 94-room motor lodge, decorated in country decor. Finally there's the Colonel Ebenezer Crafts Inn, dating back to 1786 and located about 1½ miles away; its eight rooms are furnished with antiques and reproductions. Albert Cournoyer is the innkeeper.

"Our room at the Publick House was spotlessly clean, with a high-quality reproduction canopy bed, and fine linens. Excellent value." *(Paul Steinmetz, also BJ Hensley)* "Friendly and helpful staff made our stay delightful. The sticky buns are a highlight of the breakfast buffet." *(JFI)* "The lobster pie is scrumptious. Try the 'Joe Froggers' for dessert—large molasses cookies which arrive with an explanation of their name." *(Mary & Jim Rafferty)* "Every day is Thanksgiving at the Publick House, and the traditional turkey dinner with stuffing was a traditional treat." *(MW)*

Open All year.

Rooms 11 suites, 114 doubles—all with full private bath, desk, air-conditioning, fan. Rooms in 9 buildings.

Facilities 3 restaurants, gift shop, bake shop. 60 acres with swimming pool, tennis court, playground. Boating, fishing nearby.

Location Central MA. From Mass. Pike, take Exit 9, through tolls. Take Exit 3B to lights, turn left on Rte. 131. From I-84, take Exit 2 to Rte. 131.

Restrictions No smoking in some guest rooms. Traffic, restaurant noise in some rooms.

Credit cards Amex, CB, DC, MC, Visa.

Rates Room only, $114–155 suite, $90–135 double. Extra adult, $15; children under 17 free in parents' room. 10% AARP discount. B&B, MAP packages. Alc breakfast, $5–10; alc lunch, $12; alc dinner, $22–30. Theme weekend packages.

Extras Crib, babysitting. Wheelchair access to restaurant, lodge.

SUDBURY

For additional area entries, see **Concord** and **Southborough**.

Also recommended: A nine-acre retreat in the historic center of Sudbury, **The Arabian Horse Inn** (277 Old Sudbury Road, 01776; 978–443–7400 or 800–272–2426; joanbeers@aol.com) has three guest rooms; two overlook the pastures, Arabian horses, and duck pond. At this rambling 1880 Queen Anne Victorian, you can enjoy a full breakfast with home-baked treats in the dining room, the country kitchen, or, on your room's balcony. B&B double rates for the two guest rooms sharing a bath range from $129–159; the suite runs $249. "Tucked away near the center of Sudbury; wine and chocolates provided in the room." *(Helen & Don Cohen)* "I loved the friendly, loving animals—responsive horses and comical geese." *(Patricia Giedrys)* "The suite has a king-size four-poster canopy bed, working fireplace, private bath with a double sink and dressing table, a full walk-in closet, and a two-person Jacuzzi bath. The welcoming hosts, Joan and Rick Beers, serve an imaginative breakfast that keeps you going for hours." *(Gillia Bruce)* "Key features include the ability to come and go at ease; privacy and security; and an in-room telephone with voice mail for messages." *(Elizabeth Mueller)* "The horse theme runs throughout the inn's decor. Lovely antiques, classical music, and welcoming yet unobtrusive owners create a delightful ambience. Attentive housekeeping." *(Nicole M. Miller)*

Dating back to 1716, **Longfellow's Wayside Inn** (Wayside Inn Road, 01776; 978–443–1776 or 800–339–1776; www.wayside.org) gained its present name after publication of Longfellow's *Tales of a Wayside Inn* in 1863. Now a National Historic Site, the complex is administered by a nonprofit educational trust, established by Henry Ford in 1946. After a disastrous 1956 fire, the inn was restored to its original 18th-century appearance by a Ford Foundation grant. Classic New England cooking is offered for breakfast, lunch, and dinner. B&B double rates of $85–135 include a full traditional breakfast. Lunch offers such favorites as pot roast, chicken pot pie, and crab cakes, while dinner begins with the classic relish tray, cheese spread, and crackers, followed by such entrées as prime rib, baked scrod, and chicken with cranberry-walnut stuffing. "We had breakfast by the fireside in the Back Parlor, that appears to be right out of the 1700s, wide floorboards and all. In the evening, we enjoyed drinks in the Old Bar Room with 1700s ambience and a roaring fire in the hearth. To enjoy the inn's historic ambience at dinner, be sure to request the Tap Room, Back Parlor, or Lemon Dining Room. Our room was modest in size, with a double bed, antique dresser and mirror, night stand, and stuffed chair, plus a remodeled bathroom." *(Conrad & Nancy Schilke)* "We enjoyed the self-guided walking tour of the inn's original rooms, out-buildings, and grounds." *(Maureen Wolf)* Another reader was less taken with the inn's overnight accommodations: "I could hear every word spoken in the guest room next door; my room was neither comfortable nor cheerful." *(SR)*

WARE

The Wildwood Inn ¢   *Tel:* 413–967–7798
121 Church Street, 01082   800–860–8098

Fraidell Fenster, who has owned the Wildwood Inn since 1989, describes it as "a kick-your-shoes-off inn, close to lots of activities, but far enough from the beaten path to offer quiet relaxation." A sunny breakfast room overlooks a large yard with fruit trees and a variety of birds. Rates include a breakfast of coffee, juice, cereal, muffins or popovers, and such entrées as apple pancakes, quiche, or stuffed French toast.

"A warm and friendly inn with beautiful grounds and a lovely porch." *(Natalie Feinberg)* "Just as delightful on a return visit. Comfortable bed, friendly hosts. Enjoyed a early-morning stroll through the woods before a yummy breakfast. Tasty dinner at the Whistling Swan." *(GR)* "Delicious sparkling raspberry juice. Borrowed Fredi's canoe for a peaceful, scenic paddle on the river." *(JJ)* "The fireplace, antiques, and cradles filled with books create a relaxing atmosphere. With the exception of one bedroom done in authentic Victorian pieces, the guest rooms are simply furnished with pastel-painted walls and woodwork, good bedside lighting, some with antique beds and handmade quilts. Behind the house is a river and park, nice to explore after a hearty breakfast. Fredi is full of advice about sightseeing and hiking, particularly around nearby Quabbin Reservoir, and will gladly supply you with maps and menus from nearby restaurants." (*Lisa & Thomas Signorelli, also SWS*) "I had lunch on an apple farm, browsed in a huge used bookstore/café, and learned where to spot bald eagles. I was introduced to the other guests, and didn't feel at all uncomfortable as a single person." (*A.P. Zimmerman*)

Open All year.

Rooms 9 doubles—all with private bath and/or shower, air-conditioning, fan. 5 with desk.

Facilities Parlor with fireplace, puzzles, games, books; breakfast room. 2 acres with gardens, woods, path leading to river. Canoe, sleds, basketball, games, fishing, croquet, tennis. Cross-country, downhill skiing, swimming hole nearby.

Location Central MA; halfway between Sturbridge & Deerfield, near Amherst & Exit 8 of Mass. Pike. 1½ hrs. drive W of Boston; 3⅓ hrs. drive N of NYC. ¾ m from town. Rte. 9/32 becomes Main St. in town. Turn onto Church St. at 2nd traffic light in town (South St. opposite).

Restrictions Minimal traffic noise in front rooms; limited soundproofing between rooms. No smoking. No children under 6. No TV at inn.

Credit cards Amex, MC, Visa.

Rates B&B, $50–90. Extra person, $15. No tipping. Packages.

WELLFLEET

For additional area entries, see **Eastham, North Truro,** and **Provincetown.**

The Inn at Duck Creeke ¢ 🏃 ✕ ♿   *Tel:* 508–349–9333
Main Street, P.O. Box 364, 02667   *Fax:* 508–349–0234 (summer)
     Fax: 508–349–9333 (winter)
     Email: duckinn@capecod.net
     URL: http://www.capecod.net/duckinn

Owned by Bob Morrill and Judy Pihl since 1980, the Inn at Duck Creeke is set on a knoll overlooking Duck Pond, a tidal creek, and a salt marsh. The four buildings which make up the inn complex include the Captain's House, built in the early 1800s, and the equally venerable building housing the inn's two restaurants, Sweet Seasons and the Tavern Room. The innkeepers travel each winter to Europe or the Caribbean so that Chef Judy can add new dishes to her culinary repertoire—the Tavern's steak-and-ale puff pie was learned on a recent trip to England and Ireland. Favorite entrées at Sweet Seasons include shrimp with tomatoes, feta, garlic, and ouzo; pork with citrus, cilantro, and pine nuts; and chicken with garlic, sage, and vermouth cream. Choices at the

Tavern are no less appealing, ranging from veggie and sirloin burgers to a New England boil: cod with shrimp, kale, and Portuguese sausage in vegetable broth; plus wonderful cod and salmon fishcakes. Although the inn is not a fancy place, upgrading is an ongoing process; most recently, Judy notes that they've remodeled bathrooms, added carpeting and ceiling fans, and in 1999, will have new suites in the remodeled Saltworks building.

"The delectable little town of Wellfleet, with its many art galleries and craft shops, is as charming as nearby Provincetown is gaudy and honky-tonk. The simple but comfortable guest rooms are furnished with period pieces—Boston rockers, spool beds, and the like. Breakfasts are basic—served on paper plates with plastic cutlery—with excellent coffee in real mugs." *(Hilary Rubinstein)* "A wonderful creaky old house. We were delighted with the breakfast of fresh muffins and pastries served from 8–10 A.M., along with cereal and juice. We visited during a heat wave but our un-air-conditioned room was comfortable." *(Duane Roller)* "The helpful staff arranged for wonderful babysitters. Rooms are simple and small, yet comfortable; bathrooms basic but functional." *(BF)* "Charming airy rooms. Beautiful, peaceful in the fall. The Tavern offers good food, great fun. Bob and Judy are helpful, willing to accommodate guests' requests." *(Elizabeth McGinty)* "Pleasant atmosphere; peaceful, quiet ambience. Owners sincerely interested in our comfort and enjoyment during our stay." *(Joseph Laput)*

Open Early May–mid-Oct.

Rooms 25 doubles—17 with private bath and/or shower, 8 with a maximum of 4 people sharing a bath. Some with air-conditioning; all with ceiling fan. 7 rooms in annex.

Facilities Restaurant, tavern with live music, breakfast room, common room, screened porches, veranda. Swimming, boating, fishing, hiking, bicycling nearby.

Location Cape Cod, 17 m S of Provincetown, 100 m SE of Boston. Take Rte. 6 to Wellfleet; turn left at Wellfleet Center sign at traffic lights. Go 500 yds. to inn on right. Historic district; ½ m to village.

Restrictions Traffic, restaurant noise in some rooms. No refunds late June–Labor Day; transferable credit given toward a future stay.

Credit cards Amex, MC, Visa.

Rates B&B, $65–100 double. Extra person, $15; children under 5 in parents' room, $5. 2–3 night weekend minimum in season. Alc dinner $12–20. $10 one-time charge for crib, cot.

Extras Limited handicap access. Crib, babysitting.

WEST DENNIS

For additional area entries, see **Dennis Port, Harwich Port, South Dennis,** and **West Harwich.**

Also recommended: If you are looking for an old-time family resort, **The Lighthouse Inn** (Lighthouse Inn Road, P.O. Box 128, 02670; 508–398–2244; www.lighthouseinn.com), run by the Stone family since it opened in 1938, may well be the place. This oceanfront country inn complex has accommodations in cottages with fireplaces, Cape-style houses with guest rooms, individual suites, and rooms in the main house, and offers a children's program in summer. *Paula Devereaux* writes that "the inn was just as appealing on a return visit. The grounds are well maintained with an outdoor pool, tennis courts, beach area, and playground. Fine family getaway." And from *Ron Kahan*: "For a family reunion, we stayed in a five-bedroom house next to the tennis court, and were delighted with the accommodating staff and wonderful breakfast buffets. Excellent value." The center section of the main house is officially recognized by the U.S. Coast Guard as the West Dennis Lighthouse. Per person rates range from $111–153, including breakfast and dinner; children pay $40–65 each, depending on age.

WEST HARWICH

West Harwich is on the south side of Cape Cod, 80 miles southwest of Boston, and seven miles east of Chatham. To get there, take Route 28 through the village of West Dennis into West Harwich.

For additional area entries, see **Chatham, Dennis Port, Harwich Port, South Dennis,** and **West Dennis.**

Cape Cod Claddagh Inn ✕   *Tel:* 508–432–9628
77 Main Street, Route 28, P.O. Box 667, 02671   800–356–9628
Fax: 508–432–6039
E-mail: claddagh@axscapecod.com
URL: http://www.capecodcladdaghinn.com

Jack and Eileen Connell invite guests to share their Irish hospitality in this turn-of-the-century Victorian home. They note that "we open our hearts as well as our home to our guests. We want our guests to relax and have fun, to see Cape Cod from a native's viewpoint." The authentic Irish pub has a copper-clad bar, good homemade food, and Irish beers and stout; candlelight dinners are served in the Blarney Room. Irish music occurs spontaneously with the help of musical instruments decorating the pub—or bring your own for an evening of sing-alongs or traditional Irish music. Many of the staff are Irish University students, working at Cape Cod for the summer.

"Lovely setting; exceptionally warm hospitality." (*Terry Roscoe*)

"Delicious breakfasts served at 9 A.M. Irish oatmeal (a delicious concoction of creamy oatmeal topped with cranberries, apples, and sliced almonds), bacon and Irish sausages, Irish muffins and soda bread accompanied a fluffy spinach omelet one morning and stuffed French toast the next." (*Nancy & Alan Pawlow*) "Parking is ample, and well lit at night. The candlelit breakfast was served on crystal and china, lace and linen." (*Mr. & Mrs. John LaTulippe*) "Although the inn is located on a busy street, it's very quiet at night." (*Rebecca Martone-Ward*) "Rooms cleaned daily; baths spotless, with complimentary shampoo and bubble bath." (*James Dehelmas*) "Comfortable accommodations, warm hospitality, delightful pub, bountiful breakfasts." (*TJC*)

Open April 1–Dec.

Rooms 1 cottage, 8 suites—all with private bath and/or shower, radio, TV, desk, air-conditioning, fan, refrigerator. 2 suites in cottage 50 yds. from inn.

Facilities Irish pub, 3 dining rooms, living room with fireplace, sun room, wraparound porch, guest refrigerator. 2 acres with swimming pool, patio. Swimming, fishing, hiking, bicycling, tennis, golf nearby.

Location Cape Cod. 12 m E of Hyannis, 7 m W of Chatham. Walking distance to Dennisport. From Rte. 6, take Exit 9 to right. Go left at 3rd traffic light to Rte. 28. Watch for inn sign, ½ m on right.

Restrictions Smoking in pub only.

Credit cards Amex, Discover, MC, Visa.

Rates B&B, $95–125 suite or cottage. Tipping encouraged. Weekly rates. 10% AARP, AAA discount. Prix fixe breakfast, $6.50; alc lunch, $4–7; alc dinner, $12–15.

WEST STOCKBRIDGE

For additional area entries, see **Great Barrington, Lee, Lenox, North Egremont, Richmond, South Egremont,** and **Stockbridge.**

The Williamsville Inn ✕
Route 41, 01266

Tel: 413–274–6118
Fax: 413–274–3539

For a peaceful country setting at the foot of Tom Ball Mountain, with a location convenient to all the Berkshires have to offer—both summer and winter—the Williamsville Inn is a good choice. Owned by Gail and Kathleen Ryan since 1991, the inn was built in 1797 by Christopher French, a Revolutionary War soldier; Govane Lohbauer is the longtime manager. French bought the land from Tom Ball, said to be the last Mohican Indian to sell his land in the Berkshires. The inn was a working farm until 1952; today, its restaurant offers such entrées as roast duck with blackberry sauce, pistachio-crusted breast of chicken with leeks and apples, and salmon and sea bass with lemon beurre blanc.

"Owner Gail Ryan is a lovely, vivacious, former Manhattan actress who is the heart and soul of the Inn. Although her mother, Kathleen, stays in the background, she's also a pleasure to talk to, as is manager Govane Lohbauer. Inn-dog Molly is equally hospitable; only the cat is shy. Guest rooms are pleasantly decorated with Colonial reproductions; many have four-poster or canopy beds. A winter favorite is the Louisa May Alcott Room on the third floor, tucked under the eaves; rooms in the barn are simpler in style, but have newly redone bathrooms. The excellent breakfasts offer a choice of juice, granola or oatmeal, French toast or an omelet—mine was filled with broccoli and chevre, with country-toasted bread and bacon. Highlights of my dinner included the appetizer—a spinach cake with shiitake mushrooms—and the dessert—chocolate truffle cake with whipped cream and raspberry sauce. Grounds are lovely and spacious." *(SWS)* "Lovely glass-enclosed breakfast room, with a view of the mountains and woods; we watched a fawn eating fallen crab apples, not fifteen feet from the window. Gail gave us great touring suggestions, yet was never intrusive." *(Barbara & Larry Glazer)*

Open All year. Restaurant closed Mon.–Wed., Sept.–May.
Rooms 1 suite, 15 doubles—all with private bath and/or shower, air-conditioning. 6 with fireplace/wood stove, 4 with private entrance, 1 with desk. 4 rooms in barn.
Facilities Restaurant, tavern, breakfast room, living room; most with fireplace. Sunday night storytelling/entertainment dinners Nov. 1–April 31. 10 acres with off-street parking, swimming pool, tennis court, lawns, gardens, games, barn with sheep & goats, tree swing. Fishing, hiking, skiing nearby.
Location W MA. Berkshires. Approx. 10 m S of Lenox. 5 m N of Great Barrington, via Rte. 41. From I-90 (Mass. Pike) take Exit 1, W Stockbridge & go S (left) on Rte. 41 to inn on right. From Stockbridge, take Rte. 102 5 m W to Rte. 41 & go S (left) approx. 5 m inn on right.
Restrictions Smoking in tavern only. Minimal interior soundproofing in some rooms.
Credit cards Amex, MC, Visa.
Rates B&B, $160–185 suite, $120–150 double. Extra person, $20. $2 daily housekeeping gratuity. Senior, AAA discount. 3-night minimum summer weekends; 2-night minimum June, Oct., holiday weekends. Alc dinner, $35. Sun. entertainment dinners, $20.
Extras Inquire about pets. Spanish spoken.

WEST YARMOUTH

Also recommended: A sea captain's home completed in 1827, the **Captain Farris House** (308 Old Main Street, South Yarmouth, 02664; 508–760–2818 or 800–350–9477; www.captainfarriscapecod.com) was elegantly restored in 1993. B&B double rates for the eight guest rooms range from $80–195, including a full breakfast; each room has a private bath, TV, and telephone with data port; some have double Jacuzzi tubs. "Clean and beautiful; comfortable, serene atmosphere; delicious breakfasts; careful attention to detail." *(Josef Polichino)* "Excellent food, a help-yourself kitchen open 24 hours a day, beautiful antiques, a living area with a baby grand, and a spacious front porch." *(AM)*

For additional area entries, see **Hyannis Port, South Dennis,** and **West Dennis.**

The Manor House Bed and Breakfast *Tel:* 508–771–3433
57 Maine Avenue, 02673 800–962–6679
Fax: 508–790–1186
E-mail: manorhse@capecod.net
URL: http://www.capecod.net/manorhouse

Most innkeepers survive twenty or thirty years in the corporate world before bailing out to start a second career as B&B owners; Rick and Liz Latshaw jumpstarted their life as innkeepers at the tender ages of 31 and 26 (respectively), when they discovered the Manor House in 1994. "Selling our home and everything else that wasn't nailed down," they've worked hard to renovate and redecorate this 1920s gambrel-roofed Dutch Colonial home. Judging from all reports, the energetic Latshaws made the right decision. Breakfast is served from 8:30–10 A.M.; early-morning coffee and tea can be found on the upstairs teacart around 7:30 A.M. Rick's creative menus might include cranberry-orange juice with raspberry sherbet, cinnamon crunch muffins, peaches with honey, and whole-wheat blueberry buttermilk pancakes with real maple syrup. Rates also include afternoon tea and evening turndown service with pillow chocolates.

"Liz welcomed us with tea and lemon cookies. Each room has a different theme. Done in restful shades of pink, blue, and green, the Howling Coyote Room has Southwestern decor with a queen-size golden pine cannonball bed, side chair with reading lamp, fresh flowers, and cactus plants. The charming Picket Fence Room has an actual fence used as wainscoting, lots of flowers, and garden accessories. The lovely Secret Garden is crisp in green and white, with ivy wallpaper and bedspread, a high four-poster queen-size bed, and lots of plants. Whalewatch is the largest, with a nautical theme and a bay view. The living area has a brick fireplace, pine armoire entertainment center, upholstered wicker furniture, and good lighting for reading, plus lots of magazines, area information, and menus. A comfortable, unpretentious inn." *(Rose Ciccone)* "Rick's breakfasts are awesome, and inn pets Whitesocks and Hairball were always there to greet us." *(Carol Gauthier)*

"Relaxing atmosphere; delicious breakfasts; long, hot baths." *(Chris & Emily Riley)* "The aroma of freshly baked bread was accompanied by a cart with wake-up coffee and tea set just outside our door." *(Tom & Jo Strader)* "Soft music played in the sitting room. The two inn cats add to the homey atmosphere. Our spacious room had a view of the bay, a walk-in closet, and ample drawer space." *(Georgia Moro)* "Ample parking. Quiet residential neighborhood, just a short walk to a delightful local beach." *(Larry Davis)* "Just-baked muffins, fresh flowers, flavored coffees, and an incredible raspberry sorbet punch are among our delightful memories." *(Kathy O'Reilly)*

Open All year.

Rooms 6 doubles—all with private bath and/or shower, clock/radio, fan. 3 with air-conditioning.

Facilities Living/dining room with TV/VCR, stereo, fireplace; reading nook with books; porch. ¼ acre with off-street parking, lawn games. 2 beaches in walking distance.

Location Cape Cod, 77 m S of Boston. Take Rte. 6 to Exit 7. Go left at end of exit, & 2nd left onto Higgins Crowell Rd. Go through 2 traffic lights. After crossing Rte. 28, name changes to Berry Ave. Stay on Berry, then go and turn right on Broadway. Go right on 2nd street on right, Maine Ave. to inn, 2nd house on left.

Restrictions No smoking. Children 10 and over.

Credit cards Amex, MC, Visa.

Rates B&B, $68–128 double, $58–118 single. Extra person, $20. 10% senior, AAA discount. 2-night minimum May–Oct. 10% weekly discount, summer; 4-day stay, off-season.

Extras Local airport/station pickups.

WILLIAMSTOWN

Williamstown is a beautiful country town, the home of small but prestigious Williams College, and of two fine art museums—the Clark Institute, particularly famous for its Impressionist collection, and the Williams College Art Museum, with some impressive 19th- and 20th-century paintings. The summer theater festival is also of interest. Williamstown is located in the northern Berkshires of northwest Massachusetts, 40 miles east of Albany, and 130 miles west of Boston.

Also recommended: A country estate built in 1948, the **Field Farm Guest House** (554 Sloan Road, 01267; 413–458–3135) is owned by the Trustees of Reservations, a century-old foundation whose goal is to save significant areas of open land in Massachusetts; Jean and Sean Cowhig are the innkeepers. B&B double rates for the five guest rooms, each queen- and/or twin-size beds, and private bath, are $125, including a full breakfast; guests are welcome to explore the property's 300 acres, complete with swimming pool, tennis court, hiking trails, and beaver pond. "Contemporary art and sculpture from the Bloedel Collection highlight the decor and landscape. The delicious breakfast included friendship bread, egg pie, homemade granola, and fresh fruit compote." *(June Sullivan)* "Magnificent views, classic modern Scandinavian and American furnishings from the 1950s. Friendly, helpful staff; good restaurant recommendations." *(James Salzmann, also James Bowers)*

Williamstown's most luxurious (and expensive) option is **The Orchards** (222 Adams Road [Route 2], 01267; 413–458–9611 or 800–225–1517), a 47-room hotel and restaurant. To counter its location on a busy road in a commercial zone, the inn is built around a central courtyard, highlighting the luxury of the rooms and appointments; the inn was built in 1985. The spacious rooms are individually decorated in an English country theme. The over-size rooms have bay windows, tub baths as well as showers, dressing areas, and telephones in both the bedroom and the bath. The dining room is elegant; the lounge inviting with a huge fieldstone fireplace. Double rates for the 47 guest rooms range from $125–225; facilities include an exercise room and outdoor swimming pool. "Exceptionally beautiful rooms; lovely amenities and delicious home-baked cookies; convenient location within walking distance of Williams College." *(Molly Jones, also MW)* "Elegance and perfection; top-notch restaurant. A large guest room, yet cozy; the bed was covered with a crocheted bedspread." *(Leigh Robinson)*

For authentic Colonial atmosphere, try **River Bend Farm** (643 Simonds Road [Route 7], 01267; 413–458–3121) built in 1770, and owned by Dave and Judy Loomis since 1980. The B&B double rate for the four guest rooms is $90, including a breakfast of homemade granola, breads, muffins, jam, and honey. One guest room and bath are on the first floor; a second bath and three guest rooms are on the second floor. "We were entranced by the authenticity of the house and its primitive antique furnishings, and delighted by our conversations with Dave and Judy." *(James Owens)*

The **Williamstown B&B** (30 Cold Spring Road, 01267; 413–458–9202) is located just off the circle where Routes 2 and 7 join, an easy walk to the theater, campus, and village center. This 1880 restored Victorian home is owned by Kim Rozell and Lucinda Edmunds, and has three cozy guest rooms, furnished in period oak, maple, and mahogany decor, each with a private bath. The ample common areas include the welcoming front porch, living room, and dining room. B&B double rates are $70–95. "Immaculate, well furnished, quiet, and charming. Kim and Lucinda are unobtrusive yet available to answer questions and chat. Fantastic breakfasts of delicious fresh fruit, orange juice, blueberry muffins, waffles, or eggs with toast. Afternoon lemonade and iced tea. Comfortable, uncluttered rooms, good advice on activities and restaurants." *(Susan Hanley)* Comments appreciated.

Blackinton Manor
1272 Massachusetts Avenue, North Adams, 01247

Tel: 413–663–5795
800–795–8613
Fax: 413–663–3121
E-mail: epsteind@bcn.net
URL: http://www.blackinton-manor.com

Dan and Betsey Peters-Epstein describe their inn, an 1849 Italianate Federal mansion, as being "a historic house of music in the Berkshires." Historic—because it was built by a prominent textile manufacturer, back in the days when nearby North Adams was major industrial and railroad center. Musical—because owner Dan Epstein is a concert pianist, and Betsey is an operatic soprano and cantor. Rehearsals and chamber music concerts with renowned classical musicians are not unusual at Blackinton. Last but not least is its location in the northern Berkshires, convenient for outdoor sports and a full range of cultural activities in Williamstown. Abandoned for years, Blackinton Manor was restored by the Epsteins as an elegant and romantic B&B; Charlene Hildebrand is the manager. Its wrought-iron balconies and floor-to-ceiling pocket windows are complemented by period antiques, Oriental rugs, and spacious guest rooms with queen- or king-size beds.

Breakfast is served from 8–9:30 A.M.; a recent menu included sliced mangoes and blackberries, omelets with sun-dried tomatoes, chevre, and basil, and popovers fresh from the oven; or possibly melon, blueberry buttermilk pancakes, and turkey sausage. In warmer months, guests can relax poolside amid the gardens.

"Music, personal service, and New England charm. Quaint and quiet location." *(Lawrence Ricketts)* "Wonderful atmosphere. Guests gather to visit in the large living room, but there's equal opportunity for privacy. Both Daniel and Betsey are caring people, and Daniel loves to cook." *(Dera Drosin)* "The Epsteins are real professionals yet treat their guests like friends and family. They pay attention to detail; their inn combines elegance and comfort. Everything, from the exquisitely appointed interiors to the delicious breakfasts, is done with extraordinary care." *(Mark Castillo)* "Even though our son has graduated from nearby Williams College, we will return to the area just to stay at Blackinton." *(Mr. & Mrs. Mark Federman)* "Large, sumptuous suite. A delightful performance of song on Saturday night during our visit." *(A. Norman Redlich)*

Open All year.

Rooms 1 suite, 4 doubles—all with full private bath and/or shower, clock, air-conditioning. 1 with whirlpool tub, private entrance, or piano.

Facilities Dining room, living room with fireplace, piano, books; screened porch. Concert series. ¾ acre with patio, swimming pool, gardens. ¼ m to Appalachian Trail for hiking, cross-country skiing. Golf, downhill skiing nearby.

Location NW MA. 3 hrs. N of NYC & W of Boston. 2 m E of Williamstown, just over N. Adams line. From Williamstown, go E on Rte. 2. Pass Rte. 43 entering right; watch for traffic light at Cole Ave. From light, go 1.7 m & go left on Ashton Ave. Turn right on Mass. Ave. to inn on left, at corner of Church Hill Rd.

Restrictions No smoking. Children 7 and over.

Credit cards MC, Visa.

Rates B&B, $105–125 suite, $100–125 double. Extra person, $20. 2-night weekend/holiday minimum. Advance reservations essential for major college weekends. Music appreciation weekends; writing workshops.

Extras Spanish, German spoken.

YARMOUTHPORT

Yarmouthport is located on the north side of Cape Cod, 75 miles south of Boston and 5 miles from the Hyannis airport.

For additional area entries, see **Barnstable** and **Dennis**.

Liberty Hill Inn   ♿ 🧍

77 Main Street, Route 6A, 02675

Tel: 508–362–3976
800–821–3977
Fax: 508–362–6485
E-mail: libertyh@capecod.net
URL: http://www.sunsol.com/libertyhillinn

Listed on the National Register of Historic Places, the Liberty Hill Inn is a stately Greek Revival home, restored to its original beauty and decorated with antiques and traditional furnishings. Built in 1825 by shipwrights for a whaling tycoon, the inn's spacious rooms and lofty ceilings reflect the wealth of its original owners. Many guest rooms have a queen- or king-size canopy or sleigh bed. Beth and Jack Flanagan, owners since 1986, expanded the inn in 1997 by rebuilding the original barn, which was on the verge of collapse. They were able to preserve about twenty percent of the original structure, which now houses four guest rooms, each with a fireplace built into the corner, and a TV recessed into the wall above. Although ideal for a romantic getaway (one even has a double whirlpool tub), they're also perfect for any traveler who especially likes privacy and modern conveniences.

Wake-up coffee is ready at 7 A.M., and breakfast is served from 8–10 A.M. A recent menu included fresh fruit and juice, cereal, and such entrées as baked eggs in cheese sauce, crabmeat Thermidor, or stuffed French toast. In the afternoon, the Flanagans offer complimentary setups and tea.

"Special touches in our room included fresh roses and delightful chocolates. Each morning we awoke to the aroma of fresh coffee. Morning sunshine pours in the windows of the elegant dining room, and guests are treated to generous breakfasts with Jack's French toast or a hearty casserole. Recipes are shared willingly. Gracious and informative hosts." *(Krista McGrath)* "Great location, picture-perfect room, delightful hosts." *(Dianne Engren)* "Beautiful restoration; professional service." *(Hugh Troutman)* "Impeccably clean; Beth and Jack are interesting, warm, compassionate hosts." *(Linda & Ron Lembo)* "Easy to find, convenient parking. Hosts were most helpful in answering questions and assisting with phone numbers and touring advice. Inviting veranda to enjoy the evening breezes and landscaped grounds." *(Bruce Bordelon)*

Open All year.

Rooms 1 suite, 8 doubles—all with full private bath and/or shower, radio, clock, TV, air-conditioning. 4 rooms in carriage house with TV, gas fireplace. 1 with whirlpool tub, desk, ceiling fan, balcony/deck.

Facilities Dining room with guest refrigerator, living room, library, porch. Guest use of fax, copier, dataport. ¾ acre with gardens, lawn games. 1.5 m from bay beach. 3 m from dock for fishing charters, whale-watching. Bicycle rental nearby.

Location Cape Cod. Mid-Cape, north side. On Rte. 6A. Take Rte. 6 to Exit 7 (Willow St.). Turn right at end of ramp. Follow Willow 1.1 m to inn on right, just before intersection with Rte. 6A.

Restrictions No smoking. Children in family suite.

Credit cards Amex, MC, Visa.

Rates B&B, $130–165 suite (sleeps 4), $90–190 double, $80–95 single. Extra person, $30; crib, $8. Tipping encouraged. 10% senior, AAA discount. 2-night summer weekend minimum. Honeymoon package.

Extras Wheelchair access; bathroom specially equipped. Train, plane, bus pickups from Hyannis or Barnstable.

One Centre Street Inn ¢   *Tel:* 508–362–8910
1 Centre Street & Old King's Highway   888–407–1653
Route 6A, 02675

Built in 1824 and listed on the National Register of Historic Places, One Centre Street has been owned by Karen Iannello since 1994. Chelsea, the inn's Dalmation, is slowing down a bit with age, but she doesn't let that stop her from personally welcoming each guest to her home. Furnished with Victorian antiques and reproductions, two rooms have queen-size beds plus sofa beds, accommodating four people. Karen designed the inn's newly renovated country kitchen. Guests come in all the time to watch her prepare such tempting dishes as apple-cranberry crisp or baked bananas; entrées like blueberry lemon yogurt pancakes, orange French toast, apple phyllo crêpes, or eggs Provençal; and such baked temptations as raspberry tea cakes or scones with dried cherries and candied ginger. Breakfast is served from 8–9:30 A.M. at individual tables, and the menu includes fresh fruit and juice, granola, yogurt, home-baked muffins, and coffee cake.

"Immaculate rooms, delicious breakfasts, delightful dog, helpful information on area sights and activities." *(Mary, Bill & Heidi Vance)* "A relaxing, enjoyable stay; phenomenal breakfasts." *(Sean & Larene D'Angelo)* "Tastefully appointed, comfortable inn. Only someone who loves to cook could prepare such breakfasts." *(Ginnie & Dick Carr)* "Karen's breakfasts are imaginative and refreshing; her ideas and suggestions for outings were perfect." *(Suzanne Welsh)* "Luxurious, fresh-smelling linens. Karen and I chatted about our perennial gardens; she even dug up plants for me to take home." *(Linda Blakita)* "My room, decorated in Laura Ashley fabrics, included a huge brass bed, luxurious linens, and a Tiffany lamp. Chocolates were provided each evening; sherry was always available in the lovely common room. Beautiful and tasty breakfast of quiche, cranberry walnut bread, and peach crisp." *(Rosalie Lewis)* "The oversize Carriage House Room has lovely stenciling, a brass bed, and sitting area. Karen is a delightful and attentive host." *(Rose Ellis & Steven Green)* "The suite has a large fireplace and sitting room, with antique furniture and modern amenities. Restaurant menus and helpful area information were available. Peaceful, quiet atmosphere." *(E. & J. Levy)* "Our spacious room had a bed with a wicker headboard, and matching floral fabrics on the comforter and window valances. Lovely linens, plump towels, and thick white terry robes. Convenient location, peaceful setting. Gray's Beach with its boardwalk out among the marshes is only a mile away." *(Dick & Judy MacDonald)*

Open All year.

Rooms 1 suite, 5 doubles, 1 single—5 with private bath and/or shower, 2 with maximum of 4 people sharing bath. All with clock/radio, fan. 1 with TV, fireplace. 1 room in attached carriage house.

Facilities Dining room, living room with piano, breakfast room with woodstove, screened porch. 1 acre with flower/herb gardens, off-street parking; bicycles. Bay, ocean beaches nearby.

Location Cape Cod. 70 m SE of Boston. 1 m from town. Take Rte. 6 to Exit 8, Union St. Turn left and proceed 1½ m to blinking light. Turn left onto Rte. 6A. Inn is at the corner of Centre St., third block on right ⅒ m.

Restrictions No smoking. Children 8 and over. Traffic noise possible in front rooms.

Credit cards Discover, MC, Visa.

Rates B&B, $120 suite, $75–110 double, $75–85 single. Extra person, $20. Tipping welcome. 2-night weekend minimum July–Aug.

Important Note on Area Codes

Telephone area codes are changing faster than a two-year-old's attention span. Although we've tried to incorporate all the new ones in our listings, many numbers were still in the "to be decided" state at press time. *If you dial a number listed here and get an announcement that it's not in service, we urge you to call the information operator and see if that region has been assigned a new area code.* Please forgive the inconvenience!

New Hampshire

Snowvillage Inn, Snowville

First settled in 1623, New Hampshire was originally part of the Massachusetts colony. Showing early the autonomy of spirit it maintains to this day, the colony broke away and declared its independence in January 1776, half a year before the country's Declaration of Independence was signed; today, its presidential primary officially launches the national campaign.

Although people outside New England tend to lump New Hampshire and Vermont together, the two states have very different personalities. Tourism is now vital to the economic well-being of both states, but New Hampshire has a significant industrial base, while Vermont is primarily agricultural; politically, New Hampshire is much more conservative, with far less in the way of zoning and environmental control.

There are several areas of particular tourist interest in New Hampshire. The southwest corner, also called the Monadnock region, has low mountains and lovely small lakes, as well as the "world's most climbed mountain," Mt. Monadnock. Attractive inns are found as far north as Littleton, close to St. Johnsbury, Vermont. Two major roads run north/south through New Hampshire—Interstate 93, through the center of the state, and Route 16 in the east. Both intersect the White Mountains National Forest, I-93 at Franconia Notch, and Route 16 through the Mt. Washington Valley. These two areas are home to New Hampshire's best skiing, and to many wonderful inns as well. Just south of the White Mountains is New Hampshire's Lake Region, centering around the beautiful Lake Winnipesaukee. If you're traveling to western New Hampshire, plan to take I-91 through Massachusetts and Vermont, then cross the Connecticut River into New Hampshire.

Side by side with the natural beauty of the state are cultural offerings from summer theater to the nine League of New Hampshire Craftsmen shops scattered across the state. Also worth noting are the Shaker Village at Canterbury Center, the Hood Museum of Art (part of Dartmouth College), and Strawbery Banke, a historic waterfront village in Portsmouth.

New Hampshire is popular with tourists in all seasons but "mud" (late March and April), although the demand for rooms is highest during the period of peak foliage in October, and the Christmas/New Year's holidays. Many inns either close or scale back operations during mud season.

Reader tip: "Don't miss the opportunity, if weather permits, to take the Auto Road to the top of Mt. Washington; make sure you bring a jacket, even in a heat wave, as it is always cold and windy on top. We recommended taking one of the tours, in specially equipped four-wheel-drive vehicles, available at the entrance to the Auto Road. You won't worry about your car overheating and will get a lots of information along the way. When it is clear, you can see the Atlantic Ocean to the east, and the Green Mountains of Vermont to the west. In addition to the usual gift shop and restaurant, there's a museum documenting the historic weather conditions recorded at the peak (the highest in the Northeast) and amazing film footage of the winds." *(NB)*

ASHLAND

Glynn House Inn ¢ 👫
43 Highland Street, P.O. Box 819, Ashland, 03217

Tel: 603–968–3775
800–637–9599
Fax: 603–968–3129
E-mail: glynnhse@lr.net
URL: http://www.bbonline.com/nh/glynnhouse/

Whether you arrive to see the Glynn House bright with flowers on a summer afternoon, or on a winter night with hundreds of tiny white lights reflected in the snow, Karol and Betsy Paterman will do their best to welcome you warmly to the inn they opened in 1989. A century-old Queen Anne Victorian home, its exterior is highlighted by a flower-filled wraparound veranda and conical turret, while the inside combines original oak woodwork with reproduction period wallcoverings and Victorian furnishings. Each of the romantic suites have a fireplace, whirlpool tub for two, and a queen-size canopy bed. Rates include early morning coffee, and breakfast of fresh fruit and juice, and eggs Benedict, Belgian waffles, strudel, or perhaps thick-sliced French toast.

"Gracious innkeepers who make you feel right at home without intruding on your privacy. Karol is an excellent chef, and Betsy is a delightful host, who welcomed us with glasses of wine after our long drive. The lovely guest rooms are beautifully decorated in Victorian style, right down to the old-fashioned dolls on the beds. Lots of clean fresh towels in the bath. Fireplace ready to light, with additional wood at the ready. A decanter of sherry on the table, and mints next to the bed. Coffee or tea is brought to your door in the morning to enjoy while you get ready for the day. Quiet street, beautiful front porch with wicker chairs. Great hiking and antiquing in the area." *(Patrick & Lisa McGuire)*

"Romantic and private. Breakfast served in the guest's room when requested." *(Beverly Straub)* "Menus available from nearby restaurants; the innkeeper recommended one to suit our tastes and gave us directions along with a discount card." *(Pamela Ballard)*

"Betsy and Karol do a wonderful job—their personality and pleasing manner with guests is terrific. Decor is lovely, maintenance impeccable, breakfasts delicious, and parking convenient. Better with every return visit." *(Beatrice Ferguson & Joseph Gagnon)* "Karol came out to the car to greet us and help with the bags." *(Janet Tackett)* "Thoughtful touches include mints, sherry, and maps of the local area." *(John Nicoll)* "Huge white house with impressive round tower and curving windows; beautifully appointed interior with period furniture." *(C.E. Sandelin)* "Karol was always available with offers of coffee or wine, restaurant and activities suggestions, or just pleasant company." *(Diane Moore)* "Good, firm mattress and plenty of hot water." *(Lisa Sherman)* "The delicious breakfasts were excellent, abundant, and served on time." *(Helen Brewer)*

Open All year.
Rooms 4 suites, 5 doubles—all with private bath, air-conditioning, clock radio/tape player. Most with fireplace, double Jacuzzi, TV/VCR.
Facilities Dining room, living room with fireplace, stereo; video library; wraparound porch. ½ acre. 7 m cross-country from door. 2 min. to Squam Lake for water sports; 10 min. to downhill skiing. Tennis, golf nearby.
Location Central NH, 2 hrs. NW of Boston. ¼ m from center of town. Take Exit 24 off I-93. Go E on Rte. 25 & 3⁷⁄₁₀ m into Ashland, left on Highland St.
Restrictions Smoking in living room only. Children over 6.
Credit cards Amex, Discover, MC, Visa.
Rates B&B, $125–165 suite, $85–95 double. Extra person, $10. $10 foliage surcharge.
Extras Bus station pickup. Babysitting. Polish, Russian spoken.

BETHLEHEM

Bethlehem is a quiet little town in the White Mountains of northwestern New Hampshire, 115 miles northwest of Boston. Although the town itself offers little other than a few antique shops, it makes a good touring base in any season. It's about six miles north of Franconia Notch, and about 12 from Cannon Mountain. Bretton Woods is about 18 miles east for superb cross-country skiing. Warm weather activities include hiking, canoeing, fishing, golf, and bicycling.

Adair ✕
80 Guider Lane, 03574

Tel: 603–444–2600
888–444–2600
Fax: 603–444–4823
E-mail: adair@connriver.net
URL: http://www.adairinn.com

To make a sweeping generalization (we're good at those), there are two kinds of inns: the kind that offer satisfactory accommodation to travelers and those that are themselves the essence of a vacation. Adair, a Georgian Revival Colonial home built in 1929, clearly falls into the latter category. In 1992, Adair was restored as a luxurious country inn; it was purchased by Judy and Bill Whitman in 1998. The spacious common areas include an inviting living room with several conversational groupings of comfortable furniture, an elegant dining room, and an appealing tap room with a piano, TV/VCR, pool table, and bar area. For a special-occasion getaway, Judy suggests the deluxe suite, complete with a double whirlpool tub, fireplace, king-size sleigh bed, and balcony. Landscaped by Frederick Law Olmsted, designer of New York's Central Park, the back lawn slopes down to a tennis court, a walled garden, and a reflecting pool with a gazebo. Coffee and tea are set out at 8 A.M., with guests seated for breakfast (family-style or at individual tables) from 8:30–9 A.M. A typical meal includes fruit juices, fresh fruit, yogurt, homemade granola or oatmeal, hot-from-the-oven popovers, and a hot entrée such as fruit-filled French toast with bacon, ham and cheese frittata, or perhaps pumpkin pancakes. Tea is served at 4 P.M., with bar set-ups at 5:30 P.M. Tim-bur Alley, originally a restaurant in Littleton, occupies the dining room at night, and a typical menu might include wild mushroom and Brie strudel, salmon with blue corn crust, and apple cranberry tart.

"No expense has been spared in this first-class renovation. A wonderful getaway from the cozy and inviting basement Tap Room to the third-floor guest rooms." *(SWS)* "Careful attention to detail, meticulous upkeep, friendly hosts." *(Nat & Bob Schnell)* "Idyllic setting with beautiful views and gardens. Large, comfy, inviting rooms decorated in period antiques." *(Carol & Shelly Bush)* "Relaxing setting on the terrace, scented by lilacs, with views of Mt. Washington. Gracious, friendly owners; peaceful, quiet environment." *(Carol Kerry)* "Nice people, cozy bedrooms, marvelous dining, gracious setting, wonderful weather—what more could you want?" *(GR)* "Gracious hospitality, elegant accommodations, lovely views, lots to do in the area." *(MW)*

Open All year. Restaurant open Wed.–Sun. in season.
Rooms 2-bedroom cottage, 2 suites, 7 doubles—all with full private bath, clock. 1 with double whirlpool, balcony. 5 with desk, 7 with gas fireplace.
Facilities Restaurant, dining room, living room, tap with pool table, TV/VCR, wet bar, piano. All with fireplace. 200 acres with gazebo, tennis court.
Location 155 N of Boston, 337 m N of NYC. From I-93, take Exit 40 to inn. From Bethlehem, take Rte. 302 3 m W to inn on left.
Restrictions No smoking. Children over 11.
Credit cards Amex, MC, Visa.
Rates B&B, $185–220 suite, $135–155 double. $285 cottage. Extra person, $28. Alc dinner, $25–35.

BRADFORD

Also recommended: For warm hospitality, excellent breakfasts, and affordable rates, a fine choice is the **Candlelite Inn** (5 Greenhouse Lane, 03221; 603–938–5571 or 888–812–5571). Built in 1897, this simply furnished Victorian farmhouse has six guest rooms, each with a private bath; B&B double rates range from $75–95. Owners Marilyn and Les Gordon serve tasty breakfasts, different each day—perhaps lemon sour cream-streusel muffins, eggs Benedict with asparagus, and fruit with orange yogurt sauce. "Les and Marilyn marked our anniversary with a bottle of champagne and flowers by the fireplace." *(Estella Rosmus)* "The warm flannel sheets and soft quilt made for a peaceful night's sleep." *(Joyce & Doug Rose)* "Breakfast was served from 8–10 A.M., so we didn't have to rush." *(Scott Alther)*

Rosewood Country Inn ¢ ♿
67 Pleasant View Road
RR 1, P.O. Box 235, 03221
Tel: 603–938–5253
800–938–5273
Fax: 603–938–5253
E-mail: rosewood@conknet.com
URL: http://www.bbonline.com/nh/rosewood/

Although country inns are a relatively new phenomenon in much of the U.S., they've been around for a long time in New England. Built in 1850 and an inn since 1896, the Rosewood Country Inn hosted such well-known figures as Jack London, Gloria Swanson, Mary Pickford, Douglas Fairbanks, Charlie Chaplin, and Lillian Gish in the early 1900s. In 1991, Dick and Lesley Marquis bought the inn, and have worked hard to upgrade it to meet the standards of today's inngoers. In 1998, they added five luxury suites, complete with king- and queen-size beds, fireplaces, double Jacuzzi tubs, air-conditioning, and romantic window seats. The music of Vivaldi and Mozart set the tone at breakfast, served between 8 and 9:30 A.M. A typical menu might consist of coffee, tea, and juice, plus fresh fruit cup with lemon yogurt and raspberry sauce, egg soufflé, and pumpkin nut muffins; or perhaps cranberry muffins, poached pears with orange coulis, and Belgian waffles with bananas Foster.

"Ideal balance of hospitality and privacy. Delightful afternoon tea served during the mother-daughter weekend, and delicious breakfasts with attention to special dietary requests. Dick provided delightful service with a smile." *(Patricia Santoro)* "The Dickens Christmas Weekend provided a welcome break in a harried holiday schedule." *(Audrey Jarrelle)* "A pampering, relaxing experience from the early-riser cup of coffee by the kitchen fireside to the last good-night." *(JW)* "Plenty of hot water in the morning for showers." *(Patricia & Abe Siff)* "Owners and inn are lovely; immaculate throughout with lovely stenciling and fabrics; beautifully renovated and maintained. Lovely country backroads to explore by car or bicycle." *(SWS, also Velva & Phil Lennox)*

"Lesley makes everyone who walks through the door feel like a family member coming home. Her breakfasts are fabulous. The inn is beautifully decorated with candle-lit windows and hand-stenciling throughout." *(Linda Schaeffer)* "An English country-house look enhanced by antiques and rich fabrics. Each guest room offers something special, whether it's a crocheted lace-canopy bed, pineapple four-poster, or views of a meandering stream. A three-course breakfast is served in the formal dining room at intimate tables for two." *(Carolyn Lanstat)*

"Country farmhouse atmosphere, impeccably clean, elegant but not cluttered. Fantastic breakfast of oven-baked apple pancakes with cider syrup, blueberry muffins, sausages, and juice." *(DD)*

Open All year.

Rooms 5 suites, 6 doubles—all with private bath and/or shower. Some with fireplace, TV/VCR, Jacuzzi, double shower, clock, desk, data ports, air-conditioning, fan.

Facilities Dining room with fireplace, living room with fireplace, family room with wood-stove, TV; porch, deck; conference/function room. 12 acres with off-street parking, lawn games. Stream, swimming hole, lake nearby. Cross-country skiing, snowshoeing, hiking from door; 10 min. to downhill skiing.

Location S NH, Sunapee Region. 20 m NW of Concord, approx. 6 m S of Lake Sunapee. 1½ m from town. Go W on Main St. At end of road, bear left & go up hill 1.7 m to Pleasant View Rd. on right. 3rd house on right.

Restrictions No smoking. Children over 10.

Credit cards Amex, MC, Visa.

Rates B&B, $125–150 suite, $75–99 double. Extra person, $25. Senior discount. 2-night minimum July, Aug., & holiday weekends. Llama treks, bicycle tours, ski packages, theme weekends (cooking, gardening, mother/daughter).

Extras French spoken. Wheelchair access to conference room.

CENTER HARBOR

Also recommended: A century-old brick mansion, the **Red Hill Inn** (Route 25B, RFD 1, P.O. Box 99M, 03226; 603–279–7001 or 800–5RED–HILL or www.redhillinn.com) has a restaurant with good food and 22 pleasant guest rooms, in five different buildings. "Romantic room with a Franklin stove and a double whirlpool bath. Excellent, creative dinners." *(Thelma Carpenter)* "Central location in the Lakes Region. Try the roast duck and the rack of lamb." *(Linda & John Mizesko)* "Tranquil atmosphere; period decor; accommodating staff. Recommend the onion soup and prime rib." *(Estelle & Richard Votour)* "Dinner was served in the main dining room, overlooking the White Mountains and Squam Lake." *(Janet & Bob Huie)* B&B double rates range from $105–175.

For additional area inns, see **Ashland, Holderness,** and **Moultonboro.**

CHARLESTOWN

For additional area entries, see **Claremont** and **Walpole.**

MapleHedge B&B Inn
355 Main Street, P.O. Box 638, 03603

Tel: 603–826–5237
800–9–MAPLE–9
Fax: 603–826–5237
E-mail: debrine@fmis.net

When traveling the Great Road via stagecoach in the early 1800s, passengers rested and ate at farmhouses converted into inns. Food and drink were served in the public room, while the unheated sleeping rooms were upstairs. Those traveling the Great Road today (now known as Route 12) can experience the history of this period minus the hardships of 19th-century travel. Built circa 1820 and restored as a B&B in 1990 by owners Joan and Richard DeBrine, MapleHedge balances historic ambience with modern amenities. In addition to breakfast, rates include an evening social hour with wine and local cheese, a decanter of sherry in each room, and evening turndown with Burdick chocolates. The three-course breakfast varies daily, but might include orange juice, granola, baked pears, ginger muffins, and lemon pancakes with blueberry sauce, served on fine china with crystal and silver.

"First-rate atmosphere and cleanliness combined with warm and gracious hospitality and comfort." *(Carol & Greg Iwan)* "A delightfully restored house, just across Main Street from the site of a French-and-Indian-War–era fortification. The queen-size beds are extra firm, the showers hot, the towels abundant. Our tasty breakfast included oatmeal pancakes, garden-fresh fruit, and homemade applesauce. Perfectly cool in summer, with central air-conditioning." *(Dave & Cheri Kendall)* "Attractive, spotlessly clean, and beautifully decorated. The DeBrines are friendly, warm, and caring. Rooms vary in decor, furnishings, and size, but all are appealing." *(Tiz Hamilton)* "Our room was well-lit with a comfortable reading chair. Helpful innkeepers, sensitive to our need for privacy. Lighting was ample, balanced by romantic firelight and candlelight. Good plumbing; ample hot water. Convenient location, easily reached from the interstate." *(Vicki Boyle & Craig Coleman)* "Breakfasts were excellent, and the afternoon wine and cheese was a fireside treat." *(Warren Schulingkamp)*

Open All year.

Rooms 1 suite, 4 doubles—all with private bath and/or shower, clock, desk, air-conditioning.

Facilities Dining room, living room with fireplace, stereo; library. ½ acre with horseshoes, croquet. CT River for boating; rentals nearby. Downhill, cross-country skiing, hiking nearby.

Location SW NH; CT River Valley. 1¾ hrs. N of Hartford, CT; 25 m N of Keene, 25 m S of Hanover. Historic district. On Rte. 12, S of school. From I-91 N, take Exit 7 at Springfield, VT. Go E on Rte. 11. Cross toll bridge to Charlestown, NH. Go right on Rte. 12 to inn 1 m on left.

Restrictions No smoking. Children 12 and over.

Credit cards MC, Visa.

Rates B&B, $90–100 suite, $80–90 double, $75–85 single. Extra person in suite, $20. 2-night minimum in foliage.

Extras Station pickups.

CLAREMONT

For additional area inns, see **Charlestown** as well as **Windsor** , in Vermont.

Also recommended: Located in the Dartmouth–Lake Sunapee region, the **Goddard Mansion Bed & Breakfast** (25 Hillstead Road,

03743; 603–543–0603 or 800–736–0603; Goddardmansion@usa.net) has been owned by Debbie Albee since 1986. This ten guest-room inn offers several common areas for guests, including a living room with a huge fireplace and baby grand piano, as well as a sitting room, a library, and a porch looking out to the mountains. Breakfast includes home-baked muffins with home-grown fruit preserves, fresh fruit, whole grain cereals, and such hot dishes as pancakes, French toast, or egg souf-flés. B&B double rates range from $65–125. "We stayed in the spacious Swan Room, with a king-size bed and amazingly comfortable blankets and pillows; large windows looked out to the woods. The adjoining bathroom had an old-fashioned, oversize bathtub. Delicious breakfasts were prepared by the friendly innkeeper. The mansion was in great con-dition, along with the well-manicured grounds." *(Kelly Fitzsimmons)* "Good recommendations for meals, and a wonderful, varied breakfast. Debbie Albee is most gracious." *(Nancy Hoskins)*

CONCORD

Also recommended: Ten miles northeast of downtown Concord is the 200-year-old **Wyman Farm B&B** (22 Wyman Road, Loudon, 03301; 603–783–4467), set on a hilltop surrounded by 55 acres of fields and woodlands. Each of the three guest rooms offers a sitting area, private bath, telephone, TV, and air-conditioning. Longtime owner Judith Wyman Merrow serves a full breakfast as well as a tea tray in the af-ternoon or evening. Double rates range from $55–85, including tax. "Lovely farmhouse off the beaten track. Spacious rooms, excellent breakfast. Well worth a visit, especially if you like peace and tranquil-ity." *(Pat Tanner)*

CORNISH

Reader tip: "Well worth visiting in Cornish is the Saint Gaudens Na-tional Historic Site, the home and studio of one of America's most fa-mous sculptors." *(BL, also Paula Devereaux)*

For additional area entries, see **Plainfield,** and **Windsor, Vermont.**

The Chase House ♿	*Tel:* 603–675–5391
Chase Street, Route 12A, RR #2	800–401–9455
P.O. Box 909, 03745	*Fax:* 603–675–5010
	URL: http://www.chasehouse.com

All the canopy beds in the world can't substitute for the authentic charm of a truly historic residence. A National Historic Landmark, the Chase House is an example of the early New England tradition of com-bining two houses—a 1766 Settlement Colonial-style house and a circa 1775 Federal-style house. In 1845, both houses were relocated when the railroad arrived in the Connecticut River Valley. The Chase House's most famous resident, Salmon Portland Chase, served as Lincoln's Secretary of the Treasury, a chief justice of the Supreme Court, and is the namesake of the Chase Manhattan Bank. Barbara Lewis has owned the inn since 1991, and shares innkeeping duties with her husband Ted Doyle.

"Beautiful country setting; hospitable, charming hosts; exquisite antiques throughout the house; delicious food in generous portions. Barb graciously shared her recipes with us." *(Betsy Howard)* "Excellent country breakfast with eggs, bacon, French toast, yogurt, and fresh berries and melon." *(Brigitte Schierig)* "A superb combination of history, comfort, and beautiful grounds. Barbara maintains an informal atmosphere that made it easy to enjoy the company of other guests, and goes out of her way to accommodate her guests." *(Stanley Humphries)* "Our room was decorated with simple yet elegant furniture, pale blue wallpaper, a four-poster queen-size bed with a delicately crocheted canopy, and matching blankets and quilts. Delicious breakfasts of cheese strata or buttermilk pancakes with thick-sliced bacon." *(JLM)* "History types will enjoy the parlor books on Salmon Chase. Music, interior design, and culinary types will marvel at Barbara's influence throughout." *(Rick & Melody Barker)* "I appreciated the thermostat in my room since I prefer to sleep in a chillier room than most. Breakfast was spectacular—freshly squeezed orange juice, homemade popovers, muffins or sticky buns, scrambled eggs, freshly cut fruit, or warm pineapple-banana-raisin compote. We enjoyed warm mulled cider with homemade hors d'oeuvres before a roaring fire in the great room." *(Eileen Monroe)*

Open All year. Closed Nov., Christmas
Rooms 8 doubles—6 with private bath, 2 with maximum of 4 people sharing bath. All with clock, air-conditioning.
Facilities Dining room with fireplace, living room, function room with fireplace, piano, TV/VCR, stereo, books; porch/deck. 160 acres with gardens, sleds, snowshoes; 2,000 feet CT River frontage for canoeing, fishing. 7 m to downhill, cross-country skiing.
Location W NH, Sullivan Cty. 20 m S of Dartmouth/Hanover, NH; 2 m E of Windsor, VT. From I-91 N, take Exit 8 to Rte. 131 E across CT River. Take Rte. 12A N 4 m to inn. From I-91 S, take Exit 9. Take Rte. 5 S to Rte. 44 (Windsor). Go E across covered bridge, then S on 12A 1.3 m to inn. From I-89, take Exit 20, & take Rte. 12A S 17 m to inn.
Restrictions No smoking. Children over 12.
Credit cards MC, Visa.
Rates B&B, $95–125 double. Extra person, $10. 2-night minimum, weekends, foliage.
Extras Limited wheelchair access. Airport/station pickups; Amtrak stop, car rentals available.

DANBURY

Schoolhouse Corner B&B ¢ 👥
61 Eastern District Road, 03230

Tel: 603–768–3467
Fax: 603–768–3119

Constructed on the site of a one-room schoolhouse, the Schoolhouse Corner B&B has been the home of Nancy and Donald Buebendorf since

1969. In 1993, they added a separate wing, connected by a corridor to their house, with both spacious common areas and guest rooms, and opened their B&B. Guests breakfast from 8–9:30 A.M. at individual tables, and have their choice of juice, fruit, cereal, eggs or Belgian waffles, bacon or sausage, English muffins or home-baked toasting bread, plus such daily specials as popovers, omelets, or strata. Rates also include a 5 P.M. social hour, when all gather around the fire for refreshments and to discuss dining opportunities and area activities. The Buebendorfs are happy to help with trip-planning, make reservations for dinner and golf tee times. We've heard from many Schoolhouse guests, and all are delighted with this B&B's lovely setting, cordial hosts, and excellent breakfasts.

"Nancy and Don clearly enjoy the company of their guests but are never intrusive." (Dana Burke) "The outstanding features include the view of Ragged Mountain and the friendly hosts." (Constance & D. Keith Law & others) "Wonderful views from the floor-to-ceiling windows of the great room. From the deck you can almost pick out your family members skiing down the slopes. Dr. B's popovers are to die for!" (Lucille & Ray Kelley) "We enjoyed watching the birds at the feeders." (Anne Becklean) "The skylit loft room has a comfortable king-size bed and wonderful views." (Michelle Dilorenzo) "Our four children were heartily welcomed and loved their stay. Great toy area with games, puzzles, and videos. Hosts helpful with restaurant suggestions and skiing hints." (Janne Armstrong) "Loved having a menu choice at breakfast. Nancy and Don provided maps to facilitate day trips." (Jerilyn & Kevin MacWilliam) "We especially liked finding a plate of goodies upon our return from a day of skiing." (Linda & Mike Dore)

"The rambling buildings offer a broad view of the valley below and a mountain vista in the distance, to be enjoyed from an assortment of porches." (Oliver Jensen) "The luxurious first-floor suite has a queen-size bed and pull-out couch, ideal for a family. The second-floor sitting room is stocked with toys for children and comfortable seating for supervising adults. The living room is spectacular, with a cathedral ceiling and a floor-to-ceiling Palladian window overlooking the field, pond, and mountain beyond. Coffee is ready early in the morning so guests can light the always-laid fire and enjoy the view, or in summer, take a cup of coffee to the deck." (Sherry & Herb Clark) "Rooms are immaculate, with pretty quilts and lovely antiques. A number of restaurants and pubs are nearby, but you can bring groceries to fix yourself in the guest kitchen." (Amy & John Kamb) "Easy highway access, yet off-the-beaten path location." (Rosemary McLauglin)

Open Dec.–March, June–mid-Oct.

Rooms 1 family suite, 3 doubles—2 with private bath and/or shower, 2 with maximum of 4 people sharing bath. All with clock/radio. 3 with fan, 1 with desk, TV.

Facilities Dining room, living room, TV room with VCR, family room with games, library, guest kitchen, ski storage, porches. 8 acres with lawns, pond with fountain, gardens, hammock, croquet. Trout fishing, golf, downhill, cross-country skiing nearby. Discount lift tickets for Ragged Mt. Ski Area.

Location S central NH. 2 hrs. NW of Boston; 3¾ hrs. from SE CT. 28 m NW of

Concord. 2 m to town. From I-93, take Exit 17 & Rte. 4 at Boscawen. Take Rte. 4 W to Danbury. Go right on Rte. 104. Go 2 m & turn left onto Eastern District Rd. Go 7/10 m to inn on left. From I-91, take Exit 7. Take Rte. 11/12 to Claremont. Go on Rte. 11 to Rte. 4 W to Danbury & follow as above.

Restrictions No smoking. Toilet-trained children over 3 welcome.

Credit cards Discover/Novus.

Rates B&B, $63–75 double, $58–68 single. Extra person, $20. No tipping. 2-night weekend minimum. 10% discount for 6-night stay.

DIXVILLE NOTCH

Also recommended: In northernmost New Hampshire, 390 miles north of New York, 223 miles north of Boston, and eight miles south of Canada, is a grand holdover from another age, **The Balsams Grand Resort Hotel** (Route 26, Dixville Notch, 03576-9710; 603–255–3400 or 800–255–0600; www.thebalsams.com). Although a large hotel of 232 guest rooms, we've received good reports on this grande dame of mountain resorts. Its 15,000 acres easily accommodate two golf courses, six tennis courts, a heated swimming pool, Lake Gloriette for boating, swimming, fly fishing, and trails for both downhill and cross-country skiing. Inside activities (in addition to some serious eating), include numerous public rooms, a lounge, nightclub, game room, sun room, and more. Guest rooms are sufficiently luxurious to have earned the resort four diamond/star ratings from AAA and Mobil, and all-inclusive double rates range from $250–330; numerous packages are available. "Spacious rooms, superb food at all three meals. At dinner, the different dishes are on display so you can see what they look like before you order. Friendly, helpful staff. I was impressed with the mission statement included in the information packet: it speaks of the staff being 'ladies and gentlemen serving ladies and gentlemen.' " *(Tom Wilbanks)*

DURHAM

Home of the University of New Hampshire, Durham is located in the southeast corner of the state, five miles from Portsmouth and the Maine border.

Also recommended: Recently restored in the tradition of the original 1649 homestead, the **Three Chimneys Inn–Sawyer Tavern** (17 Newmarket Road, 03824; 603–868–7800 or 888–399–9777) overlooks formal gardens and the Oyster River. The 25 guest rooms have four-poster beds, Edwardian-style drapes, and rich tapestries; all have private baths, telephones, and TVs, and many have a gas fireplace and whirlpool tub. Listed on the National Register of Historic Places and located a few blocks from the University of New Hampshire, the B&B offers double rates from $149–189 and includes a full breakfast. "A wonderful conversion of an 18th-century home and barn, furnished with a combination of authentic pieces and tasteful reproductions. Two wonderful restaurants, one elegant, the other a rustic tavern." *(Nancy DiGrezio)* "We were warmly greeted by the innkeepers, and were relaxed by the glow of the fireplace and the offer of delicious chocolate chip cookies. Rooms spacious but intimate, with comfortable beds." *(Cheryl Spadoni)*

A good choice on the University of New Hampshire campus is the **University Guest House** (47 Mill Road, 03824; 603–868–2728; www. unhguesthouse.com), decorated with antiques and collectibles, and owned by Beth Fischer. B&B rates for the four guest rooms (sharing two baths) range from $55–90. "Homemade treats, fresh fruit, and coffee available on the kitchen counter at all times. Clean, quiet, responsive, comfortable, convenient, and safe." *(Sue Grise)* "Beth offers warm hospitality and always tries to meet guests' needs. Her breakfasts are superb, usually consisting of a healthful three-course meal. Guest rooms are spotless, comfortable, and attractive, with tasty chocolates and thick terry robes." *(Mary Kay DeGenova)* "Homey atmosphere; Beth is well informed about everything from restaurants to car repairs." *(Pat Gormley)*

For additional area inns, see **Portsmouth.**

EATON CENTER

Rockhouse Mountain Farm Inn ¢ 👫   *Tel:* 603–447–2880
P.O. Box 90, 03832

The Edges—first Senior, now Junior—have operated this inn since 1946—in 1996, they celebrated fifty years of innkeeping! It's a working farm, with animals for the kids to play with, as well as a variety of outdoor activities.

"The farm sits in the foothills of the White Mountains and has its own Rockhouse Mountain, with an Indian cave at the top, for which the inn is named. The house itself is a typical old white clapboard New England farmhouse that was expanded many times as families grew larger and more space was needed. The crew is made up of college students (usually former guests), who know how to help guests enjoy themselves. The house is furnished in antiques, many of which were brought from Wales and England by the Edge family years ago. Some of the beautiful paintings are registered at the Tate Gallery in London." *(Ronald & Patricia Meyers)* "Johnny Edge is one of those quiet types who makes everything run smoothly without apparent effort, and has a wonderful sense of humor. Libby Edge greets you every morning with a bubbly smile; she has a special knack of making everyone feel as though they were cousins come to visit. Dinners are splendid and delicious; the separate dining areas for adults and children are a pleasure. My spotless room had a cozy fireplace and an enormous window affording an incredible mountain view. The lake, a short walk or drive, is lots of fun—either just relaxing or sliding down huge boulders into the water. Guests and staff are exceptionally friendly; it's as much fun to visit Rockhouse as a single person as part of a couple or family." *(Anne Leopold-Equale)*

"The sitting room offers a spectacular view, particularly during foliage season. The children are up early and out in the barn as they work up an appetite for the 8 A.M. feast. Milking cows, cuddling kittens, or teasing the peacocks and llamas are just a few choices. The barn swing is fun for all ages." *(Ronald Trieff)* "Libby's homemade relishes are not to be missed; each night there is a different just-baked bread." *(Robin Britt)* "We love the group picnic beside the rushing Swift River, and the canoe trip on the Saco." *(Ray & Pat Kerridge)* "Central location, yet far from crowds and congestion." *(Stephanie Goldstein)*

Open Mid-June–Oct.
Rooms 15 doubles, 3 bunk rooms—7 rooms with private bath and/or shower, 8 with maximum of 4 people sharing bath. All with fan.
Facilities Dining rooms, 2 living/music rooms, game room, guest refrigerators. 450 acres with private beach, row- and sailboats, canoes, children's play equipment, trout pond, farm animals, Simental cattle, peacocks, llamas, hiking trails. Tennis, golf, fishing, swimming nearby.
Location E central NH. 52 m W of Portland, ME, 128 m N of Boston, 6 m S of Conway. ½ m from center of town.
Restrictions No alcohol is served; BYOB.
Credit cards None accepted.
Rates MAP, $104–120 double, $70–80 single. Extra child, $28 (age 1–5); $34 (age 6–11); $40 (12–14). Service additional. 1-week minimum stay (Sat.–Sat.) preferred, July & Aug.
Extras Airport/station pickups for additional charge. French spoken. Crib, babysitting.

EXETER

Located in southeastern New Hampshire, 16 miles from Portsmouth, Exeter is best known as the home of Phillips Exeter Academy, one of the country's most prestigious prep schools.

Also recommended: A Federal-style townhouse built in 1809, **The Inn by the Bandstand** (4 Front Street, 03833; 603–772–6352; www.portsmouthnh.com/lodging) has been handsomely restored with much of the original woodwork and flooring intact. Located in the center of town, within walking distance of shops and restaurants, the inn is elegantly furnished. "Our handsome, uncluttered first-floor suite included a room with a comfortable queen-size canopy bed, and an additional twin-bedded room. Individual thermostats, a small refrigerator, plenty of current magazines, robes, and a bottle of sherry were among the amenities. Our mattress was extremely comfortable; pillowcases were changed nightly. Continental breakfast was well served in the living room and included fresh fruit and juice, yogurt, granola, and a variety of oven-fresh scones and muffins; many guests take a tray back to their rooms. A pot of freshly brewed coffee is set out on a sideboard for early risers. Always available are carafes of ice water, a selection of teas, coffee, and hot chocolate." *(Rose Ciccone)* B&B double rates for the eight well-equipped guest rooms—many with a gas log fireplace—range from $99–165.

Information please: Built in 1932, **The Inn of Exeter** (90 Front Street,

03833; 603–772–5901 or 800–267–0525) is the first choice of anyone connected with Phillips Exeter Academy, but is equally popular with vacationers and business travelers for its accommodations, which combine period charm and modern conveniences, its well-regarded restaurant, and its high standards of service. Double rates for the 50 guest rooms range from $88–195, depending on room size and season. "Wonderful dinners; lovely lobby and common rooms." *(Rose Ciccone)*

For additional area inns, see **Portsmouth** and **South Hampton**.

FITZWILLIAM

Fitzwilliam is a quintessential New England village, with Federal and Greek Revival buildings circling the town common. It's close to Mt. Monadnock; other area activities include skiing, hiking, rock climbing, swimming, art and craft galleries, summer theater, lakes for water sports, golf, and tennis. Antiquers will enjoy the numerous shops in town and within an easy drive. Fitzwilliam is located in south central New Hampshire, in the Monadnock Region. It's 60 miles northwest of Boston, and 75 miles north of Hartford, Connecticut.

For an additional area entry, see **Troy**.

Hannah Davis House ¢ ♦♦   *Tel: 603–585–3344*
106 NH Route 119 West, 03447

A few steps beyond the town common is the Federal-style Hannah Davis House, built around 1820. Mike and Kaye Terpstra bought the house in 1988 and have done a wonderful job of restoring it as a B&B, with wide-board pine floors, old-fashioned white iron beds, flowered wallpapers, and braided rugs. Guest rooms range from the cozy Hannah's Room to the spacious suites. The breakfast menu varies daily, and might include grapefruit or perhaps passion fruit juice, homemade granola and applesauce, blueberry muffins, sliced fresh fruit, baked apple puff, and scrambled eggs with bacon; or perhaps cinnamon-raisin and pumpkin breads, strawberries and cream, omelets filled with tomato and herbs, bacon and cream cheese, toast and asparagus, or maybe sugar snap peas.

"Although the rooms are charming, the grounds lovely, and the food tasty, here as always, the innkeepers make the inn. Kaye and Mike are exceptionally warm and welcoming innkeepers, who have a knack for making their guests feel relaxed and at home, while never intruding on their privacy. Breakfast is served in the inviting kitchen area with lots of green plants, plus dried flowers hanging from the exposed beams. A narrow screened porch overlooks flower gardens and beaver pond beyond. The inviting guest rooms are pleasantly furnished with a teddy bear here and there—nothing is overdone or cluttered. Good lighting, immaculate throughout." *(SWS)* "The spacious, cathedral-ceilinged Popovers Room is very private and quiet, surrounded by windows which let the sunlight in. The couch in front of the fireplace was our favorite spot, although you could also see the fire from the queen-size cannonball bed. The delicious breakfasts were enhanced by our conversations with Kaye and Mike, warm and friendly hosts." *(Tina Hom)* "Lovely room, outstanding breakfast. Good dinner at the nearby Fitzwilliam Inn. Excellent value, highly recommended." *(Cecille Desroches)*

"The original hardware on doors have been retained, and functional antique furniture is in all rooms. Wonderful beds with firm mattresses, goose down quilts, cotton sheets, feather and foam pillows." *(Richard Lehman)* "A welcoming bowl of popcorn and hot cider when you arrive; a stuffed animal awaits on your turned-down bed with a plate of cookies or brownies." *(M.A. Watkins)* "Mike and Kaye combine congeniality, generosity, and hospitality with such touches as lace bedding, high beds and quilts, a water carafe and glasses on the dresser, and 'insider' restaurant recommendations." *(LL)* "We loved the Terpstras' stories about Hannah Davis, a 'bachelor woman' who traveled by sleigh in the 1800s, selling her homemade hat boxes." *(SG)* "I missed my own pets, and was happy to meet the Terpstras' two dogs and beautiful Maine coon cat." *(MW)*

Open All year.
Rooms 3 suites, 3 doubles—all with full private bath, clock/radio, fan. 4 with writing tables, 4 with wood-burning fireplace, 3 with private entrance. 1 with air-conditioning, 1 with deck.
Facilities Breakfast room with fireplace, TV; living room with piano, stereo, books, TV/VCR.
Location Monadnock Region. 60 m NW of Boston. 75 m N of Hartford. In historic district on Rte. 119. Next to village center and town common.
Restrictions No smoking. Street noise possible in front room. Children welcome in suites.
Credit cards Discover, MC, Visa.
Rates B&B, $105–115 suite, $60–85 double, $50–75 single. Extra person, $20. No tipping.

FRANCESTOWN

The Inn at Crotched Mountain ¢ ⋔ ✕ ✈ ⅙   *Tel:* 603–588–6840
534 Mountain Road, 03043

John and Rose Perry have owned the Inn at Crotched Mountain since 1976. The original inn was built in 1822 and was later a stop on the Underground Railroad, with a secret tunnel built to help slaves escape. Destroyed by fire in 1936, the inn was rebuilt in its present form. Rates include a breakfast of eggs or French toast with bacon and sausage, juice, English muffins, toast and homemade jam. The dinner menu changes seasonally, and might include such entrées as cranberry pot roast, tuna aioli, roast loin of pork, and eggplant Parmesan primavera.

"Winter visits are always warm and cozy, with great cross-country skiing; summer stays offer beautiful views, a great swimming pool, and flower, vegetable, and herb gardens to explore. Rose's cooking is delicious. We return for the Perrys' generous hospitality and the beautiful views." *(Ann & Steve Burtt)* "A beautiful, peaceful haven, with marvelous views of the fall foliage. Our charming room—perhaps the nicest—had a pretty wooden bed, sofa, armchair, attractive paintings and quilts, and a welcoming fireplace." *(Caroline Raphael)* "If a pastoral setting, warm hospitality, good food, affordable rates, and a family-and-pet friendly atmosphere are more important to you than designer decor and state-of-the-art bathrooms, you'll love this inn." *(MW)*

"Although the view from the inn is spectacular, overlooking the rolling hillsides, it is owners John and Rose Perry who make this place special. Besides the appetizing entrées, with many of the vegetables and garnishes grown in the inn's garden, several desserts are prepared daily by John. His chocolate mousse cake is not to be believed. Before or after dinner, drinks are available in the pub, where a blazing fire takes away the evening chill. Guest rooms are individually decorated country-style, and supplied with extra pillows and blankets. Quiet setting, far from major roadways." *(Mary Little & Ronald Perri)*

Open May–Oct., Dec.–March.

Rooms 13 doubles—8 with private bath and/or shower, 5 with maximum of 4 people sharing bath. All with clock/radio, fan. 3 with fireplace.

Facilities Dining rooms with fireplace, sitting rooms with fireplace, pub. 65 acres with walking paths, gardens, swimming pool, wading pool, 2 tennis courts, croquet, 5½ m cross-country ski trails. ¼ m to downhill skiing. Golf, fishing, hiking, boating nearby.

Location S central NH. Monadnock Region. 75 m NW of Boston. 30 min. W of Manchester. From Manchester, take Rte. 101 W to Rte. 114 N to Goffstown. Follow Rte. 13 S to New Boston. Then take Rte. 136 W to Francestown. In Francestown, go N on Rte. 47 2½ m; turn left onto Mt. Rd., 1 m to inn.

Restrictions Smoking permitted in sitting room, tavern; prohibited in guest rooms, dining room. Possible noise from heating pipes, plumbing.

Credit cards None accepted.

Rates B&B, $70–120 double, $50–80 single. Extra person, $30. 15% service. 2-night weekend/holiday minimum. AAA, senior discount. Alc dinner, $20–30. Midweek packages.

Extras Wheelchair access. Pets permitted, $5 per day. Babysitting by arrangement. Chinese, Indonesian spoken.

FRANCONIA/SUGAR HILL

Franconia, one of New Hampshire's oldest mountain resort areas, is full of activities in both summer and winter. To get the best feel for the area, get out of your car and walk the lovely trails of Franconia Notch State Park and the White Mountains National Forest. In addition to hiking in summer, skiing in winter, mountain bikers will enjoy the trails built exclusively for bicyclists in Franconia Notch State Park.

Franconia is located in the White Mountains, 150 miles north of Boston and 75 miles north of Concord; it's about 10 miles southeast of the Vermont border, and about 20 miles from St. Johnsbury. Both **Sugar Hill** and **Easton** are nearby villages which share the Franconia mailing address. Cannon Mountain is the closest major ski area.

For additional area inns, see **Bethlehem**, six miles north.

Bungay Jar
Easton Valley Road, P.O. Box 15, 03580

Tel: 603–823–7775
800–421–0701
E-mail: info@bungayjar.com
URL: http://www.bungayjar.com

Too often charming historic structures are found in settings that today are totally unappealing. The solution in this case was to take a nearly ruined 18th-century barn and move it into the quiet mountain village of Easton, about six miles south of Franconia. There it was re-crafted from the posts, beams, and boards, and was renovated as a B&B by Kate Kerivan and Lee Strimbeck in 1983. Although the overall form and feeling of the original barn was retained wherever possible, the final effect is light and airy, both rustic and elegant. Kate notes that "although relaxed and informal, our guest rooms are lavish, some with private balconies, queen- or king-size beds with handmade quilts, and custom-made baths with antique English stained-glass windows, oak panels, skylights, and six-foot soaking tubs." Also available is Plum Cottage, a whimsical private home located in Franconia Village, within walking distance of restaurants and shops.

"Our favorite room, the Stargazer, at the top of the house, offers skylights open to the evening stars and a spectacular view of the mountains. The gardens are glorious all summer long; in the winter, skiing is near by. The innkeepers loaned snowshoes for a walk through the back woods. Breakfasts are huge and delicious with fresh fruit, baked goods, and a hot entrée. Tea is always offered with afternoon snacks. Kate is exceptionally welcoming. Even the pets are friendly and well-mannered." *(Cherry Bennett)* "I enjoyed taking the poodles, Lila and Toby, for a walk." *(Susan & Andre Dery)* "Innkeepers attentive without being overbearing. Rustic yet elegant interior." *(Joan Regensburger)* "Kate is an avid gardener, and the inn's gardens are a delight." *(MW)*

"The inn is set back far from the road, in the shadow of tall pines. Once inside the door, you are greeted by warm wood tones, exposed beams, and a large open-hearth fireplace. Great care has been given to the preparation, decoration, and interior design of each room, complemented by fresh-cut flowers from the extensive gardens. Homemade mulled cider is served in late afternoon in cool weather; iced tea in hot. Hiking paths around the grounds take you to a nearby stream, and hiking for all levels is close by. Afterward the sauna awaits to soothe aching muscles." *(Margot & Bob Balazik)* "Delicious breakfast of apple pancakes, hot-from-the-oven popovers with jam, and fresh fruit salad." *(Deborah & Dean Keyek-Franssen)* "Quirky antiques, beautiful house plants, books, interesting nooks and crannies. The breakfast table overlooks the mountains through sliding glass doors." *(Emily Dexter)*

Open All year.
Rooms 3 suites, 3 doubles, 2 cottages—all with private bath and/or shower. 1 suite with double Jacuzzi. Some with desk, balcony, terrace. 2 suites with gas fireplace. Cottage located in Franconia Village, with full kitchen, double whirlpool, fireplace.
Facilities Dining area, living room/library with fireplace, games, piano; sauna, decks; garden shop. 12 acres with woods, river, paths. Tennis, golf, cross-country, downhill skiing nearby. Garden design workshops.

Location From I-93 take Exit 38. Go S on Rte. 116 (Easton Valley Rd.) 5½ m to inn.
Restrictions No smoking.
Credit cards Amex, Discover, MC, Visa.
Rates B&B, $120–195 suite, $95–125 double. Extra person, $20.

Foxglove
Route 117 at Lovers Lane, Sugar Hill, 03585

Tel: 603–823–8840
888–343–2220
Fax: 603–823–5755
E-mail: foxgloveinn@compuserve.com
URL: http://www.foxgloveinn.com

A designer-decorated turn-of-the-century home, Foxglove is set in a park-like wooded setting. Janet and Walter Boyd, owners of the inn since 1993, report that Foxglove decorates for all holidays—from Halloween with a cobwebbed entry to Valentine's Day with a six-foot tree laden with hearts, lace, and bows. Breakfast is served between 8 and 9 A.M. in the dining room, on the enclosed porch, or, in the summer, on the terrace. The breakfast menu changes daily but might include scrambled eggs with chives, sautéed sweet potatoes, smoked salmon, and cheddar cheese biscuits; or buttermilk crêpes with fresh fruit and smoked turkey. Dinners are available by reservation; a recent meal included Cuban black bean soup; orange and red onion salad with rosemary vinaigrette; shrimp with sesame noodles; fruit tart; coffee, tea, and sherry.

"Cordial hosts, elegant decor, beautiful scenery. The Mrs. Harmes Room has a circular turret with lace-curtained windows with views of the birch forest, a tiny white church, and beautiful sunsets. Comfortable queen-size bed. Every day, Janet changes the china and linens as well as the delicious menu; she takes personal preferences into consideration whenever possible; dinners are equally special. The living room is inviting for the crackling fire in the fireplace and good conversation, but my favorite place is the glassed-in porch, with views of flowers in summer, foliage in fall, and the snow in winter." *(Mary & Ron O'Keefe)* "Warm, elegant comfort; beautifully restored and decorated home; lovely setting; gracious hospitality. Though never intrusive, the Boyds were always close by, willing to visit with guests and give helpful advice on area activities. The decor is a wonderful mixture of Victorian and country, highlighted by beautiful antique linens, perfume bottles, and dresser sets. The bathrooms are fully modernized with beautiful tiled showers, new fixtures and mirrors." *(LH)* "Complimentary appetizers and wine served in the luxurious living room. The inviting sunny porch is the perfect place to read and spend a lazy afternoon." *(Robin & Ivan Bachelder)* "Dinners accompanied by soft music and candlelight; a favorite was shrimp served on spicy sesame noodles with red and yellow peppers." *(Jacklyn & Eric Snyder)*

Open All year.
Rooms 6 doubles—all with private bath and/or shower, clock, fan.
Facilities Dining/breakfast room, 2 living rooms with fireplace, porch. 3 acres with gardens, lawn games. Skiing, hiking, tennis, golf nearby.

Location Take I-93 to Exit 38. Go right on Rte. 18 for ½ m. Go left on Rte. 117 to inn, 2.3 m on right. From I-91, take Exit 17. Follow Rte. 302 E, 16 m. Turn right onto Rte. 117 to inn 5.6 m on left.

Restrictions No smoking. Children over 12.

Credit cards MC, Visa.

Rates B&B, $85–165 double. MAP by request, $153–223 double. Prix fixe dinner, $29.

Franconia Inn ₵ 🛏 ✕ 🎿   *Tel:* 603–823–5542
Easton Road, 03580   800–473–5299
                                      Fax: 603–823–8078
                      E-mail: info@franconiainn.com
              URL: http://www.franconiainn.com

Alec and Richard Morris, owners since 1981, try to combine the atmosphere of a country inn with the facilities of a small resort. The inn dates from the mid-1800s when the Spooner family invited paying guests to stay with them during the summer months. Robert Frost once lived in the farmhouse and composed his famous "The Road Not Taken" poem here. The original building was destroyed by fire in 1934, but was rebuilt as an inn shortly thereafter. Rooms are simply furnished, with a few antiques and country touches. Although menus change frequently, some recent dinner entrées included trout with a rosemary, tomato cream sauce; duck in brandied apricot sauce; and rack of lamb with sautéed apples.

"Our favorite features include the quiet, beautiful surroundings; the inn's ample facilities, from the tennis courts to hiking trails, the cozy bar and game room to the relaxing porch; the fine food and service; the warm and helpful innkeepers; and the scenic but convenient location." *(Tom Furniss)* "Convenient to area activities. Excellent value." *(G.L. Long)* "Outstanding location, with breathtaking sunrise and sunset views from the porch. Our favorite rooms are on the third floor." *(EE)* "Relaxed and friendly, with welcoming staff who remember us from year to year. Our kids enjoy the independence of visiting the game room and adjacent skating rink on their own." *(RT)*

"Owners and staff are gracious and helpful with hiking, skiing, and dinner recommendations. The dining room is large with views of Cannon Mountain. Our spacious third floor was furnished with good reproductions. Lots of fresh flowers downstairs." *(Julia & Dennis Mallach)* "Breakfast was diverse and filling: serve-yourself pastries, fruit, granola, yogurt, cereal, plus anything off their breakfast menu, from waffles to eggs Benedict to steak and eggs. Beautiful location. You can watch gliders take off, swim in a large, heated pool, play tennis, badminton, and croquet, walk to the river, ride horses, or drive to nearby attractions. The common areas include the large porch with white wicker seating, cozy library, inviting bar, and more." *(Jennifer Ball)*

Open May 15–April 1. Restaurant closed mid-week Nov.

Rooms 3 suites, 32 doubles—34 with private shower and/or bath, 4 with a maximum of 6 sharing a bath. All rooms with desk, fan.

Facilities Dining rooms, bar/lounges, sitting room, library, TV room with movies nightly, game room, hot tub, porches. 117 acres with hiking, horseback riding, and cross-country skiing trails, heated swimming pool, 4 clay tennis courts, croquet, bikes, glider plane rides, swimming and fishing stream, horse-drawn sleigh rides, ice-skating. Golf, downhill skiing nearby.

Location E NH. From I-93 take Exit 38. Turn left off exit. Cross road to Rte. 116. 2 m to inn. 2½ m from town.

Restrictions Smoking in downstairs lounge only. Light sleepers should request back rooms.

Credit cards Amex, MC, Visa.

Rates Room only, $116–156 suite, $71–116 double, $86 single. B&B, $138–168 suite, $98–128 double, $98 single. MAP, $205–235 suite, $175–195 double, $110–130 single. Extra person $10–50. 15% service. Family rates. Alc breakfast $4–7, alc lunch $6–8, alc dinner $30. Ski packages.

Extras Bus station pickups. Crib, babysitting.

The Inn at Forest Hills
Route 142, P.O. Box 783, 03580

Tel: 603–823–9550
800–280–9550
Fax: 603–823–8701
E-mail: ss@innfhills.com
URL: http://www.innatforesthills.com

Located at the top of Franconia Notch, the English Tudor–style Inn at Forest Hills was built in 1890 as a private house connected with the Forest Hills Hotel, a grand summer hotel constructed in 1884 and razed in 1984. The house was purchased in 1993 and restored by Joanne and Gordon Haym. Coffee is ready at 7:30 A.M., and breakfast is served at 8:30 A.M. The menu changes daily, but might include freshly squeezed orange juice, homemade granola with yogurt, poached bananas, pumpkin spice bread, and French toast with orange sauce or maple syrup; or possibly sautéed apple rings, banana nut bread, and sour cream Belgian waffles with raspberry sauce. Rooms are light and airy, with simple contemporary furnishings; guest rooms have white ruffled curtains with floral comforters or quilts on the beds. Readers are consistently delighted with the food, accommodations, location, and most especially the exceptional hospitality found at this delightful B&B.

"Joanne and Gordon leave no stone unturned in their efforts to make your visit special. The large veranda has hummingbirds flitting around the hanging feeders; the interior is glorious, with classical music enhancing the huge sitting area, dominated by a roaring fire. Joanne is a master chef, and Gordon describes and then serves her sumptuous breakfasts with great enthusiasm. We feasted on warm caramelized grapefruit, extraordinary French toast with fresh maple syrup, blueberry muffins and fresh fruit. After a day of hiking, we returned to find coffee, teas, and lemonade awaiting us along with Joanne's delicious baked treats. The spacious Franklin Pierce Room offered carefully chosen decor and a comfortable sitting area; at night a chocolate was placed on each pillow." *(Sybil Marcus & Ron Berman)* "Immaculate, bright, and cheery; beautifully decorated; friendly, helpful hosts. Afternoon treats included home-baked cookies or perhaps chocolate-dipped strawberries." *(Linda Grigsby & others)* "Awesome French toast for breakfast; they keep track of menus so that you won't get the same breakfast on a return visit unless you request it." *(Steve & Jeff Soule)* "The helpful owners supplied needed area information." *(Roland St. Cyr)* "Several large common rooms offer a choice of settings to relax, read, watch a movie, or talk with other guests. We've spent hours on the porch with wine and cheese, watching the hummingbirds." *(Kenneth Batorksi)* "Breakfasts can last two hours in summer—wonderful food and conversation. Everything is clean, well-lit, and in good working order. Each guest room is different, but each is decorated with thought and care. The location is convenient, set back from the highway for quiet and charm, but convenient to sights and activities." *(Joan Nortel)* "Loved meeting Tiffany, the inn cat." *(GS)*

Open All year.

Rooms 1 suite, 6 doubles—all with private bath and/or shower, clock, fan.

Facilities Dining room with fireplace, living room with fireplace, family room with fireplace, TV/VCR, and books; solarium with TV/VCR, puzzles; porch. 5 acres with tennis court, lawn games, swing, ponds. Hiking, cross-country skiing on property. Echo Lake for swimming, boating; golf nearby. Downhill skiing, groomed free cross-country trails nearby.

Location 1.2 m to center of town. Take I-93 N to Exit 37, & turn right to inn ⁴⁄₁₀ m up hill on left. From I-93 S, take Exit 38 & follow signs to Rte. 142.

Restrictions No smoking. Children over 11.

Credit cards Amex, DC, MC, Visa.

Rates B&B, $110–150 suite (up to 4 people), $90–150 double. Extra person, $25. Senior, AAA discount. 2-night minimum high season & most weekends.

Extras Bus station pickups.

Lovett's Inn by Lafayette Brook ¢ 🚶 ✗

Route 18, 03580

Tel: 603–823–7761
800–356–3802
Fax: 603–823–8578 (call first)
E-mail: lovetts@ncia.net
URL: http://www.lovettsinn.com

Franconia Notch in the White Mountains is an ideal vacation destination in almost every season, and generations of families will attest to the delights of making Lovett's Inn their base for exploring this beautiful area. Built in 1784, Lovett's is listed on the National Register of Historic Places, and has operated as an inn for the past half-century. The inn was bought by Jan and Jim Freitas in 1998. Both the common areas and the guest rooms in the main inn are decorated with antiques, while the modern cottages have a more contemporary look with country-style furnishings.

"Wonderful hospitality and friendly service from both owners and staff. Excellent food; the chef is an artist, with original and delicious dishes. Guest rooms are attractive, quiet, and clean, with high quality appointments and accessories; common areas are lovely and charming." *(John Snyder)* "Our immaculate poolside cottage had a magnificent view of the mountains from our picture window. We also had a sitting area, a working fireplace, bright reading lamps, and a porch." *(Brooke Connors)* "Delightful inn, excellent value. Dinner included delicious salmon with Dijon mustard sauce; equally tasty breakfast." *(Carol Flint)* "Impressive hand-hewn ceiling beams, quiet nooks for reading or playing chess, and fireplaces crackling in cold weather. Our suite faced the pond; we were serenaded by a marvelous choir of spring peepers and a tumbling brook. Excellent, heart-healthy breakfasts with home-grown herbs and locally harvested mushrooms." *(Crisanne Roberts)* "Congenial owners; warm, welcoming atmosphere; lots to do right at the inn. Adults are drawn to the warm atmosphere of the pub—off limits to children in the evening. Fabulous mountain views from the dining room windows and from the swimming pool area. Tasty dinner of black bean soup, pan-fried trout, and blueberry pie." *(BNS)* "Our inn room had pink floral wallpaper, lace curtains, and a canopy bed. At night, the bed was turned down with pillow mints." *(Anne Winkler & Michael Kowalkowski)* "Plenty of videos and games are provided for the children." *(Mr. & Mrs. Thomas Godfray)*

Open June–Oct., Dec. 26–Mar.

Rooms 1 suite, 6 doubles, 15 cottages with fireplace, all with private bath and/or shower. Most with telephone, air-conditioning, fan, fireplace, porch, radio, TV, coffee maker. 1 with 3 bedrooms.

Facilities Separate dining, breakfast, living rooms, sun room; some with fireplace. Bar/lounge, recreation room with TV/VCR, Ping-Pong, piano; deck. 10 acres with swimming pool, spa, fishing pond, lawn games, cross-country skiing, rentals.

Location Exit 3 off of I-93 onto Rte. 18. Inn on left.

Restrictions Smoking permitted in cottages only.

Credit cards Amex, Visa.

Rates MAP, $115–190 cottage, $156–180 double, Children under 12 free. 3-, 5-day packages. 2-night minimum during foliage. 15% service. Picnic lunches.

Extras Pets permitted in cottages by arrangement. Cribs, babysitting.

HAMPSTEAD

Stillmeadow Bed & Breakfast ¢ 👫
545 Main Street (Route 121), 03841

Tel: 603–329–8381
Fax: 603–329–4075
E-mail: rover@tiac.net

Whether you're traveling on business or for pleasure, alone or with the kids, Stillmeadow is a convenient, affordable, and family-friendly place to stay. An Italianate-style farmhouse built in 1850, and restored by Lori and Randy Offord in 1987, the reasonable rates include a welcome glass of wine, a bottomless cookie jar, and breakfasts of fresh fruit and juice, yogurt, hot and cold cereals, and home-baked specialties. A favorite breakfast menu consists of fresh fruit sundaes followed by baked cinnamon French toast topped with apple compote; the meal is served at the dining room table between 7:30 and 9:30 A.M.

"Lori was extremely helpful in providing area information. The large and comfortable Tulip Suite—tucked under the eaves—is ideal for a family, with two queen-size beds and a day bed. Several restaurants are within an easy drive for dinner." *(Christine DeSantis)* "The Dawn Suite has a queen-size brass bed and sitting room; its cheery yellow color scheme brought the sunshine inside. Lori made us feel like part of the family." *(Patricia Turner)* "Absolutely immaculate." *(CMS)* "Lori helped us with house-hunting and suggested restaurants. Breakfast included home-baked coffee cake or perhaps scones. A friendly dog, a cat, and two children live on the premises. Beautiful yet convenient location, near woods and fields, stone walls and brilliant autumn foliage, close to larger towns and attractions." *(Benita Kane Jaro)*

Open All year.

Rooms 2 suites, 2 doubles—all with private bath and/or shower, clock, TV, fan. 1 with telephone, desk, data port. 3 with refrigerator.

Facilities Dining room, living room, family room with TV/VCR, books; guest refrigerator; porch. 2.5 acres with fenced play yard with sandbox, swing set. Croquet courts across st. Town lake beach, boat launch nearby.

Location SE NH. 43 m N of Boston, 15 m S of Manchester, NH; 8 m NW of Haverill, MA. Historic district. 3.7 m N of intersection of Rtes. 121 & 111. Convenient to I-93, I-495. From I-495, take exit for Rte. 125, Haverhill. Go N on 125, then N approx. 5 m on Rte. 121 to inn on right. From I-93 S, take Exit 4. Go E on Broadway to rotary; continue E on E. Derry Rd. 5 m to Main St. (Rte. 121). Go right to inn on left. From I-93 N, go E on Rte. 111. At Rte. 121, go N 3.7 m to inn on right.

Restrictions No smoking. Children welcome with prior approval.

Credit cards Amex, Discover, MC, Visa.

Rates B&B, $65–90 suite, $55–75 double, $45–65 single. 2–3 night holiday weekend minimum.

Extras Train, plane, bus pickup. Crib. Some French, Spanish spoken.

HANOVER

The growth of Hanover is intertwined with the development of Dartmouth College, established in 1769. A classic New England town, the village green is encircled by fine Federal and Georgian buildings. Today, the college serves as a major cultural center for the region, with a fine art museum and the Hopkins Center for the Creative and Performing Arts. There's always something of interest going on, and travelers who wish to enjoy rural pleasures without cultural deprivation would do well to stay in or near Hanover. If you're looking for a quality remembrance of your visit, stop in at the League of New Hampshire Craftsmen shop at 13 Lebanon Street.

Hanover is located in southwestern New Hampshire, about 130 miles northwest of Boston. It's just across the Connecticut River from Vermont, and is about three miles north of the intersection of Interstates 89 and 91 in White River Junction, Vermont.

Information please: We'd like current reports on the pricey but luxurious **Hanover Inn** (East Wheelock and Main Streets, P.O. Box 151, 03755; 603–643–4300 or 800–443–7024) an elegant 90-room hotel enjoying a four-diamond AAA rating, with prices to match: $217–287 double. Dating to the 1700s, the inn was rebuilt after a fire in 1887, and fully renovated in 1989 with all modern conveniences. Owned by Dartmouth College, guests are welcome to use the college's athletic facilities. Advance reservations are essential during football season, parents' weekend, graduation, and reunions. The two restaurants offer a choice of casual or fine dining. "Summer or winter, there are always people occupying the row of white rocking chairs on the wide porch of the Hanover Inn. This lovely rambling inn faces the Dartmouth College green, ringed with the original white brick buildings, the spectacular Baker Library and Hopkins Center for the Arts, and, rising above them all, the surrounding mountains." *(Jocelyn Luff)*

For additional area inns, see **Wilder** and **Windsor, Vermont.**

HARTS LOCATION

The Notchland Inn ✕ ♦   *Tel:* 603–374–6131
Route 302, 03812   800–866–6131
                              Fax: 603–374–6168
                         E-mail: notchland@aol.com
                       URL: http://www.NOTCHLAND.com

Recipe for a wonderful inn: take two terrific guys with diverse and fascinating backgrounds in the fields of dance and medicine, a first-rate chef, an adorable Bernese Mountain dog named Coco, a handsome 1862 granite mansion, and an unparalleled location in Crawford Notch in the White Mountains, *et voilà*, the Notchland Inn, purchased by Ed Butler and Les Schoof in 1993, and upgraded and improved on a constant basis ever since. Newly completed in 1998 are two luxurious suites complete with king-size beds, Jacuzzi tubs, fireplaces, and balconies.

Guests are encouraged to play the Chickering console piano in the music room or to relax in the Gustav Stickley–designed front parlor. A five-course dinner is served by candlelight with a choice of soup, appetizer, entrée, and dessert; among the options at a recent meal were Szechuan carrot soup, mussels Provençal, beef tenderloin with portobello mushrooms and Madeira, or perhaps shrimp with tomato, asparagus, and saffron, and cranberry bread pudding. Coffee and juice are ready at 7:30 A.M.; breakfast is served from 8–9:30 A.M., and includes juice, coffee, and tea, granola and cereal, and your choice of pancakes, French toast, and eggs to order. A virtual menagerie makes its home on the grounds—Dolly, a Belgian draft horse; Mork and Mindy, miniature horses; and Sid and D.C., the llamas.

"I adore Ed's sense of humor. The building is striking, the setting unmatched, and the landscaping gorgeous." *(LDS, also John & Donna Ferrara-Kerr)* "Delightful setting, high up in the mountains near Crawford Notch, with many hiking trails practically at the inn's door. The cozy common rooms are in the original mansion, while the more modern dining room is light, airy, and elegant, with large windows looking out on hummingbird feeders and the gardens. Not another building in sight. The plant-filled solarium is a perfect hideaway for afternoon reading. Excellent dinners with ample choice, well-paced service, and reasonable portion sizes, leaving one full but not stuffed. (Les assured us that seconds on dessert are always available.) We loved having a choice at breakfast, and enjoyed the strawberry pancakes and cinnamon almond French toast. Guest rooms are quiet and pleasant, with good reading lights; even the smallest is a reasonable size." *(SWS)*

"Meals are served at separate tables (a plus for us), and the food is good." *(Anita Dichter)* "The hospitable innkeepers and staff offered tips on shopping and local history. Despite the remote setting, it's less than 30 minutes to North Conway's outlets." *(Steve Kurland)* "In the evenings, we enjoyed the abundant collection of puzzles, board games, books, and magazines." *(Wendy Waite)* "Not to miss is the wood-fired hot tub overlooking the little pond." *(Cindy Reichmann)* "Ed and Les mix well with their guests and can sense whether visitors prefer privacy or socializing." *(Andrew Ward)*

Open All year.

Rooms 5 suites, 7 doubles—all with private bath and/or shower, clock, desk, fan, wood-burning fireplace. 2 suites in adjacent 1852 schoolhouse with air-conditioning. Some with balcony, Jacuzzi.

Facilities Restaurant, living room, sun room with fireplace, library with fireplace, games, puzzles; music room with piano. 400 acres with hot tub, garden, pond, gazebo, swimming holes on Saco River. Hiking, cross-country skiing, snow-shoeing, ice-skating on grounds; connects to miles of trails. Six downhill ski areas within 10–30 min. Golf nearby.

Location White Mts. 2 hrs. N of Manchester, NH, 2 hrs. W of Portland, ME. On Rte. 302 6.5 m N of Bartlett traffic light. 12 m from N. Conway.

Restrictions No smoking. Children over 12.

Credit cards Amex, Discover, MC, Visa.

Rates B&B, $170–235 suite, $150–180 double, $120–160 single. Extra person, $40. MAP, $210–285 suite, $190–220 double, $140–170 single. Extra person, $50. 15% service. 2-night weekend minimum; 3 nights holidays, foliage. Prix fixe dinner, $32. Midweek packages.

Extras Bus station pickups. Babysitting.

HENNIKER

For additional area inns, see **Hillsborough** and **Weare**.

Colby Hill Inn ✕
3 The Oaks, P.O. Box 779, 03242

Tel: 603–428–3281
800–531–0330
Fax: 603–428–9218
E-mail: info@colbyhillinn.com
URL: http://www.colbyhillinn.com

Nearly 200 years old, the Colby Hill Inn was built as a farmhouse, and has served as a tavern, church, meeting house, and private school; Ellie, John, and Laurel Day Mack bought it in 1990. The inn's antique charms prevail in its period decor, wide pine-board floors that sag and tilt, and a fireplace with a bake oven. The rates include a breakfast of juice or fruit, and a choice of such entrées as raspberry-stuffed French toast or eggs Colby Hill, with bacon, ham, or sausage, plus the always available coffee, tea, hot chocolate, and cookie jar. The dinner menu includes such entrées as filet mignon with roasted garlic, shrimp and fennel with lemon pepper linguine, and chicken breast with lobster and leeks, all created by chef Michael Mack and his team.

"Friendly innkeepers, excellent food, lovely room, relaxed and beautiful setting." *(John Bailie, also Carolyn Russell)* "Delightful, full-service inn in a charming college town. Comfortable accommodations. Inviting dining room where I enjoyed a delicious meal of lobster bisque, salad, wild mushroom raviolis and a vegetable tart, peppers, and peach cobbler. Beautiful mountain views from the lovely swimming pool. Hard-working innkeepers always working to improve their inn." *(SWS)* "Ellie, John, and Laurel immediately make you feel part of the family. The inn is charming and spotless, with outstanding breakfasts and dinners." *(Frank Youngwertl)* "Efficient and well-run, an excellent alternative for business travelers, since the guest rooms have phones and separate jacks for computers." *(Ceci Connolly)*

"Outstanding cheesecake at dinner; delicious apple pancakes at breakfast." *(R. Eric Le Gear)* "Our visit to Henniker—including lunch at Daniels overlooking the river, a romantic stroll though the nearby covered bridge, and quilt shopping—was the highlight of our New England trip. Ellie and John Day were warm and informative, though not intrusive, with a wonderful sense of humor." *(Jorge & Marisa Bustamante)* "We had a beautiful room and bath on the main floor. Looking out the window we saw a gazebo and a tree laden with apples. Lovely, non-touristy town." *(Karen Parsagian)*

Open All year.

Rooms 16 doubles—all with private bath and/or shower, telephone/data port, air-conditioning. Some with desk, fireplace. 6 rooms in carriage house.

Facilities Dining room that serves 7 evenings a week, living room with fireplace, library with books, games, TV; central air-conditioning. 5 acres with swimming pool, lawn games, ice-skating. Tennis across street. Golf, kayaking, fishing, cross-country skiing nearby. 2 m to downhill skiing.

Location SE NH. 17 m W of Concord. 1 hr. W of Portsmouth; 1½ hrs. N of Boston. From I-89 N take Exit 5. Go W on Rtes. 9 & 202 W to Rte. 114 S. Go ½ m to center of town. Go right at blinking light in center of town to inn ½ m on right.

Restrictions No smoking. Children 7 and over welcome.

Credit cards Amex, DC, Discover, MC, Visa.

Rates B&B, $85–175 double, $75–165 single. Extra person, $20. 10% service. Minimum stay some weekends. Alc dinner $35.

HILLSBOROUGH

The Inn at Maplewood Farm ¢
447 Center Road, P.O. Box 1478, 03244

Tel: 603–464–4242
800–644–6695
Fax: 603–464–5401
E-mail: j_simoes@conknet.com
URL: http://www.conknet.com/maplewoodfarm/

Guests at the Inn at Maplewood Farm often awake to the sound of cow bells—a vast improvement over the alarm clocks most of us need to jump-start our days. Owner Jayme Simoes, who bought the inn in 1992, reports that guests enjoy feeding the cows on the farm. Surrounded by hills, fields, and a creek, Maplewood Farm has welcomed guests since it was built in 1794. Guest rooms are highlighted by European and American antiques, including an antique radio (Jayme's passion). Guests can tune in to Radio Maplewood Farm to enjoy such vintage favorites as the Fred Allen Show, the Shadow, or the Lone Ranger. Between 8:30 and 9:30 A.M., breakfast is delivered in a basket to your door, or can be enjoyed in the breakfast room, on the porch, or in the orchard seating area, and includes fresh fruit and juice, cereal or yogurt, and locally made jams and pastries. Rates also include turndown service. Antiquiteas, the Simoeses' shop specializing in vintage teapots and teatime accessories, is housed in the inn's historic tavern room.

"Lovely Center Road has rustic stone walls and rolling fields interspersed with wooded forests of hemlock and pine. Our young, energetic host made us feel completely at home. We appreciated the cleanliness, the comfortable surroundings, and the warmth of crackling fires." *(Mr. & Mrs. Joseph Gasparik)* "All the little touches—such as the hot water bottle wrapped in a flannel pillowcase and tucked in the bed for added warmth—added up to a wonderful vacation." *(D. Lynne Harrison)* "Quiet farm setting; comfortable beds." *(Peg Beutel)* "Jayme ready with helpful hints and interesting tidbits about the area, like the swimming hole up the street that came as a much needed respite from an unusual heat wave." *(Sandy & Jay Schinfeld)* "Be sure to explore charming, uncommercial, Colonial Hillsborough Center, a perfect morning walk away." *(SWS)*

Open Closed Dec.–April.
Rooms 1 suite, 3 doubles—all with private bath and/or shower, telephone, radio, clock, fan. 3 with fireplace, desk, 2 with air-conditioning, deck/patio. 2 rooms in 1880 attached barn.
Facilities Dining room with fireplace, living room with fireplace, TV, books, games; guest kitchen, porch. 14 acres with lawn games, cross-country skiing. Tennis, golf nearby. 2½ m from 2 lakes, swimming hole. Horseback riding nearby. Adjoins 1,400-acre state forest.
Location S NH. 80 m N of Boston. 30 m W of Concord. 2½ m to downtown. ½ m to historic district. From Boston, take I-93 N through NH tolls. Take exit for I-89 N to Exit 5 to Rte. 9 W (left lane exit). Follow Rte. 9 to Hillsborough. From New York and Hartford take I-91 N from Hartford to Brattleboro, VT, & take exit for Rte. 9 W to Hillsborough. In center of town, at light, go N on School St. (opposite Rte. 149), to inn 2½ m on right.
Restrictions No smoking.
Credit cards Amex, Diners Club, Discover, MC, Visa.
Rates B&B, $125 suite (sleeps 4), $75–95 double. Extra person, $20. Off-season special rates. 2-night minimum holiday weekends. Theme weekends off-season.
Extras Portuguese, Spanish spoken.

HOLDERNESS

Holderness is best known for the lake it borders, Squam Lake, made famous in the movie, *On Golden Pond*. Beautiful Squam Lake is perfect for swimming, fishing, and boating in summer, skating and ice fishing in winter. Holderness is near the White Mountains National Forest, offering splendid hiking in summer and fall, and excellent cross-country and downhill skiing in winter. Plenty of tennis courts and two golf courses are also nearby.

Holderness is located in the central New Hampshire lakes region, about a two-hour drive from Boston, and 4 to 5 miles from Exit 24 of Interstate 93.

Also recommended: A century-old farm house with Victorian furnishings as well as Asian art and rugs, **The Pressed Petals Inn** (Shepard Hill Road, P.O. Box 695, 03245; 603–968–4417) has eight guest rooms, each with a private bath. B&B double rates of $85–125 include breakfasts with freshly squeezed orange juice and just-baked breads, afternoon tea and dessert, and Saturday evening hors d'oeuvres by candlelight. "This comfortable old house across the street from the Manor on Golden Pond has been renovated and beautifully decorated by owner Ellie Dewey. Colors, fabrics, and furnishings are attractively coordinated with an eye to guests' comfort and convenience. At breakfast, we enjoyed fresh fruit, homemade bread, and quiche. Our room was complete with everything from terry robes to pressed flower bookmarks." *(Carol Workman)*

For an additional area entry, see **Ashland.**

The Inn on Golden Pond ¢   *Tel:* 603–968–7269
Route 3, P.O. Box 680, 03245   *Fax:* 603–968–9226
                                             E-mail: innongp@lr.net

Bill and Bonnie Webb bought the Inn on Golden Pond in 1984 and have individually decorated the guest rooms of their 110-year-old farmhouse in country style. Across the road, behind clusters of pine trees, is Squam Lake. A typical breakfast consists of fresh fruit and juice, cereals, home-baked white or wheat bread, rhubarb muffins, sour cream coffee cake, rhubarb jam, and farm-fresh eggs-to-order or the morning special—perhaps a puffed apple pancake or baked French toast.

"Available innkeepers, ready with suggestions for dining and sightseeing. Bonnie prepares excellent breakfasts and is willing to share her recipes." *(Danielle & Russell Brubaker)* "A quiet, peaceful location for evening or morning walks. Impeccably clean." *(Ruth & Bob Cayton)* "Perfect home-away-from-home atmosphere; delightful rooms, food, and hospitality." *(Kathy & John Valentine)* "The wide front porch is furnished with rockers and chairs overlooking the front lawn." *(Nick & Jean Ellison)* "Beautiful home in a quiet, wooded area. The living room was especially cozy and inviting. Bill and Bonnie made us feel welcome and comfortable." *(Roseanne deLeon)* "The bed was made, linens and towels replaced daily, lights turned up at night, with the shades and bed covers turned down. Parking areas are well lit and cleared of snow." *(Mr. & Mrs. Edward Hagarty)* "Everything is spotless, the lighting and plumbing good." *(Sue Wallis)* "Delicious omelets, apple or blueberry pancakes, and fresh-baked breads and muffins for breakfast. The friendly innkeepers help you plan such activities as boating on gorgeous Squam Lake." *(Donald Gorczynski)*

Open All year.
Rooms 1 suite, 7 doubles—all with private bath and/or shower, fan.
Facilities Dining room; 2 sitting rooms, 1 with TV; game room, screened porch. 50 acres with lawn games. Walking/cross-country skiing trails, golf, tennis, lake nearby. Squam Lake across road.
Location 4 m from Exit 24 on I-93. 1 m from center of town.
Restrictions No smoking. No children under 12.
Credit cards Amex, MC, Visa.
Rates B&B, $125–140 suite, $95–115 double, $75–80 single. Extra person, $30. Minimum stay peak weekends.

The Manor on Golden Pond ✕ 🏕   *Tel:* 603–968–3348
Route 3 and Shepard Hill Road, P.O. Box T, 03245   800–545–2141
Fax: 603–968–2116
E-mail: manorinn@lr.net
URL: http://www.manorongoldenpond.com

Owned by David and Bambi Arnold since 1992, the Manor was built in 1907 by a wealthy Englishman, Isaac Van Horn, who spared no expense in making his new home a work of art. The carved moldings, rich wood paneling, leaded-glass windows, and grand fireplaces in the common areas are complemented by antique furnishings and rich fabrics. With a four-diamond rating from AAA, today's guests will find the inn's luxury enhanced with all modern conveniences. The inn sits atop a hill overlooking Squam Lake; extensive grounds slope down to the road that separates the inn from the lake. In 1997, the Arnolds renovated the Carriage House rooms, bringing the decor up to the same high standard as the other lovely guest rooms; in 1998, four luxury lakeview cottages were added, complete with king-size beds, wood-burning fireplaces, and Jacuzzi tubs, laid out so that you can enjoy both the fire and the TV/VCR from either the tub or bed.

Breakfast includes freshly squeezed orange juice, cereal or granola, fresh fruit and yogurt, bacon or sausage, home fries, muffins, and toast, plus a selection of such dishes as baked apples, poached eggs with Hollandaise sauce and crab meat, omelets, pancakes, and French toast; guests gather at 4 P.M. for tea and conversation. A recent five-course dinner menu included such choices as wild mushrooms with wine and garlic; crab cake with red pepper coulis; salad; lamb with porcini mushrooms and risotto; and lemon mascarpone tart with berries.

"Elegant, beautiful inn. The pool area is an idyllic setting." *(Betsy Sandberg)* "We loved the Churchill Room, done all in blue and white. Each guest room was different, but all are spotless and lovely. Bambi, David, and their staff were on top of every detail." *(Ann Marie Mason)* "Outstanding cuisine; beautiful guest rooms with antiques and Ralph Lauren fabrics; excellent service." *(Chuck Hulsey)*

Open All year. Restaurant closed Mon., Tues. in winter. Cottages, carriage house open June 1–Columbus Day weekend.
Rooms 6 2-bedroom cottages, 25 doubles—all with private bath and/or shower, radio, clock, TV, air-conditioning (except cottages), coffee pot, telephone. Most with fireplace. Some with double whirlpool tub, TV/VCR, CD player. 17 rooms in Manor House; 4 in carriage house. 2 cottages with kitchen.

Facilities Restaurant, 3 dining rooms with fireplace, living room with fireplace, books, stereo; 2 libraries, pub with piano, TV. Some weekend piano entertainment. 14 acres with swimming pool, clay tennis court, gazebo, lawn games; on lake with boathouse, private beach, canoes, paddle boat. Fishing, cross-country skiing on lake. Downhill skiing, hiking, golf, bicycling, horseback riding nearby.

Location NH Lakes region. 2 hrs. from Boston. Walking distance to Holderness. Take Exit 24 off I-93 & go 4.5 m E on Rte. 3.

Restrictions No smoking. Children over 12 in Manor House; any age in cottages.

Credit cards Amex, MC, Visa.

Rates B&B, $210–325 suite, double; service included. Room only, cottages, $950–1750 weekly. Prix fixe dinner, $38 (3 courses); $50, (5 courses).

JACKSON

You couldn't ask for a more perfect way to enter Jackson than to turn off busy Route 16, pass under a red covered bridge, and arrive in a lovely New England town, complete with white-steepled church and old farmhouses now restored as inns, with nary an outlet store or fast-food chain in sight. Located in the White Mountains of northeast New Hampshire, it lies in the Mt. Washington Valley, 8 miles north of North Conway. Jackson is 3 hours (150 miles) north of Boston via Route 16, and 1½ hours (65 miles) west of Portland, Maine. There's ample opportunity for fishing, hiking, canoeing, golf, and tennis in summer; in winter there are five downhill ski areas and several cross-country ski centers within a short drive, making up a 156-kilometer trail system.

Carter Notch Inn ¢ 👫   *Tel:* 603–383–9630
Carter Notch Road, P.O. Box 269, 03846   800–794–9434
                    URL: http://www.journeysnorth.com/carternotch

Built in 1910, the Carter Notch Inn was restored as a B&B in 1994 by Jim and Lynda Dunwell. Perched on a hillside overlooking the Wildcat River Valley, the inn has a country cottage ambience combining New Hampshire quilts, straw hats, and dried flowers with oak and wicker furnishings. In winter, you can cross-country ski right from the door. In the summer, you can cool off at nearby Jackson Falls, or spend some time on the tennis court.

"Jim and Lynda Dunwell have painstakingly restored this delightful and comfortable B&B. The inviting wraparound porch offers spectacular views of the White Mountains. The quiet country location is conducive to a good night's sleep, followed by Jim's sumptuous breakfast. Residents of Jackson for 20 years, Jim and Lynda can expertly answer questions about the area." *(Betty Norman)* "Like Grandma's house— not fancy but very comfortable. Great innkeepers, good breakfast, lovely town." *(Cecille Desroches)* "Terrific innkeepers, so kind and witty. Inn dog Tucker is a real winner, too—he's even an L.L. Bean catalog model." *(LS)*

Open All year.
Rooms 7 doubles—5 with private bath and/or shower, 2 with maximum of 4 people sharing bath. All with clock/radio, air-conditioning. 5 with desk.
Facilities Dining room; living room with fireplace, TV; family room; sun room; porch. ¾ acre with outdoor hot tub, tennis court, swing set, gazebo, lawn games. 128 km cross-country ski trails from door.
Location 8 m to North Conway.
Restrictions No smoking. Children over 4.
Credit cards Amex, Discover, MC, Visa.
Rates B&B. $59–109 double, $59–89 single. Extra person, $15. Reduced rates for children. 2-night weekend minimum.
Extras Bus station pickup. Babysitting.

The Inn at Thorn Hill ✕
Thorn Hill Road, P.O. Box A, 03846

Tel: 603–383–4242
800–289–8990
Fax: 603–383–8062
E-mail: thornhill@ncia.net
URL: http://www.innatthornhill.com

Overlooking the village of Jackson and the Presidential Mountain Range, the Inn at Thorn Hill was designed by Stanford White in 1895, and was purchased by Jim and Ibby Cooper in 1992. Rooms in the main house have a Victorian flavor with antique and reproduction furnishings, lace curtains, ruffled linens, and canopied beds, while those in the carriage house have been upgraded to an elegant country style, with Ralph Lauren fabrics, new carpeting, wall-coverings, and bathroom tiling. Overall, the luxury level is high enough to have earned the inn a four-diamond rating from AAA. Terrific views of Mt. Washington can be had from some rooms and from the front porch rocking chairs.

The varied and well-balanced dinner menu changes every two weeks, and is complemented by an outstanding wine list. A recent meal included mushroom soup with sautéed fiddleheads; greens with basil and jicama; grilled swordfish with stir-fried green beans; and lime mascarpone cannoli with wild blackberries. The breakfast menu consists of juice, cereals, granola and yogurt, a choice of chicken hash, omelets, or pancakes, plus rosemary potatoes and a breakfast meat, and is served from 8–10 A.M. Rates also include afternoon tea, served from 3:30–5:30 P.M., with lemonade in summer, mulled cider in the fall, plus freshly baked treats.

"Enjoyed inn so much we extended our stay. Our beautifully decorated room in the Carriage House had a sitting room with a pullout couch, and two comfortable chairs. The bedroom had a queen-size bed with adjustable bedside reading lights, and the full bath had a Jacuzzi tub. Fabulous dinners; breakfast included many temptingly rich choices, but my favorite was the fresh fruit with yogurt and granola. Hospitable but unobtrusive innkeepers. Wonderful selection of single malt Scotches." *(Ralph Ferguson)* "Spacious, quiet room; pleasant service. Terrific vegetarian dinner. Jim was charming, helpful with travel advice. A nice touch was the follow-up card we received from the Coopers, thanking us for our visit." *(Stephanie Roberts)* "Our spacious suite was beautifully appointed with period pieces; magnificent views. Superb meals; gracious but unobtrusive hospitality." *(Patricia Hogan)* "Quiet, relaxing atmosphere; beautifully presented meals." *(Mrs. Stephen Kasik)*

"Just off the main road, this lovely country hotel has a glorious setting on carefully landscaped grounds. The spacious living room has beautiful Oriental rugs and formal Victorian antiques. The bar is small and cozy, and the dining room is lovely, with a deep green and pale pink color scheme. Guest rooms are fresh and inviting; those in the converted barn have a more relaxed country decor, plus a more casual living room." *(SWS)* "The Victorian furnishings combine period atmosphere and comfort. The pub is a wonderful place to relax, especially in the winter. Breakfast was served in a lovely dining room, with sunlight and flowers, and large windows overlooking greenery." *(Michael Golden & Vicki Marklew)* "Accommodating innkeepers who went out of their way to say yes to our requests." *(Lynn & Beverly Detwiler)*

Open All year.

Rooms 3 cottages, 16 doubles—all with private bath and/or shower, desk, air-conditioning. 10 with telephone; 6 with desk, fan. Cottages with telephone, gas fireplace, double Jacuzzi tub/spa, air-conditioning. 6 rooms in carriage house.

Facilities Restaurant, pub with fireplace, games; parlor, sitting room with TV, great room with fireplace, TV; porch. Hot tub, swimming pool, stocked fishing pond, stream, walking paths, cross-country skiing. Golf, tennis, hiking, horseback riding, downhill skiing nearby.

Location 8 m N of North Conway. 70 m NW of Portland. 130 m N of Boston. From Jackson Village (not Intervale), take Rte. 16A through covered bridge to Thorn Hill Rd. Go right and up hill to inn.

Restrictions No smoking. Children over 9.

Credit cards Amex, DC, Discover, MC, Visa.

Rates MAP, $240–300 cottages, $160–300 suite, double, $110–250 single. 15% service. B&B rates, $15 less per person. 2–3 night weekend/holiday minimum. Weekly, midweek rates; packages. Alc dinner (outside guests), $25–40. Summer picnic lunches by reservation. Off-season "room sale."

Extras Bus station pickups.

Paisley and Parsley &. ♦️
Route 16B, Five Mile Circuit Road
P.O. Box 572, 03846

Tel: 603–383–0859
Fax: 603–383–6973

This homestay B&B is named for the owners' two favorite pastimes: paisley for their love of antiques, folk art, and textiles; parsley for their passion for cooking and gardening. Bea and Chuck Stone have owned this contemporary home since 1989. Outside, guests can drink in spectacular views of Mt. Washington; inside, a library filled with volumes on cooking, antiques, gardening, travel, and Civil War history can quench a thirst for knowledge. Hungry stomachs will be equally sated by Chuck and Bea's bountiful breakfasts: Kona coffee, assorted teas, juices, fruit—perhaps curried peaches or banana parfaits—and the daily entrée—rum raisin French toast, pecan praline waffles, vegetable frittata, or possibly mushroom crêpes. Afternoon treats include shortbread with tea or hot cider.

"From our comfortable bed, we awakened to see the sun shining on Mt. Washington." *(Ann Ritzer)* "Special touches included Poland Spring water with two wine glasses in our loft room, the music of Louis Armstrong in the background, the warm blueberry bread, and Beatrice's genuine desire to accommodate her guests." *(Natasha Sarris)* "After our hike up Mt. Washington, we were warmly welcomed by Bea. The spacious bathroom with its inviting whirlpool tub, terry robes, and mountain views provided just the pampering we craved. The king-size bed, fluffy comforters and pillows were truly luxurious. Victorian wedding dresses and hats added charm. Breakfast in the magnificent gardens capped our stay." *(Jane Hull)* "We were treated like royalty." *(Terri & Barry Weitzel)* "The collection of antique furnishings contrasts magically with this contemporary home. Outstanding views; peaceful setting. Fantastic breakfasts with special requests honored. The main-floor guest room is extremely private, with a marvelous whirlpool tub and skylight." *(Taryl Melason)*

"Like coming home to Grandma's house. Warm and welcoming atmosphere, with lots of personal attention. Cozy common areas, pretty gardens in front, spacious deck in back yard." *(SWS)* "Wonderful food made especially for our low-fat diet." *(Patricia & Gene Martino)* "The decor includes quilts, lace-canopied beds, country antiques and extensive collectibles, vintage clothing and old-fashioned toys." *(Anne-Marie Kovacs)* "We sat at the dining room table and watched the weather change continually around Mt. Washington. At sunrise, the whole mountain was aflame in pink and orange." *(Heidi Schmidt)*

Open Mid-June–mid-Oct, mid-Nov.–mid-May.

Rooms 2 suites, 1 double—all with private whirlpool, bath and/or shower, telephone, radio, desk, TV/VCR. 1 with balcony; 1 with fan, refrigerator. Suite with stereo, books.

Facilities Dining room, living room with fireplace, library, games, TV, porch. 2 acres with herb gardens, grape arbor, covered bridge. Jackson Falls nearby for swimming, fishing; golf, hiking, cross-country/downhill skiing, ice-skating, sleigh rides nearby.

Location Mt. Washington Valley. ½ m to Jackson; 5 m N of North Conway. From Rte. 16 N of North Conway, turn right across the covered bridge onto Rte. 16A. Bear right after the Jackfrost Shop in Jackson Village onto Rte. 16B. Pass Tin Mine Rd.; the inn is the third house on the right.

Restrictions No smoking. Children over 3.

Credit cards MC, Visa.

Rates B&B, $85–115 suite, $95–135 double, $65–125 single. Extra person, $15–15. 10% service. 10% senior/AAA discount. Ski, golf packages. Off-season rates. (Doubles higher than suites because of mountain views & amenities.) 6th night free except peak dates.

Extras One room wheelchair accessible; bath equipped for the disabled. Bus station pickup. Babysitting. Some French spoken.

JAFFREY

For an additional area inn, see **Rindge.**

The Benjamin Prescott Inn ¢   *Tel: 603–532–6637*
Route 124 East, 03452   *Fax: 603–532–6637*

In 1853, Benjamin Prescott built a two-story frame house on the Old
Turnpike Road; soon after, the family built an inn adjoining the homestead. The Prescotts' ownership extended for over 100 years, during
which time the property became one of the largest and most up-to-date
farms in the area. Barry and Janice Miller bought the Benjamin Prescott
Inn in 1988.

"Warm, gracious, sincere innkeepers. Delicious breakfasts; after several visits, we still have not had the same breakfast twice. Every room
spotless." *(Mr. & Mrs. Irving Baldwin)* "Picturesque, quiet area. Jan and
Barry are accommodating hosts." *(Rudy & Esther van Wingen)* "Located
on a farm road in a peaceful area." *(Pat Wetzler)* "Jan and Barry accommodated our every wish. Delicious food from the morning soufflé
and maple French toast to the heavenly bedtime chocolate truffles."
(CJE) "A handsomely restored farmhouse filled with wonderful antiques. Breakfasts are served at small tables set for two to four, or at the
larger dining room table. Fresh flowers and plants abound. The comfortable living room is cozy with an excellent variety of magazines and
other reading materials. The bedrooms have super quilts, lots of pillows, good reading lights and an abundance of thick towels. We stayed
in John Adams's Attic, a third-floor suite well worth the climb, with a
sitting room overlooking the endless field of the neighboring dairy
farm." *(Patricia Aarons)* "A good choice for families is the third-floor
suite; lots of space, with kitchenette, living room, and sleeping alcoves
for kids off the living room." *(SWS)* "The Millers were very helpful with
dinner reservations." *(Gilbert Plaw)*

Open All year.
Rooms 3 suites, 6 doubles—3 with full private bath, 6 with private shower. All
rooms with clock/radio, fan; some with telephone, TV, desk, air-conditioning.
1 suite with kitchenette.
Facilities Living room with fireplace, TV, 2 dining rooms, screened porch. Lake
swimming, trout and bass fishing, hiking, golf nearby. 5 m to cross-country skiing, 8 m to downhill.
Location S NH, Monadnock Region. 1½ hrs. to Boston & Springfield, MA, 2 hrs.
to Hartford, CT, 4½ hrs. to NYC. 2 m to town on Rte. 124. From Rte. 202, go E
on Rte. 124 to inn on left.
Restrictions Smoking in living room only. No children under 10.
Credit cards Amex, MC, Visa.
Rates B&B, $90–140 suite, $75–90 double. Extra person, $15. Gratuity appreci-
ated. 2-night weekend minimum summer, fall. 10% senior discount.
Extras Local airport pickups.

LACONIA

Ferry Point House ¢   *Tel:* 603–524–0087
100 Lower Bay Road, Sanbornton, 03269   *Fax:* 603–524–0959
         E-mail: Ferry Pt@together.net
         URL: http://www.tiac.net/users/berg

Awakening early enough on a summer morning to slip out the door, cross the lawn, and go down to the beach for a pre-breakfast swim in a refreshing mountain lake is one of our definitions of bliss. And that's just what summer visitors at the Ferry Point House can do. Painted red with a 60-foot-long veranda overlooking Lake Winnisquam and the mountains beyond, the inn has been owned by Diane and Joe Damato since 1985. Originally built in the early 1800s by the Pillsbury family as a summer retreat, the inn is furnished with antiques and collectibles. Breakfast is served at the dining room table from 8–9 A.M., and a typical meal might include granola, cheese-baked apples, stuffed French toast with blueberries and maple syrup, apple streusel muffins, and pineapple zucchini bread, or perhaps poached pears with raspberry sauce, eggs Benedict with hollandaise, strawberry rhubarb coffee cake, and lemon poppy seed bread.

"Tasty breakfast, beautifully presented. Relaxing atmosphere." *(Barbara Bria)* "Spotless, elegant, cozy, and warm, with serene lake views. The scrumptious breakfasts are accompanied by classical music. Diane, Joe, and their children always have a welcoming smile on their faces. Diane's knowledge of the area is extensive; she always can suggest new activities." *(Renee Randolph)* "After a day of antiquing, we relaxed on the front porch or sat by the lake to watch the sunset." *(Jan Gottesman)* "Guest rooms are quiet, comfortable, and spotless, with daily changes of towels and linens. The generous breakfasts always last us until dinner time. The Damato family makes a point of finding the time to talk with guests. Their helpful dining and activity scrapbooks are complemented by their personal knowledge of the area. Simply relaxing on the porch overlooking the lake, sitting in the gazebo on the point, swimming, boating, or playing games in the large, comfortable living room are always inviting options." *(Charles Copp & also Jennifer Kern)*

Open May 1–Oct. 31.
Rooms 7 doubles—all with private shower and/or bath (some tubs with hand-held showers), clock, fan; one with double Jacuzzi tub.
Facilities Dining room with fireplace, living room with fireplace, TV/VCR, games, books; veranda, gazebo. 2 acres with gardens; on Lake Winnisquam with dock and sandy beach for swimming, boating, fishing. Tennis, golf nearby.
Location SE NH, Lakes Region. 90 m N of Boston, 10 min. W of Laconia. From I-93 take Exit 20. Go N on Rte. 3 for 4½ m. Turn left on Bay Rd., right on Lower Bay Rd.
Restrictions No smoking. Children over 12.
Credit cards None accepted.
Rates B&B, $85–110 double. Extra person, $25.
Extras Local airport/station pickup. French spoken.

LITTLETON

Littleton is a nice little town in a somewhat less touristed part of New Hampshire. It has many appealing but not fancy shops; individually owned, these are not the same factory outlet clones that have sprouted in the eastern part of the state. Because of its location away from the mountains, Littleton attracts mainly cross-country skiers in winter— generally a bit quieter, slightly older group than most downhillers.

Littleton is in northwestern New Hampshire, close to all White Mountain attractions, the Vermont border, and the Connecticut River. It's about 10 miles southeast of St. Johnsbury, VT. The town is about 175 miles from Boston, 1 mile off I-93, and 20 minutes to I-91.

Reader tips: "A wonderful town to visit and use as a sightseeing base. Dedicated diner fans will love the classic Littleton Diner on Main Street." *(Sherrill Brown)* "Downtown Littleton is old-fashioned and safe; the cars even stop for pedestrians! Being from New Jersey, it was a nice change." *(KT)*

For additional area entries, see **Whitefield**, and in Vermont, see **Lower Waterford** and **St. Johnsbury**.

Thayers Inn ¢ ✕ ♠ | *Tel:* 603–444–6469
136 Main Street, 03561 | 800–634–8179
E-mail: Don@thayersinn.com

Thayers is an old-fashioned small-town hotel, a charming relic of the horse and buggy era. Its architecture is striking—four white columns in the front with porches on the second and third floors. Built in 1842 and listed on the National Register of Historic Places, the hotel is steeped in history. U.S. Grant addressed the populace from the hotel balcony shortly after being elected to the presidency, and numerous other famous (and infamous) visitors have passed through its halls. Built to the highest standards of its day, 19th-century travelers found hotels like this in county seats throughout New England. What's unusual about the Thayers is that it hasn't been torn down or converted into apartments or offices.

"The charm of this historic hotel, with its reasonable rates and clean, comfortable rooms made it a fine choice." *(Sherrill Brown)* "A cozy sitting room is downstairs; the upstairs hallways are decorated with ancient prints and photos of the surrounding area. One can climb to the cupola at the top of the building and gaze out at the surrounding community." *(Gary Weiss)* "The immaculate rooms are simply furnished in utilitarian hotel furnishings; some have old-fashioned flowered wallpaper, and the least expensive ones are small and basic. The halls are very wide, with floral paper, and comfortable seating here and there. Most of the furnishings in the hall are antiques, some original to the hotel. Take a peek into the 1842 room on the third floor (no elevator), preserved to look as it did when the hotel was built. Longtime innkeeper Don Lambert knows everything that's going on in town and the area, and will happily suggest places to eat, or do whatever he can to make your stay pleasant." *(SWS)* "The innkeeper was helpful during a heat wave, offering to fill our small ice chest to keep our lunchtime things cold." *(Duane Roller)* "Old-timey atmosphere. Efficient plumbing, comfortable accommodations. We brought in coffee and donuts and ate breakfast on the balcony overlooking the quiet street. A nice little pub in the basement is open late." *(Karen Twisler)*

Open All year.
Rooms 6 suites, 28 doubles, 1 single—34 with private bath and/or shower, 6 with maximum of 4 sharing bath. All with telephone, TV, desk, fan.
Facilities Family room with piano, TV, games; pub.
Location Center of town.
Restrictions Traffic noise in some rooms. Parents must supervise young children in cupola.
Credit cards Amex, Discover, MC, Visa.
Rates Room only, $100 suite, $30–80 double, $30–80 single. Extra person, $5. Children under 6, free.
Extras Station pickups. Pets permitted by prior arrangement. Crib.

LYME

A quiet village on the western side of New Hampshire, across the Connecticut River from Vermont, Lyme is located less than 3 hours northwest of Boston, and about 10 miles north of Hanover. Set around a classic New England green, the town church has a bell cast by Paul Revere. Visitors enjoy the peaceful pleasures of swimming, golf, canoeing, fishing, bicycling, tennis, and downhill and cross-country skiing, yet are just a short drive away from all the concerts, plays, and other events Dartmouth College offers in Hanover.

Also recommended: A tavern and inn since 1809, the **Alden Country Inn** (P.O. Box 60, On the Common, 03768; 603–795–2222 or 800–794–2296) offers fourteen guest rooms with private bath and air-conditioning along with period decor, plus a tavern and grill serving breakfast and dinner daily. B&B double rates range from $105–160. "A traditional country inn, right on the Common. Guest rooms are clean and freshly decorated, our breakfast decadent." *(Nancy Wolfe Stead)* "Food quite good, guest rooms attractive, charming common rooms, hospitable atmosphere." *(Eileen O'Reilly)*

Opened in 1997, **Breakfast on the Connecticut** (651 River Road, 03768; 603–353–4444 or 888–353–4440) is just that, with 750 feet of frontage on the Connecticut River, a private beach, dock, canoes and kayaks. This newly built Colonial-style building is set on 23 acres and has 15 guest rooms furnished with Shaker reproductions, many with a fireplace and double whirlpool bath. B&B double rates are $105–250.

Loch Lyme Lodge ¢ ♀ ✖ ♿   *Tel:* 603–795–2141
70 Orford Road, Route 10, 03768   800–423–2141
E-mail: LochLymeLodge@valley.net

Loch Lyme has been welcoming families since 1924. It overlooks Post Pond, a spring-fed lake about three quarters of a mile wide, and about the same distance in length. Paul and Judy Barker have been running the inn since 1977, and cater to the needs of vacationing families. Breakfast includes fresh fruit and juice, cereal, yogurt, and a choice of eggs, pancakes, or French toast. A light lunch is offered in summer, and dinner consists of salad, a choice of entrées—perhaps lemon tarragon chicken, leg of lamb, and baked manicotti, with fresh peach shortcake, and perhaps Tollhouse pie for dessert.

"My grandchildren are the fourth generation to stay at Loch Lyme Lodge. A great place for children, with lots of toys, games, boats. Ice in the afternoon for drinks at your cabin, wood for the fireplace." *(Joan Otto)* "A quiet, family-friendly place for consistently great vacations. A wide variety of activities, in a casual but well-run atmosphere." *(Adeeb Fadil)* "The cabins are rustic but comfortable. The service provided by the Barker family and their staff of international exchange students is friendly, responsive, and reliable." *(Mary Hopkins)* "We have been coming to the Loch Lyme since our kids were infants; they're teenagers now, and still enjoy it. Total relaxation, a perfect balance to our busy lives." *(Laura & Jon Barone)* "We swim, canoe, and windsurf on the clear waters of the lake, hike in the mountains, picnic on the waterfront, and glory in the quiet of the woods. Good food, fresh from the garden vegetables; fun shopping nearby. The owners are always helpful and available. We love the traditional Sunday picnic on the lake." *(Linda Parker)*

"Every cabin has its own setting and layout with an eclectic array of comfortable, well-used furniture." *(Judith McGaw)* "The lake is on the opposite side of Route 10 from the cabins; the children can play safely in the Little Tyke play yard." *(LF)* "Meats and fish were well-prepared and seasoned with an array of herbs and vegetables from the inn's garden." *(Mohand Abdelli)* "Staff members arrived each morning to make the beds and bring us fresh towels." *(Maggie Williamson)* "Compatible guests who appreciate simple pleasures." *(June and Matt Wolfberg)* "Kids make new friends easily here." *(Alvin Berk & Judy Brandwein)* "Outdoor grills made it easy for different families to gather together for dinner." *(JJH)*

Open All year except Thanksgiving and Christmas. Dinner served late June–Labor Day.
Rooms 4 doubles sharing 2 baths. 24 summer cabins with private bath. Most with kitchen, fireplace, screened porch.
Facilities Dining rooms, living room with fireplace, piano room, library, game room. 125 acres with 2 clay tennis courts, lawn games, children's play equipment, fields, woods, cross-country skiing. Lakefront with dock, canoes, boats, fishing, beach, ice-skating. 3½ m to downhill skiing.
Location On Rte. 10, 1 m N of town.
Restrictions No smoking in dining rooms. BYOB.
Credit cards None accepted.
Rates B&B, $56–92 double, $42–70 single. MAP, $106–122 double, $79–88 single. Extra person, $28–42. Picnic lunch, $5. Prix fixe dinner, $16. Reduced rates for children under 16. Weekly, off-season rates. 2-night weekend minimum in foliage season. Service additional.
Extras Some cabins wheelchair accessible. Pets in cabins only. Airport/station pickups, $14. Crib, babysitting. Spanish, limited French spoken.

MADISON

Maple Grove House ¢ 👫   *Tel:* 603–367–8208
Maple Grove Road, 03849   *E-mail:* maplegrove@landmarknet.net
         URL: http://www.nettx.com/maplegrove

Celia and Don Pray didn't have to worry about fixing up old plumbing when they and their two children bought the Maple Grove House in 1994—the only "facilities" to be found in this abandoned 1911 summer boarding house was a two-holer out back! A year later, they opened their fully renovated B&B, simply furnished with handsome Colonial- and Shaker-style reproductions, bright florals, contemporary and antique prints, and gleaming maple-wood floors. Celia grew up in Barbados and Jamaica, and worked as a cook on charter boats; her galley these days is a bit more spacious, allowing her to prepare breakfasts of fresh fruit and juice, home-baked breads and muffins, cereal, omelets or perhaps French toast, bacon or sausage, home fries, coffee and tea, served at the dining room table from 7–9:30 A.M.

"Lovely setting, with views of Mt. Chocorua across the valley. This rambling Victorian farmhouse commands the hill, with a broad porch and hanging plants. Guest rooms have excellent bedside lighting and sound-proofing; we never heard the other guests. Comfortable reading chairs with good lighting, too. Delicious breakfast of melon and blueberries, orange juice, scrambled eggs with chives, bacon, red potatoes, toast, and warm from the oven cinnamon-raisin scones. Celia has an artist's eye for color, pattern, and design; gorgeous original maple floors throughout the house. The decor is crisp, clean, and uncluttered. Celia is a delightful innkeeper. Third-floor suite is ideal for families, with a huge bathroom under the gables." *(Nancy & Bruce Barker)*

"The Pray family offers a warm, homey atmosphere. The aptly named Yellow Room is comfortable and cheerful. Don and Celia were hosting the inn's annual art fair, making our stay even more pleasurable. Celia's breakfasts are special—freshly baked muffins and breads, fresh organic eggs deliciously scrambled, fresh fruits and juices. Magnificent grounds with gorgeous views; we followed a trail through the extensive property past a beaver pond. We were told that occasional moose and bear sometimes wander through." *(Ron Berman & Sybil Marcus)* "Crisp and clean, immaculately kept." *(Deb & Ron Tuxbury)* "Beautiful decor, luxurious towels, incredibly comfortable beds. Bright, cheery, and immaculate throughout. Skip-lunch breakfasts, complete with homemade jam. Magnificent flowers, hummingbirds too. Wonderful to watch the sunset from the porch." *(Honey Scuterud)* "Delicious Triple Sec orange French toast." *(KK)*

Open All year.
Rooms 1 suite, 4 doubles—all with full private bath, fan, clock. Suite with TV/VCR.
Facilities Dining room, living room with TV/VCR, woodstove; library, wraparound porches. 216 acres with swings, lawn games, hiking, cross-country skiing, sledding, snowmobiling, woods, brooks, beaver ponds, apple orchards.

Near lake for water sports. Downhill, cross-country skiing, canoeing, bicycling nearby. Fine Arts show in Aug.

Location White Mts. 2½ hrs. N of Boston. 10 m S of Conway. From Rte. 16 N, go E in Chocorua on Rte. 113 (Deer Hill Rd.). Go through Silver Lake to Madison. At T-intersection, go right on E. Madison Rd. Go left on Pound Rd., & go 1 m to Maple Grove Rd. Go right to inn ½ m to inn on left.

Restrictions No smoking. Children over 4.

Credit cards Amex, MC, Visa.

Rates B&B, $150–165 suite (sleeps 4), $75–85 double, $65–85 single. Extra person, $15. 2-night minimum in foliage. 4th night free off-season.

MANCHESTER

Also recommended: About five miles west of Manchester, **The Bedford Village Inn** (2 Village Inn Lane, Bedford 03110; 603–472–2001 or 800–852–1166) was once a working farm, and is a now a luxury inn. The beautiful guest rooms are decorated with period furnishings, custom fabrics, Oriental carpets, and king-size four-poster beds. "The ample grounds are lovely with a gazebo and walking paths. My spacious room had a sitting area and marble bath. The tavern is a good choice for tasty dinners at moderate prices." *(Pam Phillips)* Rates range from $155–295; the restaurant serves three meals daily.

For an additional area entry, see following entry under **Milford**.

MILFORD

Information please: Just north of Milford is a small taste of the Alps. Charles and Anne Zahn, specializing in hiking, bicycling, and skiing tours of the European Alps, built an Austrian-style *gasthof* in 1992; Pat Berntson is the innkeeper. **Zahn's Alpine Guesthouse** (97 South Main Street, Route 13, P.O. Box 75, 03055; 603–673–2334 or 888–745–0051) offers eight guest rooms, each with a private bath, telephone, and TV. The chalet's *stube* is where guests gather in the evening, and again in the morning for a self-serve European-style breakfast of fruit, juice, muffins, toast, jam, honey, and cheese. The B&B double rate is $65. Comments?

The Ram in the Thicket ¢ 🏃 ✕   *Tel:* 603–654–6440
24 Maple Street, 03055

If you know the Bible, you'll remember the story of Abraham and the sacrifice of Isaac; Isaac's life was saved—and changed forever—when God sent a ram to take his place. When Andrew and Priscilla Tempelman left the Midwest in 1977, this turn-of-the-century mill owner's mansion became their personal "ram in the thicket," transforming their lives. Breakfast is served from 8–11 A.M. and includes fresh fruit, hot and cold cereals, homemade coffee cake, scones or muffins, boiled eggs, and yogurt. Dinner menus change frequently, but might include such entrées as pork tenderloin with bacon and brown sugar; lamb with cranberries, mushrooms, and Port; and ratatouille and noodles with an Asian accent.

"Sitting at the bar, listening to Andy's stories is most entertaining; he is a most engaging fellow. Priscilla's expertise in the kitchen is evident in the excellent food. Attention to detail and the ultimate satisfaction of their guests is the Tempelmans' goal." *(Terry Howes)* "Outstanding food, beautifully presented." *(Liz & David Wojiechowski)* "Quiet location on a peaceful lane at the top of a knoll. Housekeeping was unobtrusive but efficient. A rich and varied menu; Priscilla's food was marvelous and plentiful. Andrew was the perfect host." *(Melody Best)*

Open All year. Restaurant open Wed.–Sun., May–Oct. 31; open weekends Nov.–April.
Rooms 2 suites, 6 doubles—2 with full private bath; 6 with shared baths. All with clock, fan. 1 with fireplace. TV on request.
Facilities Restaurant, bar, breakfast room, sitting room with fireplace, TV/VCR, books, stereo; screened porch. 7 acres with swimming pool, lawn games.
Location SE NH. Eastern foothills of Monadnock Region. 20 min. NW of Nashua, SW of Manchester. Turn off Rte. 101 at signal light for Wilton Business District. Turn right on North River Rd. Turn left on Maple St. Inn is first house on the left.
Restrictions No smoking.
Credit cards Amex.
Rates B&B, $135 suite, $75 double with private bath, $60 double with shared bath, $60 single with private bath, $45 single with shared bath. Extra person, $10. Alc dinner, $20.
Extras Crib. Pets permitted.

MOULTONBORO

Olde Orchard Inn 🛉
Lee Road, RR 1, P.O. Box 256, 03254

Tel: 603–476–5004
800–598–5845
Fax: 603–476–5419
E-mail: innkeep1@aol.com
URL: http://www.oldeorchardinn.com

The earliest portion of the Olde Orchard Inn was built of handmade sun-dried bricks made from clay from an adjacent pasture, with the frame additions completed by 1812. It was restored as an inn in 1984; the decor includes antiques and reproductions, and most of the guest rooms have queen-size beds. Jim and Mary Senner purchased the inn in 1992, retiring from a world-wide career in the foreign service. In addition to putting down personal roots in New Hampshire, they've added a few to the farm, planting several hundred apple trees to the inn's orchards. Not surprisingly, apples are featured at breakfast; a recent menu included sweet cider, cranberry-apple pancakes with local maple syrup, and maple-glazed slab bacon.

"Tasteful country decor with hand-stenciled wall borders, quilts, antique beds with comfortable queen-size modern mattresses and big, fluffy comforters. Guests can feel at home next to the crackling fire as

331

they write their complimentary postcards to friends. The morning breakfast, served at two times for guests' convenience, is prepared from scratch, almost always with a homegrown apple side dish. I particularly enjoyed the light, delicious Belgian waffles and sausages. The gazebo is ideal for enjoying a cup of coffee, and the sauna and antiques shop in the adjacent barn are equally appealing." *(Mary Ellen Butkus)* "Peaceful country setting, lots to do nearby. The neighboring Woodshed Restaurant is excellent and convenient for dinner. After Mary's delicious breakfast we walked through the orchard and down the back roads, exploring this lovely area. Later, we relaxed with board games, videos, and books." *(Joanne and Dan Gingres)* "Rooms are attractive and comfortable, the food excellent, the hospitality superb." *(Suzanne Maybee)* "Friendly owners; delicious, imaginative breakfasts." *(W.J. Stenhouse)*

Open All year.
Rooms 1 cottage, 9 doubles—all with private bath and/or shower, clock/radio, TV, air-conditioning. 3 with wood-burning fireplace, whirlpool.
Facilities Dining room, family room with TV/VCR, books; porch; Barn with antique shop, sauna. 12 acres with gazebo, lawn games, pond, brook. 1 m to Lake Winnipesaukee for water sports; hiking, cross-country skiing nearby.
Location Central NH. Lakes District. 18 m N of Wolfeboro. 1 m from Rte. 25. In center of Moultonboro, go E on old Rte. 109. Take 1st right on Lee Rd. & continue ½ m to inn on right. From Wolfeboro turn left on Lee Rd. to inn on left.
Restrictions No smoking.
Credit cards Discover, MC, Visa.
Rates B&B, $60–125 double. Extra person, $25. 2-night minimum some weekends.
Extras Station pickups. Pets with prior approval in cottage. Cribs, babysitting.

NEW LONDON

In central New Hampshire, New London is convenient to ski areas in winter and many lovely New Hampshire lakes and golf courses in summer. It's also the home of Colby-Sawyer College, a group of Georgian-style buildings, set on the town green.

Also recommended: A Federal Colonial–style building dating back to 1792, **The New London Inn** (Main Street, P.O. Box 8, 03257; 603–526–2791 or 800–526–2791; www.newlondoninn.com) is set on the town green, where one can browse in the shops and walk to the London Barn Playhouse. Each of the inn's 27 rooms has a private bath, and many have sitting areas. B&B double rates include a buffet breakfast, and range from $110–140. "Attention to detail was everywhere from the charming guest rooms to the antiques in the public rooms to the tasteful Christmas decorations. Innkeepers Kimberley and Terance O'Mahoney, their children, and the staff were always available to help, but were never intrusive. Magical breakfasts appeared each morning. Warm and welcoming atmosphere." *(Dianne Muller)*

Owned by the Kidder family since it opened in 1897, **Twin Lakes Vil-**

lage (21 Twin Lake Villa Road, 03257; 603–526–6460) offers an old-fashioned summer getaway vacation. Accommodations are available in the main lodge as well as 17 cottages, and the weekly double rate of $700–850 (service additional) includes three meals daily, plus the use of all facilities. Situated on 200 acres of woods and fields on the shore of Little Lake Sunapee, the inn provides tennis courts, a nine-hole par-three golf course, row boats, sailboats, canoes and kayaks, plus a supervised children's playhouse from 9 A.M. to noon. "A great family place—like camp for the whole family. They even take dogs!" (*Jill Reeves*)

NORTH CONWAY

North Conway is an old mountain resort town, home of Mt. Cranmore, one of the country's first downhill ski areas. Located in the Mt. Washington Valley of the White Mountains, it's about 2½ hours north of Boston, and 1¼-hours' drive west of Portland, Maine. North Conway is right at the edge of the White Mountains National Forest; the area offers many opportunities for hiking, fishing, swimming, rafting, canoeing, hunting, golf, bicycling, and tennis in summer, along with concerts and summer stock theater, with a wide choice of cross-country and downhill ski areas in winter, plus outdoor ice-skating. The area has also become a haven for serious shoppers, with dozens of stores offering name-brand goods and apparel at tax-free discount prices. Even L.L. Bean has an outlet!

Worth noting: Traffic on Route 16 can be horrendous, especially in summer and fall. Ask your innkeeper for alternate route directions.

Reader tip: "We had an excellent, reasonably priced dinner at the Riverside Inn in Intervale; they serve on Fridays and Saturdays by reservation only." (*Jim & Mary White*)

For additional area entries, see listings under **Bartlett, Eaton Center, Jackson, Madison**, and **Snowville**, as well as **Fryeburg, Maine**.

The Buttonwood Inn ¢ **♦♦** **&.**
Mt. Surprise Road, P.O. Box 1817, 03860

Tel: 603–356–2625
800–258–2625
Fax: 603–356–3140
E-mail: button_w@moose.ncia.net
URL: http://www.buttonwoodinn.com

Tucked away on Mt. Surprise, a dead-end country road, it's hard to believe that the shops and restaurants of Route 16 are just two miles away from this quiet farmhouse-turned-inn. Purchased by Claudia and Peter Needham in 1993, the rates include a breakfast of juice, homemade breads—perhaps almond poppy seed muffins or low-fat cider-cranberry cake—plus such entrées as blueberry crumble French toast, ham and cheese strata, apple-cinnamon spiced waffles, or a sunrise puff with orange sauce. The guest rooms are bright and cheerful, with Waverly and Imperial fabrics on the valences and dust ruffles, handmade quilts, light-colored floral wallpapers, wide-board pine floors, custom-made Shaker-style furnishings and country antiques; most have queen-size beds. An upstairs sitting room was redone as an indoor garden room, complete with flowers stenciled as a garden all around the room and a ceiling that looks like the sky.

"Genuine, warm, funny, and hardworking innkeepers who take pride in their lovely inn. Peter's talents in the award-winning gardens and kitchen are matched only by Claudia's skill at decorating and putting guests at ease." (LDS, also Cecille Desroches) "Everything we could have wanted, including a dog to pet." (MNP) "Serene and soothing, secluded and private." (Kelly Timm) "A great night's sleep was followed by a wonderful breakfast of cornmeal waffles with homemade strawberry preserves." (Carol Montana) "Peter and Claudia's advice was always accurate and useful, from suggested hikes to the best restaurants in town. Terrific location removed from traffic yet just minutes from great hiking, skiing, and shopping. (David Miller & Jami Steinroeder) "Comfortable, high-quality mattresses; bed linens are beautifully coordinated with simple window treatments. Furnishings include locally hand-crafted pieces." (Jennifer Gray) "Wonderful mountain views; we even saw a bear wandering in the backyard. Peter is always sensitive to dietary needs when preparing his marvelous breakfasts." (Heather Hanks)

"I called to let them know I would be arriving later than planned; upon arrival, I found my bed turned down and hot tea waiting." (Melissa Wilbricht) "On the first floor is an intimate, Colonial-style parlor with a piano and selection of books, tapes, and CDs; the basement has an inviting common room with a large stone fireplace. In the morning, one is welcomed into a sunny, cheerful dining room with seating at individual tables." (Marilyn Bodnar) "The Needhams have a sweet black Lab named Emily, and two well-behaved girls who were friendly but never bothersome." (Sharyn-Michelle Smith) "Fully endorse existing entry." (Jim & Mary White)

Open All year, except Christmas Day.

Rooms 2 suites, 10 doubles—all with private bath and/or shower, telephone, clock, fan, individual thermostats. 2 with gas fireplace, 1 with Jacuzzi. Most with ceiling fan, 1 with air-conditioning.

Facilities Dining room, living room with piano, wood stove, books, stereo; sitting room with books; common room with TV/VCR, fireplace, guest refrigerator; gift shop; porch. 5 acres with gardens, lawn games, swing set, swimming pool, 65 km cross-country ski trails from door.

Location 2 m NE of village. Take Rte. 16 N to N. Conway. From traffic light in village turn right on Kearsarge St. Bear left at top of hill onto Kearsarge Rd. and go 1½ m to stop sign. Go straight through, ½ m further to inn, and watch for sign. Ask for alternative summer directions via Hwy. 112, Rte. 302, Bear Notch Rd. & Hurricane Mt. Rd. to avoid Rte. 16 traffic.

Restrictions No smoking. No children under 6.

Credit cards Amex, Discover, MC, Visa.

Rates B&B, $85–175 double, $75–165 single. Extra person, $25. Family rates. 2–3 night winter weekend/holiday minimum. Downhill ski packages. Midweek rates.

Extras Wheelchair access; 1 room fully equipped.

NORTH WOODSTOCK/LINCOLN

North Woodstock is located in the White Mountains, 60 miles north of Concord, New Hampshire, and 120 miles north of Boston. Neighboring Lincoln is home to Loon Mountain ski area.

Reader tips: "North Woodstock may be the most optimally located town in all the White Mountains. Along with its neighbor Lincoln (they're really like one town), it has a lot to offer, without the insane traffic and crass commercialism of North Conway. If shop you must, it's only a 37-mile drive down the beautiful Kancamagus Highway to the Route 16 outlets. Moreover, it's centrally located to many other White Mountain attractions." *(Brad Wheeler, also EK)*

Wilderness Inn ¢ 👫
Routes 3 & 112, RFD 1, P.O. Box 69, 03262

Tel: 603–745–3890
800–200–WILD
Fax: 603–745–6367
E-mail: wildernessinn@juno.com
URL: http://www.musar.com/wildernessinn/

Built by a local lumber baron in 1912, the Wilderness Inn has an unusual architectural design described by owners Michael and Rosanna Yarnell as "overgrown Germanic cottage–style." Breakfast is served from 7:30–10 A.M. at separate tables, and includes fresh fruit and juice, home-baked muffins, tea or the inn's blend of French Roast and Colombian coffees, plus an extensive list of entrées. Guests have their choice of such favorites as cranberry-walnut pancakes made with oatmeal, wheat germ, and yogurt; crêpes with apple sauce and sour cream; and omelets with mushrooms and Brie; chef Michael will be happy to prepare teddy bear pancakes or French toast for the kids. Rates also include afternoon tea, cider, or lemonade.

"At night, all we heard was the sound of the rushing Lost River. Wonderful breakfast pancakes, plus pineapple-coconut muffins. The Yarnell family lives in a house they've built next door, but are available by phone. Rosanna helpfully suggested a tour of Lost River's gorges and caves, plus a secret local swimming hole known as the Ladies' Bathtub." *(BNS)* "Our suite had a huge private bath, an enclosed porch, a large bedroom with a sitting area, and a small room with bunk beds—perfect for kids. Excellent location, close to skiing." *(MP)* "The inn's strongest attributes are Rosanna's efficient, polite service and Michael's delicious breakfasts." *(Brad Wheeler)* "Your description is accurate. The hosts are hospitable, the food delicious, rooms plain and simple—appropriate for a ski lodge." *(Judy & Russ Rosen)* "Our room was spacious, clean, and comfortable, with exceptional breakfasts. We enjoyed the half-mile walk to town, past shops and restaurants." *(Michael & Dina Miller)*

Open All year.
Rooms 2 suites, 5 doubles, 1 cottage—6 with private bath and/or shower, 2 with maximum of 4 sharing bath. All with fan, 2 with desk. Cottage with gas fireplace, TV, deck.

Facilities Dining room, living room with fireplace, piano, TV, books, stereo. Enclosed porch, deck. Laundry facilities. On Lost River for swimming, fishing. Downhill skiing 3 m (Loon Mt.) and 10 m (Cannon Mt.); cross-country skiing from doorstep.

Location White Mts. 120 m N of Boston, 60 m N of Concord. In center of town. From Rte. 93, take Exit 32 to Rte. 112. From Rte. 91, take Exit 17 to Rte. 302 to Rte. 112. Inn is at the intersection of Rtes. 3 & 112.

Restrictions No smoking in public areas.

Credit cards Amex, MC, Visa.

Rates B&B, $70–115 cottage, $60–105 suite, $40–95 double, $35–85 single. Extra person, $10–15. No charge for children under 6. 2–3 night holiday minimum.

Extras Bus station pickup. Crib, babysitting. French, Italian, Bengali, Amharic spoken.

PETERBOROUGH

Apple Gate B&B ¢   *Tel: 603–924–6543*
199 Upland Farm Road & Route 123S, 03458

Crisp apples and New England go together as naturally as sleigh bells and snow. When Ken and Dianne Legenhausen bought this 1832 farmhouse set amid apple orchards, and converted it into a B&B in 1990, Apple Gate was the fitting name they choose. Of course, guest rooms are named for apples, and are simply decorated with charming Colonial-style furnishings. Breakfast menus change daily, but always include apples; a recent menu contained baked apples, lemon poppy seed muffins, and spinach soufflé with English muffins.

"A classic New England bed and breakfast—small and homey, with innkeepers who personify the best of old-fashioned innkeeping traditions. Dianne and Ken are gracious and considerate hosts, offering helpful suggestions for dinner and area activities. Dianne's breakfasts were delicious and well-prepared, served at a common table in a cozy dining room. We enjoyed the quiet location on a country road, next to an apple orchard, just a couple miles outside the lovely village of Peterborough." *(John Felton)*

"Quiet country setting; inviting and well-maintained, inside and out. Friendly, welcoming innkeepers." *(SWS)* "Dianne was kind enough to share a favorite recipe." *(Joe & Elizabeth Cavanaugh)* "Beautiful gardens. The innkeepers went out of their way to help me contact a long-lost cousin." *(Robert Cashiou)* "Ken and Dianne immediately made me feel like family. Breakfasts are made to order, and Dianne is always happy to accommodate special dietary needs. Books, clippings, maps, and brochures, menus, and restaurant recommendations are available to assist guests with their travel plans." *(Kathleen Olson)* "Our room had twin beds with coordinated linens and ample magazines and books. Delightful candlelight breakfast; the table was beautifully set with red dishes and wooden-apples napkin rings. The food was delicious, ample, and well-served." *(Grace Anastasia)* "Surrounded by flowering shrubs and apples trees in full bloom. At breakfast, our hosts encouraged conversation among the guests, yet were not intrusive." *(Ann &*

Ed Dibble) "Decorated with antiques and traditional furniture, with top-of-the-line bedding. Our large corner room had a queen-size bed and views of fields, orchards, and forests. The breakfast consisted of apple pancakes and sausage, homemade muffins and quiche. Dianne and Ken clearly enjoy their work; although they make it look easy, no detail was overlooked. Peterborough served as the model for Thornton Wilder's famous play, *Our Town,* and also has a famous artists' colony." *(William Burggraf)*

Open All year.
Rooms 3 doubles, 1 single—all with private bath and/or shower, radio, fan. Some with desk.
Facilities Dining room with fireplace; living room with fireplace, stereo; library with piano, TV, books; porch. 3 acres with garden, apple orchard. Downhill, cross-country skiing nearby.
Location S central NH. Monadnock Region. 90 m NW of Boston. 2 m from town. From intersection of Rtes. 202 & 101, proceed E on Rte. 101 for 1 m. Turn right at blinking light (Rte. 123 S) & go 1.4 m to inn on right.
Restrictions No smoking. No children under 12.
Credit cards MC, Visa.
Rates B&B, $65–80 double, $60–75 single. 2-night weekend minimum in season.

PORTSMOUTH

In the pell-mell rush to Maine, many travelers zoom through New Hampshire's "don't blink or you'll miss it" seventeen-mile coastline with nary a second glance. Although it's just an hour north of Boston, those in the know will plan an overnight in Portsmouth, a historic town founded in 1623. Made wealthy in the 19th century as a shipbuilding seaport, the town has much to offer, including Strawbery Banke (the town's original name), a restoration of the original waterfront buildings (open May 1–October 31); several historic buildings turned museum; and Prescott Park, home to lovely gardens, various festivals, and a folk art museum. To placate fidgety children, we'd suggest a steamship cruise of this working harbor, and a visit to the local children's museum. For ocean swimming, beaches can be found at two nearby state parks. For details, contact the Chamber of Commerce (500 Market Street, P.O. Box 239; 603–436–1118).

Reader tip: "We enjoyed dinner at Molly Malone's and lunch at the Press Room. One of Portsmouth's best-kept secrets is the one-man show at the Player's Ring." *(Madeleine Lessard)*

Information please: A converted brick brewery, **The Bow Street Inn** (121 Bow Street, 03801; 603–431–7760) is set on the Piscataqua River, above the Seacoast Repertory Theatre. The modest decor in each of the ten second-floor guest rooms is simple country Victorian, with flowered comforters, matching curtains, fabric-covered tables, and fresh flowers. The Penthouse, at the top of the inn, has harbor views from its windows and the wraparound deck. The lower level has a bedroom, living room, and kitchen, while the skylit upper level can be used as a living room or second bedroom. Double rates range from $114–135 and include continental breakfast.

Two blocks from Market Square, **The Inn at Strawbery Banke** (314 Court Street, 03801; 603–436–7242 or 800–428–3933) is an 1800s Colonial-style inn with seven guest rooms. Proprietor Sarah Glover O'Donnell serves a breakfast of fruit, juices, homemade breads and muffins, cereals, crêpes or perhaps pancakes, and ham, bacon, or sausage. Double rates range from $75–110. "Warm hospitality, clean rooms, beautiful breakfast room, wonderful innkeeper and daughter." *(Madeleine Lessard)*

Jane and Paul Harnden, longtime owners of the **Martin Hill Inn** (404 Islington Street, 03801; 603–436–2287) since 1983, have restored the two buildings that make up their historic inn; the Main House, built in 1820, and the Guest House, dating to 1850. Each of the seven beautifully decorated and immaculate guest rooms has a sitting area (some quite compact) and a canopy, four-poster, brass or iron bed. A typical breakfast includes orange juice, sautéed bananas, French toast with almonds and Canadian ham, and good, strong coffee. The location is convenient—about a 15-minutes' walk from the center of town. Double B&B rates range from $85–115. Guests are delighted with the inn's delicious breakfasts and convenient location. Although there's no living room, guests can relax in the lovely garden. "Immaculate. At the sociable breakfast, guests chat and the innkeepers make sure you have all you need in the way of directions and information." *(Donald Brown & Elaine Smith)*

Business travelers are especially pleased with the atmosphere and amenities at the **Sise Inn** (40 Court Street, 03801; 603–433–1200 or 800–267–0525). The inn dates back to 1881, and connects the original Queen Anne Victorian structure with a modern addition that houses the majority of this small hotel's 34 guest rooms. Rooms are decorated in period with antiques and reproductions, and rates include a buffet breakfast of baked goods, fruit, cereals, granola, and juice; a toaster and microwave are available as well as snacks and drinks. B&B double rates range from $89–175. "The suites are especially nice with sitting rooms, French doors to the bedrooms and whirlpool baths." *(Pam Phillips)*

Built between 1840 and 1880 as part of a major seaside resort colony, **Rock Ledge Manor** (1413 Ocean Boulevard, Rye, 03870; 603–431–1413) is just a few miles from Portsmouth. It has four guest rooms, each with ocean views. Owners Sandi and Stan Smith provide a hearty breakfast of crêpes or perhaps omelets and home-baked sweet rolls. The wraparound porch looks out on the Atlantic, just across the street. Double rates range from $80–100. Rye is located five miles south of Portsmouth. "Friendly owners, lovely water views, adequate accommodations." *(RC)*

For additional area inns, see listings for the **Gundalow Inn**, a tenminute walk across the river in **Kittery, Maine**, plus **Durham, Exeter**, and **South Hampton, New Hampshire**, as well as **Newburyport, Massachusetts**.

SNOWVILLE

Snowville Inn ✕   *Tel:* 603–447–2818
Stuart Road, P.O. Box 68, 03832   800–447–4345
                                                Fax: 603–447–5268
                                    E-mail: snowville@nci.com
                          URL: http://www.snowvillageinn.com

The Snowvillage Inn was built as a summer estate in 1916 and offers spectacular views of the White Mountains from its quiet end-of-the-road location. It's been owned since 1994 by experienced innkeeper Kevin Flynn. The most recent addition to the inn is a barn-style annex, the Chimney House, with a two-story atrium entrance, an attractive guest lounge with a fireplace, and four guest rooms with white walls, brick corner fireplaces, scrubbed pine woodwork and floors accented with simple antiques, quilts, and Oriental or dhurrie rugs; bathrooms are generously sized, with natural pine-paneled walls and good lighting. The pine-paneled rooms in the original barn have simple but tasteful decor; rooms in the main inn, each named after a writer, are comfortable and pleasantly decorated; bathrooms are small but functional. A favorite is the Robert Frost Room; its twelve windows afford spectacular White Mountain views. A flower cutting garden is available to guests, who can fill the antique Mason jars in their rooms with a bouquet of their own chosing.

The breakfast menu changes daily, but always includes fresh fruit and juice, cereal and muffins, plus such choices as eggs Benedict or blueberry pancakes; it is served from 8–9:30 A.M. The dinner menu features fresh herbs and berries from local farms, and entrées such as grilled shrimp with a gingered tomato sauce, spinach stuffed lamb, and roast duck with blackberries, accompanied by home-baked rolls, and desserts. The dark-beamed living room has plenty of comfortable couches and chairs, often occupied by guests reading one of the inn's hundreds of books.

"The dining room has richly patterned valances at the large windows, bright brass chandeliers, and crisp white and burgundy table linens. Small pottery pitchers filled with flowers from the inn's glorious perennial gardens and Depression glass sugar bowls add just the right touch of whimsy at each table. The bar and living room have hunter green fabrics, Oriental rugs, and intimate seating areas, complete with comfy sofas, antique and reproduction armchairs. Large windows open onto the screened porch, comfortably arranged with white wicker chairs and sofas, a perfect spot for watching the sunset illuminate Mt. Washington in the distance. Our Chimney House Room had a delightfully firm queen-size canopy bed, quality linens, thick towels, and coordinating fabrics for the window treatments, the two upholstered chairs, and the bedspread. Dinner was delicious and flavorful, with an eggplant-tomato soup, a salad topped with grilled portabello mushroom in a cumin-orange vinaigrette, and spicy blackberry Chambord roast duck. Attention to detail included the proper serving of my tea in a china teapot. The location is convenient for hiking, or shopping in the busy outlets and shops of North Conway, and the inn is a quiet place to return." *(Nancy Barker)*

"Spectacular views of Mount Washington. Friendly, helpful staff." *(Richard Harrison)* "Kevin Flynn went out of his way to make sure our stay was enjoyable. Cross-country trails right outside the inn." *(Tim & Karen Chilone)* "In the shadow of Foss Mountain, where blueberries abound in late summer and the snow piles high in the winter, is serene Snowville. Host Kevin and his young daughters Caitlin and Maggie are warm and friendly, as are the staff. Guests who enjoy walking, hiking, or cross-country skiing will find well-groomed trails immediately adjacent to the inn. Crystal Lake, perfect for a refreshing swim, is just a mile down the hill. The long porch with its relaxing rockers and conversational groupings of chairs and settees, provides an ideal position to view the panoramic White Mountains. To sit quietly at sunset, enjoying a glass of wine as the light on the mountains flushes pink, then orange, and finally slides into darkness is to experience complete relaxation." *(Judith Borden)* "Great innkeeper with a sense of style, open to new ideas. Wonderful mountain views, and beautiful gardens." *(LDS)* "Comfortable queen-size bed; good reading lights; exceptional bed linens and towels. Careful consideration of guests' needs; excellent food." *(Elizabeth Holmes-Rosenberg)*

Open All year.

Rooms 18 doubles—all with private bath and/or shower, desk, fan. 6 rooms in inn, 4 with fireplace in Chimney House, 8 in converted barn.

Facilities Dining room, living room with fireplace, games; bar, screened porch. 10 acres with gardens, sauna, sleds, cross-country skiing with rentals, lessons, trails. Summer/fall: monthly llama hikes with picnic lunch; spring: music, wildflower weekends; winter: full moon cross-country skiing; cooking classes. 1 m to lake swimming, ice-skating. 6 m to downhill skiing.

Location NE NH, White Mts. 60 m W of Portland, 120 m N of Boston, 315 m N of NYC. 7 m from town. Take Rte. 16 or 25 to Rte. 153. Turn right in village at Snowville sign to inn.

Restrictions No smoking. Children over 6.

Credit cards Amex, DC, Discover, MC, Visa.

Rates B&B, $79–189 double, $59–169 single. Extra person, $30–45. Children's rates. Midweek rates. 2-night weekend minimum. MAP rates available.

SOUTH HAMPTON

The Inn at Kinney Hill 🏃‍♀️
96 Woodman Road, 03827

Tel: 603–394–0200
888–OUR–HILL
Fax: 603–394–0200
E-mail: dsoconnor@aol.com

A beautiful hilltop home built in 1979, the Inn at Kinney Hill offers magnificent views of the New Hampshire countryside and distant coast. Renovated as a B&B in 1997, its location makes it an ideal base for touring historic villages and seacoast towns from Newburyport to

Portsmouth. The extensive grounds offer a heated indoor pool and ten-person hot tub, plus a working equestrian facility. The guest rooms are decorated with antiques and designer fabrics, and have either a queen- or king-size bed. Owners Dotti Ann and George O'Connor serve breakfast in the formal dining room; afternoon tea is available in the library or drawing room and includes tempting sandwiches, scones, and cookies. Though a continental buffet breakfast is available for early risers, it's worth waiting for the gourmet selections offered at 9:30 A.M., from freshly squeezed orange juice to strawberry soup and herbed omelets with fresh salsa and roasted baby potatoes.

"Although contemporary in architecture, the inn feels like an elegant country manor home. The views are outstanding; on extremely clear days, you can actually see the coast. Dotti welcomed us to Kinney Hill, and thoughtfully asked whether we wanted to see our room first or take a tour of the house. Comfortable furnishings in the library include a leather sofa and side arm chairs, with good lighting for reading. The dining room had a large Chippendale-style table with seating for eight, a sideboard, and china cabinet. The drawing room had many family photos, upholstered chairs, and a grand piano. All have lots of large windows, overlooking the fields and horse corrals. Handsome chestnut and walnut wood trim. Downstairs is a TV room as well as exercise equipment, an indoor heated pool, and a spa hot tub.

"The Devon Room has a beautiful carved walnut queen-size bed, fine linens, down pillows and down comforter, end tables with reading lamps, a dresser, a small boudoir chair, and a closet. Hypo-allergenic pillows are offered. The color scheme is a restful hunter green, taupe, and white. The remodeled bath has a cast-iron slipper tub, an oversize shower, marble-tile floor, pedestal sink, and skylight windows. Good quality thick towels, bath robes, and Gilchrist & Soames almond soaps, shampoos, conditioners, and lotions are provided. Another lovely room has a four-poster draped canopy bed with an extremely large walk-in closet. All the bedrooms have fresh flowers, reading material and a bottle of sherry. Truffles and a bottle of Pellegrino water were included with the evening turndown. Dotti served delightful afternoon tea in the library with finger sandwiches, scones, and sweets. The delicious breakfast included fresh-squeezed orange juice, broiled grapefruit with brown sugar and granola, freshly made herb and feta omelets accented with fresh fruit and flowers, as well as a basket of tea bread and English muffins." *(Rose Ciccone)* "Easy access to lovely coastal towns with quaint shops and great antiquing. Spacious rooms with commodious baths—all very comfortable and nicely decorated. Best of all are the innkeepers themselves—their constant attention to detail and their desire to make guests feel comfortable without being fussy. Breakfasts uncommonly varied, of excellent quality, lovingly prepared and delicious." *(Marilyn & John Morrow)*

Open May 1–Nov. 1.

Rooms 1 suite, 3 doubles—all with full private bath and/or shower; 1 with whirlpool tub. All with radio, clock, fan; 1 with desk.

Facilities Dining room with fireplace, living room with piano, library with fireplace, exercise room, game room with TV/VCR, billiard room, guest refrigerator. 120 acres with heated indoor swimming pool, hot tub, equestrian facility with indoor riding rink, gazebo, hiking/riding trails, bird-watching. Golf, boating, fishing nearby.

Location SE NH. 38 m N of Boston, 18 m S of Portsmouth, 6 m NW of Newburyport. From Boston, take I-95 N to Exit 58B, Amesbury (Rte. 110). Go right at 1st light onto Elm St. toward Amesbury Center. Go right onto Rte. 150 at circle. Bear left at war memorial onto S. Hampton Rd. Go right onto Woodman Rd. Go 0.7 m to Kinney Hill Farm driveway on left. From NY/CT area, take I-91 N to I-84 E to I-90 E (Mass. Pike) to I-290 E to I-495 N to Exit 54 (Amesbury). Go right at exit onto Rte. 150 towards Amesbury. Take 2nd right out of circle in Amesbury Center onto Rte. 150 and follow as above.

Restrictions No smoking. "Well-behaved children of all ages."

Credit cards Amex, Discover, MC, Visa.

Rates B&B, $160 suite; $95–130 double. Extra person, $20. 15% service. 2-night holiday weekend minimum. Prix fixe dinner by prior reservation, $65. Afternoon tea, $15 (free to overnight guests).

Extras French spoken. Crib. Horses stabled (by reservation), $35 nightly.

TAMWORTH

The Tamworth Inn ✕ ♦   *Tel:* 603–323–7721
Main Street, 03886   800–NH2–RELAX
                                        Fax: 603–323–2026
                      E-mail: tamworth@nxi.com
                      URL: http://www.tamworth.com

Tamworth is a quiet little town, set halfway between the White Mountains to the north, and the Lakes Region to the south; down the street is the country's oldest summer stock theater. Built in 1833, the inn was purchased by Phil and Kathy Bender in 1988. Guest rooms are decorated with country wallpapers, handmade quilts, and many antiques; the Benders have gone beyond cosmetics to comfort, investing in new hot-water heaters and plumbing, and making sure each room has good reading lights. Breakfast changes daily but might consist of French toast, eggs, and homebaked breads and muffins. A typical dinner might include smoked trout with horse radish sauce; green salad; pork roasted with garlic and rosemary; and for dessert, cream puffs filled with vanilla ice cream, topped with hot fudge sauce; a lighter menu is offered in the pub.

"Just as delightful in winter as summer. Tamworth was a winter wonderland, with cross-country skiing from the front door, plus lots of helpful maps in the living room, ice-skating minutes away, and a cozy fireside welcome at the end of the day. Delightful New Year's Eve celebration, too. We had dinner on the enclosed porch, and enjoyed good food with excellent service. Kathy and Phil are wonderful innkeepers, always responsive to guests' needs; this was clear from our own experience, as well as the many comments from returning guests in the guest diaries. The staff is well-trained and always helpful with restaurant recommendations. A most peaceful village; the surrounding area offers much to see and do." *(Sally Ducot)* "The inn is painted gray, with red shutters, and is across the street from a church built in the early 19th century, with a beautiful steeple and weather vane, bordered by farmland. The breakfast was excellent and the dining room decor most inviting." *(Michael Stulbarg)* "A charming inn, with comfortable and appealing guest rooms and ample common areas. Our seven-year-old granddaughter loved this inn, because of its four cats. A thoughtful touch was the dinner menu, mailed with our confirmation." *(Ginny Watkins)*

Open Closed April. Restaurant closed Mon., Tues. in winter; Mon. in summer.
Rooms 7 suites, 9 doubles—all with private bath and/or shower, ceiling fan. Some with air-conditioning.
Facilities Restaurant, pub with fireplace, living room with fireplace, TV; library with game table and fireplace; screened porch. 3 acres with gazebo, trout stream, swimming pool, cross-country skiing. Swimming, fishing, boating, golf, downhill skiing, summer theater nearby.
Location Lakes Region. 2 hrs. N of Boston. Take Rte. 16 to Chocorua; go W on Rte. 113 to inn in center of Tamworth. From Rte. 25, take Rte. 113 N to Tamworth.
Restrictions Smoking limited.
Credit cards MC, Visa.
Rates B&B, $115–130 suite, $95–115 double. Extra person, $25. MAP, $140–160 suite, $120–140 double. 15% service. 2–3 night minimum holiday weekends. Alc dinner, $16. 3-night inn-to-inn bike tours, $249 per person.
Extras Station pickups. Babysitting. Pets permitted.

WAKEFIELD

Wakefield Inn ¢   *Tel:* 603–522–8272
2723 Wakefield Road, Wakefield Corner, 03872   800–245–0841
                     E-mail: lsisson@worldpath.net
             URL: http://www.nettx.com/wakefieldinn

The first visitors to the Wakefield Inn, built in 1803, arrived by stagecoach; the coach would pull up to the front door and the passengers would disembark while their luggage was handed up to the second floor, through a door still visible today over the porch roof. A later visitor to the inn was the poet John Greenleaf Whittier. Today's guests are welcomed by Lou and Harry Sisson, who invite you to head up the spiral staircase to one of their country-comfortable guest rooms, decorated with ruffled curtains, small-print wallpaper, quilts, and plants. At the center of the large common area is a three-sided fireplace; the windows have Indian shutters and many have the original panes. The inn is in a historic district of 28 buildings; ask for the inn's walking tour brochure, which tells what life was like in the early 1800s.

"One of the many high spots of this charmingly restored Colonial house is its three-story free-standing circular staircase. Guest rooms are delightfully decorated, thoughtfully appointed, and scrupulously maintained. Mrs. Sisson's hand-crafted quilts add to the warm and hospitable ambience of the public rooms. Innkeepers were attentive, never insistent. Wakefield offers many historic buildings, including a charming little library." *(Peter Sandberg)* "Generous, delicious, filling breakfast." *(Patricia Poole)* "In the historic center of town, surrounded by picturesque homes, churches, and the town hall. Beds are covered with quilts made by Lou, who also teaches the craft. The dining room overlooks the landscaped, well-maintained garden with flowers and birdfeeders. Lou and Harry made us feel right at home." *(Maude Mosher)* "The breakfast menu includes home-baked bread, muffins, or coffee cake. The sitting room provides visitors with the chance to chat with the other guests. The inn is spotless; towels are replenished daily. The owners are friendly and eager to offer suggestions to visitors." *(Alice Eckardt)*

Open All year.

Rooms 7 doubles—all with private bath and/or shower, ceiling fan. Some with desk.

Facilities Living room with fireplace, wraparound porch with rockers. 6 acres with patio. Swimming, fishing, hiking, golf, cross-country skiing nearby. 20 min. to Lake Winnipesaukee.

Location SE NH. Approx. 12 m E of Wolfeboro. Take Spaulding Tpke./Rte. 16 N. Watch for inn sign; go right on Wakefield Rd.

Restrictions No smoking in bedrooms. Children over 10.

Credit cards MC, Visa.

Rates B&B, $70–75 double, $55 single. Service additional. Extra person, $20. Mid-week, seasonal weekend packages. Mystery, quilting, golf packages.

WALPOLE

For an additional entry, see **Charlestown**, approximately 10 miles north.

The Josiah Bellows House ¢
Old North Main Street, 03608

Tel: 603–756–4250
800–358–6302
Fax: 603–445–1973
E-mail: bhbakery@sover.net

One look at this handsome Federal home, dating back to 1813, with 10-foot ceilings and extravagantly large windows for the period, will tell you that Josiah Bellows, its builder and first owner, was a proud and wealthy man. If he were still around today, Mr. Bellows would be pleased with the beautiful way in which his home has been restored by innkeepers Lois Ford and Lou Ciercielli. The decor is eclectic but elegant, effectively combining Colonial and Victorian motifs with Oriental carpets and brass chandeliers. Breakfast typically includes fresh berries and homemade breads and muffins served with bacon and eggs or pancakes and real maple syrup.

"Comfortable yet beautifully furnished, with excellent full breakfasts. The innkeepers are friendly, helpful, delightfully unconventional, and unobtrusive. Walpole sits on the Connecticut River and is a lovely town with beautifully maintained historic houses." *(Margaret & Barry Fogel, also Ron Berman & Sybil Marcus)* "Lou and Lois have lots of energy, coupled with great senses of humor. We spent hours with them at the breakfast table, enjoying their company and indulging in Lois's fabulous baked goods." *(Dana Miller)* "The bed was turned down at night, and a plate of delicious cookies awaited me." *(Rosemarie Shaughnessy)* "Ample common areas for relaxing; Lois's cookies; the beautifully decorated, quiet, and spotlessly clean guest rooms." *(Mary Now & Al Korostynski)*

Open All year.
Rooms 4 doubles—all with private bath, radio, desk.
Facilities Dining room with fireplace, parlor, 2 living rooms with library, TV, piano, porch. 5 acres with gardens. Hiking, golf, tennis, canoeing, fishing, cross-country and downhill skiing nearby.
Location SW NH. On CT River, just S Bellows Falls, VT. 23 m N of Brattleboro, 17 NW of Keene. From I-91, take Exit 5, cross river to Walpole. Go N on Old N. Main St. Inn is 6th house on right heading from the intersection of Old N. Main and Turnpike Sts. Walking distance to village.
Restrictions No smoking, children, or pets.
Credit cards MC, Visa.
Rates B&B, $75 double, including tax.
Extras Airport/station pickups.

WEARE

The Weare-House B&B 🛉 ¢   *Tel:* 603–529–2660
76 Quaker Street, 03281   *E-mail:* Cgold@empire.net

So where is Weare? Well, it's where your children and pets are welcome. It's where you'll find a handsome country 1819 farmhouse, with wide-plank pine floors, gunstock beams, antique furnishings, and beds with goosedown comforters. And it's where you'll find innkeepers Ellen and Curt Goldsberry, in the home they restored in 1993, along with their two young sons Nathan and Jacob, and assorted dogs, horses, miniature donkeys, and hens. Last but not least, it's where you discover nearby lakes and mountains for water sports, hiking, and skiing. Breakfast is served from 8–9:30 A.M. at the dining room table, including such entrées as buttermilk pancakes, French toast, or quiche, accompanied by freshly ground coffee, a large selection of teas, home-baked goods, and fresh fruit; eggs come fresh from the hen house. Dietary restrictions are accommodated with advance notice.

"Large barn, beautiful setting. Rooms have genuine Colonial charm, with simple country antiques." *(LDS)* "Peaceful and affordable; the Goldsberrys are charming, caring, not overbearing. A perfect place for a family or a single traveler. Hosts Ellen and Curt and their two sons are charming." *(Jude Ward)* "Wholesome, homemade breakfast ample in quantity and variety; charming, Colonial decor; friendly owners." *(Janet King)* "Excellent housekeeping and breakfasts; accommodating, pleasant hosts." *(Janet Maleski)*

Open All year.
Rooms 4 doubles—2 with full private bath and/or shower, 2 with maximum of 4 people sharing bath. 4 with fan.

Facilities Dining room, living room with fireplace, stereo, books, porch. 12 acres with tire swing. 2 m from Lake Horace for swimming, boating. 8 m from downhill skiing.

Location W central NH, approx. 20 min. from Concord & Manchester. 18 m SW of Concord. 1 m from town. From Boston: Take I-93 N to 293 N/101 W (in Manchester, NH). Follow 101 W for 5 m until it intersects with 114 N. Follow 114 N for approx. 18 m through Goffstown to Weare. After flashing light, watch for "Welcome to Weare, NH" sign on right. Take next left onto Quaker St. to inn .4 m on right. From Hartford, CT, take I-91 to Brattleboro, VT. Take exit for Rte. 9 E to Keene, NH. Follow Rte. 9 to Henniker. From Henniker, take Rte. 114 S for approx. 8 m. Watch for Weare Animal Hospital on right & go right on Quaker St. to inn is .4 m on right.

Restrictions No smoking.

Credit cards MC, Visa.

Rates B&B, $60–75 double/single. Extra person, $15.

Extras Crib. Pets welcome by reservation; not permitted in guest rooms; have their own room downstairs; $5 daily per pet.

Free copy of INNroads newsletter

Want to stay up-to-date on our latest finds? Send a business-size, self-addressed, stamped envelope with 55 cents postage and we'll send you the latest issue, *free!* While you're at it, why not enclose a report on any inns you've recently visited? Use the forms at the back of the book or your own stationery.

We Want to Hear from You!

As you know, this book is effective only with your help. We really need to know about your experiences and discoveries. If you stayed at an inn or hotel listed here, we want to know how it was. Did it live up to our description? Exceed it? Was it what you expected? Did you like it? Were you disappointed? Delighted? Have you discovered new establishments that we should add to the next edition?

Tear out one of the report forms at the back of this book (or use your own stationery if you prefer) and write today. *Even if you write only "Fully endorse existing entry" you will have been most helpful.*
Thank You!

Rhode Island

Castle Hill Inn & Resort

Rhode Island is the country's smallest state, squeezed in by Connecticut to the west and Massachusetts to the north and east. It does, however, offer many attractive shore resorts, and two well-known islands, Newport and Block Island—the former accessible by a bridge, the latter by ferry or airplane. Providence, Rhode Island's capital, is home to many colleges and universities, most notably Brown.

BLOCK ISLAND

Only 3 miles wide and 7 miles long, Block Island is 140 miles northeast of New York City, and 120 miles southwest of Boston. It's 14 miles east of Montauk Point, NY, and just about the same distance from Point Judith, RI. When making reservations ask the innkeeper for ferry information, or call 401–783–4613 or 800–MONTAUK; from Montauk, call 516–668–5700. Ferries depart from Point Judith year-round (the closest point), and seasonally from Providence, Newport, Montauk, and from New London, Connecticut. The ride can be rough, so stock up on Dramamine. Limited air service is also available; call New England Airlines at 401–596–2460 or 800–243–2460 for information on flights from Westerly to Block Island.

Most innkeepers recommend leaving your car on the mainland, but if you must bring your car on the ferry, make reservations months ahead for peak-season crossings. Many innkeepers will pick you up and return you to the ferry for free; taxis are also available, and most people rent bicycles or mopeds. High season runs from around Memorial Day through Columbus Day or the end of October. Expect two- to four-day weekend minimums in season; rates drop *substantially* off-season, and the general atmosphere is calmer and more relaxed.

347

Although Block Island was first settled in 1661, most development took place in the late 19th century, giving the island its characteristic Victorian appearance. Points of interest include "The Maze" on the bluffs overlooking Clay Head, and the Southeast Lighthouse at Mohegan Bluffs. Visitors spend most of their time exploring the many beaches and ponds, plus the 25 miles of walking trails; there are few tennis courts and no golf courses.

Reader tips: "This little island can be a mob scene on summer weekends; visit midweek or in May or October to avoid the noisy hordes of mad motorbikers." *(MW)* And: "We ate well at the Mohegan Cafe and Dead Eye Dick's." *(Gary Stuart)*

The Atlantic Inn ⵌ ✕ 🛪
P.O. Box 1788, High Street, 02807

Tel: 401–466–5883
800–224–7422
Fax: 401–466–5678
E-mail: AtlanticInn@Biri.com

Set atop a hill with commanding views of Old Harbor, the Atlantic Inn has been welcoming guests since its construction in 1879. Purchased in 1994 by Rhode Island natives Brad and Anne Marthens, the inn epitomizes Victorian summer hotel style; the Marthenses' renovations combine modern comfort with period decor. The playhouse replica of the inn is a favorite with families; parents can watch their children having fun from the wraparound veranda. Breakfast, served buffet-style from 8–10 A.M., features freshly baked pastries, fruit, homemade granola, cereals, juices, and a selection of coffees and teas. The inn's restaurant is considered one of the best on Block Island, highlighted by fresh seafood, accented with herbs and vegetables from the inn's garden; its wine cellar is also highly regarded. Dinner one evening might start with such choices as vegetable ravioli with roasted onion sauce or smoked chicken with goat cheese; followed by such entrées as beef tenderloin with wild mushrooms or grilled mahi-mahi with pistachio couscous; and concluded with a raspberry Napoleon or blackberry flan.

"The gracious atmosphere reflects the Victorian era of the island. Helpful, cordial front desk staff. Rooms have Victorian antiques; those with an ocean view are especially nice, although all are fine. We spent several hours sitting on the lawn, sipping iced tea, and enjoying the gorgeous views. A short walk to Old Harbor and local activities." *(Pam Phillips, also Kathy Banak)* "Brad and Anne really go out of their way to accommodate their guests, and set a tone of graciousness and intelligence for their staff." *(JJ)* "Quiet, relaxed atmosphere, even in the height of the season. Come early, so you can have a pre-dinner drink on the veranda and watch the sunset." *(DLG)*

Open April–Oct. Restaurant closed Nov., April.
Rooms 1 suite, 20 doubles—all with private shower and/or bath, telephone, fan. 8 with desk.
Facilities Restaurant, bar/lounge, breakfast room, living room, wraparound porch. Conference center with TV/VCR. 6 acres with 2 tennis courts, horseshoes, croquet.
Location Historic district. 7-min. walk to ferry.

Restrictions No smoking.
Credit cards Amex, MC, Visa.
Rates B&B, $165–210 suite, $99–195 double. Extra person, $25. Tipping appreciated. Children under 12 free in parents' room. 2–3 night weekend/holiday minimum. Prix fixe dinner, $40.
Extras Crib. Babysitting by arrangement.

The Rose Farm Inn ♿   *Tel:* 401–466–2034
Roslyn Road, P.O. Box E, 02807–0895   *Fax:* 401–466–2053
                        E-mail: rosefarm@blockisland.com

Five generations of the Rose family have fished and farmed on Block Island. In 1980, Judy and Robert Rose restored the family farmhouse, built in 1897, as an inn; in 1993, they added a second building, the Captain Rose House. Guest rooms have either water or country views, and are furnished with antiques and king- or queen-size canopy beds; many have old-fashioned rose-patterned wallpapers. Breakfast consists of fresh fruit and assorted juices, cereal, and coffee cake, muffins, or bagels, served on enclosed stone porch overlooking the water.

"Terrific views in a quiet, serene location away from town. Attractive, comfortable rooms; attentive staff." *(Pam Phillips)* "Judy Rose tended to her guests from early morning well into the evening. Rooms are well cared for, both on a daily and annual basis—the paint, wallpaper, and wood stain always look fresh. Its hilltop location affords an excellent view of much of the island. Old Harbor with its shops and restaurants is within walking distance, yet is far enough away that night-time noise is not a problem. After a day at the beach or of bicycling around the island, we love to sit in the comfortable wicker chairs on the front porch of the old farmhouse and read a book, while watching the ferry boats come and go in the Old Harbor." *(Charles & Ann Haaser)* "Our favorite is Room #9, where you can see the water view from the comfortable, king-size canopy bed." *(DLG)*

Open Feb.–Nov.
Rooms 10 doubles in original farmhouse; 9 in Capt. Rose House. 17 with private bath and/or shower, 2 with maximum of 4 people sharing bath. All with fan, deck/porch. 9 with double whirlpool tub, private entrance.
Facilities Enclosed breakfast porch, sitting room with TV, guest refrigerator; laundry; porch, sundeck. 20 acres with gardens. Bicycle rentals. Tennis nearby.
Location From Old Harbor, walk up High St. & go left on Roslyn Rd. to inn. Approx. 10-min. walk from ferry.
Restrictions No smoking. Children 12 and over.
Credit cards Amex, Discover, MC, Visa.
Rates B&B, $89–195 double. Extra person, $25. 2-night minimum June, Sept., Oct.; 3-night minimum July, Aug. Sept.; longer peak holiday weekends.
Extras Wheelchair access; 1 room specially equipped.

Sea Breeze   *Tel:* 401–466–2275
Spring Street, P.O. Box 141, 02807   800–786–2276

Robert and Mary Newhouse bought the Sea Breeze in 1979 and fully renovated the rooms of this shingled house and several adjacent cottages, making up a compound encircled by perennial gardens. Guest rooms are furnished with old island pieces, including some 19th-century painted furniture and English chintz fabrics. Rates include a breakfast of Viennese coffee, tea, juice, fresh fruit, and croissants or muffins. Mary Hall is the manager.

Mary describes the inn as being "close in atmosphere to an English seaside cottage. Our small staff is friendly, helpful, and available. Sea Breeze is beautifully sited on a hill overlooking our meadow and has a broad ocean panorama. Lovely perennial gardens and a quiet location on the edge of the historic district are great pluses." She describes Block Island as "a place with little organized activity or fancy shopping, small enough to explore it fully on foot or by bike—all beaches are open and there are countless paths to explore."

"Our beautifully decorated room offered great views of the pond and the gardens. Ample breakfast, with fresh, warm muffins and croissants." *(Judith Hayes)* "A secluded, romantic place." *(Marty Wray)* "The friendly innkeeper pointed out excellent restaurants for dinner and interesting sights." *(Donald Rollack)* "We stayed in Room #10, with a view of the ponds and ocean. We especially enjoyed watching the sunrise from our porch." *(Susan Ledoux)* "Peaceful location, within walking distance of town. Cozy rooms tastefully decorated with antiques and original art." *(Tom Hardy & Karen Lukas-Hardy)*

"Modern yet quaint rooms with antique furnishings, flowers, high ceilings, and fresh fruit; most have water views. Our cottage porch was a superb spot to sip wine at the end of the day." *(JCJ)* "A basket of coffee, tea, juice, fresh fruit, croissants, and muffins is delivered to your door each morning." *(Ann Riiska)* "Spotlessly clean, with firm mattresses and large, fluffy towels. Breakfast, delivered to our cottage after 8:30 A.M., was excellent with strong coffee, fresh muffins, and fruit." *(Carol Frankel)* "Mary is an artist and many of her paintings and ceramic work can be enjoyed at the inn." *(DLG)*

Open All year.

Rooms 1 suite, 9 doubles—5 with private shower bath, 5 with maximum of 6 people sharing bath. Some rooms with desk. Rooms in 3 cottages; some with private entrance, deck/patio.

Facilities Sitting rooms with games, books; guest refrigerator. Pay phone for guest use. 2½ acres with ponds for fishing; perennial gardens. Kayaks for use on pond. On the ocean.

Location 4-min. walk to town, 5 min. from ferry landing. From ferry landing, turn left on Water St. & go straight up Spring St.

Restrictions Smoking discouraged.

Credit cards MC, Visa.

Rates B&B, $240 suite (sleeps 4), $90–190 double. Weekly rates. 2–3 night weekend/holiday minimum.

BRISTOL

Bristol is located on East Bay, 15 miles southeast of Providence, and 10 miles north of Newport. Listed on the National Register of Historic

Places, it's known for having the country's oldest and largest Fourth of July parade, and is also home to Blithewold Mansion, a Newport-style cottage with beautifully landscaped grounds. A seaside bike trail goes through town.

Reader tip: "When touring the area, we found the charming town of Bristol to be an affordable and enjoyable alternative to pricey Newport. We bought a roll of ten tokens for the bridge, which cut down on the wait." *(MW)*

Also recommended: Built in 1792, and enlarged in the 1840s, the **Bradford-Dimond-Norris House** (474 Hope Street, 02809; 401–253–6338 or 888–329–6338; bdnhouse@edgenet.net) was restored as a B&B in 1994 by Suzanne and Lloyd Adams. Rooms are furnished with antiques, and double rates for the four guest rooms—each with TV, air-conditioning, and private shower bath—range from $75–120. Breakfasts are served on the garden veranda in good weather, and might include fresh fruit salad, apple-cinnamon puff pastry, and English muffins topped with ham, broccoli, and melted cheddar. "Lovely, spacious rooms with fishnet-canopy beds, good lighting, loveseat, new bathrooms with stall showers, and Oriental rugs. Charming, uncluttered common rooms with traditional furniture; charming mural of Bristol in the dining room. Lovely gardens, too." *(Rose Ciccone)*

William's Grant Inn ¢
154 High Street, 02809

Tel: 401–253–4222
800–596–4222

A five-bay Federal house with paired interior chimneys, painted a rich nautical navy blue with white trim, the William's Grant Inn was built in 1808, and was restored as a B&B in 1993 by Mary and Michael Rose. The decor combines family antiques with the work of the Roses' artist friends and relatives, including several pieces of furniture built to resemble the inn dogs, Tadger and Chloe, and a mural of Bristol Harbor in the front hall.

"Beautiful inn; gracious and hospitable hosts; atmosphere of comfortable elegance. Mike's heart-healthy, delicious breakfasts are a highlight." *(Kathy Adams, also Beatrice Sultz)* "Charming, themed rooms with very comfortable beds. Excellent breakfasts, attentively served. Friendly innkeepers, knowledgeable about the area and Rhode Island. Relaxed, homey atmosphere at the breakfast table." *(John & Anne Lee)* "Located on a quiet residential street of handsome historic homes, the inn is within easy walking distance of the harbor, local museums, restaurants, shops, and more. Innkeepers Mike and Mary are outgoing, friendly, and enthusiastic, but do not intrude. I had a key to the front door and my room, and felt free to keep my own schedule." *(Eleanor Edelstein).* "Mike and Mary took care of all our needs unobtrusively, but with warmth and humor." *(Robert Kaplan)*

"Even the inn's sign is inviting and humorous, with its seagoing innkeepers and inn dogs. Mary Rose greeted us warmly, pointing out the lovely upstairs parlor with its antiques and decanter of sherry. Although our room was just off the kitchen, we were undisturbed by cooking sounds. Our private bath was well-stocked with thick towels, soap, and other accessories. Breakfast consisted of blueberry cobbler, lemon ginger muffins, freshly squeezed orange juice, fresh fruit cup with mint, pumpkin pancakes with homemade cinnamon syrup, and wonderful coffee." *(Jay Miller)* "A nice feature is the opportunity to have breakfast at your choice of time." *(Robert & Betsy MacDonald)* "Excellent breakfast of fresh fruit, granola, cranberry orange scones, Grand Marnier French toast, or omelets with home-grown herbs, cheese, and asparagus." *(John & Carol King)*

Open All year.

Rooms 5 doubles—3 with private bath and/or shower, 2 with maximum of 4 people sharing bath. All with clock/radio, fan, fireplace.

Facilities Dining room, living room with fireplace, piano, books, magazines; porch. ½ acre with lawn games, garden, fish pond, courtyard, off-street parking. Tennis, golf nearby. 2 blocks to harbor for swimming, windsurfing, kayaking.

Location Historic district. Fourth of July parade route. 1 block from town. From I-95 N, take I-195 E to Exit 7 (Barrington/Rte. 114 S) Stay on Rte. 114 S to Bristol. Follow Hope St. through Bristol to Constitution St. Go left, go up 1 block, go right on High St. to inn on left.

Restrictions No smoking. Children over 12 welcome.

Credit cards Amex, DC, Discover, MC, Visa. 5% credit card surcharge.

Rates B&B, $65–115 double. Extra person, $15. 2-night minimum holidays, graduation, peak season.

MATUNUCK

Also recommended: Listed on the National Register of Historic Places, the **Admiral Dewey Inn** (668 Matunuck Beach Road, South Kingston, 02879; 401–783–2090 or 800–457–2090) is a four-story shingled house with a lovely wraparound porch, complete with rocking chairs to catch the off-shore breeze. The Victorian furnishings include paisley-patterned wallpapers, velvet-covered chairs, claw-footed tables, brass beds with matching brass lamps, and six-foot carved headboards; five of the guest rooms have distant ocean views. Rates of $50–130 include a buffet breakfast of fruit, juice, cereal, coffee cake, bagels, and muffins. "Lovely Victorian antiques, inviting sea breezes. Homey atmosphere with cordial innkeeper. Immaculately clean and quiet." *(Patricia Kempt, also Kathryn Mardon)*

NARRAGANSETT

Narragansett is an old-fashioned beach community, where generations of Providence-area families have been summering for years. It makes a pleasant and affordable base for touring Newport, the University of Rhode Island, and for accessing the Block Island ferry, all within a short drive.

   Also recommended: Situated on a tree-lined street two blocks from the ocean, **Murphy's Bed & Breakfast** (43 South Pier Road, Narragansett, 02882; 401–789–1824) offers two guest rooms, each with private bath and TV, tucked under the eaves on the third floor of a spacious turn-of-the-century Victorian house. B&B double rates range from $75–95. "The two guest rooms are across the hall from one another, with a small guest fridge in the hall; the set-up is ideal for two couples or one family traveling together. One room has a queen-size bed, the other twin beds which can be made up as a king. We had fresh roses in our room, from the innkeeper's garden; breakfasts were divine with scrambled eggs with cheese and green onions the first day, and pancakes the second. Martha, the innkeeper, is kind and mellow, interested in her guests, and a wonderful cook and gardener." *(Ray & Lisa Witkowski)*

NEWPORT

Newport is often mobbed with tourists during the height of the season—July through Labor Day weekend. People come to see the extraordinary mansions built in the late 19th century by the Astors, Vanderbilts, and others of the super-rich: thirty-room "cottages" are now museums open to the public. These same giants of commerce had yachts as grand as their cottages, with paid crews of 30 or more men. It was through their initial efforts that the America's Cup races were hosted in Newport for over fifty years. Newport has also created a maritime museum which has become home port to many classic sailing yachts of the last century. Often overshadowed by the glare of the grand lifestyles of the Vanderbilts and Astors is the fact that Newport contains more pre-Revolutionary houses than any other town in America; both the oldest Quaker meeting house and the oldest synagogue in North America (constructed in 1763) are located here. Walking tours of Colonial Newport are offered on Fridays and Saturdays by the local historical society; other areas of interest are the Tennis Hall of Fame, quality shops, restaurants, theater, music, beaches, sailing, fishing, tennis, and golf.

Reader tips: "Newport can be difficult in season. Summer traffic is thick, restaurants and lodging are costly, and merchants can be stressed. The mansions, however, are wonderful, and if you want to see any number of them, it is best to stay in Newport, as driving in and out of town can be unpleasant." *(SHW)* Similarly: "We visited Newport in July, and found it difficult to get around town—street signs seemed to be rationed." *(JH)* And an alternative: "Early May is an ideal time to visit Newport. It's cool, quiet, sunny, and all the great houses open for the season on May 1st." *(RSS)* And: "If you're visiting midweek, off-season, and don't mind traveling without reservations you can get some great deals—we paid $150 for a gorgeous $295 suite at a top inn." *(RC)* A suggestion: "Traffic on the bridge could be significantly reduced if one could buy a token for the return trip; consider buying a roll of ten tokens to save time." *(BNS)* Also: "Parking meters were in force until midnight. Bring lots of quarters to feed the meters." *(CM)*

Newport is 35 miles south of Providence, 90 miles south of Boston, and 115 miles northeast of New Haven, CT. Rates are highest from June through September, and two- to three-night minimums are often required. Rates drop substantially off-season.

Also recommended: In the heart of Newport's mansion area is the **Ivy Lodge** (12 Clay Street, 02840; 401–849–6865 or 800–834–6865), owned by Maggie and Terry Moy, a mansion built following the designs of Stanford White. The $95–220 rates include a hearty breakfast buffet, beach towels and chairs, and off-street parking and use of the inn's bicycles. There are eight guest rooms, including a suite in the carriage house ideal for families.

Built as a summer cottage in 1870, the **Sanford-Covell Villa Marina** (72 Washington Street, 02840; 401–847–0206) is listed on the National Register of Historic Places. The entry is highlighted by a 35-foot grand staircase, and exceptional woodwork, with eight different kinds of wood. B&B double rates for the five guest rooms range from $75–265. "Beautiful views of the Newport Bridge and the sunset. Generous continental breakfast served on English bone china and crystal. We relaxed in front of the living room fireplace, played on the two grand pianos, and enjoyed the company of their handsome standard poodle named Amadeus." (*Judy MacDonald*)

Away from the crowds in town and overlooking the ocean is **A Viewpoint** (231 Coggeshall Avenue, 02840; 401–848–7773 or www.aviewpoint.com), owned by Judy and Robert Cruz. Located at the intersection of Bellevue Avenue and Ocean Drive, the inn truly has "rooms with a view"—of Bailey's Beach, of the Atlantic, of several famous mansions. Guests can choose from B&B guest rooms with Victorian decor on the first floor or two deluxe apartments on the upper floors. Double rates of $65–150 include a full breakfast. "Spectacular views. Wonderful hospitality from gracious, attentive hosts. Thoughtful touches included bedtime candy and sherry, and a delicious breakfast of a baked apple, homemade biscuits, and more." (*Susan Goldblatt*)

Worth noting: Inns marked with the symbol ¢, denoting them as being an especially good value, are still pricey in season. For additional area entries at substantially lower rates, see **Bristol** just ten miles north of Newport via Route 114 and **Narragansett**, about 20 minutes away, depending on traffic.

Castle Hill Inn & Resort ✕ ♿
590 Ocean Avenue, 02840

Tel: 401–849–3800
888–466–1355
Fax: 401–849–3838
E-mail: castlehill@edgenet.net
URL: http://www.castlehillinn.com

For water views, posh accommodations, elegant dining, fascinating history, and the privacy provided by its location on a forty-acre promontory, an excellent choice is the Castle Hill Inn. The grande dame of Newport's inns, it has been extensively renovated, and is once again under the management of the O'Reilly family, which has owned Castle Hill since 1938. It consists of the original Victorian mansion, built in

1874 for renowned scientist and explorer Alexander Agassiz. The spacious guest rooms in the mansion are decorated in period style, with views of the Atlantic Ocean or Narragansett Bay. The Chalet was built in 1877 as a laboratory for Agassiz, and offers a handsome meeting room suite, as well as modest guest rooms. Harbor House was built in the 1940s, and was renovated in 1997; its rooms have king-size beds, gas fireplaces, Jacuzzi tubs, and porches with bay views. Families enjoy the rustic cottages; they're simply furnished but right on the beach.

Well-known for its restaurant, the inn offers a buffet-style breakfast, served from 8–10 A.M., including a variety of fresh fruit and juice, cereal and baked goods, plus a hot entrée. A jazz brunch is offered on Sunday, with such dishes as eggs Benedict, lobster ravioli, and waffles with wild mushrooms and tarragon sauce. Lunch ranges from spinach salad with scallops and bacon to smoked turkey with cranberries on a baguette. Dinner entrées include duck breast with brown vinegar glaze; striped bass with clams and Vidalia onions; and grilled veal with smoked tomato butter.

"This grand old lady is back on track. The view is as spectacular as ever, and the guest rooms have been completely refurbished and redecorated, with beautiful new queen- and king-size beds, down comforters, 100% cotton linens, goose-down pillows (with hypo-allergenic pillows in every closet). Immaculate housekeeping and attention to detail. Homemade chocolate chip cookies are set on the side table of every bed. Spotless bathrooms, new carpeting, new window screens, Castle Inn robes hanging crisply and freshly inside every closet, iron and ironing boards, hairdryers, and more. Complimentary tea is served every afternoon at 4 P.M., with a huge assorted breakfast buffet every morning. The chef is outstanding and reservations for the excellent lunches and dinners are essential. The carefully manicured grounds now have flower cutting gardens." *(Gail Gunning)* "Excellent location." *(Dennis & Donna Sachs & others)* "Outstanding staff." *(Jane Milano)* "Simple elegance and spectacular view." *(Dave Dube)* "Great view from Harbor House rooms." *(Gail Mayer)*

Open All year.
Rooms 19 cottages, 2 suites, 18 doubles—32 with private bath and/or shower, 6 with maximum of 6 people sharing bath. 6 with whirlpool tub, fireplace. All with clock. Some with telephone, radio, TV, desk, air-conditioning, fan, kitchenette, refrigerator, balcony/deck. Guest rooms in main mansion, Harbor House, Chalet & Beach Cottages.
Facilities Restaurant with fireplace, breakfast room, bar/lounge with fireplace, piano, TV; lobby with fireplace; living room, porch. Jazz Fri. evening in winter, Sun. afternoon in summer. 40 acres with private beach, lawn games. Walking trails, lighthouse.
Location From downtown Newport, take America's Cup Ave. S & go right on Thames St. (Wave statue on corner). At Wellington Ave. (across from Shell station), turn right. Follow Wellington to Ocean Dr. & turn right. Keep bearing right for approx. 3 m to inn on right.
Restrictions Smoking in lounge only. Children welcome in cottages; 12 and over in other rooms.
Credit cards Amex, MC, Discover, Visa.

Rates B&B, $136–325 suite, $125–300 double. Extra person, $25. $1.50 daily housekeeping charge per person. No charge for children under 18. 2–3 night weekend/holiday minimum. Alc lunch, $15; dinner, $45. Midweek, off-season packages. Weekly rates for cottages in season.
Extras Wheelchair access to restaurant; bathroom specially equipped.

Cliffside Inn
2 Seaview Avenue, 02840

Tel: 401–847–1811
800–845–1811
Fax: 401–848–5850
E-mail: cliff@wsii.com
URL: http://www.cliffsideinn.com

An award-winning reader favorite, Cliffside was built in 1880 as a Newport summer cottage by the governor of Maryland, and was the longtime residence of eccentric painter Beatrice Turner. This B&B is located in a quiet residential neighborhood, shielded from traffic yet within walking distance of Newport's attractions. Owned by Winthrop Baker, its very capable manager is Stephan Nicolas. Rooms are handsomely furnished with Victorian antiques, accented with delicate country floral fabrics; those on the upper floors have the best water views. The adjacent Seaview Cottage houses two luxury suites, each with a water view, vaulted ceilings, and a sundeck. B&B rates include morning in-room coffee service, breakfast, afternoon tea, and choice of newspaper.

"Charming, tasteful, and classy. Miss Kay's Room has a lovely bay window, fresh flowers, and an especially comfortable bed. Delicious goodies at tea-time. We enjoyed early morning juice and tea, then a wonderful breakfast buffet of homemade granola, fruits, muffins, breads; served to our table was an entrée of scrambled eggs and sausage in croissants. The young staff was polite, helpful, and friendly from our initial phone call through our departure." *(Pat Malone)* "Stephan and staff provide guests with impeccable, friendly service." *(Caren & George Zahn)* "The helpful staff suggested tours and made restaurant reservations." *(Barbara Wenglin)*

"Beautifully decorated for Christmas with poinsettias. The two-story Garden Suite has a spiral staircase to the bath on the lower level, with its own fireplace, double whirlpool tub, heated floors, separate shower, and French doors opening to a private patio area. The Seascape Suite on the third floor has a water view, skylights in the bedroom and over the double-whirlpool tub. The dark green and white tiles are striking, and both bath sheets and towels are provided. The queen-size plantation bed has a lovely flowered duvet with matching pillow shams and white lace accent pillows. The floral print wallpaper and coordinating border complement the bedding. Lined, rose-colored Grecian-style shades block the early morning sun. A large armoire holds a TV and VCR. Bottled water and such turndown treats as miniature Napoleons with strawberries are brought to the room each evening. The cozy sitting room has shelves with books on either side of the fireplace. Breakfast included delicious ricotta pancakes with bacon. The staff here gives 100% and all are cheerful and helpful." *(Rose Ciccone)*

"Miss Beatrice's Room, #6, is large, pleasantly decorated, with a fireplace and a huge marble bathroom with a whirlpool tub. Breakfast is served at both large and small tables, accommodating both guests who enjoy conversation and those who prefer privacy." *(Bruce Bilmes)* "The large front porch faces beautiful trees on a quiet dead-end street; a few steps beyond is the sea." *(Katina Pendleton)* "Afternoon refreshments, served from 5–6 P.M., included cheese and crackers, crudités, sliced fruit, chicken wings, iced tea, lemonade with strawberries, hot coffee, tea, and butter cookies. The breakfast entrée was pancakes with strawberry butter, fresh sliced peaches, and sausages. No sooner had we arrived home than a thank-you note arrived in the mail from Cliffside." *(RC)*

Open All year.

Rooms 6 suites, 9 doubles—all with private bath and/or shower, telephone, radio, TV/VCR, ceiling fan, air-conditioning. 11 with Jacuzzi tub, 12 with fireplace. 2 suites in Seaview Cottage.

Facilities Living room with fireplace, porch; guest refrigerator. ½ acre with off-street parking. 100 yds. to Cliff Walk, 5 min. walk to beach, 15–20 min. to wharf.

Location From Newport Bridge, exit at "Scenic Newport." Go right onto Farewell St. At 2nd set of lights, turn right onto America's Cup Ave. Follow in left lane to 7th set of lights. Go up hill; becomes Memorial Hwy. Go through 2 sets of lights. Take last right before beach onto Cliff Ave. Go left on Sea View. From end of Rte. 138A, go right on Memorial Blvd. After passing beach, take 1st left onto Cliff Ave., then left on Sea View to inn.

Restrictions No smoking. No children under 13. Non-refundable deposit; can be credited to a future stay.

Credit cards Amex, DC, Discover, MC, Visa.

Rates B&B, $285–450 suite, $185–285 double. Extra person, $30. Midweek discount, Nov.–April. 2–3 night weekend/holiday minimum.

Extras French spoken.

Elm Tree Cottage   *Tel:* 401–849–1610
336 Gibbs Avenue, 02840   *Toll-free:* 888–ELM–TREE
                           Fax: 401–849–2084
                    E-mail: elmtreebnb@aol.com
                    URL: http://www.elmtreebnb.com

When visiting Newport, it's easy to fantasize about what it would be like to stay in a grand mansion; if you stay at Elm Tree Cottage, the reality may be even better than your fantasy. Designed by noted architect William Ralph Emerson, this 1882 shingle-style house has both Queen Anne and Colonial Revival detailing. Restored as an inn in 1990 by Tom and Priscilla Malone, it offers a taste of grand Newport style. Although many Victorian antiques highlight the decor, the English and French country fabrics and the color scheme of ivory, pale pink, and green create a light and airy look. Tom creates and restores stained glass, and his artwork accents many windows. Guest rooms have queen- or king-size beds, ample bedside lighting, and comfortable seating areas. The common areas include the living room with a Steinway grand and a Victorian upright grand piano, and views of the gardens and Easton Pond; the Morning Room with Ralph Lauren wicker and upholstered furniture, and a maze of plants; and the Pub Room, created to resemble the interior cabin of a 1930s yacht.

Breakfast is served from 8:30–10 A.M.; guests are seated at individual tables. The buffet changes daily, but might include fresh fruit and juices, yogurt, homemade granola and cereal, with peach cobbler, lemon poppyseed bread, or rice pudding; a hot entrée is brought to your table—perhaps cheese blintzes in blueberry sauce; Parmesan-cheese eggs on an English muffin; or potatoes with herbed scrambled eggs.

"Attentive helpful innkeepers, who take fine care of their guests, but are never intrusive. Excellent breakfasts, comfortable room. Great restaurant recommendations and insider reservations." *(Gail de Sciose)* "Sally and Tom are charming hosts who run a smooth operation. We felt at home and comfortable immediately. A lot of thought is evident in the room amenities: books on the area, bottled water, a variety of toiletries, excellent lighting, delicious breakfasts. The Duchess of Windsor (Room #1) is the largest, with spacious living areas, a king-size bed, and fireplace. Room #5 is ample in size with a king-size bed, loveseat, two bureaus, a side chair, and charming accessories. A corner shelf unit in the bathroom provided ample space for our things." *(Sally Ducot)* "We stayed in the handsome Ralph Lauren–style room on the main floor, but had a chance to see several other rooms, and all were lovely, even the least expensive." *(Lauren & Al Kenney)* "Phenomenal attention to detail. Immaculate housekeeping, ample hot water, convenient parking. My favorite entrée is an egg dish with Parmesan cream sauce; the Malones were happy to accommodate our vegetarian diet." *(Kathryn Lashendock)* "The beds are especially comfortable; the rooms unusually well-equipped—wine glasses, corkscrews, matches for the fireplace. Always thinking of ways to make their guests' stay more comfortable, Tom and Priscilla bring a much-appreciated enthusiasm to their work." *(Kim & John Guman)* "The Malones greeted us warmly, and showed us to our room, #4. We thought we had made the best choice until we saw the rest of the rooms, which were equally lovely. The location is quiet and serene, yet within minutes of the harbor, shops, and historic sites." *(Linda & Tom Ferri)*

Open All year. Closed Christmas, month of January.
Rooms 1 suite, 5 doubles—all with private bath and/or shower, clock/radio, air-conditioning, fan. Most with fireplace, desk. TV on request.
Facilities Dining room with fireplace, living room with fireplace, pianos; sitting room, pub (BYOB). 1 acre with gardens, gazebo, off-street parking. 2 blocks from First Beach, Cliff Walk.
Location 1 m from harbor. From Newport Bridge, exit at "Scenic Newport" sign & turn right onto Farewell St. At 2nd set of lights turn right onto America's Cup Ave. Follow in left lane to 7th set of lights; proceed up hill (divided hwy.) which becomes Memorial Blvd. Continue through two sets of traffic lights; take 4th left onto Gibbs Ave. to first stop sign. Inn is third house on right.
Restrictions No smoking. Children over 14.
Credit cards Amex, MC, Visa.
Rates B&B, $275–350 suite, $175–250 double. 2–3 night weekend/holiday minimum.

The Francis Malbone House Inn ♿
392 Thames Street, 02840

Tel: 401–846–0392
800–846–0392
Fax: 401–848–5956
E-mail: innkeeper@malbone.com
URL: http://www.malbone.com

An impressive Georgian-style stone mansion, the Francis Malbone House Inn was built in 1760, designed by the same architect responsible for the Touro Synagogue and the Redwood Library. Legend says that Malbone enhanced his profits by building a tunnel from underneath the house to the waterfront, enabling him to avoid paying duty to the King. The original part of the house was restored in 1990; a newer section was added in 1996; both surround the courtyard, where breakfast is served in warmer weather. The inn is handsomely furnished with antiques and reproductions; Will Dewey is the longtime manager. Breakfast is served from 8:30–10 A.M.; a typical menu consists of cereal, yogurt, apple crisp or perhaps poached pears in Melba sauce, bread pudding with maple syrup or carrot raisin muffins, plus such entrées as raspberry cream cheese French toast or pumpkin waffles. Rates also include afternoon tea.

"Beautifully decorated yet not overdone; warm and friendly staff." *(Deborah Spagnoletti)* "Rooms wonderfully equipped; monogrammed linen sheets, large, fluffy towels. Fantastic breakfast and elegant, personal service." *(H.R. Drackett)* "Like staying with the wealthy relatives (you wish you had) for the weekend." *(Frank Haas)* "Perfect location for shopping, walking, visiting the mansions, and strolling along the Cliff Walk." *(Vining Bigelow & Frank Libby)* "We were shown to the Counting House suite by the friendly, gracious hostess. Given its name back in 1760, the suite included a living room, dining room, bedroom, and bath with Jacuzzi. In the morning, fires were crackling throughout the house as Will Dewey prepared a wonderful breakfast for us. I wanted time to stand still." *(Gail Gunning)* "The innkeepers willingly provided excellent recommendations for activities, food, and fun. The friendship extended by the friendly staff enhanced our stay. The backyard garden is an ideal escape from the busy harbor area, and is perfect for relaxing, reading, visiting with other guests and staff, and for enjoying an afternoon snack." *(Marvin Blum)* "An oasis in the middle of town. Though located directly on the street, the inn is extremely quiet and private. Impeccably maintained; handsomely decorated. I was transported to another era upon entering the front door." *(Betsy Sandberg)*

Open All year.
Rooms 2 suites, 16 doubles—all with private bath and/or shower, telephone, radio, clock, air-conditioning. 10 with whirlpool tub, TV, desk; 15 with working fireplace; 2 with refrigerator.
Facilities Dining room, breakfast room, living room—each with fireplace. Library with fireplace, TV, games. Guest kitchen, refrigerator. 1 acre with garden patio, fountain. Off-street parking.
Location Harborfront district. From Newport Bridge, go right on America's Cup Ave. at 2nd set of lights. Go to 6th set of lights & turn right onto lower Thames St. at Perry Mill Market/Newport Bay Club. Inn is 3 blocks down on

left. For guest parking, go left onto Brewer St. (3rd left off Thames) to 1st driveway. From Rte. 138 S, follow to Thames St., go left; follow directions above.
Restrictions No smoking. Children over 12. Some summer traffic noise in front rooms.
Credit cards Amex, MC, Visa.
Rates B&B, $225–355 suite, $175–245 double. Extra person, $30. Tipping envelopes. Off-season promotions.
Extras Limited wheelchair access; 1 room specially equipped.

The Inn at Shadow Lawn ¢ ♁
120 Miantonomi Ave, Middletown, 02842

Tel: 401–847–0902
800–352–3750
Fax: 401–848–6529
E-mail: randy@shadowlawn.com
URL: http://www.shadowlawn.com

History and hospitality are key components of most B&Bs, and the Inn at Shadow Lawn is amply supplied with both. Built as a private home in 1856, the inn was designed by Richard Upjohn, generally regarded as the "father" of the Gothic Revival movement in American architecture; Trinity Church in New York City is one of his best-known designs. Said to be the first Italianate stick-style house in the U.S., the inn features original woodwork, lovely stained-glass windows, wall stenciling, and period wallpapers. In 1994 it was purchased and restored by Selma Fabricant and her son Randy. Named for Victorian women writers, the guest rooms are well-equipped and spacious—18 by 20 feet or larger. Breakfast is served from 8–10 A.M., and includes apple or blueberry pancakes, or perhaps Belgian waffles, plus juice, cereal, croissants, and pastry. Splits of wine are placed in guest room refrigerators upon arrival.

"Selma and Randy are gracious hosts, providing information on their beautiful Victorian home. Much time and attention to detail was put into the restoration. Elegant and impressive common areas, comfortable sitting room, plus guest rooms which balance modern convenience and Victorian design. Enjoyed a breakfast of French toast, sausages, and sliced pears. I felt very welcome, and enjoyed talking with the Fabricants." *(Susan Goldblatt)* "Exceptional restoration, hospitality, and attention to detail. Homey atmosphere, lovely decor. Skip-lunch breakfast." *(Mrs. T. Natale & others)* "Comfortable bed, quiet and peaceful. Good water pressure in the shower." *(GR)*

Open All year.
Rooms 8 doubles—all with full private bath and/or shower, telephone with data port, radio, clock, TV/VCR, air-conditioning, ceiling fan, fireplace, refrigerator. Some with kitchen.
Facilities Dining room, living room with piano, library; each with fireplace; veranda. 2 acres with gazebo, lawn games, off-street parking. 5 min. to water sports.
Location Historic district, 5 min. from town center. From N, take I-93 S to 24 S to 114 S, through Portsmouth & Middletown. Left onto Miantonomi Ave. at the Gateway Motel traffic light. At 1st stop sign watch for inn sign diagonally to left. From S, take I-95 N to Exit 3A (138 E). Follow Rte. 138 over Jamestown & Newport Bridges. Take Exit 2 off Newport Bridge towards Fall River. At bot-

tom of exit ramp, turn left at light & go up hill through 2 sets of lights. Becomes Miantonomi Ave. Watch for inn sign at 1st stop sign.
Restrictions No smoking.
Credit cards All major.
Rates B&B, $50–$175. Extra person, $15. 10% senior discount. 2–3 night weekend summer/holiday/special event minimum. Extra charge for kitchen use.
Extras Crib, babysitting.

The Melville House ¢
39 Clarke Street, 02840

Tel: 401–847–0640
Fax: 401–847–0956
E-mail: innkeeper@ids.net
URL: http://www.melvillehouse.com

The Melville House, built in 1750, was purchased by Vince DeRico and David Horan in 1993; rooms are simply furnished in traditional Colonial style. Colonial troops were quartered here during the Revolutionary War; Washington, Lafayette, and Rochambeau met just across the street. David, a culinary school graduate, prepares hearty breakfasts of Yankee cornbread, Irish scones, stuffed French toast, Portuguese quiche, or Rhode Island johnnycakes, and homemade granola. Rates also include afternoon tea or sherry and biscotti.

"The inn's authentic furnishings, wall coverings, rugs, and wide-board floors make it easy to imagine what a house was like back in the Revolutionary period. Our small but spotless bathroom had ample lighting, hot water, and a good supply of soft towels." *(Mrs. & Mr. Ted Proehl)* "Gracious hosts, great dinner recommendations, delicious breakfasts with sour cream pancakes, Portuguese sausage, or broccoli and eggs in puff pastry, and wonderful music. Thoughtful touches included the chocolate and apples in our room, fresh flowers, and first-rate housekeeping." *(GR)* "Our cozy room had such thoughtful amenities as fresh fruit, magazines, flowers, even a tiny board game in the bedside table drawer." *(JO)* "We were welcomed by Dewey, the inn cat, and David, who offered us peanut butter cookies, iced nut bread, and cheesecake. After a wonderful breakfast of ginger waffles with blueberries, we took Vince's advice and followed the Cliff Walk to the Breakers." *(MSG)* "Typical Colonial-era home, with low ceilings and doorways; neither cluttered nor fussy. The garden and off-street parking are definite pluses. The quiet, pretty gaslit street is just a block away from Thames Street shops and restaurants." *(Rose Ciccone)* "Our room had an antique wooden bed covered with a lace comforter and pillows. Reading lamps, plus an excellent supply of books and magazines in the hall library, enhanced our stay." *(Roseanne Cuccinello)* "Compact, comfortable rooms." *(Lon Bailey)*

Open All year.
Rooms 7 doubles—5 with private shower, 2 with maximum of 4 people sharing bath.
Facilities Breakfast room, sitting room with games, books. Garden, picnic table, bicycles, parking area. 1 m to beach; charter boats nearby.
Location Historic Hill section. 1 block from center. From Newport Bridge, exit at "Scenic Newport." Turn right onto Farewell St. Go through 2 sets of lights.

Bear right onto Thames St. At light, go left onto Touro St. Take 2nd right onto Clarke St. to inn on right.
Restrictions No children under 12.
Credit cards Amex, Discover, MC, Visa.
Rates B&B, $165 winter fireplace suite; $85–145 double; $60–100 off-season. 2–3 night weekend/holiday minimum.
Extras 3 blocks to bus station.

The Old Beach Inn
19 Old Beach Road, 02840

Tel: 401–849–3479
888–303–5033
Fax: 401–847–1236
E-mail: oldbeachinn.com
URL: http://www.oldbeachinn.com

Cynthia and Luke Murray have done more than a little "reviving" of the 1879 Gothic Revival home they bought in 1989. Their renovations have extended to every corner of the house and beyond to their property as well. Rates include a breakfast of fresh-squeezed juice, fresh fruit (berries are a favorite in season), muffins, bagels, pastry, specially blended coffee, and tea, plus a hot entrée on Sundays; the guest pantry is kept stocked with coffee and tea makings.

"An elegant, charming inn, an easy walk from many shops and restaurants. Breathtaking gardens, gazebo, lily pond, and more. Cyndi and Luke are perfect innkeepers—warm, hospitable, and welcoming; Cyndi is a talented decorator. The handsome parlor is done in a navy and cranberry motif. The dining room is set up with small tables covered with rose-flowered lace tablecloths. Each beautiful guest room has a flower theme. The Wisteria Room is done in lilac, white, cranberry, and sea-spray green. Upstairs is the Lily Room with an 1879 cottage bed and a peach and ivory color scheme; the Rose Room with a queen-size canopy bed, wicker furniture, and straw hats; the Forget-Me-Not Room is done in wicker, with powder blue, yellow, and white accents; and the more masculine Ivy Room done in green and dark red tones with a hunting theme and twig furniture. Cindy did all the stenciling, faux painting, and free-hand painting herself." *(Gail Gunning)* "Luxurious decor, quiet and clean, perfect location, wonderful innkeepers." *(Deborah Waiserman)* "Meticulous attention to detail. Wonderful breakfast room with classical music, and a 'secret garden' backyard. The Murrays happily provide sightseeing and restaurant advice." *(Maureen Murphy)*

Open All year.
Rooms 7 doubles—all with private bath and/or shower, air-conditioning, fan. 4 with gas fireplace. 2 rooms in carriage house with private entrance.
Facilities Dining room with fireplace, parlor with fireplace, books, games; guest pantry, porches. ½ acre with garden, gazebo, fish pond, patio, off-street parking.
Location 30 m SE of Providence. 2 blocks off Bellevue Ave. From Newport Bridge, take America's Cup Ave., which becomes Memorial Blvd. At 2nd light on Memorial, go left on Bellevue, then right after the art museum onto Old Beach Rd.
Restrictions No smoking. Children over 12.
Credit cards Amex, Discover, MC, Visa.

Rates B&B, $85–175 double. Extra person, $20. 2–3 night weekend, holiday minimum.
Extras Bus station pickups.

Stella Maris Inn ¢ &   *Tel: 401–849–2862*
91 Washington Street, 02840

Built in 1861 with redstone shipped from Connecticut, the Stella Maris was restored as an inn in 1990 by Dorothy and Ed Madden. Its name dates to the 1920s when the Sisters of Cluny used the mansion as a convent, naming the mansion Stella Maris, meaning star of the sea. Breakfast is served at individual tables, and includes homemade breads and muffins—perhaps peach melba muffins, strudel, or Irish bread—with cereal, orange juice, fresh fruit, fresh-brewed coffee and tea.

"Spacious yet intimate, with welcoming innkeepers. You can socialize with the other guests, or maintain your privacy. If you enjoy walking, there's no need for the car. The atmosphere, the grounds, the wide porch, the fireplaces in winter, and the home-baked breads, cakes, scones, and strudels keep drawing us back." *(Egon Klohe)* "A charming old Victorian inn with comfy beds and great breakfasts. Dorothy and Ed Madden are hospitable, friendly hosts who are well-traveled and knowledgeable about art, music, and literature." *(Mary Johnstone)* "The Irish theme is intriguing and inspiring. Mrs. Madden's Irish soda breads and New England muffins make breakfast a treat." *(Rev. John Chalmers)* "The sign over the front door reads *Cead Mile Failte*, Gaelic for 'A hundred thousand welcomes'; the inn truly lives up to its motto. The magnificent back garden is a delight to relax in." *(Mary & John Hannon)*

"Beautiful antiques, yet homey and comfortable. We enjoyed a fire in the fireplace and wonderful magazines to read. Delicious breakfast, elegantly served on a beautiful table with antique china." *(Pamela Ellis)* "Our lovely room was well-appointed with antique wicker furniture, Ralph Lauren comforter, lace curtains, overstuffed chairs, abundant books and magazines, plus a wonderful view of the bay. Dorothy's kitchen garden provided fresh herbs for her muffins and breads. We enjoyed breakfast on the porch with a soft bay breeze, and in the garden among Ed's flowers. Dorothy and Ed provided many suggestions for restaurants and tours." *(Kathryn & Elmer Lippmann)* "Quiet area within walking distance of the busy downtown district. Delicious afternoon tea, complete with homemade apricot bread; complimentary wine before dinner. My husband played the inn's grand piano; we both took advantage of the large assortment of books in the parlor." *(Elizabeth Lichera)* "Guest rooms are named for Irish writers, with books by the respective authors in each room." *(Eileen O'Reilly)*

Open All year.
Rooms 10 doubles—all with private bath and/or shower, radio, fan. 4 with fireplace.
Facilities Breakfast room, living room with TV, books; piano; wraparound porch; elevator. 1½ acre with gardens. Off-street parking.
Location From Newport Bridge, exit at "Scenic Newport." Turn right onto Farewell St. At 1st light, turn right to harbor. Go left on Washington St. to inn on left.

Restrictions No smoking. No children under 10.
Credit cards None accepted.
Rates B&B, $75–175 double. Extra person, $20. 2–3 night weekend/holiday minimum.
Extras Limited wheelchair access. Bus station pickup. French spoken.

The Victorian Ladies   *Tel:* 401–849–9960
63 Memorial Boulevard, 02840   *Fax:* 401–849–9960

Three elegant porcelain figurines were given to Helene O'Neill when she left her banking career, and it is these same "Victorian Ladies" that lent their name to the B&B Don and Helene O'Neill bought in 1985. The inn consists of three buildings, the main building constructed circa 1850, decorated with Victorian, Colonial, and country antiques and reproductions. Breakfast is served from 8–9:30 A.M. at individual tables and includes cereal, fresh fruit, bagels, muffins, and coffee cake, plus eggs with ham or sausage, rice pudding or bread pudding, or perhaps stuffed French toast or eggs Benedict.

"Helene has given every inch of this inn a special touch with beautiful fabrics, wallpaper, lace canopied beds, Indian and Oriental carpets, and mahogany, pine, oak, and wicker furniture. The living room is decorated in varying shades of dusty blue and mauve, with fresh flowers everywhere, while the dining room has a huge 18th-century Welsh oak sideboard and matching tables and chairs. Everything is impeccably clean throughout and in perfect condition. All the window treatments are exceptional, with wonderful fabrics. There are no doors on the closet, as Helene wanted to use fabrics in her clever way and it is definitely eye-catching; she made the bed skirts and matching pillows with equal flair. The effect is light and airy, neither fussy nor cluttered. The inn is comfortable, not intimidating, and Helene and Don are enthusiastic, hospitable owners. When I visited, the charming English courtyard garden was in full bloom with daffodils, tulips, and other spring flowers. The inn's buildings have over 30 window boxes that overflow with flowers all summer." *(Gail Gunning)* "Well located a few blocks from fine shops, convenient to the mansions, and away from the touristy waterfront area. Room #8 is located in the carriage house, and was charmingly decorated in blue and white with rose and yellow accents, with comfortable reading chairs and excellent lighting. Spotless housekeeping; spacious bathroom with ample storage space. At breakfast, we enjoyed scrambled eggs with sausage and frittata plus yummy raspberry bread pudding." *(Carolyn Myles)* "Excellent maintenance. Donald is ready to make repairs at a moment's notice if necessary. Helene is bubbly, effervescent, warm, and caring." *(Michael & Dina Miller)*

Open Feb.–Dec.
Rooms 11 doubles—all with full private bath, clock, radio, TV, air-conditioning. Some with telephone, desk. 5 rooms in main building, 6 rooms in two cottages.
Facilities Dining room, living room with fireplace, books; ½ acre with brick walkways, courtyards, fish pond, gardens, gift shop. Off-street parking. 3 blocks to beach, town.
Location ½ m to harbor area. From Newport Bridge, take America's Cup Ave., which becomes Memorial Blvd.

Restrictions No smoking. Children over 10 welcome. Traffic noise possible in one room.
Credit cards MC, Visa.
Rates B&B, $105–215 double, $95–205, single. 2–3 night weekend minimum.

PROVIDENCE

Capital of Rhode Island, Providence is home to several well-known colleges and universities, including Brown University and the Rhode Island School of Design. Founded in 1636 by Roger Williams, many of its historic buildings have been restored in recent years.

Reader tip: "Fabulous Italian dinner at Walter's in the Federal Hill district. Enjoyed walking in the adjoining piazza and surrounding neighborhood before dinner. Not all Providence neighborhoods are safe for night-time strolls, so be sure to ask for advice." *(Sally Ducot)*

For excellent area recommendations, be sure to check our **Massachusetts** chapter under **Middleborough** and **Rehoboth**, just a short drive east of Providence.

Historic Jacob Hill Farm B&B 🦌
120 Jacob Street, Seekonk, MA, 02771

Tel: 508–336–9165
888–336–9165
Fax: 508–336–0951
E-mail: jacobhillfarm@juno.com
URL: http://www.travelguides.com/inns/full/RI/3824.html

In the 1920s, the socially prominent elite of Providence came to the Jacob Hill Hunt Club in Seekonk to ride horses in what was then farmland. A large farmhouse, dating back to 1722, served as the hunt clubhouse. In 1991, Bill and Eleonora Rezek bought the property and painstakingly restored it, opening their B&B in 1995. Handsome floors of Southern pine were found buried under orange shag carpeting and layers of paint, while new plumbing was installed to ensure guest comfort. Fresh wallpaper, paint, and fabric create a color scheme of ivory and taupe, accented with mauve, green, or blue, complemented by Colonial and Victorian antiques and reproductions. The hunt club motif is reflected by horse designs and hunting motif paintings. Guest rooms are spacious, most with sitting areas and king-size beds, and several with fireplaces and/or Jacuzzi tubs. Additional renovations in 1997 produced a lovely room—the Mansion Suite—with a delightful floor-to-ceiling mural of the farm, painted around the entire room by a local artist from the Rhode Island School of Design; another spacious room has a king-size pillow-top bed, French doors opening to a marble bath with a double Jacuzzi, and a wood-burning firestove, angled so you can see the flames from the bed or tub, and done in French country decor with hand-painted furniture. Breakfast is served from 7–9:30 A.M., and might include blueberry pancakes, stuffed French toast, or perhaps omelets; with bacon or sausage, fruit, muffins, bagels, and cereal.

"Attractively decorated, meticulously clean, bright and comfortable, with many lovely antiques. Quiet location, close to antiquing, shopping, and the ocean. Best of all are the hosts, who put their hearts into redoing this beautiful farm house." *(Larry & Rosemary Williams)* "Bill and Eleonora are delightful hosts and great conversationalists. Be sure to ask Bill the story behind the old heart-shaped bottles." *(David Goldsmith)* "Comfortable, immaculate rooms; upgraded plumbing in prime condition; tasty, generous breakfast." *(Philip K. Hathaway)* "Our charming room was light and fresh with a lace-topped canopy bed and an ivory-colored love seat." *(MW)* "Delightful innkeepers who go all-out to ensure their guests' comfort. Immaculate housekeeping. Extremely comfortable king-size bed, triple-sheeted quality linens and fluffy pillows. Tasty breakfast of fresh fruit salad with delicious papaya, raspberry-stuffed French toast, bagels and muffins, endless coffee and juice. In the evening, we enjoyed wine and cheese, iced tea and cookies on the porch, and watched the sun set behind meadows and woods, and distant hills. Almost impossible to believe that this serenely pastoral scene is literally minutes from downtown Providence." *(SWS)* "Attentive, savvy innkeepers with high standards of careful stewardship, as evidenced by the interior, exterior, and well-kept grounds of this stunning B&B. Careful renovation evidenced by the use of seven coats of polyurethane on the beautiful pine floors. Wonderful recommendations and directions to area restaurants, bakeries, hiking and bicycling trails, and other activities. Equally pleasant to just read and relax by the pool or in the gazebo." *(Michael Cronin)*

Open All year.
Rooms 1 suite, 6 doubles—all with full private bath, clock, radio, air-conditioning, telephone. 3 with double whirlpool tub, fireplace. 1 with private gazebo porch.
Facilities Dining room with fireplace; living room with fireplace, TV, stereo; den/library with TV, fireplace; screened porch; gazebo; deck. 5 acres with swimming pool, tennis courts. Horseback riding, golf, canoeing, fishing, walking, cross-country skiing nearby.
Location SE MA. 3 m from E. Providence, RI. From I-195, take Exit 1 in MA. Follow Rte. 114A N. Go right on Rte. 44 E for 1.5 miles. Go left on Jacob St.
Restrictions No smoking. Children 12 and older.
Credit cards Discover, MC, Visa.
Rates B&B, $95–225 suite, double, $75–125 single. Extra person, $25. 2–3 night weekend holiday minimum.
Extras Airport/station pickups. Polish spoken.

State House Inn ¢ 👭
43 Jewett Street, 02908

Tel: 401–351–6111
Fax: 401–351–4261

A "country-style B&B in the city" is how Frank and Monica Hopton, longtime owners of the State House Inn, describe their Colonial Revival home, built in 1890 and restored as an inn a century later. The inn is located on Smith Hill, an urban neighborhood of Victorian homes—some handsomely restored—nominated for National Historic District status. Close to the State Capitol building (hence its name), the inn is within walking distance of Brown University, the Rhode Island School of Design, and downtown.

Guest rooms are simply decorated with Colonial and Shaker reproduction furnishings, with handmade quilts or down comforters on the queen- or king-size beds (some four-posters, some with canopy). Rates include a breakfast of muffins, breads, bagels, fresh fruit, cereal, and hot entrée of the day—from pancakes to omelets.

"Convenient location, cordial hosts, comfortable room." (*Carol Cocke*) "A pleasant stay; secure environment; spacious, well-decorated room." (*Sally Ducot*) "Beds were comfortable, and the owners most cooperative. We were provided with helpful information about local restaurants and treated to an excellent breakfast prepared by our hostess." (*Robert Boas*) "We enjoyed chatting with the other guests over a tasty meal." (*RAB*) "A neat, clean, and civilized place, owned and operated by friendly and considerate people. Breakfast is available from about 7 A.M.—good for business people who have to get an early start." (*Edward Matthews*) "Spacious rooms, comfortable beds, homey atmosphere. Healthy breakfast with lots of fruit." (*Anthony Graham*) "Warm and friendly, attention to special needs. My favorite room has a fireplace, and a down comforter on the bed." (*Trine Bech*)

Open All year.

Rooms 10 doubles—all with full private bath, telephone, radio, TV, air-conditioning. Some with desk, 2 with fireplace.

Facilities Breakfast room with fireplace, living room with library, laundry facility, porch, fax machine. Garden, off-street parking. Beach nearby.

Location Smith Hill. 4 blocks to Capitol; 10–15 min. walk to downtown, Brown, RISD. Take Exit 22 off I-95. Go left at light onto Francis St. Bear left at 2nd light around Capitol. Go left on Smith St. After going under Interstate take 2nd left onto Schaffer St. to inn on left at corner of Jewett.

Restrictions No smoking. Common rooms locked after 9:30 P.M.

Credit cards Amex, MC, Visa.

Rates B&B, $99–129 double, $89–109 single. Extra person, $10. 10% discount for 3 nights. Midweek corporate rates. 2-night minimum weekends May, Oct.

Extras Crib.

WEEKAPAUG

Weekapaug Inn 🚶 🐾 ♿
25 Spring Avenue, 02891

Tel: 401–322–0301
Fax: 401–322–1016

Celebrating its centennial in 1899, the Weekapaug Inn has been owned by the Buffum family for four generations, and is managed by Jim and DeeDee Buffum. Many special events are planned for the inn's 100th anniversary, from parties to a special book on the Weekapaug's history. The inn was originally located on the neighboring private crescent-shaped barrier beach, but was destroyed in the fall of 1938 by a massive hurricane (which caused major destruction along the whole Rhode Island and Connecticut shore). The inn was completely rebuilt, in time for the 1939 summer season, on a slightly more protected spit of land just behind the beach. In addition to the beach, guests have the use of an adjacent salt pond, ideal for protected kayaking, windsurfing, sailing, and canoeing. Breakfast includes fresh fruit and juice; muffins, toast, and bagels; cereal and granola; blueberry pancakes, oatmeal raisin French toast, and eggs-to-order—from omelets to shirred eggs; breakfast meats; plus a daily special. The lunch buffet includes soups, such hot entrées as striped bass with tarragon mustard or beef with shiitake mushrooms, plus sandwich makings and salads; box lunches can be ordered the night before. The sophisticated, creative dinner menu includes a variety of choices—perhaps corn jalapeño fritters with crème fraîche and caviar, chilled kiwi and plum soup, boiled or stuffed lobster or grilled chicken breast with mango-nectarine relish, and pumpkin roulade or vanilla crème brûlée for dessert.

"The quintessential summer resort. It is a tribute to the inn that both guests and staff return year after year. The atmosphere is casual and friendly with a touch of elegance, as befits an institution dating from the turn of the century. The inn has done a commendable job of attracting younger families, and there are many activities and programs for children. Rooms are simply furnished with rock maple beds and dressers, good mattresses and spotless chenille bedspreads, white ruffled curtains, and old-fashioned baths. The common areas of the inn are a delight: the pine-paneled Pond Room with honor bar, piano, and comfortable seating; the Sea Room facing the ocean with moss-green furnishings; and much more. Fresh flowers are in abundance. Situated on a beautiful point of land, rolling lawns lead to tennis courts, the pond; it's a short stroll to the ocean-side beach. New or short-term guests are greeted as warmly as longtime regulars. The staff, from the front desk to the chambermaids, are friendly, professional, and courteous. The full meal plan is the centerpiece of the inn's reputation. Assigned tables and wait staff assure you of consistent, friendly service. The food is excellent, with a buffet lunch, and tempting dinner offerings that change nightly. " *(Constance & Donald Reder, SWS)*

"Waking up to see the sun rising over the pond where swans are floating is my idea of complete relaxation. Lots to do at the inn, or order a picnic for the beach or a drive. People return year after year and become friends. The staff is well-trained and pleasant. They obviously enjoy themselves and want guests to do the same. Do not go if you must have an in-room television, radio, phone, or air-conditioning; the guests never miss them." *(Arne & Helen Hovdesven)* "A one-of-a-kind place. Superb food, delightful ambience, unlocked doors, upbeat college students as staff. Understated upscale." *(Allen H. Seed)* "I first visited as a teenager, and now vacation there with my own family. Low-key, understated elegance—high-quality people, excellent food, beautiful setting." *(James G. Rogers)*

"Comfort, not decor, is the key concept at Weekapaug. The food is prepared from scratch using fresh, local ingredients, and the facilities are terrific. No liquor is sold here; guests bring their own and set-ups are provided." *(SB)* "Low-key, spotless, quiet, beautiful, spectacular location, outstanding food and service, delightful management and staff. Great for families, offering a bingo night, a movie night, a cookout night, a lecture night." *(Claire Kretschmer)*

Open Mid-June–Labor Day weekend.

Rooms 7 suites, 35 doubles, 12 singles—all with full private bath, desk. 6 with refrigerator. 1 studio cottage. 10 singles with shared bath.

Facilities Lobby, sitting rooms, TV/VCR room, game room, play room, deck. Movies, bingo, bridge, speakers, travelogues. 2 Omni tennis courts, 1½ m private beach, bocce, shuffleboard. Children's program (ages 3–10, included in rate), play equipment. Windsurfers, sailboats, kayaks, canoes, rowboats. Golf nearby.

Location SW RI coast; close to CT border. 2 hrs. S of Boston, 40 min. W of Newport, 40 m SE of Providence, RI, 20 min. to Mystic Seaport. 5 m from town. Take I-95 to CT Exit 93, Clarks Falls, to Rte. 216 S. Follow to Rte. 3. Go left on Rte. 3 & quick right back onto 216 S. Follow Rte. 216 S & go right onto Rte. 91 S. Follow 91 S to center island in rd. Enter island, go to stop sign. Go straight onto Dunn's Corners/Bradford Rd. Go straight to Dunn's Corners traffic light (Mobil Gas Station on corner). Go straight across Rte. 1 onto Langworthy Rd. Go straight at next stop sign onto Weekapaug Rd. Bear right at next stop sign; follow along shore to inn, staying on paved road.

Restrictions Minimal interior soundproofing. Jackets suggested in the dining room. Smoking allowed in lobby.

Credit cards None accepted.

Rates Full board, $350–370 suite, double; $185–210 single. 15% service. Children's rates, $35–125. 3-night minimum stay. Box lunches available. Prix fixe meals: $15 lunch; $35 dinner, plus 15% service.

Extras Limited wheelchair access. Crib, babysitting. Airport/station pickups, $15–175.

We Want to Hear from You!

As you know, this book is effective only with your help. We really need to know about your experiences and discoveries. If you stayed at an inn or hotel listed here, we want to know how it was. Did it live up to our description? Exceed it? Was it what you expected? Did you like it? Were you disappointed? Delighted? Have you discovered new establishments that we should add to the next edition?

Tear out one of the report forms at the back of this book (or use your own stationery if you prefer) and write today. *Even if you write only "Fully endorse existing entry" you will have been most helpful.*
Thank You!

Vermont

Inn at the Round Barn Farm, Waitsfield

Vermont is a lovely state filled with lovely inns. Winters and summers are beautiful in Vermont, although inns are most crowded (and rates are at their highest) during the first half of October. In general, peak-season rates apply in winter and during fall foliage season. Summer is still considered off-season in many ski towns, and rates are often extremely reasonable. Many lodges offer lower "ski-week" rates from Sunday through Friday nights, except during Christmas and February vacation periods. A number of establishments close or scale back their activities in the early spring and late fall, when the state is not at its best.

Northeast Kingdom: The northeastern section of Vermont comprises most towns north and east of Stowe, and mixes pastoral beauty, picturesque charm, and occasional rural poverty. Rates for both food and accommodation are extremely reasonable. Entries in the Northeast Kingdom include **Coventry, Craftsbury Common, Derby Line, East Burke, Greensboro, Hardwick, Lower Waterford, Lyndonville, St. Johnsbury,** and **Wolcott.**

Lake Champlain: Separating Vermont and New York State, beautiful Lake Champlain offers views of the Green Mountains to the east, and the Adirondacks to the west. It's worth taking the ferry from Burlington to the New York side for the vistas alone, although a stop at Ausable Chasm is worthwhile.

For inns on or near the lake, see (going from north to south): **Alburg, North Hero, South Hero, Burlington, Shelburne,** and **Vergennes.**

Reader tips: Bicycle tours are extremely popular in Vermont, and a number of companies arrange delightful ones from inn to inn. However, "if you are traveling independently, looking for peace and quiet, don't hesitate to ask if a tour will be staying overnight during your visit." *(Ed Okie)* "My favorite time to travel in Vermont is after Labor Day weekend and before foliage; rates are reasonable, there are no crowds, and the weather is often perfect, with warm, sunny days, and crisp, cool nights." *(MW)* "Bring insect repellent; the river and wooded sections of Vermont do get buggy, especially in spring and early summer." *(JC)*

"Much of the beauty of Vermont can be found on lightly traveled country roads. To navigate these with confidence, carry a copy of the *DeLorme Atlas & Gazetteer*. During the cold of winter two welcome Vermont treats are good coffee and delicious pastry. Virtually every gas station and convenience store offer aromatic blends of Green Mountain Coffee. Outstanding bakeries include: the Otter Creek Bakery, Middlebury; Rainbow Sweets, Marshfield Village; La Brioche, Montpelier; Queen of Tarts and Mirabelles, Burlington; Bridge Street Cafe, Waitsfield; and the Vermont Country Deli & Cafe, Brattleboro." *(Joe Schmidt)*

Worth noting: Smoking is prohibited in virtually all Vermont B&Bs and inns. Many full-service Vermont inns add a 15% service charge to the entire rate, not just the allocated food cost.

ALBURG

For more inns near Lake Champlain, see (going from north to south): **North Hero, South Hero, Burlington, Shelburne,** and **Vergennes.**

Thomas Mott Homestead B&B ¢ *Tel:* 802–796–3736
Blue Rock Road, Route 3 800–348–0843
P.O. Box 149-B, 05440 *Fax:* 802–796–3736
URL: http://www.virtualcities.com/ons/vt/a/vta3502.htm

Guaranteed at the Thomas Mott Homestead are breathtaking views of Lake Champlain, especially lovely at sunset or by the light of a full moon. On clear days, you can see beyond the lake to the Green Mountains of Vermont, the Adirondacks of New York, and even to the White Mountains of New Hampshire. Guaranteed in warm weather is the peaceful sound of waves lapping at the shore. In fact, the only thing that Patrick Schallert, who has owned the Thomas Mott Homestead since 1987, can't guarantee you is a sighting of Champ, the legendary monster of Lake Champlain.

Built in 1838, the inn features the original beamed walls, ceilings, and floors, complemented by antique furnishings and hand-crafted Vermont quilts. Breakfast is served at guests' convenience between 6:30 and 9 A.M., and includes guests' choice of such treats as raspberry pancakes, French toast, Maine crab omelets with home-baked bread, or vegetable quiche, plus fresh fruit and juice.

"Pat is a fantastic cook and a great storyteller; plenty to do nearby." *(Cynthia Perdigao)* "Outstanding location on the lake; guests can swim and canoe right off the front lawn." *(Jane Somers)* "Incredible location; Ransom's Nest has an especially stunning view. The Ben & Jerry's ice cream outstanding. Pat is helpful and friendly, always going out of his way for guests, adding thoughtful touches from complimentary spring water to chocolates on the pillow." *(Judith Evans)* "Looking out my win-

371

dow, I saw a beautiful blue heron standing on the shore of the lake. Memorable breakfasts of French toast, quiche, and shrimp omelets." *(Jacilyn Fricks)* "Amazing view of the lake from the bed of the corner suite. Pat was relaxed, friendly, and welcoming; interesting fellow guests, too." *(T. Bayly)* "Beautiful views of the fall foliage during the day, the full moon reflected off the lake at night. In the evening, Pat offered us free dishes of Ben & Jerry's ice cream; after returning home, Pat sent us photos he had taken of us." *(Susan Cooper)* "The house is full of fabulous books on fine wines, travel, food, and more. The frozen lake was utterly quiet and peaceful. Loved all the breakfast choices." *(Rhoda Flaxman)* "We enjoyed feeding the quail which Pat raises and releases each year." *(MW)*

Open All year.
Rooms 5 doubles—all with private bath and/or shower, clock/radio, desk, fan. 2 with fireplace, 1 with balcony. Telephone on request.
Facilities Dining room, living room, library with TV, family room with bumper pool, darts; guest freezer; porches. 2½ acres on Lake Champlain with gazebo, gardens, lawn games, dock, canoes, fishing, cross-country skiing (40 m of trails). Tennis nearby.
Location NW VT. Approx. 5 m S of Canadian border. 1 hr. S of Montreal, 1 hr. N of Burlington. Take I-89 N to Swanton exit. Take Rte. 78 W for 1 m (past drawbridge) to Blue Rock Rd. Go S (right) at B&B sign & drive to end.
Restrictions No smoking inside. Prefer children over 6.
Credit cards All major.
Rates B&B, $75–95 double. Extra person, $10.

ANDOVER

Inn at High View 👫
East Hill Road, RR 1, P.O. Box 201A, 05143

Tel: 802–875–2724
Fax: 802–875–4021
E-mail: hiview@aol.com

The Inn at High View is a rambling 150-year-old farmhouse restored as a B&B in 1987; in 1991 Greg Bohan purchased this hilltop property; Sal Massaro is his partner and chef. Breakfast is served from 8–9 A.M. at the large dining room table, and includes juice, fruit, coffee, and such entrées as fruit pancakes or waffles. Dinner is served on Saturday nights, and a sample menu might consist of prosciutto and melon, pasta with sun-dried tomatoes and pesto, gingered chicken with asparagus and wild rice, and homemade cheesecake.

"Greg and Sal are friendly, welcoming, sincere hosts. Breakfasts are bountiful and varied. Our weekend also included a great gourmet barbecue, served on beautiful china. Charming rooms, too." *(H. Bussey)* "Cozy, warm, and inviting with a large stone fireplace and sectional sofa in the living room. Well-presented, tasty breakfast, while accommodating to special dietary needs. Dinners are memorable; Sal specializes in Italian cuisine. When dining elsewhere, we always found their recommendations helpful." *(Ross & Ginger Ludeman)* "A quiet place to retire after a day of skiing at Okemo. Guest rooms are decorated with canopy beds and antiques." *(Robert Fucci)* "The porch faces south and overlooks the swimming pool, with rolling hills beyond;

rocking chairs make it perfect for a quiet evening." *(Ted & Laura Brum-leve)* "Down comforters, terry robes, and brandy in each room. Greg and Sal are attentive to every need: renting your favorite movie; ready with hot coffee; welcoming you on cold days with a warming fire." *(Anne & Jim Ragone)* "Lots of extra-thick bath towels. Public rooms have a personal tone with family photos and collectibles tastefully displayed." *(Marjorie DeWeese)* "At night, decanters of punch or mineral water, and small chocolates await you." *(RR)* "A relief to find an inn that is not overly pink and frilly. Fantastic French toast filled with cream cheese and walnuts, dipped in cinnamon batter." *(Gayle Joseph)*

Open All year. Closed 2 weeks in April, Nov.

Rooms 2 suites, 6 doubles—all with private bath. 5 with balcony, 2 with desk, air-conditioning.

Facilities Dining room, living room, both with fireplace, piano, stereo, books; game room, guest refrigerator, screened porch. Conference room with TV/VCR, business equipment. 72 acres with swimming pool, treehouse, gazebo, lawn games, hiking trails, cross-country skiing. Tennis, golf nearby. 7 miles to downhill skiing.

Location S VT. 90 m E of Albany, NY; 110 m N of Hartford, CT; 130 m from Boston, MA. 7 m W of Chester, 5 m E of Weston. From S take I-91 N to Exit 6, then take Rte. 103 N to Chester. Go W on Rte. 11 to Andover-Weston Rd. & turn right at sign to inn. From N (Ludlow) go S on Rte. 100 for 3.4 m, turn left at Andover sign. Go 5 m to inn; ½ m past Cobb Rd.

Restrictions No smoking. Over age 12 preferred; younger children in suites.

Credit cards MC, Visa.

Rates B&B, $95–155 suite, $95–135 double, $80–125 single. MAP, $205 suite, $185 double, $140 single. Extra person, $20. 2–3 night fall/winter, holiday weekend minimum. Prix fixe dinner, $30 (Sat.).

Extras Station pickup. Crib, babysitting by arrangement. Italian, Spanish spoken. Small pets possible.

ARLINGTON

A quiet village set along Route 7A, Arlington is in southwestern Vermont, 3½ hours north of New York City and about the same distance northwest of Boston. It's 15 miles north of Bennington and 8 miles south of Manchester. Of particular interest is the Norman Rockwell Exhibition, housed in an 1875 church. More than 1,000 magazine covers and illustrations are on display, many of them pictures of local residents who modeled for Rockwell during the fourteen years he lived here. Arlington is intersected by the Battenkill River, one of Vermont's best trout-fishing streams.

Reader tip: "Arlington is a charming, peaceful town minutes from busy Manchester." *(Joe Schmidt)*

Arlington Inn ✕ 🐾 👪 ⚥ ¢   *Tel:* 802–375–6532
Route 7A at Route 313, P.O. Box 369, 05250   800–443–9442

To imagine the power and wealth of the 19th-century railroad barons, one must think of the vast fortunes and influence of today's computer moguls—a picture of America's railroads today just doesn't summon the right image. In 1848, one such magnate, Martin Chester Deming, built himself an imposing Greek Revival mansion, framed by Doric columns on two levels. In 1888, the building became an inn, and has offered food and lodging to travelers ever since. Owned by Deborah and Mark Gagnon since 1994, the inn has characteristics unusual in snowy Vermont; the structure's roof is flat and the windows are oversize. Inside, guests find rooms done in period antiques, and tongue-in-groove paneled ceilings similar to those found in railroad cars of the period. Most guest rooms have queen- or king-size four-poster, canopy, or sleigh beds. The Gagnons have also renovated the 1830 parsonage next door, which now houses six guest rooms, four with wood-burning fireplaces.

Breakfast is served in the charming solarium from 8–9:30 A.M., and includes a choice of eggs any style with home fries, the omelet du jour, French toast, plain or blueberry pancakes, plus bacon or sausage, muffins, cereal, and fresh fruit and juice. Local produce and native Vermont products are used whenever possible for the dinner menu. Although menus change often, possible entrées include roast duck with sage and red wine sauce, dilled salmon with citrus butter, and grilled pork tenderloin medallions with bourbon and candied fruit.

"Exceptionally good food and service at dinner." (*Flora Neumeister*) "Mark and Debbie are enthusiastic, hard-working, skillful innkeepers who maintain a first-rate facility. My room in the main house was spotless, with the original wide-planked floors and period furniture, maintaining the spirit of this 150-year-old house. In the comfortable restaurant, the number of evening diners is limited to ensure a relaxed and unhurried meal." (*Joe Schmidt*)

Open All year.

Rooms 6 suites, 14 doubles—all with full private bath and/or shower, air-conditioning, clock, fan. 1 with whirlpool tub. Some with telephone with data port, TV, desk, fireplace, balcony/deck. 7 rooms in main building, 7 in carriage house, 6 in Old Parsonage.

Facilities Restaurant with fireplace, solarium, living room, library with books, games, TV/VCR; porch. 4 acres with off-street parking, tennis court. Golf, hiking, fishing, skiing nearby.

Location Center of town, at junction of Rtes. 7A & 313.

Restrictions No smoking. Children welcome on a "case by case" basis.

Credit cards Amex, MC, Visa.

Rates B&B, $160–205 suite, $70–90 double. Extra person, $20. MAP, $230–275 suite, $140–160 double, $105–125 single. Extra person, $55. 2-night minimum most weekends. Alc dinner, $25–30. Tips appreciated.

Extras Wheelchair access; bathroom specially equipped. French, Spanish spoken. Crib, babysitting.

Hill Farm Inn 🐾
Hill Farm Road, RR 2, P.O. Box 2015, 05250

Tel: 802–375–2269
800–882–2545
Fax: 802–375–9918
E-mail: hillfarm@vermontel.com
URL: http://www.hillfarminn.com

Sometimes it seems that Vermont is filling up with "designer inns" faster than the proverbial woods with snow. So it's nice to see that an old-fashioned inn is still doing what it does best—providing families with comfortable accommodations in a comfortable country farm atmosphere.

The Hill family began farming this area in 1775; in 1905, Mettie Hill, a widow with young children, opened the farmhouse to paying guests in summer. Craig and Kathleen Yanez, along with Kathleen's parents Anne and Rob Weber, bought the inn in 1998. They're all experienced innkeepers; the Webers own the Inn at Covered Bridge Green (see entry), while Craig and Kathleen owned the Country Willows B&B. Accommodations are available in the main farmhouse built in 1830 and an adjacent guest house dating from 1790. Guest rooms are bright and cheerful, simply furnished with flowered wallpaper, hand stenciling, quilts, and Vermont country antiques. Breakfast is served from 7:30–9:30 A.M., and includes juice, home-baked muffins, granola or oatmeal, and a choice of eggs, French toast, or blueberry pancakes, plus bacon or sausage; snacks and beverages are available in the afternoon and evening. Guests enjoy a four-course dinner on Saturday nights at 7 P.M., with homemade soups, breads, and desserts, plus vegetables from the inn's gardens.

"Scenic area, with lovely mountain views, and lots to do nearby. The inn is quiet, clean, bright, and airy; the innkeepers are friendly and helpful. Tasty breakfast with great coffee. The goats and sheep add to the inn's friendly charms. The Lilac Suite is a two-unit building apart from the main inn with a little kitchenette and ample country charm, right down to the quilt on the bed." (*Mr. & Mrs. Robert Duarte*) "Quilts and stuffed animals give each room a homey feel; most enjoyable is the living room with its huge fireplace, lit in the wintertime at 5:30 P.M. The inn is located off a main road, far enough away from traffic noise yet on the way to Manchester (about eight minutes) and all the shops." (*Jennifer Karchmer*) "Great location for fishermen with access to the Battenkill River." (*GR*) "Immaculately clean inn located in a quiet, rural setting. We were particularly pleased with the warm welcome extended to our children." (*John McNally*)

"Special touches in each room include a little basket of apples, herbal soap, a complete notebook of area information, and a night-light in the bathroom. Breakfasts are satisfying, and the granola is superb. The comfortable guest rooms have lovely quilts, padded rocking chairs, and ruffled curtains. The porch has comfortable wicker furniture and beautiful views of Mt. Equinox." (*Steven & Rita Bendix*) "Our room and bathroom were kept immaculate by an invisible housekeeper." (*Diane & Robert Dunn*) "We were offered fresh cider and cookies on arrival." (*David Loomis & Wendy Gross*) "The unobtrusive innkeepers respected our privacy." (*Jeffrey & Terry McKown*) "Plenty of time is allowed for breakfast, so I could sleep in and not miss a good meal; several choices, plus wonderful muffins and endless coffee." (*Rita Cummins Sapppenfield*)

Open All year. Cabins open late May–late Oct.

Rooms 2 suites, 11 doubles, 4 cabins—12 with private shower and/or bath, 5 rooms sharing 3 baths. 6 rooms in annex. All with clock/radio, fan. 6 with porch/deck, 3 with refrigerator, 1 with fireplace, TV.

Facilities Living room with fireplace, TV; sitting room with Franklin stove; dining room with fireplace; screened porch. 50 acres with lawn games, swings; 1 m frontage on Battenkill River for tubing, fishing, canoeing, swimming; conservation, bird-nesting area. Cross-country and downhill skiing nearby.

Location SW VT. From Arlington go 4 m N on Rte. 7A. Turn right on Hill Farm Rd. and go ½ m to inn on right.

Restrictions No smoking indoors.

Credit cards Amex, Discover, MC, Visa.

Rates B&B, $155–186 suite, $80–155 double, $70–145 single. Extra adult, $20. MAP, $198–230 suite, $125–198 double. Children's, weekly rates. Mid-week specials in winter/spring. Tax included; 15% service charge. 2-night minimum most weekends. Prix fixe dinner, $20.

Extras Pets permitted in cabins, May–Oct. Cribs.

The Inn on Covered Bridge Green
3587 River Road, RD 1, P.O. Box 3550, 05250

Tel: 802–375–9489
800–726–9480
Fax: 802–375–1208
E-mail: cbg@sover.net
URL: http://www.bestinns.net/usa/vt/cbg.html

What could be more quintessentially Vermont than a 200-year-old Colonial farmhouse, overlooking a little white church and a red wooden covered bridge? Possibly the fact that this old house, built in 1792, was for 12 years the home of Norman Rockwell, America's beloved illustrator of small-town American life.

In 1987, Anne and Ron Weber moved to Vermont, where they embarked on a major renovation of the house. Rooms are named for Rockwell prints that adorn the walls, but guests coming for a longer stay can soak up the Rockwell atmosphere in either of his two studios, which the Webers have converted into housekeeping cottages. Most rooms have four-poster or canopy queen-size beds. Breakfasts of baked French toast with walnuts or baked egg in tomato, with fresh fruit and juice, are served on bone china, with Waterford crystal, and sterling silver.

"This is the kind of B&B I like most, where one feels 'at home' but not 'home'; not a guest so much as a distant relation or new acquaintance; a place that is cozy and charming without being self-consciously quaint. The Corn Crib is a rustic efficiency apartment with a sleeping loft, perfect for the person who relishes peace, privacy, independence, and simple creature comforts. It was originally the studio of Norman Rockwell's son Jarvis; Rockwell's own studio is right next door. A fine spread is laid at breakfast, with fresh fruit and often such Southern specialties as grits and corn pone. The Webers also recommended excellent restaurants and walks amid beautiful scenery." *(Julie Li)*

"Anne and Ron are exceptionally friendly and generous innkeepers. Their B&B is comfortable and tranquil, a place for great conversations with interesting fellow guests." *(Holly Dinsmore)* "Comfortable and homey; exceptional furnishings; warm and welcoming hosts." *(Carolyn & Paul Meyer)* "The owners' knowledge of Norman Rockwell makes staying in his former home a personal experience. Large rooms, filled with wonderful antiques; candles were lit in all the windows. I stayed in Norman's room, called the Spooners (after the painting); clean and quiet, with great water pressure in the modern baths. Anne and Ron are excellent cooks and breakfast is different every day." *(Dianne Crawford)* "We loved the location, the history, and the hospitality. Relaxing, yet with much to do nearby. Wonderful blueberry bread at breakfast." *(Diane Vogt)*

Open All year.
Rooms 1 suite, 2 cottages, 4 doubles, 1 single—6 with private bath. All with desk, air-conditioning. 2 Rockwell studios with fireplace, kitchen, laundry, TV. 1 with whirlpool tub, 4 with fireplace.
Facilities Dining room with fireplace, living room with fireplace, TV/VCR, stereo, games; library. 5½ acres, tennis court, picnic/barbecue area. On Battenkill River for fishing, swimming, canoeing, tubing. Golf nearby. 20–40 minutes to cross-country, downhill skiing, ice-skating.
Location From Rte. 7A in Arlington, go W on Rte. 313 opposite Arlington Inn. Go 4½ m to red covered bridge & white church on left. Turn left through bridge; inn is straight ahead.
Restrictions No smoking.
Credit cards None accepted.
Rates B&B, $145–165 suite, $110–145 double, $110–130 single. 15% service. Extra person, $25. 2-night minimum foliage, holidays, most weekends, June–Oct.

Keelan House ☏
Rte. 313, RD 1, P.O. Box 1272, 05250

Tel: 802–375–9029
Fax: 802–375–1103
URL: http://www.keelan.com

The Keelan House is a spacious Federal home built in 1820 and restored by Don and Verrall Keelan in 1986. Their intimate B&B is decorated with exceptional Colonial antiques, early American crafts and collectibles, beautiful colors and fabrics, and the original wide-planked flooring. There's a table and chairs for picnicking out back, and a path leading down to the Battenkill River. Breakfast is served at 8:30 A.M. sharp, and includes fresh fruit and juice, bacon, ham or sausages, and eggs.

"Although we visited on a hot muggy weekend, efficient central air-conditioning kept our immaculate room cool and made sleeping easy. Breakfast was great—fresh blueberries and melon, chocolate chip muffins, Green Mountain Roasters coffee, and generous servings of ham and eggs—served at a table for eight." *(Jane Mattoon)* "The lovely grounds have shaded seating, paths, and bridges for exploring this scenic section of the Battenkill River. We saw blue heron hunting minnow, and muskrats on the banks." *(Robert Stedman)* "Provides for children with toys, books, and taller chairs." *(Donna Bernier)* "Embroidered linens, beautiful quilts, and colorful pillows highlight the decor. A perfect setting—you can see foxes running through a frosted corn field or go for a stroll along the river path at dusk." *(Meredith Schultz)* "Beautifully kept house and grounds; immaculate housekeeping; beautiful antique furnishings." *(SWS)* "Absolutely immaculate, with pristine white linens and lots of towels. Warm welcome; the Keelans are helpful with suggestions for restaurants and sights. We followed the trail along the river for perfect foliage views. Don has two aerated pools where he breeds trout. The Carlin Room and the Herbert Room at the back of the house are especially quiet." *(Michael Miller)*

Open All year. Closed Christmas Day–New Year's Day.
Rooms 5 doubles—all with private bath and/or shower, fan, central air-conditioning.
Facilities Dining room with fireplace, living room with fireplace, porch. 17 acres on river, walking paths, pond for swimming, fishing; children's play equipment, canoeing, tubing, trout fishing, cross-country skiing. ½ hr. to downhill skiing.
Location ½ m W of town. Go W on Rte. 313 opposite Arlington Inn.
Restrictions Smoking restricted to living room.
Credit cards None accepted.
Rates B&B, $95–125 double, $70–85 single, including tax.
Extras Crib.

BARNARD

Also recommended: Vermont's most luxurious inn is **Twin Farms** (Barnard, 05031; 802–234–9999 or 800–TWIN–FAR[MS]), a pastoral retreat on a 235-acre estate once owned by Sinclair Lewis. Renovated, restored, and refurbished at a cost of millions, Twin Farms offers every conceivable amenity that the sophisticated traveler could enjoy in an elegant but unpretentious and informal house-party atmosphere. It's one of the few properties to receive a five-star rating from Mobil. The Point, in Saranac Lake, is the only comparable property in the East. The all-inclusive rates start at $800 for a double and climb to $1500 for the incredible cottages (plus 15% service and 8% tax), and cover everything from meals to drinks to tennis and skiing. In this atmosphere of complete relaxation, we figure the only stress comes when you have to pay the bill. "The accommodations were impeccable, the meals prepared and presented to perfection, and the staff most efficient and hospitable. The atmosphere is totally stress-free and guest privacy is a top priority." *(Nancy Cannata)* "The staff is extraordinary, the food is incomparable, the art is fabulous and irreverent." *(David Kramer)*

The Maple Leaf Inn ♿   *Tel:* 802–234–5342
Route 12, P.O. Box 273, 05031   800–51–MAPLE
E-mail: mapleafinn@aol.com
URL: http://www.mapleleafinn.com

Antique charm balanced with modern convenience, personal attention tempered with concern for privacy—that's the atmosphere Gary and Janet Robison sought to create when they built the Maple Leaf Inn in 1994 as a romantic getaway for couples. This reproduction turn-of-the-century Victorian farmhouse has guest rooms highlighted by king-size beds, stenciling, stitchery, and hand-made quilts. Guests are welcomed with afternoon refreshments, served by the parlor fireplace or on the porch rocking chairs, depending on the weather. Evening turndown service includes chocolates and replenished bathroom towels. Breakfast is served from 8:30–10 A.M. at individual tables; in addition to a choice of fruit juices, hot beverages, and homemade granola, a typical menu might include apple fritters with warm maple syrup, sautéed bananas, and stuffed French toast; followed the next day by cinnamon rolls, warm citrus compote, and Dijon egg puff with homemade toasted challah bread.

"Gary and Janet visited dozens of inns to develop their list of amenities for their own inn. Individual heating zones provide guests with finger-touch temperature control, including luxuriously heated bathroom floors. On a cold snowy night we lounged snugly in our room, enjoying the fireplace and a movie from the inn's tape collection. Delicious breakfast of egg soufflé with homemade bread and maple-leaf–shaped spiced pears." (Sheila & Joe Schmidt) "A beautiful home surrounded by flowers and trees. After our arrival, a tray with crackers, cheese dip, and apple cider was brought to our room. After dinner at a nearby restaurant (Gary and Janet had made the reservation for us), we found a personally written note and a package of Vermont wildflower seeds on the pillow. Fresh flowers in the bath; a small bag of homemade chocolate chip cookies upon departure. Superb breakfast with homemade challah bread." (Pat Malone) "Little touches mean so much—afternoon hot cider and treats, the collection of romantic videos, great dinner recommendations, expert advice on cross-country ski trails." (Amy Joges) "Huge smiles, warm handshakes, and a heartfelt desire to ensure your welcome." (Philip Pearlman)

"Exceptional hospitality. Perfectly situated well off the quiet road in a grove of magnificent birches. Each room is luxuriously comfortable, from the top-of-the-line mattress to the fireplace awaiting the strike of a match, to the complimentary sweets, to the heated bathroom floors. We were treated to bananas sautéed in lemon butter, melt-in-your-mouth cranberry biscuits, and French toast stuffed with flavored cream cheese. The lactose intolerance of one of us was wonderfully and cheerfully accommodated by an equally scrumptious feast. No one is rushed and the servings are limitless." (Barbara & Dennis Jarry) "Beautiful inn with a wraparound porch, set in the snowy woods, with small white Christmas lights in every window." (Kimberly & Michael Kelliher) "Gary's story-telling skills entertained us during breakfast. We stayed in the Winter Haven Room, with stenciled scenes of snow-capped cottages." (Michelle Spiller) "The wraparound porch is our favorite place to relax. Exceptional attention to detail was seen in the fresh flowers throughout the inn; the linen closet for extra pillows and blankets; the ample information on area activities; the room diaries; and the thoughtful personal note left with the evening turndown service." (Kimberly Kelly)

Open All year.
Rooms 7 doubles—all with full private bath, telephone, radio, clock, TV/VCR. Most with whirlpool tub, wood-burning fireplace.
Facilities Living room with fireplace; dining room with fireplace; library; wraparound porch/gazebo. 16 acres with lawn games, cross-country skiing &

hiking. Downhill skiing, golf, tennis, lake nearby for swimming, boating, fishing.

Location Central VT. 270 m N of NYC; 175 m N of Hartford, CT; 157 m NW of Boston. Take I-89 to Exit 1. Take Rte. 4 W to Woodstock. Go 9 m N on Rte. 12 to Barnard. Inn is ¼ m S of Barnard General Store.

Restrictions No smoking. No children.

Credit cards Amex, CB, DC, DSC, JCB, MC, Visa.

Rates B&B, $125–175 double.

Extras Wheelchair access; bathroom specially equipped.

BENNINGTON

Bennington is located in the southwestern corner of Vermont, just 30 miles east of Albany, New York, and 25 miles south of Manchester, Vermont. Its role in the Revolutionary War is commemorated in the Bennington Battle Monument, an obelisk offering lovely views; also worthwhile is the Bennington Museum, home to a substantial collection of Grandma Moses paintings. Visit Old First Church to see a classic New England Congregationalist Church dating back to 1805.

Reader tip: "The town of Old Bennington contains dozens of meticulously preserved homes and churches constructed between 1730 and 1830. In the cemetery behind Old First Church, headstones mark the graves of poet Robert Frost and soldiers of the Revolutionary and Civil Wars."

The Four Chimneys Inn ✕   *Tel:* 802–447–3500
21 West Road, Route 9, 05201   800–649–3503
              Fax: 802–447–3692
       E-mail: chimneys@vermontel.com

After many years of corporate life and extensive travel, Judith and Ron Schefkind fulfilled their lifelong dream and purchased the Four Chimneys Inn in 1996. A magnificent Georgian Revival mansion, the inn is set amid expansive lawns, huge trees, and beautiful gardens. Its history goes back to 1793, when it was built by Reverend David Avery, pastor of the Old First Church. Unable to afford its upkeep, he sold the estate to Nathaniel Brush, a participant in the Battle of Bennington. Brush had financial difficulties as well, and turned the mansion into a boarding-house and general store. Restored to its original grandeur in 1870, the structure burned to the ground in 1910. Rebuilt by a prominent Bennington businessman, the building opened as an inn and restaurant after his death in 1949.

The Schefkinds have upgraded and updated the guest rooms and common areas, improving comfort levels while preserving the inn's historic appeal. The restaurant is open to the public and has built a strong culinary reputation; Four Chimneys is also a popular spot for weddings, hosted in tents in the lovely gardens. Lunch choices range from salmon burgers on croissants to chicken pot pie; a recent prix fixe dinner included such courses as salmon terrine, Caesar salad, rack of lamb or chicken in wild mushroom cream sauce, and a selection from the dessert tray with espresso or cappuccino.

"Clean, attractive rooms; excellent location, close to the attractions of charming Old Bennington. Our spacious upper-floor room had large closets, a comfortable sitting area, a whirlpool bath, and a gas fireplace. Breakfast included a colorful serving of fresh fruit, cereal, and just-baked croissants." (*Joe Schmidt*) "While waiting to be seated for dinner, we relaxed with the other diners and overnight guests in the inn's handsome living room, then were shown to our table for an excellent meal." (*MW*) Comments appreciated.

Open All year. Restaurant closed Mon.
Rooms 1 suite, 10 doubles—all with full private bath, telephone, radio, clock, TV, air-conditioning. Most with whirlpool tub, desk, fan, fireplace, data port. 2 rooms in carriage house, ice house.
Facilities Restaurant with fireplace, living room with TV/VCR, books. 11 acres with off-street parking, gardens, pond; wedding/banquet facilities. Fishing, swimming, canoeing, hiking, golf, tennis, skiing nearby.
Location Historic district. On Rte. 9, 1 m from town; walking distance to Bennington Museum & Battle Monument.
Restrictions No smoking. Children 12 and over.
Credit cards All major.
Rates B&B, $105–185 suite, double, $85–125 single. Extra person, $15. 2–3 night weekend/holiday minimum. Alc lunch, $8–12; alc dinner, $34. Children's portions. MAP rates on request; 12% service.
Extras Wheelchair access; bathroom specially equipped. Spanish spoken.

Molly Stark Inn ¢ 🛉   *Tel:* 802–442–9631
1067 East Main Street, 05201   800–356–3076
                                           Fax: 802–442–5224
                              E-mail: mollyinn@vermontel.com
                              URL: http://www.mollystarkinn.com

Reed Fendler bought and renovated the Molly Stark Inn in 1988. In 1996, Cammi Fendler made the transition from guest to innkeeper when she and Reed got married; they first met in 1989 when Cammi and her family stayed at the inn on vacation. A large Victorian home dating back to 1860, rooms are simply decorated with antiques, hand-stitched antique quilts, and stenciling. The saltbox-style guest cottage has a loft with a king-size brass bed, skylights, and a double Jacuzzi tub. Breakfasts include such favorites as homemade granola and puffed apple pancakes.

"Reed and Cammi Fendler are a delightful couple who let you know they are happy to have you as a guest. They were helpful with area information, and directed us to sights, places to eat, and scenic drives to see the beautiful fall colors and covered bridges. Attentive housekeeping; all is fresh and clean; convenient parking. The inn is located on a busy street but sits on a large lot with the neighbors far enough away that you feel you are in the country. Breakfast consisted of apple pancakes, waffles with maple syrup, bacon, and a variety of muffins; local products are used whenever possible. Every evening freshly baked cookies were served to the guests." *(Janet Tackett)*

"Painted gray-blue with white trim, the porch was adorned with pumpkins and corn husks during my October visit. Hot cider was served in the afternoon, and a fire in the woodstove kept us cozy and warm. My room was large, with a firm queen-size bed, good bedside lighting, plump pillows, and an antique quilt. The other guests were agreeable company, and Reed was helpful with restaurant recommendations. The inn is surrounded by trees, and a babbling brook borders the rear of the property." *(Sarah Connors)* "Our spacious room had an antique quilt and tons of pillows on the bed; the ceiling fan made sleeping comfortable. Wonderful breakfasts with fresh fruit, great muffins, and delicious entrées." *(Melissa Rossi)* "Samples of Reed's photography hang in many of the rooms. Molly, the inn's darling dog-in-residence, is obedient and loving." *(Alice Vacca)*

Open All year.
Rooms 1 cottage, 6 doubles—all with private bath and/or shower, air-conditioning, fan; 2 with Jacuzzi, desk. Cottage with TV, stereo, woodstove, double Jacuzzi, wet bar, refrigerator, ceiling fan.
Facilities Dining room; den with woodstove, games, TV; parlor. 1 acre with stream.
Location SW VT. 130 m NW of Boston. ½ m E of Bennington Village Center on S side of Rte 9.
Restrictions No smoking. Traffic noise in front rooms. Common room noise in downstairs guest room.
Credit cards Amex, Discover, MC, Visa.
Rates B&B, $145 cottage, $65–95 double. Extra person, $15. 6% gratuity. Family rate. 10% senior discount. Ski package. 2-night minimum most weekends. Dinner packages.
Extras Station pickup. Crib.

BOLTON

Also recommended: Twenty minutes drive east of Burlington and west of Stowe, at an elevation of 2,000 feet, is **The Black Bear Inn** (Mountain Road, 05477; 802–434–2126 or 800–395–6335; www.blkbearinn. com). Guests can ski right to the door, as Bolton Valley Ski Resort wraps around the inn, providing both downhill and cross-country skiing. Each of the 24 guest rooms has a private bath; some also have private balconies, fireplaces, and/or whirlpool tubs. The inn's restaurant is run by innkeeper/owner Ken Richardson, a graduate of the Culinary Institute of America; other amenities include the tennis courts, outdoor hot tubs, heated swimming pool, plus golf, hiking trails, bicycling, and fly fishing. B&B double rates range from $75–135; the rate with both breakfast and dinner runs from $120–180. Ask about golf and skiing packages.

For additional area inns, see **Burlington** and **Waterbury**.

BRANDON

Brandon is located in west-central Vermont, on Route 7, halfway between Middlebury and Rutland, 60 miles south of Burlington and 15 miles north of Rutland, and makes a great base for hiking in the Green Mountains.

For additional area inns, see **Goshen** and **Middlebury**.

Churchill House Inn   *Tel:* 802–247–3078
RR 3, Route 73 East, P.O. Box 3265, 05733   *Fax:* 802–247–6851
                                 E-mail: rciatt@sover.net
                         URL: http://www.inntoinn.com

This inn was built by the Churchill family in 1871 and served as a stopover point for farmers bringing grain and lumber to the mills. Roy and Lois Jackson have owned the inn since 1982, and operate a 12-mile ski-touring center in the winter months. In addition, they run inn-to-inn hiking, bicycling, and cross-country skiing tours. The Jacksons also pride themselves on their creative cuisine. A typical single-entrée dinner might include Mexican corn soup, avocado and grapefruit salad, rack of lamb, roast potatoes, broccoli, and maple-walnut pie.

"Our family was warmly welcomed by our hosts and fellow guests. Outstanding food, too. Excellent cross-country skiing. Our first time at an inn, but not the last." *(Sue Razaire)* "Lois and Julie are geniuses in the kitchen; with advance notice, they accommodated our vegan diet with delicious meals with lovely flower garnishes. Each evening Ray suggested hiking adventures with valuable tips from first-hand experience." *(Leigh Hunt)* "Spacious, airy quarters hand-stenciled by Lois. Before dinner we gathered on the porch and enjoyed hot crabmeat spread while we chatted with other guests. Dinner included homemade French bread and an especially tender rack of lamb. After a good night's sleep we were treated to delightful cottage cheese pancakes with all the accompaniments." *(Janet Beall)* "Lovely flagstone porch, with weather-tight sliding glass doors and skylights to make it bright and airy in summer, and sunny and cozy in winter. Especially appreciated were the before-dinner appetizers and set-ups, cheery fires in the woodstove on chilly mornings and evenings, and the forever-full coffeepot." *(Joan & Dave Riley)* "Ample common areas for guests to relax and play games. The innkeepers are knowledgeable about the area, and can always suggest the best places to ski." *(ET)* "Attractive hand-stitched quilts. The Jacksons are cordial, welcoming us with iced tea and just-baked chocolate chip cookies." *(SWS)*

Open May–Oct., late Dec.–mid-March.
Rooms 8 doubles—all with full private bath, fan. Some with whirlpool tubs, desk.
Facilities Dining room; 2 sitting rooms with open wood-burning stoves, piano, books, games; enclosed porch. ½ acre with swimming pool, sauna, children's play equipment, borders Green Mt. National Forest. Hiking, biking, fishing, cross-country skiing; bicycle rentals. Golf, tennis nearby.

Location W central VT. 4 m E of Brandon on Rte. 73.
Restrictions No smoking. Children over 5 welcome.
Credit cards MC, Visa.
Rates MAP, $150–200 double, $90–135 single. Extra person, $75–85. 15% service. ½ price for children under 13 in parents' room. 2-night weekend minimum, fall, winter, holidays. Picnic lunch, $7. Package rates.
Extras Station pickup.

Lilac Inn ✕ ♿ ♀   *Tel:* 802–247–5463
53 Park Street, 05733   800–221–0720
                         Fax: 802–247–5499
                E-mail: lilacinn@sover.net
                URL: http://www.lilacinn.com

Built in 1909 as a private summer cottage overlooking tree-lined Park Street, the elegant Lilac Inn has been restored to its original elegance by Michael and Melanie Shane, who bought the inn in 1992. Improvements to the inn are ongoing, from the cobblestone courtyard that wraps around the ballroom and extensive landscaping, to the improved decor of the guest rooms. Michael reports: "My favorite room continues to be Albert's Room, decorated in golds and purples with its step-up pine bed; our guests' favorite room is the Kimble Room, a playful, patriotic interpretation of American folk art and Warren Kimble's studio—one of Brandon's most famous residents." Breakfast is served from 8–9 A.M. on weekdays, and includes muffins, fruit, eggs-to-order with sausage, ham, or bacon, plus juice and coffee. The dinner menu changes frequently, but possible entrées include peppered tuna with leeks and garlic, shrimp Dijon, grilled ginger chicken, and sun-dried tomato–artichoke ravioli.

"Beautifully restored Greek Revival inn, designed with classical symmetry. Ample common areas for overnight guests, restaurant patrons, and wedding groups. The delightful Sunday brunch is served in the solarium-style dining room, and included a wonderful buffet of assorted salads: sugar snap peas with mushrooms, tomatoes with mozzarella, zucchini and peppers, fresh fruit salad, plus blueberry and corn muffins. Next, you're invited into the kitchen where breakfast chef Michael prepares your choice of Belgian waffles with whipped cream and strawberries, omelets, eggs Benedict, plus delicious apple-cured ham and home fries. Good coffee and juice, too. Guest rooms are located on the second floor, and even the smallest is spacious, light, and airy. Each has a different color scheme, keyed by the floral border in each room. Beautifully done bathrooms, each with deep soaking tub, some with a regular shower, others with a European-style hand-held shower. Hospitable, welcoming innkeepers, Michael and Melanie, have done a wonderful job here, and continue to work to improve their inn." *(SWS)*
"Furnished with elegance, comfort, and charm; relaxed atmosphere; delightful proprietors." *(Frank Morley)* "Excellent facilities for weddings in a charming setting." *(RR)*

Open All year. Restaurant open Wed.–Sat. for dinner, plus Sun. brunch, May–Oct.

Rooms 9 doubles—all with full private bath, telephone, clock/radio, TV, desk, air-conditioning, ceiling fan. 1 with whirlpool tub, 3 with wood-burning fireplace. Some with hand-held shower.

Facilities Restaurant, bar, library with books, fireplace; lobby/parlor, banquet/ballroom with piano; cobblestoned patio with gazebo. Feb., March book readings, jazz/classical concerts. 2¼ acres with patio courtyard, gazebo, 5-hole putting green. Hiking, cross-country skiing, lake for swimming, boating, fishing nearby. 20 m to downhill skiing.

Location In historic district, 1 block to center of town. From Rte. 7, go E 1 block on Rte. 73 (Park St.) to inn on right.

Restrictions No smoking.

Credit cards Amex, MC, VISA.

Rates B&B, $100–250 double, $60–120 single. Extra person, $25. MAP, $175–325 double, $98–158 single. Extra person, $60. 2–3 night holiday weekend minimum. Alc lunch, $10; alc dinner, $30; Sunday brunch, $15. Weddings most weekends April–Oct.; inquire for details.

Extras Wheelchair access. Crib.

BRATTLEBORO

Located in southeastern Vermont, Brattleboro is located in Windham County, on the Connecticut River, at the junction of Route 9 and Interstate 91 (Route 5). It's about 2½ hours northeast of Boston, and four hours north of New York City. While not a tourist town, its many appealing shops and restaurants are fun for browsing and grazing, and all of Vermont's outdoor activities—from hiking to skiing—are within a short drive.

For additional area inns, see **Newfane**.

40 Putney Road Bed & Breakfast   *Tel:* 802–254–6268
40 Putney Road, 05301   800–941–2413
                                                                         Fax: 802–258–2673
                                                   E-mail: frtyptny@sover.net
                        URL: http://www.putney.net/40putneyrd/

Although any visitor will be delighted with a visit to 40 Putney Road, business travelers will especially appreciate its ideal balance of gracious hospitality, elegant environs, and sensitivity to professional needs. Built in 1931 in the style of a French château, this B&B has been owned by Peter and Joan Broderick since 1994. Joan notes: "Our property is classically landscaped and surrounded by mature trees. Inside, our home is decorated with antiques, hardwood floors, detailed woodwork, and Oriental carpets. Our proximity to southern Vermont's corporate centers make our inn an ideal place for business travelers. To accommodate them, we offer early breakfasts, laundry and dry cleaning service, and fax machines. Most importantly, we offer privacy, comfort, and respectful attention to all our guests, business travelers and tourists alike."

Breakfast is served from 7–9 A.M. in front of the dining room fireplace, or in warm weather, on the garden patio. In addition to a variety of hot and cold cereals, fresh fruit, and homebaked pastries, the daily entrée might be Swedish pancakes, apple crêpes, Grand Marnier French toast, eggs Benedict, or spiced buttermilk pancakes. Special diets are accommodated with advance notice.

"A beautiful home, with well-maintained grounds bordering the West River, yet only a few blocks' walk to downtown. Pete and Joan are extremely helpful—from making restaurant reservations to brushing snow off guests' cars." *(Lewis W. Coghill)* "After days on the road, the iron and ironing board in the large closet were a welcome sight, as was the digital telephone system, designed to work with laptop computers. Delicious cranberry yogurt muffins." *(Joe Schmidt)* "Be sure to follow the path down to the river." *(Marty & Barbara Mueller)* "Warm and inviting, yet mercifully uncluttered." *(MW)* "Every room is meticulously decorated in French country style. Gorgeous floral wallpapers and comforters; French Impressionist prints on the walls. Original bath fixtures with modern conveniences." *(Robert & Evangeline Bourgeois)* "Our inviting suite had a cozy fireplace and fresh flowers, and a view of the inn's gardens. A comfortable wing chair by the fireplace had a good light for reading, and an ottoman for resting one's feet. Chocolates, fresh towels, and robes were provided daily. A sitting room near the guest rooms held a refrigerator with a variety of juices, available to guests at their convenience. In the living room guests could help themselves to complimentary port." *(Dana & Angel Logan, also RSS)* "Decorated impeccably with interesting antiques, eclectic artwork, lovely fabrics and linens. Attention to detail includes baskets of chocolates and fruit in the sitting areas, and magazines and videos." *(Rita Gerber)* "A good night's sleep is essential, especially when facing a day of back-to-back meetings. 40 Putney provides wonderful pillows, all-cotton sheets, and cushy down comforters. Pete and Joan accommodate my wishes for a breakfast of fresh fruit, whole grain cereal, and skim milk, although their omelets and pancakes are most tempting." *(Katherine McDonnell)* "Immaculately clean, lovingly cared for, and carefully maintained." *(Michael Spring)* "The Brodericks' anticipation of guests' preferences are exceptional. They balance friendliness and hospitality with privacy needs." *(Peter Agur)* "We'll return in warm weather to canoe the river—right in the inn's backyard." *(Robert & Nancie Marti)* "The Brodericks make sure there are extra blankets to keep this Southerner toasty warm at night." *(Dale Tepp)* "The breakfast feast is served in an elegant dining room by hosts who seem to spend every waking moment thinking of more delightful ways to create a perfect stay." *(Grace & Frank Whittemore)* "Upon our arrival, we were greeted by Joan, who took our bags to our room and toured us through the house." *(John Lunt)*

Open All year. Closed Dec. 24–25.

Rooms 1 suite, 3 doubles—all with full private bath, telephone, radio, clock, TV, desk, air-conditioning, ceiling fan, data port, iron/ironing board, robes. 2 with fireplace.

Facilities Dining room with fireplace, living room with fireplace, sun room, library, upstairs sitting room with TV/VCR, books, video library, guest refrigerator; porch. Business services: laundry, dry cleaning, fax; small corporate meetings. 1 acre with gardens, fountains, lawn games, path to river. River for swimming, ice-skating, ice fishing. ½ m from canoe rentals. Hiking, skiing nearby.

Location Take Exit 3 off I-91. Turn right onto Rte. 5 S to inn on the right, 1.8 m down the road. Historic district, ½ m from center.

Restrictions No smoking. Children 12 and over.

Credit cards Amex, Discover, MC, Visa.

Rates B&B, $155–175 suite, $105–135 double, $80–135 single. Extra person, $18. 10% senior discount. 2-night minimum holiday weekends, Christmas week.

Extras Train, bus station pickup.

Latchis Hotel ¢ 👬 ✕ ♿
50 Main Street, 05301

Tel: 802–254–6300
Fax: 802–254–6304
URL: http://www.brattleboro.com/latchis

Considering the number of historic buildings destroyed during the 1950s and '60s, it's always a pleasure to find a classic in-town hotel saved from the wrecking ball. Built by the Latchis family in 1938, the Latchis Hotel is one of only two truly Art Deco buildings in Vermont, and is listed on the National Register of Historic Places. Managed by Elizabeth Latchis, its 1989 restoration won an award for excellence from the Vermont Preservation Trust. The adjacent movie theater shows first-run movies and independent films. The original 1938 main theater has a mural of the Greek myths, a zodiac ceiling, and elaborately worked terrazzo floors; renovations now permit live performances once again. The in-house Windham Brewery offers ales, porters, and lagers, plus seasonal specialty brews. Dinner entrées at the Latchis Grille might include sesame-ginger chicken and duck roulade, shepherd's pie, squash Napoleon, or wild mushroom polenta. Breakfast is a simple affair, with juice, milk, and the makings for coffee and tea in the in-room refrigerator while a basket of warm muffins is brought to your door in the morning.

"Ask for an upper-floor room facing the street; the view is better, and double-glazed windows keep out the noise. Guest rooms have been redone in soothing green and peach colors and many have handsomely restored lacquered furnishings, original to the hotel. Ask about the hotel's fascinating history, and visit the handsome old theater." *(SWS)* "Outgoing, friendly staff." *(Mark & Cecilia Acheson)* "Reasonably priced, attractive hotel, enhanced by the quality of both the food and the beer in the adjacent Grille." *(Jim & Mary White)*

Open All year.

Rooms 3 2-bedroom suites, 17 doubles, 6 singles—all with full private bath, telephone, TV, desk, air-conditioning, refrigerator, coffee-maker.

Facilities Restaurant with live jazz or classical music, bar/lounge, deli, movie theater, micro brewery, elevator, off-street parking.

Location Take Exit 2 off I-91. Turn left onto Rte. 9. Follow Rte. 9 to downtown; turn right at 1st light onto Main St. Hotel at corner of Main & Flat Sts.

Restrictions Traffic noise in some rooms. Non-smoking rooms. Children over 8 preferred.

Credit cards Amex, MC, Visa.

Rates B&B, $125 suite; $62–99 double; $55–90 single. Extra person, $10. No charge for children under 12 in parents' room. Weekly, corporate rates. Alc lunch, $6–10; alc dinner, $15–25.

Extras Limited wheelchair access to guest rooms, not restaurant. Crib. French, Spanish, some Japanese spoken.

BRIDGEWATER CORNERS

October Country Inn ¢
Upper Road, P.O. Box 66, 05035

Tel: 802–672–3412
800–648–8421
E-mail: oci@vermontel.com
URL: http://www.vermontel.com/~oci

A rambling Vermont farmhouse with assorted additions of different vintages, the October Country Inn has been owned by Richard Sims and Patrick Runkel since 1987. They continue to improve the inn, remodeling and restoring it, adding skylights and refurbishing the comfortable country decor.

Dinners are served family-style around big tables, with a different cuisine featured nightly—Italian, Greek, Mexican, and French country are favorites, but Scandinavian, African, and Eastern European recipes have also been featured. A sample Greek dinner might include egg lemon soup; braided pepper bread; spicy chicken with braised red cabbage; spinach pie; rice pilaf with red pepper; salad with artichokes and feta cheese; and honey walnut cake. Breakfasts are more traditional, with granola, muffins, blueberry pancakes or eggs and bacon.

"In these days of ever-more glizty and high-priced inns, it's special to find a country inn still doing what country inns do best—providing genuine hospitality, comfortable accommodations, wonderful food, and congenial fellow guests—all at an affordable price. Guest rooms and common areas are comfortable and inviting, with good lighting. Richard is the people person; bushy-whiskered Patrick stayed mostly in the kitchen preparing meals that kept guests purring as contentedly as their cat." (*SWS*) "Richard was the perfect host; Patrick's meals were delicious. Our fellow guests were a delightful bunch." (*Audrey Levine*) "We sat around the fireplace with the other guests, laughing, playing games, conversing, and reading." (*Dan Coyle*) "The best eggplant Parmesan I've ever tasted." (*Barbara Wolfe*) "Richard is an attentive host, supplying coffee or wine as guests relax by the fireplace." (*Susan Landon*) "Patrick cooked innovative and incredible vegetarian meals for us." (*Gail DeSciose*) "Patrick bakes fresh cookies every day, and you'll want to grab a couple, along with a mug of tea, hot chocolate, or coffee, before you proceed to the living room to relax with a puzzle or magazine. Later on, ask Richard to surprise you with a beer from his collection of brews. Dinner is served family-style at 7 P.M., and always starts with soup and just-baked bread, and concludes with a wonderful dessert. Dinner conversations usually continue over coffee or tea, then on to a game of Scrabble or Uno. Coffee is ready at 7:15 A.M., with breakfast from 8–9:30 A.M. Patrick makes wonderful mini-muffins in different flavors, with scrambled eggs with cheddar, pancakes, or French toast among the main dishes." *(Bruce Wells)*

Open Open Nov. 21–April 1, May 1–Oct. 31.
Rooms 10 doubles—8 rooms with private bath and/or shower, 2 rooms with maximum of 4 people sharing bath. All with fan. 2 with air-conditioning.
Facilities Dining room, living room with fireplace, wood-stove; deck. 5 acres with swimming pool, hot tub (May–New Year's). Downhill, cross-country skiing, fishing, swimming, summer theater nearby.
Location Central VT. 21 m E of Rutland, 8 m W of Woodstock. Barn is at intersection of Rtes. 100A and 4; inn is on dirt road up behind barn.
Restrictions No smoking.
Credit cards Amex, MC, Visa.
Rates B&B, $75–95 double, $45–85 single. Extra person, $30. MAP, $124–160 double, $80–95 single. Extra person, $45. 8% service. Family rates. Discount for 3-night stay. Prix fixe dinner, $20.
Extras Station/airport pickup, $30. Babysitting by arrangement.

BROOKFIELD

Also recommended: About 25 minutes south of Montpelier and a few miles south of Northfield is the **Green Trails Inn** (By the Floating Bridge, Brookfield, 05036; 802–276–3412 or 800–234–3412; www.quest-net.com/fti). Dating back to 1790, the inn is located in the center of the village, overlooking Sunset Lake and the longest floating bridge east of the Mississippi. Sue and Mark Irwin have owned the property since 1995 and have worked hard to upgrade the inn, and expand its cross-country ski and snowshoeing trails. Most of the thirteen rooms offer a private bath. Breakfast, served between 8 and 9 A.M., is included in the double rates of $79–150. "The innkeepers are full of energy and have worked hard to upgrade the accommodations. It would be hard to find a more peaceful setting. During the restoration of my room, Sue and Mark discovered and meticulously restored hand-stenciled patterns created in the distant past by a traveling artist. An interesting feature of the inn is Mark's old clock collection. Cross-country skiers will particularly enjoy having private trails at their back door." *(Joe & Sheila Schmidt)*

BURLINGTON/ESSEX JUNCTION

Vermont's largest city is a charming place, overlooking beautiful Lake Champlain and the Adirondack Mountains of New York to the west, and Mt. Mansfield and the Green Mountains to the east. Home to the University of Vermont, Champlain College, and nearby St. Michael's College in Winooski, it offers an appealing pedestrian mall, and lots of intriguing shops and inviting restaurants and clubs.

Reader tip: "Favorite eateries include the Muddy Waters Coffee Shop, Queen of Tarts Bakery and Tavern, Leunig's Bistro, and Sweetwaters." *(Joe Schmidt)*

Also recommended: Having broken through restrictive zoning barriers, Burlington finally has an appealing inn, the **Willard Street Inn** (349 South Willard Street, 05401; 802–651–8710 or 800–577–8712; www.willardstreetinn.com), adjacent to Champlain College. Built of brick and marble in 1880 in a combination of Queen Anne and Georgian Revival styles, the inn has fifteen guest rooms, most with private bath, in-room TV and telephone, antique and reproduction decor, and down comforters. B&B double rates of $75–200 include a full breakfast and afternoon tea. "A short walk from downtown. The rooms are bright, comfortable, and clean. Homemade cookies are on the nightstand. My breakfast, served in the sun room, included fruit and tasty waffles. Particularly enjoyable was the opportunity to chat over coffee with other guests." (*Joe Schmidt*)

For additional area inns, see **Richmond, Shelburne,** and **Vergennes**.

The Inn at Essex ✕ ⅁ ♦	*Tel:* 802–878–1100
70 Essex Way, Essex Junction, 05452	800–727–4295
	Fax: 802–878–0063
	E-mail: info@innatessex.com
	URL: http://www.innatessex.com

Completed in 1989, and completely renovated in 1998, the Inn at Essex was built in the style of an English manor house. General manager Jim Lamberti and his knowledgeable staff really know what a good inn is all about. Rooms are individually decorated with high-quality Colonial reproductions in cherry or pine, designed to combine luxury hotel amenities with country inn charm. Mauve, soft greens, and ivory key is the color scheme, and each room has distinctive floral wallcovering, bedspreads, and draperies.

Prepared by students of the New England Culinary Institute, the inn's cuisine has been winning rave reviews from guests and critics alike. At a recent dinner, the entrées included such choices as black pepper polenta cake with shiitake mushrooms and red pepper coulis; rack of lamb with goat cheese soufflé; or poached halibut with scallop dumplings. Lunch entrées are equally creative and very affordable.

"Friendly, courteous staff; family atmosphere despite its size. I was given a tour of the inn, and allowed to select a favorite room. Dining is superb; the Culinary Institute is truly innovative in its cuisine and artistic in its presentation. Beautiful ice sculptures at the Sunday buffet." (*Jacqueline Fitzgerald*) "This is the inn to captivate anyone who claims not to like inns. It has the size, facilities, and amenities of the finest hotels (and a 4-diamond rating from the AAA), yet the individual charm and personal concern of an inn. Rooms are delightful—some more formally decorated, others less so—but even the least expensive is charming and eminently acceptable. Equally appealing are the spacious common rooms." (*SWS*) "The front desk staff knew us by name, and did everything possible to make our stay a pleasant one. Delicious food." (*Doris Modesitt*) "Fully endorse entry. Delicious dinner at the hotel and a delightful meal at the Cafe Shelburne." (*Hilary Cheney*) "Genuine hospitality, from the front desk staff to the housekeepers." (*Emma Morris*)

Open All year.

Rooms 2 suites, 95 doubles, all with telephone (modem/fax hookups), radio, TV, desk, air-conditioning. 30 rooms with fireplaces.

Facilities 2 restaurants; library, 2 parlors, lounge/bar. 18 acres with heated swimming pool, gardens, tented patio, gardens, hiking trails. Health club privileges nearby. 8 m to Lake Champlain for water sports. 20–60 min. to downhill/cross-country skiing.

Location NW VT. 8 m NE of Burlington. From I-89, take Exit 11 (Richmond). Go to stop sign & go right. Take immediate hard right onto Rte. 117. Go 6 m & go right onto I-289 W. Take Exit 10 to Essex Way. Bear left to inn on left.

Restrictions No smoking in public areas, restaurants, some guest rooms.

Credit cards Amex, DC, Discover, JCB, MC, Visa.

Rates Room only, $180–380 suite; $139–199 double. Extra person, $15. Alc breakfast, $5–10; alc lunch, $6–12; alc dinner, $25–35; prix fixe dinner, $25; 17% service. Off-season rates; packages available.

Extras Wheelchair access; 10 rooms equipped for disabled. French, Spanish, German spoken. Cribs, babysitting by prior notice. Free airport/station pickup. Member, Someplace(s) Different, Summit Hotels & Resorts.

CHELSEA

Reader tips: "A worthwhile detour on the road to Chelsea is South Royalton, home of the University of Vermont Law School. The South Royalton House serves modestly priced meals in a pleasant cellar pub. Highly recommended is the Stone Soup Restaurant in the pleasant town of Stratford; pretty garden, nice decor." (*JS*)

Shire Inn ♿
Main Street, P.O. Box 37, 05038

Tel: 802–685–3031
800–441–6908
Fax: 802–685–3871
E-mail: info@shireinn.com
URL: http://www.shireinn.com

A farming community dating to 1781, Chelsea is noted for its unusual twin town commons and handsome brick buildings, most dating to the early 1800s. Built in 1832 by a successful chair manufacturer, the Federal-style Shire Inn was constructed of red brick, with granite window lintels, pumpkin pine floorboards, ten-foot ceilings, and a grand spiral staircase. Restored as an inn in 1977, it's been owned by Jay and Karen Keller since 1992. Rooms are handsomely furnished with genuine Colonial charm, including antiques, quilts, and lace-canopied queen-size beds.

Breakfast is served from 8:30–9:30 A.M. at individual tables, and might include cinnamon scones or oatmeal maple muffins, apple pancakes or perhaps zucchini red pepper omelets, with bacon or sausage. Dinner is served at 7 P.M., and is not open to the general public, creating an intimate, leisurely atmosphere. The menu changes nightly, but might consist of three-vegetable terrine; sorbet; broccoli, rice pilaf, and a choice of pork with maple/mustard sauce, sea scallops with tomato coulis, or carrot curry linguini; a salad of greens, kiwi, and pecans with balsamic dressing; and chocolate torte with raspberry sauce.

"A gorgeous example of Federal design. Inside, it's equally impressive with classic proportions, yet unpretentious. This fine inn has only improved since the Kellers took over. Exceptional dining, with a well-set table and handsome food presentation, while maintaining a comfortable, unstuffy atmosphere. An excellent value, equally appealing for special occasions or as a home base for nearby scenic country drives and area attractions." *(Ed Okie)* "In warm weather, the back porch is a quiet spot to savor the beauty of rural Vermont. For romantic hearts, the handsome living room houses a delicately carved walrus tusk that reads 'To my dear Kathleen, The bark Veronica out of New Bedford, 1849.' " *(Joe Schmidt)* "Immaculately clean, meticulously maintained. Homey country charm with family antiques, yet mercifully devoid of cutesy country clutter. Friendly and welcoming from our first phone call to our departure. The surrounding roads are pleasant for walking, and the grounds are inviting for reading and relaxing. Very good food; dinner is an excellent value. Our comfortable, quiet room had large windows to let in the cool night air. Good towels, too." *(DBS)*

"Careful attention to detail: nice soaps, bath oil, even locally made maple syrup and strawberry jam in the rooms. We dined by candlelight each evening and a fire welcomed us to the parlor. The town of Chelsea is quiet and picturesque, great for hiking, cross-country skiing, and antiquing." *(Debbie & Kevin Crawford)* "Extensive information on area sights, fishing, restaurants, and more. Lovely spacious guest rooms, beautiful music, and delicious omelets." *(Diana & Bill deFigueiredo)*

Open All year.

Rooms 6 doubles—all with private bath and/or shower, clock, desk, fan. 4 with wood-burning fireplace.

Facilities Dining room, living room with fireplace, stereo, games, books; porch. 23 acres on river for swimming, canoeing, fishing; gardens, lawn games, bicycles, cross-country skis & trails. Hiking, bicycling, antiquing, golf, tennis, horseback riding, downhill skiing nearby.

Location Central VT, 25 m S of Montpelier. 30 min. from I-91 & I-89. Take I-91 N to I-89 N. Take Exit 2 at Sharon & go left. After ⅛ mile, go right on Rte. 14. Go approx. 6 miles, & turn right on Rte. 110. Go 13 miles to Chelsea & inn on left.

Restrictions No smoking. Children over 6 preferred.

Credit cards Discover, MC, VISA.

Rates B&B, $95–145 double, $90–140 single. Extra person, $30. MAP, $145–205 double, $115–175 single. Extra person, $55. 15% service. 3rd night free most months (B&B).

Extras Limited wheelchair access; 1 bathroom partially equipped. Some French, Spanish spoken.

CHESTER

Incorporated in 1764, Chester is home to two National Historic Districts, including the Stone Village, a group of 19th-century buildings faced in gleaming mica schist. Six downhill ski areas are within a 25-minute drive; in warm weather, the area offers ample opportunities for golf, hiking, antiquing, and summer music and theater. This quiet town is located in southeastern Vermont, about 30 miles north of Brattleboro, and is best reached by taking I-91 to Exit 6, Rockingham; take Route 103 northwest 10 miles to Chester. Where 103 takes a sharp right in the village, continue straight on Route 11 (Main Street) to the village green.

For additional area entries, see **Andover, Grafton,** and **Weathersfield.**

The Hugging Bear Inn ¢ 🐾
244 Main Street, 05143

Tel: 802–875–2412
800–325–0519
Fax: 802–875–3823
E-mail: georgette@huggingbear.com
URL: http://www.huggingbear.com

If the idea of a thousand cuddly bears waiting to be hugged appeals to you, then the Hugging Bear Inn will head your list of favorite inns. Children are special guests at this comfortable 140-year-old Victorian home, owned and operated since 1983 by Georgette Thomas. In refreshing contrast to the many inns where breakfast assumes nearly ceremonial status, things are far more loose and casual here, with Monty, the puppet bear, greeting guests as they arrive at the table.

"Our room, #2, was comfortable with a very clean shower and bathroom. The sink was in the room, supplied with liquid soap and plenty of towels. A basket on the dresser held more towels, soaps, and Tupperware glasses, plus two postcards and a cute bumper sticker reading 'Greetings from the Hugging Bear Inn.' We had two double beds, a chair, two dressers, extra blankets, and plenty of lights. Wonderful bears all over the place. One sitting room is filled with books, games, and an antique crib filled with bears. Georgette cooked us breakfast to order, with eggs, toast, bacon and pancakes, juice and coffee. Georgette welcomed us with glasses of juice; hot water was always available for hot chocolate, coffee, or tea. Georgette and her entire staff were accommodating and friendly." *(Julie Phillips)* "Our room was decorated with a panda theme, and had a most comfortable bed; the bathroom had a claw-foot tub. We loved the shop with its endless variety of bears." *(Stefany Soutor)* "Plenty of children's videos, combined with the bears, puppets, and games made our daughter's stay extra-special." *(Lydia Gladstone)*

Open All year.
Rooms 6 doubles—all with private bath and/or shower, fan. 1 with balcony.
Facilities Dining room, living room, den/library with fireplace, TV, piano; porch, teddy bear shop. Town tennis courts across street; ½ m to town pool. Cross-country and downhill skiing, golf nearby.
Location In center of town, across from village green. From I-91, take Exit 6, Rockingham. Take Rte. 103 10 m W to Chester. Do *not* turn right when Rte. 103 turns in Chester. Stay on Main St. to inn on right.
Restrictions Some traffic noise. No smoking.
Credit cards Amex, Discover, MC, Visa.
Rates B&B, $85–115 double, $60–75 single. Extra adult, $25; child under 15, $10. 2-night holiday/fall weekend minimum.
Extras Station pickup. Crib.

CHITTENDEN

Tulip Tree Inn   *Tel:* 802–483–6213
49 Chittenden Dam Road, 05737   800–707–0017
Fax: 802–483–2623
E-mail: ttinn@sover.net
URL: http://www.TulipTreeInn.com

Too often, readers are disappointed when the quiet country inn they'd dreamed about sits right on a busy highway. Fortunately, this is *not* the case with the Tulip Tree Inn. Chittenden itself is well off the beaten path, and the inn is a half mile from the center of this tiny town. Innkeepers Rosemary and Ed McDowell have decorated their inn with Victorian antiques, Oriental carpets, and soft plush couches. The comfortable guest rooms are cheerfully furnished and have queen-size beds.

Rosemary's ample breakfasts, served from 8:30–9:30 A.M. (coffee is available earlier), include fluffy buttermilk pancakes or French toast, country sausage, cereal, fruit and yogurt, and home-baked sweet breads. Dinners are served by candlelight, with background music playing, and Ed personally seats each guest at the tables for eight, so that "our guests can get to know each other and we can get to know them."

"Cocktails start around 5 P.M., served in the spacious den before a roaring fire in the handsome river rock fireplace; Ed and Rosemary will gladly join you, offering Vermont cheddar and crackers. At 7 P.M. Ed rings the dinner bell and tells you what will be served for dinner. I especially enjoyed the herbed tomato soup finished with a swirl of cream and a dash of gin, and pork loin with a warm bourbon sauce. Conversations continue after dinner, in the den, over coffee and cordials." *(John Rafner)* "Ed and Rosemary are extremely gracious hosts— engaging, attentive, and informative. Ed's storytelling is appealing and amusing too." *(James & Heidi Maggs)* "A short walk away is the Chittenden Reservoir where one can boat, fish, or swim." *(Sandra & Matthew Keysers)* "Cozy, clean, and quiet, with complimentary sherry and chocolates in our room. Wonderful food at breakfast and dinner. Enjoyed relaxing in the den, chatting with Rosemary, Ed, and our fellow guests." *(Lori Pollock)*

Open Mid-May–March.
Rooms 8 doubles—7 with full private bath, 1 with private shower. All with fans, some with air-conditioning. 5 with Jacuzzi, 2 with fireplace.
Facilities Dining room, library/pub, living room and den with fireplace, porch. 5 acres with trout stream. Canoeing, swimming, skiing, golf, tennis, horseback riding nearby.
Location 7 m N of Rutland. From Rutland, take Rte. 7 to fork in rd. At fork, bear right on Chittenden Rd. 6 m. At fire station, go straight ½ m to inn.
Restrictions No smoking. No children.
Credit cards MC, Visa.
Rates B&B, $100–140 double. MAP, $140–299 double. 15% service. 2–3 night holiday/weekend minimum; midweek discounts.

COVENTRY

Heermansmith Farm Inn ¢ ✕ ♦   *Tel:* 802–754–8866
Hermanville Road, P.O. Box 7, 05825

Although the recipes on file at the Heermansmith Farm Inn have helped to bring it well-deserved acclaim, the inn itself is a recipe for a relaxing Vermont vacation. First, take a scenic farm in the heart of the Northeast Kingdom, owned by the same family since 1807, and add two equally historic homes to provide guest accommodations. Season liberally with activities ranging from hiking to antiquing to skiing, and flavor with the hospitality of longtime owners Louise and Jack Smith. Simmer slowly—a couple of generations should do it—and *voilà*—a peaceful, affordable country getaway.

A hearty farm breakfast is served at guests' convenience; the inn's restaurant offers a surprisingly extensive and creative dinner menu. While menus change often, recent entrées included roast duck with a strawberry Chambord sauce, cornmeal-crusted Atlantic salmon with green peppercorn-mustard sauce, and steak Diane. Guest rooms are in the farmhouse, dating to 1853, with additional accommodations in the renovated 1809 House, a three-bedroom home adjacent to the inn, that is ideal for families.

"A prime example of down-home country comfort without a bit of pretense. Jack and Louise are gentle, caring folks who share their family homestead with guests. Food at the inn's spacious restaurant is delightful. Each night offers ample choices, satisfying in quality and quantity. Guest rooms are small but neat as a pin. For those who enjoy country walks or jogging along a winding gravel road, this area is sheer beauty, with a waterfall in one direction, and a covered bridge in another." *(Ed Okie)*

Open All year, except for 1 week in Nov. and 1 week in April. Restaurant open daily July–Oct, Wed.–Sun. from Nov.–June.
Rooms 13-bedroom cottage with kitchen, 6 doubles—all with full private bath and/or shower, clock, fan.
Facilities Restaurant, bar/lounge, library; porch. 125 acres with gardens, lawn; 8 acres of strawberry fields. River with waterfall borders property for trout fishing, swimming. 30 min. to cross-country, downhill skiing. 3 lakes 5–10 m away for sailing, canoeing.
Location Northeast Kingdom. 5 m S of Newport. Short walk to village. Take I-91 N to Orleans, then Rte. 5 N to Coventry. From Canada, take I-91 S to Newport, then Rte. 5 S to Coventry. In Coventry, look for church-turned-antique store, Holy Cow. Straight across st., up short hill, is rd. to inn, about ⅓ m ahead.
Restrictions No smoking.
Credit cards Amex, MC, Visa.
Rates B&B, $75 double, $50 single. Cottage (sleeps 6), $125 daily, $500 weekly. Extra person, $10. Alc dinner, $25–30.
Extras Limited wheelchair access; bath specially equipped. Pets only with prior approval.

CRAFTSBURY COMMON

In the heart of Vermont's remote Northeast Kingdom, the hamlet of Craftsbury Common is about as quintessentially Vermont as one could wish, with classic white-painted homes surrounding the deep green of the common. Area activities include tennis, hiking, bicycling, golf, and water sports at Lake Eligo and Caspian Lake in summer; cross-country skiing in winter.

Also recommended: The **Inn on the Common** (Craftsbury Common, 05827; 802–586–9619 or 800–521–2233; www.innonthecommon. com) occupies three early–19th-century buildings. Rooms are handsomely furnished with antiques, hand-crafted country furnishings, quilts, and original art. Double rates for the 16 guest rooms range from $230–290 (15% service and 9% tax added to all inn charges), including a full breakfast, a five-course dinner, and evening turndown service; children are welcome, and pets are permitted with prior approval plus a $15 daily charge. "The inn has a swimming pool, tennis court, and exceptionally handsome gardens that alone are worth the journey. Summer activities include weekly concerts, wine walks, and gourmet weekends; in winter, a complete cross-country touring center awaits. The inn menu, which varies daily, includes items like sautéed breast of pheasant, roasted wild boar, and blackened tofu. Rooms were fresh and clean; the inn and grounds meticulously maintained." *(Joe Schmidt)*

For additional area entries, see **Coventry, Greensboro, Hardwick,** and **Wolcott.**

DANBY

Settled in 1765, Danby is the home of the world's largest indoor marble quarry; its marble was used to build the Jefferson Memorial in Washington, D.C. Renowned author Pearl Buck chose it as her summer home years ago; its quiet charms have changed little since then. Located about 12 miles north of Manchester and 20 miles south of Rutland, Danby occupies a few peaceful streets just off busy Route 7. Since it's a bit off the beaten path, it makes a most affordable base for visiting Manchester's outlet shops, area restaurants, theaters, and antique stores, and is equally convenient for hiking, swimming at Emerald Lake State Park (3 miles away), and skiing at one of several nearby areas. Also available in the area are tennis, golf, horseback riding, hunting, and fishing.

Reader tip: "About two miles north of Danby is the White Dog Tavern. Superb seafood stew—cioppino—and grilled salmon. Simple, unpretentious, and terrific. Beautifully restored 1812 house with a handsome fireplace of local marble." *(Eric Friesen)*

For additional area inns, see **Dorset** and **Wallingford.**

The Quail's Nest Bed & Breakfast
P.O. Box 221, Main Street, 05739

Tel: 802–293–5099
800–599–6444
Fax: 802–293–6300
E-mail: quails_nest@compuserve.com
URL: http://ourworld.compuserve.com/homepages/quails_nest

Creativity is a hallmark of many B&Bs, and you'll find it in ample supply at the Quail's Nest, a Greek Revival home built in 1835 and restored as a B&B by Nancy and Greg Diaz, formerly from the corporate computer world. Shifting from high-tech to high-touch, they have decorated the inn with Nancy's quilts, her son Jeff's hand-crafted woodwork, and original artwork by Nancy's aunt Jenny Berson, a well-known Massachusetts artist. Nancy's passion for sewing is evident in the handmade quilts throughout the inn; she also fashions period clothing which she wears when serving breakfast. She's equally enthusiastic about cooking; in addition to the inn's usual vegetarian fare, she is pleased to cater to special diets, from macrobiotic to vegan (with advance notice). Breakfast is served family-style from 7:30–9 A.M., and typically includes fresh fruit or a smoothie, home-baked scones, muffins, or biscuits, hot cereal, and such entrées as Vermont cheddar pie or pancakes.

"Located across the street from a quaint library and within easy distance of the restaurants and outlets of Dorset and Manchester. The guest rooms are cozy, and a joy to a quilt lover. Breakfast started with a hot cereal, great for the cool mornings, followed by a filling second course. Evenings brought homemade cookies and other treats." *(Deborah Siders)* "Top-notch hospitality; quiet and comfort; picturesque setting; easy access to area activities; knowledgeable, hospitable, friendly innkeepers." *(Michael Murray)* Comments appreciated.

Open All year.
Rooms 6 doubles—4 with private shower bath; 2 rooms share bath. All with radio, clock, fan. 1 with desk.
Facilities Dining room; living room with fireplace, piano, TV/VCR, stereo, books, games. 1 acre.
Location 13 m N of Manchester. Take I-91 to Brattleboro. Take 2nd Brattleboro exit for Rte. 30, Manchester. Follow Rte. 30 to Manchester, then take Rte. 7 N to Danby. Turn left on Main St. to inn on left. From I-87, exit at NY Rte. 7. Go E on Rte. 7 to VT; becomes Rte. 9. In Bennington, N on Rte. 7 to Danby.
Restrictions No smoking. Infants & children 8 and over.
Credit cards Amex, Discover, MC, Visa.
Rates B&B, $60–95 double, $45–95 single. Extra person, $10. 10% AARP discount.
Extras Airport/station pickup, $20.

Silas Griffith Inn ¢ ℟ ✕
South Main Street, RR 1, P.O. Box 66F, 05739

Tel: 802–293–5567
800–545–1509
Fax: 802–293–5559

Vermont's first millionaire, Silas Griffith, made his fortune in lumber. When he built a mansion for his bride in 1891, he didn't stint on expenses. Today, guests of the Silas Griffith Inn—and of owners Paul and Lois Dansereau—can enjoy the careful attention the house received so long ago. Special care was lavished on the woodwork, with such unusual touches as an eight-foot-wide rounded sliding pocket door. Equally handsome are the original stained-glass windows and embossed tin ceilings. The carriage house has been turned into a restaurant, and a recent dinner included such choices as spinach and roasted garlic ravioli, salad with buttermilk garlic dressing; salmon filet with artichokes and sun-dried tomatoes; and white chocolate mousse pie for dessert. Breakfast includes cereal, juice, fruit, home-baked muffins and scones, and an entrée such as multi-grain pancakes or Spanish omelets with Vermont cheddar.

"A wonderful front porch with rocking chairs looking out on tall old trees, a small white church, and the mountains beyond. The spacious library has lots of comfortable chairs and an inviting fireplace." *(James Ellis)* "Lois and Paul are warm and friendly innkeepers; a down-home feeling." *(Nancy & Tom Keyes)* "Clean, comfortable, and homey, with a fire going every night, homemade cookies in the afternoon, plus a corner where guests could make themselves a cup of tea or coffee. Our spacious room had a walk-in closet, private bathroom, and a second sink outside of the bathroom." *(Alicia Berfield)* "We enjoyed dinner in front of the fireplace in the carriage house, and breakfast was equally pleasant, with self-service fruit and cereal and a choice of entrées." *(Judy Powell)* "Spacious common rooms; guest rooms in the main house have handsome Victorian furniture. Quiet location in a charming village, yet minutes from Route 7 and Manchester. Delicious cream scones at breakfast." *(SWS)* "Our comfortable carriage house room was simply furnished with Colonial-style maple furniture." *(Rose Ciccone)* "Lovely gardens; friendly, knowledgeable hosts, who helped us find local hiking trails and galleries. Lemonade, iced tea, and cookies were set out in the reading room each afternoon." *(Eric Friesen)*

Open All year. Dinner by reservation only.

Rooms 17 doubles—14 with private bath and/or shower, 3 with a maximum of 6 people sharing bath. Most with fan, 3 with radio, 1 with desk, air-conditioning. Some with deck. 8 rooms in carriage house.

Facilities Dining room, living room with fireplace, library; restaurant with fireplace, bar; parlor with TV/VCR; guest pantry; porch. 11 acres with swimming pool.

Location From Rte. 7, turn onto Main St. to inn in center of village.

Restrictions No smoking.

Credit cards MC, Visa.

Rates B&B, $72–94 double. Extra person, $20; children under 10, free. MAP, 2–3 night weekend/holiday minimum; $15 surcharge during foliage season/holiday weekends. Alc dinner, $28, prix fixe, $22. Theme weekends.

Extras Rutland airport pickup, $5.

DERBY LINE

Straddling the Vermont/Québec border in the Northeast Kingdom is the town of Derby Line, which also carries the distinction of being at the midway point between the equator and the North Pole. International 32-mile-long Lake Memphremagog is nearby for all water sports, several golf courses are nearby in Vermont and Canada, and downhill skiing awaits at Jay Peak, Burke Mountain, and Owls Head. The town is also home to the Haskell Free Library and Opera House, with its stage in Canada and the seats in the U.S.

Information please: A 1920s Colonial Revival home, **The Birchwood B&B** (48 Main Street, P.O. Box 550, Derby Line 05830; 802–873–9104; birchwd@together.net) offers three guest rooms, each with private bath, at B&B double rates of $75. "Charming B&B in the Northeast Kingdom, furnished with antiques collected by innkeepers Betty and Dick Fletcher. Efficient service; immaculate and well-equipped guest rooms; delicious breakfasts with homemade muffins or croissants, French toast, or fruit-filled crêpes." *(Mary Selby)*

Derby Village Inn ¢ ♙   *Tel:* 802–873–3604
46 Main Street, P.O. Box 1085, 05830   *Fax:* 802–873–3047
E-mail: dvibandb@together.net
URL: http://homepages.together.net/~dvibandb

An imposing Neo-classical home, the Derby Village Inn was built in 1902 by General Butterworth, a Civil War officer, and is notable for its magnificent woodwork. Catherine McCormick and Sheila Steplar bought the inn in 1997 and have worked hard to restore it to its original elegance. Rooms are decorated with traditional furnishings and some period pieces. The Passageway guest room has bird's eye maple woodwork, a gas fireplace, queen-size bed, and three large windows providing light for the two comfortable reading chairs; the suite has a quilt-topped queen-size bed with built-in bookshelves, and magnificent sunset views of Jay Peak. Breakfast is served at 8:30 A.M. at the dining room table, and includes fresh fruit, granola, and a daily entrée, perhaps French toast, pancakes, or waffles.

"Catherine and Sheila have done much of the renovation work themselves, with excellent results. The rooms are large and well-decorated. On the first floor is a kitchen and dining area where they serve an excellent full breakfast. A great place to relax and enjoy the local lakes and scenery." *(Walt & Elinor Hermanson)* "Relaxing atmosphere, delicious breakfasts with endless coffee. After recovering from a challenging day of bicycling up and down hills (mainly up!) along a lovely route laid out by the hostesses, I went to a wonderful local restaurant where they had made reservations for me." *(Carolyn Alexander)* "Immaculate inside and out. Plush towels in the bathroom. Perfect stopover en route to/from Québec City." *(Jane & Glenn Karuschkat)* "Four separate downstairs common areas enable guests to find their favorite spots: the TV room, for those who simply can't go for a night without it; the formal living room; the drawing room with a baby grand piano, and several tables on which to work a puzzle or play cards; and my personal favorite, the lovely sun porch with a table and chairs, a sofa, and easy chairs. Outside, the beautiful grounds offer ample seating as well. We were welcome to store a bottle of wine in the guest refrigerator (glasses are provided) and help ourselves to hot and cold drinks. In the evening, we were asked about dietary restrictions and breakfast times. Breakfast was superb and elegantly served. Catherine and Sheila are delightful and do their best to make guests feel welcome and at home." *(Monica Gohm)*

Open All year.
Rooms 1 suite, 4 doubles—all with private bath and/or shower, clock, fan. 1 with gas fireplace.
Facilities Dining room, living room with fireplace, library with TV/VCR, stereo, books; sun porch with guest refrigerator. 2.5 acres with off-street parking, lawn games.
Location 2 hrs. N of Burlington VT & S of Montréal, Québec. Take I-91 N to Exit 29, at Canadian border. Follow signs to Derby Line. Go left onto Rte. 5, Main St. & watch for inn sign about ½ m on right.
Restrictions No smoking.
Credit cards Amex, Discover, MC, Visa.
Rates B&B, $100 suite, $75–85 double. Extra person, $15. 2–3 night weekend/holiday minimum.
Extras Airport/station pickups.

DORSET

A picture-postcard New England country village, Dorset is listed on the National Register of Historic Places. Activities include the country's oldest nine-hole golf course, tennis, hiking, quarry swimming, and cross-country skiing. The Battenkill River and Lake St. Catherine are nearby for fishing and boating. In summer there is good theater as well as concerts and art exhibits at the Southern Vermont Arts Center. Shopping, antiquing, and art galleries await year-round. Dorset is located in southwestern Vermont, 1½ hours northeast of Albany, 4 hours north of New York City, and 3½ hours northwest of Boston. It's 6 miles north of Manchester Center on Route 30, and 12 miles to downhill skiing at Bromley, 22 to Stratton.

Reader tips: Our correspondents have been delighted with the food at the **Dorset Inn,** right on Route 30. "Inviting common rooms, appealing tap room and restaurant. Popular with sophisticated, savvy locals." *(Flora Neumeister)* "Second the comments on Dorset Inn: service excellent, delicious meals with good vegetarian selections. Reservations essential on weekends—the dining room was full and loud when we were there." *(Diane Inman)*

Barrows House 🛏 ✕ 🐾 ♿
Route 30, 05251

Tel: 802–867–4455
800–639–1620
Fax: 802–867–0132
E-mail: innkeepers@barrowshouse.com
URL: http://www.barrowshouse.com

The Barrows House combines an inviting setting with the amenities of a small resort, with an atmosphere that is both romantic and "family-friendly." Bought by Linda and Jim McGinnis in 1993, the inn includes the main house, built in 1784 in the Federal style, plus eight outbuildings converted for use as accommodations after Barrow House became an inn in 1900. The staff will help you choose the appropriate accommodation, whether you're vacationing with the kids or looking for a quiet, romantic getaway. Well-known for the American regional cuisine served in its restaurant, the menu offers dishes and portions to suit a variety of tastes and appetites. A typical dinner might consist of broccoli and cheddar soup, grilled halibut with roasted corn-tomato relish, and peach tart; or mussels and leeks in white wine, filet mignon with Dijon Madeira sauce, and mango cheesecake.

"Extremely good service; owners and staff have positive can-do attitudes. Jim went out of his way to lend a hand when we had car troubles. A lovely, peaceful getaway." *(GR)* "A delightful dinner, with Linda in attendance to ensure that guests were pleased. We were allowed to see a number of unoccupied guest rooms, and thought they looked charming." *(Rose Ciccone)* "Accommodating innkeepers, comfortable accommodation, delicious food. A special treat was the sleigh ride." *(Daemon Heckman)* "We stayed in the Shubert House, Room #1, and found it to be comfortable, warm, and cozy, with ample firewood." *(MA)* "The library-like pub was my favorite room—warm and intimate, with backgammon boards on some tables." *(Ann Brown)* "The dining room is beautiful, with a fully heated, enclosed greenhouse; our table overlooked moonlit, snow-covered fields." *(Judy Margolin)* "We stayed in the Carriage House, with a bedroom and living room downstairs, and a bunkroom upstairs for our kids. Lots of nooks and crannies, ample privacy, and quiet." *(David & Leigh Jenkins)*

Open All year.

Rooms 10 suites, 18 doubles, 1 single—all with private bath or shower, air-conditioning. 6 with fireplace. Most rooms with TV; suites with TV/VCR. Some with desk. 28 rooms in 9 separate buildings.

Facilities Dining room, living room, restaurant, tavern with TV, piano; game room, library, sitting room with fireplace; small conference facility. 6 acres with lawn games, gazebo, heated outdoor swimming pool, sauna, 2 tennis courts, badminton court, gardens (perennial, herb, children's "please pick"). Complimentary bicycles, cross-country skis, sleds. Downhill skiing nearby. Golf, boating, fishing 10–30 min.

Location Walking distance to town. 6 m N of Manchester Center on Rte. 30.

Restrictions Smoking in two guest rooms only.

Credit cards Amex, Discover, MC, Visa.

Rates B&B, $180–240 suite, $165–200 double, $145–185 single. MAP, $220–275 suite, $205–235 double, $165–205 single. Children's rates. Extra adult, $50. 15% service. 2–3 night minimum holidays/some weekends. Theater special, $18; alc dinner, $30; children's menu. Theater, golf, family, and midweek packages. Midweek skiing specials.

Extras Limited wheelchair access. Station pickup, crib, babysitting by prior arrangement. Dogs OK in 2 guest rooms, $20/day, by prior arrangement.

Cornucopia of Dorset
Route 30, 05251

Tel: 802–867–5751
800–566–5751
Fax: 802–867–5753
Email: cornucop@vermontel.com
URL: http://www.CORNUCOPIAofDORSET.com

Many innkeepers arrive at this profession after having their fill of the corporate rat race, while others (less typically) prepare for this field through study and work in the travel/hospitality industry. Bill and Linda Ley, owners of the Cornucopia since 1987, fall into this second category. Linda worked in airline marketing, while Bill studied at the Cornell School of Hotel Management, then went on to work for Marriott. In restoring and redecorating their 19th-century Colonial-style home, they've worked hard to combine the amenities one expects in a well-equipped hotel room with the personal touches found only in an owner-operated inn. Guests are greeted with champagne, then are shown to their room, furnished with either a queen- or king-size four-poster or canopy bed, and a sitting area. In addition to redecorating guest rooms and refurbishing the baths, Linda and Bill have now added fireplaces to all but one of the guest rooms.

Breakfast is served at the large table in the dining room, at guests' choice of time. Among the varied breakfast menus are juice and fruit, followed by such entrées as baked croissants à l'orange; fresh berries and cream crêpes; Belgian waffles; baked ham, egg, and Vermont cheddar cheese soufflé; or maple egg nests with fresh dill and hollandaise. Sweets and an assortment of hot and cold beverages are always available; light hors d'oeuvres are served every evening before dinner.

"The building, grounds, guest rooms, and common areas are immaculate, attractive, and comfortable. Linda and Bill have seemingly anticipated just about every conceivable need of their guests. Our room was large, comfortable, and quiet, with a lovely view of the gardens. Breakfasts were delicious and beautifully presented. Linda and Bill offered helpful suggestions for area touring, and were on hand to answer questions, but did not smother us with attention." (*John Felton & Marty Gottron*) "Inviting common areas, from the cozy library to the plant-filled sun room. Our room was furnished with great attention to detail, from the excellent reading lights, to the fluffy quilt, and the Crabtree & Evelyn toiletries." (*SWS*) "We enjoyed Kitt, the genuine Vermont inn-dog, a well-behaved fixture in the common room. The nightly turn-down service is complete with a menu of the next day's breakfast, chocolates, and a lighted oil lamp. Excellent restaurant recommendations." (*Caroline & Jim Lloyd*) "Our spacious room overlooked the beautiful gardens." (*Hilary Cheney*) "The inn is clean, charming, and well furnished. Every amenity is of the best quality; breakfast is beautifully presented and delicious. Bill and Linda's conversational skills are unsurpassed." (*Laura Simoes*)

Open All year.

Rooms 1 cottage suite, 4 doubles—all with private bath, air-conditioning, telephone. 4 with fireplace. Suite with air-conditioning, fireplace, fully equipped kitchen, loft bedroom, patio.

Facilities Dining room, living room with fireplace, study/library with fireplace; sun room with TV/VCR; porch, patio. Gardens with comfortable seating.

Location SW VT. 6 m N of Manchester Center on Rte. 30. Walking distance to village green, restaurants, theatre.

Restrictions No smoking. Appropriate for discerning adults.

Credit cards Amex, MC, Visa.

Rates B&B, $200–225 cottage, $115–155 double, $115–145 single. Weekend/holiday minimum; seasonal specials.

EAST BURKE

For additional area entries, see **Lower Waterford, Lyndonville,** and **St. Johnsbury.**

The Inn at Mountain View Creamery ✕ ♙   *Tel:* 802–626–9924
Darling Hill Road, P.O. Box 355, 05832   800–572–4509
                                                                                      Fax: 802–626–9924
                                      E-mail: innmtnvu@plainfield.bypass.com

"The Northeast Kingdom of Vermont is best suited for outdoor enthusiasts," suggests innkeeper Laurelie Welch, and longtime owners Marilyn and John Pastore. "In our remote but easy-to-access location, we are close to a full range of summer and winter sports." On this gentleman's farm, built in 1883 by wealthy Vermont architect Elmer Darling, accommodations are provided in the fully renovated Creamery, where workers once made butter and cheese to be shipped to Mr. Darling's hotel in New York City. Breakfast is served from 8–9 A.M. at individual tables, and includes fresh fruit, cereal, granola, yogurt, juice, homemade breads and a hot entrée. At dinner, a choice of entrées might include bouillabaise of scallops, mussels, and haddock in a saffron tomato broth; lemon Moroccan chicken with garbanzo beans, onions, and prunes; and polenta layered with roasted vegetables and feta cheese.

"Beautiful, tranquil setting, with views of Burke Mountain and Willoughby Gap; welcoming, hospitable owners and manager; tasty breakfasts." *(Shirley & Lew Segal)* "Despite mud from the spring thaw, the inn was spotlessly clean. Marilyn Pastore gave me a tour of the property. Pleasant dining room in the old creamery boiler room; guest rooms, originally used by Darling's visitors, are bright and simply furnished. The farm's magnificent views are best enjoyed by walking, skiing, bicycling, or riding on the horse-drawn sleigh." *(Joe Schmidt)* "Photography buffs will love the bright red barns and yellow farm houses." *(Roseanne Buckman)*

"Among the properties on the site is the original creamery, a classic red brick building in the Georgian Colonial style, now a B&B. Across the courtyard is the original main house, housing several beautiful larger units. Completing the large courtyard periphery is a series of red barns, home to cows, turkeys, and the horses who pull the winter sleighs and summer haywagons for guests' enjoyment. Lush gardens produce fruits and vegetables used to prepare meals. The property offers both rough and well-groomed trails, leading to meadows of wildflowers, the riding stable, and to the center of East Burke. Owners Marilyn and John Pastore devote meticulous attention to their inn. Each guest room is named for a local town, decorated with handmade quilts and antiques, modern baths, and decorative colors and fabrics. Our East Haven Room was done in blue and white coordinated stripes and prints; the night-light was a typically thoughtful touch. I was able to sink into a plushy cushioned chair in the inn's library and get lost in a book. The dining room overlooks the gardens and the threshing barn, a fine example of antique barn architecture. Using a giant black iron stove as a buffet table, the innkeepers graciously served a delicious country breakfast with just-picked blueberries and strawberries on a flowered linen tablecloth with matching napkins." *(Mary Fiorentino)*

Open All year. Restaurant open Thurs.–Sat.

Rooms 1 2-bedroom condo unit, 1 suite, 9 doubles—all with private bath and/or shower, clock, desk, fan. Condo with kitchen, fireplace, Jacuzzi.

Facilities Dining room with fireplace, living room, family room with fireplace, piano, TV/VCR, stereo, books; porch. 440 acres with gardens, tree swing, lawn games, farm animals, riding stable, cross-country ski trails, sleigh rides, hiking. 15 min. to Lake Willoughby for fishing, boating; 5 min. to downhill skiing at Burke Mt.

Location Northeast Kingdom. 3 hrs. NW of Boston, 90 m NE of Burlington. 2½ hrs. SE of Montreal. Take I-91 N to Exit 23. Take Rte. 5 N to Rte. 114. Bear right & follow for 4.4 miles. Turn left at Burke Hollow sign, bearing left to go straight up hill. At top, turn left onto Darling Hill Rd. to B&B, 100 yds. on right. 1 m to center of town.

Restrictions No smoking. Children welcome with parental supervision.

Credit cards Amex, MC, Visa.

Rates B&B, $165–185 condo, $95–140 double, $80–130 single. Extra person, $25. 2-night minimum weekends, holidays, foliage.

Extras Crib. Some Russian spoken.

GRAFTON

The Old Tavern at Grafton ✗ ♿
Main Street, Route 121, 05146

Tel: 802–843–2231
800–843–1801
Fax: 802–843–2245
E-mail: tavern@sover.net
URL: http://www.old-tavern.com

With its hand-hewn beams, wide pine flooring, pewter and brass, the Old Tavern looks very much the way it did in the old days, when it accommodated Daniel Webster, Oliver Wendell Holmes, Ulysses S. Grant, Nathaniel Hawthorne, Ralph Waldo Emerson, and Henry David Thoreau. The Windham Foundation operates the Old Tavern, as well as seven separate restored Colonial houses. Rooms are well-furnished with four-poster or canopied beds, antiques, and soft wing chairs; some recently have been refurbished with updated fabrics, wallpapers, and renovated bathrooms. Rates include a full country breakfast. Dinner menus change frequently, but might include such entrées as cheddar and ale soupe, trout with almond lemon butter or venison with apricot wild rice, and for dessert, apple crisp with homemade maple walnut ice cream or apple pie with Grafton cheddar.

"A picture-postcard setting; a classic Vermont town beautifully restored, in a quiet, out-of-the-way, yet not inconvenient setting. Lots of common rooms in which to socialize or enjoy a private moment; guest rooms quite lovely with many antiques." *(SWS)* "Welcoming and accommodating staff; superb food." *(Matthew Brandt)* "My room was in a beautifully restored farmhouse, three-quarters of a mile from town; when I arrived, a flock of wild turkeys was grazing in the adjacent field." *(Richard Stephan)* "Our room was beautifully furnished with a four-poster bed and antiques; the bathroom was immaculate and modern. We enjoyed tea and cocktails by the warmth of the fireplace." *(Mrs. Arthur P. Ferrier)* "We enjoyed a flavorful vegetarian entrée of baked, stuffed squash." *(Gail deSciose)* "The garden restaurant is bright and pretty, service friendly, food wonderful, especially the light and crunchy fish and chips." *(Flora Neumeister)* "The guest rooms have wonderful mattresses, extra pillows, luxurious towels, and fine antiques. Dining by candlelight is always a treat, as is strolling by the inn and seeing the glow of the candles from the outside. If there is a nip in the air the fireplace is ablaze, and in warmer weather, 'front-porch rocking' is equally pleasant." *(Beth Wallach)*

Open May–March.
Rooms Main tavern, 14 doubles; Windham and Homestead Cottages, 20 doubles; 7 guest houses—all with private bath/shower, fan.
Facilities Restaurant, tavern, 2 TV rooms, library, living rooms, game room. Pond, 2 tennis courts, platform tennis, shuffleboard, billiards, Ping-Pong, stables, 30 km of cross-country ski trails with snow-making. Mountain and road bikes available. 30–40-min. drive to 4 major downhill ski areas.
Location SE Vermont. 2½ hrs. to Boston, 5 hrs. to NYC. 12 m W of I-91 in center of town.
Restrictions Children under 7 welcome in 3 guest houses. No smoking in dining room.
Credit cards MC, Visa.
Rates B&B, $500–790 guest house (sleeps 7–9 persons), $180–190 cottage, $125–205 double. Extra person, $35. Senior, frequent guest, midweek, off-season discounts. Alc breakfast, $5; alc lunch, $10; alc dinner, $35; children's menu. Weekly rates; midweek, off-season rates.
Extras Wheelchair access to all public facilities. One handicap room available. Horses boarded.

GREENSBORO

For additional area entries, see **Craftsbury Common, Hardwick,** and **Wolcott.**

Highland Lodge 🏃 ✕ 🚲 ♿   *Tel:* 802–533–2647
Caspian Lake, RR 1, P.O. Box 1290, 05841   *Fax:* 802–533–7494
                                    E-mail: hlodge@connriver.net
                    URL: http://www.pbpub.com/vermont/hiland.htm

"A warm and friendly place—one of the few country inns that cater to children," is how Wilhelmina and David Smith, along with their son Alex, describe the inn they've owned since 1979. "We are in an area that is still the real Vermont—far from population centers and tourist areas." The inn is set above the shores of deep-blue Caspian Lake, in an area of green rolling hills. Guests enjoy a wide variety of activities right at the inn, as well as exploring the country roads of the Northeast Kingdom. Breakfast is served from 8–10 A.M., and includes fresh fruit and juice, cereal, daily muffin and waffle specials, and a choice of pancakes, French toast, or eggs; lunch includes a variety of sandwiches; and a typical dinner might consist of white bean and kale soup, salad and home-baked bread, grilled chicken with pear chutney, and chocolate cake with mocha icing for dessert.

"The cottages are clean and comfortable, simple and rustic; both #1 and #2 have porches with beautiful views of Caspian Lake and the mountains beyond. Housekeeping staff is friendly and helpful. Wonderful food: memorable dishes included maple pecan muffins, waffles, fruit salad, cream of zucchini soup, Parmesan potatoes, duck with plum mustard sauce, deviled crab, blueberry pie, carrot cake, and more. Beautiful beach, with clean air and water; on Mondays, a lunch-time cookout is held here." *(MSC)* "Pretty, easy-to-walk trails above the lodge in the pine forest. Lovely flower and herb gardens." *(Andrew & Paula Rosen)* "Although the lake is a ⅓ mile down from the lodge, it's a pleasant hike through the forest—a great way to exercise and not at all inconvenient (although car parking is available). The lake's sloping sandy shore is great for small children, while a swimming raft in deep water awaits older kids. The menu offers home-style dishes as well as creative offerings for both breakfast and dinner." *(Brad Lockner)* "Immaculate, comfortable, and well-maintained, providing everything from beach toys for the kids to sophisticated board games and books for the adults. Our girls loved the play program, and so did we, since it gave us time to play tennis, and hike and canoe around the lake." *(Patricia Killorin)* "Guest rooms are plain and compact, but clean and cheery. Small modern baths. " *(SWS)*

Open Memorial Day weekend–mid-Oct., Dec. 23–mid March.

Rooms 10 doubles, 1 single, 11 cottages, all with full private shower and/or bath. 2 with desk, all with fan; some cabins with kitchen.

Facilities 2 dining rooms, 4 living rooms, playroom. 120 acres with gardens, croquet, badminton, playhouse (with supervised children's [age 4–9] program in A.M.), swing set, tennis court, self-guided nature trail, hiking trails, lake with beach, rowboats, paddleboats, canoes, sailboats, fishing. Cross-country skiing. Golf nearby. Sept. quilting workshops.

Location Northeast Kingdom. 30 m NE of Montpelier, 70 m NE of Burlington. Take Rte. 16 to E. Hardwick, then turn W & follow signs to Greensboro. Leaving Greensboro, bear left & keep left, 2 m to lodge. Lodge is at N end of Caspian Lake on Greensboro/E. Craftsbury Rd.

Restrictions No smoking.

Credit cards Discover, MC, Visa.

Rates MAP, $230–420 cottage (2–4 adults), $180–230 double, $100–130 single. Extra adult in room $98; extra child, $20–65; infants free. Family rates. Alc lunch, $6–8. Includes 15% service.

Extras Ground-floor rooms, 1 cottage wheelchair accessible. Crib, babysitting. Dutch, French spoken.

HARDWICK

For additional area entries, see **Craftsbury Common, Greensboro, St. Johnsbury,** and **Wolcott.**

Reader tip: "Try J.D. Elliots Restaurant on Main Street for a variety of tasty entrées and light fare at reasonable prices." *(Joe Schmidt)*

Also recommended: Built during Hardwick's granite boom, complete with hardwood floors, cypress staircase, oak woodwork, and crystal chandeliers, is **Carolyn's Victorian Inn** (15 Church Street, P.O. Box 1087, 05843; 802–472–6338). B&B double rates for the two guest rooms and one suite (some with shared bath) range from $85–110, including afternoon tea and breakfasts of lemon poppyseed French toast or banana-walnut pancakes with homemade bread and strawberry jam. "Owner/innkeeper Carolyn Richter welcomed us with fresh apple pie and ice cream. Carolyn has furnished her cozy guest rooms with the softest of feather beds. Fabulous egg soufflé and croissants for breakfast. She suggested several restaurants in town, and offered us just-baked cookies and friendly conversation in front of a roaring fire after dinner. Carolyn is an exceptionally warm, friendly, caring, interesting person, with a wide variety of interests and activities, from mountain biking and skiing to children's play therapy." *(Bill & Sheryl Martinez, also JS)*

JEFFERSONVILLE

Located in north-central Vermont, Jeffersonville is home to Smugglers' ski area, and is connected to the better known town of Stowe via Route 108. This beautiful mountain road passes through ruggedly handsome Smugglers' Notch, open to cars in summer, skiers in winter. The town is located 35 miles northwest of Burlington, 90 miles southwest of Montréal.

Reader tip: "Route 108 is closed to automobiles in winter making the town much quieter than Stowe, its busy cousin to the south." *(JS)*

Smugglers' Notch Inn ¢ ✗ ♦   *Tel:* 802–644–2412
Church Street, P.O. Box 280, 05464   800–845–3101
       Fax: 802–644–2881
E-mail: smuginn@pwshift.com
URL: http://www.smugglers-notch-inn.com

In the early 1800s, smugglers en route to Canada followed a trail through the gap between Mount Mansfield and Sterling Peak, giving this scenic mountain pass its name. Later, Smugglers' Notch was used by escaping slaves, and during Prohibition, smugglers followed the road south with contraband liquor. The eponymous inn, located in the historic village of Jeffersonville, dates back to 1791. Used as an inn since 1854, it was purchased by the husband-and-wife team of Cynthia

Barber and Jon Day in 1995. Guest rooms are simply but pleasantly decorated with contemporary oak or pine furnishings and quilt-topped beds. Breakfast is served from 8–9 A.M.; the menu varies daily, but might include orange juice, cereal, cornflake-oatmeal-raisin cookies, orange blueberry bread, cranberry pecan bread, and baked eggs with Swiss cheese and ham.

"Charming setting, yet convenient to major roads. The guest rooms are clean, homey, and comfortable." *(Frank J. Auriemmo, Jr.)* "A front-porch swing created a sense of nostalgia. The color-coordinated linens were of exceptionally good quality. Guests gather in the small, well-stocked bar before or after dinner." *(Margaret McNamara)* "The friendly innkeepers are pleased to offer sightseeing advice, and are responsive to requests." *(Mr. & Mrs. Ulrich Henning)*

"The spacious dining room has the feel of an old-fashioned hotel, with original wood floors and quilts hung on the walls. Service was prompt and friendly, and we enjoyed a fine dinner of salad with tasty home-made, low-fat dressing, and such entrées as delicious pork Dijonaise and chicken breast stuffed with cheddar and apples; the pecan pie was well worth the calories for dessert. The extensive and very reasonably priced wine list was also a pleasant surprise. After dinner, we relaxed in the spacious parlor, and dawdled over a waiting jigsaw puzzle." *(SWS)* "Guest rooms are clean and simply furnished. Our family found the inn and the nearby ski area an attractive alternative to Stowe, with a variety of well-groomed slopes for skiers of all skill levels. The innkeepers are accomplished bicyclers and cross-country skiers and are happy to offer advice on both sports." *(Joe Schmidt)*

Open All year.

Rooms 1 suite, 10 doubles—all have full private bath, fan, clock. 1 with whirlpool tub, gas fireplace.

Facilities Restaurant, bar, living room with fireplace, TV, books; screened dining porch; open porch with swing, deck with hot tub. 1.4 acre with swimming pool, lawn games. Canoe rentals, fly fishing instruction, downhill skiing, cross-country skiing, hiking, bicycling nearby.

Location NW VT, Lamoille Cty. 26 m E of Burlington, 290 m N of NYC, 220 m NW of Boston. Take I-89 to Exit 11. Go right at end of ramp. Take immediate right onto Rte. 117 & right again onto Gov. Peck Rd. Go 2 m. At stop sign go left onto Brown's Trace & go 5 m. At stop sign, go right onto Rte. 15 E. Go 15 m & go right onto Rte. 108 (opposite Mobil station) to inn on right in ¼ m.

Restrictions No smoking in common areas.

Credit cards Amex, MC, Visa.

Rates B&B, $60–125 double. Extra person, $15. Inquire for single rates. Children under 2, free; under 12, $10. 2-night minimum foliage season, holiday weeks.

KILLINGTON/MENDON

Best known for its outstanding downhill ski area, the Killington area offers a variety of activities year-round, including ice-skating, snowmobiling, and cross-country skiing in winter, plus such warm weather activities as golf, tennis, hiking, the alpine slide, concerts, and more.

For additional area entries, see **Bridgewater Corners** and **Woodstock**.

Red Clover Inn ✕
Woodward Road, Mendon, 05701

Tel: 802–775–2290
800–752–0571
Fax: 802–773–0594
E-mail: redclovr@vermontel.com
URL: http://redcloverinn.com

Under the capable ownership of Sue and Harris Zuckerman is the charming Red Clover Inn, well known for its comfortable rooms, excellent food, and attractive country setting. Built in 1840, the main house holds the restaurant, keeping room with fireplace, and country-comfortable bedrooms with queen-size beds, handmade quilts and antique accents. Completed in 1997 was an addition to the carriage house with three spacious guest rooms, each with a king-size bed, sitting area, double whirlpool tub, gas fireplace, air-conditioning, and beautiful mountain views. The upstairs room has French doors leading to a deck facing Pico and Killington.

Served in the breakfast room, recently redone in teal colors, the morning meal consists of coffee and tea, fresh fruit, cereals, and a daily special—perhaps Vermont cheddar omelets, lemon ricotta pancakes, cinnamon raisin French toast, or Swedish oatmeal pancakes. The main dining room is charmingly painted in yellow and white with hand-painted free-form floral stencils. Under the supervision of chef Francis Clogston (formerly of Hemingway's), the dinner menu changes nightly, but might include such entrées as rosemary-crusted rack of lamb with eggplant rolls and garlic mashed potatoes; ginger-honey glazed duck breast with wild mushrooms and Vermont cheddar polenta; and boneless Vermont trout stuffed with rosemary potato soufflé and baby squash.

"Our attractively decorated room had a gas fireplace, a whirlpool tub for two, and windows on three sides with mountain views. The bath towels were thick and fluffy. My dietary restrictions were easily and thoughtfully accommodated; the food was superb." *(Jill & Marty Post)* "The food, wine, service, and decor all reflect the truly caring attitude and professional competence of Sue and Harris Zuckerman and their staff. Each charming room has a diary for guests to record their thoughts—enjoyable to read. The keeping room is the social center of the inn, a perfect place to socialize, play a game, watch TV, or enjoy a cocktail in the cozy bar." *(Norma & Fred Spina, also Joyce Burkhardt)* "Improves with every return visit. The outstanding wine cellar Harris has developed rivals many New York City restaurants." *(Merrie Kelly)* "A casual, sophisticated country inn for adults, with charming folk art. Imaginative menu; vegetarians are always accommodated. Our favorite room is the main inn, and looks out on Pico Peak." *(Kathy Baum)*

"Exceptional dinner; welcoming owners; likable English bulldogs, Lily and Hoadie." *(Patricia Hughes)* "Surrounded by woods and fields. Terrific location on a peaceful little road, just minutes from Route 4 and the Killington access road. The cozy pub is inviting for pre-dinner

409

drinks. My room (#10), done in handsome shades of forest green, had a gas fireplace, double Jacuzzi tub, lots of windows with great mountain views, and separate bathroom with shower. Other rooms varied in size, but all were lovely, one with an antique rope bed, another with white iron and brass bed. Our delicious dinner included a lobster sushi roll, followed by swordfish garnished with addictive sweet potato hay, and concluded with a sinfully rich chocolate truffle in phyllo." *(SWS)* "Meticulous attention to detail; superb food; relaxing country atmosphere; immaculately maintained." *(Carol Ann Tonken)*

Open Closed mid-April until late May. Restaurant closed Sun. (except holidays).

Rooms 5 suites, 9 doubles—all with private bath and/or shower, radio, clock, fan. Some with air-conditioning, desk, gas fireplace, whirlpool tub, TV/VCR. Rooms in 2 buildings.

Facilities Breakfast room, 2 dining rooms, bar/lounge, keeping room with fireplace, TV, piano, stereo, books; wine cellar. 13 acres with swimming pool, badminton, croquet.

Location S central VT. 5 m NE of Rutland. From Rte. 7 in Rutland, take Rte. 4 E for 5.2 m. Turn right on Woodward Rd., go ½ m to inn on left.

Restrictions No smoking. Children over 10 welcome.

Credit cards Discover, MC, Visa.

Rates MAP, $160–350 suite, $150–285 double. Extra person, $60. B&B, $110–310 suite, $100–245 double. 15% service. 2–3 night weekend, holiday minimum. Midweek package rates, excluding holidays. Alc dinner, $35.

Extras Rutland airport/station pickup. Pets in carriage house with approval.

The Vermont Inn 🏃 ✕ 🐾 ⅖
Route 4, 05751

Tel: 802–775–0708
800–541–7795
Fax: 802–773–2440
E-mail: vtinn@aol.com
URL: http://www.vermontinn.com

A longtime favorite, the Vermont Inn was purchased in 1995 by Megan and Greg Smith, along with their two daughters, Molly and Lisa. The Smiths have used their years of experience to make a good inn even better; most of the inn's staff have stayed on board, including the inn's fine chef, Stephen Hatch. The inn's acclaimed restaurant is open to the public, and a recent dinner included such entrées as scallops Dijon, roast turkey, pan-fried trout, or pasta primavera.

"Delicious food, beautiful mountain views. Megan, Greg, and their terrific staff made us feel right at home. Cheery, comfortable, clean guest rooms of varying size." *(Judith Kane)* "The atmosphere of the common rooms is warm and friendly. A nice touch was the fresh apples, cider, and cookies in the lobby. The innkeepers are friendly, gracious, and have a wonderful sense of humor." *(Dorothy M. Hoffman)* "Wonderful ambience, exceptional food, cordial innkeepers who make each guest feel special." *(Melanie Horne)*

"Cleanliness is a top priority and it shows. Lighting is good, plumbing is country and adequate, parking is convenient, and the location, although on a busy highway, is set so far back from the road that all is peaceful and quiet. The first-rate dining is intimate in the evening with soft background music and a cozy fire in winter; at breakfast all is cheery and bright. Desserts—when one still has room—are great, including superb pecan pie. Breakfast is informal with a serve-yourself bar. Also available are pancakes, French toast, eggs, bacon, and more. In summer lighter fare is offered: fresh fruit, hot homemade muffins, cold cereal, and assorted juices. A family atmosphere is encouraged by the TV and VCR where many guests congregate to watch a program or free movie. Good lighting and comfortable seating encourage reading or conversation in the living room." *(Mr. & Mrs. Frank Washburn)* "Firm, comfortable mattresses. I loved the little touches—a welcoming flask of sherry, fresh flowers in mid-winter, the strawberry candies in my room, and the fragrant bath soaps. Excellent food, especially the salads, vegetables, and soups—the spinach and bacon, and the cheddar and ale soups are stand-outs." *(Ann Conway)*

Open Closed May 25–April 15.
Rooms 18 doubles—all with private bath and/or shower. Some with fireplace, air-conditioning, ceiling fan.
Facilities Dining room, living room, game room, bar, porch. Heated outdoor swimming pool, hot tub (winter), sauna, tennis court, lawn games, gardens.
Location Central VT, 6 m E of Rutland on Rte. 4. 4 m W of Killington ski area, 2 m W of Pico ski area.
Restrictions Children 6 and over. No smoking.
Credit cards Amex, DC, MC, Visa.
Rates MAP, $115–240 double, $65–125 single. Extra person, $25–60. 15% service. B&B rates available. Seasonal packages.

LOWER WATERFORD

For additional area entries, see **East Burke, Lyndonville,** and **St. Johnsbury,** plus **Littleton, New Hampshire.**

Rabbit Hill Inn ✕ ᕱ
Pucker Street, Route 18, 05848

Tel: 802–748–5168
800–76-BUNNY
Fax: 802–748–8342
E-mail: Rabbit.Hill.Inn@ConnRiver.net
URL: http://www.RabbitHillInn.com

In the 1790s, an active trade route developed between Portland, on the Maine coast, and interior New England and Montréal. Dozens of passing wagon teams carried produce, Fairbanks scales, and maple syrup eastward; spices, molasses, textiles, and general merchandise journeyed west. To accommodate the travelers, the home built by Jonathan Cummings in 1795 was converted into an inn. Not a great deal has changed in Lower Waterford since then.

Brian and Leslie Mulcahy report that "ours is a classic country inn offering gentility, period decor, and a romantic atmosphere. Our restored 150-year-old village has no traffic lights or shops. Everything is white clapboards and dark green shutters. Our hiking trails lead over a country bridge spanning the stream that feeds our swimming pond, continue by a meadow where cows graze and end up at a beaver colony." Four diamond/star awards from both AAA and Mobil are acknowledgment of the innkeepers' hard work and attention to detail.

Meals are prepared under the supervision of chef Russ Stannard; care is taken to include heart-healthy and vegetarian selections. On a winter evening, one diner might select scallop spoon bread with spinach, baby greens with balsamic vinaigrette, duck breast with cassis and leek jam, and chocolate torte; while a companion might prefer venison and sweet potato pie, cumin-spiced roasted halibut, and cherry-pear strudel. Breakfast includes a buffet of fruit, pastries, juices, yogurt and granola, plus a choice of two entrées—perhaps egg crêpe soufflé with goat cheese, asparagus, and triple-smoked bacon; and lemon poppy-seed waffles with raspberry maple syrup, Grand Marnier butter, and Canadian bacon.

"Our spacious fairytale room, the Loft, was wonderfully decorated with a vaulted ceiling and exposed wooden beams. The food was exceptional, from the candlelit breakfasts, to the afternoon tea by the fire in the sitting room, to dinner in front of another beautiful fireplace. I collect rabbits, so I noticed every subtle bunny accent. After dinner, we ascended the hidden stairway to our room to find the fireplace glowing, candles burning around the Jacuzzi, soft music playing, and the bed turned down with a special gift on the pillow. A light outside our Palladian window lit up the snow falling outside." *(Denise Hyatt)* "We stayed in a suite that was once a tavern; the original door was still in use as the front door to our suite." *(Deann & Michael Collins)* "The buildings and grounds are impeccably clean, the service exceptionally gracious. The turndown service with its soft music, candlelight, and delicate surprises (like rose petals strewn across a crisp, white pillowcase) provide a civilized and gently pampering close to the day." *(Amy MacDonald-Persons)* "Brian and Leslie have improved upon perfection. The attention to detail is astounding, yet the atmosphere is comfortable and friendly." *(Phyllis Mackey)*

"Molly's Promise is a beautiful room done in mauve and beige tones. The comfortable king-size bed had good reading lamps on both sides; plenty of current magazines and books were supplied. We could have spent the day on the couch in front of the gas fireplace. Wonderful afternoon tea, excellent dinner. The entire staff made us feel at home." *(Tina Hom)* "Outstanding breakfasts. Tavern's Secret is a marvelous room, complete with fireplace and whirlpool tub. A nice, quiet, relaxed atmosphere with puzzles, Scrabble, and a pub." *(Patricia Sinacole)* "A fire blazed on the hearth, and everywhere were exquisite Christmas decorations. Each room has reading lights on both sides of the queen- and king-size beds, plus comfortable seating with good lighting for those times when you want to relax in your room. A short drive away are the shops of Littleton and the Victorian painted ladies of St. Johnsbury and its eccentric museums." *(SWS)* "Upon returning to our room, we found a lighted candle, soft music playing, and a tiny heart pillow gift on the turned-down beds." *(Gladys & Bob Dunn)*

Open All year.
Rooms 5 suites, 16 doubles—all with full private bath, air-conditioning, cassette player, radio, fan, coffee maker. 12 with fireplace. All suites with fireplace, double Jacuzzi tub. 5 rooms in separate building.
Facilities Dining room; parlor with fireplace; pub; sitting room with fireplace; lounge with fireplace, TV/VCR, games; library; covered porches. 15 acres with herb and flower gardens, gazebo, greenhouse, lawn games, pond for swimming, fishing, cross-country skiing. Canoes for use on nearby CT River. Golf, downhill skiing, hiking nearby.
Location NE VT, Northeast Kingdom, 10 m from St. Johnsbury and Littleton, NH. From I-93 N, take Exit 44. Follow Rte. 18 2 m N to inn on left, across from church. From I-91 S, take Exit 19 onto I-93 S. Take Exit 1 (VT) to Rte. 18 S. Go 7 m to inn on right.
Restrictions No smoking. Not recommended for children under 12. Proper attire required for dinner.
Credit cards Amex, MC, Visa.
Rates MAP, $250–300 suite, $200–250 double. 15% service. Extra person, $70. Prix fixe dinner, $39. Mid-week winter discounts. Honeymoon packages.
Extras Wheelchair access; 1 room specially equipped.

LUDLOW

Ludlow is in south-central Vermont, 4½ hours north of New York City and 2½ hours northwest of Boston. From I-91, take Exit 6 to Route 103 west to Ludlow. It's 22 miles southeast of Rutland and about 20 miles from I-91. Okemo is 1 mile from the center of Ludlow, and Killington is 16 miles north. Eight golf courses lie within 30 miles of Ludlow, and five lakes are nearby for all water sports; hiking, bicycling, and horseback riding are also popular activities.

Also recommended: An 1829 village colonial home, set on a quiet side street, the **Andrie Rose** (13 Pleasant Street, P.O. Box 152, 05149; 802–228–4846) combines Victorian oak antiques and reproductions with designer fabrics and wallcoverings, for a light and airy look. The 20 guest rooms have designer linens and color-coordinated window treatments, many with views of Okemo's ski trails, fireplaces, and double Jacuzzi tubs. B&B double rates range from $80–285; ask about the family suites which sleep up to six.

Information please: Originally built as a Victorian summer hotel in 1840, **Echo Lake Inn** (P.O. Box 154, 05149; 802–228–8602 or 800–356–6844 or www.vermontlodging.com/echolake.htm) has been owned by Yvonne Pardieu and Chip Connolly since 1993. Recent renovations to the four-story building include a six-person Jacuzzi; an outdoor swimming pool is also available. The restaurant, open to the public, offers such entrées as grilled pork tenderloin, rainbow trout with artichokes, and chicken with black raspberry sauce. Accommodations are available in the original building as well as adjacent condo units; double rates range from $90–199.

For additional area entries, see **Andover, Chester, Weathersfield,** and **Weston.**

LYNDONVILLE

Information please: Set on 550 acres, **The Wildflower Inn** (Darling Hill Road, Lyndonville, 05851; 802–626–8310 or 800–627–8310) is a working dairy farm with accommodations in the main house, converted carriage barn, a neighboring home, and a one-room schoolhouse (with a double whirlpool tub). The breakfast might include pancakes with applesauce, along with a buffet of cereals, yogurt, fruit, and granola. There's a heated swimming pool and tennis court, horse-drawn wagon rides, and cross-country skiing and sledding in winter, plus lots for kids to enjoy at this family-oriented inn. "Set atop a hillside with spectacular views of the Green Mountains; beautiful sunsets. Our room and meals were adequate. Animal lovers will enjoy the friendly critters in the barn." *(James Burr)* "Lovely setting; delightful accommodations in the Schoolhouse." *(Emma Morris)* B&B double rates range from $95–110, with suite rates to $220; children under 5 stay free, and those under 12 pay $8 daily.

For additional area entries, see **East Burke, Lower Waterford,** and **St. Johnsbury.**

MANCHESTER

Manchester is located in southwestern Vermont, 1½ hours northeast of Albany, 3 hours northwest of Boston, and 4½ hours north of New York City. The town is about 25 miles north of Bennington and 30 miles south of Rutland via Route 7 or 7A. Manchester Center is the area which surrounds the village of Manchester, near the intersection of Routes 30, 7/7A, and 11.

It's a 10- to 25-minute drive to Bromley, Stratton, and Magic Mountain for downhill skiing, and there are four cross-country ski centers within a 20-minute drive. Summer activities cover Vermont's full range of hiking, bicycling, antiquing, golf and tennis, lake and quarry swimming, trout fishing in the Battenkill River, canoeing, and summer theater. Shopping is a favorite year-round activity, with a supply of discount stores to rival those in North Conway or Freeport. For a change of pace, visit the American Museum of Fly Fishing, or Hildene, the summer home of Abraham Lincoln's son.

Reader tip: "Our tour of Hildene, Robert Lincoln's home, was the best of its kind we have ever taken—our guide was both knowledgeable and opinionated." *(Brad Lockner, also SWS)*

Worth noting: Although some of Manchester's inns are fairly close to Route 7A, nighttime traffic noise is rarely a problem, since through traffic, especially trucks, take Route 7, a divided, limited-access highway in this section. If Manchester's inns are out of your price range, see our entries in **Arlington, Danby,** and **Dorset.**

Also recommended: The beautifully restored **Equinox** (Route 7A, P.O. Box 46, 05254; 802–362–4700 or 800–362–4747), a 200-year-old Vermont classic, has 183 rooms and full resort/spa facilities, including an 18-hole golf course; rates range from $179–319, with various packages available. For the person who has everything, consider enrolling in the British School of Falconry or even the Land Rover Driving School (living in Greenwich, CT, is not required for enrollment). "Expensive but first class all the way." *(BJ Hensley)* "Great service, well-appointed, and charming; the spa treatment is worth every penny." *(LDS)* "Delicious casual dinners, great atmosphere at the pub at the Equinox." *(Hilary Soule)*

The Battenkill Inn   ♿   *Tel:* 802–362–4213
Route 7A, P.O. Box 948, 05254   800–441–1628
Fax: 802–362–0975
E-mail: innfo@battenkillinn.com
URL: http://www.battenkillinn.com

Sometimes, when an inn changes hands, readers are concerned that it won't be as good. More often, as in the case of the Battenkill Inn, it only gets better. Laine and Yoshi Akiyama bought this B&B in 1996, and judging from the rave reports we received from their guests, they made the right choice when they decided to leave longtime careers with Walt Disney Imagineering, load their two golden retrievers into the back of the truck, and leave southern California for Vermont.

A Victorian farmhouse built in 1840, painted yellow with white trim, the inn is decorated with antiques and reproductions, with high ceilings and marble fireplaces. Breakfast is served from 8–9:30 A.M., and might include poached pears in citrus glaze, pepper and onion quiche, turkey bacon, and eggs-to-order; or perhaps fresh fruit cup, huevos fandangos, and chicken-apple sausage. Granola, home-baked muffins, and eggs-to-order are always available, and dietary restrictions are accommodated with advance notice.

"Charming, knowledgeable, well-traveled hosts. Wonderful mountain views looking out the back of the inn. Breakfast is served in one of two dining rooms, one with two tables for four, the other room seating about ten at one large table. On the first morning, we were offered a choice of an omelet or French toast and sausage; the next day, we enjoyed eggs Benedict. Around four every afternoon, the sideboard is set up with red and white wine, hors d'oeuvres, and fresh fruit." *(Barbara Walsh)* "Coffee and tea always available. Welcoming hosts." *(Laurel Bailey)* "Yoshi and Laine are gracious hosts—friendly but not overbearing." *(JI)* "The chocolate kisses an added touch. Yoshi accommodated our dietary needs at breakfast. Don't miss the granola." *(Gila Pollack)* "Exceptionally well-presented breakfast and late-afternoon snacks. The hosts' energy and enthusiasm encouraged a relaxed atmosphere and conversation among the guests." *(Sylvia & Tom Smith)* "Warm, friendly, homey atmosphere." *(Margaret Noone)* "Norman Rockwell charm. Each morning, Laine and Yoshi greeted us with a most artistic presentation of fruit. The hot entrées guaranteed farm-fresh." *(Elizabeth Noone)* "The constant supply of tasty hot coffee and yummy home-baked cookies, as well as the big dish of pistachios, made us feel right at home in front of the blazing fire. Wonderful scenery and shopping." *(Melinda & Mike Andreski)* "The decor is fresh and inviting, with crisp new fabrics and floral wallpapers, firm mattresses, and good bedside lighting. Wonderfully helpful guide to area sights, hikes, activities, and more given to each guest." *(SWS)*

Open All year. Closed Dec. 24 & 25.
Rooms 11 doubles—all with private shower bath, clock/radio, air-conditioning. 10 with fan, 4 with fireplace, 3 with porch.
Facilities 2 dining rooms, living room with TV/VCR, library with books; porch; guest refrigerator. 7 acres with lawn games, pond. Canoe rentals next door.
Location Take I-91 N to Brattleboro, Exit 2. Take Rte. 30 N to Rte. 7A in Manchester Center. Turn left on 7A & drive S 4.5 m to inn on left.
Restrictions No smoking.
Credit cards MC, Visa.
Rates B&B, $90–165 double. 2-night weekend/holiday minimum. Midweek packages with dinner. Theme weekends: maple sugaring, antiquing, Ethan Allen days. Picnic baskets, Equinox spa packages.
Extras Wheelchair access; 1 guest room specially equipped.

1811 House	*Tel:* 802–362–1811
Route 7A, P.O. Box 39, 05254	800–432–1811
	Fax: 802–362–2443
	E-mail: stay1811@vermontel.com

The 1811 House offers elegance, quiet, and relaxation in a lovely setting. Though the rooms are beautifully decorated, the inn is still casual enough that you are free to wander into the kitchen to make yourself a cup of tea. Built in the late 1700s, the house has been operated as an inn since 1811, except for a brief period when it was a private residence of Mary Lincoln Isham, Lincoln's granddaughter; it's been owned by Bruce and Marnie Duff since 1990. Breakfast, served from 8–9:30 A.M., includes fresh fruit and juice, home-baked goods, and a daily special— perhaps waffles and bacon or eggs Benedict and Vermont ham; hot and cold cereal and egg-white veggie omelets are always options. On weekends, a traditional English breakfast is served with fried eggs, scones, bacon, grilled tomatoes, apples, and mushrooms.

"Beautiful antiques and impeccable taste. Even the selection of magazines in each room include not only a variety of the latest issues, but also such collector's items as a 1939 issue of *Home and Garden*. The pub is a delightful place to meet the other guests and catch up on local activities. Adam and Marnie's wonderful breakfasts are served on beautiful china, silver, and crystal. Bruce's gardens make me want to go home and dig up my whole backyard. The staff will go out of their way to make dinner reservations and arrange for almost anything a guest might want to do." *(Dennis & Nancy Studrawa)* "Outstanding service, friendliness, and comfort. Homey rooms decorated with fine furnishings." *(Peter Van Ness Philip)* "The owners and staff are loving, caring people who make each guest feel at home and special. Comfortable king-size canopy beds ensure a sound night's sleep. Beautiful Oriental rugs and antique brass. The pub is open nightly from 5:30–8 P.M. with the largest selection of single malts I've ever seen." *(Antonio De Grasse)*

"On a quiet evening, we spent a fascinating hour in the inn's cozy pub, as Bruce taught us all about single malt whiskies." *(Dave Shea)* "Marnie and Bruce were extremely knowledgeable about the inn and area. Marnie's homemade chocolate-chip cookies are irresistible. Breakfast was delicious and varied, with pancakes, and eggs done just right. The entire inn was impeccably clean, and our room, the Jeremiah French Suite, was lovely." *(Dottie Erikson)*

"The common rooms are beautiful and inviting. Decanters of port and brandy are set out along with plenty of reading materials, games, and comfortable chairs." *(Rose Ciccone)* "Quality antiques, original art, excellent reproductions, antique silver and crystal." *(MJF)* "Marnie makes a perfect pot of tea. The recently built adjacent carriage house is a good choice for couples traveling together." *(Pam Phillips)* "Rooms are priced at three different levels, depending on size and amenities, but even the smallest are inviting. Most have queen-size, lace-canopied beds, with the nicest ones at the back of the inn, overlooking the lovely gardens, pond, and mountains beyond." *(SWS)*

Open All year.

Rooms 1 suite, 13 doubles—all with full private bath, air-conditioning, fan, desk. 6 rooms with fireplace, 1 with porch. 3 rooms in annex.

Facilities Dining room, living room, library, pub—all with fireplace; game room with pool table, TV/VCR. 7 acres with flower gardens, pond.

Location S VT. 1.1 m S of blinking light at main intersection in town.

Restrictions No smoking. No children under 16. Traffic noise possible in front rooms.

Credit cards Amex, Discover, MC, Visa.

Rates B&B, $160–220 suite, double. 2-night weekend/holiday/foliage minimum. Ask about mid-week off-season rates.

Inn at Ormsby Hill ♿

Historic Route 7A, RR 2, P.O. Box 3264, 05255

Tel: 802–362–1163
800–670–2841
Fax: 802–362–5176
E-mail: ormsby@vermontel.com
URL: http://www.ormsbyhill.com

The Inn at Ormsby Hill dates to the 1700s when it was little more than a log cabin. In the late 19th century, the building was expanded substantially to become the manor house of a large estate; the original keeping room with cooking fireplace is now one of the three inviting common areas. Chris and Ted Sprague, formerly of the Newcastle Inn in Maine, purchased the inn in 1995, and are working hard to make a lovely inn even more so. For an especially romantic escape, ask about the new guest rooms; in addition to the lovely garden and mountain views, you can see the fireplace both from your king-size bed and from the double Jacuzzi.

The breakfast buffet is available from 8–10 A.M., and consists of homemade granola, yogurt, fresh fruit, English muffins and jam, plus such treats as raspberry streusel cake, currant scones, or lemon almond bread. At 9 A.M., Chris serves such entrées as eggs Benedict bread pudding or risotto with bacon, eggs and cheddar cheese, followed by a New England dessert—perhaps apple-cranberry-almond crisp or warm gingerbread with vanilla ice cream. Dinners are offered on weekends. Friday night supper is a casual affair, available from 6:30–8:30 P.M. Guests are invited into the kitchen to help themselves to soup, stew, or pasta; a recent meal included penne pasta baked with portobello mushrooms, prosciutto, tomatoes and cheese, with home-baked sourdough bread, plus carrot cake for dessert. Saturday night four-course dinners are a more formal affair, served at 7 P.M.; a spring menu might offer risotto with arugula and Fontina, salad, cream biscuits, rack of lamb with shiitake mushrooms, and triple chocolate truffle torte with white chocolate sauce.

"A great getaway—charming inn, appealing town. We signed up for the full breakfast at 9 A.M., and it was well worth it. Super comfortable beds, beautifully redone rooms." *(Barbara Walsh, also HS)* "Chris and Ted are creating a world-class inn in a spectacular setting. The inn offers a lovely, convenient location; a genuinely historic home; all modern amenities; ample common areas and inviting guest rooms; wonderful food; and the genuine hospitality of two involved, hands-on innkeepers. My favorite room is the beautiful, spacious conservatory-style dining room with wraparound windows, French doors leading out to the terrace, and wonderful mountain views." *(SWS)*

"We loved staying at the Spragues' inn in Maine, and are even more delighted with their new Vermont venture. The rooms are tasteful, luxurious, warm, and comfortable. The Library Room has a working fireplace and book-lined walls." *(Edward M. Westerman)* "Our beautiful room had a spectacular view of the sunrise. Saturday morning Chris served us white chocolate pound cake followed by orange slices with cranberry sauce, then a baked pancake with sausage and maple syrup. Dinner Saturday was just as delightful. Ted and Chris are amicable hosts; they welcome you into their home and you immediately feel like longtime friends." *(Larry Webb)*

Open All year.
Rooms 10 doubles—all with full private bath, clock/radio, air-conditioning. 10 with fireplace, double whirlpool tub.
Facilities Dining room with fireplace, parlor with fireplace, TV room, library with fireplace, stereo; guest refrigerator, porch, terrace. 2½ acres with lawn games.
Location S VT. 2 m S of historic district.
Restrictions No smoking. Children 10 and over preferred. BYOB.
Credit cards Discover, MC, Visa.
Rates B&B, $115–290 double, $95–270 single. Extra person, $25. 2-night weekend minimum. Prix fixe dinner: $15 Fri. night; $32.50 Sat. night. Package weekends.
Extras Wheelchair access. 1 bathroom fully accessible.

Meadowbrook Inn ✗
RR 1, P.O. Box 145, Landgrove, 05148

Tel: 802–824–6444
800–498–6445
Fax: 802–824–4335
E-mail: tony@meadowbinn.com
URL: http://www.meadowbinn.com

"You can't have your cake and eat it too," we were all taught, but at the Meadowbrook Inn, renovated by Madeline and Tony Rundella in 1996, you can sure try. Like to spend your days hiking or skiing in the Green Mountains but would rather soak away your aches and pains in a double Jacuzzi tub? Enjoy a wilderness setting with cross-country skiing right outside your door yet be minutes from Manchester outlet shopping? The Rundellas are working hard to make it all happen for you in their gambrel-roofed inn, built in the 1930s. Guests can relax in the pine-paneled living room, dining room, and bright solarium breakfast room overlooking the forest setting. Named for flowers, the fully refurbished and spacious guest rooms have queen-size beds, hardwood floors, and Oriental carpets. Larkspur has an iron bed, brick fireplace, seafoam green walls, and floral fabrics, while Delphinium has knotty pine paneling, vaulted ceilings, a maple bed, and a Vermont Castings woodstove.

Breakfast is offered from 8–9 A.M. on weekends (8:30–9 A.M. weekdays), and begins with home-baked muffins and juice, followed by a hot entrée; one morning it might be Grand Marnier French toast with home-baked bread; the next day might feature vegetable omelets with Vermont cheddar and fresh herbs. A recent dinner menu included such entrées as herb-crusted rack of lamb, grilled salmon with risotto, penne à la vodka with seafood and mushrooms, and hazelnut-crusted chicken with sun-dried tomatoes.

"Gracious hosts Madeline and Tony have done a superb job of renovating the inn. The delightful breakfast room looks out over beautiful trees and well-kept lawns. Our delicious breakfast of blueberry pancakes with bacon and real maple syrup was beautifully garnished with fresh fruit and edible flowers. The Lilac Room has colorful and cozy down pillows and comforter on the exceptionally comfortable bed; the immaculate bathroom was spacious." *(Ray & Ginnie Salminen)* "Inviting nature walks, with a variety of birds and flowers." *(Teresa Cellucci)* "Madeleine's meals are delicious from breakfast to dinner, to afternoon biscotti and cider." *(Sharon Turner)* "One morning while at breakfast, we watched a visiting moose through the solarium windows." *(Diane & Jeremy Zung)* "Wonderful hospitality and food." *(Isabel & Joseph Medeiros)* "White linen tablecloths at breakfast and dinner, flowers everywhere, warm fireplaces, and even a full-service bar." *(Mrs. Owen Ash)* "Rooms are inviting, and immaculately clean." *(Carolee Brisson)*

Open May–March. Restaurant open Wed.–Sun. from May–Oct.; weekends, Dec.–March.

Rooms 7 doubles—all with full private bath and/or shower. 3 with double whirlpool tub, fireplace/firestove. All with clock, fan.

Facilities Restaurant with fireplace, pub with fireplace, living room with fireplace, patio. Acoustic guitar some Sats. during dinner. 8.5 acres with pond, trails. Ski touring center with instruction, rentals, 26 km of trails for cross-country skiing, snowshoeing; hiking, bicycling in summer. Close to Appalachian, Catamount, Long Trails. 4 m to downhill skiing. Guided fishing, canoe trips.

Location 10 m E of Manchester, between Peru & Londonderry. From I-91, take Exit 6 (Rockingham) to Rte. 103 W to Chester. Take Rte. 11 W to inn. From I-87, take Exit 23 to I-787 to Rte. 7 E; becomes Rte. 9 E in VT. In Bennington, take Rte. 7 N to Exit 4. Turn right onto Rte. 11 E to inn.

Restrictions No smoking. Children 12 and over.

Credit cards Amex, CB, DC, Discover, MC, Visa.

Rates B&B, $95–185 double; MAP, $165–255. 2–3 night weekend/holiday minimum. Alc dinner, $35.

Village Country Inn ✕
Route 7A, P.O. Box 408, 05254

Tel: 802–362–1792
800–370–0300
Fax: 802–862–1792
E-mail: vci@vermontel.com
URL: http://www.villagecountryinn.com

Anne and Jay Degen left the corporate world behind in 1985 when they bought the Village Country Inn. Built a century ago as the summer home of the Kellogg family, it was converted into an inn in the 1920s. Several hundred yards of flowered fabric later, the Degens had created the charming atmosphere of a country hotel. The living room, for example, combines the original fieldstone fireplace with muted rose linen couches; a flat wooden sleigh makes a unique coffee table. Each guest room is different, done perhaps in dusty blue and white wicker, pale apricot, or varying shades of mauve, Anne's favorite color. Some recently redecorated rooms have elaborately draped canopy beds; decor ranges from subdued and elegant to the delightfully outrageous. Renovation and upgrading is an ongoing process throughout the inn; one recently renovated suite, the Rose Noir, has a king-size canopy bed, mini-bar, double soaking tub, and a sitting area. The "standard" rooms, though small, are charming, with canopy beds, and are an excellent value.

Breakfast consists of juice, muffins or pastry, coffee or tea, and your choice of eggs, pancakes, waffles, cereal, or one of the chef's breakfast specials. Dinner choices include citrus-marinated, charcoal-grilled salmon, pan-roasted duckling with apricot brandy sauce, and roasted rack of lamb with couscous.

"My room was done in shades of rose and deep green, and had a king-size bed, a comfy chaise lounge with a good reading light and telephone. The large bathroom had great lighting, a large glassed-in shower, and a claw-foot tub, while the cozy sitting room had a white wicker settee and a small TV. Service at breakfast was fast and friendly. I had a delicious artichoke, tomato, and cheese omelet with home fries and oatmeal toast." *(SWS)* "Our small corner room had four windows, and overlooked the flower garden, with a view of Mt. Equinox. Decor was light and airy—an ecru-on-mauve, petite floral wallpaper, and wonderful lace on the windows and bed. Brass reading lamps were mounted on either side of the bed; two Windsor chairs sat beside a round table. Anne and Jay are a hardworking couple who love their work; they were visible the whole time we were there, from the front desk to the dining room." *(Rose Ciccone)* "Attentive, responsive owners and staff. Beautiful gardens." *(Sally Ducot)* "The gardens alone are worth a visit; even in the bustle of Manchester, you feel like you've been transported to an English country setting. Available but unobtrusive staff." *(LOS)*

Open All year.
Rooms 33 suites, doubles—all with private shower and/or bath, air-conditioning. 22 with TV. 2 with refrigerator.

Facilities Restaurant with fireplace, tavern with fireplace, living room with fireplace, gift shop, porch. Swimming pool, terrace, perennial garden with fountains.
Location In center of village.
Restrictions No smoking. No children.
Credit cards Amex, Discover, MC, Visa.
Rates MAP, $205–350 suite, $145–185 double. Extra person, $65. 15% service.

Wilburton Inn ✗ ♠ ⚛ ♿
River Road, P.O. Box 468, 05254

Tel: 802–362–2500
800–648–4944
Fax: 802–362–1107
E-mail: wilbuinn@sover.net
URL: http://www.wilburton.com

Manchester was a popular summer resort at the turn of the century, and many wealthy families built summer "cottages" in which to escape the city heat. The Wilburton Inn dates back to this period, when James Wilbur, treasurer of the New Haven railroad, purchased this imposing brick mansion on a high knoll with beautiful views. Wilburton was converted into an inn in 1945 and has been owned by Georgette and Albert Levis since 1988. Rooms are furnished with period antiques, some original to the house, and Oriental rugs. Breakfast is served from 8–10 A.M. in the Terrace Room, overlooking the Battenkill Valley, and usually includes fresh fruit and juice, cereal and muffins, and a choice of eggs, pancakes, and waffles; rates also include afternoon tea, cookies, wine, and cheese and crackers. Dinner entrées include cornmeal-crusted trout, lamb with garlic rosemary sauce, and chive fettuccini and shrimp. A strikingly unusual aspect of the inn's buildings and grounds is Dr. Levis's modern art collection, most connected to his psychiatric theories of conflict resolution and male-female relationships.

"Our family group of eight was superbly accommodated in a cottage with a large living room with a fireplace, a den area with a piano, two large bedrooms and two full baths. Delicious lobster-stuffed sole and a mouth-watering sirloin steak at dinner. The Levises' sons Oliver and Max waited on us at dinner and made a lasting impression." *(Lauren Buday)* "Georgette and Albert don't so much check you in as invite you to share their mansion and its grounds. Century-old Persian carpets of heroic proportions peacefully co-exist with gooey chocolate chip cookies and lemonade." *(Brian Saipe)* "Highlights include the magnificent views and lovely grounds, the extensive facilities, the convenient location, and the friendly, casual owners and staff. Appealing for both families and romantic getaways." *(Hilary Soule)* "Like visiting relatives in the house you wish they had. Beautiful setting, yet close to town." *(Margaret Hedberg)* "Our room was decorated in shades of blue; the comfortable four-poster bed featured a down comforter and quality linens. The fainting couch, placed in the bay window overlooking the mountains, was ideal for reading the Sunday papers and napping. The resident English setter visited our table at breakfast, wearing a red bandana ascot with the aplomb one would expect of a dog spending his days amid such grandeur." *(Elaine Trehub)*

Open All year. Restaurant closed mid-week off-season.

Rooms 12 suites, 23 doubles—all with full private bath and/or shower. 3 with whirlpool tub. All with telephone, radio, clock, desk, air-conditioning. 24 with TV, 8 with fireplace, 10 with refrigerator, 12 with balcony/deck. Rooms in 6 buildings.

Facilities Dining room, terrace, library, living room with fireplace, grand piano; game room with TV/VCR, porch. 17 acres with swimming pool, 3 tennis courts, gazebo, barbecue, cross-country skiing. Fishing, golf, downhill skiing nearby.

Location 1 m S of village; follow Rte. 7A to River Rd. Go ½ m on River Rd. past Hildene on right to inn on left. Turn at stone pillars & go uphill to inn.

Restrictions No smoking.

Credit cards Amex, MC, Visa.

Rates B&B, $145–265 suite, $115–190 double. MAP, $200–330 suite, $180–255 double. 15% gratuity. Children less $15. 2–3 night weekend/holiday minimum. Alc dinner, $35.

Extras Wheelchair access; bathroom specially equipped. Crib. Babysitting by arrangement. Spanish, French, German, Greek, Romanian spoken.

MIDDLEBURY

Middlebury is, of course, home to Middlebury College, and also makes a good base for touring this area of Vermont; area attractions include the Sheldon Museum, the Morgan Horse Farm, and the State Craft Center at Frog Hollow.

Reader tips: "Great hiking in the Green Mountain National Forest, past waterfalls, mountain and lake views. An enjoyable trail for the literary-minded is the Robert Frost Interpretive Trail; to honor this local poet, sections of his poems are etched into wood plaques and posted along the trail." *(Judy & Don Hayes)* "Go to Mr. Ups for a great salad bar and burgers, and Woody's for excellent food at reasonable prices. For a fun experience, try the Dog Team Tavern, a few minutes' drive north of town and a college tradition. While the food is so-so, the prices are extremely reasonable, the casual ambience is fun, and dinner includes sticky buns to die for." *(SWS)* "For deliciously sinful treats, try the Otter Creek Bakery; for sinful treats of a different kind, tour and sample the beer at the Otter Creek Brewery." *(Hilary Soule)*

Also recommended: A charming country inn, the historic **Waybury Inn** (Highway 125, East Middlebury, 05740; 802–388–4015 or 800–348–1810; www.wayburyinn.com) offers an inviting bar, an appealing restaurant, and upstairs, old-fashioned guest rooms. B&B double rates for the 14 guest rooms range from $80–115. "Consistently good meals in an elegant, quiet, old-inn atmosphere. Gracious, helpful service. Exceptionally good swordfish with black bean, corn, and shrimp salsa." *(SWS)* "Our room was small but comfortable. On a return visit, I'd request the Green Mountain House Room. The pub is a cozy place, with locals coming to both dine and drink. Good breakfast menu; we enjoyed strawberry pancakes and eggs, French toast, and ham." *(RC)*

For additional area inns, see **Goshen** and **Vergennes**.

Note: The Middlebury Inn is not listed in this edition.

The Annex ¢ 👫   *Tel:* 802–388–3233
Route 125, P.O. Box 520
East Middlebury, 05740

A simple farmhouse built in 1830, the Annex has been owned by Josie Bartlett and Teedee Hutchins since 1987; it was originally an "annex" to the Waybury Inn across the street.

"An unpretentious building in the Greek Revival style, with wonderful pine antiques, hand stenciling, and Teedee's handmade quilts on the beds. Bathrooms are simple, but spotless and functional. The dining room, warm and welcoming, looks out over a partially wooded field, with a creek and perennial garden." *(John & Sheila Burrell)* "Teedee is informative about points of interest; many guidebooks and trail maps, plus a variety of interesting books and magazines are available for leisure reading." *(Christian Rieseberg)* "The essence of what a B&B should be: warm, welcoming, hospitable, unpretentious, and an excellent value. Teedee is a charming and gracious hostess. The living room is small but cozy; guests gather for breakfast in the spacious dining room, added to the back of the house. We sat with the other guests at a large table, and enjoyed grapefruit, hot or cold cereal, freshly baked blueberry muffins, and coffee cake. While not fancy, the guest rooms are inviting, cheery, and charming. Many have one double bed and a twin, perfect for college visits. Lots of repeat guests." *(SWS)* "Comfortable atmosphere. Teedee offers warm hospitality." *(Barbara Hill)*

Open All year.
Rooms 1 suite, 5 doubles—4 with shower only, 2 with maximum of 4 people sharing bath. All with clock, 4 with air-conditioning, 3 with balcony/deck, 2 with fan.
Facilities Breakfast/family room with TV, living room, unscreened porch. 1 acre with croquet. Lake for water sports, cross-country skiing, hiking nearby.
Location W central VT. 42 m S of Burlington, 5 m SE of Middlebury. From Rte. 7 S, go E 1 m on Rte. 125 to inn.
Restrictions No smoking.
Credit cards None accepted.
Rates B&B, $90–115 suite, $60–75 double, $50–60 single. Extra person, $10. Family rates. 2-night weekend minimum.
Extras Bus station pickup. Babysitting.

Swift House Inn 🍴 ♿ 👫   *Tel:* 802–388–9925
25 Stewart Lane, 05753   *Fax:* 802–388–9927
                 E-mail: shi@together.net
           URL: http://www.swifthouseinn.com

Swift House was built in 1815 and expanded in 1890. Along with her father, the governor, Jessica Swift moved to the house at the age of 5 and lived there until she died in 1981 at the age of 110. John Nelson bought Swift House in 1985 and restored it as an inn; Karla Nelson-Loura is the innkeeper. Rooms are decorated with Queen Anne and Chippendale antiques, Oriental rugs, four-poster beds, and handmade quilts. A continental breakfast buffet of granola, fresh fruit and juice, and homemade popovers is served from 7:30–10 A.M.; for an extra fee, you can enjoy French toast, pancakes, omelets, or corned beef hash. Dinner is served by candlelight on white linen; Vermont products are used whenever possible. A recent dinner included potato-onion soup, salad with balsamic vinaigrette, grilled quail, marinated in citrus juices, and for desert, coffee toffee pecan torte.

"Great staff. The Mansfield Room in the Carriage House is our favorite, with a king-size bed, fireplace, sitting area, huge bathroom, and French doors opening to a private terrace bordered by flowers." *(Mary Lou Graper, also David Bennett)* "Our beautiful Carriage House room had a fireplace, Jacuzzi tub, four-poster bed, beautifully coordinated fabrics, good lighting, coffeemaker, terry robes, hairdryer, and convenient parking just outside the door. Everything is spotless and fresh. Convenient to downtown but removed enough to ensure quiet. Lovely, well-maintained grounds with flower beds and inviting seating. Welcoming dining room with friendly but respectful service. Rooms in the main inn are smaller but lovely as well, with compact bathrooms." *(Rosemary Pousson)* "A quiet, elegant oasis. Superb service; plush towels in the well-appointed bathrooms. Depending on the season, I've relaxed on the porch, in the garden swing, or before the fireplace. Excellent coffee at breakfast." *(Stephanie Alexander)* "An armoire hid the TV, and wood was laid in the fireplace, needing only a match to light." *(Linda Phillipps)* "A lovely place, with the ambience of a small hotel; accommodating staff." *(Debra LaBerge)* "Our cozy room in the main house was an excellent value." *(LF)*

Open All year.
Rooms 6 suites, 15 doubles—all with private bath and/or shower, telephone, radio, desk, air-conditioning, fan, hairdryer. Some with TV, fireplace, whirlpool bath. 11 in 2 separate buildings.
Facilities Dining room, bar, living room with fireplace, TV room, library, family room; most with fireplaces. Screened and open porches. Sauna, steam room. 3 acres with formal garden, children's play equipment. Swimming, fishing, hiking, golf nearby. Downhill, cross-country skiing 10–45 min. away.
Location W central VT. 45 min. S of Burlington on Rte. 7. 2 blocks N of village green, at corner of Stewart Lane and Rte. 7.
Restrictions Some after-dinner noise from restaurant in one guest room. Cancellation policy.
Credit cards Amex, DC, Discover, MC, Visa.
Rates B&B, $90–195 suite, double. Alc dinner, $15–30. $5 extra for full breakfast.
Extras Wheelchair access. Crib.

MONTPELIER

With a population of 8,000, Montpelier is the smallest state capital in the U.S.; the gold dome of the capitol building is framed by the dark green of the surrounding mountains. Creative cuisine can be found at reasonable prices at the two restaurants run by students of the New

England Culinary Institute, the Main Street Grill and the Chef's Table. Nearby are lakes and rivers for water sports, trails for hiking and cross-country skiing, and within a 45-minute drive, several downhill ski areas. Montpelier is located in north-central Vermont, 40 miles east of Burlington, and 180 miles west of Boston.

Betsy's B&B ¢ 👭
74 East State Street, 05602

Tel: 802–229–0466
Fax: 802–229–5412
E-mail: betsybb@plainfield.bypass.com
URL: http://www.central-vt.com/business/betsybb

A creatively "painted lady," Betsy's B&B is a Queen Anne Victorian built in 1895, and restored as an inn in 1991 by Jon and Betsy Anderson, now joined by their son Tyler. This handsome home has a turret and many gables, plus intriguing "keyhole" openings on the veranda, and is painted several shades of pink and dusty rose with blue accents. Inside, the high ceilings and carved woodwork complement the period decor. Breakfast is served from 7:30–9:30 A.M. at the dining room table; a typical menu includes fruit compote, orange pancakes, maple link sausages, and home-baked lemon pound cake; or perhaps scrambled eggs with green chile and cheese, cornmeal muffins, refried beans, and home fries.

"We shared the breakfast table with a Boston teacher/author/lecturer, a young lawyer interviewing for a clerkship with the Vermont Supreme Court, a traveling auditor, and a new student from the New England Culinary Institute. Later, we all joined Betsy in clearing 10 inches of fresh snow from our cars. Guest rooms are bright, and clean, with excellent bathroom lighting." *(Sheila & Joe Schmidt)* "Betsy accommodated my late arrival and other special needs. A friendly place." *(Richard Lavery)* "Excellent heating, even in January; ample hot water, too." *(Douglas Grant)* "Daily linen change and light cleaning. Convenient location." *(Avis & Terry Tidwell)* "Wonderfully accommodating hosts, who helped us find a babysitter, and went far beyond the call of duty to ensure that we had a good stay." *(Carol Fox)*

"Quiet residential street close to the main shopping/business area. Our room, #1, had a queen-size tiger maple poster bed, oak floors with pink area rugs, wing chairs, and a desk." *(SC)* "Betsy willingly answered questions about activities and provided transportation to the train station." *(Francela Davies)* "Great blueberry French toast. Charming Victorian atmosphere." *(Lois Mountzoures)* "We appreciated being able to use the kitchen, and enjoyed meeting guests from other countries." *(Carol Steele)* "For our first visit, we had a clean, comfortable room in the house next door which shared a lovely sitting room and small kitchenette with another room. The kitchenette was stocked with tea, coffee, and more, so you could fix a snack or refreshing drink. For our return stay, we were just as pleased with a room in the main house; it was equally comfortable and the shared bath was clean and convenient. Best of all are the excellent, generous breakfasts. Betsy and her husband are cordial without being overbearing." *(Mary-Ann & Anthony Palmieri)*

Open All year

Rooms 1 2-bedroom suite with kitchen, 11 doubles—all with private shower/tub, telephone, clock/radio, TV, desk, fan. 9 with refrigerator. Suite in carriage house, 8 guest rooms in adjacent home.

Facilities Dining room, living room with piano, fireplace; TV room, exercise room; guest pantry/refrigerator. Yard with gardens, off-street parking.

Location 3 blocks to center of town. Take Exit 8 off I-89. Continue on access rd. (Memorial Dr.) to 4th set of lights. Go left on Main St. Go to next light & turn right on E. State St. Inn is 3 blocks from Main on left.

Restrictions No smoking.

Credit cards Amex, Discover, MC, Visa.

Rates B&B, $95–170 suite, $55–85 double, $50–80 single. Extra person, $5.

Extras Crib. Station pickups. Some Spanish spoken.

NEWFANE

For additional area inns, see **Brattleboro** and **West Townshend**.

Four Columns Inn ✕ 🛉
230 West Street, P.O. Box 278, 05345

Tel: 802–365–7713
800–787–6633
Fax: 802–365–0022
E-mail: Frcolinn@sover.net
URL: http://www.FourColumnsInn.com

Rooms for romance, rooms for families, rooms for your golden retriever, wonderful food, a perfect location in a picture-postcard setting, woods to hike, plus shops, skiing, and even the interstate just a 15-minute drive away—why go anywhere else? Built in 1832, the Four Columns is a longtime reader favorite, and innkeepers Gorty and Pam Baldwin, who bought the inn in 1996, have made the inn even more appealing with their exceptionally warm and hospitable style.

Breakfast is served at individual tables from 8–9:30 A.M., and includes fresh fruit, yogurt, home-baked scones, breads, and muffins, local cheddar cheese, and homemade granola. Before dinner, guests can enjoy their favorite beverage in the Tavern Room with a 40-foot mural of historic Newfane and an antique pewter bar. Greg Parks is the longtime chef; possible entrées might include seared tuna with caponata, veal with peppercorns, steamed halibut with lemon grass, and sirloin with Roquefort and portabellos.

"Our gorgeous room had a double Jacuzzi tub, sitting area, fireplace, and balcony overlooking a pretty little pond. Pam and Gorty were exceptional hosts. Worth every penny for our anniversary getaway." (*Kate & Gopal Ramakrishna*) "Lovely, peaceful setting; attractively furnished rooms; quiet, restful atmosphere. Our favorite room is #17, with a fireplace, and adjacent to one of the gardens. Another drawing card is chef Greg Parks, who prepares delicious dinners, graciously served in a charming dining room." (*Esther & Nicolas Deminger*) "The atmosphere is warm and informal, devoid of stuffiness and pretension. The innkeepers have a young child of their own and do everything they can to accommodate families with children, without disturbing couples enjoying an adult getaway. Pets are welcome in selected rooms. Our English sheep dog runs on the hiking trails, splashes in the mountain stream, slurps a bowl of water on the front porch while we have a cocktail, and sobs loudly when we have to leave. Pam and Gorty are always available to help a guest, respond to a request, or suggest area activities. At dinner, fresh local ingredients are used when possible, health-conscious choices are always available, and the wine list has been carefully chosen for quality and affordability. The pool and hiking trails are a good way to work off the superb cooking. The two newest rooms are #10 and #12, with lovely views and a whirlpool tub and fireplace in each; #12 is our favorite for special occasions, but we also like the simpler rooms #2, #17, and #18; all have gas fireplaces and are cozy cold-weather retreats." *(Nancy & Frank Burke)* "Convenient to shopping in Manchester, Brattleboro, and Putney." *(Robert Ahlstrom)* "Amenities include great toiletries, soft but adequate lighting, comfortable beds with good linens, careful housekeeping. Inviting hammocks and Adirondack chairs to read and relax." *(Steve Lott)*

"Set on the village green, with a classic four-columned façade, perfect for an after-dinner stroll. I like to walk around the square after dinner. Very few cars pass this way at night, and often the bullfrogs provide the only summer sounds. The inviting guest rooms have modern bathrooms supplied with plenty of thick, thirsty towels." *(Helen & Ron Mayrbaurl)* "Pam and Gorty make it look so easy: running a charming B&B and first-class restaurant yet somehow seeming so relaxed. Our blood pressure drops ten points just pulling into their driveway." *(Joanne Lund)* "On our most recent trip, the kitchen cheerfully accommodated our macrobiotic friends, who eat neither meat nor dairy products." *(John Rosenthal)* "The outdoor pool has the prettiest setting I've ever seen." *(MM)* "There's a rushing stream, and trails leading into the woods and up the hill behind the inn. One favorite room is the suite just under the roof of the front building, done country-style in brick red and natural wood, with a spacious bedroom, cozy sitting area, and a glassed-in porch overlooking the town common." *(SWS)*

Open All year. Restaurant closed Tues.

Rooms 5 suites, 10 doubles—all with private bath and/or shower, telephone, clock/radio, fan, air-conditioning, desk, hairdryer. 9 with fireplace. 4 suites with Jacuzzi or soaking tub. Rooms in 2 buildings.

Facilities Restaurant with fireplace; tavern with antique pewter bar and murals; living room with fireplace, TV, books, games; porch. 150 acres with swimming pool, hiking, stream, gardens. Cross-country, downhill skiing, horseback riding, golf, tennis nearby.

Location SE VT. 11 m N of Brattleboro, via Rte. 30.

Restrictions No smoking. Jackets recommended at dinner.

Credit cards Amex, CB, DC, Discover, MC, Visa.

Rates B&B, $140–225 suite, $110–140 double. $100–130 single. MAP (required late Sept.–Oct. 15), $240–325 suite, $210–240 double, $175–205 single. Alc dinner, $40–50; 2-night weekend/foliage minimum. 1 child per room free under 12. Extra person, $25.

Extras Some Spanish spoken. Pets welcome with prior permission, $10 nightly.

NORTH HERO

Located in northwestern Vermont, the Champlain Islands stick down into Lake Champlain like a long skinny finger pointing south, and are connected to the mainland by bridges on Route 2. The area is also accessible by ferry from Plattsburg, New York, across to Grand Isle. Visitors often alternate days enjoying the water with area explorations on both the New York and Vermont sides of the lake—Ausable Chasm, Burlington, and Shelburne are all within an easy drive.

Information please: A three-story Colonial-style structure, built in 1891, the **North Hero House** (Route 2, Champlain Islands, 05474; 802–372–4732 or 888–525–3644; www.northherohouse.com) has undergone a recent multi-million dollar renovation. Offering magnificent views across the lake to the Green Mountains, the property includes twenty-six guest rooms in the historic inn and several smaller buildings at the water's edge. Some rooms have Jacuzzi tubs and porches with lake views. Other amenities include a tennis court, sauna, game room, sandy beach with dock, boat rentals, and a full-service restaurant. Possible entrées from the summer menu include pan-seared rainbow trout, yellow fin tuna with penne pasta; and mint-crusted rack of lamb. "Wonderfully transformed from a rundown property to an inviting getaway. Special packages include a five-day session devoted to the history of the Broadway musical theater." *(Linda Trevillian)* B&B double rates range from $99–160; MAP rates from $109–210. The inn is a 35-mile drive northwest of Burlington, and a short ferry ride from Plattsburgh, New York.

For an additional area entry, see **Alburg.**

QUECHEE

Quechee is located in east-central Vermont, about 150 miles northwest of Boston. It's 4½ miles on Route 4 from Exit 1, I-89, and about 2 miles from the intersection of I-89 and I-91 at White River Junction. Woodstock is 15 minutes farther west on Route 4, and Hanover, New Hampshire, is a short drive north on I-91.

Information please: Built in 1819, the **Country Garden Inn** (87 Main Street, 05059; 802–295–3023 or 800–859–4191; www.country-garden-inn.com) has earned a four-diamond rating from the AAA. In addition to a natural rock and waterfall-fed wading pool and a fitness club, guests also have access to the facilities of the nearby Quechee Club. A full three-course breakfast is included in the double rates of $110–200; imported teas and enticing desserts are served Wednesday through Sunday, by reservation. Reports welcome.

For additional area inns, see **Woodstock.**

Quechee Bed & Breakfast   *Tel: 802–295–1776*
Route 4, Waterman Hill, P.O. Box 80, 05059

Spectacular cliff-edge views of the Ottauquechee River and valley await
guests at this B&B, located in a 1795 Colonial home. A short walk away
is the village, covered bridge, waterfall, and the shop/restaurant of
glassblower Simon Pearce. Susan and Ken Kaduboski, who have owned
this B&B since 1985, have decorated the rooms with four-poster and
sleigh beds and antiques. In 1998, they opened the Shop, featuring the
work of Vermont artisans. Breakfast specialties include fresh fruit and
apple-cinnamon pancakes, stuffed French toast, or cheese omelets with
homemade muffins. A beverage menu is available daily from 3–8 P.M.
and includes beer and wine.

   "The decor? I 'stole' at least twenty ideas. The food? I'll never enjoy
French toast again until I return for Susan's." *(Carol Ann Thebarge)*
"Spectacular views. Hospitable innkeeper. Impeccable housekeeping."
(Annette Bollinger) "Filled with charm from the large, elegant, and comfortable rooms to the views of the Ottauquechee River and green hillside beyond. The dining room is lighted by a wall of windows facing
perennial gardens and the patio. A covered bridge crosses the river a
few hundred feet from the inn, offering a scenic stroll in this enchanting town." *(Janet Thompson)* "The beautiful garden, abounding with
flowers, overlooks a bend in the river and the hilly countryside. Our
room was beautifully decorated, with lots of closets and a modern
bathroom with double sinks and ample place to set things. The living
room with a fireplace is welcoming and warm. It was nice to have the
possibility of a light snack in the late afternoon. Susan was warm,
friendly, and helpful." *(Birgit & Jerry Scott)* "Set back from the highway;
grounds are restful, safe, and well-lit." *(Shirley Cook)*

   "My room had a mahogany four-poster bed, with lacy ruffled sheets
and pillows, topped by a quilted down puff; an antique dresser; bedside table with reading lamp; and a settee. The dining room is plant-
filled, sunny place, with well-spaced tables set with colorful linens."
(Mrs. E.P. Scriggins) "Excellent bedside and bathroom lighting. Ample,
convenient parking, yet positioned so that one didn't disturb other
guests. Breakfasts were superb; the presentation excellent and unrushed." *(Marilyn & Henry Brook)*

Open All year.
Rooms 8 doubles—all with private bath and/or shower, radio. 8 with air-
conditioning.
Facilities Dining room, living room with fireplace, craft shop. 2½ acres with
patio, gardens. Cross-country skiing nearby; downhill 20–45 min. Guest privi-
leges at Quechee Club for golf, tennis, swimming & fitness center. Fishing
nearby.
Location Short walk to village. 6½ m E of Woodstock, ½ m W of Quechee
Gorge on Rte. 4.
Restrictions No smoking. No children under 12.
Credit cards MC, Visa.

Rates B&B, $109–179 double. 2-night minimum, weekends in season, fall foliage, holidays.
Extras Airport/station pickup. Spanish spoken.

RICHMOND

The Richmond Victorian Inn ¢

191 East Main Street, Route 2, 05477

Tel: 802–434–4410
888–242–3362
E-mail: gailclar@together.net

An 1880s Queen Anne Victorian house, the Richmond Victorian Inn has been owned by Gail Clark since 1997. Each of the guest rooms is decorated in a country Victorian style, with light floral fabrics and Victorian antique furnishings. Breakfast, served at the dining room table between 7:30 and 9:30 A.M., includes fresh fruit, bacon or sausage, juice, and such entrées as baked oatmeal, cheese strata, or blueberry cream cheese toast casserole.

"An extremely clean, bright, cheerful inn, just minutes from I-89, and extremely convenient to the Burlington area. In the winter, the lights in the windows give a welcoming glow. Gail Clark combines a personal and professional approach to her new role. She accommodates special dietary needs and serves a 'skip-lunch' breakfast." (*Jude Hersey*) "Sunny and pretty with beautiful furnishings, fluffy and plentiful towels, and lots of personal touches. When I wanted an afternoon nap, there were plenty of pillows, a quiet room with shades to block the light, and even a wonderful soft throw in which to snuggle up. Off-street parking is ample, with good outdoor lighting. The views from the yard were lovely, with a spectacular spring sunset. On a chilly afternoon, Gail served us hot tea and cookies. I know I'll be making Gail's stuffed French toast at home, because she gave me a copy of the recipe." (*Donna Martin*) "Gail Clark takes special care of her guests in a way that encourages friendship; quiet location." (*Daryl Impey*) "Immaculately clean. Gail is an exceptionally warm and caring person." (*Joann Cavenaugh*)

Open All year.
Rooms 6 doubles—all with private shower bath, clock/radio, clock, fan.
Facilities Dining room, living room with TV/VCR, games, books; porch. ¼ acre with gardens, off-street parking. Fishing, swimming, canoeing, hiking nearby. 5 m from downhill, cross-country skiing.
Location 12 E of Burlington. From I-89, take Exit 11 to Rte. 2 to inn, 2 blocks from center of town & historic round church.
Restrictions No smoking. Children 12 and over.
Credit cards Amex, MC, Visa.
Rates B&B, $80–100 double, $75–95 single. Extra person, $20. 2-night holiday/special event minimum.
Extras Free airport/station pickups. Some German spoken.

ST. JOHNSBURY

The center of Vermont's Northeast Kingdom, St. Johnsbury owes much of its 19th-century prosperity to the invention of the Fairbanks platform scale and to the maple sugar industry. The town's wonderful Victorian homes are a legacy from this period.

Reader tip: "Worth visiting is the Fairbanks Museum, a marvelous and quirky collection of items housed in a thoroughly old-style manner. While low-key and low-tech, the planetarium show is wonderfully entertaining and informative." *(Brad Lockner)* "We enjoyed our visit to the St. Johnsbury Athenaeum, with its romantic 19th-century paintings from the Hudson River School." *(MW)*

Information please: Built in 1850 as the Simeon Hill Tavern, the **Moonstruck Inn** (RR 3, P.O. Box 199, 05819; 802–748–3052 or 800–579–3644) is a mansard-roofed brick Victorian home which first provided food and lodging to those traveling between Vermont and Maine. Formerly known as the Looking Glass Inn, it has been owned by Megan Fletcher since 1996. Each of the five guest rooms has a private bath; four have a queen-size bed, and one has twin beds. The B&B double rates of $70–90 include a full breakfast and afternoon tea. Reports please.

For additional area entries, see **East Burke, Lower Waterford, Lyndonville,** and **Littleton, New Hampshire**.

SHELBURNE

Shelburne is located on Lake Champlain, five miles south of Burlington, and is home to Vermont's premier museum, the Shelburne Museum, consisting of 37 buildings spread over 45 acres, collected over many years by Electra Havemeyer Webb. Offering a fascinating lesson in New England life since the 1700s, it includes everything from an early settler's cabin to a private railroad car to a Lake Champlain sidewheeler; collections range from circus memorabilia to toys to farm implements. Also worth visiting is Shelburne Farms, a 1400-acre farm estate originally owned by William Seward and Lila Vanderbilt Webb; see below for information on the Inn at Shelburne Farms. If all that old money puts you in the mood to spend some of your own, take a tour of the Vermont Teddy Bear Company, also on Route 7 in Shelburne.

Reader tip: "During the American Revolution, Lake Champlain served as a travel route for British and American armies, including forces led by Benedict Arnold. The lake bottom is littered with 200-year-old watercraft. Some have been raised and are displayed at the nearby Shelburne and Champlain Maritime Museums." *(Joe Schmidt)*

Information please: An 1886 Queen Anne Victorian home, the **Heart of the Village Inn** (2130 Shelburne Road, P.O. Box 953, 05482; 802–985–2800) is adjacent to the library and town green. The three-story main house has five guest rooms, each with a private bath; the renovated carriage barn houses four additional rooms, including a suite with a double whirlpool bath, and a wheelchair accessible room. Owners Bobbe Maynes and Pam Pierce feature Vermont products at breakfast and include a hot entrée accompanied by a sideboard of homemade granola, muffins, fresh fruit, and coffee. Afternoon tea and cookies are served every day but one, which is reserved for a catered traditional English tea. The entire staff is knowledgeable about area activities, but Bobbe is especially well-informed, having served as Vermont's tourism commissioner for five years. B&B double rates range from $95–150.

It would be hard—if not impossible—to find a more spectacular inn and setting than **The Inn at Shelburne Farms** (Shelburne, 05482; 802–985–8498). This 1400-acre estate overlooks Lake Champlain, and was created in the late 1880s by Dr. William Seward Webb and Lila Vanderbilt Webb as their summer residence. The grounds were designed by the noted landscape architect Frederick Law Olmsted, of Central Park fame. Shelburne House, a 60-room brick-over-wood Queen Anne mansion, was constructed between 1889 and 1899. A National Historic Site, Shelburne Farms has been owned since 1976 by a nonprofit educational corporation; the barn is so imposing you will at first think you are seeing the inn. Families should plan to tour the farm, even if they won't be visiting the inn itself. Contributing editor *Susan Schwemm* recommends the Rose Room, the W. Seward Webb Room, the Overlook Room, and the Brown Room; all are on the second floor, facing the lake and are decorated with fine antiques. If you're on a tight budget, a good choice is one of the third-floor rooms with garden views and shared baths; your room will be modest, but you'll be able to experience this incredible place, with its evocative common areas, at a reasonable price. Double rates for the 25 guest rooms range from $95–350 (food is extra), depending on size of room and view. Although reports on the food have been very good, and comments on the room furnishings generally favorable, readers felt there was room for improvement in terms of the upkeep, housekeeping, and maintenance, and especially the level of friendliness and hospitality amongst the staff. The inn is open from mid-May to mid-October, and has neither heat nor air-conditioning; although the latter is rarely missed, Vermont can be quite chilly in May and October, so plan accordingly.

STOWE

Stowe, a well-known resort town since the 19th century, calls itself the "Ski Capital of the East" and offers superb downhill skiing at Mt. Mansfield and Spruce Peak. Stowe also has four cross-country ski touring centers; the Trapp Family Lodge is the best-run and most well-known. Summer and fall are equally lovely, with many special activities in addition to the usual summer mountain sports and pleasures: golf, tennis, mountain biking, gliding. A 5-mile paved recreation path offers cross-country skiers, walkers, and joggers a delightful car-free experience. Stowe is located in north-central Vermont, 35 miles from Burlington. It's about 6½ hours north of New York City, 4 hours northwest of Boston, and 2½ hours south of Montréal.

Also recommended: Readers have generally been delighted with **Topnotch at Stowe** (Mountain Road, P.O. Box 1458, 05672; 802–253–8585 or 800– 451–8686; www.topnotch-resort.com/spa). This luxurious full-service resort and spa with 114 rooms plus assorted condominiums has a four-diamond rating from AAA; rates range from $150–650, with many packages available. "Complete spa facility, with a gorgeous indoor pool and a wonderful hot tub with a waterfall. The Buttertub Bar is perfect for a relaxing drink and pleasant music; the hotel's relaxed elegance makes it a good choice for families as well as couples. Be aware that Topnotch does book bus tours during foliage season. Some rooms have better sound-proofing than others; some have mountain views, others overlook the parking lot, so inquire for details." *(SWS)* "Inviting living room with fireplace, mountain views, and baskets of apples; several sitting rooms with lots to read. Excellent service and food in the dining room; the creative low-fat menu included the freshest of fish, fruits, and vegetables, with home-made pasta." *(Harriet Krivit)* "First-rate spa experience." *(Roseanne Buckman)*

Another resort alternative is the famous **Trapp Family Lodge** (42 Trapp Hill Road, 05672; 802–253–8511 or 800–826–7000; www.trappfamily.com), with wonderful cross-country ski trails, a fitness center with indoor pool, restaurant, and more. Accommodations are available in the main lodge, lower lodge, and time-share units, at rates ranging from $98–380, meals extra. "Wonderful views from the private deck on our lower lodge room. Beautiful foliage views from the hiking trails. Excellent dinners and breakfasts; we enjoy the extras such as the harpist at dinner and the sing-a-longs." *(Tom Wilbanks)*

Information please: Guests can don their cross-country skis and head directly out the door of **The Siebeness Inn** (3681 Mountain Road, 05672; 800–426–9001 or 802–253–8942; www.stoweinfo.com/saa/siebeness) to one of the major local trail systems, or drive a short distance to downhill skiing at Mt. Mansfield. At the end of a day of hiking, skiing, or just relaxing, guests enjoy a soak in the outdoor hot tub or (in summer) the swimming pool. Each of the twelve guest rooms has a private bath; some offer gas fireplaces. Owners Sue and Nils Andersen provide a hearty breakfast, included in the rates of $70–180; most rooms have a queen-size bed, the suites have a double Jacuzzi tub, fireplace, TV, and mountain-view deck.

Andersen Lodge: An Austrian Inn ¢ 🚶 🎿

3430 Mountain Road, 05672

Tel: 802–253–7336
800–336–7336

Andersen's is a contemporary-style lodge, long owned by Trude and Dietmar Heiss, an Austrian couple. "Trude and Dietmar Heiss are key to this cozy and delightful Austrian country inn. Our kids love the basement game room; for adults, there's an adjacent set-ups bar with cheese and crackers." *(Margot & Ken Walker)* "The rooms are clean and comfortable—each with its own thermostat for heating and cooling."

(Miriam Schleich) "The inn's hillside location keeps it out of sight of both the road and, for the most part, the parking lot." *(Robin DeWeese)*

"Great food and atmosphere in the large, airy dining room. Dinner included cream of celery soup, home-baked bread, mixed salad, roast beef, roast potatoes, broccoli with cheese sauce, and apple strudel. Our vegetarian was accommodated with broiled sole. The friendly patient waiter (the same each night) was a great source of information about local skiing, and in case anyone could take another bite, Trude always comes around with seconds on potatoes and vegetables. Needless to say, breakfast is just as good and no less filling." *(Anne Wichman)* "Considerate, professional innkeepers. Staff is carefully selected and well-trained." *(Ruth & Arthur Mintz)*

"Its location is convenient to everything, yet totally private. The food is excellent, with the kind of professional service you'd find in an Austrian country hotel; the furnishings are serviceable, and the value is unbeatable. Two of the guest rooms are much bigger than the rest; the best one is exceptionally spacious, with a separate pull-out couch, and a balcony overlooking the swimming pool and tennis court; the other is nearly as big, but overlooks the parking lot." *(SWS)* "Clean, comfortable, and friendly." *(Anne-Liese Kaufmann)*

Open June 1–Oct. 25, Dec. 15–April 15. Restaurant closed Thurs.; also in June.
Rooms 17 doubles—all with private bath and/or shower, TV, desk, air-conditioning. 1 room has bath across the hall. Some with telephone, refrigerator.
Facilities Dining room, lobby with fireplace, game room with Ping-Pong, bumper pool, cable TV, guest refrigerator; hot tub, sauna. Heated swimming pool, tennis court, play equipment. Off-street parking with winter plug-ins. Cross-country skiing across road. 3 m to downhill skiing. Recreation path nearby.
Location From Rte. 100, turn left in Stowe Village onto Rte. 108 (Mountain Rd.). Go 3½ m to inn on right.
Credit cards Amex, MC, Visa.
Rates Room only, $50–132 double. MAP, $100–190 double. Family rates. 10% senior discount. Prix fixe dinner, $20–25.
Extras German, French spoken. Crib, baby-sitting. Station pickup.

The Brass Lantern Inn ¢
717 Maple Street, 05672

Tel: 802–253–2229
800–729–2980
Fax: 802–253–7425
E-mail: brasslntrn@aol.com
URL: http://www.brasslanterninn.com
United Kingdom: 0–800–962–332

"I stopped counting after the 300th roll of wallpaper," reports Andy Aldrich, who restored the Inn at the Brass Lantern in 1988, and hasn't stopped improving it since. This early 1800s farmhouse and carriage barn offers ample common areas comfortably furnished with soft couches, fireplaces, stenciled walls, and antiques, while the guest rooms have fluffy quilted comforters, ruffled curtains, softly flowered wallpaper, and, in some cases, fireplaces. Upgraded bathrooms, some with double whirlpool tubs, ensure that modern amenities complement the inn's antique charms. Rates include breakfast—perhaps thick-sliced bacon and apple crêpes or a veggie omelet—and afternoon cookies and lemonade or hot drinks. A typically thoughtful touch is the availability of a post-checkout shower—after a day on the slopes, you can come back to the inn to shower and change before heading home.

"Andy was attentive, informative, friendly, and unobtrusive. Attractive antique oak decor." *(Lyn Caruso)* "Inviting, relaxed atmosphere; clean, well-cared-for rooms; convenient location close to town. Breakfasts were beautifully presented, hot and delicious, served in the spacious dining room with views of Mt. Mansfield. Our room had a canopy bed, whirlpool tub, and wonderful mountain views." *(Judy Pigman)* "As an architect, I appreciated the care and detail with which Andy has renovated the inn. As a guest, I appreciated the quiet but friendly welcome, the assistance given whenever needed." *(William Moffet)* "The inn is fresh and crisp, inside and out, with lovely flower gardens. The immaculate rooms are beautifully done with handmade quilts and country antiques. In any season, the views of Mt. Mansfield from the common areas and from most of the guest rooms are among the best of any inn in Stowe." *(SWS)*

Open All year.
Rooms 9 doubles—all with private bath and/or shower, radio, air-conditioning. TV on request. Most with double whirlpool tub and/or fireplace.
Facilities Dining room, living room with fireplace, TV room, mud room, deck. 1½ acres with off-street parking. Guest privileges at health club.
Location On Rte. 100, ½ m N of Village. On right, just before Grand Union.
Restrictions No smoking.
Credit cards Amex, MC, Visa.
Rates B&B, $80–225 double. Extra person, $25. Ski, golf, hiking, bicycling, honeymoon, romance, adventure, spa packages.

The Gables Inn ¢ ✕ ♿
1457 Mountain Road (Route 108), 05672

Tel: 802–253–7730
800–GABLES–1
Fax: 802–253–8989
E-mail: Inngables@aol.com
URL: http://www.Gablesinn.com

An old farmhouse converted into an inn, the Gables has long been owned by Lynn and Sol Baumrind. "The living room is small but inviting; the dining room is casual, with pine tables; and the tiny solarium is cozy in winter. Families will especially enjoy the spacious downstairs den, complete with fireplace and lots of comfortable seating, a TV, and a big supply of games—soup and generous quantities of hors d'oeuvres are served here in winter. The guest room decor is country, comfortable, with both antiques and reproductions, lots of canopy beds, pretty flowered wallpapers, and white woven bedspreads. Guest rooms in the main house are most affordable; those in the carriage house have cathedral ceilings, fireplaces, and whirlpool tubs. A neighboring farmhouse was renovated in 1993, and has two spacious suites; both are lovely and private, but the upstairs one is our favorite with cathedral ceilings in both the living room and bedroom, and wonderful mountain and river views.

"Breakfasts are delicious, from the freshly squeezed orange juice to the cinnamon bread they use for the French toast; a favorite is the Greek omelet with spinach, garlic, and feta cheese. In summer, you sit at tables with bright yellow umbrellas spread over the lawn, with gorgeous views of Mt. Mansfield; lunch is offered as well. Dinner is served in winter, with an extensive menu; you can sit with your own group or mingle with the other guests. Choices include beef stew baked in a bread bowl, chicken with shallots in cider sauce, or salmon with roasted red pepper sauce. And of course, Lynn and Sol are two of the nicest people you'll ever meet." *(SWS)*

"Lynn and Sol are friendly and concerned innkeepers. Our favorite features include the food, the mountain views, the carriage house suite, cleanliness, friendly staff, and convenient parking." *(Nicholas Graben)* "The Baumrinds continually improve and expand the facilities without losing that personal touch and attention to detail. The staff is always friendly and helpful, genuinely glad to have your family as guests. The food has always been exceptional comfort food; nothing so fancy that you can't pronounce it, but always a delicious adventure. A relaxing getaway for the entire family." *(Leslie Petrichko)* "My breakfast of peach pancakes with Vermont maple syrup was delicious, as was my wife's cinnamon raisin French toast." *(Max Hansen)* "Ideally located on the Mountain Road, and close to the wonderful walking path." *(Rita & Ed Collins)*

Open All year. Dinner served during ski season.
Rooms 6 suites, 12 doubles—all with private bath and/or shower, air-conditioning. 1 with fireplace, 5 with TV. 4 suites in annex with whirlpool, TV, fireplace; 2 suites in farmhouse with fireplace, kitchenette.
Facilities Dining room, living room, den, game room, solarium. 1½ acres with swimming pool, hot tub. Cross-country skiing from door. 4 m to downhill skiing.
Location 1.5 m from village. From red blinker stop sign at intersection of Rtes. 100 & 108, go 1.5 m on Rte. 108 (Mt. Rd.) to inn.
Restrictions No smoking. No pets.
Credit cards Amex, Discover, MC, Visa.
Rates B&B, $65–195 suite, double; Extra person, $25. 12% service. Family rates. Packages available.

Timberholm Inn 🚶
452 Cottage Club Road, 05672

Tel: 802–253–7603
800–753–7603
Fax: 802–253–8559

Built in 1949 as a ski lodge, the Timberholm was bought by Louise and Pete Hunter in 1993, switching from the corporate world of New York City and Dallas to life as Vermont innkeepers. Guests gravitate to the living room's huge fieldstone fireplace to relax after a hard day of skiing or hiking, and to enjoy the beautiful mountain views from the inn's large picture windows and deck. Louise's buffet breakfasts include fresh fruit and juice, cereal and granola, muffins or coffee cake, an egg dish or French toast with Vermont maple syrup, and a bottomless coffee pot.

"Quiet mountain setting, yet a short walk, bike ride, or drive to restaurants and recreational facilities. We love the clean, well-maintained, and spacious suites. The mountain breezes lull us to sleep at night, along with the soft sound of birds and tree frogs. Louise's pepper and onion quiche is a breakfast favorite, along with the fresh fruit and nut breads. Breakfast is also a good time to visit with the other guests and share experiences about planned activities. Equally enjoyable is the afternoon lemonade and home-baked cookies, and a relaxing soak in the hot tub after a day of hiking or bicycling." *(Sharon & Tom Templeton)* "Gracious innkeepers, welcoming hospitality. We return each year at Christmas with our extended family and take over the whole inn. Wonderful common room with fireplace, couches, lots of books, music, and breakfast tables, and a wonderful view. Comfortable, cozy guest rooms." *(Mrs. Paul Morriseau)* "The beautiful deck outside the common area looks out to Stowe Pinnacle, a favorite hiking spot. Tasty breakfasts of home-baked breads and rolls, with a different egg dish each morning. In winter, Pete and Louise offer a delicious homemade soup to warm you up after a day of skiing." *(Suzanne Reed)* "Shimmering trees with colorful foliage fill the distant valley and mountain slopes with a vibrant glow. The beautiful garden and expansive lawns are maintained meticulously by Pete. Fires lit each night in the large stone fireplace welcome you to evenings of quiet conversation or reading; the game room downstairs awaits for livelier moments. Our upstairs suite had an adequate bathroom and a sitting room overlooking the lovely garden." *(Maxine Greer)* "Friendly innkeepers and lots of nice guests from all over the U.S." *(Sally & David Thompson)* "All of the set-ups for cocktail hour were in readiness—an ice bucket, lemons, mixed peanuts and pretzels, and mixers." *(Natalie Baumer)*

Open All year.

Rooms 2 2-bedroom suites, 8 doubles—all with private shower and/or bath. Some with air-conditioning.

Facilities Living room and library with fireplaces, books, TV/VCR, stereo; game room. 4 acres with deck, hot tub, flower gardens.

Location 2 m from Stowe Village. From village, take Rte. 108 N to Cottage Club Rd. Turn right (E) on road, ½ m to inn on right.

Restrictions No smoking.

Credit cards Discover, MC, Visa.

Rates B&B, $110–150 suite, $80–120 double. Extra person, $15. Children's discount in ski season.

Extras Cribs.

TOWNSHEND

Boardman House ¢ 👫　　　　　　　　　*Tel:* 802–365–4086
On the Green, P.O. Box 112, 05353

The Boardman House, a white clapboard house with black shutters, has a picture-postcard setting on the town green, across from a typically

New England white-steepled church. Entering the inn, many visitors find the decor a pleasant change from the cluttered country look favored by many inns. The walls are plain white, with simple prints here and there, and several of the beds have barn-red headboards with red and white geometric fabric pillow and duvet covers. Most have brass swing-arm lamps which provide reading lights on both sides of the bed. Owned by Sarah Messenger and Paul Weber since 1987, Boardman House is known for Sarah's creative breakfasts: perhaps warm fruit compote, apple butter muffins, and baked eggs with mushrooms, cheddar cheese, and sausage.

"Idyllic setting, warm and friendly hospitality, great breakfasts." *(Bruce & Liz McKinnon)* "A quaint inn set next to one of the most photographed churches in Vermont. Sarah and Paul were kind and hospitable, and went out of their way to make our stay special. Our room was clean and comfortable; breakfast was delicious." *(Sue Ming Jue)* "Ideal balance of privacy and recommendations for places of interest in the area." *(Dolores Welber)* "Rooms are spacious, charming, and scrupulously clean, with an abundance of reading material." *(Elroy Berkowitz)* "We love the porch where we can sit and watch the autumn leaves swirl across the church lawn next door; the exceptional breakfasts; the quaint, comfortable, and clean rooms; the proprietors' knowledge of the area including bike routes and restaurants; and most importantly, Sarah and Paul's hospitality." *(Kathryn Inouye)* "Our well-furnished room overlooked the commons and gazebo, with the mountains in the distance. It was so quiet we thought we were the only ones there." *(Audreyann Spatafora)*

Open All year.

Rooms 1 suite, 5 doubles—all with private bath, fan.

Facilities Breakfast room, living room, library with TV, piano; sauna. 1 acre, children's play equipment. Watersports nearby. 10–23 min. to downhill, cross-country skiing.

Location SE VT, approx. 17 m NW of Brattleboro, at intersection of Rtes. 30 & 35.

Restrictions No smoking.

Credit cards None accepted.

Rates B&B, $100–130 suite, $70–85 double, $60–75 single. Extra person, $10. 10% senior, AAA discount.

VERGENNES

The town of Vergennes is in western Vermont, 22 miles south of Burlington, and borders Lake Champlain. Vergennes is one of the oldest cities in the U.S., and with only 2,500 residents, one of the smallest. The area is very flat (for Vermont) and excellent for biking.

For additional area entries, see **Middlebury** and **Shelburne**.

Basin Harbor Club ✕ 🏹
Basin Harbor Road, 05491

Tel: 802–475–2311
800–622–4000
Fax: 802–475–6545
E-mail: res@basinharbor.com
URL: http://www.basinharbor.com

The Basin Harbor Club has been owned by the Beach family since its founding in 1886; some families have summered there for almost as long. Located at the southeastern end of Lake Champlain, this old-fashioned family resort is also home to the Lake Champlain Maritime Museum, and a 150-year-old stone schoolhouse, with exhibits documenting the Revolutionary War and War of 1812. There are guest rooms in three buildings, and 77 cottages (each different), along with a multitude of resort activities, from golf to water sports. Classic American cuisine highlights the menus in the three dining rooms, and local Vermont farms provide fresh produce, meat and game; the extensive wine list has earned awards from *Wine Spectator* magazine.

"Situated on a picturesque inlet of Lake Champlain, this family-oriented resort has beautifully groomed grounds and lots of activities for families." *(Mimi Cohen)* "Our cottage, recently redone, had light green carpeting, a coordinating floral fabric for curtains, pillows, and upholstered chair, good lighting, a large table with chairs, and a sliding glass door opening to a deck that had unobstructed views of the lake. The furniture was scrubbed pine, and a white woven bedspread covered the king-size bed. Staff was pleasant and most helpful at all times. The main lodge was very inviting, with fires lit each chilly evening and many pleasant seating areas. The bar area was light wood and very attractive, though unobtrusive; a library is located in another of the lodge/guest house buildings. The dining room is a glassed-in semi-circle facing the Basin Harbor, and is only about three tables deep, so all have a nice view. From the extensive menu, we chose cold peach soup, polenta with Vermont jalapeño cheese, arugula and pear salad, and beef tenderloin; service was gracious and unhurried. Breakfast was an extensive hot and cold buffet, with attentive waiters to serve hot beverages." *(Susan Schwemm)*

Open Early May–mid-October.
Rooms 77 cottages, 38 doubles—all with private bath, telephone. Cottages with heating, air-conditioning, refrigerator; some with deck, screened porch, fireplace.
Facilities 3 dining rooms (1 with evening entertainment), bar/lounge, lobby, library, sitting rooms, meeting rooms. 700 acres with gardens, beach, 18-hole golf course, putting greens, driving range, pro shop, gift shop, recreation center, fitness center, rope course, bicycle rentals, 5 tennis courts, croquet, shuffleboard, jogging & biking trails, swimming pool, playground, 3,200-ft. airstrip, museum. Summer children's program; also weekends in fall. On lake with all watersports, fishing; equipment rentals. Boat tours. Maritime museum.
Location W VT. From town, follow Rte. 22A over bridge. Go right on Panton Rd., then right on Basin Harbor Rd. Go 6 m to resort.
Restrictions Men over age 12 must wear coat & tie after 6 P.M. in all public areas, except 1 dining room. Proper tennis attire required.

Credit cards MC, Visa.

Rates Cottages: Full board (summer), $290–405 double; MAP (early & late season), $235–285 double; B&B (early & late season), $175–220 double. Rooms: Full board (summer), $200–265 double; MAP (early & late season), $180–225 double; B&B (early & late season), $119–165 double. Extra person, $70. Special children's rates; no charge for children's program. 15% service. Seasonal golf, tennis, vacation packages. Corporate, group rates.

Extras Small, well-trained pets in cottages, $6.50/day. Airport/station pickups.

Strong House Inn
82 West Main Street, 05491

Tel: 802–877–3337
Fax: 802–877–2599
E-mail: shi@flinet.com
URL: http://www.flinet.com/~bargieleer/shi_inn.htm

Strong House is an 1834 Federal-style house, with Greek Revival influences, listed on the National Register of Historic Places, and bought by Mary and Hugh Bargiel in 1992. The inn sits on a slight ridge, with views of the Green Mountains to the east, and the Adirondacks to the west. Breakfast menus vary with the season; perhaps hot apple crumble in winter, minted melon in summer, followed by homemade breads and muffins, and such entrées as crêpes with fresh strawberries or herb and cheese frittata. Sundays from noon until 4 P.M. (by reservation), Mary serves a delightful English tea complete with salmon pâté and water crackers, crumpets with honey and butter, tea sandwiches, scones with cream and strawberry jam, and a dessert buffet. A harpist plays throughout tea-time; house tours are offered afterwards.

"Mary welcomed us graciously, and gave us a room-by-room tour of the inn, starting with the kitchen, where the aroma of baking bread was hard to ignore. She invited us to make ourselves at home by helping ourselves to drinks and snacks, and showed us through the elegant dining room and the comfortable but formal living room. Mary's catering background was clear; the delicious food was beautifully presented. Breakfast began with an elegant stemmed glass, layered with yogurt, sliced bananas and kiwi, followed by scrumptious French toast and bacon. For the Quilting in Vermont seminar, Mary had arranged for a teacher; all fourteen women set up their machines in the library and the foyer to sew and talk quilting." *(Sally Malley & Nancy Bischoff)*

"Our favorite is the Vermont Room, with a queen-size country pine bed, French doors opening to a balcony and private entrance, and beautiful mountain views. Mary knows our tastes and makes great recommendations to local establishments." *(Paul Brundaue)* "Our suite had a magnificent library with a sofa bed, many books and magazines, fireplace, a table set for chess, and several additional comfortable chairs, plus a bedroom and bath as well as a small sun room." *(Catherine Arnott)* "Guests are welcome to come into the kitchen to fix tea, coffee, cocoa from the instant hot water dispenser, and to help themselves to crackers and cookies. The spacious Empire Room has a beautiful queen-size lace-canopy rice bed, and is done in a white, yellow, blue color scheme, with good lighting, a day bed, and two blue leather wing chairs before the fireplace." *(SWS)*

Open All year.

Rooms 2 suites, 6 doubles—all with private bath and/or shower, clock, air-conditioning. 6 with desk, 3 with TV, 2 with fireplace (Duraflame logs). 1 suite with TV, gas fireplace, sunporch.

Facilities Dining room, living room with fireplace, piano; guest refrigerator. 6 acres with walking paths, gazebo, gardens, lawn games, skating pond, snowshoeing, toboggan run, walking trails. 2 miles to hiking, 20 miles to skiing.

Location ¼ m S of town, on W side of Rte. 22A.

Restrictions No smoking. Children over 10 preferred. Air-conditioning masks traffic noise in front rooms.

Credit cards Amex, MC, Visa.

Rates B&B, $120–175 suite, $75–150 double. Extra person, $20. English teas, $15. Prix fixe dinner, by arrangement, $25 per person. Quilting seminars winter, spring.

Whitford House Inn 👫
Grandey Road, Addison
Mailing address: RR 1, P.O. Box 1490
Vergennes, 05491

Tel: 802–758–2704
800–746–2704
Fax: 802–758–2089
E-mail: whitford@together.net

Some tourists think that a vacation means rushing around from one place to the next, driving for hours each day, and sleeping in a different inn each night. Experienced travelers are smarter, and head for an oasis like the Whitford House. Dating back to the 1790s, Barbara and Bruce Carson bought this nearly abandoned farmhouse, and have done a beautiful job of renovating and restoring it. Guests come to enjoy the Adirondack mountain vistas, relax on the shady porch, borrow a bike to pedal down country lanes, or paddle the Carsons' canoe in the creek. Whitford House also makes a perfect base for area explorations, from lively Burlington, to the Shelburne Museum, to nearby Middlebury and its college, and of course, beautiful Lake Champlain. The book-filled library has comfortable Mission-style chairs and good reading lights for a quiet evening, and the original attached carriage house has been renovated as the light and airy living room, with mountain views, a handsome slate floor, and twelve-foot ceilings with hand-hewn beams, Oriental rugs, and a majestic stone fireplace. The inn's decor includes Colonial and Victorian antiques, hand-wrought iron railings, chandeliers, and sconces, plus the Carsons' handsome modern art collection.

Breakfast is served at guests' convenience at the dining room table, with menus of fresh fruit, homemade honey-coconut granola, and perhaps Belgian waffles one morning, and baked eggs Florentine the next. Rates also include afternoon refreshments, evening hors d'oeuvres, turndown service, and the use of the inn's bicycles and canoe. Candlelight dinners are served by advance reservation.

"Distant hills framed the evening sunset. In winter, the aurora borealis often splashes the sky with color. Two friendly dogs, a cat, and a newborn lamb were in residence. My room, in the cottage, was exceptionally pleasant with luxurious touches like zoned heating, a stereo, heated floors, and towel warmers in the bathroom." *(Joe Schmidt)* "A private location, off a quiet dirt road; comfortable, immaculate farmhouse and guest house; gentle hospitality." *(Gill Barlow)* "Gracious, articulate, warm innkeepers; comfortable lodging; beautiful setting; wonderful food." *(Sarah & Frank Vattano)* "Sophisticated country decor, with lots of fresh flowers and careful attention to detail." *(Felicia & Joshua Holtz)* "A remote location with fine views, privacy, friendly staff, gracious proprietors, outstanding accommodations and service." *(Stanley Ebner)* "Located on a charming country road looking out towards Lake Champlain and the Adirondacks. Complete privacy; unhurried, relaxing atmosphere; generous breakfasts. The Carsons know how to make their guests feel at home yet are never invasive." *(Peter & Ruth Burnstone)* "The filled bookshelves tempt you to browse in the company of two friendly beagles, while the country lanes beckon for long walks. The student staff are efficient and courteous. After enjoying the magnificent fall foliage, I returned to find hot cider and tasty canapés." *(Anna Biegun)*

Open All year.

Rooms 1 cottage with kitchenette, stereo. 1 suite, 3 doubles—all with full private bath and/or shower, clock, fan. 2 with telephone, desk.

Facilities Dining room; living room with fireplace, baby grand piano, books, stereo; library with fireplace, books, stereo; porch; decks. 37 acres with swings, lawn games, trails, bicycling, canoeing. Hiking, skiing nearby.

Location W central VT. Approx. 5 m NW of Middlebury, 10.5 m S of Vergennes, 30 m S of Burlington. From Rte. 7 N, go through Middlebury. Approx. 2 m N of town, go left on Rattlin' Bridge Rd., or next left, Town Line Rd. Go approx. 1.5 m & go right on Grandey Rd. to inn on left. From Rte. 7 S, go 1.9 m S of Addison (at intersection with Rte. 17), & go left on Nortontown Rd. for 2.5 m to Grandey Rd. Go left on Grandey for .9 m to inn on right.

Restrictions No smoking.

Credit cards MC, Visa.

Rates B&B, $150–175 suite, $110–135 double. Extra person, $25. No charge for infants. Prix fixe dinner, $35. Gardening, kayaking workshops; culinary weekend.

Extras Pet OK in guest house by arrangement. Crib. Babysitting on request.

WAITSFIELD

Waitsfield is located in north-central Vermont, close to excellent downhill and cross-country skiing at Sugarbush, Sugarbush North, and Mad River. Summer and fall attractions include hiking, bicycling, gliding, canoeing, golf, tennis, horseback riding, and swimming, plus exploring Vermont's antique and craft shops and auctions. Don't miss the nearby Bundy Gallery of art and outdoor sculpture, with evening concerts on the grass on summer Sundays. Waitsfield is 4 hours northeast of Boston, 6 hours north of New York City, and 35 miles southeast of the Burlington airport.

Also recommended: Not surprisingly, every guest room at **The Featherbed Inn** (Route 100, RD 1, P.O. Box 19, 05673; 802–496–7151) has a featherbed; the decor also includes antiques and family heirlooms, accented with stenciling and hand-crafted furnishings. A Greek Revival–style home built in 1806, this farmhouse was extensively renovated by

Tracey and Clive Coutts, who opened it in 1993. Rates for the two suites and five doubles (most with private bath) are $85–125 and include a full breakfast and afternoon goodies; maybe cheese and crackers with hot tea or warm cider in winter or iced tea or lemonade with cookies in the warmer months. "Lovely gardens; beautiful hikes nearby. Innkeepers go out of their way to make guests feel at home. Wonderful breakfasts with home-baked cakes, juice, fresh fruit, and French toast with crème anglaise, or possible fruit-filled crêpes." *(Paula Rosen)*

Reader tips: "If you pass through Waitsfield don't miss the "Bridge St. Bakery." A tiny eating place with arguably the best soup in Vermont. Certainly the best chocolate caramel pecan tart." *(Joe & Sheila Schmidt)* "For funky glass jewelry, and incredible sale prices, visit Baked Beads, at the corner of Route 100 and Bridge St." *(SWS)*

Inn at the Round Barn Farm	*Tel:* 802–496–2276
East Warren Road, RR 1	*Fax:* 802–496–8832
P.O. Box 247, 05673	*E-mail:* roundbarn@madriver.com
	URL: http://www.innattheroundbarn.com

Designed by the Shakers, this round (actually 12-sided) barn has been a Waitsfield landmark since it was built in 1910, and is one of only six such structures still standing in Vermont. In the ownership of the Joslin family for over a century, the farm was bought by the Simko family in 1986; Anne Marie Simko DeFreest is the longtime innkeeper. After extensive renovation of both the farmhouse (built in 1810) and the barn, the Simkos opened their elegant country inn, furnished with antiques and many luxurious extras. Wide-planked pine floors, ceiling medallions, and hand-carved moldings combine with king-size canopy beds, good reading lights, steam showers, and zoned heating to give guests the best of old and new. Fluffy cottage cheese pancakes with raspberry-maple sauce are a breakfast favorite, often accompanied by baked apples and blueberry muffins; guests are served in the handsome attached restored barn with its hand-hewn beams, and can enjoy their meal around the large English pine table, or at small tables for two or four.

"The entire complex has been completely and tastefully updated and restored. While the rooms are all delightfully furnished with antiques, there is nothing antique about the amenities, which include individual heat controls for each room, large fluffy towels and robes, well-placed reading lights, soft down comforters, comfortable beds, Jacuzzi tubs or steam showers. Guests are asked to remove their boots upon entering, and are given floppy slippers to wear during their visit. The spacious Richardson and Joslin Rooms have gas fireplaces, sitting areas, whirlpool tubs, and separate steam showers; the English, Sherman, and Dana Rooms are less extravagant, but still have mountain views and relaxing steam showers. The diminutive Jones Room is tucked cozily under the eaves." *(David Kendall)*

"Beautiful hooked rugs. Attention to detail included the special makeup remover mitts and cream in the bathroom." *(LDS)* "Delicious breakfasts, including graham walnut muffins. Even the mailbox is in the shape of the Round Barn." *(Tina Hom)* "The library is lovely, with an inviting fire going constantly, a decanter of sherry to be enjoyed and plenty of reading material. The Barnard Room, done in peach with green accents, has Shaker-style furniture with a pencil-post queen-size bed with a crocheted canopy and a wonderful down comforter. Our breakfast included wonderful, crisp French toast with sautéed apples, pears, and cranberries, plus maple syrup, and an apple cake." *(Rose Ciccone)* "The inn is reached by driving up a country road and through an old covered bridge." *(SWS)* "The Dana Room has high wooden ceilings, a queen-size canopy bed, huge Oriental rug, and a black wicker fainting couch near the fireplace. The steam shower was a real treat after a day's skiing, complemented by fluffy towels, quality soaps, big terry robes, and a lighted makeup mirror." *(Wendy McGrath)* "On the lower level, a patchwork rooster props open the door to the game room. Well-equipped with games, puzzles, and books, this area has a mini-kitchen for guests, stocked with complimentary soda and snacks, plus the makings for coffee, tea, and hot chocolate." *(Krista Irmischer)*

Open All year. Closed three weeks in April.

Rooms 11 doubles—all with private bath and/or shower, some with whirlpools tubs, steam showers, desk, ceiling fan, air-conditioning, gas fireplace.

Facilities Breakfast room, library with fireplace, lounge with TV, billiards, refrigerator, stocked guest pantry; game room with TV/VCR. Barn with 60-foot indoor lap pool, meeting rooms, greenhouse. 235 acres with ponds for swimming, ice-skating; river for fishing, canoeing; cross-country ski touring center with 30 km trails, rentals, lessons.

Location 1½ m to town. From Rte. 100 in Waitsfield, drive through covered bridge, up East Warren Rd. to inn on left.

Restrictions No smoking. No children under 14. No shoes in house; slippers provided.

Credit cards Amex, MC, Visa.

Rates B&B, $125–250 double, $10 less for singles. 2-night minimum some weekends. Midweek package available for 4 guest rooms, $99 per night, 3-night minimum. Cooking classes.

Extras Airport/station pickups, $35–50.

The Mad River Inn ¢ 👪 &

Tremblay Road, P.O. Box 75, 05673

Tel: 802–496–7900
800–832–8278
Fax: 802–496–5390
E-mail: madriverinn@madriver.com

For those who feel that country inns and kids don't mix, a stay at the Mad River Inn may change your mind. Luc and Rita Maranda bought this 1860 farmhouse in 1989 and converted it into an inn, furnishing the rooms with period antiques and country Victorian floral fabrics. Breakfast, served outdoors on the back porch in warmer weather, includes home-baked muffins, fresh or baked fruit, and a hot entrée; afternoon tea is served from 4–7 P.M. daily. Much of the food comes from the inn's extensive gardens of vegetables, fruits, herbs, and edible flowers. The Mad River Recreation Path runs just behind the inn and meanders for miles along the river with pastoral views of dairy farms, corn fields, and mountains.

"Beautiful setting, warm and friendly inn. Delicious breakfasts, individually prepared and served." *(Carole Somol)* "Although the inn is great for families, we found it to be equally appealing to couples. It's unpretentious and extremely accommodating to serious skiers like ourselves. Amazing breakfasts in terms of quantity and quality—they kept us going all day on the slopes." *(Diane Elam)* "Our charming two-room suite had flowered Victorian-style wallpaper and floral fabrics, lace curtains, and cozy European featherbeds. Meals are served at a long table in the dining room, and the guests chat amiably before heading off for their day's outings." *(Brenda Viehe-Naess)* "The Angelina Mercedes Room had a quilt on the antique maple four-poster queen-size bed, lots of light, and a little private bath made from a closet. An etched glass decanter and water glasses were set on a round table, along with maps, area guides, magazines, and a candle in a crystal holder. Downstairs is the spacious family room, with a little playroom for kids. Delicious breakfast of blueberry banana muffins, broiled pears with maple syrup and whipped cream, fresh-squeezed orange juice, and eggs Benedict with tomatoes and roast potatoes." *(Merryl Woodard, also SWS)* "Our favorite was the Lucy Alexander Room with a white wicker queen-size bed and rocker, with rose and teal accents. Tasty afternoon tea and pie; good advice on area restaurants and hiking trails." *(MM)*

Open All year.

Rooms 10 doubles—all with private bath and/or shower, fan.

Facilities Dining room, living room with fireplace, library; lounge with woodstove, billiards, TV/VCR, BYOB bar, stereo, games; children's playroom; deck with hot tub; porches. Swimming hole in river, canoeing, gazebo, gardens. Massage therapy by appointment. Downhill nearby; recreation path at back door for cross-country skiing, snowmobiling. Weddings/catering.

Location Go approx. 1 m N of town on Rte. 100 & turn right onto Tremblay Rd., opposite Rest Area, to inn on left.

Restrictions No smoking.

Credit cards Amex, MC, Visa.

Rates B&B, $69–125 double, $59–115 single. Extra person, $20. Child, family rates. 2–3 night minimum peak holidays.

Extras Limited wheelchair access. Crib, babysitting. French spoken.

WALLINGFORD

For an additional area entry, see **Danby.**

    Reader tip: "Pricey but superb dinner at the Victorian Inn." *(Eric Friesen)*

The I.B. Munson House
7 South Main Street
P.O. Box 427, 05773

Tel: 802–446–2860
888–519–3771
E-mail: ibmunson@vermontel.com
URL: http://www.ibmunsoninn.com

Isaac Munson, a wealthy sheep farmer, needed a home with many bedrooms to house his twelve children, so in 1856 he constructed this imposing Italianate-style Victorian house. With nine bedrooms, it became a natural choice for conversion to an inn, and was listed on the National Register of Historic Places in 1992. The inn was purchased in 1996 by Phillip and Karen Pimental, who note that "our inn is most appreciated by guests who yearn for the warmth, grace, and romance of a bygone era." Period furnishings, crystal chandeliers, Waverly fabrics and wallcoverings, and Oriental rugs highlight the decor. Breakfast is served around the oak dining room table, or on the garden deck, from 8–9:30 A.M., and a typical meal includes juice, fresh fruit cup, just-baked muffins, and such entrées as blueberry pancakes with sausage or a ham and apple strata with country potatoes. Tea and snacks are offered in the late afternoon; in the evening, the player piano and Victrola in the parlor provide a musical backdrop while guests savor a glass of wine.

"Charming antiques, soothing colors. We enjoyed the company of the other guests at breakfast. Phil and Karen recommended the restaurant across the road, where we had a delicious dinner. Though our room was one of the least expensive, we slept well and found it quiet and charming." (*Anthony Barone*) "Delightful, polite, kind innkeepers. Lovely room with fireplace." (*Sonia Isabella*) "Beautifully restored in lavish Victorian style. Scrupulously clean, beautifully appointed, warm and cozy. Karen and Phil were welcoming and knowledgeable about the town and the inn's history. At breakfast, we were seated by the bay window, with a fire going in the fireplace, and were served a delicious meal." (*Belinda Muse*)

Open All year.

Rooms 1 suite, 6 doubles—all with private shower and/or bath. 2 with desk, wood-burning fireplace; 3 with fan.

Facilities Dining room, living room, library—all with fireplace; library, living room with TV/VCR, stereo; porch, deck. ¾ acre. Golf nearby. Near lakes for swimming, boating, fishing. 10–30 min. to hiking, cross-country, downhill skiing.

Location SW VT, 10 m S of Rutland. On Rte. 7, ⅒ m S of Rte 140.

Restrictions No smoking. Children over 12.

Credit cards Amex, Discover, MC, Visa.

Rates B&B, $145–160 suite, $85–135 double. Extra person, $25. 2-night holiday, foliage season minimum.

Extras Some pets by prior arrangement.

WARREN

Warren is a tiny village located 3 miles south of Waitsfield on Route 100. It doesn't contain much more than the Warren Store, which once sold little more than bologna and white bread, but has developed into gourmet emporium over the last 30 years. About a mile north of the village, the Sugarbush access road extends east from Route 100 to Sugarbush Village and the ski area; many inns and restaurants are located along here. Area activities include the usual Vermont outdoor pleasures, from downhill and cross-country skiing in winter to such warm weather favorites as a rather difficult Robert Trent Jones golf course, plus gliding, polo, and, in late July and early August, the Sugarbush Grand Prix Horse Show.

Warren is 200 miles northwest of Boston, 300 miles north of New York City, and 45 miles south of Burlington, in north-central Vermont.

Beaver Pond Farm Inn ¢
Golf Course Road
RD Box 306, 05674

Tel: 802–583–2861
Fax: 802–583–2860
E-mail: beaverpond@madriver.com
URL: http://www.beaverpondfarminn.com

A restored Vermont farmhouse, Beaver Pond Farm Inn is surrounded by cross-country ski trails in winter; in the summer, golfers are challenged by the adjacent Robert Trent Jones course. Betty and Bob Hansen are the longtime owners. Rates include breakfast and afternoon refreshments; a prix fixe dinner, including wine, is served three nights weekly in winter. A recent meal included goat cheese soufflé, salad with coriander-mint vinaigrette, rack of lamb, potatoes au gratin, and chocolate raspberry torte.

"Bob and Betty are wonderful hosts. We had afternoon snacks on the deck, enjoying gorgeous views of the golf course, lush meadows, beaver pond, and mountains." *(Bruce Grossman)* "Betty is a super cook. Marvelous dinners with good food and interesting conversation. Bob offered excellent advice on cross-country and downhill skiing. Great location for walking quiet country lanes and hiking in the mountains nearby." *(Lucy Guillet-Boyden, also Leo & Mary Drewes)* "The location is great, only five minutes from the Sugarbush ski area and ten minutes to Warren and Waitsfield." *(Arthur Capella)* "A golfer's heaven—the inn is bordered by the Sugarbush Golf Club and even has its own practice tee; Betty is a knowledgeable golfer, and can offer advice and arrange tee times. Bob is an avid fisherman, and is pleased to help guests with similar interests. The dining room is highlighted by a beautiful Oriental rug, while the living room is spacious and inviting, an ideal spot to curl up with a cup of tea and Betty's yummy cookies. Cheerful, homey guest rooms, all with good lighting, some tucked under the eaves. A warm, welcoming, old-fashioned B&B." *(SWS)*

"Betty was most helpful in accommodating my food allergy." *(Kerstin Rav)* "The wet bar adjacent to the living room is stocked with mixers and ice; we joined other guests at this oasis before heading out to one of many great restaurants. Equally appealing were our dinners at the inn; Betty knows her French cuisine and Bob is excellent as host and wine connoisseur." *(Lynda Dartnell)* "Our delicious breakfast included a choice of salmon and scallion omelets or orange yogurt pancakes, accompanied by a whipped banana and orange juice drink, lemon muffins, mixed berry salad, toast, English muffins, cereal, and a variety of teas and coffee, served at a large round table on the deck, overlooking the beautiful gardens and mountains beyond." *(Al & Lauren Kenney)*

Open Memorial Day weekend–Oct., Thanksgiving–April.
Rooms 6 double rooms—4 with full private bath, 2 with maximum of 4 people sharing bath. All with radio, hairdryer; 1 with patio.
Facilities Living room with fireplace, TV room, BYOB bar, deck. Flower gardens, pond. Adjacent to Sugarbush golf course, 25 km of groomed cross-country skiing. Fishing, swimming nearby; trout-fishing guide service.
Location 1 m from Warren village. From I-89, take Exit 9 to Rte. 100. Go S on Rte. 100 to Sugarbush Access Rd. Turn left at Sugarbush Ski Area parking lot onto Inferno Rd. Go 1.3 m, then left at mailboxes onto Golf Course Rd. to inn on right.
Restrictions No smoking. Children 7 and over.
Credit cards Amex, MC, Visa.
Rates B&B, $72–104 double, $52–84 single. 15% service. Extra person, $25. 20% discount for 2-night midweek stays. 2-night weekend minimum. 3–5-night ski, golf, July 4th, Thanksgiving packages. Christmas dinner on request. Prix fixe dinner, $25.
Extras French spoken. Airport/station pickups.

Hamilton House

German Flats Road, RR 1, P.O. Box 74, 05674

Tel: 802–583–1066
800–760–1066
Fax: 802–583–1776
E-mail: james@hamiltonvt.com
URL: http://www.hamiltonvt.com

Hamilton House offers a first-rate experience in the caliber of the accommodations, inviting common areas, lovely setting, personable hosts, delicious food, and overall ambience. Constructed in the 1960s as a private home by the builder of the nearby Sugarbush Inn, Hamilton House was remodeled as a vacation and retirement home by James and Joyce Plumpton. When they became innkeepers in 1994, they named their inn for Joyce's Scottish ancestors (the Hamiltons) and furnished each guest room to reflect their past, from the colleges of their native England and Scotland, to the "India Room" reminiscent of their years near Bombay. The drawing room and dining room are classically elegant with English antiques and reproductions.

Breakfast is served at the large dining room table or informally in the conservatory, and includes fresh fruit and juice, cereal, freshly baked rolls and muffins, croissants and toast, and such entrées as scrambled eggs with cheddar and onions, sautéed mushrooms and bacon, or perhaps spiced apple pancakes with maple syrup. Afternoon tea features home-baked cakes, tea sandwiches or hot buttered crumpets. By advance reservation, three-course dinners are offered; some sample entrées include roast beef with Yorkshire pudding, poached salmon with asparagus, Greek lamb kebabs, and Cornish pasties.

"Charming, gracious owners make you feel like you are their personal guests, yet never intrude on your privacy. Elegant yet unpretentious." *(Linda Phillipps)* "We were welcomed with sherry and tea with dainty sandwiches, served in the drawing room. A silver bowl of chilled grapes awaited in our splendid guest room. In the morning, we were served a tasty breakfast in the conservatory, complemented by freshly cut flowers from their garden. James and Joyce are helpful in making dinner reservations, suggesting activities, and booking tennis courts at a nearby club. We were soothed, pampered, and felt utterly special." *(Leigh Mackenzie Taylor)* "Isolated setting with wonderful views, yet conveniently located." *(Mary Kaufmann)* "We enjoyed afternoon tea on the back lawn, enjoying the view of mountains ablaze with crimson, orange, and yellow foliage." *(Dale Hill)*

Open All year.
Rooms 2 suites, 2 doubles—all with full private bath, clock, desk, fan. 1 suite with TV.
Facilities Dining room with fireplace, drawing room with fireplace, stereo, library; guest pantry, conservatory/sun room, terrace. 25 acres with gardens, lawns, hiking trails, cross-country skiing, snowshoeing (snowshoes provided).
Location Between Sugarbush & Sugarbush North ski resorts. From Waitsfield, take Rte. 17 W & go 2 m to German Flats Rd. Turn left & go 3 m up the mountain. Pass Pepper's Lodge on right & restaurant on left. Go past crest in rd. 100 yds. to driveway to inn. From Sugarbush Access Rd., turn right on German Flats Rd. to inn on right.
Restrictions No smoking. No children.
Credit cards Amex, Discover, MC, Visa.
Rates B&B, $180–200 suite, $140–160 double. 2–4 night minimum. Ski, golf packages; returning guest discount. No tipping or service charge.
Extras Limited French, reasonable American, superb English spoken.

The Pitcher Inn ✕ ♿
Main Street, P.O. Box 347, 05674

Tel: 802–496–6350
888–867–4824
Fax: 802–496–6354
E-mail: pitcher@madriver.com
URL: http://www.pitcherinn.com

Originally built in the 1800s, the original Pitcher Inn was a convenient stopover for loggers and wayfarers. By the 1980s, it was a popular local breakfast spot, with a dozen inexpensive but run-down shared bath guest rooms. In 1993, a dramatic fire consumed the original building. Four years later, Winthrop and Margaret Smith had the inn rebuilt from the same footprint as the original structure, incorporating the luxuries of a first-class hotel, while respecting its history and architecture. The Smiths' daughter and son-in-law, Heather and John Carino, are the innkeepers.

Breakfast is served to overnight guests, as well as the public, from 7:30–11:30 A.M. House-made granola, omelets, and smoked salmon with poached eggs are just a few of the house specialties. Under chef Tom Bivins, formerly of the Inn at Shelburne Farms, the dinner menu changes frequently, and a recent mid-winter menu included such entrées as venison with sun-dried tomato butter sauce; salmon with ginger purée; and polenta and tomato lasagna with carmelized onions, fennel, and olives. Many dishes are available in smaller portion sizes to accommodate reduced appetites and/or wallets.

"The 1993 fire that consumed the original Pitcher Inn was a severe blow to the economy of this small, picturesque town. As a 'thank you' to the community, Maggie and Win Smith, long-term summer residents, employed a team of architects, designers, local craftsmen, and artists to create a multi-million dollar showcase inn on the original site. Like a stage setting, the theme of each room has been developed using fine wood floors and cabinets, hand-carved king-size beds, murals, window boxes, antiques, and mood lighting. The bathrooms are finished in marble; many have double whirlpool tubs, Jacuzzis, and steam rooms. Antique objects—snowshoes, skis, photographs, and paintings—are found in great profusion. Decorating themes vary from the busy School Room with chalk board, desk, and library; to the rustic Mountain Room with the mood of a hiker's hut; to the Trout Room, with a birch-log bed and stone wood-burning fireplace, a sculptured fly-tying table, and a collection of canoe paddles. The bright cheerful dining room overlooks bubbling Freeman Brook. Our tasty breakfast included lemon scones, blueberry muffins, and delicious pumpkin pancakes. Charming, enthusiastic staff; outstanding facilities and maintenance." *(Joe Schmidt)* "Having visited the Pitcher Inn in 1988, and again in 1998, I felt like Rip Van Winkle re-awakened. Other than the inn's name and location, I didn't recognize a thing. Where I once crashed for $50 a night has been transformed into a fantasy suite." *(MW)*

Open All year. Closed early May, early Nov.

Rooms 4 suites, 6 doubles—all with full private bath and/or shower, whirlpool tub, telephone, radio, TV, desk, air-conditioning. 8 with fireplace, 3 with refrigerator, 4 with balcony/deck. 2 two-bedroom suites in barn with living room and fireplace.

Facilities Restaurant with fireplace, piano; living room with fireplace, stereo; game room with fireplace, stereo; library with fireplace; screened porch, deck. 2 acres with croquet, off-street parking.

Location Center of village, ½ m off Rte. 100.

Restrictions No smoking.

Credit cards MC, Visa.

Rates B&B, $250–325 suite, $165–300 double. Extra person, $50. 9% service charge. 2-night weekend/holiday minimum. 5-night minimum at Christmas.

Extras Wheelchair access; bathroom specially equipped.

The Sugartree
Sugarbush Access Road
RR Box 38, 05674

Tel: 802–583–3211
800–666–8907
Fax: 802–583–3203
E-mail: sugartree@madriver.com
URL: http://www.sugartree.com

A 1960s ski lodge restored as a country inn in the 1980s, the Sugartree was bought by Frank and Kathy Partsch in 1992; when not improving and upgrading the inn, Frank enjoys woodcarving (his whimsical Santas are delightful), while Kathy has taken up quilt-making. The guest rooms have a country decor with ruffled curtains, floral wallpapers, and lace-canopy or brass beds with handmade quilts. Breakfast, served at several tables from 8–9:30 A.M., might consist of a farmer's omelet, quiche with hash-brown potato crust, fruit crisps, and soda bread.

"Frank and Kathy welcomed us with lemonade and lemon squares in the inviting sitting area." *(Katherine & David Lamartire)* "Frank and Kathy always had time to talk or give advice on activities from Ben & Jerry's to breathtaking Texas Falls to Kennedy Brothers in Vergennes with floors of woodcrafts and antiques. Our second-floor room was decorated with a lace-canopy bed, a sturdy rocking chair, and an antique sewing table. Each morning's breakfast was different, but Kathy's gingerbread pancakes with lemonade were my favorite. Each afternoon, guests were offered apple cider and freshly baked cookies." *(Marilyn Smith)*

"The inn is set back from the road at the top of a hill and while the grounds are not expansive, the landscaping is lovely. Perennials and annual flowers were in bloom all over, including flower boxes on the windows. Tasty breakfast of peach crisp, bacon, thick-sliced French toast with homemade honey-orange syrup and Vermont maple syrup. Our country-comfortable third-floor room felt like it was in a tree house. Guest rooms are done with pretty wallpapers; canopy, brass, or four-poster queen-size beds (some rooms have an additional twin-size bed); handmade curtains and quilts, electrified oil lamps; and reproduction and antique dressers, armoires, and end tables. Frank is an accomplished cabinet maker who has built many of the bathroom vanities and other interior woodwork." *(Rose Ciccone)*

"Frank and Kathy are just as warm, welcoming, and friendly as they can be, working hard to maximize their guests' enjoyment and comfort." *(SWS)* "Immaculately clean and comfortable. From the dining/living area we watched birds clustered at the feeders, and squirrels scooting about." *(Diane Shaughnessy)* "My favorite spot is the large but cozy living room, ideal for reading from their excellent collection of Vermont and New England books, doing a puzzle, or playing checkers. Frank, an avid woodcarver, will teach you with pieces he has readily available." *(Harold Burnell)* "Our children felt totally welcome—Frank challenged our son to a game of chess." *(Susan Wells)* "We enjoyed early morning coffee in the gazebo; Kathy's brownies tempted us in the evening." *(Susan & Ronald Townsend)*

Open All year.

Rooms 1 suite, 8 doubles—all with private bath and/or shower, telephone, hairdryer. 7 with fan, 2 with air-conditioning, 1 with desk, fireplace. Clock on request.

Facilities Dining room, living room with fireplace, pump organ, stereo, games, library, guest refrigerator; porch, gazebo. Off-street parking, lawn games. Woodcarving lessons. ¼ m to Sugarbush sports center.

Location 3 m from town. Go N on Rte. 100 for 1 m to Sugarbush Access Rd. Turn on access rd. & go 2½ m to inn on right.

Restrictions No smoking. Children over 7.

Credit cards Amex, Discover, MC, Visa.

Rates B&B, $100–135 suite, $85–135 double, $75–90 single. Extra person, $25. Senior, AAA discount. 2–3 night winter weekend/holiday minimum. Midweek, off-season rates. Mid-April–mid-Sept., 4th night half-price or 5th night free. Free ski shuttle to Sugarbush. Ski packages.

West Hill House
West Hill Road, RR 1, P.O. Box 292, 05674

Tel: 802–496–7162
800–898–1427
Fax: 802–496–6443
E-mail: westhill@madriver.com
URL: http://www.westhillhouse.com

Dotty Kyle and Eric Brattstrom call West Hill House a B&B, but we think they're being too modest—bed and breakfast and tea and cookies and hors d'oeuvres and drinks is a more accurate name. Plus warm and welcoming hospitality, beautiful decor, and comfortable accommodations, of course. As Dottie describes the 1850s farmhouse she and Eric bought in 1993: "We seem to attract adults of all ages who have an active lifestyle, read more than most, enjoy movies (we have an extensive VCR film library), and relish lively table conversations. The atmosphere here is informal and relaxed, and feelings of warmth and friendship amongst innkeepers and guests is the norm." Eric is a master renovator who has added space without changing the character of this 1850s farm house; Dottie is an artist whose skills are displayed in the B&B's decor, and in her cooking as well.

Breakfast is served at guests' convenience, starting at 8 A.M., at the oversize antique English table, and includes fresh fruit with granola and yogurt, or perhaps baked bananas; ginger lemon muffins or possibly pecan-orange scones; followed by baked apple pancakes with local maple syrup, or maybe scrambled eggs with Vermont cheddar and just-picked herbs. Afternoon refreshments include iced tea and cookies, or in winter, hot cider or mochaccino and bread pudding. Cocktail hour brings chips and dips, crackers and cheese, flatbreads from the inn's wood-fired oven, or home-baked soft pretzels with honey mustard. The guest fridge is kept stocked with wine, beer, and soft drinks.

Guest rooms have good reading lights, down comforters, and modern bathrooms with lots of amenities; most have a queen-size bed; two have twin beds convertible to a king-size beds. The Wildflower Room has a fireplace angled into the corner, a double Jacuzzi tub, a beautiful floral quilt, and walls sponge-painted to match. The cozy Blue Room has a hand-sewn quilt on the queen-size bed and a matching hand-painted floral spray on the wall, wide-board pine floors, antique furnishings, and an Oriental rug.

"Outstanding warmth and hospitality. Have never tasted such light muffins and pancakes. Upon our 4:00 arrival, Dotty presented us with wonderful cookies, scones, cream and jam. After dinner, we enjoyed a complimentary glass of sherry. We sat out on the veranda watching squirrels and chipmunks. In our peaceful room, we fell asleep to the sounds of croaking frogs." *(P. Tanner)* "The innkeepers are full of fun and have worked all sorts of magic to create comfortable guest rooms and private baths in this old house and barn. We particularly enjoyed the large public spaces. On a cold winter night two wood stoves and the kitchen bread oven make them cozy and warm." *(Joe & Sheila Schmidt)* "Talented hosts; secluded, peaceful location. The inn is clean and well-kept with constant upgrades from year to year." *(Don Bauman)* "Gets better and better with every return visit. Interesting guests from all over the world." *(Tillie Akin)* "Dottie and Eric are skilled and sophisticated hosts, knowledgeable about a great many subjects. Lots to read, too. Spotless rooms, scrumptious breakfasts and evening treats; comfortable beds. Dottie's artistry gives the rooms a special charm." *(Margaret Scott)*

Open All year.

Rooms 1 suite, 6 doubles—all with private bath and/or shower, clock/radio, ceiling fan. Some with double whirlpool tub, TV, air-conditioning, fireplace.

Facilities Great room, sun room, library—each with fireplace, stereo, books, TV/VCR; guest refrigerator; porch, deck. 9 acres with gardens, meadows, beaver pond, off-street parking, hiking, sledding, cross-country skiing, snowshoeing. Golf course adjacent. 1 m to downhill skiing at Sugarbush resort.

Location 1½ m to Warren, 1 m to Sugarbush. From Rte. 100 in Warren, turn onto Sugarbush Access Rd. (W). Go 3 m & go left onto Inferno Rd. Go 1 m & turn right onto West Hill Rd. to inn, 1st house on right.

Restrictions No smoking. Children 10 and over.

Credit cards Amex, MC, Visa.

Rates B&B, $125–155 suite, $100–145 double, $90–145 single. Extra person, $20. 2–3 night weekend/holiday minimum. Sat. night prix fixe dinner, by reservation, in season, $22–30.

WATERBURY

Waterbury is conveniently located at the junction of Route 100 and I-89. If you're visiting in winter, it makes a good base to sample skiing at Stowe to the north, Bolton Valley to the west, and Sugarbush and Mad River to the south. In summer or fall, it's equally central for explorations of northern Vermont. If you're going to visit Ben & Jerry's famous ice cream factory, go early in the day, especially if it's raining, to avoid the crowds. No less appealing are the exquisite chocolates of Green Mountain Chocolates, and Cold Hollow Cider Mill in Waterbury Center, to the north. If you need to work off all those goodies, hike to the top of Camel's Hump, one of Vermont's tallest mountains.

Grünberg Haus B&B and Cabins ¢ ♚
Route 100 South, RR 2
P.O. Box 1595-AW, 05676

Tel: 802–244–7726
800–800–7760
Email: grunhaus@aol.com
URL: http://www.bestinns.net/usa/vt/grun.html

A Tyrolean-style chalet hand-built in 1972, Grünberg (German for green mountain) Haus has been owned by Chris Sellers and Mark Frohman since 1989. Chris is an accomplished musician and often plays for guests at breakfast on his Steinway grand piano. The inn's common areas include a pub area with booths perfect for playing board games, a spacious living/dining area with a handsome fieldstone fireplace and a wall of windows looking over woods and mountains. Outside is a lovely deck and hot tub area, where breakfast is served in fine weather; also available are two rustic cabins in the woods along the hiking trails, and a spacious suite on the second floor of the carriage house. Though not large, the lodge guest rooms are cozily furnished with country antiques, comforters and quilts. Breakfast is served from 8–10 A.M., featuring such creative menus as maple-broiled grapefruit, peach gingerbread muffins, and spinach frittata; or spiced oranges, applesauce oatmeal muffins, and lemon ricotta pancakes.

"Chris is a pleasant, friendly host. The spacious suite is ideal for a longer stay, complete with two quilt-topped queen-size beds, kitchen, living area, cathedral ceiling, and skylights. If you'd like to be tucked away in the woods and don't mind a short but steep hike, the simple, rustic cabins are cozy and a great value." *(SWS)* "Great character, from the main entrance to the distinctive guest rooms." *(George Geoffroy)* "Charming bedrooms, each with a different color scheme and own resident bear. A roaring fire in a lovely big old fireplace welcomed us." *(Janet Thompson)* "On my comfy bed was a cuddly teddy bear (the stuffed kind) and a friendly gray-striped tabby cat (the purring kind)." *(MW)*

"A warm, wonderful home-away-from-home with relaxed, hospitable hosts." *(Glenn Alterman)* "A charming Austrian chalet, off the beaten path yet easily accessible. Friendly staff and guests, wonderful view, beautiful mountains. Our room had a comfortable bed, lovely quilt, and a balcony. We enjoyed relaxing in the hot tub and by the fireplace. Friendly resident cats. Light-as-air pumpkin pancakes for breakfast; Mark was kind enough to share his recipe." *(Carol Reinheimer)* "We loved the food, accommodations, and music, plus the cats, chickens, and teddy bears." *(RM)*

Open All year.

Rooms 2 cabins, 1 suite, 14 doubles—10 with private shower and/or tub, 5 with maximum of 4 people sharing bath. All with clock, fan. Most with balcony/deck. 4 with desk. Cabins with fireplace. Suite in carriage house.

Facilities Dining room, living room with fireplace, piano; pub (BYOB); family room, library, guest refrigerator; deck. 54 acres with tennis court, hot tub, lawn games, cross-country ski trails, hiking. Golf, Mad River swimming holes nearby. 20 min. to Stowe, Sugarbush, Mad River, and Bolton Valley ski areas.

Location N VT. 25 miles E of Burlington. 3 m S of town. From I-89, take Exit 10 to Rte. 100 S 4 m to inn on left.

Restrictions No smoking except near chicken coop. Children over 3.

Credit cards Discover/Novus, MC, Visa.

Rates B&B, $89–145 suite, $69–115 cabin, $59–125 double, $44–110 single. Extra person, $7. 10% senior discount.

Extras Airport/station pickups, $5–30. Pet boarding nearby.

Inn at Blush Hill ¢ 🏃

Blush Hill Road, RR 1, P.O. Box 1266, 05676

Tel: 802–244–7529
800–736–7522
Fax: 802–244–7314
E-mail: innatbh@aol.com
URL: http://www.blushhill.com

"What do I look for in a Vermont B&B? A quiet yet convenient rural setting, with meadows and mountain views; a vintage farmhouse that carries its years well; affordable rates; and a pervasive feeling of the owners' warmth and hospitality reflected in the inn as a whole. We're pleased to report that the Inn at Blush Hill succeeds admirably on all counts. Though it's just a short drive from the interstate and busy Route 100, its hilltop setting provides beautiful views of the Worcester Range. Built in 1790, the inn has a large and welcoming living room, and a delightful breakfast area tucked into a bay off the kitchen, where guests gather around a large harvest table for breakfasts of perhaps honeydew compote, cheddar cheese strata, and sausages, served with homemade biscuits. Although owners Pam and Gary Gosselin ensure that the entire inn is warm and inviting, our favorite guest room is the Mountain View Room over the breakfast area. In addition to being the largest, it combines breathtaking vistas with an elegant decor—a queen-size bed with Battenburg lace canopy, with white linen Roman shades on the windows. Though smaller, another favorite is done in handsome blue prints and plaids, with a queen-size bed, sitting area, and Jacuzzi tub in the bathroom." *(SWS)*

"We enjoyed reading books in the cozy parlor while munching on Pam's cookies and hot chocolate. Breakfast in the beautiful large kitchen with the fantastic hilltop view was great!" *(Pamela Sisson)* "Thoughtful touches included the robes and bottled water in our room." *(Trisha Elliott)* "Spectacular mountains views." *(Neil McLaughlin)* "Pleasant and accommodating hosts." *(Karen & Matt Ritterbusch)* "Memorable, varied, healthy, delicious breakfasts." *(Diane Cary)* "The owners and their children always helpful and courteous. Immaculate housekeeping. Beverages always available in the large, attractive kitchen. We particularly liked the side porch with its rocking chairs." *(Alice Davis)* "Roomy common areas. Enjoyed watching the goldfinches at the bird feeder during breakfast." *(Beth Standen)* "Warm welcome, great-smelling sheets." *(Maria & Steven Cabot)* "The huge living room has lots of comfortable seating, a table set up for chess, good lighting, and lots to read. Beautiful yard and gardens; rocking chairs on the front porch invite guests to relax." *(Nancy Grayson)* "Pam was warm, friendly, and informative." *(Nikki Knepp)* "Delicious homemade cookies and herbal teas in the evening." *(Carole Rupnik-Brown)* "It was hard to leave the breakfast table, with lively conversations amongst the guests; laughter prevailed." *(Halvor Franco)*

Open All year.
Rooms 5 doubles—all with private bath and/or shower, radio, fan. 1 with fireplace, ceiling fan, air-conditioning, Jacuzzi tub.
Facilities Dining room, breakfast room, both with fireplace. Parlor with fireplace, piano, TV, stereo, games; porch, deck. 5 acres with lawn games. ½ m to lake for swimming, canoeing, hiking in Mount Mansfield State Forest. 9-hole golf course across rd.
Location 1 m from town center. From I-89, take Exit 10 to Rte. 100 N. At Holiday Inn, turn left onto Blush Hill Rd. Continue ¾ m to inn on right.
Restrictions No smoking. No children under 6. Some guest rooms tucked under eaves, with limited head room; some have hooks but no closet.
Credit cards Amex, Discover, MC. Visa.
Rates B&B, $65–130 double. Extra person, $15. Family rates. Midweek 2-night ski packages; summer ice cream packages. Weekly discount.
Extras Station pickup. Babysitting.

WEATHERSFIELD

For additional area entries, see **Windsor.**

The Inn at Weathersfield ✕ ㏒ ⴑ
Route 106, P.O. Box 165, 05151

Tel: 802–263–9217
800–477–4828
Fax: 802–263–9219
URL: http://www.weathersfieldinn.com

The Inn at Weathersfield started as a four-room farmhouse in the 1780s and was expanded many times over the past 200 years. It was used as a stagecoach inn, served as a stop on the Underground Railroad during the Civil War, was returned to use as an inn in 1961, and has been owned by Mary and Terry Carter since 1995. The rooms are now luxurious enough to have earned a four-star rating from Mobil, with four diamonds from AAA for its dining experience.

A breakfast buffet is available from 8:30–10 A.M., consisting of cereals, fresh fruit and juice, bacon, cheddar eggs, or perhaps Grand Marnier French toast. This will usually last you to afternoon tea—salmon mousse on bread rounds, vegetables with dip, and a sweet such as English trifle. The five-course dinner menu, prepared by chef Michael McNamara, changes nightly; a recent meal included a choice of such entrées as swordfish with roasted red pepper sauce, pork tenderloin with maple mustard glaze, and breast of pheasant with an orange bourbon sauce.

"Mary is a remarkable innkeeper; she seemed to be everywhere, making sure all her guests were cared for, yet still found time for pleasant conversation with each one." *(Michael Kaplan)* "In the keeping room, a huge fire was burning, with an iron kettle of hot cider warming, and a plate of homemade cookies. Our room was spotless, with a canopy bed, antiques, and wide-plank pine floors, plus nice, fluffy towels in the bath. Every night we had a fire in the wood-burning fireplace, with candles and classical music playing softly in the background. Tea at 5 P.M. was outstanding, with wine and champagne, delicious pastries, and fruit and cheese trays." *(Sue & Joe Plaskas)*

"The dining room looked lovely with antique china, crystal, silver, and fresh flowers. Our third-floor suite was reached by a spiral staircase; the small sitting room held a love seat, desk, and two beautifully restored trunks (one used as a coffee table). The bedroom was decorated in coordinated floral chintz fabrics, with a comfortable king-size bed draped with netting, plenty of pillows, good reading lights, a remote-control gas fireplace, and a private rooftop deck." *(Rose Ciccone)* "Just the right amount of intermingling; lots of socializing at tea and breakfast, but privacy at dinner." *(Betsy Madero)*

Open All year.
Rooms 3 suites, 9 doubles—all with private shower and/or bath, desk, fan. 8 with fireplace; 2 with deck. 1 with whirlpool tub.
Facilities Living room with library; keeping room; dining room with piano; gathering room; all with fireplace. Fitness/game room with exercise bike,

weight machine, sauna, billiards, TV/VCR; greenhouse; porches. 21 acres with amphitheater, walking trails, lawn games, berry picking, English gardens, sleigh/carriage rides. Pond for swimming, fishing, boating, skating; canoeing, golf nearby. 15–20 m to cross-country, downhill skiing.

Location SE VT. ½ m S of Perkinsville. Take Exit 7 (Springfield) off I-91. Take Rte. 11/106 N to Springfield, then right on Rte. 106 toward Perkinsville.

Restrictions No smoking. Children over 8.

Credit cards Amex, DC, Discover, MC, Visa.

Rates B&B, $95 suite, $85 double, $65 single; extra person, $20. MAP, $195–225 suite, $175–195 double, $145 single. Extra person, $75. 17% service. 2–3 night minimum high-season weekends/holidays. Prix fixe dinner, $35. Thanksgiving, Christmas packages.

Extras Wheelchair access; inquire for details. Local airport/station pickups. Babysitting.

WEST DOVER

West Dover is in south-central Vermont, about 25 miles west of Brattleboro and east of Bennington, and 5 miles north of Wilmington, at Route 9. It is about a 4-hour drive north of New York City, and about 3 hours northwest of Boston. To get there, take I-91 or Route 7 to Route 100, then go north on 100 to West Dover. Many of West Dover's inns are right on Route 100, a scenic but busy north-south route. If you're a light sleeper, be sure to ask your innkeeper for a quiet room.

West Dover is the closest town to Mt. Snow, the largest ski area in southern Vermont, with both downhill and cross-country skiing available. Stratton and Bromley are a 45-minute drive north. Summer activities include hiking and tennis at Mt. Snow, plus the well-known golf and mountain bicycling schools, with many lakes and streams nearby for swimming, fishing, and boating, as well as the summer music festival at Marlboro.

Reader tip: "Excellent lunch at Julie's Cafe, casually and artistically decorated with painted floors and floral tablecloths. Mouthwatering dishes, many with a Southwestern accent. Excellent grilled chicken with homemade salsa in a soft tortilla; delicious hummus and chevre rolled in Armenian flatbread." *(Betsy Sandberg)*

For additional area entries, see **Wilmington**.

Austin Hill Inn	*Tel:* 802–464–5281
Route 100, P.O. Box 859, 05356	800–332–RELAX
	Fax: 802–464–1229
	E-mail: austinhi@sovernet.com
	URL: http://www.austinhillinn.com

A Colonial-style home built in 1930, the Austin Hill Inn began accepting paying guests in 1955, and is decorated with a comfortable mix of antiques and traditional pieces. In December, 1997, it was purchased by Debbie and John Bailey, their sons Marshall and Nicholas, and their black lab Shannon. Growing up, both Debbie and John worked in resorts in New England, and they met while employed at the Ritz-Carlton in Boston. The Baileys are pleased to combine their favorite elements at the Austin Hill Inn: careers in the hospitality industry; love of sports and the outdoors; and the opportunity for family togetherness.

Upon arrival, guests are welcomed with wine and cheese or, in summer, perhaps iced tea, lemonade, or a fruit smoothie served poolside. Breakfast is served at individual tables from 8–9:30 A.M., and includes home-baked muffins and breads, a choice of grapefruit or possibly cranberry-apple compote, as well as a two entrées—blueberry stuffed French toast or cheese strata, or perhaps orange-cranberry pancakes or eggs Benedict. After a busy day, guests are welcomed back to the inn with afternoon tea, fruit, and hot-from-the-oven cookies. Beds are turned down at night, with softly glowing candles to welcome guests back to their rooms.

"Warm, relaxing atmosphere; friendly innkeepers; clean, comfortable accommodations; delicious breakfasts. Great dog, too." (GR, also Cheryl & Tim Gielow) "Welcoming hospitality, personable service." (Andrea & Steve Weeks)

Open All year.
Rooms 12 doubles—all with private shower and/or tub. 5 with balcony.
Facilities 2 dining rooms, 1 with fireplace; 2 living rooms with fireplace; 1 with TV/VCR, tapes, games, books. 5 acres with heated swimming pool.
Location ½ mile from historic district. On Rte. 100. 2.5 m from Mt. Snow.
Restrictions No smoking. Well-behaved children welcome.
Credit cards Amex, Discover, MC, Visa.
Rates B&B, $115–130 double. Extra person, $30. 2-night weekend minimum. Off-season, mid-week discounts; golf and ski packages.

Deerhill Inn ✖
Valley View, P.O. Box 136, 05356

Tel: 802–464–3100
800–99DEER9
Fax: 802–464–5474
E-mail: deerhill@sover.net
URL: http://www.deerhill.com

Built in 1954, the Deerhill Inn has been owned by Linda and Michael Anelli since 1984. Linda describes the inn as a "romantic refuge for couples looking to decompress for a few days—luxurious but not pompous or intimidating—offering real Vermont hospitality for real people." Breakfast is served at individual tables between 8 and 9:30 A.M., and Michael's dinners might include such entrées as veal with wild mushrooms and lemon cream sauce or chicken breast with pesto and sun-dried tomatoes. Many of the guest rooms have queen- or king-size beds with views of the gardens and swimming pool.

"Some inns just happen to have a restaurant on the premises; others are restaurants offering rooms as an afterthought. Then there's the Deerhill Inn, which has perfected the art of doing both. Owners Linda and Michael Anelli set the tone immediately with their warm, hospitable welcome. When we arrived, Michael had just returned from fishing—his true passion, along with cooking. One night we feasted on portabello mushrooms stuffed with crab and lobster, crisp duckling with lingonberry sauce, and concluded with Amaretto crème brûlée and homemade peanut butter-chocolate chip ice cream in a homemade cookie shell. The next night we had a difficult time deciding between grilled loin of pork with wild mushrooms and five-layer veal with roasted red-pepper sauce. Breakfast didn't disappoint either with freshly squeezed orange juice, light blueberry or strawberry pancakes, divine French toast, omelets, or eggs any style. Warm muffins (blueberry one morning, apple-cinnamon the next) are brought to the table in a basket, with refills if desired. Each meal is artistically presented, often garnished with nasturtiums. Linda is a wonderful gardener, and flowers bloom everywhere on the grounds; she's an equally talented decorator, and guest rooms mix and match charming floral designs. Rooms are comfortable, pristine, with good lightning, and comfortable sitting areas. Ours had a queen-size bed, several chairs, and a large dresser. A balcony led down one flight to the swimming pool. Appealing common areas, with lots of plants and flowers, and a handsome stone fireplace in the living room; extensive variety of games and books. Incredible views, beautiful in any season. Exceptionally pleasant staff; friendly inn dogs." *(Betsy Sandberg)*

Open All year. Restaurant closed Wed.

Rooms 2 suites, 13 doubles—all with private bath and/or shower, clock, fan. 8 with balcony, 5 with TV, 4 with fireplace, 1 with desk.

Facilities Restaurant with fireplace, bar/lounge, 2 living rooms with fireplaces; library, porch. 3 acres with swimming pool, croquet court, lawn games. 1 m to Mt. Snow resort.

Location From intersection of Rtes. 9 & 100, go N on Rte. 100 to W. Dover. After 6.2 m, turn right on Valley View Rd. & go ¹⁄₁₀ m to inn on right.

Restrictions Smoking permitted in guest rooms. Children over 8.

Credit cards Amex, MC, Visa.

Rates B&B, $198–260 suite, $117–190 double. Extra person, $30. MAP, $268–330 suite, $187–260 double. Extra person, $65. 15% service. 3-night holiday minimum. Fishing packages, with guide. Alc dinner, $40–45. Midweek packages.

Extras Airport pickup. Russian, German spoken.

Snowgoose Inn 🛉 ⚭
Route 100, P.O. Box 366, 05356

Tel: 802–464–3984
888–604–7964
Fax: 802–464–5322
E-mail: gooseinn@aol.com
URL: http://www.snowgooseinn.com

The Snow Goose Inn, a clapboard Colonial-style home, was built in 1959, expanded in 1990, and renovated in 1998 by new owners Karen and Eric Falberg. Breakfast is served from 8–9:30 A.M. and includes coffee, tea, fresh fruit, muffins, cereals, and a choice of three entrées: perhaps French toast stuffed with bananas; herb-mushroom scrambled eggs, or bagels with cream cheese and lox, plus bacon or sausage. Rates also include early-bird coffee and evening refreshments.

"We relaxed on the porch, enjoying the fresh Vermont air, explored the lovely gardens, sat in the Adirondack chairs, and watched the birds. Karen and Eric welcomed us warmly and proudly gave us a tour of their newly renovated inn. Our room was tastefully decorated with antiques, Victorian lace, and beautiful fabrics, plus a cozy featherbed. We awakened in the morning to the aroma of fresh coffee brewing, and joined the other guests in the spacious dining room for a leisurely breakfast with 'imported' H&H New York City bagels and lemon ricotta pancakes with fresh berries and Vermont maple syrup. Eric and Karen's warm hospitality was also apparent during the evening wine and hors d'oeuvres, served in front of a crackling fireplace. Guests shared stories, listened to jazz playing softly in the background, or borrowed books from the library." *(Teri Karpe)* "Our welcoming corner room in the new wing featured a whirlpool tub and fireplace, perfect lighting, and excellent plumbing. The location was convenient to everything in the area, yet was surprisingly quiet." *(L.A. Vaulancourt)* "Set back and above the road, the inn has a lovely garden and comfortable, immaculate rooms." *(CK)*

Open All year.

Rooms 11 doubles—all with shower and/or tub, clock, TV. 6 with whirlpool tub, 7 with wood-burning fireplace, 5 with deck, 3 with refrigerator, 2 with air-conditioning. Clock on request.

Facilities Dining room with fireplace, parlor, living room with fireplace, stereo, books; game room with TV/VCR; patio. Sat. evening jazz, chamber music concerts. 3 acres with gardens, off-street parking. Tennis across street.

Location S central VT. 7 m N of Wilmington on Rte. 100; just S of Mt. Snow access rd.

Restrictions No smoking. Children 10 and over.

Credit cards Amex, DC, MC, Visa.

Rates B&B, $110–210 double. Extra person, $25. 15% service. 2–3 night weekend/holiday minimum.

Extras Wheelchair access; 1 room specially equipped. Crib, babysitting by arrangement.

West Dover Inn ✕
Route 100, P.O. Box 1208, 05356

Tel: 802–464–5207
Fax: 802–464–2173
E-mail: wdvrinn@sover.net
URL: http://www.westdoverinn.com

Constructed in 1846 as a stagecoach stop and tavern, the West Dover Inn celebrated its 150th year of continuous operation in 1996; it was purchased by Greg Gramas and Monique Phelan in 1995. A splendid example of the Greek Revival style of architecture, complete with two-story columned porch, it offers country-comfortable guest rooms furnished with antiques and hand-sewn quilts, and Oriental rugs topping the wide-plank pine floors. Breakfast, served from 8–9 A.M. (to 9:30 on weekends) at individual tables, includes such offerings as pancakes, thick-sliced French toast or eggs-to-order, plus bacon or sausage. Guests are welcomed with afternoon tea and coffee, often accompanied by other treats. The seasonally changing dinner menu at Gregory's restaurant features such entrées as duck with honey Hoisin sauce, jerk-spice pork tenderloin, shrimp-stuffed phyllo, and spinach-roast garlic ravioli. "Monique and Greg get to know their guests on a one-to-one basis. Our well-maintained room was cozy yet spacious with a fireplace and

Jacuzzi." *(Larry Smith)* "Pleasant innkeepers, convenient location." *(BNS)* "Monique and Greg were friendly and helpful, offering advice and suggesting activities. Breakfast was served in a pleasant nook and included Amaretto French toast and strawberry pancakes. The atmosphere was casual and relaxed; we chatted with Monique while we ate. She was an equally gracious hostess at Gregory's, where Greg tends the bar. Well-chosen dinner menu; the salmon with ginger and scallions was especially tasty." *(Katherine Knappenberger)* "Excellent dining; simple, spotless furnishings; exceptional staff." *(Dr. Tamra Mohan)* "Friendly inn dogs Sam and Zoe made us dog lovers feel right at home." *(W.E. Goss)*

Open Mid-May–Oct., mid-Nov.–mid-April. Restaurant open Wed.–Sun. in winter; Thurs.–Sat. in summer; nightly in foliage season and holidays.

Rooms 4 suites, 8 doubles—all with private bath and/or shower, clock, TV, fan. 2 with fireplace. Some with shared balcony. Suites with fireplace, double whirlpool tub.

Facilities Restaurant with fireplace, bar/lounge with TV, stereo; common room with fireplace, library; VCR; 2 porches, patio. 1 acre with lawn games, off-street parking.

Location In historic district, on Rte. 100.

Restrictions No smoking in public areas. Children over 8.

Credit cards Amex, Discover, MC, Visa.

Rates B&B, $135–200 suite, $90–125 double. Extra person, $25–35. MAP, $245 suite, $170 double. 15% service. 2–3 night weekend/holiday minimum. À la carte dinner, $25–35. Ski, golf packages.

WESTON

Weston is a lovely Vermont town, centered around a classic village green. In addition to Vermont's usual warm-weather attractions—swimming, hiking, golf, tennis, fishing, and so on—Weston is also home to the Weston Priory, a Benedictine monastery famous for its singing monks. It also offers a particularly nice selection of craft shops and art galleries, and the Weston Playhouse. In winter, there's cross-country skiing right in town, and Bromley, Magic, Stratton, and Okemo are all within easy driving distance for downhill skiers.

Weston is located in south-central Vermont, on Route 100. From Manchester, take Route 11 east to Londonderry, then Route 100 north to Weston. From Brattleboro, take Route 30 west to Rawsonville, then Route 100 north to Weston. It's about 2½ hours northwest of Boston, and 4 hours north of New York City.

The Wilder Homestead Inn ¢   *Tel:* 802–824–8172
25 Lawrence Hill Road, 05161   *Fax:* 802–824–5054
       E-mail: innkeeper@wilderhomestead.com
       URL: http://www.wilderhomestead.com

In 1985, Peggy and Roy Varner bought the Wilder home, built of brick by Judge Wilder about 160 years earlier. They've restored it as a B&B,

furnishing it with antiques and preserving the original 1830 Moses Eaton wall stencils. Breakfast, served from 8–9:30 A.M., includes fruit and juices, cereal, homemade biscuits and jam, eggs-to-order, blueberry pancakes, home fries, bacon and sausage.

"Canopy beds, handmade quilts, lace sheets and large, fluffy towels. Homemade biscuits and jams, delicious blueberry pancakes. Hot cider and cheese and crackers set up in the afternoon. When a blizzard made the local restaurants inaccessible, Roy and Peggy—innkeepers extraordinaire—prepared a spaghetti dinner for fourteen." (*Judy & Gary Wagner & others*) "Roy welcomed us warmly, showing us the lovely guest rooms and the marvelous keeping room, with its Colonial charm. Beautifully located in a wonderful village." (*Sally Ducot*) "Roy and Peggy are friendly, personable, and gracious folks who have lovingly restored this historic landmark." (*Allyn & Diana Foster*)

"A huge tree and a waterfall is on the left, a beautiful little white church on the right, and then the inn—a stately brick home, with welcoming rockers on the front porch. The decor includes furnishings made by Roy, and original artwork by local Vermont artists." (*Mary & Hal Portner*) "Our immaculate room had a canopy bed covered with a beautifully made quilt, and a fireplace with antiques upon the mantel." (*Harvey & Karen Rosenberg*) "Peggy and Roy are knowledgeable about the history of their home and the town. Top-quality mattresses and towels; bathrooms are supplied with extras in case you forgot shampoo or a toothbrush. Sherry and crackers are placed in each guest room, with cheese and crackers on the bar every afternoon. The company at breakfast is as delightful as the food, and guests sit around chatting long after they've finished eating. Parking is ample, with a large private space across from the inn." (*Dawn & Kevin Ruehle*)

Open May–March.

Rooms 7 doubles—5 with private bath and/or shower, 2 with maximum of 4 people sharing bath.

Facilities Living room with TV; sitting room with fireplace, books, guest refrigerator; common room with games, player piano; dining room with fireplace. Craft shop. 2 acres.

Location From village green, turn left onto Landgrove/Lawrence Hill Rd., cross river to second house on right.

Restrictions No smoking. No children under 6.

Credit cards MC, Visa—$5 per night surcharge.

Rates B&B, $75–110 double. Extra person, $25. 2-night winter weekend minimum. Midweek winter/spring discount. Call for fall foliage rates.

WEST TOWNSHEND

Windham Hill Inn ✕ ♿   *Tel:* 802–874–4080
RR 1, P.O. Box 44, 05359   800–944–4080
                                    Fax: 802–874–4702
                         E-mail: windham@sover.net
                         URL: http://windhamhill.com

Set into the mountainside, the Windham Hill Inn provides lovely views of the valley and the surrounding mountains from its hillside location.

Built in 1825, the inn's decor complements this quiet mood perfectly. Most guest rooms have king- or queen-size four-poster beds, some locally crafted from solid cherry, and are simply done in soft colors, with careful attention to guest comfort. Grigs and Pat Markham, who bought the inn in 1993, have expanded the dining room, added fireplaces and central air-conditioning, renovated guest rooms, built a tennis court and swimming pool, and in 1997, built a state-of-the-art conference room.

Breakfast is served from 8–9:30 A.M. while dinner is served from 6–8:30 P.M. Guests are seated privately for meals, though some choose to gather at the "big table" in a dinner party atmosphere. On a recent spring evening, choices included such appetizers as wild mushroom ravioli or crab cakes with papaya-lime sauce; followed by asparagus bisque and a salad of mesclun greens and saffron-currant bread; entrées included beef tenderloin with rosemary Cabernet sauce; arctic char with Pernod; vegetarian shepherd's pie with lentil-filled phyllo; and lamb with minted port wine sauce. The meal concluded with lemon soufflé with raspberries, chocolate peanut butter torte, or raspberry-cassis sorbet.

"Pat and Grigs have worked hard to make a wonderful inn even more so. Cramped bathrooms are now light and luxurious spaces. The swimming pool and tennis court were carefully sited so as not to interfere with the views. Landscaping and outdoor lighting enhance the beautiful setting. Despite all the changes, this still feels like the friendly country inn we first visited years ago. The staff is top-notch. Chef Cameron Howard deserves special mention for the high quality of her fresh ingredients, and her superb soups and fish dishes." *(Linda & Nick Rizopoulos)*

"The rooms are beautiful—one has a maple cannonball four-poster bed, and another is done in scrubbed pine, while a third has an old-fashioned tub in front of the bedroom fireplace; a welcome basket had bottles of spring water and juices. Plenty of areas to sit and read or mingle in the ample common areas. The dining area has a number of tables with valley views." *(Rose Ciccone)* "A sitting area under the eaves was a cozy place for gazing through a tree to the hills beyond; the view is spectacular from many spots in the inn." *(Sally Ducot)* "We stayed in General Fletcher's Room in the White Barn, with its wonderful views of the valley; a tray of coffee and/or tea is brought out early each morning." *(Gail De Sciose)*

Open All year except April, Christmas.

Rooms 21 doubles—all with private bath and/or shower, telephone, desk, air-conditioning. 16 with fireplace/Vermont Castings gas stove. Some with balcony, soaking tub, Jacuzzi. 8 rooms in restored barn.

Facilities Dining room; 3 common rooms with fireplaces; conference room/great room with fireplace; library; bar/lounge. 160 acres with flower gardens, swimming pool, tennis court, pond, lighted ice-skating, hiking trails, cross-country skiing trails; skis, snowshoes provided. Horsedrawn carriage rides/picnics. Golf, fishing, downhill skiing nearby.

Location SE VT. Approx. 15 m NW of Brattleboro, 25 m SE of Manchester. From I-91, take Exit 2 to Rte. 30 W for 21 m. Go right at the red country store in W. Townshend and go 1½ m up hill to inn.

Restrictions No smoking. "Not appropriate for children under 12."

Credit cards Amex, Discover, MC, Visa.
Rates MAP, $245–370 double, $190–315 single. Service included. 2-night week-end/foliage-season minimum. Seasonal specials available.
Extras Wheelchair access; 1 room equipped for disabled.

WILMINGTON

Wilmington is located in south-central Vermont, 19 miles west of Brattleboro, 19 east of Bennington, on Route 9, a major east-west route. It is approximately 4 hours north of New York City, and 2½ hours northwest of Boston. West Dover and Mount Snow lie about 5 miles north of Wilmington, up Route 100. Four downhill ski areas are within a 15-minute drive; four cross-country areas are 10 minutes away. Summer pleasures include golf at Haystack or Mt. Snow; hiking in the surrounding mountains; swimming, boating, and canoeing in Lake Whitingham; and theater and music in Wilmington and Marlboro.

For additional area entries, see **West Dover.**

Nutmeg Inn *Tel:* 802–464–3351
Route 9 West (Molly Stark Trail) 800–277–5402
P.O. Box 818, 05363 *Fax:* 802–464–7331
E-mail: nutmeg@sover.net
URL: http://www.nutmeginn.com

The Nutmeg is an early 1800s Vermont farmhouse, with connecting carriage house, converted to a country inn in 1957, and purchased by Dave and Pat Cherchio in 1996. Breakfast is served at individual tables from 8–9:30 A.M., and includes a choice of juices, cereal, bacon or sausage, eggs with toast or English muffins, pancakes, or French toast, and is highlighted by Dave's wonderful thick-crust natural yeast breads and cookies. The well-insulated guest rooms have queen- or king-size cherry or oak four-poster or brass and white iron beds with quilts and comforters. Summer visitors will enjoy the lovely flower garden that can be seen from the dining room and several guest rooms.

"Beautiful gardens and lots of trails behind the inn. Inviting entrance, with flowering plants, and a front hall with dried flowers hanging from the beamed ceiling. Nicely decorated, air-conditioned guest rooms. Dave is a great baker, from his breakfast breads to his melt-in-your-mouth double chocolate chip cookies." *(Betsy Sandberg)* "Friendly, hospitable innkeepers who helped us with travel plans, and dinner reservations." *(Piet Haanstra)* "Excellent food; enthusiastic innkeepers." *(TOH)* "A classic Vermont farmhouse with low ceilings and exposed beams. Convenient to town and all southern Vermont attractions. Plenty of menus on hand from local restaurants." *(Amanda Howe)* "Homemade chocolate chips in the evening; freshly baked breads accompany breakfast." *(Catherine Cimini & Mary Powderly)* "The truffled eggs and blueberry pancakes out of this world." *(Audrey & Dave Schmidt)* "Spotless and well-maintained. The wood was laid for a fire in our room's fireplace; all we had to do was strike a match. Dave's breakfasts are so good that we skied all day without stopping for lunch." *(Lauren & Richard Grubb)* "Truly interested in making every aspect of our getaway memorable, the innkeepers mailed us information about the area prior to our visit." *(Sandra Yook)*

"We were greeted warmly by Dave and Pat. After cookies and lemonade, we were given a tour of the inn and grounds. Our room was bright, charming, and immaculate; the bath was spacious and modern. From the adjoining deck, we had a view of the expansive back lawn and the hills beyond. After dinner, we returned to the inn and found a delicious lemon tart, fresh from Dave's oven, waiting in our room. Great French toast with maple syrup for breakfast, plus tasty anise whole wheat bread." *(Larry Weber)* "The living room was rustic with a lovely old brick fireplace, plenty of comfortable chairs for reading, and a bar with ice, refrigerator, and glasses always available, plus coffee, tea, hot chocolate (and lemonade in summer)." *(Alice McCarthy)* "The inn, although located on a major east-west route, has a large acreage behind that gives a real country feeling. Although full when we were there, it was quiet, with plentiful, well-lit parking conveniently close to the inn." *(Kathleen & Jack DiMaggio)*

Open All year.
Rooms 4 suites, 10 doubles—all with private bath and/or shower, air-conditioning. 1 suite with double whirlpool. 1 with deck. 10 with fireplace, TV; 4 with VCR.
Facilities Dining room; living room with fireplace, library, (BYOB) bar. 3 acres with flower garden, picnic area, lawn games, brook, toboggan hill.
Location On Rte. 9, 1 m W of Wilmington.
Restrictions No smoking. Children over 12 preferred.
Credit cards Amex, Discover, MC, Visa.
Rates B&B, $149–259 suite; $88–199 double. Extra person, $30. 2–3 night weekend, holiday minimum.

The Red Shutter Inn ✗
41 West Main St, P.O. Box 636, 05363

Tel: 802–464–3768
800–845–7548
Fax: 802–464–5123
E-mail: redshutr@sover.net
URL: http://www.redshutterinn.com

Built in 1894, the Red Shutter Inn is a Colonial-style building, set high above the road and framed by maples, pine oaks, and evergreens. An inn since 1955, it was purchased by Renee and Tad Lyon in 1995, who report "the only changes of substance we've made are making all desserts ourselves (Renee is a trained chef), and moving the office upstairs. We've also brought along Taffy, the quietest, sweetest cocker spaniel ever to run an inn!" Breakfast, served from 8–10 A.M. at individual tables, includes a daily special, which might be an omelet, French toast, blueberry pancakes, or quiche. Candlelight dinners are served both to guests and the public from a well-balanced menu; summertime brings al fresco dining to the inn's awning-covered deck. Although the menu changes often, possible entrées include trout with pecans, smoked chicken and artichoke ravioli, and venison with green peppercorn sauce.

"Tad is friendly and likeable, and immediately puts one at ease. Cozy dining room with dark paneled walls, soft lighting, and a stone fireplace. A creative and appealing menu is listed on a chalkboard at the entrance to the dining room." *(BNS)* "Homey atmosphere. Attentive, welcoming innkeepers, who were pleased to make dinner reservations for us. Enjoyed the honor bar set up in the main house. Our room was extremely well-furnished and impeccably clean. Breakfast was ready at the time we requested, and consisted of coffee, juice, a choice of omelets, home fries, sausage, and melt-in-your-mouth poppyseed glazed muffins." *(Madeleine Ferrucci)*

"The Joseph Courtemanche Suite has a high exposed-beam ceiling with skylight, a sitting room with pull-out sofa, good reading lights, a wood-burning fireplace, bay window, stereo, remote-controlled TV, whirlpool tub in the bath, and even games, books, and magazines. The bedroom had a brass bed with a lovely quilt, and a sliding glass door leading to a private balcony overlooking the hillside. The bathroom was good-sized with an attractive color scheme, fragrant soaps and bath gel, and a night light. Dinner was served in a richly paneled dining room, large enough for about six or seven tables, each intimate and private. Breakfast was served in a small, sunny room off the dining room." *(Carole Joslin)* "We enjoy the cozy ambience in the dining room, friendly service, and excellent food." *(Sally Ducot)*

Open Mid-May–mid-April. Restaurant closed Mon.
Rooms 2 suites, 7 doubles—all with private bath and/or shower. Suites with radio, TV, wood-burning fireplace, private deck. 1 suite with double whirlpool tub. 4 guest rooms in carriage house.
Facilities Restaurant with fireplace; living room with fireplace, piano, books; pub; TV room with VCR; porch. 5 acres with lawn.
Location On Rte. 9, W of intersection of Rtes. 9 & 100.
Restrictions No smoking. No children under 12.
Credit cards Amex, Discover, MC, Visa.
Rates B&B, $125–210 suite; $98–105 double; $93–100 single. Extra person, $25. 15% service. Golf, ski packages. 2–3 night weekend/holiday minimum. 2–5 night mid-week discount except peak periods. Alc dinner, $28–35.

Trail's End, A Country Inn 🦌
5 Trail's End Lane, 05363

Tel: 802–464–2727
800–859–2585
Fax: 802–464–5532
E-mail: trailsnd@together.net
URL: http://www.trailsendvt.com

Trail's End combines the drama of a ski lodge with the warmth of a country inn, and the amenities of a small resort. It was purchased by Debby and Kevin Stephens in 1997, ably assisted by inn-dog Bailey, a chocolate lab. The 22-foot stone fireplace in the living room, and loft above, create a dramatic setting, while the guest rooms provide more intimate spaces. The interior of this 1950s-era lodge has been gutted, rebuilt, redecorated, and refurbished. Guest rooms sparkle with light-colored walls and wall-to-wall carpeting (and individual thermostats), and are furnished with reproduction brass or country pine beds and antique chests. Breakfast, served at several large tables, includes fruit and juice, homemade granola, cereal, English muffins or wheat toast, bacon or sausage, and a choice of eggs, pancakes, French toast, Belgian waffles, or the daily special. Rates also include an afternoon treat: perhaps iced tea and oatmeal raisin cookies in summer, hot chocolate with fruit, cheese and nuts in winter.

"An unusual contemporary inn, with a distinct ski-lodge feel. Several sitting areas surround the fireplace, both on the lower and upper levels. Rooms freshly decorated. Wonderful amenities from a clay tennis court to a heated swimming pool. A most relaxing, serene location." *(Betsy Sandberg)* "We were warmly welcomed by the innkeepers, and greeted by the aromas of just-baked cake and a fire crackling in the fireplace. Our three-level suite had a four-poster bed, kitchenette, fireplace, couch and chair, TV, an extra bed in a separate area, and a Jacuzzi. Ideal balance of privacy and innkeeper interaction. They keep local restaurant menus on hand, gave wonderful directions on all local sights, and made themselves available at all times. It was my dream of a White Christmas come true, complete with chestnuts roasting on an open fire, carols, a horse-drawn sleigh ride, snowman, and more." *(Cynthia & Michael Cothran)* "The wonderful fireplace area is where the warm and friendly guests gather to socialize at this quiet and restful inn. Excellent breakfasts. Appealing town with lots of good restaurants within a twenty-minute drive." *(Lynn Scull)* "Wonderful setting, attentive service, extremely friendly innkeepers." *(C. Breiner)* "The delightful guest rooms are cozy with mini-printed wallpaper, matching thick comforters and lovely little personal touches. In late afternoon, guests enjoy light hors d'oeuvres and mulled cider or tea." *(Bonnie Nalwasky)*

Open All year.

Rooms 2 suites, 13 doubles—all with private bath and/or shower, clock. 4 with wood-burning fireplace, TV. Suites with whirlpool tub, fireplace, refrigerator, microwave oven, wet bar, TV. 1 with balcony/deck.

Facilities Dining room, living room with fireplace; loft family room with TV, stereo; library, guest refrigerator, deck. 10 acres with stocked trout pond, heated swimming pool, clay tennis court, hiking paths.

Location 4 m from town. From Rte. 100 take East Dover Rd. Go right on Smith Rd. to inn.

Restrictions No smoking.

Credit cards Amex, Discover, MC, Visa.

Rates B&B, $145–185 suite, $95–155 double. Extra person, $30. 15% service. 2–3 night weekend/winter holiday minimum. Discount for 7-night stay (summer), 5-night midweek (winter); excluding holidays.

WINDSOR

Vermont's constitution was adopted in Windsor in 1777, making the town the "Birthplace of Vermont." It's located in southeastern Vermont, on the Connecticut River, close to Mt. Ascutney, about 2½ hours from Hartford and Boston, about 25 minutes south of Hanover, New

Hampshire. The area is ideal for canoeing on the Connecticut River, plus bicycling, hiking, and skiing in winter.

For additional area entries, see **Weathersfield**, plus **Claremont** and **Cornish, New Hampshire.**

Mill Brook B&B ¢ **♦♦**　　　　　　　　　　　*Tel:* 802–484–7283
Route 44, P.O. Box 410　　　　　　　　　　　*Fax:* 802–674–5926
Brownsville, 05037　　　*E-mail:* millbrook@outboundconnection.com
　　　　　URL: http://www.outboundconnection.com/millbrook.htm

Built in the late 1800s, Millbrook was originally the home of mill-owner Wilber Sykes, who also owned a steam-operated circular sawmill, producing thousands of hardwood chairstocks. The B&B has been owned by the Carriere-Zito family since 1986; Kay Carriere is the innkeeper. Guests are kept well-nourished with a hearty breakfast, normally served from 8–9 A.M.; from 4:30–6:30 P.M. in winter, hungry skiers can help themselves to bowls of homemade soup—corn or fish chowder, onion soup au gratin, or turkey soup. Tea and sweets are served year-round. Kay describes the Mill Brook as "a visit to a great-aunt's house. We've heard from many of Kay's guests, and all praise her exceptional hospitality and cooking, the immaculate housekeeping, and ample supplies of hot water."

"Afternoon tea with home-baked apple pie and made-from-scratch chocolate-orange cake. Breakfast feasts of homemade oatmeal with fruit and maple syrup, Dutch pancakes, or orange crêpes with strawberry filling, or farm-fresh eggs. Ample space for sitting and great hospitality." *(Jan Getek)* "Kay was a wonderful hostess to both us and our dog." *(Mr. & Mrs. Frank Farina)* "My bed was so comfortable that I hated to get up in the morning. The afternoon soups, stews, and desserts were delicious." *(Lauren Ford)* "Charming setting in the shadow of Mt. Ascutney. Neat and tidy. Plentiful, delicious variety of food prepared and served by a caring hostess." *(Frank Warner)* "When we walked in, we found the hospitable Kay in the kitchen baking a strawberry marble cake. We wanted to take her back with us to South Africa to cook for us." *(BJ Visser)* "Kay was always ready to offer information on activities, dinner reservations, etc. Pampering hospitality, country atmosphere." *(Bob Miller)*

"Our room was comfortable and quiet, our privacy respected. Cleanliness, lighting, plumbing, parking, and location were excellent. Service was personal and most pleasant; breakfasts delightful." *(AM)* "What a breakfast—oatmeal, muffins, and popovers; waffles, pancakes, French toast with Vermont syrups; any type of eggs desired, plus cider, juices, and bottomless cups of coffee." *(Ed Finnegan)* "Several sitting rooms allowed people to spread out. The small hot tub was great for after skiing." *(Kim Hendrickson)*

Open All year.
Rooms 3 suites, 2 doubles—all with private bath and/or shower, fan.
Facilities Dining room, living room with wood-stove, parlor with TV/VCR, original kitchen with guest refrigerator/microwave; TV room with books. 1½ acres with hot tub, picnic area, hammock, lawn/children's games, screen house. Brook for swimming, fishing. Pool, tennis, golf, downhill, cross-country skiing nearby.

Location From I-91 N, take Exit 9 to Rte. 5 S to Windsor. At second traffic light turn right onto Rte. 44. Take Exit 8 from I-91 S to Rte. 5 N. Turn onto Rte. 44A to Rte. 44. Go through Brownsville to inn .2 m from center on right.

Restrictions No smoking. Traffic noise in front rooms. Limited storage space in some rooms.

Credit cards Amex, MC, Visa for final payment on non-discounted rates.

Rates $97–107 suite, $67–97 double. Extra adult, $20; up to 2 children free with 2 parents in suitable rooms. Low-season discount, single rate, weekly rate. Add 3rd night to weekend at half-price, 4th night free. 2–3 night minimum weekends/holidays, foliage, Christmas.

Extras Pets by arrangement. Playpen, crib, high chair; babysitting by arrangement.

Juniper Hill Inn ✕
Juniper Hill Road, RR 1, P.O. Box 79, 05089

Tel: 802–674–5273
800–359–2541
Fax: 802–674–2041
E-mail: innkeeper@juniperhillinn.com
URL: http://www.Juniperhillinn.com

Juniper Hill was built at the turn of the century by Maxwell Evarts of Windsor as his private residence. It's not hard to imagine the gatherings of prominent railroad and shipping magnates of the day who were entertained in this Georgian-style Colonial mansion. Evarts was also a friend of President Teddy Roosevelt, who stayed at Juniper Hill when touring the Northeast. Robert and Susanne Pearl purchased the inn in 1992, and have refurbished both common areas and guest rooms, keeping guests' needs for comfort and privacy always in mind. In addition to fresh fruit, juice and coffee, breakfast includes a choice of oatmeal with fruit toppings, bagels and cream cheese, apple or berry pancakes, French toast, strata, or eggs Benedict. Dinners, served at 7 P.M., offer a choice of three entrées; a recent menu included mushroom soup, salad with chevre and poppyseed dressing, herb-crusted rack of lamb, and chocolate raspberry truffle cheesecake.

"A Vermont gem. Sue and Rob Pearl create an atmosphere of friendliness and comfort in the most professional way." *(Andreas & Ann Marie Harrington-Hagenow)* "Warm, relaxing, romantic atmosphere created by innkeepers who make you feel like a family member come to visit, yet never intrude on one's privacy. Superb cleanliness; our room was made up daily with fresh sheets and towels." *(Troy Squires)* "Breakfast is served in a room full of windows with river and mountain views. Incredible oatmeal and pancakes. Guests can socialize in the great room, or retreat to the intimate library for quiet moments." *(Laura Julier)* "We enjoyed Rob and Susanne's personal touch and impeccable taste. Our comfortable room had antique furnishings, a four-poster bed, sitting area facing the fireplace, and a reading chair and desk. Breakfasts were particularly tasty, with eggs Benedict and raspberry pancakes." *(Susan Snyder)* "Wonderful little extras in the room—sherry, mints, fresh flowers." *(Susan & John Hillery)* "Beautiful grounds with a lovely swimming pool, manicured lawns and gardens, mountain and water views. Peaceful hilltop setting, yet convenient location." *(Suzanne LaBine)*

"Great hot water pressure, ample wood for the fireplace. Even great inn dogs, Welsh Corgis named Jane and Tucker." *(Andrea Harmin)* "Bedrooms were quiet, with good soundproofing." *(Peggy Dorson)* "Beds are firm and comfortable, lighting attractive and adequate. At breakfast, we could choose whether to mix with the other guests or not." *(Gail Charpentier)*

Open May–March. Closed April. Restaurant open by reservation Mon.– Sat.
Rooms 16 doubles—all with private bath and/or shower, ceiling fan. 9 with wood-burning fireplace; 2 with gas fireplace. Some with desk.
Facilities Dining room, library with games, bar; 2 parlors, TV room. 14 acres with swimming pool, nature trails, croquet, snowshoeing; bicycle rentals. 1 m from CT River for canoeing; rentals available. Golf, tennis, fishing, horseback riding, hiking, downhill and cross-country skiing nearby.
Location 2 m from town. Take Exit 9 off of I-91. Go 2.7 m S on Rte. 5. Turn right on Juniper Hill Rd., go ¼ m to fork, go left. Go ¼ m to driveway & inn on right.
Restrictions No smoking. No children under 12.
Credit cards Discover, MC, Visa.
Rates B&B, $90–150 double. 2-night minimum, holidays/fall foliage/fireplace rooms. Bicycling, canoeing packages. Midweek, extended stay discounts. By reservation, prix fixe dinner, $27–30, plus 15% service.
Extras Station pickup.

WOLCOTT

For additional area entries, see, **Craftsbury Common, Greensboro,** and **Hardwick.**

Golden Maple Inn ¢
Route 15, 05680

Tel: 802–888–6614
800–639–5234
Fax: 802–888–6614
E-mail: GoldnMaple@aol.com
URL: http://members.aol.com/GoldnMaple

A good example of Vermont's indigenous style of "continuing architecture" (otherwise known as "big house, little house, back house, barn"), the Golden Maple Inn is a Greek Revival farmhouse built in 1865. The unusual star-shaped attic vents were designed by the original owner, H.B. Bundy, to celebrate the return of his sons from the Civil War. Restored in 1990 as an inn by Dick and Jo Wall, its location on the Lamoille River makes it a popular spot for combining the delights of fly-fishing with explorations of Vermont's Northeast Kingdom. The Walls have decorated the inn with Vermont country antiques, simple floral wallpapers and fabrics; wide-board floors are topped with Oriental and braided rugs. In addition to innkeeping, Dick and Jo have a fly-fishing school and provide professional guiding in spring, summer, and fall.

Breakfast is served with sterling silver, English bone china, and crystal. A typical menu might include poached pears with brown sugar, homemade maple granola, juice, croissants layered with scrambled eggs, smoked ham, apples, and Vermont cheddar; or oven-baked French toast with blueberries and local maple syrup. Candlelit dinners are served on weekends, and might include Caesar salad, chicken baked with garlic, wild rice, fresh vegetables, home-baked rolls, chocolate Amaretto mousse, and cappuccino or espresso.

"The Walls went out of their way to ensure that our stay was pleasant, easy, and relaxing. Wonderful breakfasts with freshly brewed coffee, home-baked lemon raisin scones, fresh fruit, and eggs baked with maple-smoked bacon." *(Craig Chandler)* "Wonderful site along the river provides a peaceful setting for tea among the flower beds. Great canoe access, too. We were lulled to sleep by the sound of the water." *(Mary & Chip Chapman)* "The book-lined living room is a wonderful place to relax with tea. Cozy and comfortable beds, with beautiful linens." *(S. Lyons)* "Our favorite room is the Geneva Suite with gas fireplace and huge cast-iron bathtub. Soft classical music in the common rooms created a soothing atmosphere." *(Deborah Owens & Kevin Underwood)* "Immaculate. At night, we slept with open windows, with a gentle breeze stirring the lace curtains. The Walls are inviting, warm, and cultured; they made us feel special and welcomed." *(Nancy Redman)* "Dick and Jo knew just when we wanted company and when privacy was preferred. Dick was helpful with suggested activities, and provided maps to guide us." *(Brent & Heather Glossinger)*

Open All year.
Rooms 2 suites, 2 doubles—all private bath, radio, desk, fan.
Facilities Dining room, library, parlor with TV/VCR. 1 acre on Lamoille River for fly-fishing, canoeing. Canoe rentals, shuttle. Fly-fishing instruction; guided fishing trips. Cross-country skiing nearby; 35 min. to downhill.
Location NE VT, Northeast Kingdom. On Rte. 15, just W of village.
Restrictions No smoking. Children over 12.
Credit cards Amex, Discover, MC, Visa.
Rates B&B, $69–79 suite, $59–69 double, $49–59 single. MAP, $107–117 suite, $97–107 double, $68–78 single. Extra person, $15–34. Tipping not encouraged. 10% senior discount. 2-night holiday/peak season weekend minimum. Prix fixe dinner, $23 (by reservation). Fly-fishing school, bike-touring packages.

WOODSTOCK

An archetypal New England town, Woodstock offers a picture-perfect village green, surrounded by beautifully restored 18th- and 19th-century homes and an ample supply of tasteful shops—even a covered bridge. Skiers stay here in winter (it's 4 miles to Suicide Six and 12 miles to Killington and Pico, plus cross-country skiing at the Woodstock Country Club), while summer offers hiking, fishing, golf, and tennis. Woodstock is set on Route 4 in east-central Vermont, about 10 miles west of the intersection of I-91 and I-89 at White River Junction. Boston is 153 miles southeast, while New York is 280 miles southwest.

Woodstock's picturesque beauty owes much to the generosity of longtime patrons Laurance and Mary Rockefeller, who helped to preserve the town's historic charms, create the Billings Museum, rebuild the Woodstock Inn, and most recently, have made a gift of their former estate. Now Vermont's first national park, the Marsh-Billings National Historic Park is dedicated to the history of the environmental conservation movement, and comprises the original estate mansion and 550 acres of meadows and woodlands, including many trails on Mt. Tom. You enter the park through the Billings Museum.

Worth noting: Traffic noise can be a problem for any inn located close to busy Route 4. In summer, insist on a room away from the road unless you plan to keep the air-conditioning on.

Reader tip: "The Billings Museum is well worth seeing; kids will love the animals, especially lambs and calves in spring, and all, especially adults, will enjoy the farm exhibits, with exceptionally clear and informative signage. The docents provide a good picture of 19th-century life during the farmhouse tours." *(RSS)*

For additional area entries, see **Barnard, Bridgewater Corners, Killington/Mendon,** and **Quechee.**

Deer Brook Inn ¢ 🕴	*Tel:* 802–672–3713
Route 4 West, HCR 68	*URL:* http://www.bbhost.
P.O. Box 443, 05091	com/deerbrookinn

Once the main house of a dairy farm, the Deer Brook Inn is owned by Brian and Rosemary McGinty, who renovated this 1820 Colonial home in 1987. They polished the original wide pine floors, and accented them with braided rugs. Guest rooms feature Rosemary's homemade quilts atop queen- or king-size beds, and hand-painted stencils. You can relax on the porch and watch the Ottauquechee River meander by; in cooler weather, lounge in front of the fire in the living room. Breakfast, served at your choice of a large table or small, includes juice, coffee, fresh fruit, homemade muffins, and an egg dish, pancakes, waffles, or French toast.

"We truly appreciated the inn's cleanliness, as our toddler often plays on the floor. The simple but lovely bedroom decor is another plus for parents who don't want to worry about their children breaking priceless antiques. Delicious breakfasts, accompanied by delightful conversation with the other guests. One day we had muffins and an egg soufflé; zucchini bread and French toast the next. Rosemary even made small portions of each entrée for my daughter. In the evenings, we enjoyed a roaring fire in the sitting room, and played Trivial Pursuit with newfound friends. Rosemary was very helpful in directing us toward area activities; her children are charming. Convenient location for exploring Woodstock, hiking the nearby trails, and rummaging through local antique shops." *(Cora Sparwasser)*

"A charming old farmhouse overlooking a brook; peaceful setting, great pancakes." *(Georgia Alder)* "We awoke to the soothing sound of the river, yet were within minutes from Woodstock and area attractions. Gracious hosts, immaculate home." *(Susan Becerra, also SWS)* "After a good night's sleep on the king-size bed, we were served a scrumptious breakfast of warm banana-chocolate muffins and omelets; soft music played in the background." *(Joan Legath)*

Open All year.

Rooms 1 suite, 4 doubles—all with full private bath, clock, air-conditioning. Suite with TV.

Facilities Dining room, living room with fireplace, TV/VCR, books. 4.5 acres. Hiking nearby.

Location 5 m W of town. From Rte. 100, take Rte. 4 E to inn.
Restrictions No smoking.
Credit cards MC, Visa.
Rates B&B, $90–125 suite, $75–105 double, $60–80 single. Extra person, $15. Children under 2 free in parents' room.
Extras Crib.

The Jackson House Inn ✕ &

37 Old Route 4 West, 05091

Tel: 802–457–2065
800–448–1890
Fax: 802–457–9290
E-mail: innkeeper@jacksonhouse.com
URL: http://www.jacksonhouse.com

"An elegant, romantic, quiet country inn, with personal yet unobtrusive service" is how world travelers and native Argentines Juan and Gloria Florin describe the inn they purchased in 1997 and expanded, adding four suites, a fine dining restaurant, and a fitness center with exercise machines and a steam room. Guest rooms and common areas are beautifully furnished in French, American, and English antiques, with hand-crafted cherry and maple woodwork, and Oriental rugs. Although the decor of each room varies—French country, Empire, Victorian, and New England country—each has fresh flowers, bottled spring water, fresh fruit, plush terry robes, and Gilchrist & Soames toiletries. Some have queen-size sleigh or four-poster beds, gas fireplaces, Italian marble bathrooms, and French doors opening to decks overlooking the inn's gardens.

Breakfast is served at the large table in the breakfast room, or at individual tables in the restaurant from 8–9:30 A.M. Menus vary daily, but might feature such choices as orange or grapefruit juice; warm fruit compote or bananas with crème fraîche; granola, oatmeal, or eggs with mushroom sauce on English muffins; plus orange poppyseed cake, chocolate croissants, and banana muffins. Rates also include an evening reception from 6–7 P.M., with hors d'oeuvres, wine, and champagne. At the Jackson House Restaurant, a double-sided, floor-to-ceiling granite fireplace, cathedral ceiling, and picture windows overlooking the formal English gardens set the stage for chef Brendan Nolan's creations. A recent chef's tasting menu included smoked-rabbit ravioli, grilled sea bass with kiwi-orange relish, passion fruit sorbet, duck breast with truffled mashed potatoes; cheese and fruit plate, and chocolate brandy soufflé; also available is an equally tempting vegetarian tasting dinner.

"All of the charm of an old house with beautiful antiques plus the luxuries of an elegant small hotel—magnificent linens and down comforters, fireplaces, Jacuzzi baths, and evening champagne. The chef's prix fixe dinner, embellished by local ingredients, was topped off by a memorable chocolate hazelnut soufflé. Gets our vote for the best New England restaurant north of Boston. We can't wait to go back." *(Jevin & Janine Eagle)* "Impeccable service and housekeeping; warm, welcoming, genuine, relaxed hospitality." *(Rick & Carolyn Gilligan)* "The management, ambience, service, and the food all exceptional." *(Frank Keegan)*

Open All year. Restaurant open Thurs.–Mon.

Rooms 6 suites, 9 doubles—all with private bath and/or shower, air-conditioning. Some with whirlpool tub, fan, telephone, clock/radio, clock, gas fireplace, desk, balcony/deck/patio, private entrance.

Facilities Restaurant with fireplace; parlor with fireplace; TV room with TV/VCR; library; fitness center/spa with steam room; guest refrigerator; veranda. 5 acres with gardens, brook, swimming pond, croquet.

Location 1½ m W of village just off Rte. 4 (Senior Lane).

Restrictions No smoking. Children 14 and over.

Credit cards Amex, MC, Visa.

Rates B&B, $216–260 suite, $153–190 double. 2–3 night minimum some holidays/weekends/foliage. Prix fixe dinner, $42–50.

Extras Wheelchair access; 1 suite specially equipped. Spanish, French, Italian spoken.

The Woodstock Inn and Resort 🛏 ✕ ⚕
14, The Green, 05091

Tel: 802–457–1100
800–448–7900
Fax: 802–457–6699
E-mail: Woodstock.Resort@connriver.net
URL: http://www.woodstockinn.com

Dating back to 1793, the Woodstock Inn originally catered to travelers transferring from one stagecoach line to another. The original building was replaced in 1892 when Woodstock became known as a summer resort. Updated many times over the years, it was purchased by Laurance Rockefeller in 1967, and when renovations proved impracticable, a new inn was built on the site in 1969, then expanded in 1990. The ideal man to re-create the Woodstock Inn, Mr. Rockefeller had long-term ties to the community, having married a local girl, Mary Billings French; the financial assets required to create a first-class resort, as the grandson of John D. Rockefeller; and first-class qualifications, having developed top-quality resorts in the Caribbean, Wyoming, and Hawaii. Tom List is the inn manager; before coming to Woodstock, Tom was the innkeeper at the well-known Old Tavern at Grafton.

A well-known full-service luxury resort, the inn is an imposing white building centrally located on Woodstock's green, offering easy access to everything the town has to offer, as well as a full range of recreational facilities at the nearby Sports Center and golf course. A wide variety of activities will keep children occupied on weekends and during vacations; business conference facilities are equally extensive. All travelers should inquire about the inn's many packages, which can make a stay more affordable. Guest rooms are decorated with reproduction furnishings and handmade quilts; those in the new wing are most luxurious. Not all have mountain or forest views, so be sure to ask for details when booking.

Meals at the inn are served at the casual Eagle Café, Richardson's Tavern, and the more formal inn dining room. A recent menu sampling at the Tavern turned up such specialties as sole with vegetable couscous; maple-roasted chicken with apples; and shrimp and scallops with fettuccine and roasted red pepper sauce. Afternoon tea is served in the lounge from 4–5 P.M. and is accompanied by live piano.

"Friendly, accommodating, longtime staff, who remember our family and make us and our children feel right at home. Among our favorite pleasures are: the comfortable, homey guest rooms, morning coffee, afternoon tea and pre-dinner wine in the Wicker Lounge, reading in the library, the beautiful grounds, the golf club, Mt. Tom, Billings Farm, and the village. Under chef Tom Guay, the food and service in the dining room is exceptional." *(Charles O'Neill)* "Spacious, spotless rooms with parking right outside the front door. Exceptional year-round sports to suit any athletic preference, ability, or age. Woodstock is a New England picture-perfect postcard." *(Elaine Lasoff)* "The food is great, the service and staff are super. Complete facilities. A wonderful place to relax and enjoy the flowers." *(Cynthia & Richard Cummings)*

Open All year.

Rooms 7 suites, 137 doubles—all with full private bath and/or shower, telephone, radio, clock, TV, desk, air-conditioning. 23 with working fireplace. 45 with refrigerator. 3 with balcony/deck. Data port upon request. 2 townhouses; 1 full house.

Facilities 2 restaurants, tavern with piano music, dining room, living room, game room, library, porch. 3 acres with swimming pool, putting green, bicycle rentals, nature walks. 1.5 m to fitness center with exercise rooms, 12 tennis courts (2 indoor), croquet, indoor swimming pool, sauna, steam room, hot tub, paddle tennis; ski touring center; 18-hole golf course. Downhill skiing nearby.

Location On village green.

Restrictions Smoking only in designated rooms, also Richardson's Tavern.

Credit cards Amex, MC, Visa.

Rates B&B, $325–525 suite, $110–305 double. Extra person, $15–25. Children 14 & under free in parents' room. 2–3 night weekend/holiday minimum. Prix fixe dinner $28–42. Alc lunch $16–19. Alc dinner $28–42. Golf, tennis, skiing, theme packages.

Extras Wheelchair access; bathrooms specially equipped. Cribs, babysitting. Spanish, French, German spoken.

Important Note on Area Codes

Telephone area codes are changing faster than a two-year-old's attention span. Although we've tried to incorporate all the new ones in our listings, many numbers were still in the "to be decided" state at press time. *If you dial a number listed here and get an announcement that it's not in service, we urge you to call the information operator and see if that region has been assigned a new area code.* Please forgive the inconvenience!

_____*MAPS*

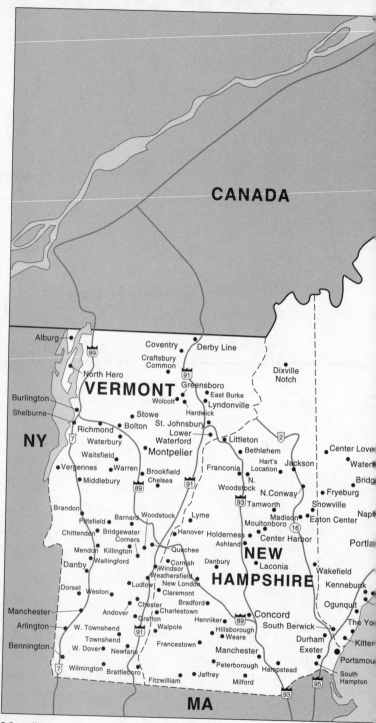

Map #1

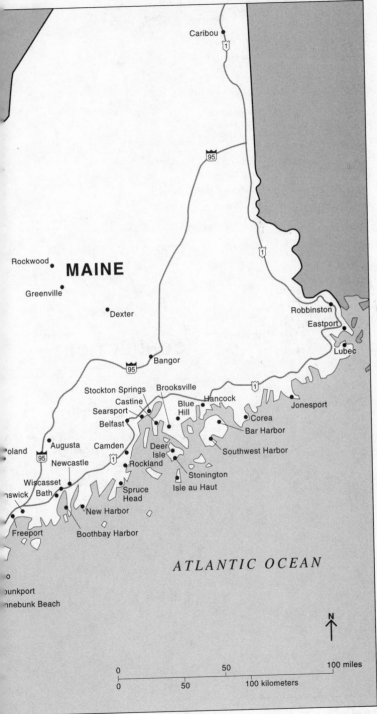

Map #1

Map #2

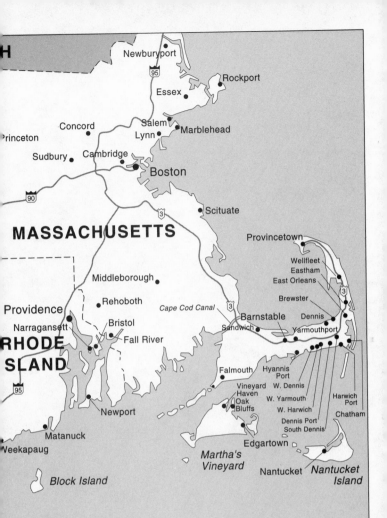

Map #2

Index of Accomodations

Hotel/Inn Report Forms

The report forms on the following pages may be used to endorse or critique an existing entry or to nominate a hotel or inn that you feel deserves inclusion in the next edition. Don't feel you must restrict yourself to the space available; feel free to use your own stationery or e-mail. All nominations (each on a separate piece of paper, if possible) should include your name and address, the name and location of the hotel or inn, when you have stayed there, and for how long. Please report only on establishments you have visited in the last eighteen months, unless you are sure that standards have not dropped since your stay. Please be as specific as possible, and critical where appropriate, about the character of the building, the public rooms, the accommodations, the meals, the service, the nightlife, the grounds, and the general atmosphere of the inn and the attitude of its owners. Comments about area restaurants and sights are also appreciated.

Don't feel you need to write at length. A report that merely verifies the accuracy of existing listings is extremely helpful, i.e., "Visited XYZ Inn and found it just as described." There is no need to bother with prices or with routine information about the number of rooms and facilities, although a sample brochure is very helpful for new recommendations.

On the other hand, don't apologize for writing a long report. Although space does not permit us to quote them in total, the small details provided about furnishings, atmosphere, and cuisine can really make a description come alive, illuminating the special flavor of a particular inn or hotel. Remember that we will again be awarding free copies to our most helpful respondents—last year we mailed over 500 books.

Please note that we print only the names of respondents; addresses are never published or sold. Those making negative observations are not identified. Although we must always have your full name and address, we will be happy to print your initials, or a pseudonym, if you prefer.

Reports should be sent to P.O. Box 150, Riverside, CT 06878 or afi@inns.com.

To: *America's Favorite Inns, B&Bs, and Small Hotels*,
P.O. Box 150, Riverside, CT 06878 or ssoule@msn.com.

Name of hotel _____

Address _____

Telephone _____

Date of most recent visit _____ Duration of visit _____

☐ New recommendation ☐ Comment on existing entry

Please be as specific as possible about furnishings, atmosphere, service, and cuisine. If reporting on an existing entry, please tell us whether you thought it accurate. Unless you tell us not to, we shall assume that we may publish your name in the next edition. Thank you very much for writing; use your own stationery if preferred.

I am not connected with the management/owners.
I would stay here again if returning to the area. ☐ yes ☐ no
Have you written to us before? ☐ yes ☐ no

Signed _____

Name _____
                        (Please print)

Address _____
                        (Please print)

_____